The **Rough Guide** to

Iceland

written and researched by

David Leffman and James Proctor

ROUGH
GUIDES

NEW YORK • LONDON • DELHI

www.roughguides.com

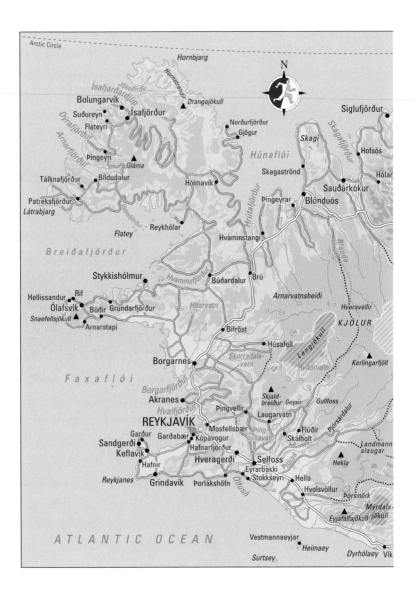

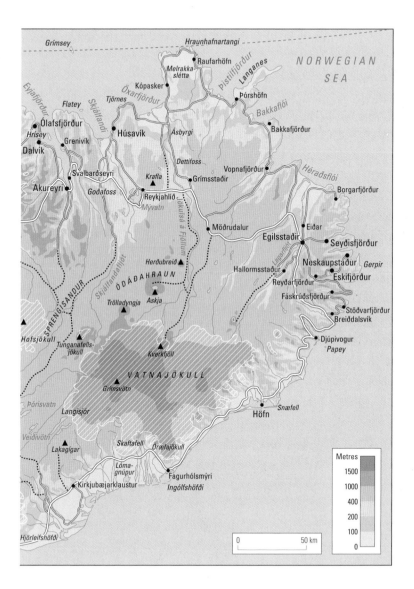

Grímsey   Hraunhafnartangi

Raufarhöfn

NORWEGIAN SEA

Melrakka-slétta

Kópasker   Pistilfjörður   Langanes

Öxarfjörður   Þórshöfn

Flatey   Tjörnes

Bakkaflói

Eyjafjörður   Skjálfandi

Ólafsfjörður   Húsavík   Ásbyrgi   Bakkafjörður

Hrísey   Grenivík

Dalvík

Dettifoss

Svalbarðseyri   Krafla   Vopnafjörður   Héraðsflói

Akureyri   Goðafoss   Grímsstaðir

Reykjahlíð   Borgarfjörður

Mývatn   Jökulsá á Fjöllum

Möðrudalur   Eiðar

Egilsstaðir   Seyðisfjörður

Lagarfljót

Herðubreið   Neskaupstaður   Gerpir

ÓDÁÐAHRAUN   Hallormsstaður   Eskifjörður

Reyðarfjörður

Trölladyngja   Askja   Fáskrúðsfjörður

Skjálfandafljót

SPRENGISANDUR   Stöðvarfjörður

Breiðdalsvík

Hofsjökull   Tungnafells-jökull   Kverkfjöll   Djúpivogur

Papey

VATNAJÖKULL

Grímsvötn

Þórisvatn   Langisjór   Snæfell

Höfn

Veiðivötn

Lakagígar   Skaftafell   Öræfajökull

Lóma-gnúpur

Kirkjubæjarklaustur   Fagurhólsmýri

Ingólfshöfði

Hjörleifshöfði

Metres	
1500	
1000	
400	
200	
100	
0	

0   50 km

Introduction to
Iceland

Resting on the edge of the Arctic Circle and sitting atop one of the world's most volcanically active hotspots, Iceland is nowadays thought of for its striking mix of magisterial glaciers, bubbling hot springs and rugged fjords, where activities such as hiking under the Midnight Sun are complemented by healthy doses of history and literature.

It's misleading, then, that one of the country's earliest visitors, the Viking **Flóki Vilgerðarson**, saw fit to choose a name for it that emphasized just one of these qualities, though perhaps he can be forgiven in part: having sailed here with hopes of starting a new life in this then uninhabited island, he endured a long hard winter in around 870 AD that killed off all his cattle. Hoping to spy out a more promising site for his farm he climbed a high mountain in the northwest of the country, only to be faced with a fjord full of drift ice. Bitterly disappointed, he named the place **Ísland** (Ice Land) and promptly sailed home for the positively balmy climes of Norway.

A few years later, however, Iceland was successfully settled and, despite the subsequent enthusiastic felling of trees for fuel and timber, visitors to the country today will see it in pretty much the same state as it was over a thousand years ago, with the **coastal fringe**, for example, dotted with sheep farms, a few score fishing villages and tiny hamlets – often no more than a collection of homesteads nestling around a wooden church. An Icelandic town, let alone a city, is still a rarity and until the twentieth century the entire nation numbered no more than 60,000. The country remains the most sparsely populated in Europe, with a population of just 283,000 – over half of whom live down in the southwestern corner

Fact file

• Though geographically as big as England, Iceland's **population** is tiny. At barely 283,000, it's no bigger than many towns in other countries. Three out of five Icelanders live in and around the capital, Reykjavík.

• Iceland sits atop the **North Atlantic Ridge**, the fault line where two of the Earth's tectonic plates are slowly drifting apart. As a result Iceland is getting wider at a rate of roughly 1cm per year. Either side of this ridge, from the northeast to the southwest, **earthquakes** and **volcanic activity** are commonplace.

• There are no motorways or railways in Iceland. The country's one and only main road, the **Ringroad** which circumnavigates the island, was only completed thirty years ago following several unsuccesful attempts to bridge treacherous glacial rivers on the south coast.

• Iceland is home to the third-biggest **glacier** in the world, Vatnajökull, covering an area equal to that of the English county of Yorkshire. One of the country's greatest sources of **geothermal energy**, the Grímsvötn caldera, sits directly beneath the icecap.

• Thanks to the existence of countless medieval documents, many Icelanders can trace their ancestors back to the time of the **Viking Settlement**, around 800 AD. Low **immigration** over the centuries means that today's Icelanders have one of the purest gene pools in the world, providing an invaluable research opportunity for scientists.

around the surprisingly cosmopolitan capital, **Reykjavík**. **Akureyri**, up on the north coast, is the only other decent-sized population centre outside the Greater Reykjavík area.

If the coast is thinly populated, Iceland's **Interior** remains totally uninhabited and unmarked by humanity: a starkly beautiful wilderness of ice fields, infertile lava and ash deserts, windswept upland plateaux and the frigid vastness of Vatnajökull, Europe's largest glacier. Even in downtown Reykjavík, crisp, snow-capped peaks and fjords hover in the background, evidence of the forces that created the country. And Iceland's location on the Mid-Atlantic ridge also gives it one of the most volcanically active landscapes on Earth, peppered with everything from naturally occurring hot springs, scaldingly hot bubbling mud pools and noisy steam vents to a string of unpredictably violent volcanoes, which have regularly devastated huge parts of the country. It's something that Icelanders have learned to live with: in June 1998, when Reykjavík was rocked by a major earthquake, the ballet dancers at the National Opera performed right through it without missing a step.

Historically, the **Icelanders** have a mix of Nordic and Celtic blood, a heritage often held responsible for their character-istically laidback approach to life – taps in hotels often drip, buses don't depart to the stroke of the driver's watch, and every-body, including the President and the Prime Minister, is known by their first name. The battle for survival against the elements over the centuries has also made them a highly self-reliant nation, whose dependence on the sea and fishing for their economy is virtually total – hence their refusal to allow foreign trawlers to fish off Iceland during the diplomatically tense 1970s, sparking off three "Cod Wars", principally with Britain. However, their isolated location in the North Atlantic also means that their island is

Getting legless for an arm and a leg

It's one of Iceland's greatest paradoxes: how can a country that charges some of the highest prices for alcohol in Europe also support such an eclectic scene of bars and clubs? Put simply, spending vast amounts of money on everyday items is a fact of life in Iceland, a country where import taxes and inflation have caused prices to soar; and even though alcohol prices in real terms have fallen in recent years, a half litre of beer in Reykjavík will still cost at least double what you're used to paying at home. Icelanders get round the astronomical cost of booze by drinking at home before hitting the town. Buying beer and wine in the state-run alcohol store, the **vínbúð**, is the homegrown way of cutting costs – and even then, although prices are considerably lower than in bars, the store charges for the plastic bag to take your booty home in.

To whale or not to whale

The Icelandic government's decision to resume **commercial whaling** for scientific purposes, in August 2003, drove a wedge through Icelandic public opinion. The majority of the country views whaling as a virtual birthright and is only too keen to turn a nationalistic blind eye to international protest; but it is also true that the nation's burgeoning **tourism industry** has led to a decline in its near-total dependence on the fishing industry. Consequently, promoters of tourism lost no time in pointing out that foreigners have flocked to Iceland in recent years to **watch whales** in their natural habitat, not to see them unceremoniously sliced up for the dinner table – and despite a seeming nonchalance, Icelanders are painfully aware that their tiny country on the very edge of Europe can ill afford any kind of international boycott.

frequently forgotten about – Icelanders will tell you that they've given up counting how many times they've been left off maps of Europe – something that deeply offends their strong sense of national pride. For all their self-confidence though, they can seem an initially reserved people – until Friday and Saturday nights roll around, when the *bjór* starts to flow, and turns even the most monosyllabic fisherman into a lucid talkshow host, right down to reciting from memory entire chunks of medieval sagas about the early settlers.

Where to go

It's difficult to imagine the emptiness of a country that is as large as England or the US State of Kentucky yet has a population of barely over a quarter of a million (in comparison with

England's 48 million). Route 1, the **Ringroad**, runs out from **Reykjavík** to encircle the island, with all long-distance buses and domestic planes beginning their journeys from the city. It may be small, but what Reykjavík lacks in size it more than makes up for in stylish bars, restaurants and shops, and the nightlife is every bit as wild as it's cracked up to be – during the light summer nights, the city doesn't sleep. The world's most northerly capital also boasts cinemas, an opera, a symphony orchestra and a dance

company, as well as the usual string of museums and galleries. Reykjavík makes a good base for visiting **Geysir**, the original geyser that gave its name to all other such hot springs, and the spectacular waterfalls at **Gull-foss**. The **Reykjanes Peninsula**, home to the country's only international airport at Keflavík and therefore the first sight most travellers get of Iceland, is renowned for its teeming birdlife and its whales, which are frequently spotted off the peninsula's western tip.

Outside the relatively densely populated **southwestern** corner, the wilder side of Iceland begins – open spaces of vivid green edged by unspoilt coastlines of red and black sands all set against a backdrop of brooding hills and mountains. The main draw of the **West Coast** is the towns of **Borgarnes** and **Reykholt** and the surrounding countryside, where there's barely a feature that's unassociated with the **sagas**, such as **Keldur**, a farm where dramatic scenes from *Njal's Saga* were played out.

Away from the Ringroad, the **Snæfellsnes Peninsula** with its dramatic views of the glacier at its tip is one of the country's most accessible hiking destinations. Arguably Iceland's most dramatic scenery is found in the far northwest of the country, the **West Fjords**, where tiny fishing villages nestle at the foot of table-top mountains or are tucked away in the neck of narrow fjords which offer protection from the ferocious Arctic storms that batter this exposed part of the country. **Ísafjörður** is the only settlement

of any size in the region and makes a good base from which to strike out on foot into the wilderness of the **Hornstrandir Peninsula**. Beautifully located at the head of **Eyjafjörður** on the north coast, **Akureyri** is rightfully known as the capital of the north and functions as Iceland's second city. With a string of bars and restaurants it can make a refreshing change from the small villages elsewhere on the north coast. From here it's easy to reach the island of **Grímsey**, the only part of Icelandic territory actually within the **Arctic Circle**, and nearby **Siglufjörður**, for an insight into the twentieth-century herring boom that once made this tiny village the country's economic powerhouse.

The country's biggest tourist attraction outside the capital is **Lake Mývatn**, an hour to the east of Akureyri. The lake is a favourite nesting place for many species of duck and other waterfowl and is surrounded by an electrifying proliferation of volcanic activity, including long-dormant cinder cones and the still-steaming lava fields at **Krafla**, which last burst forth in the 1980s. North of Mývatn, the small town of **Húsavík** is one

of the best places in the country to organize summer whale-watching cruises, while just inland to the east, the wilds of **Jökulsárgljúfur National Park** offer superlative hiking along deep river gorges to the spectacular **Dettifoss**, Europe's most powerful waterfall. Across on the east coast, the **Eastfjords** centre on **Egilsstaðir** and the port of **Seyðis-fjörður**, where Iceland's only international ferry docks, and offer further walking opportunities – both coastal and around the fjords, and inland to the volcanic spire of **Snæfell** – in a part of the country which regularly receives the driest and warmest weather. The small town of **Höfn** in the southeast corner is a good base from which to visit Europe's biggest glacier, the mighty Vatnajökull, either on a skidoo trip or on foot through **Skaftafell National Park**. Further to the west the nearby glacial lagoon, **Jökulsárlón**, offers the surreal chance to cruise alongside floating icebergs which were once part of the glacier itself. Iceland's most rewarding long-distance hiking route is also found in this corner of the country – the **Þórsmörk** trail is one of the world's most exhilarating walking paths.

The **south coast** is marked by vast stretches of black, volcanic coastal

sands punctuated by tiny villages that unfortunately are prone to some of the country's foulest weather – the town of **Vík** is Iceland's wettest but boasts teeming seabird colonies. Just off the south coast, and easily reached by ferry from Þorlákshöfn, the **Vestmannaeyjar** (**Westman Islands**) sport the world's largest puffin colonies and were propelled into the world headlines during the 1960s and 1970s by a series of volcanic eruptions that created a new island, **Surtsey**, and also threatened to bury the town of **Heimaey** under lava and ash.

Sexual equality in Iceland

Regardless of the tongue-twisting name, Vigdís Finnbogadóttir was the person who put Iceland on the map when she became the world's first female president in 1980, high-profile proof of Iceland's approach to **sexual equality**. However, treating women as equals was nothing new in Iceland. Ever since Viking times, when every pair of working hands was required to farm, fish and simply exist in such a harsh climate, the nation's small population base has catapulted women into positions that for centuries were seen solely as a man's preserve in many other countries . Today, things are no different; both women and men often work long hours, fulfilling several roles, to keep the Icelandic economy ticking over. Generous childcare facilities provided by the Icelandic welfare state have also enabled women to re-enter the labour market shortly after having children and work their way up the career ladder, often to the very top. Even the Icelandic **language** reflects the equal nature of society; there's often no specifically male or female word for a profession – just one term applied to both women and men.

Iceland's barren **Interior** is best tackled as part of a guided tour – it's much easier to let experienced drivers of all-terrain buses pick their way across lavafields and cross unbridged rivers than to try it yourself. Parts of the Interior's fringes are also feasibly explored on foot, however, and even by bus it's perfectly possible to break your journey anywhere and camp – you'll be sharing the stunning scenery with only the ghosts of the early settlers who perished in its bleak, grey-sanded lava deserts.

When to go

Though milder than you might think, Icelandic **weather** is notoriously unpredictable. In **summer** there's a fair chance of bright and sunny days and temperatures can reach 17°C but these are interspersed with wet and misty spells when the temperature can plummet to a chilly 10°C. Generally speaking, if it's wet and windy in the southwest it'll be sunny and warm in the northeast, which receives more than its fair

share of sunshine in the summer months, much to the dismay of city slickers at the other end of the country. Most budget accommodation is only open from late May to early September, and it's at these times, too, that buses run their fullest schedules. Many bus routes through the Interior don't start until late June or early July when the snow finally melts. Although Iceland lies south of the Arctic Circle and therefore doesn't experience a true **Midnight Sun**, nights are light from mid-May to early August across the country. In the north the sun never fully sets during June. Between September and January the Aurora Borealis or **Northern Lights** can often be seen. They appear as an eerie, oscillating curtain of green, blue or pale orange light in the night sky.

Winter temperatures fluctuate at 7–8°C either side of freezing point and heavy snowfall and avalanches block many of the roads. There's little chance of accommodation other than in the large hotels in Reykjavík and the other main towns, and hiking and camping are out of the question. However, a stay in the capital at this time means a lack of crowds and at Christmas its streets are bathed in the glow of candles burning behind every window. Bear in mind though that daylight in midwinter is limited to a few hours – in Reykjavík, sunrise isn't until almost 11am in December; the sun is already sinking slowly back towards the horizon after 1pm; and by 3.30pm, it'll be dark again. Further north in Ísafjörður, reckon on around one and a half hours' less daylight than in Reykjavík.

Reykjavík temperatures

	Jan	Feb	Mar	Apr	May	Jun	Jul	Aug	Sep	Oct	Nov	Dec
Average daily temperatures (°C)												
Maximum temp	2	3	4	6	10	12	14	14	11	7	4	2
Minimum temp	-2	-2	-1	1	4	7	9	8	6	3	0	-2
Rainfall (mm)												
Rainfall	89	64	62	56	42	42	50	56	67	94	78	79

things not to miss

It's not possible to see everything that Iceland has to offer in one trip – and we don't suggest you try. What follows is a selective taste of the country's highlights: outstanding buildings, natural wonders, historic sites and abundant wildlife. They're arranged in five colour-coded categories, which you can browse through to find the very best things to see and experience. All highlights have a page reference to take you straight into the guide, where you can find out more.

01 The Blue Lagoon Page **98** • A dip in the sublime waters of the Blue Lagoon is a quintessentially Icelandic experience.

02 Geysir Page **111** • See the original geyser at Geysir, after which all other such features are named.

03 The sagas Page **68** • Reykjavík's Culture House boasts some of Europe's oldest and finest medieval manuscripts.

04 Akureyri Page **241** • The best place outside Reykjavík to enjoy a spot of urban sophistication.

05 **Lake Mývatn** Page **265** • Curious geological features and rich birdlife come together to make Lake Mývatn one of Iceland's biggest draws.

06 **Independence Day** Page **208** • The birthplace of Iceland's independence leader, Jón Sigurðsson, Hrafnseyri is undoubtedly the best place to be for national day events.

07 **Hallgrímskirkja** Page **71** • Hallgrímskirkja is undoubtedly Reykjavík's best known landmark and offers unsurpassed views of the world's most northerly capital from its tower.

08 **Flatey** Page **179** • This island retreat is renowned for its beautifully restored houses and teeming birdlife.

09 **Puffins**
Page **141** •
Found in vast
numbers during
the long summer
months, this
comical bird is
always a delight
to spot.

10 **Sprengisandur** Page **330** • A trip into the desolate, uninhabited Interior is a humbling experience.

11 **Iceland's birds** Pages **352–354** • Iceland has around 300 bird species, and while it's unlikely that you'll be able to spot the lot, you'll probably see some of the following at the very least.

Red Shank

Gyrfalcon

Fulmar

Golden plover

Guillemot

Raven

Puffin

Whooper swan

Pink footed goose

Kittiwake

Ptarmigan

Snipe

Arctic tern

Red necked Phalarope

Gannet

12 Þingvellir Page **107** • Human history and geological activity meet at Þingvellir, site of both Iceland's ancient parliament and the rift between the European and North American plates that form the earth's crust.

13 Phallological Museum Page **71** • A distinctly Icelandic take on how to present a wildlife museum – an eye-opening exhibition of penises, big and small, from every kind of the country's mammals.

14 Grettislaug Page **101** • Don't leave Iceland without taking a dip in a geothermally heated hot pool.

xxi

15 Landmannalaugar Page **122** • The Interior's best known feature, Landmannalaugar offers terrific hiking and a chance to bathe in naturally heated waters.

16 Askja Page **333** • The Askja caldera in the Interior, containing a geothermal lake, Víti, is perfect for a quick dip.

Contents

Using this
Rough Guide

We've tried to make this Rough Guide a good read and easy to use. The book is divided into six main sections, and you should be able to find whatever you want in one of them.

Colour section

The front colour section offers a quick tour of Iceland. The **introduction** aims to give you a feel for the place, with suggestions on where to go. We also tell you what the weather is like and include a basic country fact file. Next, our authors round up their favourite aspects of Iceland in the **things not to miss** section – whether it's great food, amazing sights or unmissable wildlife. Right after this comes a full **contents** list.

Basics

The Basics section covers all the **pre-departure** nitty-gritty to help you plan your trip. This is where to find out which airlines fly to your destination, what paperwork you'll need, what to do about money and insurance, about Internet access, food, security, public transport, car rental – in fact just about every piece of **general practical information** you might need.

Guide

This is the heart of the Rough Guide, divided into user-friendly chapters, each of which covers a specific region. Every chapter starts with a list of **highlights** and an **introduction** that helps you to decide where to go, depending on your time and budget. Likewise, introductions to the various towns and smaller regions within each chapter should help you plan your

itinerary. We start most town accounts with information on arrival and accommodation, followed by a tour of the sights, and finally reviews of places to eat and drink, and details of nightlife. Longer accounts also have a directory of practical listings. Each chapter concludes with **public transport** details for that region.

Contexts

Read Contexts to get a deeper understanding of what makes Iceland tick. We include a brief **history**, articles about geology and wildlife, and a detailed further reading section that reviews dozens of **books** relating to the country.

Language

The **language** section gives useful guidance for getting by in Icelandic and pulls together all the vocabulary you might need on your trip, including a comprehensive menu reader. Here you'll also find a glossary of words and terms peculiar to the country.

small print + Index

Apart from a **full index**, which includes maps as well as places, this section covers publishing information, credits and acknowledgements, and also has our contact details in case you want to send in updates and corrections to the book – or suggestions as to how we might improve it.

Map and chapter list

○ Colour section

● Contents

Ⓑ Basics

❶ Reykjavík

❷ Southwestern Iceland

❸ The west coast

❹ The West Fjords

❺ Northwest Iceland

❻ Mývatn and the northeast

❼ The Eastfjords and the southeast

❽ The Interior

Ⓒ Contexts

Ⓛ Language

Ⓘ Index

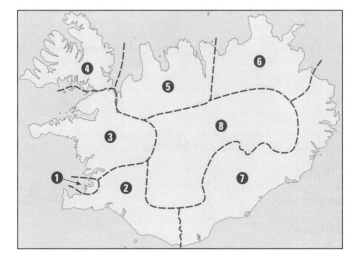

Contents

Colour section i–xxiv

Colour map of the country ....ii–iii
Introduction iv
Where to go viii

When to go xii
Things not to miss ....xiv–xxiv

Basics 7–45

Getting there 9
Visas and red tape 16
Insurance 17
Travellers with disabilities 18
Costs, money and banks 20
Health 21
Information and maps 22
Getting around 24
Accommodation 31

Food and drink 34
Post, phones the and Internet 37
The media 38
Opening hours, holidays
    and festivals 39
Sports and outdoor activities 40
Gay and lesbian travellers 43
Police, crime and sexual harassment 44
Directory 45

Guide 47–334

❶ **Reykjavík**............................49–92
    Arrival and information...................53
    City transport 54
    Accommodation 58
    Central Reykjavík 63
    Laugavegur and around 68
    Laugardalur and around 76
    Eating and drinking 77
    Nightlife and entertainment 80
    Activities 83

    Listings 86
    Around Reykjavík: Hafnarfjörður
        and the islands 87

❷ **Southwestern Iceland**
   93–148
    The Blue Lagoon and Keflavík 97
    From Hafnir to Krísuvík 100
    Þingvellir and around 104
    Skálholt, Geysir and Gullfoss 110

Hverageði 114
Selfoss and around 116
Þjórsárdalur, Hekla and
    Landmannalaugar 119
Njal's Saga country 125
Skógar and Þórsmörk 131
From Mýrdalsjökull to Vík 136
Vestmannaeyjar: Heimaey
    and Surtsey 140
Hverageði and around 80
Selfoss and around 82

❸ **The west coast** 149–188
Akranes and around 154
Borgarnes and around 158
Reykholt and around 162
The Snæfellsnes Peninsula 173

❹ **The West Fjords**...........189–221
Ísafjörður 193
Around Ísafjörður 196
Hornstrandir 201
From Ísafjörður to the
    southwestern peninsula 205
The southwestern peninsula 210
The south coast: Bjarkalundur
    and Reykhólar.............................215
Hólmavík and the Strandir coast....217

❺ **Northwest Iceland** 223–259
From Brú to Akureyri 228

Akureyri 241
Western Eyjafjörður 254
Eyjafjarðardalur valley 255
Grímsey 25

❻ **Mývatn and the northeast**
   261–289
Reykjahlíð and the lake 268
Bjarnarflag, Krafla, Leirhnjúkur
    and around 274
Húsavík and around......................277
Jökulsárgljúfur National Park 281
The northeast coast......................284

❼ **The Eastfjords and the**
    southeast 291–324
Egilsstaðir and around 295
The Eastfjords 303
Lón and Höfn 312
Skálafellsjokull and Skaftafell
    National Park 315
Across Skeiðarársandur to
    Kirkjubæjarklaustur 320

❽ **The Interior** 325–334
Across Sprengisandur:
    the F26 330
Across Kjölur: the F35 331
Herðubreið and Askja: the F88 332
Routes to Kverkfjöll 334

Contexts

335–358

Some history 337
Landscape and geology 347

Wildlife and the environment 351
Books and sagas 355

Language

359–367

small print and Index

389–398

Basics

Basics

Getting there 9

Visas and red tape 16

Insurance...17

Travellers with disabilities 18

Costs, money and banks...20

Health...21

Information and maps...22

Getting around 24

Accommodation..31

Food and drink...34

Post, phones and the Internet 37

The media 38

Opening hours, holidays and festivals...........................39

Sports and outdoor activities.......................................40

Gay and lesbian travellers..43

Police, crime and sexual harassment...........................44

Directory...45

Getting there

Given the long distances involved in reaching Iceland, flying is by far the quickest and cheapest option. Iceland's newly revamped and extended international airport, Keflavík, is where all planes from the US and most from the rest of Europe land. Between May and September it's also possible to reach Iceland by sea onboard the new Faroese superferry *Norröna*, which performs a once-weekly circuit of the North Atlantic calling at Lerwick in Shetland for UK connections.

Since there are neither direct air nor ferry links between **Ireland** and Iceland, all routes from Belfast and Dublin to Reykjavík lead first to London or Glasgow. Flights from **Australia** and **New Zealand** also go via London. There are direct flights from the **US** but travellers coming from **Canada** will need to go via the US.

Airfares always depend on the **season**, with the highest being around June to August, when the weather is best; fares drop during the "shoulder" seasons – September to November and April to June – and you'll get the best prices during the low season, November to March (excluding Christmas and New Year when prices are hiked up and seats are at a premium).

You can often cut costs by going through a **specialist flight agent** – either a consolidator, who buys up blocks of tickets from the airlines and sells them at a discount, or a **discount agent**, who in addition to dealing with discounted flights may also offer special student and youth fares and a range of other travel-related services such as travel insurance, rail passes, car rentals, tours and the like.

If Iceland is only one stop on a longer journey, you might want to consider buying a **Round-the-World** (RTW) ticket. Some travel agents can sell you an "off-the-shelf" RTW ticket that will have you touching down in about half a dozen cities; others will have to assemble one for you, which can be tailored to your needs but is apt to be more expensive.

Booking flights online

Many discount travel websites offer you the opportunity to book flight tickets and holiday packages **online**, cutting out the costs of agents and middlemen; these are worth going for, as long as you don't mind the inflexibility of non-refundable, non-changeable deals. There are some bargains to be had on auction sites too, if you're prepared to bid keenly. Almost all airlines have their own websites, offering flight tickets that can sometimes be just as cheap, and are often more flexible.

Online booking agents and general travel sites

Ⓦ **www.cheapflights.co.uk** (in UK & Ireland), Ⓦ **www.cheapflights.com** (in US), Ⓦ **www.cheapflights.ca** (in Canada), Ⓦ **www.cheapflights.com.au** (in Australia). Flight deals, travel agents, plus links to other travel sites.

Ⓦ **www.cheaptickets.com** Discount flight specialists (US only). Also at ☎1-888/922-8849.

Ⓦ **www.ebookers.com** Efficient, easy to use flight finder, with competitive fares.

Ⓦ **www.etn.nl/discount.htm** A hub of consolidator and discount agent links, maintained by the nonprofit European Travel Network.

Ⓦ **www.expedia.co.uk** (in UK), Ⓦ **www.expedia.com** (in US), Ⓦ **www.expedia.ca** (in Canada). Discount airfares, all-airline search engine and daily deals.

Ⓦ **www.flyaow.com** Online air travel info and reservations.

Ⓦ **www.gaytravel.com** US gay travel agent, offering accommodation, cruises, tours and more. Also at ☎1-800/GAY-TRAVEL.

Ⓦ **www.geocities.com/thavery2000** An extensive list of airline websites and US toll-free numbers.

Ⓦ **www.kelkoo.co.uk** Useful UK-only price-comparison site, checking several sources of

low-cost flights (and other goods & services) according to specific criteria.
Ⓦ www.lastminute.com (in UK),
Ⓦ www.lastminute.com.au (in Australia),
Ⓦ www.lastminute.co.nz (in New Zealand). Good last-minute holiday package and flight-only deals.
Ⓦ www.opodo.co.uk Popular and reliable source of low UK airfares. Owned by, and run in conjunction with, nine major European airlines.
Ⓦ www.priceline.co.uk (in UK),
Ⓦ www.priceline.com (in US). Name-your-own-price website that has deals at around forty percent off standard fares.
Ⓦ www.skyauction.com Bookings from the US only. Auctions tickets and travel packages to destinations worldwide.
Ⓦ www.travelocity.co.uk (in UK),
Ⓦ www.travelocity.com (in US),
Ⓦ www.travelocity.ca (in Canada),
Ⓦ www.travelshop.com.au Australian site offering discounted flights, packages, insurance, and online bookings. Also on ☎ 1800/108 108.
Ⓦ travel.yahoo.com Incorporates some Rough Guides material in its coverage of destination countries and cities across the world, with information about places to eat and sleep.
Ⓦ www.zuji.com.au (in Australia). Destination guides, good fares and deals for car rental, accommodation and lodging.

From Britain

Iceland Express fly daily from London Stansted to Keflavík (2hr 50 min) all year round, with lowest return fares at any season starting at £118. They planning to increase the flight frequency to twice daily from April 2004.

Icelandair operate from both London Heathrow and Glasgow to Keflavík. From April to September, the Heathrow flights (3hr) operate twice daily; from October to March, the frequency is reduced to one daily on Monday and Saturday, but remains at two daily for the rest of the week. From Glasgow (2hr), they fly four times a week, on Sunday, Tuesday, Thursday and Friday. Summer (April–Sept) return fares from London range from £150 to £280; outside summer peak season (June–Aug) it's worth checking with Icelandair directly, or visiting its Web site, for any **special offers** – deals can see prices fall to just £134 including tax. Cheapest flights from Glasgow all year round cost around £150.

One of the best ways to find **discounted flights** to Iceland is to look on the Internet (see pp.9–10); other options include the classified sections of the Sunday newspapers. If you live in London, *Time Out* magazine and the *Evening Standard* occasionally throw up good offers. It's always worth calling one of the **discount flight agents** (see below), who sell slightly reduced Icelandair flights as part of package deals, such as STA Travel for youth and student reductions, although such discounts with Icelandair only amount to £30 or so.

Airlines

Icelandair ☎ 020/7874 1000,
Ⓦ www.icelandair.co.uk.
Iceland Express ☎ 0870/8500 737,
Ⓦ www.icelandexpress.com.

Agents and tour operators

Arctic Experience 29 Nork Way, Banstead, Surrey SM7 1PB ☎ 01737/214214, Ⓦ www.arctic-experience.co.uk. Well-established wildlife holiday specialist, with groups led by naturalists to Iceland, plus city breaks, fly/drive holidays and independent travel.
Bridge the World 47 Chalk Farm Rd, London NW1 8AN ☎ 020/7911 0900,
Ⓦ www.bridgetheworld.com. Good deals aimed at the backpacker market.
Explore Worldwide 1 Frederick St, Aldershot, Hants, GU11 1LQ ☎ 01252/760 000,
Ⓦ www.explore.co.uk; brochure requests ☎ 01252/760 100. Small-group tours, treks and expeditions and safaris on all continents, with few supplements for single travellers; the emphasis is on small local hotels.
Flynow.com 214 Edgware Rd, London, W2 1DH ☎ 0870 444 9911, Ⓦ www.flynow.com; 1 Brunswick Court, Bridge St, Leeds LS2 7QU ☎ 0870 444 9922; 16 Reform St, Dundee DD1 1RG ☎ 0870 444 9933. Large range of discounted tickets.
Flight Centre 143 Earls Court Rd, London SW5 9RH; branches nationwide ☎ 0870/499 0040,
Ⓦ www.flightcentre.co.uk. UK arm of large Australian discount flight specialists.
North South Travel Moulsham Mill Centre, Parkway, Chelmsford, Essex CM2 7PX ☎ & ℻ 01245/608 291, Ⓦ www.northsouthtravel.co.uk. Friendly, competitive travel agency, offering discounted fares worldwide – profits are used to support projects in the developing world, especially the promotion of sustainable tourism.

Regent Holidays 31 High Street, Shanklin, Isle of Wight PO37 6JW ☎01983/86 4212. Good package operator specialising in Iceland and Greenland.
STA Travel ☎0870/1 600 599, ⓦwww.statravel.co.uk; 86 Old Brompton Rd, London SW7 3LQ; 117 Euston Rd, London NW1 2SX; 85 Shaftesbury Ave, London W1 5DX; 38 Store St, London WC1E 7BZ; 11 Goodge St, London W1P; plus branches; 222 Corporation Street, Birmingham B4 6QB ☎0121/236 6791;38 North St, Brighton ☎01273/728 282; 43 Queens Rd, Bristol BS8 1QQ ☎08701/676 777; 38 Sidney St, Cambridge CB2 3HX ☎01223/366 966; 75 Deansgate, Manchester M3 2BW ☎0161/839 3253; 88 Vicar Lane, Leeds LS1 7JH ☎08701/686 878; 78 Bold Street, Liverpool L1 4HR ☎0151/707 1123; 9 St Mary's Place, Newcastle-upon-Tyne NE1 7PG ☎0191/233 2111; 36 George St, Oxford OX1 2BJ ☎018701/636 373; 27 Forrest Road, Edinburgh ☎0131/226 7747; 184 Byres Rd, Glasgow G12 8SN ☎0141/338 6000; 30 Upper Kirkgate, Aberdeen ☎01224/658222. Specialists in low-cost flights and tours for students and under-26s, though other customers welcome.
Trailfinders 1 Threadneedle Street, London EC2R 8JX ☎020/7628 7628, ⓦwww.trailfinders.co.uk; 215 Kensington High St, London W6 6BD ☎020/7937 1234; 58 Deansgate, Manchester M3 2FF ☎0161/839 6969; 7–9 Ridley Place, Newcastle-Upon-Tyne NE1 8JQ (☎0191/261 2345; 254–284 Sauchiehall St, Glasgow G2 3EH ☎0141/353 2224; 22–24 The Priory Queensway, Birmingham B4 6BS ☎0121/236 1234; 48 Corn St, Bristol BS1 1HQ ☎0117/929 9000; 105–106 St Aldates, Oxford OX1 1BU ☎01865/261000; 22 Sidney St, Cambridge CB2 3HG 01223/461600. One of the best-informed and most efficient agents for independent travellers.

By ferry

Although it's possible to travel by sea to Iceland, the journey is recommended only to those with a cast-iron stomach, since the frequent gales, storms and unsettling swell of the North Atlantic can well and truly quash romantic images of riding the waves to your destination. However, the luxurious new ferry *Norröna*, which came into service in 2002, has made things more comfortable with en-suite cabins, a swimming pool, a shopping arcade and even a fitness centre. It also offers an opportunity to break your journey and take in the stunning beauty of the Faroe Islands.

The Faroese shipping company **Smyril Line** operate a once-weekly car and passenger **ferry** between early May and early September from Lerwick, in Shetland, to Seyðisfjörður, in eastern Iceland, departing on Wednesday at 2am and arriving on Thursday at 8am. To reach Lerwick from the rest of the UK, you can take the nightly **NorthLink Ferries** service from Aberdeen to Lerwick, departing at 7pm on Mondays, Wednesdays and Fridays and at 5pm on other days, arriving in Lerwick at 7am the next day. Though NorthLink's ships are also new and well-equipped, travelling by this route can be a real endurance test depending on where you're coming from: from London, for example, the entire journey takes three and a half days.

High season is defined as the months of July and August. During this time, one-way **fares** from Aberdeen to Lerwick are £29.50 for a single couchette (£19.25 in low season) and £26 (£17) per person to share a four berth cabin; return tickets cost double these prices, and taking a **car** on this route costs an extra £105 (£78.50). For an onward ticket with Smyril Line from Lerwick to Iceland, costs are £116 in high season for a single couchette (£84 in low season) and £148 per person for an inside four-berth cabin (£108), though it frequently doesn't work out much more expensive to take your car than to travel as a foot passenger. Once again, returns cost double.

Ferry companies

Smyril Line ☎01595/690 845, ⓦwww .smyril-line.com/uk.
NorthLink Ferries ☎0845/6000 449, ⓦwww.northlinkferries.co.uk.

Package tours

An all-inclusive **package tour** can sometimes turn out to be the cheapest way of doing things, and may be a much easier way of reaching remote areas of Iceland, particularly in winter. The specialist operators listed opposite provide deals ranging from a visit to Reykjavík and the Golden Circle attractions of Geysir and Gullfoss to all-singing, all-dancing adventure holidays involving snowmobiling across Vatnajökull and whale watching in Húsavík.

City breaks invariably work out less costly than arranging the same trip independently: prices include return travel, transfer from Keflavík to your hotel, hotel accommodation and often a city sightseeing tour of Reykjavík. Out of season, prices can be as low as £299 per person for a weekend – contact Icelandair, the main operator of city breaks, for the latest details on dates and prices.

From Ireland

By **plane**, it's most straightforward to buy a return ticket to London Heathrow or London Stansted (see box for operators) and then connect on to an Icelandair or Iceland Express flight to Iceland (see p.10). If you wish to connect onto the Smyril Line **ferry** (see p.11), you'll first have to make your way to Aberdeen for the ferry to Shetland, though of course this just extends an already lengthy trip.

When it comes to **packages**, you're best off contacting one of the British-based companies listed on pp.10–11.

Airlines

Aer Lingus ☎0818/365000,
Ⓦwww.aerlingus.com.
British Midland ☎+44/1332/854 854,
Ⓦwww.flybmi.com.
Ryanair (☎0818/30 30 50), Ⓦwww.ryanair.ie.

Agents and tour operators

STA Travel 92–94 Botanic Ave, Belfast BT7 1JR ☎02890/241469; Ⓦwww.statravelgroup.com; Trinity College Students' Union, House 6, Trinity College, Dublin 2 ☎01/677 7957.
Trailfinders first floor, Waterstones, 42–44 Fountain St, Belfast BT1 5EE ☎028/9027 1888; 4–5 Dawson St, Dublin 2 ☎01/677 7888, Ⓦwww.trailfinders.com.
USIT Now Call Centre ☎0818/200020; Ⓦwww.usitnow.ie. Fountre Centre, College St, Belfast BT1 6ET ☎028/9032 7111; 66 Oliver Plunkett St, Cork ☎021/427 0900; 19/21 Aston Quay, Dublin 2, ☎0818/200020; Unit 4, Tallaght Retail Centre, Tallaght, Dublin 24 ☎01/459 7800; 16 St Mary's St, Galway ☎091/565 177; Central Buildings,O'Connell St, Limerick ☎061/415 064; 36–37 Georges St, Waterford ☎051/872 601.

From the US

From North America, Iceland is served only

by **Icelandair** (☎1-800/223-5500, Ⓦwww .icelandair.com), Iceland's national carrier, who fly out of a handful of airports in the US but none in Canada. All flights go to Keflavík international airport.

From the US Icelandair flies five times weekly all year round to Keflavík from Baltimore (US$545/298; 5hr 40min), six times weekly from Boston (US$545/298; 5hr); four times weekly from Minneapolis (US$725/348; 6hr); and twice weekly from Orlando (US$725/348; 7hr 10min). From April to early November only, Icelandair flies six times weekly direct to Keflavík from New York JFK (US$545 high season, US$298 low season; 5hr 35min),

Discount travel companies and travel clubs

Airtech Suite 204, 588 Broadway, New York NY 10012 ☎212/219-7000, Ⓦwww.airtech.com. Standby seat broker; also deals in consolidator fares and courier flights.
Airtreks.com High Adventure Travel, 442 Post St, 4th Floor, San Francisco CA 94102 ☎1-877/AIRTREKS, Ⓦwww.airtreks.com. Round-the-world tickets; Web site features interactive database that lets you build and price your own RTW itinerary.
Educational Travel Center 438 N Frances St, Madison WI 53703 ☎1-800/747-5551 or 608/256-5551, Ⓦwww.edtrav.com. Student/youth and consolidator fares.
STA Travel incorporating Council Travel. 10 Downing St, New York NY 10014 ☎1-800/781-4040; Ⓦwww.sta-travel.com; plus branches in Los Angeles, San Francisco, Miami, Chicago, Seattle, Philadelphia, Washington DC, Boston. In Canada, branches at 200 Bloor St West, Toronto (☎1-888/427 5639) Ottawa, Calgary, Vancouver. Worldwide discount travel firm specializing in student/youth fares, student IDs, travel insurance, car rental etc.
Student Flights Suite A104, 5010 E Shea Blvd, Scottsdale AZ 85254 ☎1-800/255-8000 or ☎480/951-1177, Ⓦwww.isecard.com. Student/youth fares, student IDs and rail passes.
TFI Tours International 34 W 32nd St, New York NY 10001 ☎1-800/745-8000 or 212/736-1140; Ⓦwww.lowestairprice.com. Consolidator.
Travac Tours ☎1-800/TRAV-800; Ⓦwww.thetravelsite.com. Consolidator and charter broker with offices in New York and Orlando.
Travel Avenue Suite 1404, 10 S Riverside Plaza, Chicago IL 60606 ☎1-800/333-3335 or

Ⓣ 312/876-6866, Ⓦ www.travelavenue.com.
Discount travel agent.
Travel CUTS 187 College St, Toronto ON M5T 1P7
Ⓣ 1-888/FLY-CUTS in Canada or Ⓣ 866/246-9762
in US, Ⓦ www.travelcuts.com; plus other branches
throughout Canada. Student travel organization
specializing in student fares, IDs and other travel
services.
Travelers Advantage 100 Connecticut Av,
Norwalk, CT Ⓣ 1-877/259-2691,
Ⓦ www.travelersadvantage.com. Travel club;
annual membership fee.
UniTravel Ⓣ 1-800/325-2222;
Ⓦ www.unitravel.com. Consolidator.
Worldtek Travel 111 Water St, New Haven CT
06511 Ⓣ 1-800/243-1723 or Ⓣ 203/772-0472,
Ⓦ www.worldtek.com. Discount travel agency.

Round-the-world tickets

If you are travelling to Iceland as part of a
longer trip, consider buying a **Round-the-
World** (RTW) ticket, although as Icelandair
has a monopoly on flights to and from
Iceland, fares that allow stopovers for anything over three days are not discounted.
Since Iceland is not one of the more obvious
destinations for round-the-world travellers,
you would probably have to have a custom-
designed RTW ticket (rather than an "off-
the-shelf" RTW ticket) assembled for you by
a travel agent, which can be quite expensive. For example, New York–San Jose de
Costa⸱ Rica–Caracas–Paris–Glasgow–
Rejkavík–Boston–New York will set you back
$2879.

Packages and organized tours

There are a number of companies operating
organized tours of Iceland, ranging from de
luxe cruises to cycling holidays. Group tours
can be very expensive, and occasionally
don't include the airfare, so check what you
are getting. Reservations can often be made
through your local travel agent; most of the
tour operators listed below also have informative Web sites that allow you to book online.

Tour operators in North America

Adventure Center Ⓣ 1-800/228-8747, or
510/654-1879, Ⓦ www.adventurecenter.com.
Ten-day Land of Fire and Ice tour throughout Iceland,
starting at US$1620, land only.

Adventures Abroad Ⓣ 1-800/665-3398 or
360/775-9926, Ⓦ www.adventures-abroad.com.
Canadian-based company with a variety of packages,
specializing in small group tours. A twelve-day
Iceland tour starts around CAN$3857, land only.
Borton Overseas Ⓣ 1-800/843-0602,
Ⓦ www.bortonoverseas.com. Adventure-vacation
specialists, offering a variety of Iceland tours with
biking, hiking and rafting activities, plus farm and
cabin stays.
Brekke Tours Ⓣ 1-800/437-5302,
Ⓦ www.brekketours.com. Sightseeing and cultural
tours of Iceland, such as the three-day "Iceland
Stopover Adventure" starting at US$320. Call for a
brochure.
Icelandair Holidays Ⓣ 1-800/779-2899. Iceland
tour specialists, offering a variety of tours from basic
airfare plus hotel packages to fully escorted tours.
**International Gay and Lesbian Travel
Association** Ⓣ 1-800/448-8550,
Ⓦ www.iglta.org. Trade group with lists of gay-
owned or gay-friendly travel agents, accommodation
and other travel services.
Passage Tours Ⓣ 1-800-548-5960,
Ⓦ www.passagetours.com. Nine day Icelandic
Quartet tours , from $2,518 airfare included.
Optional five-day extensions to Greenland.
Scanam World Tours Ⓣ 1-800/545-2204,
Ⓦ www.scanamtours.com. Group and individual
tours and cruises, plus cheap weekend breaks. Four-
day tours of Iceland start at US$575.
Scantours Ⓣ 1-800/223-7226,
Ⓦ www.scantours.com. Numerous mini breaks and
longer tours of Iceland; their eight-day Iceland
Panorama starts from $2015, land only.
Vantage Deluxe World Travel Ⓣ 1-800/322-
6677, Ⓦ www.vantagetravel.com. De luxe group
tours and cruises. Their 13 day Iceland: Landscapes
and Legends tour starts from $2499, round trip
airfare from Boston included.

From Australia and New Zealand

There are no direct flights to Iceland from
Australia or New Zealand, and by far the
cheapest way of getting there from down
under is to find a discounted airfare to
London and arrange a flight to Reykjavík
from there (see p.10). As London is a major
destination for most international airlines
flying out of Australia and New Zealand, the
high level of competition ensures a wide
choice of routes worldwide, with flights via
Southeast Asia being the cheapest option.
Prices quoted below are for travel to

London; see p.10 for the add-on fare for London–Reykjavík flights.

There are a couple of companies offering all-inclusive **tours to Iceland** from Australia, though not New Zealand – we've listed them on pp.15–16.

From Australia

Depending on the route and transfer time, **flight times** between Australia and Britain are 22–28 hours via Asia, and 25–30 hours via North America. All **airfares** to London from Australian east-coast gateways such as Brisbane, Sydney, and Melbourne are equally priced, with the domestic carrier Ansett or Qantas providing a shuttle service to the point of international departure. If you're going via Asia, note that scheduled flights from Perth or Darwin are going to cost A$100–200 less than if departing from eastern gateways, though you'll also spend A$400 more if going via the USA from these places.

The cheapest deals are **via Asia** and may involve a night's free overnight stop in the carrier's home city, with accommodation, meals and transfers included in the ticket price – often a welcome break on long-haul flights. The cheapest fares are usually offered by Garuda, Japan Airlines and Royal Brunei, all costing between A$1650 and A$2400. Virgin Atlantic have teamed up with Malaysian Airlines to offer no-frills London flights via Kuala Lumpur for around A$1800–2300 in low season and around A$2600 in high season. Mid-price carriers flying to London include Korean Airlines, Malaysia Airlines, Thai Airways, Singapore Airlines, Cathay Pacific, Qantas, British Airways and Air New Zealand: prices range from A$2169 to A$2600. More expensive, but faster and entailing only a short refuelling stop or a quick change of planes, are Thai Airways, Singapore Airlines, Cathay Pacific, Qantas, British Airways and Air New Zealand, coming in at A$2200–2800.

Flights to London are pricier **via North America**, and all require a change of planes en route (via LA or San Francisco with United Airlines and Air New Zealand, and via Toronto or Vancouver with Canadian Airlines); expect to pay A$2300–3000.

From New Zealand

Fewer carriers fly from New Zealand than from Australia; however, **routes** are just as varied. Japan Airlines, Malaysia Airlines, Thai Airways and Korean Air all fly from Auckland, with a transfer or overnight stop in the carrier's home city, for between NZ$2200 and NZ$2500; Qantas and British Airways, who go **via Sydney**, **Bangkok** or **Singapore**, are more expensive at NZ$2500–$3100, but will get you there about six hours faster.

The most direct route (though still requiring a change of planes) is **via the Pacific and North America**. Air New Zealand and United Airlines fly via LA for between NZ$2200 and NZ$3000. British Airways, going via LA, and Canadian Airlines, via Vancouver, offer flights for about NZ$2700 to NZ$3200. **Via South America**, a normal return fare with Aerolineas Argentinas via Buenos Aires is quite expensive, with a year-round flat rate of NZ$3800; an RTW ticket is a better bet (see p.16). Another option is to fly to an Australian gateway city and then on to London (see p.10 & p.13); you'll get a greater choice of airlines and routes this way.

Airlines

Air Canada Australia ☏ 1300/655 747 or 02/9286 8900, New Zealand ☏ 09/379 3371, ⊛ wwww.aircanada.com.

Air New Zealand Australia ☏ 13/2476; New Zealand toll-free ☏ 0800/737 000, or ☏ 09/357 3000; ⊛ www.airnz.com. Six flights weekly to London Heathrow via Auckland and Los Angeles with connections from major Australian and New Zealand cities.

British Airways Australia ☏ 1300/767 177, New Zealand ☏ 0800/274 847 or 09/356 8690, ⊛ www.britishairways.com. Daily flights to London Heathrow from Sydney or Melbourne, via Singapore or Bangkok, some operated by codeshare partner Qantas.

Cathay Pacific Australia ☏ 13 17 47, ⊛ www.cathaypacific.com/au, New Zealand ☏ 09/379 0861 or 0508/800 454, ⊛ www.cathaypacific.com/nz. Daily flights to London Heathrow from Auckland, Sydney and Melbourne; several weekly from Brisbane, Perth, Cairns and twice weekly from Adelaide; all with a transfer in Hong Kong.

Garuda Indonesia Australia ☏ 02/9334 9970,

New Zealand ☏ 09/366 1862, 🖥 www.garuda-indonesia.com. Several flights weekly from Melbourne and Sydney in Australia and Auckland in New Zealand to London Gatwick, mostly routing via Denpasar and Jakarta and either Frankfurt or Amsterdam. Auckland flights route via Denpasar and Kuala Lumpur.

Icelandair The Australian agent is Nordic Travel (see p.16) and Bentours (see below) can also issue tickets for London–Reykjavík fares; there is no New Zealand agent.

Japan Airlines Australia ☏ 02/9272 1111, New Zealand ☏ 09/379 9906, 🖥 www.au.jal.com. Daily flights to London Heathrow from Brisbane and Sydney, plus several flights a week from Cairns and Auckland, all with either a transfer or overnight stop in Tokyo or Osaka. Code-share with Air New Zealand and Qantas.

Korean Air Australia ☏ 02/9262 6000, New Zealand ☏ 09/914 2000, 🖥 www.koreanair.com.aa. Several flights weekly to London Heathrow from Sydney and Auckland, plus once a week from Brisbane with either a transfer or overnight stop in Seoul.

Malaysia Airlines Australia ☏ 13 26 27, New Zealand ☏ 0800/777 747, 🖥 www.malaysiaairlines.com.my. Several flights weekly to London Heathrow from Sydney, Melbourne, Perth and Auckland, with either a transfer or overnight stop in Kuala Lumpur.

Qantas Australia ☏ 13 13 13, 🖥 www.qantas.com.au, New Zealand ☏ 0800/808 767, 🖥 www.qantas.co.nz. Daily flights to London Heathrow from major cities in Australia, either direct (with a short refuelling stop) or with a transfer in Sydney, Singapore or Bangkok; daily flights from major cities in New Zealand to London Heathrow via Sydney, and with a transfer in Singapore or Bangkok.

Royal Brunei Airlines Australia ☏ 07/3017 5000, 🖥 www.bruneiair.com. Four weekly flights to London Heathrow from Perth and three each from Brisbane and Auckland, plus two weekly from Darwin and Perth, all via Abu Dhabi or Dubai and with a transfer or overnight stop in Brunei.

Singapore Airlines Australia ☏ 13 10 11, New Zealand ☏ 0800/808 909, 🖥 www.singaporeair.com. Daily flights to London Heathrow from Brisbane, Sydney, Melbourne, Perth and Auckland, either direct or with a transfer in Singapore, and four times weekly from Adelaide.

Thai Airways Australia ☏ 1300/651 960, New Zealand ☏ 09/377 0268, 🖥 www.thaiair.com. Daily flights to London Heathrow from Auckland, Sydney and Melbourne, four times weekly from Perth and three times weekly from Brisbane, with either a transfer or overnight stop in Bangkok.

United Airlines Australia ☏ 13 17 77, 🖥 www.unitedairlines.com.au, New Zealand ☏ 09/379 3800 or 0800/508 648, 🖥 www.unitedairlines.co.nz. Daily flights to London Heathrow from Sydney, Melbourne and Auckland, with a transfer in LA or San Francisco.

Virgin Atlantic Airways Australia ☏ 02/9244 2747, New Zealand ☏ 09/308 3377, 🖥 www.virgin-atlantic.com. Daily flights to London Heathrow from Sydney, with a transfer or overnight stop in Kuala Lumpur. Code-share with Malaysia Airlines.

Discount travel agents

Anywhere Travel 345 Anzac Parade, Kingsford, Sydney ☏ 02/9663 0411, www.anywheretravel.com.au.

New Zealand Destinations Unlimited New Zealand ☏ 09/414 1685 🖥 www.holiday.co.nz.

Flight Centre Australia ☏ 13 31 33 or 02/9235 3522, 🖥 www.flightcentre.com.au. New Zealand ☏ 0800 243 544 or 09/358 4310, 🖥 www.flightcentre.co.nz. 350 Queen Street, Auckland ☏ 09/358 4310, toll-free ☏ 0200/354 448. Also has branches nationwide.

Holiday Shoppe New Zealand ☏ 0800/808 480, 🖥 www.holidayshoppe.co.nz.

Northern Gateway Australia ☏ 1800/174 800, 🖥 www.northerngateway.com.au.

STA Travel Australia ☏ 1300/733 035, 🖥 www.statravel.com.au. 260 Hoddle St, Abbotsford, Victoria; 855 George Street, Sydney; 240 Flinders Street, Melbourne; plus other offices in state capitals and major universities. New Zealand ☏ 0508/782 872, 🖥 www.statravel.co.nz. Level 8, 229 Queen St, Auckland; plus branches in major cities and university campuses.

Student Uni Travel Australia ☏ 02/9232 8444, 🖥 www.sut.com.au. New Zealand ☏ 09/379 4224, 🖥 www.sut.co.nz.

Trailfinders Australia ☏ 02/9247 7666, 🖥 www.trailfinders.com.au. 8 Spring Street, Sydney, NSW 2000 ☏ 02/9247 7666; 372 Lonsdale Street, Melbourne, VIC 3000 ☏ 03/9600 3022; 3 Hides Corner, Lake Street, Cairns, QLD 4870 ☏ 07/4041 1199; 91 Elizabeth Street, Brisbane, QLD 4000 ☏ 07/3229 0887; 840 Hay Street, Perth, WA 6000 ☏ 08/9226 1222.

Specialist tour operators

Bentours Level 7, 189 Kent Street, Sydney NSW 2000 ☏ 02/9241 1353, ☏ 9251 1574, www.bentours.com.au. Handles Icelandair ticket sales; also offers fly/drive and 7 day Iceland complete packages from $2500.

Nordic Travel 600 Military Road, Mosman, NSW 2088 ☎02/9968 1783. The regional Icelandair agent and representative for most major Icelandic tour agents, this long-established operator can book you onto pre-existing tours within Iceland or tailor special-interest packages – from driving, hiking or cycling around the highlights to snowbmobiling across Vatnajökull.

Round-the-World tickets

If you're planning to visit Iceland as part of a longer trip, then you'll find that a **Round-the-World** (RTW) airfare offers greater flexibility and is better value than a straight-forward return flight. However, as with standard returns from Australia and New Zealand, you'll have to add the airfare to Reykjavík from London or New York to the following prices.

As a guideline – prices are very volatile – a RTW ticket from Sydney or Auckland to Singapore or Bangkok, then on to London, New York, Los Angeles, Auckland and back to Sydney starts at around A$2500 /NZ$3000; a ticket from Sydney to Auckland, Santiago, Rio, London, Paris, Bangkok, Singapore and back to Sydney starts at A$2750/NZ$3400.

Visas and red tape

Citizens from the European Economic Area (comprising the EU, Switzerland and Liechtenstein), US, Canada, Australia and New Zealand need only a passport valid for at least three months after the planned date of arrival to enter Iceland for up to three months.

European Economic Area nationals, however, may stay longer than three months on condition that they secure work for a further period of three months minimum. Once in employment, there is no time limit on the length of stay in Iceland but **residence and work permits** are required, normally valid for five years, and available from the **Icelandic Statistical Bureau** (Hagstofa Íslands, Pjóðskrá, Skuggasund 3, Reykjavík; ☎560 9850). Non-EU nationals can only apply for residence permits before leaving home, and must be able to prove they can support themselves without working. For further information, contact the relevant embassy in your country of origin or the Icelandic **Ministry of Foreign Affairs** at www.mfa.is.

As regards **customs regulations**, all visitors to Iceland, irrespective of country of origin, can bring in the following: either one litre of spirits and one litre of wine, or one litre of spirits and six litres of beer, or one litre of wine and six litres of beer or two litres of wine. In addition to this, 200 cigarettes, or 250g of other tobacco products, are also permitted.

Icelandic embassies abroad

Australia and New Zealand Contact the Icelandic Embassy in China: Landmark Tower 1, 802, 8 North Dongsanhuan Road, Chaoyang District, 100004 Beijing ☎86/106590 7795.
Canada Constitution Square, 360 Albert Street, Suite 710, Ottawa, Ontario, K1R 7X7 ☎613 482 1944, ⊛www.iceland.org/ca. Consulate General, One Wellington Crescent,
Winnipeg, Manitoba
Canada R3M 3Z2, ☎204 284-1535, ⊛www .iceland.org/ca/win. Plus consulates in Edmonton, St John's, Halifax, Toronto, Montreal and Regina.
Republic of Ireland Contact the Icelandic Embassy in the UK.
UK 2A Hans St, London, SW1X 0JE ☎020/7259 3999, ⊛www.iceland.org/uk.

US 1156 15th Street NW Suite 1200 Washington DC 20005-1704 ☎202/265 6653, ⓦwww.iceland.org/us; Consulate General, 800 3rd Ave, 36th Floor, New York, NY ☎212-593-2700; plus consulates in Phoenix, Tallahassee,

Anchorage, San Francisco, Miami, Chicago, Atlanta, Louisville, New Orleans, Boston, Detroit, Minneapolis, Kansas City, New York, Harrisburg, Dallas, Houston, Norfolk and Seattle.

Insurance

A typical travel insurance policy usually provides cover for the loss of baggage, tickets and – up to a certain limit – cash or cheques, as well as cancellation or curtailment of your journey. Most of them exclude so-called dangerous sports unless an extra premium is paid: in Iceland this can mean whitewater rafting and trekking. Read the small print and benefits tables of prospective policies carefully; coverage can vary wildly for roughly similar premiums.

Many policies can be chopped and changed to exclude coverage you don't need – for example, sickness and accident benefits can often be excluded or included at will. If you do take medical coverage, ascertain whether benefits will be paid as treatment proceeds or only after return home, and whether there is a 24-hour medical emergency number. When securing baggage cover, make sure that the per-article limit – typically under £500 equivalent – will cover your most valuable possession. If you need to make a claim, you should keep receipts for medicines and medical treatment, and in the event you have anything stolen, you must obtain an official statement from the police. Bank and credit cards often have certain levels of medical or other insurance included and you may automatically get travel insurance if you use a major credit card to pay for your trip.

Travel agents and **tour operators** are likely to offer some sort of insurance when you book a package holiday, though according to UK law they can't make you buy their own (other than a £1 premium for

Rough Guide Travel Insurance

Rough Guides Ltd offers a low-cost travel insurance policy, especially customized for our statistically low-risk readers by a leading British broker, provided by the American International Group (AIG) and registered with the British regulatory body, GISC (the General Insurance Standards Council). There are five main Rough Guides insurance plans: **No Frills** for the bare minimum for secure travel; **Essential**, which provides decent all-round cover; **Premier** for comprehensive cover with a wide range of benefits; **Extended Stay** for cover lasting four months to a year; and **Annual Multi-Trip**, a cost-effective way of getting Premier cover if you travel more than once a year. Premier, Annual Multi-Trip and Extended Stay policies can be supplemented by a "Hazardous Pursuits Extension" if you plan to indulge in sports considered dangerous, such as scuba-diving or trekking. For a policy quote, call the **Rough Guides Insurance Line**: toll-free in the UK ☎0800/015 09 06 or ☎+44 1392 314 665 from elsewhere. Alternatively, get an **online quote** at ⓦwww.roughguides.com/insurance

"schedule airline failure"). If you have a good all-risks home insurance policy it may cover your possessions against loss or theft even when overseas. Many private medical schemes such as BUPA or PPP also offer coverage plans for abroad, including baggage loss, cancellation or curtailment and cash replacement as well as sickness or accident.

Americans and **Canadians** should also check that they're not already covered. Canadian provincial health plans usually provide partial cover for medical mishaps overseas. Holders of official student/teacher /youth cards are entitled to meagre accident coverage and hospital in-patient benefits. Students will often find that their student health coverage extends during the vacations and for one term beyond the date of last enrollment. Homeowners' or renters' insurance often covers theft or loss of documents, money and valuables while overseas, though conditions and maximum amounts vary from company to company.

Travellers with disabilities

Iceland is fairly well prepared for disabled travellers. Several hotels in Reykjavík and Akureyri have rooms specially designed for disabled guests, larger department stores are generally accessible to wheelchair users, while transport – including coastal ferries, airlines, and a few public tour buses – can make provisions for wheelchair users if notified in advance.

The best idea is to contact the service operators, either directly or through your travel agent; tourist information offices in Reykjavík (see p.54) also have copies of the Icelandic Hotels and Guesthouses brochure, which includes a list of hotels accessible to disabled visitors. The Accessible Reykjavík booklet produced by **Sjálfsbjörg**, Reykjavík's Disabled Association, is available for free from the main tourist office in Reykjavík.

For advice before you go, there are two US-oriented **Web sites** for disabled travellers, both of which have comprehensive links to other similar sites. Access Able Travel (www.access-able.com) has a bulletin board for passing on tips and accounts of accessible attractions, accommodation, guides and resources around the globe. Disability Travel (www.disabilitytravel.com) deals in arranging all aspects of travel for the mobility impaired and will at least be able to offer advice on Iceland. Though they are not geared specifically to visitors, ÖBÍ, the Organisation of Handicapped in Iceland (English-language homepage at www.obi.is/ensk/) also have a Web site with links to various organizations for disabled people in Iceland, who again will have information on available services.

There are also **organized tours and holidays** specifically for people with disabilities – the contacts in the box opposite will be able to put you in touch with specialists for trips to Iceland. It's important to know where you may expect help and where you must be self-reliant, especially regarding transport and accommodation. It's also vital to be honest with travel agencies, insurance companies, and travel companions, plus you should think about your limitations, making sure others know about them too. If you don't use a wheelchair all the time but your mobility is limited, remember that you are likely to need to cover greater distances while travelling – sometimes over rougher terrain and in different temperatures to those you are familiar with. If you use a **wheel-**

chair, have it serviced before you go and carry a repair kit.

People with pre-existing medical conditions are sometimes excluded from **travel-insurance policies**, so check the small print carefully. A **medical certificate** of your fitness to travel, provided by your doctor, is pretty well essential, as some insurance companies or transport operators may insist on it. Make sure that you have extra supplies of drugs, and a prescription including the generic names in case of an emergency. If there's an association representing people with your disability, contact them early in the planning process for advice.

Contacts for travellers with disabilities

In the UK and Ireland

Holiday Care 2nd floor, Imperial Building, Victoria Rd, Horley, Surrey RH6 7PZ ☎0845/124 9971, minicom ☎0845/124 9976, ⊛www.holidaycare .org.uk. Provides free lists of accessible accommodation abroad – European, American and long haul destinations – plus a list of accessible attractions in the UK. Information on financial help for holidays available.
Irish Wheelchair Association Blackheath Drive, Clontarf, Dublin 3 ☎01/818 6400, ⊛www.iwa.ie. Useful information provided about travelling abroad with a wheelchair.
Tripscope Alexandra House, Albany Rd, Brentford, Middlesex TW8 0NE ☎0845/7585 641, ⊛www.tripscope.org.uk. This registered charity provides a national telephone information service offering free advice on UK and international transport for those with a mobility problem.

In the US and Canada

Access-Able ⊛www.access-able.com. Online resource for travellers with disabilities.
Directions Unlimited 123 Green Lane, Bedford Hills, NY 10507 ☎1-800/533-5343 or 914/241-1700. Travel agency specializing in bookings for people with disabilities.
Mobility International USA 451 Broadway, Eugene, OR 97401 ☎541/343-1284, ⊛www.miusa.org. Information and referral services, access guides, tours and exchange programmes. Annual membership $35 (includes quarterly newsletter).
Society for the Advancement of Travelers with Handicaps (SATH) 347 5th Ave, New York, NY 10016 ☎212/447-7284, ⊛www.sath.org. Non-profit educational organization that has actively represented travelers with disabilities since 1976.
Wheels Up! ☎1-888/38-WHEELS, ⊛www.wheelsup.com. Provides discounted airfare, tour and cruise prices for disabled travelers, also publishes a free monthly newsletter and has a comprehensive website.

In Australia and New Zealand

ACROD (Australian Council for Rehabilitation of the Disabled) PO Box 60, Curtin ACT 2605; Suite 103, 1st floor, 1–5 Commercial Rd, Kings Grove 2208; ☎02/6282 4333, TTY ☎02/6282 4333, ⊛www.acrod.org.au. Provides lists of travel agencies and tour operators for people with disabilities.
Disabled Persons Assembly 4/173–175 Victoria St, Wellington, New Zealand ☎04/801 9100 (also TTY), ⊛www.dpa.org.nz. Resource centre with lists of travel agencies and tour operators for people with disabilities.

Costs, money and banks

Due to its small consumer base and dependency on imports, Iceland is an expensive country to visit, even compared to the rest of Europe and Scandinavia. There are ways to minimize costs, whether you're planning to stay in hotels and rent a car, or simply travel between campsites on public buses, but expect to pay substantially more than you're used to for all food, transport and accommodation.

Iceland's **currency** is the **króna** (krónur in the plural), abbreviated to either Isk, Ikr or kr. Notes come in 5000kr, 2000kr, 1000kr and 500kr denominations, and there are 100kr, 50kr, 10kr, 5kr, and 1kr coins, decorated with fish. At the time of writing the **exchange rate** was approximately 127kr to £1; 89kr to €1; 76kr to US$1; 57kr to CAN$1; 52kr to AU$1; and 45kr to NZ$1.

Basic costs

The best way to minimize costs in Iceland is to be as **self-sufficient** as possible, and bring in full camping equipment, some food and a sleeping bag for camping, or to use the cheapest unfurnished hostel-style beds (see p.31), and make use of the various **bus passes** on offer (see p.25). A **Hostelling International Card** (p.32) will also get you a few hundred krónur a night off official Youth Hostel rates. Bear in mind too that **seasons** affect costs: places to stay and car-rental agencies drop their prices between October and May, though at that time inexpensive summer-only accommodation will be shut, campsites will probably be under snow, and bus services are infrequent or suspended.

Taking all this into account, budget travellers can keep **daily costs** down by camping out every night – mixing campsites with free camping in the wilds – using a bus pass and cooking for themselves, keeping average daily costs for accommodation, travel and food down to around 3500kr (though cyclists can cut this in half) a day. Throw in a few nights in hostel-style accommodation and the occasional pizza and you're looking at 4500kr. Mid-range travel still means using a bus pass to get around, but, favouring hostels and eating out cheaply

most of the time, this will set you back about 6000kr a day. Staying only in guesthouses or hotels and eating in restaurants for every meal means that you're looking at daily expenses of anything upwards of 12,000kr.

If you need **car rental** at any stage, your best bet is to try and organise a package deal when you book your ticket to Iceland, which will almost certainly work out cheaper than the minimum 5500kr a day, plus fuel, that rental costs in Iceland – see p.26 for more about this. None of the above takes into account additional costs for entertainment such as tours, entry fees, drinking (an expensive pastime in Iceland – see p.35), or alternative transport such as flights and ferries, for which we've given prices in the guide.

If you do incur any serious expenses – or even just buy a souvenir woollen sweater – take advantage of the fact that visitors can get a partial Value-Added Tax, or **VAT refund** on purchases exceeding 4000kr, provided departure from Iceland is within 90 days of the purchase. The VAT itself totals 24.5 percent of the cost price, though the refund is only 15 percent. The goods (except woolens) must be sealed in a bag at the time of purchase, when you also fill out a form; this is handed over with all receipts at the currency-exchange booth upstairs by the duty-free shop at Keflavík airport (see p.53), where you'll receive your refund in cash; you can ask for this in any currency. If you leave by ferry from Seyðisfjörður (see p.11), get your form stamped at customs and then apply for a refund within three months to Global Refund, Kaplahraun 15 IS-220, Hafnarfjörður (☎555 2833, ☞555 2823, ⊛www.globalrefund.com).

Banks and exchange

Branches of Iceland's three **banks** – Íslandsbanki, Landsbanki Ísland and Búnaðarbanki – are found right around the country, including in many single-street villages, and most sport an **ATM**, often located in a weatherproof lobby that can be accessed outside opening hours. Normal **banking hours** are Monday to Friday 9.15am to 4pm, though a few branches in Reykjavík have longer hours.

All banks handle **foreign exchange**, with the Íslandsbanki charging no commission and the others a nominal fee per transaction. Outside banking hours, you could also try major hotels – rates, however, are poor and commissions high in both cases. Banks can also arrange **international money transfers**, though you should expect a service charge in the region of 2000kr and for the transfer to take at least a few days.

Travellers' cheques and Cards

Travellers' cheques, available in advance through banks and travel agents, are the safest way to carry your funds around, as they can be cashed in all Icelandic banks and many hotels, and can be replaced if lost or stolen – keep a list of the serial numbers separate from the cheques. Take US dollar, Euro, or UK sterling denomination cheques, as it's not possible to cash Australian or New Zealand dollar travellers' cheques in Iceland. Some stores and accommodation in Reykjavík also accept US dollar, Euro, or British notes, though elsewhere you'll have to exchange foreign currency into krónur first.

Credit cards are widely used in Iceland for just about everything. MasterCard and Visa are the major brands, valid not just for shopping but also for **cash advances** over the counter at all banks and a few of the larger post offices. Íslandsbanki also advance cash on Diners' Club, while the American Express agent is Úrval-Útsýn Travel Agency, at Lágmúli 4, Reykjavík. You should also check whether your credit card or home **ATM card** has Cirrus/Maestro/Electron connections, which will allow it to draw funds directly from your home account through Icelandic ATMs. The fee for this depends on your bank, but can work out as the cheapest way of all to access your money.

Health

Iceland is by and large a healthy country to be in – a small industrial output means that pollution levels are very low. Health care is also excellent and available in most communities, and while language is unlikely to be a problem, tourist offices can also recommend doctors and hospitals – all of whom will anyway be English speaking. No vaccinations are required for visitors to Iceland.

If you're spending much time out of doors, be aware that the weather and distance might cause difficulties if you need medical attention in a hurry, and it's wise to carry a first-aid kit. Two important items to include are a roll of elasticated sticking plaster (band aids) and crepe bandages – both vital for supporting and splinting sprained muscles or broken bones.

Most problems you'll encounter, however, are minor. Though you might not think the northern sun would be much trouble, it's still strong enough to cause sunburn and eyestrain – especially when reflected off ice or snow – so use **sunscreen** and **sun glasses**. Some sort of hand cream or **moisturiser** and **lip balm** are a good idea too, as the cold dry air, wind and dust can painfully crack exposed skin. **Eye drops** will also relieve irritation caused by dust. **Flies** are not the problem in Iceland that they can be in Scandinavia; Mývatn (see p.265) is the only place you'll encounter them in plague proportions, though very few bite.

About the most serious thing to worry about is **hypothermia**, wherein your core body temperature drops to a point that can be fatal. In Iceland, it's obviously most likely to occur if you get exhausted, wet and cold whilst out hiking or cycling; symptoms include a weak pulse, disorientation, numbness, slurred speech and exhaustion. If you suspect someone is suffering from hypothermia, seek shelter from the wind, rain, and snow, get the patient as dry as possible, and prevent further heat loss – aside from clothing, a foil "space blanket" available from camping stores will help. Sugary drinks can also help (alcohol definitely doesn't), but serious cases need immediate hospital treatment. The best advice is to avoid

hypothermia in the first place: while hiking, ensure you eat enough carbohydrates, drink plenty of water and wear sufficient warm and weatherproof clothing, including a woolen **hat** – most body heat is lost through the head – and gloves. During the colder parts of the year, **motorists** should always carry a blanket and warm gear too, in case they get stranded by snow.

Pharmacies and medical treatment

There's at least one pharmacy, or **apotek**, in every town in Iceland, as well stocked as any chemist you'll find at home. Most open during normal business hours, though some in Reykjavík and Akureyri stay open longer. **Doctors** are similarly distributed, though if you need **hospital treatment**, you'll need to get yourself to a major regional centre – Reykjavík also has several **health centres** with general practitioners on hand through the day.

Information and maps

For information before you go, the Icelandic Tourist Board maintains several promotion offices abroad, as do Icelandair and their agents, where you'll be able to pick up brochures of the highlights, plus information on tours, transport and accommodation. There's also heaps of information available about Iceland on the Internet – see p.24 for useful Web sites.

Once you're in the country, Reykjavík's **tourist information centre** (see p.54) has information and brochures for the whole country, with independent tourist information offices in almost every other town, often housed in the bus station. Wherever you are, your accommodation is another good source of local details; for instance, families may have lived on particular farms for generations, and have very thorough knowledge of the region.

Icelandic tourist board offices abroad

Australia and New Zealand There are no

Icelandic tourist or airline offices in either Australia or New Zealand; instead, contact Bentours or Nordic Tours (see the "Specialist operators" on pp.15–16).

Canada There are no Icelandic tourist or airline offices in Canada; contact the US office instead.

Ireland There are no Icelandic tourist or airline offices in Ireland; contact the UK office instead.

UK Icelandair, 172 Tottenham Court Road, 3rd Floor, London W1P 9LG ☎ 020/7338 4499 or 7874 1000, ⊛ www.goiceland.co.uk, ⊛ www.icelandair.co.uk.

US Iceland Tourist Board, 655 3rd Ave, 18th Floor, New York, NY 10017-5689 ☎ 212-885-9700, ⊛ www.icelandtouristboard.com.

Maps

A range of excellent **maps** of the country, costing between 800 and 1100kr, is available for all types of use – if you can't find what you want overseas, you'll be able to pick it up in Reykjavík and Akureyri, or sometimes from local tourist offices and fuel stations. In addition to the maps detailed below, Iceland's hiking clubs (see p.41) and National Parks put out a few maps of varying quality for popular nature reserves and national parks (available from park offices on-site).

For **general orientation**, try the widely available Íslandskort series published by Mál og menning bookshop in Reykjavík, which provides a single 1:600,000 sheet of the entire country, along with four separate 1:300,000 maps covering each quarter. Landforms, roads and road types are well defined, and there's a clear distinction made between farms and small settlements – so you can accurately gauge where the next shops are. The back of each sheet also has a thumbnail sketch of the region's main sights. In addition, they publish a range of **specialist** titles, including a bird-watchers' map with a species key and prime twitching sites indicated; their geological and tectonic maps of Iceland, plus a sheet of Surtsey, the world's newest island, seem to be currently unavailable.

Alternatively, there's Landmælingar Íslands, the Icelandic National Land Survey. Their most popular products are the 1:500,000 **road map**, also available as a booklet; and a series that splits the country into six sections, covered by three 1:250,000 sheets (there are maps on both sides). In both cases their contour detail is far superior to Íslandskort's, and the 1:250,000 set are suitable for most **hiking** demands. Landmælingar also publish excellent small-scale maps of Þingvellir, Hornstrandir, the Húsavík-Mývatn area, Mývatn, Skaftafell, Þórsmörk-Landmannalaugar (including Hekla) and Vestmannaeyjar.

Finally, Uppdráttur Íslands covers the entire country on 115 sheets using a very detailed 1:50,000 scale, obviously of more interest to hikers than general users. The major bookshops in Reykjavík should have the complete set; otherwise they're hard to find.

Specialist map and guide outlets

In the UK and Ireland

Stanfords 12–14 Long Acre, London WC2 ☎020/7836 1321, ⊛www.stanfords.co.uk. Also at 39 Spring Gardens, Manchester ☎0161/831 0250, and 29 Corn St, Bristol ☎0117/929 9966.
Blackwell's Map Centre 50 Broad St, Oxford ☎01865/793 550, ⊛www.maps.blackwell.co.uk. Branches in Bristol, Cambridge, Cardiff, Leeds, Liverpool, Newcastle, Reading & Sheffield.
The Map Shop 30a Belvoir St, Leicester ☎0116 /247 1400, ⊛www.mapshopleicester.co.uk.
National Map Centre 22–24 Caxton St, London SW1 ☎020/7222 2466, ⊛www.mapsnmc.co.uk.
National Map Centre Ireland 34 Aungier St, Dublin ☎01/476 0471, ⊛www.mapcentre.ie.
The Travel Bookshop 13–15 Blenheim Crescent, London W11 ☎020/7229 5260, ⊛www.thetravelbookshop.co.uk.
Traveller 55 Grey St, Newcastle-upon-Tyne ☎0191/261 5622, ⊛www.newtraveller.com.

In the US and Canada

110 North Latitude US ☎336/369-4171, ⊛www.110nlatitude.com.
Book Passage 51 Tamal Vista Blvd, Corte Madera, CA 94925 ☎1-800/999-7909, ⊛www.bookpassage.com.
Distant Lands 56 S Raymond Ave, Pasadena, CA 91105 ☎1-800/310-3220, ⊛www.distantlands.com.
Globe Corner Bookstore 28 Church St, Cambridge, MA 02138 ☎1-800/358-6013, ⊛www.globecorner.com.
Longitude Books 115 W 30th St #1206, New York, NY 10001 ☎1-800/342-2164, ⊛www.longitudebooks.com.
Map Town 400 5 Ave SW #100, Calgary, AB, T2P 0L6 ☎1-877/921-6277, ⊛www.maptown.com.
Travel Bug Bookstore 3065 W Broadway, Vancouver, BC, V6K 2G9 ☎604/737-1122, ⊛www.travelbugbooks.ca.
World of Maps 1235 Wellington St, Ottawa, ON, K1Y 3A3 ☎1-800/214-8524, ⊛www.worldofmaps.com.

In Australia and New Zealand

Map Centre ⊛www.mapcentre.co.nz.
Map Shop 6–10 Peel St, Adelaide ☎08/8231 2033, ⊛www.mapshop.net.au.

Map World 173 Gloucester St, Christchurch ☎ 0800/627 967, ⊛ www.mapworld.co.nz.
Map World 371 Pitt St, Sydney ☎ 02/9261 3601, ⊛ www.mapworld.net.au. Also at 900 Hay St, Perth ☎ 08/9322 5733.
Mapland 372 Little Bourke St, Melbourne ☎ 03/9670 4383, ⊛ www.mapland.com.au.
Speciality Maps 58 Albert Street, Auckland ☎ 09/307 2217.
Travel Bookshop Shop 3, 175 Liverpool Street, Sydney ☎ 02/9261 8200.
Worldwide Maps and Guides 187 George Street, Brisbane ☎ 07/3221 4330.

Iceland online

Iceland Review ⊛ www.icelandreview.is. Daily round-up of local news stories in English, all reported with an Icelandic quirkiness – gives a good feel for the country.
Icelandic Tourist Board ⊛ www.icetourist .is. Comprehensive regional run-down of the

country, listing the main sights and recommended services.
Iceland Worldwide ⊛ www.iww.is. Some excellent photos but lightweight text on travelling around Iceland, plus a monthly newsletter on practically any topic – such as politics, sport, or travel – to do with the country and a Yellow Pages-style service directory.
Natural Iceland ⊛ www.nat.is. Web-guide with regional breakdown of the country; includes info on tours, transport, activities, sights, and has discount online booking.
Reykjavík City ⊛ www.visitreykjavik.is. Net-zine for Reykjavík, with all upcoming attractions, parties, bands and events.
Travelnet ⊛ http://travelnet.is. Tourist brochure with snippets of history, plus practical information on transport, accommodation and tours.
What's On In Iceland ⊛ www.whatson.is. Reykjavík-centric rundown on current nightlife and events, with heaps of practical links for accommodation, car hire, and tours.

Getting around

Iceland's small scale makes getting around fairly straightforward – at least during the warmer months. From Reykjavík, it's possible to fly or catch a bus to all major centres, and in summer there are even scheduled buses through the Interior. In winter, however, reduced bus services and difficult road conditions might make flying the only practical way to travel. It's also easy enough to hire cars or four-wheel-drives, though those on a budget will find cycling a cheaper alternative.

On the ground, whether you're planning to take buses around the country, hire a car or cycle about, you'll probably spend a good deal of time on **Route 1**, or *Hringbraut*, the **Ringroad**, which largely follows the coast in a 1500-kilometre circuit of the country via Reykjavík, Akureyri and Egilsstaðir. With the exception of a long gravel run in the northeast between Mývatn and Egilsstaðir, most of the Ringroad is surfaced, and in winter snow-ploughs do their best to keep the route accessible to conventional vehicles, though you'll still need to take care and use snow tyres.

Elsewhere, while stretches around towns might be surfaced, the majority of Icelandic

roads are gravel. Some of these are perfectly decent if bumpy to travel over, while many others – such as most **roads through the Interior** – are only navigable in high-clearance four-wheel-drives. Note that interior roads are only open between June and August: exactly when each one opens and closes each year – or whether some open at all – depends on the weather, and the going can be difficult even then.

You can check on the **current road conditions** anywhere in Iceland by logging on to ⊛ www. vegag.is, a continually updated website in English and Icelandic that shows maps of the country with roads colour-coded according to their state.

Flights

Flying in Iceland is good value: the single airfare from Reykjavík to Egilsstaðir, for instance, is 8675kr – around two-thirds the price of the bus fare for the same journey – and takes just one hour instead of two days. As an added bonus, you'll get a different take on Iceland's unique landscape from above – flying over Vatnajökull's vast expanse of ice is about the only way to get a grasp of its scale.

Aside from minor carriers concentrating on day-tours (details are given through the Guide), the main **domestic airline** is Flugfélag Íslands (ⓦwww.airiceland.is), who, in cooperation with the smaller Ice Bird, fly all year from Reykjavík to Akureyri, Bíldudalur, Egilsstaðir, Gjögur, Ísafjörður, Sauðárkrókur, Vestmannaeyjar, and Höfn (Hornafjörður) almost daily. From Akureyri, they have less regular connections between April and October to Grímsey, Vopnafjörður and Þórshöfn. They offer various **ticket types**: Priority, which are the most expensive and are valid for a year; Bonus, valid for a month and some twenty percent cheaper; Standby, available for under 25s at less than half the Priority fare; and other special rates for children, students, seniors, and the disabled. **Bookings** can be made through an agent, or online through their website, where you'll often find additional discounts on advertised fares – just note that **bad weather** can cause cancellations at short notice and that it's best to book well ahead for summer weekends and holidays. **Luggage allowance** is 20kg, and you need to **check in** thirty minutes before departure.

Sample Bonus fares for one-way tickets from Reykjavík are: Akureyri 7675kr; Egilsstaðir 8675kr; Hornafjörður 8675kr; Westman Islands 5700kr.

Buses

Buses are pretty much the most convenient way to get around a large chunk of Iceland, and Iceland's umbrella long-distance-bus organisation, **BSÍ** (ⓦwww.bsi.is), based at the bus station in Reykjavík, puts out a free, comprehensive **timetable** of scheduled

departures and tours run by various companies. Between May and October, scheduled services cover the entire Ringroad and many other routes, with regular tours tackling interior destinations once the roads open around June – about the only way you'll get to see these remote places unless you've considerable off-road driving experience and the right vehicle.

On the down side, bus travel is expensive, especially for the relatively small distances involved: one-way **fares** from Reykjavík are 6250kr to Akureyri; 7650kr to Höfn; and around 13,400kr to Egilsstaðir. In purely point-to-point terms it costs less to fly (see above), and if you can get a group together, car rental (see below) might work out cheaper, depending on how far you're going and for how long. Between October and May, the range of buses is also greatly reduced: interior roads close, local services dry up, and even along the Ringroad buses only run as far east as Höfn and Akureyri.

Bookings for main-road services can be made at the BSÍ terminal in Reykjavík, though they're not really necessary as you can always pay on board, and – according to BSÍ – extra buses are laid on if more than one busload of passengers turns up. Buses into the Interior, or local tours (even if advertised through BSÍ), will probably require advance booking, however.

Bus passes

Bus passes available from BSÍ and other outlets in Akureyri, Seyðisfjörður, and Egilsstaðir, will save you money on extended bus travel, and also get you **discounts** at many campsites, and five percent off ferry tickets and selected bus tours when booked through BSÍ in Reykjavík. Passes are not valid on city bus services, nor on Interior routes.

The **Full Circle Pass** costs 21,900kr and lets you orbit the country using scheduled services along the Ringroad, with no time limit. However, you're not allowed to double back on your route, and have to pay extra if you detour off the Ringroad – through the Golden Circle, Interior, or Westfjords for instance – but overall you save around a third of the cost of simply paying fares as you go. A **Full Circle-Westfjords Pass**

(32,900kr) is essentially the same as the Full Circle, with a Westfjords extension that also allows free passage on the Stykkishólmur–Brjánslækur ferry. The **West Iceland and Westfjords Pass** (14,395kr) has similar conditions again, and is valid for a return circuit through the Westfjords from Reykjavík.

Alternatively, the **Omnibus Pass**, valid from between 7 days (24,940kr in summer, 15,147kr in winter when there are no buses on the Höfn–Akureyri stretch) and 28 days (49,020kr, summer only), allows you to change direction, and covers the entire Full Circle-Westfjords route as well as the Golden Circle. You also get a five percent discount on buses through the Interior, but only if you pay on board.

Bus tours and buses through the Interior

BSÍ and its operatives also run **tours**, from year-round excursions along the Golden Circle (see p.103), to multi-day explorations of the **Interior** during summer. Passes are not valid on these routes, but you can get off along the way and pick up a later bus – tell them your plans in advance so a space can be reserved for you. Make sure too that you know when the next bus is due – some parts of the country are only covered once or twice a week.

Interior routes covered by buses from the BSÍ terminal include the two Fjallabak routes, which take you past Landmannalaugar's thermal springs and a wild gorge system (see p.122); and traverses across the country to Mývatn either via the impressively barren Sprengisandur route, or easier and slightly more scenic Kjölur route (see p.331).

In addition, you can find buses or day-trips elsewhere to tackle the short and stark Kaldidalur route in the west (see p.168); the trip to the mighty Askja caldera south of Mývatn (see p.333); easterly Snæfell, Iceland's highest free-standing peak (see p.301); and Lakagígar, site of a massive eighteenth-century eruption in the south of the country (see p.323).

Driving

Driving around Iceland allows far greater flexibility than taking the bus. **Car-rental** is expensive for solo travellers – especially if left until you're actually in Iceland – but might work out a reasonable deal in a group, and it's also possible **to bring your own vehicle** in to the country for a limited time. Depending on whether you're in Reykjavik or out in the wilds, **fuel** costs 90–110kr per litre for standard (95 Octane) unleaded petrol (*blýlaust*). UK, US, Canadian, Australian and New Zealand **driving licenses** are all valid for short-term visits.

Contrary to expectations, you don't necessarily need a four-wheel-drive to experience the heart of the country, at least in summer, when both the Kjölur (F35) and the Kaldidalur (F550) open up to carefully-driven conventional vehicles – though check with your car-rental policy to ensure you're covered for these highland roads. Four-wheel-drive is essential for other Interior routes, however, most often because of sticky sand and numerous river crossings. Whatever you're driving, and wherever you are, note that you must not drive or pull off the road or track, apart from at designated passing places or car parks – aside from often unstable verges, you can cause serious erosion damage to the landscape.

Car rental

Car-rental agencies, offering everything from small economical runarounds to gas-guzzling four-wheel-drives, are found right around Iceland. In smaller places the selection will be limited, and rental counters are usually located at the local airport or bus terminal. Avis, Hertz and Europcar are the most widespread of the international companies, with plenty of indigenous operators who might give slightly better rates. Agencies' contact details are given throughout the guide, but hiring in Iceland is very expensive and you'll almost certainly save a good deal of money by organising things **in advance**: your travel agent or nearest specialist operator might be able to offer a discount **fly-drive** package; while rental agencies themselves often advertise slight discounts on their **websites** – we've given a few in the list below, or try ⓦ www.arctic.is.

Rental-rate options boil down to two types: a **daily rate**, which covers the first

100km, after which you pay upwards of 30kr per additional kilometre; or an **all-inclusive rate**, which fixes a flat daily fee – obviously of benefit if you're planning a relatively short-term, long-range excursion. Check that advertised prices include **tax and insurance**, known as CDW (Collision Damage Waiver) – they often don't – and note that if you're planning on a **one-way rental** (hiring the car in Reykjavík and leaving it in Akureyri, for instance) you'll have to pay an additional relocation fee. It's always worth bargaining, especially if you're planning a lengthy rental period or are in Iceland outside the tourist season; some companies even wait until you return the car before working out which rental option will give you the best rate for the time and distance covered.

Including CDW, **prices** for a small sedan start around 3900kr per day, plus additional kilometre fees, rising to 6000–8000kr per day for unlimited kilometres. Even after factoring in petrol costs, the lower end of this scale works out favourably over a week for two or more people, compared to bus travel on a Full Circle Pass. For a four-wheel-drive, however, you're looking at 12,000kr per day at the very least, plus heavy fuel consumption.

Car rental agencies

In Iceland
ÁG ☎587 5504, ⊛www.ag-car.is.
Avis ☎591 4000, ⊛www.avis.is.
Bílaleiga Íslands, ☎545 1300,
⊛www.carrental.is.
Europcar ☎591 4050, ⊛www.europcar.is.
EuroRent ☎568 6915, ⊛www.eurorent.is.
Hertz ☎505 0600, ⊛www.hertz.is.

In the UK and Ireland
Avis ☎0870/606 0100; Northern Ireland ☎0990/900 500; Eire ☎01/874 5844, ⊛www.avis.com.
Budget ☎0800/181 181; Eire ☎0800/973 159, ⊛www.budgetrentacar.com.
Europcar ☎0345/222 525; Eire ☎01/676 7476, ⊛www.europcar.com.
Hertz ☎0870/844 8844; Northern Ireland ☎0990/996 699, Eire ☎01/676 7476, ⊛www.hertz.com.
Holiday Autos ☎0870/400 0011; Northern Ireland ☎0990/300 400; Eire ☎01/872 9366, ⊛www.kemwel.com.

In the US and Canada
Auto Europe ☎1-800/223-5555, www.autoeurope.com.
Avis ☎1-800/331-1084, ⊛www.avis.com.
Budget ☎1-800/527-0700, ⊛www.budget.com.
Europcar ☎1-877-940-6900, ⊛www.europcar.com.
Hertz US ☎1-800/654-3001; Canada ☎1-800/263-0600, ⊛www.hertz.com.
Kemwel Holiday Autos ☎1-800/422-7737, ⊛www.kemwel.com.

In Australia and New Zealand
Avis Australia ☎1800/225 533; New Zealand ☎09/526 2800, ⊛www.avis.com.
Budget Australia ☎1300/362 848; New Zealand ☎0800/652 227 or ☎09/375 2270, www.budget.com.
Hertz Australia ☎1800/550 067; New Zealand ☎09/309 0989 or 0800 655 955, ⊛www.hertz.com.

Bringing your own vehicle

The vehicle ferry from Scandinavia and Scotland to Seyðisfjörður in the Eastfjords (see p.11) makes **bringing your own vehicle** into Iceland fairly straightforward. Assuming you have been living outside Iceland for the previous twelve months, you're allowed to import the vehicle and 200 litres of fuel duty free for a period of one month starting from date of entry. You'll also need to produce proof that the vehicle has third-party insurance (this can be purchsed on arrival) and to bring along its registration certificate and your driving licence, before a duty-free import permit is granted. Permits can often be extended for up to three months after arrival, but overstay your permit and you'll be liable to full import duties on the vehicle.

Driving regulations and road conditions

Icelanders have a cavalier attitude to **driving** in conditions that most other people would baulk at – they have to, or would probably never get behind the wheel – and take dirt tracks and frozen twisting mountain roads very much in their stride, barely slowing for any hazards. Native drivers also tend to gravitate towards the road's centre and don't slow down much or move over for oncoming traffic, which can be very disconcerting at first. Aside from the weather and potential road conditions, however, low-volume traffic makes for few problems.

Cars are left-hand drives and you drive on the right as in the US, though the opposite to the UK, Australia and New Zealand. The **speed limit** is 50km an hour in built-up areas, 90km an hour on surfaced roads, and 80km an hour on gravel. **Seat belts** are compulsory for all passengers, and **headlights** must be on at least half-beam all the time.

Two **roadsigns** you'll soon become familiar with out in the country – even if you stick to the Ringroad – are "Einbreið bru", indicating a single-lane bridge sometimes also marked by flashing yellow beacons; and "Malbik endar", marking the end of a surfaced road. Along the southeast coast, the northeast and some interior roads, **sandstorms** can be a serious hazard and have been known to overturn vehicles and strip the paint off cars; stretches of the Ringroad where these might occur are marked with orange warning signs.

Otherwise, the most common hazard is having other vehicles spray you with windscreen-cracking **gravel** as they pass; slow down and pull over to minimize this, especially on unsurfaced roads. When there's snow – though you'd be unlucky to come across much around the Ringroad during the summer – you'll find that the road's edges are marked by evenly spaced yellow poles; stay within their boundaries. The trick to **driving on snow or ice** is to avoid skidding by applying the brakes slowly and as little as possible, and to remember that momentum is key: even if you're barely crawling along, while you're still moving forward you should keep the wheels spinning and resist the temptation to change gear, as you'll lose your impetus by doing so. In winter, everyone fits studded **snow tyres** to their cars to increase traction, so make sure any vehicle you rent has them too. Pack a good blanket or sleeping bag in case you get stuck by snow in your car, and always carry food and water.

Four-wheel-driving and rough roads

Iceland's **interior routes,** plus some shorter

gravel tracks off the Ringroad to Þórsmörk and elsewhere, can be really rough. While some of these tracks are generally negotiable in conventional cars, **four-wheel-drive-only roads** – on which you may encounter stretches of sand, boulders, ice or river crossings – are designated with an "F" on road maps (for instance, the Sprengisandur route is F26), and should only be attempted in a suitable vehicle.

Even on remoter roads, however, you'll probably see some traffic as recreational four-wheel-driving is very popular in Iceland – witness the numbers of "super jeeps", with jacked up heavy-duty chassis and giant wheels. Most years, convoys of these monsters manage to cross eastwards over Vatnajökull, successfully dragging each other over the ice, crevasses and half-frozen rivers along the way.

Precautions include not tackling any four-wheel-drive roads alone; being properly equipped with all rescue gear and tools (and know in advance how to use them); and always carrying more than enough fuel, food and water. It's also wise to tell someone reliable where you're going and when you'll be back, so that a rescue can be mounted if you don't show – but don't forget to contact them when you do get back safely. You'll also need **advance information** on road and weather conditions; check out Ⓦwww.vegag.is and try local tourist offices, or the Reykjavík BSÍ bus terminal (see p.54). Above all heed **local advice** and don't take chances – many people have drowned in their cars attempting to ford rivers in the Interior.

Rough roads have their own hazards. To minimize them, stay on any marked tracks; you'll also prevent further damage and erosion to Iceland's fragile environment this way. Vehicles easily bog down in deep snow, mud or soft sand, so maintaining forward momentum is vital for getting through all these. If you stop moving forward, your spinning wheels will quickly dig the vehicle in, so take your foot off the accelerator immediately. Hopefully you'll be able to reverse out in low range, otherwise you'll have to start digging.

Rivers are potentially very dangerous, and come in two types. **Spring-fed rivers** have a constant flow; **glacial rivers** can fluctuate considerably depending on the time of day and prevailing weather conditions. These are at their lowest during the early morning and after a dry spell of weather; conversely, they can be much deeper in the afternoon once the sun has melted the glacial ice that feeds them, or when it's raining. Some rivers are bridged but many are not; **fords** are marked with a "V" on maps. You need to assess the depth and speed of the river first to find the best crossing point – never blindly follow other vehicle tracks – and to wear a **life-jacket** and tie yourself to a lifeline when entering the river to check its depth. If the water is going to come more than halfway up the wheels, slacken off the fan belt, block the engine's air intake, and waterproof electrics before crossing. Be sure to engage a low gear and four-wheel-drive before entering the water at a slow, steady pace; once in, don't stop (you'll either start sinking into the riverbed or get swept away), or change gear (which lets water into the clutch). If you stall mid-stream in deep water, turn off the ignition immediately, disconnect the battery, winch out, and don't restart until you've ensured that water hasn't entered the engine through the air-filter – which will destroy the engine. If in doubt, it's much better to wait for the river to subside or for the weather to improve than to take risks.

Cycling

Bad roads, steep gradients and unpredictable weather don't make Iceland an obvious choice for a **cycling** holiday, but nonetheless there are plenty of people who come here each summer just to pedal around. And if you're properly equipped, it's a great way to see the country close-up – you'll also save plenty of money over other forms of transport.

You'll need solid, 18- or 24-speed **mountain bikes** with chunky tyres. You can **rent** these from various hostels in Iceland, or at the BSÍ bus terminal in Reykjavík, for around 1500kr a day. If you're **bringing your own bike** to Iceland by plane, or getting it from one end of the country to the other by air, you'll need to have the handlebars and pedals turned in, the front wheel removed and strapped to the back, and the tyres deflated.

There are bike shops in Reykjavík, Akureyri and a couple of the larger towns, but otherwise you'll have to provide all **spares** and carry out **repairs** yourself, or find a garage to help. Remember that there are plenty of areas, even on the Ringroad, where assistance may be several days' walk away, and that dust, sand, mud and water will place abnormal strains on your bike. You'll definitely suffer a few **punctures**, so bring a repair kit, spare tyre and tubes, along with the relevant tools, spare brake pads, spokes, chain links and cables.

Weather has the most capacity for ruining your enjoyment if you're not prepared for it. In summer, expect a few days of rain, a few of sunshine, a storm or two, and plenty of wind. Around the coast you shouldn't need excessively warm **clothing** – a sweater and waterproof in addition to your normal gear should be fine – but make sure it's all quick-drying. If travelling through the Interior, weatherproof jackets, leggings, gloves and headware, plus ample warm clothing, are essential. Thick-soled neoprene surf **boots** will save cutting your feet on rocks during river crossings.

It's not unfeasible to cover around 90km a day on paved stretches of the Ringroad, but elsewhere the same distance might take three days and conditions may be so bad that you walk more than you ride. Give yourself four weeks to circuit the Ringroad at an easy pace – this would average around 50km a day. Make sure you've worked out how far it is to the next store before passing up the chance to buy **food**, and and don't get caught out by supermarkets' short weekend hours (see p.39). Note that **off-road cycling** is prohibited in order to protect the landscape, so stick to the tracks.

If it all gets too much, you can put your bike on a **bus** for a few hundred krónur. If there's space, bikes go in the luggage compartment: otherwise it will be tied to the roof or back. Either way, protect your bike by wrapping and padding it if possible.

For help in planning your trip – but not bike rental – contact the **Icelandic Mountain Bike Club** (Íslenski Fjallahjólaklubbúsins, or ÍFHK), who organize club weekends and also have heaps of advice for cyclists. You can download most of this and contact them through their Web site at ⓦ www .mmedia.is/~ifhk, which has English text.

Hitching

Hitching around Iceland is possible, at least if you have plenty of time. Expect less traffic the further you go from Reykjavík, and even on the Ringroad there are long stretches where you may go for hours without seeing a vehicle. Leave the Ringroad and you might even have to wait days for a lift, though in either case it's likely that the first car past will stop for you.

Having said this, holidaying Icelanders will probably already have their cars packed to capacity, so make sure you have as little gear as possible – without, of course, leaving behind everything you'll need to survive given the climate and long spaces between shops (see p.36). And though Iceland may be a safer place to hitch than elsewhere in Europe, Australia, or the US, doing it still carries inherent risks, and the best **advice** is not to do it.

If you must hitch, never do so alone and remember that you don't have to get in just because someone stops. Given the wide gaps between settlements it will probably be obvious where you are heading for, but always ask the driver where they are going rather than saying where it is you want to go.

The best places to line up lifts are either at campsites, hostels, or the fuel stations which sit on the outskirts of every settlement; it's possible, too, that staff in remoter places might know of someone heading your way.

Tours

Everywhere you go in Iceland you'll find **tours** on offer, ranging from whale-watching cruises, hikes, pony treks and snowmobile trips across southern glaciers, to bus safaris covering historic sites, interior deserts, hot springs and volcanoes or even joy flights over lakes and islands. Some of these things you can do independently, but in other cases you'll find that tours are the only practical way to reach somewhere.

They can last anything from a couple of hours to several days, with the widest range offered between June and September, though some, such as whale watching, are seasonal. **Booking in advance** is always a good idea, especially in the peak tourist months of July and August, when you may have to wait a couple of days before being able to get on the more popular excursions. Details of tours and operators are given throughout the guide. In winter – which as far as tourism is concerned lasts from September to May – many operators close completely, and those that remain open concentrate on four-wheel-driving and glacier exploration along the fringes of the southern icecaps, as the Interior itself is definitely off-limits by then. While bigger agents in Reykjavík offer trips almost daily in winter, don't expect to be able to just turn up at a small town off-season and get onto a tour – most will require a few days' advance warning in order to arrange everything.

Accommodation

Icelanders love exploring their country and travel all over it for work and play, and – in summer – almost every settlement has somewhere to stay in the shape of a hotel, guesthouse, hostel or campsite. In addition, farms and some rural schools provide accommodation where you might not expect it. Almost all formal lodgings are found around the settled coastal band; if you're heading into the wilds at any stage, you'll need to camp or make use of huts.

Before setting out, pick up the Accommodation in Iceland **brochure** from tourist information outlets, which lists most places to stay – though not all – and official campsites, along with their facilities. Hotels tend to stay open year-round, but many other places **shut down** from September to May, or need advance notice of your arrival outside the tourist season. Where places do stay open, **winter rates** are around 25 percent cheaper than summer ones.

In addition to a range of rooms, several types of places to stay offer **budget** accommodation. Where **made-up beds** are offered, you basically pay for a bed, not the room, so might end up sharing with strangers but for less than the price of a single room. **Sleeping-bag accommodation** is much the same thing and even cheaper, except only a bare bed or mattress is provided, hostel style, and you supply all the bedding – so even if you don't intend to camp, it's worth bringing a sleeping bag.

Accommodation organizations

Contact details for specific places to stay are given throughout the guide, many of which are run by the following organisations:

Edda Hlíðarfótur IS-101, Reykjavík ☎ 444 4000, ℻ 444 4001, ﹫ www.hoteledda.is. See p.32 for details.

Fosshótel Skipholt 50, 105 Reykjavík ☎ 562 4000, ﹫ www.fosshotel.is. Association of thirteen mid-range hotels located at strategic points around the country, including Reykjavík and Akureyri.

Icelandair ☎ 505 0910, ﹫ www.icehotels.is. Eight upmarket hotels, mostly in southern Iceland.

Icelandic Farm Holidays Síðumúla 13, 108 Reykjavík ☎ 570 2700, ﹫ www.farmholidays.is. Agent for 120-odd farms offering accommodation around Iceland.

Icelandic Youth Hostel Association Sundlaugavegur 34, 105 Reykjavík ☎ 553 8110, ﹫ www.hostel.is.

Kea Hotels Hafnarstræti 87-89, 600 Akureyri ☎ 460 2000, ﹫ www.keahotels.is. Five top-notch hotels in Akureyri, Mývatn, and Reykjavík.

Hotels and Guesthouses

Icelandic **hotels** are for the most part uninspiring places, typically elderly and gloomy or bland, modern, business-oriented blocks, though rooms are comfortable and well furnished as a rule. Bigger establishments

---

Accommodation price codes

Throughout this guide, prices given for **youth hostels** and **sleeping-bag accommodation** are per person unless otherwise specified. **Hotel** and **guesthouse** accommodation is graded on a scale from ❶ to ❽; all are high-season rates and indicate the cost of the cheapest double room. The price bands to which these codes refer are as follows:

❶ Up to 4000kr   ❹ 8000–10,000kr   ❼ 15,000–20,000kr
❷ 4000–6000kr   ❺ 10,000–12,000kr   ❽ Over 20,000kr
❸ 6000–8000kr   ❻ 12,000–15,000kr

might have their own pool, gym, sauna or even casino, and there will always be a restaurant, with breakfast included in the cost of a room. Hotels don't usually have any budget options, though you do occasionally find made-up beds or even sleeping-bag accommodation on offer in country areas, especially out of season. Room **rates** depend on the location and facilities, and start around 9000–12,000kr for a double with en-suite bath, 6000–9000kr without, and about two-thirds of these prices for a single room with and without bath.

Guesthouses (*gistiheimiliý*) tend to have a lot more character than hotels, as they're often just converted, family-run homes. Rooms range from the barely furnished to the very comfortable, though facilities are usually shared, and you'll often find some budget accommodation available too. A breakfast of cereal, toast, cheese, and coffee is sometimes included, or offered for an extra 750kr or so; some places can provide all meals with advance notice. As for **prices**, doubles cost 5500kr or more; made-up beds are around 2500kr per person and sleeping-bag accommodation will be about 2000kr.

Farms

You'll find plenty of **farms** in Iceland, some with histories going back to saga times, which offer accommodation of some kind, ranging from a room in the farmhouse to hostel-style dormitories or fully furnished, self-contained cabins. Many also encourage guests to take part in the daily routine, or offer horse riding, fishing, guided tours, or even four-wheel-drive safaris.

For the most part, farm **prices** are the same as for guesthouses; cabins usually sleep four or more and can work out a good deal for a group at around 8000-10,000kr. Come prepared to cook for yourself, though meals are usually available if booked in advance.

Summer hotels and Edda

In Iceland, many country schools open up during the summer holidays as **summer hotels**, fourteen of which come under the Icelandair-owned **Edda** banner (see p.31 for contact details). They're aimed at the budget end of things – though they very seldom have self-catering facilities – and usually have a few rooms, large dormitory space, and mattresses on the classroom floors. Facilities are shared, though most have a thermally heated pool in the grounds and there's always a restaurant.

Costs at summer hotels are around 8000kr for a double, 4000kr for a single, 3000kr for a made-up bed, and 1300-1700kr for sleeping-bags.

Hostels

The Icelandic Youth Hostel Association (see below for details) runs 24 **hostels** around Iceland, ranging from big affairs in Reykjavík to old farmhouses sleeping four out in the country. All are owner-operated, have good self-catering kitchens and either offer bookings for local tours or organize them themselves. Some can also provide meals with advance notice and have laundry facilities. Quite a few are open all year too, though you'd be hard-pushed to reach remoter ones until winter was well and truly over – turn up out of season, however, and you'll often receive a warm welcome.

Whatever the time of year, you should **book in advance**; in summer, hostels are often full, and at other times, even if officially open, owners may simply lock up the house and head off somewhere for a few days if they're not expecting guests. Dormitory accommodation is the norm, either in made-up beds (up to 2250kr) or sleeping bags (1900kr), with around a 25 percent **discount** for holders of a Hostelling International card – these have to be bought before you leave home (see contact details below).

Youth hostel associations

Australia Australian Youth Hostels Association, PO Box 314, Camperdown, NSW 2050 ⓦ www.yha.com.au.
Canada Hostelling International Canada ⓣ 1-800/663 5777 or 613/237 7884, ⓦ www.hostellingintl.ca.
Iceland Bandalag Íslenskra Farfugla Sundlaugavegur 34, 105 Reykjavík ⓣ 553 8110, ⓦ www.hostel.is.
Ireland Irish Youth Hostel Association ⓣ 01/830 4555, ⓦ www.irelandyha.org.

New Zealand Youth Hostels Association of New Zealand, PO Box 436, Christchurch 1 ☎03/379 9970, ⓦ www.yha.co.nz.
UK Youth Hostel Association (YHA) ☎0870/770 8868, ⓦ www.yha.org.uk; Hostelling International Northern Ireland ☎028/9032 4733, ⓦ www.hini.org.uk; Scottish Youth Hostel Association ☎0870/155 3255, ⓦ www.syha.org.uk.
US Hostelling International-American Youth Hostels ☎202/783-6161, ⓦ www.hiayh.org.

Camping

Camping is a great way to experience Iceland, especially during the light summer nights, when it's bright enough in your tent at midnight to feel like it's time to get up. You'll also minimize expenditure, whether you make use of the country's 150 or so campsites or set up for free in the nearest field. Just be aware that camping is really a **summer-only** option: in winter, campsites and fields alike will probably be buried beneath a metre of snow.

Most official **campsites** are only **open** between June and some point in September – though you're welcome to use them out of season if you can live without their facilities (just shower at the nearest pool). They vary from no-frills affairs with level ground, a toilet and cold running water, to those sporting windbreaks, hot showers (always extra), laundry, powerpoints, and sheltered kitchen areas. On-site shops are unusual, however, so stock up in advance. Campsites in the Interior are very barely furnished, usually with just a pit toilet. While some town campsites are free, **prices** come in at around 600kr per person per day, though sometimes you'll pay per tent, or even a fixed, one-off fee regardless of how long you stay.

If you're doing extensive hiking or cycling there will be times that you'll have to **camp in the wild**. The main challenge here is to find a flat, rock-free space to pitch a tent over. Where feasible, always seek **permission** for this at the nearest farmhouse before setting up; farmers don't usually mind – and often direct you to a good site – but may need to keep you away from pregnant stock or the like. Note too, that in a few reserves such as Skaftafell and Jökulsárgljufur, camping is only permitted at designated areas.

When camping wild, you can bury anything bio-degradeable but should carry other rubbish out with you.

Camping equipment

Aside from bringing in your own equipment, you can **buy** good camping gear from outdoor supply shops such as Nanoq (see Reykjavík "Listings", p.86), or **rent** it from the BSÍ bus terminal.

Your **tent** is going to be severely tested, so needs to be in a good state of repair and built to withstand strong winds and heavy rain – a good-quality dome or tunnel design, with a space between the flysheet and the tent entrance where you can cook and store your backpack and boots out of the weather, is ideal. Whatever the conditions are when you set up, always use guy ropes, the maximum number of pegs, and a flysheet as the weather can change rapidly; in some places, especially in the Interior, it's also advisable to weight the edge of the tent down with rocks.

Also invest in a decent **sleeping bag** – even in summer, you might have to cope with sub-zero conditions – and a **sleeping mat** for insulation as well as comfort. A waterproof sheet to put underneath your tent is also a good idea. Unless you find supplies of driftwood you'll need a **fuel stove** too, as Iceland's few trees are all protected. Butane gas canisters are sold in Reykjavík and many fuel stations around the country, but you're probably better off with a pressure stove capable of taking a variety of more widely available fuels such as unleaded petrol (*blýlaust*), kerosene (*steinolía*), or white spirit/shellite ("white spirit").

Mountain huts

At popular hiking areas and throughout interior Iceland you'll encounter **mountain huts**, which are maintained by Iceland's hiking organisations (see p.44). These can be lavish, multistorey affairs with kitchen areas and dormitories overseen by wardens, or very basic wooden bunkhouses that simply offer a dry retreat from the weather, and **cost** 1100–1700kr accordingly. You'll always have to supply bedding and food and should **book well in advance** through the relevant organisation, particularly at popular sites such as Þórsmörk and Landmannalaugar (see pp.122–135). If you haven't booked you may get in if there's room, but otherwise you'll have to pitch a tent; wardens can be very strict about this, so if you don't have a tent to fall back on, you might find yourself having to hike to the next available hut late in the day.

Emergency huts, painted bright orange to show up against snow, are sometimes not so remote – you'll see them at a few places around the Ringroad where drivers might get stranded by sudden heavy snowfalls. Stocked with food and fuel, and run by the SVFÍ (Iceland's national life-saving association), these huts are for emergency use only; if you have to use one, fill out the guestbook stating what you used and where you were heading, so that stocks can be maintained and rescue crews will know to track you down if you don't arrive at your destination.

Food and drink

Although Iceland's food is unlikely to be the highlight of your trip, things have improved from the early 1980s when beer was illegal and canned soup supplemented dreary daily doses of plain-cooked lamb or fish. The country's low industrial output and high environmental conciousness – the use of hormones in livestock feed is forbidden, for instance – means that its meat, fish and seafood are some of the healthiest in Europe, with hothouses now providing a fair range of vegetables and even some fruit.

While in Reykjavík and Akureyri the variety of food is pretty well what you'd find at home, menus elsewhere are far less exciting – with sheep outnumbering the people by four to one, there's a lot of **lamb** to get through. You'll often find some variety to the standbys grills or stews, however, even if **salads** have yet to really catch on; otherwise fast food or cooking for yourself will have to see you through.

Traditional foods

Iceland's cold climate and long winters meant that the settlers' original diet was low in vegetables and high in cereals, fish and meat, with **preserved foods** playing a big role. Some of the following traditional foods are still eaten on a daily basis, others crop up mainly at special occasions such as the mid-winter Þorramatur feasts, though restaurants may serve them year round.

Something found everywhere is **harðfiskur**, wind-dried haddock or cod, which you'll see airing on huge racks outside fishing villages; it's commonly eaten as a snack by tearing off a piece and chewing away, though some people like to spread butter on it first. Most Icelandic **seafood** is superb – there are restaurants in Reykjavík, Hafnarfjörður and Sokkseyri which specialise in **lobster** – and even everyday things like a breakfast of **síld** (pickled herrings) are worth trying. **Hákarl** (Greenland shark), is a more doubtful delicacy, as it can only be consumed after being buried for up to six months in sand to break down the high levels of ammonia and neurotoxins contained in its flesh. Different parts of the rotted shark yield either white or dark meat, and the advice for beginners is to start on the milder-tasting dark (*gler hákarl*), which is translucent – rather like smoked glass. Either way, the flavour is likely to make your eyes water, even if connoisseurs compare the taste and texture favourably to a strong cheese. Don't feel bad if you can't stomach the stuff, because neither can many Icelanders.

As for meat, there's ordinary **hangikjöt**, which is hung, smoked lamb, popular in sandwiches and as part of a traditional Christmas spread; **svið**, boiled and singed sheeps' heads; haggis-like varieties of **slátur** ("slaughter"), of which blood pudding (*blóðmör*) is a favourite; and a whole range of scraps pressed into cakes and pickled in whey, collectively known as **súrmatur** – leftover svið is often prepared like this, as is *súrsaðir hrútspungar*, or pickled rams' testicles.

Game dishes include the grouse-like ptarmigan (*rjúpa*), which takes the place of turkey at Icelandic Christmas dinners; an occasional reindeer (*hreindýr*) in the east of the country; and puffin (*lundi*) in the south, which is usually smoked before being cooked. In a few places you'll also come across whale or seal meat, as both are still hunted in limited numbers. Rather more appealing to non-Icelandic palates, **salmon** (*lax*), **trout** (*silingur*), and **char** (*bleikja*) are all superb and relatively inexpensive. In addition to smoked salmon or trout, try the similar-looking *gravað*, whereby the fish is marinated with herbs until it's soft and quite delicious.

About the only endemic **vegetable** is a type of lichen that's dried into almost tasteless, resilient black curls and snacked on raw or cooked with milk. Home-produced **cheese** and dairy products are very good, and it's worth trying yogurt-like **skyr**, sold all over the country plain or flavoured with fruit. **Pancakes** known as *flatbrauð* or *laufabrauð* are traditionally eaten at Christmas, and a few places – notably near Mývatn in north-eastern Iceland – bake a delicious **rye bread** called *hverabrauð* in underground ovens (see p.274).

Drinks

It's been said with some justification that Iceland runs on **coffee**, with just about everyone in the country firmly hooked, a definite café culture in the cities, and decent quality brews offered even at rural cafés. In some supermarkets, hot thermoses of free coffee are laid on for customers to help themselves, and wherever you pay for a cup,

the price usually includes a refill or two. The only place you're likely to experience bad coffee is in service stations, whose machines inevitably produce foul brews – ask for fresh or go elsewhere. **Tea** is also pretty popular, though not consumed with such enthusiasm. **Bottled water** and familiar brands of **soft drinks** are available everywhere. **Milk** comes in a bewildering range of styles, making a trip to the supermarket fridge quite a challenge if you can't read Icelandic. *Mjolk* is normal full-fat milk; *Lettmjolk* is skimmed, *AB Mjolk* is plain runny yoghurt, and *G-Mjolk* is UHT milk.

Alchohol

When it comes to **alcohol**, you'll find that it's expensive – you might want to bring a bottle of duty-free in with you to save costs – and, with the exception of beer, only sold in bars, clubs, restaurants and state-owned **liquor stores**. A state liquor store is a *vínbúð*, and they are often tucked out of sight in distant corners of towns and cities, taking some effort to find. Most Icelanders drink very hard when they put their minds to it, most often at parties or on camping trips – the August bank holiday weekend is notorious. It's surprising, then, to find that full-strength **beer** was actually illegal until March 1989, when the seventy-five-year-old prohibition laws were revoked. In Reykjavík, March 1 is still celebrated as Bjórdagurinn, or **Beer Day**, with predictably riotous celebrations organized at bars throughout the capital. Beer is available in many supermarkets, and comes as relatively inexpensive, low-alcohol pilsner, and more expensive, stronger lagers.

All **wine** and most **spirits**, naturally enough, are imported, though hard-liquor enthusiasts should try **brennivín**, a local spirit distilled from potatoes and flavoured with caraway seeds or angelica. It's powerful stuff, affectionately known as *svarti dauði* or "black death", and certainly warms you up in winter – you'll also welcome its traditional use to clean the palate after eating fermented shark.

Restaurants, cafés and bars

Just about every settlement in Iceland, from

BASICS | Food and drink

villages upwards, has a **restaurant** of some sort. In Reykjavík, and to a lesser extent Akureyri and the larger towns, there's a variety of formal establishments offering everything from traditional Icelandic fare to Mexican, Thai, Chinese, and Italian- and French-inspired dishes, and even a couple of **vegetarian** places. This is the most expensive way to dine – expect to pay upwards of 1500kr per person – though keep your eyes peeled for lunch-time **specials** offered, or inexpensive fixed-price meals of soup, bread, and stew. All-you-can-eat **smorgasbords** or buffets also crop up, especially around Christmas, when restaurants seem to compete with each other over the calorie contents of their spreads of cold meats and **cakes** – the latter something of a national institution.

In the country, pickings are far slimmer, however. Some **hotel restaurants** have fine food, though it's more often filling than particularly memorable; prices can be as high as in any restaurant, but are generally lower. Otherwise, the only place offering cooked food might be the nearest **fuel station café**, which will whip up fast fodder such as burgers, grills, sandwiches and pizzas for a few hundred krónur. Indeed, at times it seems that pizza is Iceland's national dish, and there's even a widespread chain called **Pizza 67**.

Found all over the country, **bars**, besides being somewhere to have a drink, also usually sell meals and are frequently decorated along particular themes – decked out 1950s-style, for example, or hung with fishing memorabilia. **Coffee houses** are less widespread, confined mostly to the cities and a couple of towns, offering light meals, coffee, and cakes.

Self-catering

Self-catering will save a lot over eating out, though ingredients still cost more than they do at home – again, you might want to bring in some supplies (especially camping rations) with you to save money. There are few specialist food shops besides **fishmongers** and **bakeries**, but at least one **supermarket** – often run by co-operative organisations – in all villages, towns and cities. Don't expect to find them attached to campsites, however, and when travelling about buy supplies when you can, don't get caught short by weekend shop hours, and know where the next supermarket is. There are no shops in the Interior.

Larger supermarkets can be well stocked with plenty of fresh fruit and vegetables – especially in "hothouse towns" such as Hveragerði in southern Iceland – plus fish and meat. Rural stores, however, may have little more than a few imported apples and oranges and a shelf or two of canned and dried food. Iceland grows its own capsicums, mushrooms, tomatoes and cucumbers, plus plenty of berries and a few bananas, but most other things are imported and therefore fairly expensive.

Post, phones and the Internet

Iceland may be remote but its communications are modern and reliable, making it easy to keep in touch with home.

Post offices are located in all major communities and are open from 9am until 4.30pm Monday to Friday, though a few in Reykjavík have longer hours. **Domestic mail** will generally get to the nearest post office within two working days, though a recipient living out on a farm might not collect it so quickly. For **international post** count on three to five days for mail to reach the UK or US, and a week to ten days to Australia and New Zealand. Anything up to 20g **costs** 45kr within Iceland, 60kr to Europe, and 85kr to anywhere else; up to 50g costs 55/115/160kr. **International parcels** aren't outrageously expensive – check ⓦ www.postur.is for rates – but not particularly fast; ask at any post office about Express Mail if you're in a hurry, though you'll pay far more than for the normal service.

Post restante facilities are available at all post offices; have mail sent to the relevant office marked "to be collected" in English and turn up with your passport. If you can't find an expected letter, check that it hasn't been filed, Icelandic-style, under your Christian name; it might help to have your surname underlined on the letter.

Phones

Landssíminn (Iceland Telecom) offices are usually inside the local post office, where you'll be able to place local and international calls. You'll also often find a row of **payphones** outside – if not, head to the nearest fuel station. You can make **international calls** on payphones too, and they accept either coins or **phonecards** of 500kr and 1000kr values, which you can buy in post offices. Calling from a hotel will be very expensive, and beware of **hotel payphones**, which will start gobbling your money even if the call goes unanswered. You pay **reduced rates** on domestic calls at weekends and Mon–Fri 7pm–8am; on calls to Europe daily

at 7pm–8am; and to everywhere else daily at 11pm–8am.

If you're bringing in a **mobile phone**, Iceland uses both GSM and NMT networks – ask your provider about whether your phone is compatible. GSM has a restricted range but works around most towns and villages, while NMT covers almost everywhere except a few bits of the Interior. You can buy **prepaid cards** for GSM at Landssíminn offices and most service stations; mobile phone calls to Europe, the US, and Canada cost from 19.90kr a minute.

All **phone numbers** in Iceland are seven digits long, with no regional codes. If you need to use the **phone book** (which you should be able to find chained to the phone box), remember that listings are arranged in order of Christian name – Gunnar Jakobsson, for instance, would be listed under "G", not "J".

Operator services and international calls

Operator services in Iceland

Emergencies Fire, ambulance or police ☎ 112
International directory enquiries ☎ 114
International operator ☎ 115
National directory enquiries ☎ 118

Phoning Iceland from abroad

To call Iceland from overseas, dial your international access code (see below), then ☎ 354, then the phone number.
Australia ☎ 0011
Canada ☎ 011
New Zealand ☎ 00
UK ☎ 00
US ☎ 011

Phoning overseas from Iceland

Note that the initial zero is omitted from the area code when dialing the UK, Ireland, Australia and New Zealand from abroad.

USA and Canada 00 + 1 + area code.
Australia 00 + 61 + city code.
New Zealand 00 + 64 + city code.
UK 00 + 44 + city code.
Republic of Ireland 00 + 353 + city code.

The Internet

Iceland is one of the highest per-capita users of the Internet, with most homes and businesses connected. There are several **Internet cafés** in Reykjavík and Akureyri costing around 500kr an hour; elsewhere, **public libraries** or **tourist offices** often have access for 200-700kr an hour. If all else fails, accommodation or even tour agents might allow you to use their facilities if asked nicely, though they're certainly not obliged to.

If you don't have one already, it's worth signing up for a **free email account** with a

Time difference

Iceland is on **Greenwich Mean Time** (GMT) throughout the year. GMT is 5 hours ahead of US Eastern Standard Time and 10 hours behind Australian Eastern Standard Time.

company such as Yahoo (www.yahoo .com) or Hotmail (www.hotmail.com), which will allow you to send and receive email messages from anywhere in the world that has Internet access – a good alternative to phones or poste restante. To sign up, log on to the relevant Web site, and follow the instructions; any email sent to you will then stack up in the inbox waiting to be read.

The media

Iceland's main **daily paper** is the right-wing *Morgunblaðið*, available all over the country and giving thorough coverage of national and international news. The only real competition is the left-ish *Dagur*, though many Icelanders don't consider it such a good read. If your Icelandic isn't up to it, you can get a roundup of the main stories through the *Iceland Review*, an English-language newsheet giving good outlines about main national stories – it's available in Reykjavík's newsagents or online at www.icelandreview.is. Ryekjavík's bookshops – and libraries around the country – also have copies of **British and US newspapers**, though supply is erratic

and sometimes a week or more out of date. **International magazines** such as Time and National Geographic are also available from the same sources.

There are also several **radio stations** with a menu of commercial pop, classical music and talk-back shows. Between late May and early September, the news is also broadcast in English on Radio 1, daily at 8.55am. The three **television channels** show a familiar mix of soaps, dramas, films and documentaries. All these media are predominantly Icelandic-language only, though films and TV shows are screened in their original language with subtitles.

Opening hours, holidays and festivals

Shops are generally open Monday to Friday 9am–6pm and Saturday 10am to mid-afternoon, though you might find that many close for the weekend through the summer. In cities and larger towns, supermarkets are open daily from 10am until late afternoon; in smaller communities, however, weekend hours are shorter, and some places don't open at all on Sundays.

Out in the country, **fuel stations** provide some services for travellers, and larger ones tend to open daily from around 9am to 11pm. Office hours everywhere are Monday to Friday 9am to 5pm; **tourist offices** often extend these through the weekends, at least in popular spots.

Holidays and Festivals

Though Iceland's calendar is predominantly Christian, many official holidays and festivals have a secular theme, and at least one dates from pagan times. Some are already familiar: **Christmas** and **Easter Monday** are both holidays in Iceland and are celebrated as elsewhere in the Western world, as is **New Year**.

Harking back to the Viking era, however, þorrablót is a mid-winter celebration originally honouring the weather god Þorri, and became something to look forward to during the bleakest time of the year. It is held throughout February, when people throw parties centred around the consumption of traditional foods such as *svið* and *hákarl* (see p.34), with some restaurants also laying on special menus.

Sjomannadagur, or Seamen's Day (June 4), unsurprisingly, is one of the biggest holidays of the year, with communities organising mock sea-rescue demonstrations, swimming races and tug-of-war events. This is followed by another break for **Independence Day** (June 17), the day that the Icelandic state separated from Denmark in 1944. Þingvellir (see p.104), the seat of the original parliament east of Reykjavík which hosted the original 1944 event is a good place to head for, though everywhere throws some sort of celebration. Though not an official holiday, **Jónsmessa**, on June 24, is the day that elves and other magical creatures are said to be out in force, playing tricks on the unwary; some people celebrate with a big bonfire, though it's also meant to be good for your health to run around naked.

Verslunnarmannahelgi, the Labor Day Weekend, takes place around the country on the first weekend in August. Traditionally, everybody heads into the countryside, sets up camp, and spends the rest of the holiday drinking and partying themselves into oblivion; hit any campsite in the country at this time and you'll be sharing it with thousands of drunken teenagers. On Heimaey in the Westman Islands, **Þjódhátið** is held on the same day and celebrated in the same way, though it nominally commemorates Iceland's achieving partial political autonomy in 1874.

One event to look out for, though it's not a single festival as such, is the annual stock round-up, or **rettir**, which takes place in rural areas throughout September. This is when horses and sheep are herded on horseback down from the higher summer pastures to be penned and sorted; some farms offering accommodation allow guests to watch or even participate.

Sports and outdoor activities

Iceland has its own wrestling style, called glíma – a former Olympic sport where opponents try to throw each other by grabbing one another's belts – and there's a serious football (soccer) following; the Reykjavík Football Club was founded in 1899, and an Icelandic consortium owns the English-league club Stoke City. Otherwise, there's not a great obsession with sport as such, with most people here getting outside not to play games but to work or enjoy the Great Outdoors.

The lava plains, black-sand deserts, glacier-capped plateaus, alpine meadows, convoluted fjords and capricious volcanoes that make Iceland such an extraordinary place scenery-wise also offer tremendous potential for outdoor activities, whether you've come for wildlife or to hike, ride, ski, snowmobile or four-wheel-drive your way across the horizon. Further information on these activities is always at hand in local tourist offices, while you can find out more about the few national parks and reserves from the Department of Forestry or various Icelandic hiking organisations (see opposite). Many activities can be done on an organized tour, sometimes with necessary gear supplied or available for rent. Before you set out to do anything too adventurous, however, check your insurance cover (see p.17).

Swimming and hot pots

You probably won't be coming to Iceland to **swim**, but in fact this is a major social activity year-round with Icelanders, and it's a great way to meet people or just see them unwinding – it seems mandatory for businessmen to have a dip on their way to work. Just about every town and village has a swimming **pool**, usually an outdoor affair and heated by the nearest hot spring to around 28°C. In addition, there are almost always one or two spa baths or **hot pots**, providing much hotter soaks at 35–40°C – another great Icelandic institution, and particularly fun in winter, when you can sit up to your neck in scalding water while the snow falls thickly around you. Out in the wilds, hot pots are replaced by natural hot springs – a great way to relax trail-weary muscles. Note that at all official swimming pools you are required to shower with soap before getting in the water.

Fishing

As Iceland is surrounded by the richest fishing grounds in the North Atlantic, **sea fishing** has always been seen as more of a career than a sport, though there are limited opportunities out of Keflavík in the southwest.

The country's rivers and lakes, however, are also well stocked with **salmon** and **trout**, pulling in hordes of fly fishers during the **fishing season** (April 1 to September 20 for trout, June 20 to mid-September for salmon). Both fish are plentiful in all the country's bigger waterways, though the finest salmon are said to come from the Laxá (which means Salmon River), in northeast Iceland, and the Rangá in the south. During the winter, people cut holes in the ice and fish for **arctic char**; the best spots for this are east of Reykjavík at Þingvallavatn, and Mývatn, in the northeast (see p.109 & p.265).

You always need a **permit** to fish, which is generally available from local tourist offices and some accommodation, especially on farms. Permits for char or trout are fairly inexpensive and easy to obtain on the spot, but those for salmon are always pricey and often need to be reserved months in advance, as there is a limit per river. For further information, contact the **National Angling Association**, Bolholt 6, IS-105 Reykjavík (℡553 1510, ℻568 4363, 🖳www.angling.is); or Icelandic Farm Holidays (see "Accommodation", p.31), who publish a free English-language booklet about trout and salmon fishing in Iceland.

Hiking

Hiking gets you closer to the scenery than anything else in Iceland, and exploring the countryside on foot is how many locals and visitors alike spend much of their time off. In reserves and the couple of national parks you'll find a few **marked trails**, and where they exist you should always stick to them in order to minimize erosion. Elsewhere you'll need to be competent at using a map and compass to navigate safely over the lava, sand, rivers and ice you'll find along the way.

If you're unsure of your abilities, there are two **hiking clubs** to get in touch with: **Ferðafélag Íslands** (The Touring Club of Iceland, Mörkin 6, IS-108 Reykjavík; ☏568 2533, ☎568 2535, ⊛www.fi.is); and **Útivist** (Hallaveigarstigur 1, IS-101 Reykjavík; ☏561 4330, ☎561 4606, ⊛www.utivist.is). Both run guided treks of a couple of days duration to a week or longer – though groups can be very large – and maintain various mountain huts in reserves and the Interior where you can book a bunk (see p.33). Local tourist information offices can also put you in touch with guides.

Whether you're planning to spend a weekend making short hikes from camp in a national park, or two weeks hiking across the Interior, come properly equipped for the likely conditions. **Weather** changes very fast in Iceland, and while there are plenty of sunny summer days, these will be spaced by rain, storms and the real possibility of snow on high ground or in the Interior, and you can get caught out easily even on brief excursions. Always carry warm, weatherproof **clothing**, food, and **water** (there are plenty of places in Iceland where porous soil makes finding surface water unlikely), as well as a torch, lighter, penknife, **first aid kit**, a foil **insulation blanket** and a whistle or mirror for attracting attention. The country is also carpeted in sharp rocks and rough ground, so good quality, tough **hiking boots** are essential – though an old pair of sports shoes, or a pair of **neoprene surf boots** with thick soles are useful to ford rivers.

On lava, watch out for **volcanic fissures**, cracks in the ground ranging from a few inches to several metres across, which are usually very deep. These are dangerous enough when you can see them, but blan-

keted by snow they'll be invisible – take care not to catch your foot or fall into one. Another hazard is **river crossings**, which you'll have to make on various trails all over the country. Rivers levels are at their lowest first thing in the morning, and rise through the day as the sun melts the glacial ice and snow that feed into them. When looking for a crossing point, remember the river will be **shallowest** at its widest point; before crossing, make sure that your backpack straps are loose so that if necessary you can ditch it in a hurry. Face into the current as you cross and be prepared to give up if the water gets above your thighs. Never attempt a crossing alone, and remember that some rivers have no safe fords at all if you're on foot – you'll have to hitch across in a vehicle.

When and where to hike

For the country as a whole, the **best months** for hiking are from June through to August, when the weather is relatively warm, wildflowers are in bloom, and the wildlife is out and about – though even then the Interior and higher ground elsewhere can get snowbound at short notice. Outside the prime time, weather is very problematic and you probably won't even be able to reach the area you want to explore, let alone hike around it.

One of the beauties of Iceland is that you can walk just about anywhere, assuming you can cope with local conditions, though there are, of course, some highlights. Close to Reykjavík, the **Reykjanes Peninsula** (see p.97) offers extended treks across imposingly desolate lava rubble; there are some short, easy hikes along steaming valleys near **Hveragerði** (see p.114); while trails at **Þingvellir** (see p.104) include historic sites and an introduction to rift valley geology. Further east, **Laugavegur** (see p.124) is an exceptional four-day trail; and **Þórsmörk** (see p.133) is one of the most popular hiking spots in the country, a wooded, elevated valley surrounded by glaciers and mountain peaks with a well-trodden network of paths.

Along the west coast, the **Snæfellsnes Peninsula** (see p.173) is notoriously damp but peaks with the ice-bound summit of Snæfellsjökull, the dormant volcano used as a fictional gateway into the centre of the Earth by writer Jules Verne. Further north there's **Hornstrandir** (see p.201), the wildest and most isolated extremity of the Westfjords, a region of twisted coastlines, sheer cliffs and rugged hillwalks. Those after an easier time should head to **Mývatn** (see p.265), the shallow northeastern lake where you can make simple day-hikes to extinct craters, billowing mud-pits, and still steaming lava flows; longer but also relatively easy are the well-marked riverside trails around nearby **Jökulsárgljúfur National Park** (see p.281), which features some awesome canyon scenery. Over in the east, the best of the hikes take in the highland moors and glaciated fringes of the massive Vatnajökull ice cap: at **Snæfell** (see p.301), a peak inland from Egilsstaðir; **Lónsöræfi reserve** (see p.312) near Höfn; and **Skaftafell National Park** (see p.315), another riotously popular camping spot on Vatnajökull's southern edge.

Horse riding

Horses came to Iceland with the first settlers, and, due to a tenth-century ban on their further import to stop equine diseases arriving in the country, have remained true to their original stocky Scandinavian breed. Always used for **riding**, horses also had a religious place in Viking times – a famous example was the stallion Freyfaxi in Hrafnkel's Saga (see p.300) – and were often dedicated or sacrificed to the pagan gods; with the advent of Christianity, eating horse meat was banned, being seen as a sign of paganism. Nowadays, horses are used for the autumn livestock round-up, and for recreational purposes.

Icelandic horses are sturdy, even-tempered creatures, and in addition to the usual walk, trot, and canter, can move smoothly across rough ground using the gliding **tölt** gait. The biggest breeding centres are in the country's relatively mild south, but horses are available for **hire** from farms all over Iceland, available with **guides** as needed for anything from an hour in the saddle to two-week-long treks across the Interior. Places to hire horses are given throughout the guide, but if you need to sort something out in advance, contact **Íshestar** (Sörlaskeið 26, 220 Hafnarfjörður; ☎555 7000, ☏555 7001, ⒲www.ishestar.is), who run treks of all lengths and experience levels right across the country.

Snow and action sports

Snow sports – which in Iceland are not just practised in winter – have, surprisingly, only recently begun to catch on. Partly this is because the bulk of Iceland's population lives in the mild southwestern corner of the country, but also because snow was seen as just something you had to put up with; **cross-country skiing**, for instance, is such a fact of life in the northeastern winters that locals refer to it simply as "walking", and were baffled when foreign tour operators first brought in groups to do it for fun.

The possibilities for cross-country skiing are pretty limitless in winter, though you'll have to bring in your own gear. **Downhill skiing and snowboarding** are the most popular snow sports, with two major centres – winter slopes at Bláfjöll (see p.85), only 20km from Reykjavík; and summer skiing at Kerlingarfjöll, close to Hofsjökull glacier in the central interior – accommodation at the latter needs to be booked well in advance, and **rental gear** is available at both.

For something different, plenty of tour operators offer glacier trips on **snowmobiles** or skidoos, which are like jet-skis for snow – the only way for the inexperienced to get a taste of Iceland's massive ice fields, and huge fun. If you're more water-oriented, several of southwestern Iceland's larger rivers have caught the attention of **rafting** enthusiasts (contact Arctic Rafting, ☎487 5557, ⒲www.arcticrafting.is, for more information); while Iceland also has surprisingly good **scuba diving** potential, the prime sites being in Þingvallavatn's cool but amazingly clear waters, on various shipwrecks, and at seal colonies around the coast – Arctic Diving (Grandagarði 14, 101 Reykjavík, ☎699 4556, ⒲www.ArcticDiving.com) can sort out the details, though you'll need dry-suit skills.

Gay and lesbian travellers

Iceland is a very small and closely knit society whose population is barely bigger than that of any average-sized European or American town. In fact, it's generally said that two Icelanders meeting for the first time can usually find people they know in common after just a couple of minutes of conversation – not exactly ideal conditions for a thriving gay scene to develop and indeed for years many gay people upped and left for the other Nordic capitals, most notably Copenhagen, where attitudes were more liberal and it was easier to be anonymous.

However, two things have begun to change all that. First was the establishment of the Icelandic gay and lesbian association in 1978, **Samtökin 78** (Laugavegur 3, ☎552 7878), to promote awareness of homosexuality and gay rights at a political level. This professionally run organisation also offers a support network, not only in Reykjavík, but also out in the tiny towns and villages in the countryside, where attitudes towards homosexuality are not nearly as enlightened. Despite this, there are still many men and women in far-flung villages stuck in the closet because they fear the reaction of people around them should they come out.

The countryside also lacks the effects of the second factor that has changed the lives of so many gay men and women living in the capital – the advent of the bar. The legalization of beer in 1989 meant that **bars** began springing up throughout Reykjavík, bringing people out onto the streets in larger numbers than had ever been the case before. This change in the law made it possible for gay men and women to socialize in pubs in a way that they could only have dreamt of before. Over the past decade, a bar culture has slowly but surely developed in Reykjavík and the city is now confident enough to boast three gay bars (see p.82), though there isn't a single gay bar or any gay scene to speak of in the provinces.

Samtökin's efforts have certainly paid off at the political level – after much lobbying, Iceland's politicians not only agreed to allow gay marriage in 1996 (in effect the right to register legally a partnership between two same-sex partners thus granting legal parity with straight couples), but also to allow gay men and lesbians to adopt children, making Iceland the first country in the world to pass such progressive legislation.

Police, crime and sexual harassment

Iceland is a peaceful country, and it's unlikely that you'll ever even see the police. Most public places are well lit and secure, people are friendly and helpful, if somewhat reserved, and street crime and hassles are extremely rare.

It's foolish, however, to imagine that problems don't exist, though they mainly revolve around **petty crime** and are largely confined to Reykjavík. Many criminals are drug addicts or alcoholics after easy money; keep tabs on your cash and passport (and don't leave anything visible in your car when you park it) and you should have little reason to visit the **police**. If you do seek them out, you'll find them unarmed, concerned and usually able to speak English – remember to get an insurance report from them in the event you have anything stolen.

As for **offences** you might commit, **drink-driving** is taken extremely seriously here, so don't do it: catch a taxi rather than risk being caught. Being drunk in public in Reykjavík might also get you into trouble, but in a country campsite you probably won't be the only one, and (within reason) nobody is going to care. **Drugs**, however, are treated as harshly here as in much of the rest of Europe.

Sexual harassment

In general, Iceland is an egalitarian society, and, though **women** still sometimes get paid less than men for comparable work, they enjoy a higher economic and social status than in most other European countries. Kvennréþindahreyfingin, the **Women's Rights Movement**, was founded in the early twentieth century and drove through women's right to vote and receive an equal education and, when needed, still assists with the latter.

Sexual harassment is less of a problem here than elsewhere in Europe. You can move almost everywhere in comparative comfort and safety, and although in Reykjavík clubs you might receive occasional unwelcome attentions – or simply be taken aback by the blatant atmosphere – there's very rarely any kind of violent intent. Needless to say, hitching alone, or wandering around central Reykjavík late at night, is unwise. If you do have any problems, the fact that almost everyone understands English makes it easy to get across an unambiguous response.

Addresses Addresses in Iceland are always written with the number after the street name.

Books There are bookshops with English-language publications in Reykjavík and Akureyri, but prices are extortionate – about 2000kr for a paperback novel.

Electricity is 240v, 50Hz AC. Plugs are round pin with either two or three prongs; appliances fitted with overseas plugs need an adaptor.

Laundry Outside of Reykjavík, which has a public laundromat (see p.86), you'll only find laundry facilities at accommodation or better-equipped campgrounds.

Names Icelanders have a given name, plus the name of (usually) their father with an attached "-son" for boys and "-dóttir" for girls. So, Jón's son Gunnar is called Gunnar Jónsson, and his daughter Njóla is called Njóla Jónsdóttir. Because of this lack of family names, telephone directories are arranged by given names – using the above example, you'd find Gunnar Jónsson under "G", and Njóla Jónsdóttir under "N" in the phone book. In an effort to preserve national identity, all foreigners taking Icelandic citizenship must also take an Icelandic name.

Photography Print and slide film and processing are readily available in Reykjavík, Akureyri, and most supermarkets elsewhere, but like everything else, are very expensive – bring all you'll need.

Souvenirs Icelandic woollen sweaters are a practical memento of your trip, and cost around 8000kr. Their characteristic patterns derived around a century ago from Greenland's traditional costumes. As almost all are made in cottage industries, consistent patterns, colours, sizes, shapes and fittings are nonexistent – shop around until you find the right one. Woollen hats and mittens are also good buys; as are proverbially warm eiderdown duvets, stuffed with locally collected duck feathers (very expensive, however); and better-value smoked salmon.

Guide

Guide

1 Reykjavík 47–92

2 Southwestern Iceland..93–148

3 The west coast...149–188

4 The West Fjords...189–221

5 Northwest Iceland 223–259

6 The Mývatn and the northeast 261–289

7 The Eastfjords and the southeast 291–324

8 The Interior 325–334

Reykjavík

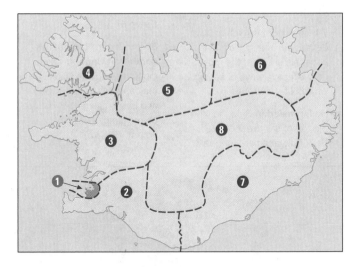

CHAPTER 1 # Highlights

✳ **Friday night in Reykjavík**
Join the locals on their *runtúr*,
a good-natured pub-crawl,
and wind your way round
some of the city's top bars
and clubs. See p.81

✳ **Culture House** Get to grips
with Iceland's stirring past
through this magnificent and
accessible collection of
ancient sagas and documents.
See p.68

✳ **Whale watching** With handy
departures from the city harbour, this is one of the most
cost-effective ways of seeing
whales up close. See p.83

✳ **Hallgrímskirkja** Ride the lift to
the top of the tower of this
Reykjavík landmark for one

of the most awe-inspiring
views in the whole country.
See p.71

✳ **Puffin tours, Akurey** With
more than thirty thousand
puffins nesting on the island's
cliffs during the short Icelandic
summer, boat trips around this
island are an amazing experience, allowing you to see the
birds up close as they fish for
food and nest in their burrows.
See p.87

✳ **Swimming in Nauthólsvík
geothermal lagoon** Take a
dip in the sublime waters of
the capital's open-air lagoon
and laze on its golden sands
before jumping into the
hotpot. See p.74

Reykjavík

The world's most northerly capital, **Reykjavík** has a sense of space and calm that comes as a breath of fresh air to travellers accustomed to the bustle of the traffic-clogged streets of Europe's other major cities, and often literally so. Although unrepresentative of the majority of the country for its relative urbanization, a visit here is a good place to obtain as true a picture as possible of this highly individual, often apparently contradictory society, secluded on the very edge of the Arctic. While it's true, for example, that Friday- and Saturday-night Reykjavík has earned the place a reputation for hedonistic revelry, with locals carousing for as long as the summer nights allow – despite the legendarily high price of alchohol here – the pace of life is in fact sedate. The tiny centre, for example, is more of a place for ambling around, taking in suburban streets and cornerside cafés set against mountain and ocean scenery, rather than somewhere to hurtle around between attractions. Similarly, given the city's capital status, Reykjavík lacks the grand and imposing buildings found in the other Nordic capitals, possessing instead apparently ramshackle clusters of houses, either clad in garishly painted corrugated iron or daubed in pebbledash as protection against the ferocious North Atlantic storms. This rather unkempt feel, though, is as much part of the city's charm as the blustery winds that greet you as you exit the airport, or the views across the sea to glaciers and the sheer mountains that form the backdrop to the streets. Even in the heart of this capital, nature is always in evidence – there can be few other cities in the world, for example, where greylag geese regularly overfly the busy centre, sending bemused visitors, more accustomed to diminutive pigeons, scurrying for cover.

Today, amid the essentially residential city centre, with its collection of homes painted in reds, yellows, blues and greens, it is the **Hallgrímskirkja**, a gargantuan white concrete church towering over the surrounding houses, which is the most enduring image of Reykjavík. Below this, the elegant shops and stylish bars and restaurants that line the main street and commercial thoroughfare of **Laugavegur**, busy with shoppers seemingly undaunted by the inflated prices of goods – import taxes and cuts by middlemen are to blame – are a consumer's heaven, even if window-shopping is all you can afford. It's within this central core of streets that the capital's most engaging **museums** are also to be found, containing, amongst other things, superb collections of the medieval **sagas**.

With time to spare, it's worth venturing outside the city limits into **Greater Reykjavík**, for a taste of the Icelandic provinces – suburban style. Although predominantly an area of dormitory overspill for the capital, the town of **Hafnarfjörður**, is large enough to be independent of Reykjavík and has a couple of museums and a busy harbour, though it's for its **Viking feasts** that

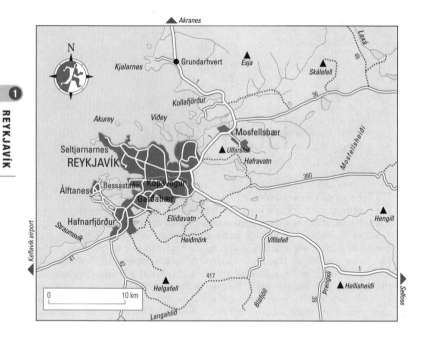

the town is perhaps best known. Alternatively, the flat and treeless island of **Viðey**, barely ten minutes offshore of Reykjavík, is the place to come for magnificent views of the city and of the surrounding mountains – there are also some enjoyable walking trails here, which lead around the island in an hour or so.

The city also makes a good base for excursions around Reykjavík, including to three of Iceland's most popular attractions: the site of the old parliament, **Alþingi**, at Þingvellir (see p.104), the waterspouts and waterfalls of **Geysir** and **Gullfoss** (see pp.111 & 112), and **Skálholt** (see p.111) cathedral – all within simple reach by public transport – or, more expensively, on day-long guided tours from the city. Also worthwhile is the **Reykjanes peninsula** (see p.97), a bleak lavafield that's as good an introduction as any to the stark scenery you'll find further into Iceland, and home to the mineral-rich waters of the **Blue Lagoon** (see p.97) – the most visited attraction in the country.

If you're only in the city for a short break, or flying on to either the US or Europe, Reykjavík is also the place to fix up adventure activities such as **snow-mobile tours** or **jeep safaris** on nearby glaciers or **whitewater rafting** on the Hvítá river in the north (see box, p.235).

Some history

As recounted in the ancient manuscripts *Íslendingabók* and *Landnámabók*, Reykjavík's origins date back to the country's first settler, **Ingólfur Arnarson**, who arrived in 874 AD, brought here by his high seat pillars – emblems of tribal chieftainship, tossed overboard from his boat – and settling, in pagan tradition, wherever they washed up. He named the place "smoky bay" (*reykja* meaning "of smoke", *vík* meaning "bay", cognate with English *wick*), mistakenly thinking that the distant plumes of steam issuing from boiling spring water were smoke caused by fire. It was a poor place to settle, however, as the soil was too infertile to support successful farming, and Reykjavík remained barely inhabited until an early seventeenth-century **sea-fishing** boom brought Danish traders here, after which a small shanty town to house their Icelandic labour force sprang into existence. Later, in the middle of the eighteenth century, **Skúli Magnússon**, the official in charge of Reykjavík's administrative affairs (*landfógeti*), a man today regarded as the city's founder, used Reykjavík as a base to establish Icelandic-controlled industries, opening several mills and tanneries, and importing foreign craftspeople to pass on their skills. A municipal charter was granted in 1786, when the population totalled a mere 167 – setting the course for Reykjavík's acceptance as Iceland's capital. At the turn of the eighteenth century, the city replaced Skálholt as the national seat of religion and gained the Lutheran Cathedral, Dómkirkjan; eighty years later, with the opening of the new Alþingi building, it became the base of the national parliament.

Since independence in 1944, **expansion** has been almost continuous. As a fishing harbour, a port for the produce of the fertile farms of the southwest and a centre for a variety of small industries, Reykjavík provides employment for over half the country's population. The city has also pioneered the use of geo-thermal energy to provide low-cost heating – which is why you have to wait for the cold water instead of the hot when taking a shower, and why tap water always has a whiff of sulphur.

Over the past decade or so there's been a substantial boom, too, in **tourism**. The ever-increasing visitor numbers to Reykjavík are largely due to the recent advent of a couple of homegrown low-cost airlines, and although the city's infrastructure is struggling to keep up with this rapid pace of expansion there are few inhabitants who disapprove, aware that contact with the outside world is what Reykjavík depends and thrives on.

Arrival and information

Reykjavík is served by two **airports**: Keflavík (information on ☎425 0200), 52km west of Reykjavík at the tip of the Reykjanes peninsula, where most international flights arrive and depart; and Reykjavík city airport (☎570 3030), built by the British when they occupied Iceland during World War II and adjacent to *Hótel Loftleiðir* on the edge of the city centre, served by all domestic flights as well as international services from Greenland and the Faroe Islands, and essentially little more than a glorified bus station. Keflavík, however, is a much larger affair with two currency-**exchange** offices, both offering the same rates – one on either side of pass-port control – plus there's an **ATM** in the arrivals hall after customs. Brace yourself as you leave the tiny terminal building for howling wind and accompanying horizontal rain.

A **taxi** from Keflavík airport into Reykjavík will set you back around a whopping 8000kr, so it's far better to take one of the Flybus **coaches** (☎562 1011, ⓦwww.re.is), which leave from immediately outside the terminal; you'll see departure times, which coincide with arrivals, displayed on monitors by the baggage reclaim. Tickets for the coach, which can be bought from the Flybus desk in the arrivals hall or on the coach, cost 1000kr one way (1800kr return) and are also payable by credit card and in major foreign currencies, including UK sterling and US dollars. The journey lasts around 45 minutes and terminates at the *Loftleiðir* hotel (see p.59), 2km from the city centre; from there a shuttle bus (same ticket) takes you to all other major hotels in the city, as well as several guesthouses, the youth hostel and the campsite (see p.61). Alternatively, taxis from here cost around 900kr, while bus #7 (220kr) goes directly into the centre. Failing that, it's around a thirty-minute walk; the hotel can provide you with a map, but bear in mind that bad weather can make this impractical, particularly if laden with heavy luggage.

Long-distance buses finish their journeys at the BSÍ bus terminal, at Vatnsmýrarvegur 10, halfway between the city centre and *Hótel Loftleiðir*. Inside is a travel agency, a bus-ticket office (June to late Aug daily 7.30am–8pm; Sept–May Mon–Fri 7.30am–7pm, Sat & Sun 9am–7pm; ☎591 1020, Ⓦww.dice.is), a fairly decent café and a left-luggage office (*Vöruafgreiðsla*; Mon–Fri 7.30am–7pm, Sat 9am–2pm, June to late Aug Sat & Sun 7.30–4pm; ☎552 6292; 500kr for one day, 700kr for 2 days, each additional day 150kr, 1 week 1300kr). There are also an ATM, postbox and public telephones here. All bus **timetables** are published on the net at Ⓦwww.dice.is.

Information

The city's busy **official tourist information office**, at Aðalstræti 2, lies close to the Parliament in the heart of the old town (June–Aug daily 8.30am–6pm; Sept–May Mon–Fri 9am–5pm, Sat & Sun 10am–2pm; ☎562 3045, Ⓦwww.visitreykjavik.is, Ⓦww.icetourist.is), is the best source of up-to-date information on both Reykjavík and the rest of the country; you can get untold amounts of brochures and maps, including the excellent free *Enjoy more of Reykjavík* and an Iceland **map**. If you're travelling independently, you can check your itinerary here with the staff before setting off for the remoter regions; there's also a tourist gift shop in the same complex (same times). Alternatively, there's unofficial tourist office, the **Central Reykjavík Travel Service** (June–Aug daily 9am–10pm, Sept–May Mon–Sat 10am–6pm; ☎511 2442, Ⓦwww.icelandvisitor.com), at Lækjargata 2. Run by students, this place is not only much friendlier than the official tourist office but its younger staff also have up-to-the-minute information on the ever-changing Reykjavík bar and restaurant scene. The office can also fix up **bike** and **car rental** (see opposite).

City transport

Reykjavík is easy to get around. The heart of the city is the low-lying quarter between the harbour and the lake, busy with shoppers by day and with young revellers by night. Most of the sights are within walking distance of here.

The Reykjavík Tourist Card

Available for 24hr, 48hr or 72hr, the **Reykjavík Tourist Card** gives you unlimited transport on buses within Greater Reykjavík, access to the main museums and galleries, plus admission to seven swimming pools in the capital and the Reykjavík park and zoo. Available at the tourist office in Aðalstræti (see above), the City Hall information desk (see p.62), the BSÍ bus terminal (see above) as well as at the Laugardalur swimming pool, it costs 1000kr for 24-hours' validity, 1500kr for 48 hours, and 2000kr for 72 hours.

Orange **city buses** known as *Strætó* (℡540 2700, ⓦwww.bus.is), depart from the two main terminals: Lækjartorg (Mon–Sat 7.20am–11.30pm, Sun 10am–11.30pm; ticket office Mon–Fri 9am–6pm); ℡510 9805), at the junction of Lækjargata and Austurstræti; and Hlemmur (Mon–Fri 8am–8pm, Sat & Sun noon–8pm; ticket office Mon–Fri 8am–6pm, Sat & Sun noon–6pm; ℡540 2701), at the eastern end of Laugavegur. Services run from 7am to midnight Monday to Saturday, and from 10am to midnight on Sundays: frequencies are roughly every twenty minutes throughout the day and every thirty minutes in the evenings and at weekends. **Night buses** run on Friday and Saturday nights only from midnight to roughly 4am. There's a flat, single-trip fare of 220kr that must be paid for with exact change; when boarding, simply throw the money into the box by the driver. Tickets are only issued if you're changing buses, in which case ask for a *skiftimiði*, valid for 45–60 minutes, as you pay.

Other ticket options include a strip of nine tickets, a *farmiðaspjald*, for 1500kr; the **Gula kortið** (Yellow card; 2500kr) which gives two weeks unlimited bus travel in the Greater Reykjavík area, which covers the surrounding satellite towns, including Hafnarfjörður; the **Græna kortið** (Green card; 4500kr) valid for one month and the **Rauða kortið** (Red card; 10,500kr) good for three months' unlimited travel. All these tickets are bought from the terminals' ticket offices (see above).

Two useful **routes** are #5, which runs from Lækjartorg via Suðurgata to the city airport; and #7, which travels from Lækjartorg via Hringbraut and the BSÍ bus terminal to *Hótel Loftleiðir*. If you want to see the city cheaply, bus #5 is excellent – as well as running to the airport, it also operates in the opposite direction from Lækjartorg east via the central Hverfisgata, Hlemmur and the swimming pool, youth hostel and campsite in Laugardalur, before swinging west to the Kringlan shopping centre; change here for route #6 to take you back into town.

Taxis, parking and cycling

Travelling by **taxi** across the city centre is not as expensive as you might think – 700–800kr should be enough to take you where you want to go from any one point to another. The main ranks are centrally located on Lækjargata, between the junctions with Bankastræti and Amtmannsstígur, as well as opposite Hallgrímskirkja church on Eiríksgata and Hlemmur. It's also possible to call one of the main operators for a taxi: Hreyfill (℡588 5522) are best, or try Borgarbíll (℡552 2440), BSR (℡561 0000) or BSH (℡555 0888). Remember that Icelandic taxi drivers aren't usually tipped.

Parking in Reykjavík is a relatively straightforward business and certainly not the nightmare you might expect in a capital city. Most residential streets, although often full with residents' cars, are unmetered, whereas in the city centre parking meters are in use. Multistorey **car parks** are dotted around the city centre, most conveniently at Skólavörðustígur. Once again they're all marked on the tourist office's Reykjavík map. Although the city's **traffic** is generally free-flowing, even at rush hours, it can be busy on Friday and Saturday nights, when it's wise to avoid Laugavegur, which mutates into a long snaking line of slow-moving cars.

Bike rental is centrally available from Borgarhjól, at Hverfisgata 50 (℡551 5653), or at the youth hostel (see p.61) or the campsite in Laugardalur (see p.76) as well as at the Central Reykjavík Travel Service (℡511 2442); all places charge around 2000kr per day. For more on cycling around the city, see p.77.

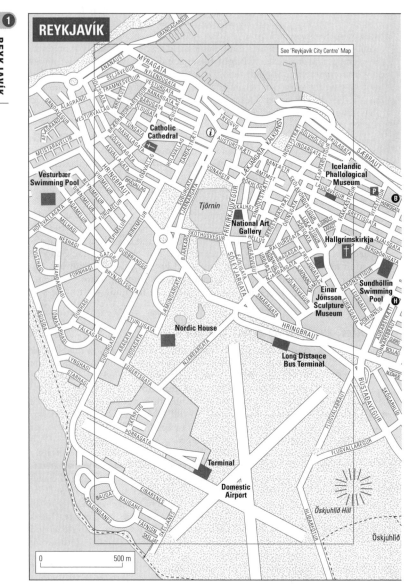

REYKJAVÍK

See 'Reykjavík City Centre' Map

GRANDAGARDUR

ANANAUST
MYRAGATA
SELJAVEGUR
NÝLENDUGATA
VESTURGATA
FRAMNESVEGUR
RÁNARGATA
ÖLDUGATA
ÁGÚSTGATA

Catholic Cathedral ⓘ AUSTURSTRÆTI

HÁVALLAGATA
SÓLVALLAGATA
ÁSVALLAGATA
HRINGBRAUT
BRÁVALLAGATA

Vesturbær Swimming Pool

Icelandic Phallological Museum Ⓟ Ⓑ

LAUGAVEGUR
GRETTISGATA
NJÁLSGATA
BERGÞÓRUGATA

Tjörnin

National Art Gallery

Hallgrímskirkja †

SKOTHÚSVEGUR

Einar Jónsson Sculpture Museum

Sundhöllin Swimming Pool Ⓗ

HRINGBRAUT

Nordic House

Long Distance Bus Terminal

BÚSTADAVEGUR

ÞORRAGATA

FLUGVALLAREGUR

Terminal

Domestic Airport

BAUGATANGI
BAUGANES
EINARSNES

Öskjuhlíð Hill

SKELJANES
FÁFNISNES
SKELJAT

Öskjuhlíð

0 —————— 500 m

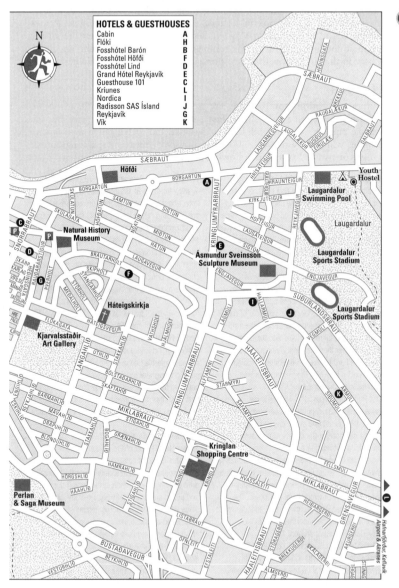

HOTELS & GUESTHOUSES

Cabin	A
Flóki	H
Fosshótel Barón	B
Fosshótel Höfði	F
Fosshótel Lind	D
Grand Hótel Reykjavík	E
Guesthouse 101	C
Kríunes	L
Nordica	I
Radisson SAS Ísland	J
Reykjavík	G
Vík	K

N

SÆBRAUT

Höfði

BORGARTÚN

Youth
Hostel

Laugardalur
Swimming Pool

Laugardalur

BORGARTÚN

SÆBRAUT

BORGARTÚN

A

HRAUNTEIGUR

KIRKJUTEIGUR

HOFTEIGUR

REYKJAVEGUR

KRINGLUMÝRARBRAUT

LAUGARNESVEGUR

LAUGALÆKUR

BUGÐA

TEIRULÆK

RAUÐALÆKUR

HRÍSATEIGUR

SÚÐAVOGUR

HERÐISGATA

DALBRAUT

BRE KKU

SKÚLAGATA

SAMTÚN

SIGTÚN

MÝRAGATA

MIÐTÚN

HÁTÚN

LAUGAVEGUR

LAUGATEIGUR

SIGTÚN

Natural History
Museum

Ásmundur Sveinsson
Sculpture Museum

Laugardalur
Sports Stadium

C

P

P

D

E

ENGJAVEGUR

ENGJAVEGUR

BRAUTARHOLT

SKIPHOLT

STANGARHOLT

STÓRHOLT

MEÐALHOLT

SKARP

KARLAG

VITASTÍG

SNORRABRAUT

ÞVERHOLT

G

F

HÁTEIGSVEGUR

Háteigskirkja

SUÐURLANDSBRAUT

Laugardalur
Sports Stadium

I

J

LAGMÚLI

HALLARMÚLI

Kjarvalsstaðir
Art Gallery

FLÓKAGATA

LANGAHLÍÐ

ÚTHLÍÐ

STAKKAHLÍÐ

VATNSHOLT

HJÁLMHOLT

HÁALEITISBRAUT

VEGMÚLI

ÁRMÚLI

SÍÐUMÚLI

K

BÓLSTAÐARHLÍÐ

SKAFTAHLÍÐ

ÁLFTAMÝRI

STARMÝRI

SAFAMÝRI

REYKJAHLÍÐ

BARMAHLÍÐ

MÁVAHLÍÐ

DRÁPUHLÍÐ

STAKKAHLÍÐ

BOGAHLÍÐ

GRÆNAHLÍÐ

MIKLABRAUT

STIGAHLÍÐ

KRINGLUMÝRARBRAUT

BLÖNDUHLÍÐ

HAMRAHLÍÐ

Kringlan
Shopping Centre

KRINGLA

KRINGLA

HVASSALEITI

MIKLABRAUT

FELLSMÚLI

HÖRGSHLÍÐ

HÁAHLÍÐ

Perlan
& Saga Museum

STIGAHLÍÐ

LISTABRAUT

HEIÐARGERÐI

GRENSÁSVEGUR

AKURGERÐI

L

BÚSTAÐAVEGUR

BEYKIHLÍÐ

VESTURHLÍÐ

OFANLEITI

EESTALEITI

HÁALEITISBRAUT

STÓRAGERÐI

BREKKUGERÐI

SKALAGERÐI

ALMGERÐI

STEINAG

TEIGAG

Hafnarfjörður, Keflavík
Airport & Akranes

Accommodation

Reykjavík's **accommodation** has been unable to keep up with the escalating tourist influx encouraged by the increased frequency of flights between Iceland and European cities (notably Copenhagen and London), which means that it's always a good idea to book in advance, especially in July and August. **Prices** rise by around third between May and September; those given here are for the cheapest double room during the summer months. If you can't find anywhere to stay in the city centre, there are alternatives in the suburb of Hafnarfjörður.

Hotels

Without exception, **hotels** in the city are heavy on the pocket. Standards are uniformly high and a buffet **breakfast** is always included in the price, but the average rate for a double with bath is 15,000kr, and even a single with private facilities will be upwards of 10,000kr. If, however, you fancy splashing out for a night or two of luxury, the following are the city's best-value options.

Borg Pósthússtræti 11 ☎551 1440, ⓦwww .hotelborg.is. The city's very first hotel, opened in the 1930s and ever since the unofficial home of visiting heads of state. Reeking with atmosphere, the fifty rooms are all individually decorated in Art Deco style with period furniture. The service can be somewhat unctuous, however, and the prices astronomic. ❽

Cabin Borgartún 32 ☎511 6030, ⓦwww .keyhotel.is. Modern hotel with fantastic views from the front rooms of the sea and Mount Esja. Bright colours are the key here, with lots of reds, yellows and blues making the décor quite lurid. Unusually, several rooms look onto the central corridor rather than the great outdoors – handy if you find it hard to sleep in the bright midnight sun. These cost a little less than normal doubles. Doubles with shower ❺

City Ránargata 4a ☎511 1155, ⓦwww .icelandichotels.is. A homely place close to the centre, though not one of the city's cheaper options considering the quality of the rooms: uninspiring but adequate. ❻

Fosshótel Barón Barónsstígur 2–4 ☎562 3204, ⓦwww.fosshotel.is. En-suite doubles, plus apartments (all with wooden floors, microwaves and showers), most of which have sea views. The apartments can vary greatly in size, so look before you choose. One-bed apartment 12,980kr May–Oct, less out of season. ❺

Fosshótel Höfði Skipholt 27 ☎552 6477, ⓦwww.fosshotel.is. An odd location for this former student hostel (in the middle of a business area), a rather a 25min walk from the town. There are few creature comforts in the cramped rooms here, but it is cheap and the doubles come with or without private facilities. ❺–❻

Fosshótel Lind Rauðarárstígur 18 ☎562 3350, ⓦwww.fosshotel.is. Bright, modern, functional hotel about a 20min walk from the centre. Rooms are plain and rather too expensive for the elevated price. Doubles with shower. ❼

Frón Klapparstígur 35a ☎511 4666, ⓦwww.hotelfron.is. If you're self-catering, this hotel right in the city centre should be your first choice. Offering nine stylish, modern studios and six two-room apartments, each with bath, kitchenette and TV, this place offers exceptional value for money. Breakfast is an extra 800kr. Studios ❺, two room apartments ❻

Grand Hotel Reykjavík Sigtún 38 ☎514 8000, ⓦwww.grand.is. A good choice for its stylish rooms of marble floors, chrome fittings and wood panels, though for the money you may wish to be closer to the centre – it's a good 25min walk from here. Also has a romantic restaurant with an open fire in the centre of the dining area. Doubles with shower ❽

Holt Bergstaðastræti 37 ☎552 5700, ⓦwww.holt.is. Part of the French Relais & Châteaux group of hotels and consequently the most expensive hotel in Iceland. Over three hundred paintings by Icelandic artists adorn the rooms and public areas of this luxury, centrally located place where rooms are of the Persian-carpet, dark-wood-panelling, red-leather-armchair and chocolate-on-the-pillow variety. Breakfast costs a whopping 1625kr extra. ❽

Klöpp Klapparstígur 26 ☎511 6062, ⓦwww .centerhotels.com. Despite its bizarre name, one of central Reykjavík's better hotels and a sound choice, modern throughout with tasteful natural black slate floors, oak furniture and wall panelling in all rooms. Unlike many places, the thick curtains here are effective at cutting out daylight at midnight. The breakfast room, though, is a little cramped. **❼**

Leifur Eiríksson Skólavörðustígur 45 ☎562 0800, ⓦwww.hotelleifur.is. Perfect location overlooking Hallgrímskirkja, right in the heart of the city. A small and friendly neatly furnished place; the top-floor rooms, built into the sloping roof, are particularly worthwhile for their excellent views. Good value for the location. Doubles with shower **❻**

Loftleiðir Reykjavík city airport ☎505 0900, ⓦww.icehotel.is. Icelandair-owned hotel stuffed with stopover travellers, though frankly not remotely worth the high prices. The quiet, carpeted rooms are a little on the small side but perfectly adequate – the atmosphere, though, is dull and business oriented. The only hotel in Reykjavík to have an indoor swimming pool, it also has separate-sex saunas. A longish walk into the city centre, however – reckon on about half an hour. Doubles with shower **❽**

Nordica Suðurlandsbraut 2 ☎505 0950, ⓦwww.icehotel.is. Another Icelandair moneyspinner and the largest hotel in Iceland, with around 300 rooms. Although this place, formerly the *Esja*, has had a serious Nordic makeover – glass, chrome and natural wood everywhere you look, it still conspires to be overly big, impersonal and unjustifiably expensive. Make sure to at least get a room at the front, with views over the sea to Mount Esja. The walk into town from here is a good 25min. Doubles with shower **❻**

Óðinsvé Þórsgata 1 ☎511 6200, ⓦwww.hotelodinsve.is. Great place that's stylish, relaxed and within an easy trot of virtually everything. Rooms here have wooden floors, Scandinavian-style minimalist furniture and a homely atmosphere. Doubles with shower **❻**

Plaza Aðalstræti 4 ☎511 1155, ⓦwww.icelandhotels.is. If you want to stay in the centre of town, this friendly hotel is an excellent choice. The style is Nordic minimalism meets old-fashioned charm, with the heavy wooden floors, plain white walls and immaculately tiled bathrooms complementing the high-beamed ceilings in this recently renovated old building a stone's throw from Austurstræti. Avoid the noisier rooms at the front which overlook the taxi rank. **❼**

Reykjavík Rauðarárstígur 37 ☎562 6250, ⓦwww.hotelreykjavik.is. Functional and uninspiring hotel, roughly twenty minutes' walk from the centre. Rooms are plain and simple but clean and presentable, though you might find some disturbingly pink furniture in them. Doubles with shower **❼**

Radisson SAS Ísland Ármúli 9 ☎595 7000, ⓦwww.radissonsas.com. Too far from the centre to be a serious opponent to its sister hotel, the *Saga* (about 2.5km), the stylish, light and airy Scandinavian-designed rooms here, with lots of wood panels and glass and chrome, are popular with businessmen and rich tourists. **❽**

Radisson SAS Saga Hagatorg ☎525 9900, ⓦwww.radissonsas.com. Swanky, large business hotel, usually packed with conference delegates dashing up to admire the view from the top-floor restaurant. The rooms, although cosmopolitan in feel and design, with bureaux and comfortable armchairs, are nothing special for the price. Doubles with shower **❽**

Skjaldbreið Laugavegur 16 ☎511 6060, ⓦwww.centerhotels.com. Plain rooms with floral and net curtains and dull grey carpets, but this is the only hotel on Reykjavík's main shopping street, and is therefore unbeatable for its location. Doubles with bath **❼**

Vík Síðumúli 19 ☎588 5588, ⓦwww.hotelvik.is. One of the capital's cheapest hotel options, the simple but pleasant rooms in this hotel are popular with German tour groups. It's oddly located in a business district, 30 minutes' walk from the centre but is perfect for good-value, upmarket self-catering, since half the rooms have a kitchen and cost just 500kr more than an ordinary double. Doubles with shower **❻**

Guesthouses and apartments

Always cheaper than hotels, but still by no means a bargain at 6000–10,000kr for a double, **guesthouses** usually provide kitchens – though breakfast is sometimes included in the price – but rooms are always on the simple side, with little to distinguish between them. Other than those we recommend, a central location is as good a reason as any to choose one over another, though bear in mind that many are fully booked weeks in advance throughout July and August. If the recommended places listed here are full, look out for signs in windows advertising rooms or ask at the tourist office for their lengthy official list.

Anna Smáragata 16 ☎ 562 1618, ✉ anna.s@mmedia.is. Run by the animated and friendly Anna, who lived in the States for 25 years and so speaks excellent English. Excellent value and very handy for the long-distance bus station, and definitely one of Reykjavík's better guesthouses. ❹

Baldursbrá Laufásvegur 41 ☎ 552 6646, ✉ baldursbra@centrum.is. Friendly, modern guesthouse with a fantastic location, right in the city centre and overlooking Tjörnin, though with rather narrow beds and unfortunate floral curtains. ❹

Flóki Flókagata 1 ☎ 552 1155, ⊛ www.eyjar.is/guesthouse. A pebble-dashed modern block with uninspiring rooms stuffed with furniture and cheesy fittings; however, it is close to the centre and is useful if elsewhere is full. Sleeping-bag accommodation 2300kr; ❺

Guesthouse 101 Laugavegur 101 ☎ 562 6101, ✉ guesthouse101@simnet.is. Expensive and soulless place at the eastern end of the main shopping street with cheap furniture and cell-like rooms. Worth a look if everything else is full. ❺

Ísafold Bárugata 11 ☎ 561 2294, ⊛ www .randburg.com/is/isafold. An excellent choice in a quiet suburban street in the western part of town. The tastefully appointed rooms all have shared bath and are decorated with paintings and stylish furniture. ❹

Jörð Skólavörðustígur 13a ☎ 562 1739, 🖷 562 1735. Central location in an old but basic house, just off the main shopping street. The plain, dull rooms are a steal for the centre of town, though breakfast costs an extra 600kr. ❸

Krían Suðurgata 22 ☎ 511 5600, ⊛ www.krian.is. Bright, airy and comfortable – and above all spacious – rooms in this good central guesthouse overlooking Tjörnin. Well

worth the slightly higher prices, which include breakfast. ❹

Kríunes Lake Elliðaárvatn ☎ 567 2245, ⊛ www.kriunes.is. A 15min drive southwest of the city, this is a truly fantastic lakeside choice, a former farmhouse surrounded by high trees and with views of the lake, kitted out with South American-style fittings and furnishings, including brightly coloured rugs. Self-catering facilities available. ❺

Luna Spítalastígur 1 ☎ 511 2800, ⊛ www.luna.is. Good gay-friendly and newly renovated guesthouse in the heart of the city, offering six tastefully decorated but expensive en-suite apartments and studios ❺–❼

Room with a View Laugavegur 18 ☎ 552 7262, ⊛ www.roomwithaview.is. Another recommended gay-friendly and operated venture, with sixth-floor flats on the main shopping street that are excellently appointed and have incredible panoramic views from the shared balcony. Kitchen, shower and steambath available. ❹–❻

Salvation Army Guesthouse Kirkjustræti 2 ☎ 561 3203, ⊛ www.guesthouse.is. The cheapest guesthouse in Reykjavík, often fully booked, despite the narrow rooms with clanking pipes, paper-thin walls and lack of private bath. Although there can be some slightly eccentric local characters in residence, it's a good sensible choice if you're on a tight budget, and it's dead central. Breakfast is an extra 800kr. Sleeping-bag accommodation from 1900kr; ❷

Travel-Inn Sóleyjargata 31 ☎ 561 3553, ⊛ www.dalfoss.is. One of Reykjavík's top three guesthouses in a tastefully renovated old house with good-sized, comfortable rooms overlooking the southern end of Tjörnin and handy for the long-distance bus station on Vatnsmýrarvegur. The rooms with shared bath are good value. ❸

B&Bs

Some homeowners rent out one or two rooms for **B&B** in summer, often giving an excellent insight into Icelandic family life: rates are slightly lower than at guesthouses. Recommended owners include Hólmfríður Guðmundsdóttir, on the fourth floor at Skólavörðustígur 16 (☎ 562 5482, ✉ holmfridur@holmfridur.is; 8500kr), right in the heart of the city; Eiríkur Rauði, Eiríksgata 6 (☎ 552 1940, ✉ eric@eric.is; 9900kr), behind Hallgrímskirkja church; Sigrún Ólafsdóttir, Skeggjagata 1 (☎ 562 2240, ✉ guest@guest.is; 6500kr), off the busy Snorrabraut, a ten-minute walk from the centre; and Monika Blöndal, Aflagrandi 20 (☎ 552 3644, ✉ monikab@simnet.is; 5000kr), in the west of the city, a 25-minute walk from the centre but exceptionally good value. If the recommended **B&Bs** or **guesthouses** listed here are full, look out for signs in windows advertising rooms or ask at the tourist office for their lengthy official list.

The city campsite and the youth hostel

The cheapest place to stay in Reykjavík is the busy city **campsite** (June to mid-Sept; ☎568 6944; 700kr per person), at Sundlaugavegur 34. Cooking and shower facilities are available on site. Next door, also at Sundlaugavegur 34, is the excellent **youth hostel** (☎553 8110, ⓦwww.hostel.is; 1550kr per person, bed linen 500kr extra), next to Reykjavík's largest swimming pool. As with other forms of accommodation in the capital, the hostel's 160 beds quickly fill in summer and advance booking is recommended; **reservations** are generally held until 6pm unless otherwise requested. The small modern **dorms** sleep between two and six people each, some also have private facilities (3000kr per person per double room). There's also Internet access, a laundry and kitchen here, while buying breakfast here will set you back 700kr. Bus #5 runs here from the central Lækjartorg and Hlemmur terminals every twenty minutes; the Flybus to and from Keflavík airport (see p.53) also stops here. Allow forty minutes to walk into town.

The City

Although small for a capital (the population is barely 110,000), compared with Iceland's other built-up areas, Reykjavík is a throbbing urban metropolis; the Greater Reykjavík area is home to three out of every five Icelanders. If you're planning to visit some of the country's more remote and isolated regions, you should make the most of the atmosphere generated by this bustling port, with its buzzing nightlife and highbrow museums. The collections in the centrally located **National Museum**, **Culture House** and **Saga Museum**, for example, offer a fine introduction to Iceland's stirring past, while you'll find the outstanding work of sculptors **Ásmundur Sveinsson** and **Einar Jónsson** outdoors in the streets and parks, as well as in two permanent exhibitions – indeed, contemporary art has a high profile in a whole host of art shops and galleries. And yet even with all of this around you, you can never forget that you're bang in the middle of the North Atlantic, with your nearest neighbours being Greenland and the North Pole – a remoteness that is at the core of Reykjavík's appeal.

The city centre is split roughly into two halves by the brilliant waters of the large, naturally occurring lake **Tjörnin**. To the north and west of this lie, respectively, the busy fishing **harbour**, full of modern hi-tech trawlers and Iceland's whaling fleet, and **Vesturbær**, the city's oldest district, dating back in parts to the Settlement, now largely given over to administration, eating, drinking and entertainment. It's also one of the city's most likeable and picturesque quarters, comprising a spread of well-to-do residential streets, at odds with the concrete apartment blocks on the eastern outskirts of the city. Another gaggle of bars and restaurants are located on **Austurstræti** and **Hafnarstræti** from where **Vesturgata**, bordered by picture-postcard houses with multicoloured rooves and facades, reaches up the hill that begins at Tjörnin's western edge. East of the lake, things become altogether more commercial, as the gently sloping main drag, **Laugavegur**, the city's main shopping street, packed with glitzy designer boutiques and the location for most of the city's bars, restaurants, shops and cinemas, leads towards the bus terminal, Hlemmur, which marks the city's edge.

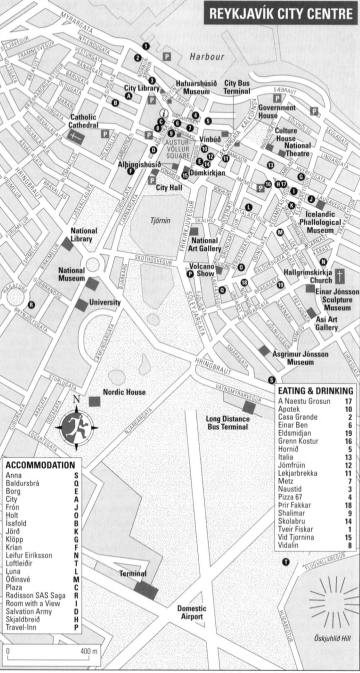

REYKJAVÍK CITY CENTRE

Harbour

MYRARGATA
NÝLENDUGATA
SELJAVEGUR
FRAMNESVEGUR
VESTURGATA
BÁRUGATA
HOLTSGÖTU
BRÆÐRABORGARSTÍGUR
ÖLDUGATA
RÁNARG
TUNGATA

City Library
Hafnarhúsið Museum
City Bus Terminal
SÆBRAUT
TRYGGVG

Catholic Cathedral
Government House
SÖLVHÓLSG
SKULAGATA

Culture House
National Theatre
LINDARGATA

HÁVALLAGATA
SÓLVALLAGATA
ÁSVALLAGATA
GARÐASTR
HRINGBRAUT
BRÁVALLAG
LJÓSVALLAGATA
FURUMELUR
HOLATORG
GRANDANESG
BRYNJÓLFSG
HÁGATORG
SÓLEYJARGATA

Vínbúð
Alþingishúsið
AUSTUR VÖLLUR SQUARE
Dómkirkjan
BANKASTR
HVERFISGATA
LAUGAVEGUR
KLAPPARSTÍG
AMTMST
City Hall
BÓKHLÖÐ

Tjörnin

National Library

FRÍKIRKJUVEGUR
SKÁLHST
SKOTHUSVEGUR
BJARKARG
BJARNARG

National Art Gallery

Volcano Show

National Museum
University

Icelandic Phallological Museum

Hallgrímskirkja Church

Einar Jónsson Sculpture Museum

Ásí Art Gallery

Ásgrímur Jónsson Museum

SKÚLAGATA
SÓLEYJARGATA
NJARÐARGATA
BERGSTAÐASTRÆTI
ÓÐINSGATA
BALDURSGATA
BRAGAGATA
NÖNNUGATA
URÐARST
BALDURSGATA
FRÍKIRKJUVEGUR
FJÖLNISVEGUR
BJARGARSTÍG
LOKASTÍG
SPÍTALAST
NJÁLSGATA
EIRÍKSGATA
BARÓNSSTÍGUR
GRETTISGATA
NJARÐARG

Nordic House

Long Distance Bus Terminal

HRINGBRAUT
VATNSMÝRARVEGUR

STURLUGATA
ARAGATA
ODDAGATA
EGGERTSGATA
SUÐURGATA
SÆMUNDARGATA
NJARÐARGATA

N

Terminal

Domestic Airport

FLUGVALLARVEGUR
HLÍÐARFÓTUR

Öskjuhlíð Hill

Nautholsvik geothermal beach ▼

0 — 400 m

ACCOMMODATION

Anna	S
Baldursbrá	Q
Borg	E
City	A
Frón	J
Holt	O
Ísafold	B
Jörð	K
Klöpp	G
Krían	F
Leifur Eiríksson	N
Loftleiðir	T
Luna	L
Óðinsvé	M
Plaza	C
Radisson SAS Saga	R
Room with a View	I
Salvation Army	D
Skjaldbreið	H
Travel-Inn	P

EATING & DRINKING

A Naestu Grosun	17
Apotek	10
Casa Grande	2
Einar Ben	6
Eldsmidjan	19
Grenn Kostur	16
Hornið	5
Italia	13
Jómfrúin	12
Lekjarbrekka	11
Metz	7
Naustid	3
Pizza 67	4
Þrir Fakkar	18
Shalimar	9
Skolabru	14
Tveir Fiskar	1
Vid Tjornina	15
Vidalin	8

Central Reykjavík

You'd be hard pushed to find another capital city as diminutive as Reykjavík, and a leisurely walk of just an hour or two will take you around almost the entirety of the centre. Such smallness accounts for the city's lack of contrasting and well-defined areas: for simple convenience, we've divided the central portion into two sections separated by the lake, **Tjörnin**, and the road, **Lækjargata**, which runs from the lake and Reykjavík's main square, **Lækjartorg**, down towards the harbour. Even the few things of note further out from the centre can be reached in a few minutes on public transport.

Lækjartorg and around

The best place to get your first taste of Reykjavík is the area around **Lækjartorg** and the adjoining pedestrianized **Austurstræti** on its western side – a general meeting place for Reykjavík's urbanites, where people stroll, strut and sit on benches munching cakes, ice creams and burgers bought from the nearby snack stands and the 10–11 supermarket. The square has always been at the heart of Reykjavík life, indeed, it was here that farmers bringing their wares to market ended their long journey from the surrounding countryside and set up camp from where they could carry out their business in town. Lækjartorg was once overlooked from its western end by the headquarters of the main daily newspaper, *Morgunblaðið*, the implication being that journalists needed only to look through their windows to discover what was happening in the city – which was usually very little. Today, however, the area can be one of the most boisterous in the city. On Friday and Saturday evenings, particularly in summer, hundreds of drunken revellers fill the square when the clubs empty out at 5 or 6am, jostling for prime position – although the noise from the throng can be deafening, the atmosphere is good hearted and not at all intimidating. By day, the area resumes its busy commercial air as people dash in and out of the post office or pop in to one of the city's two main bookshops, Eymundsson. Beyond its junction with Pósthússtræti, Austurstræti gives itself over solely to pleasure, as this is where some of the city's best bars and restaurants can be found (see p.77). This is also the location for the *vínbúð* state alcohol store (see Listings, p.86) a futuristic glass-and-steel structure at no. 10a, where those who want to drink at home have to come and part with vast amounts of cash (see Basics, p.35, for more on this).

Austurvöllur square and the Alþingishúsið

Pósthússtræti, running south from Austurstræti, leads into another small square, **Austurvöllur**, a favourite place for city slickers from nearby offices to catch a few rays during their lunch breaks, stretched out on the grassy lawns edged with flowers. Yet the square's modest proportions and nondescript apartment blocks – where Blur's Damon Albarn is rumoured to have a flat – belie its historical importance. This was the site of Ingólfur Arnarson's farm; it's thought he grew his hay on the land where the square now stands, and as such it marks the original centre of Reykjavík. Similarly, the square's central, elevated **statue** of the nineteenth-century independence campaigner **Jón Sigurðsson**, entitled *The Pride of Iceland, its Sword and Shield*, faces two of the most important buildings in the country – the Alþingi and the Dómkirkjan – though you'd never realise their status from their appearance.

The **Alþingishúsið** (Parliament House) is ordinary in the extreme, a slight building made of grey basalt quarried from nearby Skólavörðuholt hill with the date of its completion, 1881, etched into its dark frontage — yet this unremarkable structure played a pivotal role in bringing about Icelandic independence. In 1798, the parliament moved to Reykjavík from Þingvellir (see p.104), where it had been operating virtually without interruption since 930 AD. Within just two years, however, it was dissolved as Danish power reached its peak, but with great pride and after much struggle, the Alþingi regained its powers from Copenhagen as a consultative body in 1843, and a constitution was granted in 1874, making Iceland self-governing in domestic affairs. The Act of Union, passed in this building in 1918, made Iceland a sovereign state under the Danish Crown although the act was open for reconsideration at any time after 1940, but by then Denmark was occupied by the Nazis and the Alþingi had assumed the duties normally carried out by the monarch, declaring its intention to dissolve the Act of Union at the end of the war. Today, the modest interior, illuminated by chandeliers, more resembles a town council chamber than the seat of a national parliament.

The adjacent **Dómkirkjan** (Mon–Fri 10am–5pm; free), Reykjavík's Lutheran cathedral, is a neoclassical stone structure shrouded against the weather in corrugated iron, built between 1787 and 1796 after Christian VII of Denmark scrapped the Catholic bishoprics of Hólar in the north, and Skálholt in the south, in favour of a Lutheran diocese in what was fast growing into Iceland's main centre of population. The church may be plain on the outside, but venture inside and you'll discover a beautiful interior: perfectly designed arched windows punctuate the unadorned white-painted walls at regular intervals, giving an impression of complete architectural harmony. The cathedral is now deemed too small for great gatherings and services of state, and the roomier Hallgrímskirkja (see p.71) is preferred for state funerals and other such well-attended functions, although the opening of parliament is still marked with a service in the Dómkirkjan followed by a short procession along Kirkjustræti to the Alþingishúsið.

Aðalstræti and Hafnarstræti

From the southwestern corner of Austurvöllur, Kirkjustræti runs the short distance to Reykjavík's oldest street, **Aðalstræti**, which follows the route taken in the late ninth century by Ingólfur Arnarson from his farm at the southern end of the street down to the sea. Immediately in front of you is the city's oldest building, a squat timber structure at no. 10 which dates back to 1752, formerly a weaving shed and a bishop's residence, now the *Vídalín* bistro bar (see p.80), where once lived Skúli Magnússon (see p.53), High Sherrif of Iceland, who encouraged the development of craft industries here. On the opposite side of the street, a few steps north towards the sea outside the present no.9, is Ingólfur Arnarson's **freshwater well**, Ingólfsbrunnur, now glassed over for posterity, which was discovered by sheer fluke when the city council carried out roadworks here in 1992. Just beyond, at the junction with Fischersund, is the new location for the **tourist information office**.

Opposite the tourist office, at the junction of Aðalstræti and **Hafnarstræti**, is another of Reykjavík's beautifully restored timber buildings (covered in corrugated iron for protection), **Fálkahúsið**, one of three buildings in the city where the King of Denmark once kept his much-prized Icelandic falcons before having them dispatched by ship to the Court in Copenhagen. There was outrage recently when the building was converted into a bistro-bar, the *Café Viktor* (see p.78), inevitably subjecting the ancient timbers to the wear and tear of hundreds of stomping feet. Despite this, its turret-like side walls and sheer size still impress, especially when you consider the huge amount of timber that was imported for the job, as Iceland had no trees of its own. Cast an eye to the roof and you'll spot two carved wooden falcons still keeping guard over the building, either side of a garish modern representation of a Viking longboat.

Many of the buildings on the south side of Hafnarstræti were formerly owned by Danish merchants during the Trade Monopoly of 1602–1855 (for more on this, see p.343), and indeed, this street, as its name suggests (*hafnar* means "harbour"), once bordered the sea and gave access to the harbour, the city's economic lifeline and means of contact with the outside world. Today, though, the street is several blocks from the ocean after landfill extended the city foreshore. Instead, it is home to some excellent bars and restaurants, which, together with Austurstræti to the south and Tryggvagata to the north, makes up a rectangular block of eateries and drinking-holes, well worthy of exploration (see "Eating and drinking", p.77).

Tryggvagata and the harbour

Tryggvagata, one block north of the bustle of Hafnarstræti, is remarkable for two things other than the number of consonants in its name: the imposing multi-coloured mosaic mural close to its junction with Pósthússtræti, portraying a busy harbour scene complete with fishing trawlers and cranes, which livens up the otherwise frightfully dull **Tollhúsið** (Customs House); and the **Hafnarhúsið** (Harbour House), part of the **Reykjavík Art Museum** (daily 11am–5pm, Thurs til 7pm; 500kr; ⓦ www.listasafnreykjavikur.is), at Tryggvagata 17. This large, austere building was constructed in the 1930s as warehouse storage and office space for the Port of Reykjavík but has now been converted into six spacious exhibition halls connected by a corridor running over a central courtyard. Although there's certainly plenty of space here, the layout is less than obvious since the confusing array of corridors, which once linked the former warehouse's storage areas, twists and turns around the museum's supporting concrete and steel pillars, leaving the visitor quite lost at times (there are no guides available). Although the museum plays host to frequently changing displays of contemporary Icelandic and international art, the only permanent exhibition is that dedicated to the multicoloured cartoon-like work of Icelandic artist **Erró**. His vibrant collages, depicting everything from Viking warriors to spaceage superheros all seemingly caught up in the same explosive battle, are certainly striking, if somewhat eye-blinding and not to everyone's taste. Born Guðmundur Guðmundsson in Ólafsvík on the Snæfellsnes peninsula in 1932, Erró grew up in Kirkjubæjarklaustur before moving abroad to study at the art academies of Oslo, Florence and Ravenna and finally settling in Paris where he still lives today. In 1982 Erró (even the museum staff are at a loss as to why he chose this name, although he was forced to change from Ferró to Erró in 1967 after being sued) donated about two thousand of his works, including oil paintings, prints and sculptures, to the City of Reykjavík which chose to dedicate this exhibition to him. There's also a café, where it's worth taking time out to enjoy the view of the harbour and Mount Esja through the floor-to-ceiling windows.

From the museum, a two minute walk down **Grófin** leads to **Geirsgata**, the busy main road that runs along the southern side of the **harbour**, which has been built around reclaimed land – the beach where vessels once landed their foreign goods is now inland from here. Street names around here, such as Ægisgata (Ocean Street) and Öldugata (Wave Street), reflect the importance of the sea to the city, and a stroll along the dockside demonstrates Iceland's dependence on the Atlantic, with fishing trawlers being checked over and prepared for their next battle against the waves, and plastic crates of ice-packed cod awaiting transportation to village stores around the country.

Above all, you'll see the five black **whaling vessels**, each with a red "H" painted to its funnel (*hvalur* is Icelandic for "whale"). Roped together, they stood idle here for fourteen years after Iceland abandoned whaling in 1989. After its contentious resumption in 2003, it remains to see what will become of them.

Tjörnin and around

From the harbour, Pósthússtræti leads south over the pleasure meccas of Tryggvagata, Hafnarstræti and Austurstræti to Vonarstræti and **Tjörnin**, invariably translated into English as "the lake" or "the pond". *Tjörn* and its genitive form of *tjarnar* are actually old Viking words, still used in northern English dialects as "tarn" to denote a mountain lake. Originally formed by a lagoon inside the reef that once occupied the spot where Hafnarstræti now runs, this sizeable body of water, roughly a couple of square kilometres in size, is populated by 40–50 varieties of birds – including the notorious **arctic tern**, known for its dive-bombing attacks on passers-by, and found at the lake's quieter southern end – whose precise numbers are charted on notice boards stationed at several points along the bank. A walking path leads all around the lake and can make a pleasant hour's stroll, though be careful not to slip on the large amounts of duck droppings at the lake edge.

Occupying prime position on the northern edge of Tjörnin is **Ráðhúsið** (Reykjavík City Hall; Mon–Fri 8am–7pm, Sat & Sun noon–6pm; free). Opened in 1992, it's a showpiece of Nordic design, a modernistic rectangular structure of steel, glass and chrome that actually sits on the lake itself. Inside, in addition to the city's administration offices, is a small café and a fabulous self-standing **topographical model** of Iceland, to be found in one of the small exhibition areas. It gives an excellent idea of the unforgiving geography of Iceland – marvel at the sheer size of the Vatnajökull glacier in the southeast (as big as the English county of Yorkshire) and the table mountains of the West Fjords and gain instant respect for the people who live amid such landscapes.

One of the best **views** of Reykjavík can be had from Suðurgata, a street running parallel to the western shore of Tjörnin and reached from the city hall by walking west along Vonarstræti, crossing Tjarnargata. However, before continuing up to Suðurgata have a quick look at **Ráðherrabústaðurinn** (Minster's Residence) at Tjarnargata 32, an impressive wooden structure first built at Sólbakki in Önundarfjörður in the West Fjords and formerly owned by a rich Norwegian businessman who's said to have either given it or sold it to Iceland's first Home Rule minister, Hannes Hafstein, in 1904 for the princely sum of 1kr; today it is used by the Icelandic government for official receptions. One block to the west, Suðurgata is lined with tidy little dwellings, but from it you can see across the lake to the suburban houses of the city centre, whose corrugated iron rooves, ranging in colour from a pallid two-tone green to bright blues and reds, have been carefully maintained by their owners – the familiar picture postcard view of Reykjavík.

National Museum

At the junction of Suðurgata and the busy Hringbraut, the closest thing Iceland has to a motorway, is the entrance to the **National Museum** (þjóðminjasafn Íslands; daily 10am–6pm; 600kr; ⓦwww.natmus.is), offering a comprehensive historical overview of Iceland's past from the days of the Settlement right up to the birth of the Republic in 1944. Following extensive renovation work lasting six years, the former exhibition, previously little more than a rag-tag of curious finds and knicknacks, has reopened, transformed into a thoughtful and informative historical account worthy of a national capital. Particularly engaging is the section devoted to the early Viking period, detailing the use of DNA testing of bones excavatated from graves. The rich finds unearthed after the Hekla eruption of 1104 are also given due prominence. Elsewhere, a reconstruction of a medieval church helps to bring to life an extensive collection of religious artefacts, chiefly from the eleventh to thirteenth centuries. The prime exhibit, however, is undoubtedly a carved wooden door, that dates to around 1200 and depicts an ancient warrior on horseback slugging it out with an unruly dragon.

Norræna húsið

Opposite the university at Sturlugata 5 is the **Norræna húsið** (**Nordic House**; Mon–Fri 8am–5pm, Sat & Sun noon–5pm; free; ☎551 1161, ⓦwww.nordice.is), designed by renowned Finnish architect Alvar Aalto in 1961 and buzzed over by aircraft landing at the nearby city airport. Devoted to Nordic culture, with an extensive library of books written in all the Nordic languages, it holds books on virtually any aspect of Nordic life you choose to mention, from Faroese knitting to Greenlandic seal hunting. There are also temporary **exhibitions** (often photographic) in the hall and basement (daily except Mon same hours; 300kr) and frequent evening events, from classical **concerts** to **talks** covering topics from history to politics to music (sometimes in English). Check what's on from the posters inside or from the free tourist magazines at the Tourist Office (see p.54). For speakers of non-Nordic languages, the best part of Nordic House is its **café** (Mon–Sat 8am–5pm, Sun midday–5pm), which serves up a cheap fish lunch (around 850kr) as well as delicious homemade cakes with coffee.

Listasafn Íslands and Lækjargata

A few minutes' walk north from the Nordic House along Sóleyjargata, which runs along the eastern side of Tjörnin towards **Lækjargata**, passing the offices of the Icelandic president (at the corner of Skothúsvegur), is the **Fríkirkjan**, the Free Lutheran Church, a simple wooden structure painted bright white, whose best feature is its tall tower, useful as a landmark to guide you to the neighbouring former ice house, known as **Herðubreið** at Fríkirkjuvegur 7 (Fríkirkjuvegur is the continuation of Sóleyjargata). Once a storage place for massive chunks of ice, hewn in winter from the frozen lake and used to prevent fish stocks rotting, the building has been completely redesigned and enlarged and now houses the **Listasafn Íslands** (National Gallery of Iceland; Tues–Sun 11am–5pm; 400kr, free on Wed; ⓦwww.listasafn.is). Icelandic art may lack worldwide recognition, but all the significant names are to be found here, including Erró, Jón Stefánsson, Ásgrímur Jónsson, Guðmundur Þorsteinsson and Einar Hákonarson – though disappointingly, lack of space (there's only two small exhibition rooms containing barely 20 or so paintings each) means that the works can only be shown in strictly rationed portions from the museum's enormous stock of around 10,000 pieces of art. You can, however, get an idea of the paintings not on display by glancing through the postcards for sale at reception. Drop in, but expect to leave with your artistic appetite no more than whetted; also, note that on entry you have to leave your coat and bag in the lockers provided.

A walk from here back towards Lækjartorg leads on to **Lækjargata** (effectively a continuation of Fríkirkjuvegur), which once marked the eastern boundary of the town; Tjörnin still empties into the sea through a small brook (*lækjar* comes from *lækur*, Icelandic for "brook") which now runs under the road here, and occasionally, when there's an exceptionally high tide, sea water gushes back along the brook pouring into Tjörnin. The cluster of old timber buildings up on the small hill parallel to the street is known as **Bernhöftstorfan** and, following extensive renovation, they now house a couple of chi-chi fish restaurants. Named after T.D. Bernhöft, who ran a bakery in nearby Bankastræti, they're flanked by two of Iceland's most important buildings: the elegant old Reykjavík Grammar School, Menntaskólinn, built in 1844, which once had to be accessed by a bridge over the brook, and housed the Alþingi before the completion of the current Alþingishúsið in nearby Austurvöllur square (see p.63); and a small unobtrusive white building at the bottom of Bankastræti, which is, in fact, **Stjórnarráðshúsið** (Government House), another of Iceland's very parochial-looking public offices. One of the oldest surviving buildings in the city, built in 1761–71 as a prison, it now houses the cramped offices of the Prime Minister. Up on **Arnahóll**, the grassy mound behind the building, a statue of Ingólfur Arnarson, Reykjavík's first settler, surveys his domain; with his back turned on the National Theatre, and the government ministries to his right, he looks out to the ocean that brought him here over eleven centuries ago. Experts believe this is the most likely spot where Ingólfur's high seat pillars finally washed up; according to *Landnámabók* they were found "by Arnarhvál below the heath".

Laugavegur and around

From Lækjartorg, turn right into the short Bankastræti and on, up the small hill, into Laugavegur (hot spring road), the route once taken by local wash-erwomen to the springs in Laugardalur. This is Iceland's major commercial artery, holding the main shops and a fair sprinkling of cafés, bars and restau-rants. Not surprisingly therefore, on Friday and Saturday evenings in summer it's bumper to bumper with cars, their horns blaring, and with well-oiled revellers hanging out of the windows. However, before you give yourself over to extensive retail therapy, there are a couple of more cerebral attractions worthy of your time and attention in this part of town: the grand former National Library, now the **þjóðmenningarhúsið** (**Culture House**; daily 11am–5pm; 300kr; ⓦ www.thjodmenning.is), at Hverfisgata 15, one block north of and parallel to Laugavegur, has the country's largest and best exhi-bition of **medieval manuscripts**. What makes this display of treasures par-ticularly engaging is its accessibility; gone is the tedious intellectual pontificating which so often accompanies Icelandic history, instead you can get close up to these documents and see for yourself what all the fuss is about – an erudite account beside each manuscript serving as an adequate summary. A warren of darkened exhibition halls on the ground floor, illumi-nated only for a few minutes at a time by soft overhead lighting, contain about a dozen ornately decorated documents, themselves in glass cases, including the magnificient *Flateyjarbók* which was finally returned to Iceland in 1971 after spending three centuries in Denmark. The largest of all medieval Icelandic vellums preserved today, the book was written towards the end of the fourteenth century and recounts mostly sagas of kings. However, it is also the only document to contain the *Saga of the Greenlanders*, which relates Leifur Eiríksson's exploration in Vínland. Look out, too, for the *Staðarhólsbók Grágásar*, one of the earliest existing manuscript, dating from around 1270, which runs through laws from the period of the Icelandic Commonwealth, several of which are still in force today, and for the two grubby pages full of grease stains and dirty finger marks of *Kálfalækjarbók* which contains fragments of *Njáls Saga*, one of the most widely read of all the sagas and preserved in more than fifty different manuscripts; this version dates from the mid-fourteenth century. The exhibition also contains a video of the original black and white live television coverage of the manuscripts arriving back in Iceland from Denmark; it's easy to see from the sheer size of the crowds that had gathered at the harbour to welcome the ship, the total fascination Icelanders have with this element of their past – just count, for example, how many streets in Reykjavík alone are named after heros from the sagas. Naturally, the Culture House's other exhibits pale into insignificance; however, it's worth devoting a few minutes to the **Jón Sigurðsson** room on the first floor (Sun only) dedicated to the independence leader Jón Sigurðsson, though you probably have to be a national to appreciate fully some of the finer details of his bitter struggle with the Danes, and labelling of exhibits here is in Icelandic only anyway. In Iceland at least, the oil painting on the wall here depicting Jón bravely standing up in the presence of the Danish king and other top officials, putting his nation's case for independence, is much talked about and revered. Close by on the same floor another small exhibition shows how Iceland has been perceived by the outside world, and, if the collection of oddly shaped ancient maps on display here is anything to go by, knowledge was pretty scarce. On the top floor, a permanent display on **Viking history**, *Vikings and the New World*, tells how Iceland was discovered by Vikings from Norway who then, under the leadership of Eirík the Red, went on to settle Greenland before finally discovering America around the year 1000 AD. Maps, charts and pictures bring the quest for new land in the west to life, and this shouldn't be missed by anyone even vaguely interested in Icelandic history.

Magnusson's manuscripts

Despite so many of Iceland's sagas and histories being written down by medieval monks for purposes of posterity, there existed no suitable means of protecting them from the country's damp climate, and within a few centuries the unique artefacts were rotting away. Enter **Árni Magnússon** (1663–1730), humanist, antiquarian and professor at the University of Copenhagen, who attempted to ensure the preservation of as many of the manuscripts as possible by sending them to Denmark for safekeeping. Although he completed his task in 1720, eight years later many of them went up in flames in the Great Fire of Copenhagen, and Árni died a heartbroken man fifteen months later, never having accepted his failure to rescue the manuscripts, despite braving the flames himself. As he noted at the time of the blaze, "these are the books which are to be had nowhere in the world"; the original **Íslendingabók**, for example, the most important historical record of the settlement of Iceland, written on calfskin, was destroyed, though luckily it had been copied by a priest in Iceland before it left the country.

The manuscripts were to remain apart from their country of origin until long after Icelandic independence in 1944. In 1961, legislation was passed in Denmark decreeing that manuscripts composed or translated by Icelanders should be returned, but it took a further ruling by the Danish Supreme Court, in March 1971, to get things moving, as the Danes were reluctant to see these works of art leave their country. Finally, however, in April that year, a Danish naval frigate carried the first texts, **Konungsbók Eddukvæða** and **Flateyjarbók**, across the Atlantic into Reykjavík, to be met by crowds bearing signs reading *"handritin heim"* ("the manuscripts are home") and waving Icelandic flags. Even so, the transfer of the manuscripts wasn't completed until 1997.

Back on Laugavegur and a couple of blocks further east, an altogether more earthy exhibition that causes the staff at the tourist office to blush with embarrassment, is the **Icelandic Phallological Museum** at no. 24 (2–5pm: May–Aug Tues–Sat; Sept–April Tues & Sat; 400kr; Ⓦ www.phallus.is), the most offbeat of all the country's museums. Inside is a collection of the penises of virtually every mammal found either in Iceland or its offshore waters, with over eighty of them on display in jars of formaldehyde and alcohol, from the sizeable member that once belonged to a young male blue whale, now hollowed out, salted, dried and placed on a wooden plaque, to that of a rogue polar bear found drifting on pack ice off the West Fjords, shot by Icelandic fishermen and then unceremoniously butchered. Nor have testicles been forgotten: a lampshade made of ten rams' scrotums sees to that. Although a human specimen has escaped the collection to date, the museum does have several close seconds: a certificate signed by Páll Arason, a farmer in his eighties from Bugi near Akureyri, who's agreed to donate his apparently ample wedding tackle to the museum on his death; the mishapen foreskin of a 40 year old Icelander, nameless to save his blushes, donated by the National Hospital after an emergency circumcision operation; and plaster casts of three erect former museum visitors which leave nothing to the imagination.

Hallgrímskirkja church

If, after the Phallological Museum, you're in need of spiritual relief, help is close at hand, since from the lower end of Laugavegur, the tongue-twisting Skólavörðustígur streaks steeply upwards to the largest church in the country, the magnificient **Hallgrímskirkja** (daily: May–Sept 9am–6pm; Oct–April 10am–4pm; viewing platform daily 9am–5pm, May–Sept until 6pm). This is a modern concrete structure, whose neatly composed space-shuttle-like form dominates the Reykjavík skyline. Work began on the church, named after the renowned seventeenth century religious poet Hallgrímur Pétursson, immediately after World War II but was only finally completed a few years ago, the slow progress due to the task being carried out by a family firm – comprising one man and his son. Opinions on the church's architectural style – the work of state architect Guðjón Samúelsson – not least the 73-metre phallic steeple – have split the city over the years, although nowadays locals have grown to accept rather than love it. Most people rave about the organ inside, the only decoration in an otherwise completely bare Gothic-style shell; measuring a whopping 15m in height and possessing over 5000 pipes, it really has to be heard to be believed. The cost of installing it called for a major fundraising effort, with people across the country sponsoring a pipe – if you fancy putting money towards one yourself, for which you'll receive a certificate, have a word with the staff. The tower has a **viewing platform** (300kr), accessed by a lift from just within the main door, from where there are stunning panoramic views across Reykjavík; if you come up here in winter, remember to bring a warm hat and scarf because the viewing platform is open to the elements. Incidentally, don't expect the clock at the top of the tower to tell the correct time – the wind up there is so strong that it frequently blows the hands off course. In fact, it's rare for any two public clocks in Reykjavík to tell the same time because of the differing wind conditions throughout the city.

With his back to the church and his view firmly planted on Vínland, the imposing, if somewhat green **statue** of Leifur Eiríksson, Discoverer of America, was donated by the US in 1930 to mark the Icelandic parliament's thousandth birthday. It's a favourite spot for photographs and makes as good a place as any to survey your surroundings – this is one of the highest parts of

Reykjavík and on a clear day there are great **views** out over the surrounding streets of houses adorned with multicoloured corrugated-iron facades.

The Einar Jónsson museum

The heroic form of the Leifur Eiríksson statue is found in several others around the city, many of them the work of **Einar Jónsson** (1874–1954), who is remembered more officially by the pebbledash building to the right of the church. Looking like three large adjoining cubes, the **Einar Jónsson museum** (June to mid-Sept Tues–Sun 2–5pm; mid-Sept to May Sat & Sun 2–5pm; 300kr; Ⓦ ww.skulptur.is) is entered from Freyjugata, the street behind the museum. Einar was Iceland's foremost modern **sculptor**, and this structure was built by him between 1916 and 1923. He worked here in an increasingly reclusive manner until his death in 1954, when the building was given over to displaying more than a hundred of his works – many based on religious and political themes – to the public. A specially constructed group of rooms, connected by slim corridors and little staircases, takes the visitor through a chronological survey of Einar's career – and it's pretty deep stuff. Einar claimed that his self-imposed isolation and total devotion to his work enabled him to achieve mystical states of creativity, and looking at the pieces exhibited here, many of them heavy with religious allegory and all dripping with spiritual energy, it's a claim that doesn't seem far-fetched; look out for *The Guardian*, a ghost keeping watch over a graveyard to make sure the dead receive a decent burial. If the museum is closed, you can peek into the garden at the rear of the museum, where several examples of Einar's work are displayed alfresco, or admire his most visible work, the statue of independence leader, Jón Sigurðsson, found in front of the Alþingishúsið in Austurvöllur square (see p.63).

The ÁSÍ and Ásgrímur Jónsson art galleries

Another, equally admired, modern Icelandic sculptor, Ásmundur Sveinsson, once lived further down the same street as the museum, a short walk away at Freyjugata 41, in a striking if somewhat now past-its-prime functionalist building designed in 1933 by the sculptor and the architect Sigurður Guðmundsson. At the time, the combination of the building's uncompromising squat, building-block style, together with Ásmundur's array of in-your-face sculptures in the garden, caused many heads to turn, but these sculptures have since gone to the Ásmundur Sveinsson museum (see p.75), and the building now seems an integral part of the cityscape, serving as the **ÁSÍ (Icelandic Labour Unions) Art Gallery** (Tues–Sun 2–6pm; Ⓦ www.asi.is; free). This trade-union art collection includes a worthy permanent stock of Icelandic masters, backed up by regular exhibitions of more contemporary fare on the second floor. It's a rather dry place to while away a wet afternoon.

The area between here and Tjörnin is one of the more affluent parts of the city, with houses flourishing a wooden turret or two. From the ÁSÍ museum, trace your steps back to Hallgrímskirkja before heading down Njarðargata, and after about five minutes you'll come to one of the best preserved and less ostentatious abodes, now the **Ásgrímur Jónsson museum** (June–Aug Tues–Sun 1.30–4pm; 250kr; Ⓦ ww.listasafn.is), at Bergstaðastræti 74, the former home of an artist who became a seminal figure in twentieth-century Icelandic painting. Born on a farm in southern Iceland, Ásgrímur (1876–1958) grew up beside the Hekla volcano until leaving for Copenhagen, then the capital of Iceland, in 1897, to study at the Academy of Fine Arts. Six years later, having developed a style and subject matter that drew heavily from Icelandic landscapes and folklore, he returned to his home country and staged an influential exhibition of his work, reflecting the growing nationalistic mood in the country. The ground floor of this small house is kept as the artist left it when he died in 1958, including his piano which he loved to play; upstairs, you'll find a selection of thirty or forty of his canvases, mostly touching though occasionally violent. Especially pleasing are his paintings from around Húsafell where he depicts knotty birch trees struggling for life on the red volcanic soil set against lush green meadows and the whites of the ice caps.

The Kjarvalsstaðir art gallery

From the Ásgrímur Jónsson Museum it's a fifteen-minute walk east to the main highway, Hringbraut, beyond its junction with Snorrabraut and then north into Rauðarárstígur, to reach another of Reykjavík's excellent modern-art museums. Despite being surrounded by birch trees and grassy expanses, however, at first sight the **Kjarvalsstaðir Art Gallery** (daily 10am–5pm; 500kr; Ⓦ www.listasafnreykjavikur.is), part of the Reykjavík Art Museum and devoted to the work of Iceland's most celebrated artist, Jóhannes Kjarval (1885–1972), is an ugly 1960s-style concrete structure, but inside it's a surprisingly bright and airy place. After working during his youth on a fishing trawler, Jóhannes moved abroad to study art, spending time in London, Copenhagen, France and Italy, but it was only after his return to Iceland in 1940 that he travelled widely in his own country, drawing on the raw beauty he saw around him for his quasi-abstract depictions of Icelandic landscapes which made him one of the country's most popular twentieth-century painters. Painted in oils, much of his work is a surreal fusion of colour: his bizarre yet pleasing Krítik from 1946–7, a melee of icy blues, whites and greys measuring a whopping 4m in length and 2m in height, is the centrepiece of the exhibition, portraying a naked man bending over to expose his testicles whilst catching a fish, watched over, rather oddly, by a number of Norse warriors. The museum is divided into two halls – the east one shows Kjarval's work, whilst the west hall is dedicated to visiting temporary exhibitions. Whilst it may take a while for his style to grow on you, it's certainly worth dropping by – note, though, that the entrance to the museum, which is actually located in a small area of parkland, is on Flókagata, off Rauðarárstígur.

Öskjuhlíð and the Saga Museum

If you arrive in Reykjavík from Keflavík airport, it's hard to miss the space-age-looking grey container tanks that sit at the top of the wooded hill, **Öskjuhlíð**, immediately south of Kjarvalsstaðir, across Miklabraut and southeast along Bústaðavegur. Each contains 4000 litres of water at 80°C for use in the capital's homes, offices and swimming pools; it's also from here that water is pumped, via a network of specially constructed pipes, underneath Reykjavík's pavements to keep them ice- and snow-free during winter. The whole thing is topped by a revolving restaurant, *Perlan*, a truly spectacular place for dinner – if your wallet can take the strain. The restaurant is, however, one of Reykjavík's best-known landmarks and is the best place for a 360-degree panoramic **view** of the entire city; simply take the lift to the fourth floor and step outside for free. On a clear day you can see all the way to the Snæfellsjökull glacier at the tip of the Snæfellsnes peninsula, as well as the entirety of Reykjavík.

On the ground floor the excellent **Saga Museum** (daily 10am–6pm; 800kr; Ⓦ www.sagamuseum.is) housed in one of the empty water tanks is Iceland's answer to Madame Tussaud's; this popular portrayal of medieval Icelandic life uses expertly crafted **wax models** of characters from the sagas and their reconstructed farms and homes to superbly enliven this often confusing period of history. Although the entrance fee is steep in comparison to Reykjavík's other museums, it's worth splashing out to get a genuine sense of what life must have been like here centuries ago; indeed, all the big names are here: Snorri, Eirík the Red, Leifur Eiríksson, even his sister, Freyðis, realistically portrayed slicing off her breast as a solitary stand against the natives of Vínland who, after killing one of her compatriots, turned on her – according to the sagas, however, on seeing Freyðis brandish a sword against her breasts, they immediately took flight.

Before leaving, make sure you see the artificial indoor **geyser simulator** that erupts every few minutes from the basement, shooting a powerful jet of water all the way to the fourth floor: it's a good taste of what's to come if you're heading out to the real thing at Geysir (see p.111).

Öskjuhlíð itself was also an important landmark in the days when the only mode of long-distance transport was the horse, as it stood out for miles across the barren surrounding plains – and more recently served as a military base for the British army during World War II. Today though, it's a popular recreation area for Reykjavíkers who, unused to being surrounded by expanses of woodland, flock here by foot and with mountain bikes to explore the **paths** that crisscross its slopes. Although it can be pretty crowded here on a sunny day, you'll easily be able to find a shady glade to call your own.

In fact, Öskjuhlíð has only been wooded since 1950, when an extensive forestation programme began after soil erosion had left the area barren and desolate. Today the western and southern areas of the hill are covered with birch, spruce, poplar and pine. At the southern end of the hill at **Nauthólsvík**, on Nauthólsvegur road close to the Reykjavík Sailing Club, is an artifical **geothermal beach** of bright yellow sand where it's possible to swim in a sea-water lagoon (the water temperature is generally 18–20C°), thanks to the addition of hundreds of gallons of geothermally heated sea water into the open-air **pool** (free; though changing room facilities cost 200kr) next to the beach, where there's also a hotpot (30–35C°) built into the sand. As with the rest of Reykjavík, the hot water is piped here from the tanks atop the hill.

The Museum of Natural History and Höfði house

From Öskjuhlíð, it's a ten-minute walk north along Snorrabraut to the **Museum of Natural History** (Tues, Thurs, Sat & Sun: June–Aug 1–5pm; Sept–May 1.30–4pm; ⓦwww.ni.is; 300kr) at Hlemmur 5. Inside is an impressive collection of virtually every fish (including the turbot, depicted on the 100kr Icelandic coin), bird and egg found in Iceland – all preserved for posterity – including a rare stuffed specimen of the flightless Great Auk which became extinct in 1844 when the last two were killed on the island of Eldey off the Reykjanes peninsula. The museum's example was killed in 1820, although it didn't return to Iceland until 1971 after being bought at auction at Sotheby's in London. However, without a doubt, the museum's most striking exhibit is the whopping two-metre-long leatherback turtle, weighing in at 375kg, found dead in Steingrímsfjörður in the West Fjords in 1963 – it's exhibited in a glass cabinet on the staircase. Sadly the rest of the museum is of remote interest, a baffling selection of rocks and lava samples vying for your attention, although it's worth having a quick glance at the photographs and rock fragments of the Surtsey eruption in the Westman Islands. Although labelling throughout the museum is only in Icelandic, an English language information sheet containing the names of the exhibited birds and fish is available.

From the museum, continue north the short distance to the junction with Sæbraut, and bear left along the sea front to the striking *Sólfar* (Sun Voyager) **sculpture**, a sleek contemporary portrayal of a Viking-age ship, made of shiny silver steel by Jón Gunnar Árnason (1931–89) that is fast becoming one of the most photographed of Reykjavík's attractions – and, indeed, forms the eye-catching cover of *Colloquial Icelandic* (see Language, p.363).

A similar distance east of the junction of Snorrabraut and Sæbraut is **Höfði**, a stocky white wooden structure built in 1909 in Jugend style, which occupies a grassy square beside the shore, between the roads Sæbraut and Borgartún. Originally home of the French consul, the house also played host to Winston Churchill in 1941 when he visited British forces stationed in Iceland. However, Höfði is best known as the venue of the **Reagan–Gorbachev snap summit** of 1986, called at the suggestion of the former Soviet President, Mikhail Gorbachev, to discuss peace and disarmament between the two super-powers. Although agreement was reached in Reykjavík on reducing the number of medium-range and intercontinental missiles in Europe and Asia, the thornier question of America's strategic defence initiative of shooting down missiles in space remained a sticking point. However, the Summit achieved one major goal – it brought the world's attention on Iceland, which, in the mid-1980s, was still relatively unknown as a destination for travellers, in effect marking the beginning of the tourist boom that Iceland is still enjoying today.

Whether Gorbachev and Reagan were troubled by the resident Höfði **ghost** isn't known, but it's said to be that of a young girl, who poisoned herself after being found guilty of incest with her brother. Between 1938 and 1951 the house was occupied by diplomats, including one who was so troubled by the supernatural presence that one dispatch after another was sent to the Foreign Office in London begging for a transfer until he finally got his way. In recent years, lights have switched themselves on and off, paintings have fallen off walls and door handles have worked themselves loose. Today – apart from interna-tional summitry – the principal purpose of the house is as a centre for the city's municipal functions.

The Ásmundur Sveinsson museum

If sculpture is more your thing, particularly if you've already seen the man's house up on Freyjugata, you'll want to check out the domed **Ásmundur Sveinsson museum** (daily: May–Sept 10am–4pm; Oct–April 1–4pm; 500kr; Ⓦ www.listasafnreykjavikur.is), part of the Reykjavík art museum, at Sigtún, a ten-minute dog-leg walk from Höfði; first head east along Sæbraut, then south into Kringlumýrarbraut and east again into Sigtún where you'll see the pecu-liar white igloo shape beyond the trees on your right hand side.

Ásmundur Sveinsson (1893–1982) was one of the pioneers of Icelandic sculpture, and his powerful, often provocative, work was inspired by his coun-try's nature and literature. During the 1920s he studied in both Stockholm at the State Academy and in Paris, returning to Iceland to develop his unique sculptural cubism, a style infused with Icelandic myth and legend, which you can view here at his former home that he designed and built with his own hands in 1942–50. Look also at his soft-edged, gently curved monuments to the ordinary working people of the country in the grounds of the museum, many of which once stood outside his house in Freyjugata (see p.72). In case you're wondering why the museum assumes such an uncommon shape for Reykjavík, it's because when Ásmundur planned it, he was experimenting with Mediterranean and North African themes, drawing particular inspiration from the domed houses common to Arabic countries. Inside, a couple of stark white rooms contain more examples of the sculptor's work, including several busts from his period of Greek influence, but the original of his most famous sculpture, Sæmundur on the Seal, is not on display here but, appropriately, stands outside the main university building on Suðurgata. It shows one of the first Icelanders to receive a university education, the priest and historian Sæmundur Sigfússon (1056–1133), astride a seal, psalter in hand.

Laugardalur and around

After rambling through central Reykjavík for a good couple of kilometres, Laugavegur finally comes to an end at the junction with the main north-south artery, Kringlumýrarbraut, actually Route 40 leading to Hafnarfjörður. Beyond here **Suðurlandsbraut** marks the southern reaches of **Laugardalur**, a valley containing hot springs known since the time of the Settlement as a source of hot water for washing, hemmed in between the low hills of Grensás to the south and the northerly Laugarás, just behind Sundahöfn harbour. Although the springs, Þvottalaugarnar, are still here, the spot commemorated by the Ásmundur Sveinsson statue, *þvottakonan* (The Washerwoman), it's for Iceland's best **sports ground**, Laugardalsvöllur, superb outdoor **swimming complex** (see Activities p.84), Laugardalslaug, and **youth hostel** that the area is best known. The green expanses beyond the sports ground contain the country's most impressive **botanical garden** as well as a **zoo**.

The botanical garden and zoo

Barely ten minutes on foot from the Ásmundur Sveinsson sculpture museum, reached by walking east along Engjavegur, the **botanical garden**, part of the Laugardalur, contains an extensive collection of native Icelandic flora, as well as thousands of imported plants and trees. This place is particularly popular with Icelandic families who come here not only to enjoy the surroundings but also to show kids the adjoining **family park** (Fjölskyldugarðurinn) and **zoo** (Húsdýragarðurinn; both mid-May to Aug daily 10am–6pm; rest of the year daily 10am-5pm; 450kr; Ⓦ www.mu.is), where seals, foxes, mink, reindeer and fish caught in Iceland's rivers and lakes are all on hand to keep them happy. Once the attraction of the animals starts to wane, there's a small duck lake, complete with replica Viking longboat, along with other activities based loosely on a Viking theme: a fort, an outlaw hideout and even a go-cart track in the surrounding family park. Buses #2, 5, 10, 11, 12 and 15 all run here from the city centre.

The Árbæjarsafn open-air museum

From the botanical garden, it's a short bus ride on #10 (originating at the Hlemmur bus terminal) to the Árbæjarsafn Open-Air Museum (June–Aug Mon 11am–4pm, Tues–Fri 9am–5pm, Sat & Sun 10am–6pm; Sept–May Mon, Wed & Fri 1–2pm; 400kr; Ⓦ www.arbaejarsafn.is), a collection of turf-roofed and corrugated-iron buildings on the site of an ancient farm that was first mentioned in the sagas around the mid-1400s. The buildings and their contents record the change that occurred as Iceland's economy switched from farming to fishing – the industrial revolution being heralded by the arrival of the fishing trawler – and Reykjavík's rapid expansion. The pretty turf church here, dating from 1842, was carefully moved to its present location from Skagafjörður (see p.236) on the north coast in 1960. Next to it, the farmhouse is dominated by an Ásmundur Sveinsson sculpture, the *Woman Churning Milk*, illustrating an all-but-lost traditional way of life.

The Seltjarnarnes–Heiðmörk Trail

When the wind isn't blowing too strongly, the flat surrounds of Reykjavík lend themselves to **cycling** and an excellent, well-marked **trail** has been laid from the western suburb of Seltjarnarnes via the city airport, Öskjuhlíð (see p.73) and the Elliðaárdalur valley, named after the Elliðaá, one of Iceland's best salmon-fishing rivers, to Heiðmörk, a forested city park immediately southeast of the city centre declared a nature reserve in 1948 – this route is clearly marked on the excellent Map of Reykjavík available from the tourist office (see p.54); for bike rental, see p.55. The salmon season itself runs from April to September and **fishing permits** must be ordered several months in advance of your arrival in Iceland via the tourist office in Reykjavík – reckon on a hefty 6000kr to 10,000kr per day depending on location. Trout fishing is much cheaper – generally 500kr to 6000kr per day – and permits can be obtained at short notice.

East of Öskjuhlíð, the path itself follows the river as it flows into Elliðaárvatn, the largest lake within Greater Reykjavík. Formed thousands of years ago when an outflow of lava dammed the glacial valley here, the lake is 174m above sea level and therefore surrounded by Arctic flora; a walking trail leads around Elliðaárvatn and takes around three hours to complete. Elliðaárdalur is one of Reykjavík's main **horse-riding** areas – riding tours are booked through the tourist office in Reykjavík with trips varying in length from under an hour to a full day. Bordering the eastern shores of the lake, Heiðmörk, the largest and most popular recreational area in the city, is set between mountains, craters and lavafields and offers 2800 square hectares of forested expanses ideal for mountain biking or hiking – extensive planting began in 1949 to try to avert severe soil erosion from overgrazing and the harsh climate. Walking and cycle paths criss-cross the wooded expanses, dotted with picnic sites, making the area a favourite spot during summer weekends for Reykjavík's inhabitants.

Eating and drinking

Eating in Reykjavík is expensive, although there are ways to reduce costs a little. Naturally, self-catering is the least costly of all, and the best **supermarkets** in the city centre include: *10–11*, close to the Austurvöllur square at Austurstræti 17, which, confusingly, is open from 8am until midnight from June to August; the larger *Bónus*, at Laugavegur 59; and the best-stocked and largest supermarket in the country, *Nýkaup*, in the Kringlan shopping centre, at the junction of Miklabraut and Kringlumýrarbraut and reached either on foot in about forty minutes or by taking bus #6 from the city centre. If you're looking to buy booze simply to take away, the *vínbúð* **alcohol stores** are at Austurstræti 10a (Mon–Thurs 11am–6pm, Fri 11am–7pm, Sat 11am–2pm; ☏562 6511); and on the lower level of the Kringlan shopping centre (Mon–Thurs 11am–6pm, Fri 11am–7pm, Sat 11am–4pm; ☏568 9060). Supermarkets are also the best source of **breakfast** if your accommodation isn't providing any, since cafés generally don't open until around 10am – closing time is variable. Otherwise, expect to pay through the nose for it at one of the city's hotels, reckoning on at least 900kr a head for an extensive buffet selection of cold fish, smoked meats, toast, jam, cereals and coffee. For coffee and snacks during the day, use any of the numerous **cafés** dotted around, many of which mutate into **bars** from 6pm onwards, though this will leave a serious hole in your pocket – expect to pay around 1100kr per head for a cup of coffee, a sandwich and a cake. For a half-litre of beer be prepared to pay 500–600kr.

For full meals, some **restaurants** offer lunch specials from 11.30am to 2.30pm. These may be either set dishes or help-yourself buffets costing around 1100kr. These generally include a starter such as soup, a meat or fish dish, followed by coffee. If your budget stretches to it (upwards of 5000kr a head), however, you can dine in style in small, atmospheric and high-quality restaurants, though you'll often need to make a reservation for Friday or Saturday evenings in summer, and dress fairly smartly. Most open for dinner around 6.30pm or 7pm and stay open until midnight or 1am on weekday evenings and Sundays, extending their hours until around 3am on Friday and Saturday evenings. There are some decent restaurants around the city serving international cuisines, such as Mexican or Mediterranean, and these will generally be cheaper than the Icelandic ones though a few do surprise. If you're longing for a curry, you'll only be disappointed – Indian food is generally bland in the extreme, aimed at the Icelandic palate, which has yet to come to grips with lots of spices. There are also a number of similarly priced fast-food outlets serving burgers and pizzas, but none is particularly cheap: the *McDonald's* in the Kringlan shopping centre, for example, is one of the most expensive of its kind in the world.

Cafés

Brennslan Pósthússtræti 9. Good-value Parisian-style brasserie overlooking Austurvöllur square, with excellent sandwiches from 750kr, chicken and chips 1000kr, or fish dishes for around 1100kr. It's a good place for an evening drink, with over 100 different beers to choose between.

Café Paris Austurstræti 14. Over the years this French-style café has become a Reykjavík fixture, with outdoor seating in summer overlooking the Alþingi. Fine central choice for a cup of coffee or a light snack.

Café Victor Hafnarstræti 1–3. An exceptionally good value bistro bar and café in one of the capital's oldest buildings, which once served as the Danish king's falcon house (see p.64). Pasta and noodle dishes are 950–1200kr, chicken burritos 1150kr or there's deep-fried haddock with bacon and chips for 1290kr. Great ambience by evening, when the café turns into a bar.

Grái Kötturinn Hverfisgata 16a. Smoky, friendly basement café, good for meeting young Reykjavíkers who come here for the excellent coffee. Open from 7am for breakfast.

Kaffi List Laugavegur 20A. Immediately recognisable by its huge pink neon sign over the door. Locals love this smart café with a Spanish touch, serving tapas and open sandwiches. Count on 1350kr for lunch. Also a lively spot for an evening drink or two.

Kaffi Reykjavík Vesturgata 2. An excellent and popular choice for lunch or dinner.

Kaffi Sólon Bankastræti 7a. One of Reykjavík's most popular cafés, enjoying a perfect position on the main shopping street for people watching. Marble tables and gilt mirrors make for a truly relaxing afternoon over a cafetière and a piece of chocolate cake.

Kaffibarinn Bergstaðastræti 1. Trades on the rumour that Damon Alburn of Blur has shares in the place – however unlikely. A single ugly building covered in red corrugated iron with green window frames and brown wooden blinds though worth it for the curiosity value. The owners claim it attracts Iceland's jetset and arty crowd, a tall order in such a small city, though definitely a trendy place for a beer or two.

Kaffitár Bankastræti 8. Resembling a cosy Icelandic version of *Starbucks*, this is *the* place in Reykjavík to find real coffee. The owner is renowned across the capital for her exceptional choice of beans and her wide array of fresh home-ground speciality blends. Gorgeous cakes are also on offer in this non-smoking place at the foot of the main shopping street. Don't leave town without dropping in.

Kaffivagninn Grandargarður 10. A little shack down by the harbour, popular with local fishermen who come here for an early morning breakfast – indeed, this is the only place serving breakfast so early, opening at 6am. The menu changes daily but generally offers fish, stew and soup dishes of the day, and while the food may be plain and unadorned, the working atmosphere is great. Open until 7pm.

Mokka Skólavörðustígur 3a. Opened in 1958, the oldest café in Reykjavík, with a changing display of black-and-white photographs adorning the walls. The place makes a point of not playing music and was the first café in the country to serve espressos and cappuccinos to its curious clientele.

Póstbarinn Pósthússtræti 13. An unadorned down-to-earth café overlooking the cathedral and parliament in one corner of Austurvöllur square offering excellent value for money. Open sandwiches are 850kr, soups, salads and stuffed baguettes 990kr and panfried haddock is just 1190kr.

Thorvaldsen Austurstræti 8. A little bistro café that takes itself rather seriously – and hence is full of Reykjavík's trendy young things posing in the windows which look out over Austurvöllur square. A limited menu with the emphasis on snacks such as chicken sandwiches and noodle dishes from around 1290kr.

Restaurants

Á Næstu Grösum Laugavegur 20b, close to the junction with Klapparstígur. Also known as *First Vegetarian*, this place has been serving tasty vegetarian food for years, with most of the ingredients coming from geothermally heated greenhouses in southern Iceland. There's always one vegan and one wheat-free dish on the menu; a full meal here goes for less than 1000kr. Open Mon–Fri 11.30am–10pm, Sat 1pm-10pm, Sun 5–10pm.

Casa Grande Tryggvagata 8. A decent and relatively inexpensive Mexican place – if you don't mind the fake cacti everywhere – at the corner of Norðurstígur and Mýrargata. Nachos for 1000kr or enchiladas for 1500kr.

Apótek Austurstræti 16 ☎575 7900. Housed in the capital's former pharmacy, this stylishly modern café, bar and grill restaurant with an Art Deco interior of white-panelled chairs, and wooden flooring specialises in top-notch, if expensive, fusion dishes combining the best of western and oriental cuisines: Thai chicken salad with wonton for 2300kr is the cheapest dish on the menu.

Einar Ben Veltusund 1 ☎511 5090. Named after one of Iceland's finest poets, Einar Benediktsson, this is the place to come for elegant dining with chandeliers, heavy red drapes, soft lighting – and prices to match. Roast fillet of salmon with sweetcorn and fennel at 2750 is the least expensive dish, with roast chicken breast in a Bordelaise sauce at 2950kr coming a close second.

Eldsmiðjan Bragagata 38a. The best pizzas in Reykjavík, from 955kr, made in a pizza oven that burns Icelandic birchwood. In a backstreet near the Hallgrímskirkja church but definitely worth looking out for. There's also a takeaway service available.

Grænn Kostur Skólavörðustígur 8. Fantastic spicy vegan eat-in meals and takeaway, using fresh ingredients and offering a wide variety of dishes. It is annoyingly hard to find, however – from

Skólavörðustígur turn right into Bergstaðastræti then immediately right again towards the multistorey car park, and it's on your right hand side in the small parade of shops. The resident cat, Antonio, is the only one treated to milk-based products.

Hornið Hafnarstræti 4 ☎511 3233. A very popular place with young Reykjavíkers, who flock here for the excellent pizzas (1200–1500kr) and pasta (from 1650kr). The fish here is also good: dishes are often Italian-inspired, such as the salmon with basil oil and capers (1890kr). Wine here can be inordinately expensive – check carefully before ordering.

Ítalía Laugavegur 11 ☎552 4630. Expensive and average Italian restaurant serving pizzas and calzone from 1600kr and pasta from 1500kr.

Lækjarbrekka Bankastræti 2 ☎551 4430. *The* place in Reykjavík to sample lobster: the lobster feast (5280kr) includes cream of lobster soup with cognac, grilled lobster en croûte and grand marnier ice cream. The game feast (5380kr) features reindeer steak and puffin breast, whereas the lamb menu (4380kr) has delicious roast lamb in mountain herbs as a main dish. Other à la carte fish and meat dishes start around 3000kr. Undoubtedly expensive, though the tasteful décor does give the place a wonderful homely feel – perhaps one for a special occasion or your last night in Iceland.

Jómfrúin Lækjargata 4. Prices have shot up over the past year or so at this Danish-influenced place specialising in open sandwiches. Rye bread with fried plaice, smoked salmon with caviar, shrimps, asparagus and lemon is 1200kr – choose carefully to make sure you're not paying over the odds for what you get.

Metz Austurstræti 9. With an interior still showing remnants of the original Sir Terrence Conran design, featuring ornate roof supports dressed in bronze mosaic tiles, this chi-chi brasserie wouldn't look out of place in London or New York. Surprisingly, the food here is very reasonably priced: vegetarian quiche 900kr, spinach salad with olives and mozzarella also 900kr, burgers 1300kr and canneloni 1700kr. There's also a daily seafood special for 1700kr.

Naustið Vesturgata 6–8 ☎551 7759. Top-quality fish restaurant serving up expense-account meals in a high-seas atmosphere, the dark interior strewn with fishing nets. Baked salmon with spinach and monkfish in a red wine and bacon sauce are both 2350kr. Wine here starts at a totally disgraceful 4000kr per bottle.

Pizza 67 Tryggvagata 26. Although the dark and dingy interior is not immediately appealing, this is

❶

REYKJAVÍK | Eating and drinking

one of the cheaper pizzerias in Reykjavík with pizzas and pasta dishes from around 1000kr. Simple fish dishes start at 1300kr, burger and chips is 800kr, a Tex Mex chicken breast with fries and salad is 1690kr.

Shalimar Austurstræti 4. Good-value Indian and Pakistani fare spiced exactly to your taste – just tell them how hot you like it – in this small café-like restaurant at the western end of Austurstræti. Lunch here is a totally fabulous 850kr, the set dinner 1090kr including rice and salad. Alternatively you can choose your favourite from the menu – vegetarian mains cost 1390kr, chicken dishes 1590kr, lamb is 1690kr.

Skólabrú Skólabrú 1, ☎562 4455. An old wooden building from 1906, covered in corrugated iron, houses this renowned fish restaurant. Inside, the grandfather clock and lace curtains give a homely feel to the restaurant whose fish is especially succulent – try the fried catfish with sautéed tomatoes, almonds and shrimps in garlic dill butter for 2450kr.

Tveir Fiskar Geirsgata 9, ☎511 3474. Reykjavíkers are still raving about this culinary gem down by the harbour. Owned by chef Gissur Guðmundsson, the President of the Icelandic Chefs Organisation, so you can rest assured that the fish served here is of the very best quality. All main courses, everything from roast monkfish with wild mushrooms and port wine balsamic glaze to sea bass with a warm parsnip and citrus apple salad and marsala sauce, cost upwards of 3000kr. Wine here, sadly, is likely to be out of most people's

reach – don't even think about ordering a bottle before speaking to your bank manager.

Vegamót Vegamótastígur 4 ☎511 3040. A favourite hangout for Reykjavík's trendy young things, who come here for the excellent brunches (around 1190kr for the works) and the outstanding value for money lunches – chicken burritos are 1090kr or a burger with bacon, pineapple and tomato salad goes for 890kr. A popular place for dinner, too, reckon on 1300kr for a main fish or meat dish.

Vídalín Aðalstræti 10. An atmospheric bistro bar located in the oldest building in Reykjavík from 1752, with small wooden tables and a very low ceiling, serving expensive seafood and lamb. Open for dinner only from 6pm.

Við Tjörnina Templarsund 3 ☎551 8666. One of the best fish restaurants in Reykjavík, divided into quaint, cluttered rooms – the interior design reminiscent of an Icelandic grandmother's front room. Daring and delicious cuisine: everything from pan-fried fish cheeks on a bed of cajun-spiced vegetables (3200kr) to sautéed breast of guillemot (3100kr).

Þrír Frakkar Baldursgata 14 ☎552 3939. Don't be put off by the name (*Three Overcoats*), there's nothing fusty about this backstreet French-style bistro using purely Icelandic ingredients for its traditional dishes: whale peppersteak 2890kr or pan-fried cod with shrimp gratin 2090kr. The traditional plokkfiskur (fish and potato mash; 1880kr) is excellent, as is the grilled catfish with cream pepper sauce 2150kr.

Nightlife and entertainment

Thanks to some cunning publicity from the Icelandic Tourist Board, **nightlife** in Reykjavík is now deservedly known across Europe and the States for its partying. Although the scene is actually no bigger than that of any small-sized town in most other countries, what sets it apart is the northerly setting and location for all this revelry – in summer, it's very disorientating to have entered a nightclub in the wee small hours with the sun just about to set, only to emerge a couple of hours later (and several thousand krónur poorer) into the blinding and unflattering daylight of the Icelandic morning. Very few people are out much before 10pm, after which time crowds fill the streets and queues develop outside the most popular joints. The light nights mean that summer partying rarely winds up before 5am or 6am, and it's certainly not uncommon to see hordes of youngsters staggering around Lækjartorg at 4am shivering in the cold air dressed, fashion-consciously, only in their latest T-shirts and jeans – and often in much less.

You'll need plenty of cash for even a few **drinks** (a beer in a club costs upward of 600kr) – and don't be tempted to leave your drink on the bar whilst you go dancing, as the chances are it'll have been drunk by the time you

Wrecked in Reykjavík

A rite of passage for all Icelandic teenagers, the **runtúr** (literally "round tour") is a drunken pub crawl that generally takes place between at least half a dozen bars and pubs, whatever the weather. Intent on searching out the place with the hottest action, groups of revellers, already well oiled after downing several generous vodkas before setting out, maraud the city centre, particularly on Friday nights. If you come across them, expect to be engaged in conversation or to see some rather unrestrained behaviour – but then nightlife in Iceland isn't known for its subtleties.

return. **Admission fees** to clubs are not too steep, generally around 500–1000kr. As you'd expect, things are liveliest on Friday and Saturday nights, when most places swing until 5 or 6am; closing time the rest of the week is around 1am.

Bars, pubs and clubs

The best spots to start socializing are bars and pubs, as well as some of the cafés listed on p.78 that turn into bars after 6pm. Remember that, whatever your tradition at home, you won't be expected to buy a round of drinks if you're in company, since that would be virtually ruinous, and that it's quite permissible to nurse one drink through the entire evening. Some of the bars listed below are attached to restaurants but you can always drink without eating.

Don't expect to get into a club in style-conscious Reykjavík if you turn up in full hiking gear – the dress code is generally smart and Icelandic men often don a tie to go out clubbing. For foreigners things are more relaxed, but you'll feel more comfortable if you're smart-casual. At some places, jeans and sneakers aren't allowed. However you're kitted out, don't be surprised if you're approached and chatted-up as soon as you've set foot through the door – Reykjavík is a small city and new faces will always draw attention.

22 Laugavegur 22. Bar on the main street, with a small dancefloor on the second floor. Once very popular, it's now rather quiet and so is a good place if you want to chat over a beer.

Broadway Inside *Radisson SAS Hótel Ísland*, Ármúli 9. Prone to Vegas-style singing and dancing spectaculars, though occasionally with more interesting fare and popular with people of all ages, from teenagers to pensioners. Entrance 1000kr.

Dubliner Hafnarstræti 4. Traditional Irish bar with wooden tables and floor. A popular place for an evening pint of Guinness or a beer (600kr). There's also a decent selection of whiskies at 500kr per shot.

Gaukur á Stöng Tryggvagata 22. The closest thing to a traditional British watering hole, billing itself as Iceland's oldest pub – true enough since it's been plying liquor to the masses since 1983. There's live bands here most nights of the week playing everything from Britney to the Beatles. Evening entrance fee 1000kr.

Hverfisbarinn Hverfisgata 20. Consistently Reykjavík's most popular bar over the past couple of years and still going strong. This place attracts all the city's young in-crowd who come to pose and pout in the large glass windows overlooking Hverfisgata. If you're young and beautiful, or just think you are, you'll love it here. Often long queues to get in. Entrance 500kr.

Nasa Austurvöllur square. Housed in a former theatre, this is Reykjavík's biggest and best club next to Kaffi Thorvaldsen in Austurvöllur square – the entrance is to the left of the wooden house covered in corrugated iron. This is *the* place to be seen with wild dance music all night long. Entrance 1000kr.

Nellys Þingholtsstræti 2. American-style bar with a mixed gay and straight crowd, especially at weekends, open till 1am daily and serving Iceland's cheapest beer – so understandably popular. Entrance 500kr.

Samtökin Laugavegur 3. The best place for gay men and women to meet up – if the other places listed are quiet, the chances are there'll always be someone here.

Sirkus Klapparstígur 31. Reykjavík's first French

wine bar, in an unprepossessing building off Laugavegur. French wine is available by the glass, as is pastis and calvados. Busy at weekends with a Bohemian clientele who don't mind queuing to get in.

Spotlight Hafnarstræti 17. One of Reykjavík's busiest nightclubs, with a sizeable dancefloor. Popular also with the capital's gay population on Friday and Saturday nights. The place to be seen, and something of a pickup joint, with lots of dark corners hiding roaming hands. Entrance 500kr.

Þjóðleikhúskjallarinn Hverfisgata 19. Despite its unpronounceable name, the basement café underneath the National Theatre transforms itself into a popular club playing 1970–80s music on Fri and Sat nights (midnight to 3am).

Gay Reykjavík

Although a **gay scene** does exist in Reykjavík, it is very small and at times crashingly provincial in style and scale. There are just two exclusively gay **bars** in the capital and one mixed place– the best choice is the **Samtökin** bar, café and gay library all rolled into one at Laugavegur 3 (⌾552 7878, Ⓦwww.gay-iceland.com), which welcomes lesbians and gay men. To enter, walk through the arch with the red postbox, take the first door to the right and ride the lift to the fourth floor. The only other option is the smoky, male-only *MSC* leather bar (⌾562 1280, Ⓦwww.this.is/msc) in Ingólfsstræti – ring the bell through the black metal gate opposite *Kaffi Sólon* to gain entrance here. Other than the predominantly straight clubs and bars (see p.81), which attract a small but dedicated gay following on Friday and Saturday nights, the only other place to meet gay men is the sauna at the *Vesturbæjarlaug* **swimming pool** (see p.85).

Gay Pride (Ⓦwww.this.is/gaypride) is generally held over the second weekend sometime in August. It's a relatively small-scale though fun affair, with a procession of floats along Laugavegur topped by scantily-clad drag queens shivering from the cold, an evening of dancing and merrymaking and other cultural activities. For further information contact Samtökin (see p.43).

Live music, theatre and cinema

There's been a strong **rock music** network in Reykjavík for over two decades, represented originally by Björk and the Sugarcubes, and more recently by groups such as Sigur Rós, though decent venues have always been thin on the ground, with most gigs taking place in one of the city's restaurants. Besides the local talent, a lot of British and American acts use Icelandair as a cheap way to cross the Atlantic and they often do a show here on the way. Find out what's on by checking with the tourist information office (see p.54) or by looking through their free handout *What's on in Reykjavík*. The following establishments (pubs and hotel) often have live music at weekends, offering anything from jazz to rock: *Café Amsterdam* (⌾551 3800) at Hafnarstræti 5; *Dubliner* (⌾551 3233) at Hafnarstræti 4; *Gaukur á Stöng* (⌾551 1556) at Tryggvagata 22; and the *Hótel Borg* (⌾551 1440) at Pósthússtræti 11.

Remarkably, for such a small city, Reykjavík boasts several **theatre** groups, an opera, a symphony orchestra and a dance company. Unfortunately, major theatre productions and classical concerts, by the **Icelandic Symphony Orchestra**, are a rarity in summer, but throughout the rest of the year there are full programmes of both. Events are chiefly held at the *Þjóðleikhúsið* (⌾551 1200, Ⓦwww.leikhusid.is), the National Theatre at Hverfisgata 19, or the *Háskólabíó* cinema complex (⌾562 2255), home to the Symphony Orchestra, at Hagatorg off Suðurgata. The **Icelandic Opera** (⌾511 4200) is at Ingólfsstræti, and the **City Theatre** (⌾568 8000) at Listabraut 3.

The **cinema** is a better bet if you have time on your hands and little money in your pocket: new international releases are screened with subtitles.

Admission is generally 800kr; see any of the newspapers (see Basics, p.38) for full listings or call the following cinemas direct: *Bíóborgin*, Snorrabraut 37 (☎551 1384 or ☎552 5211); *Regnboginn*, Hverfisgata 54 (☎551 9000); *Háskólabíó*, on Hagatorg, off Suðurgata (☎530 1919); and Stjörnubíó, Laugavegur 94 (☎551 6500). *Háskólabíó* is the biggest and best but they're all of a high standard. More unusual is the worthwhile **Volcano Show** at Hellusund 6a (☎551 3230), a two-hour set of films in two showings of recent Icelandic eruptions from daringly close quarters filmed largely by the engaging Villi Knudsen (part one 750kr, parts one & two 950kr). During July and August part-one screenings in English (Villi Knudesen's volcano adventures) begin at 11am, 3pm and 8pm year round, with additional shows in summer, with part two (Heimaey and Surtsey eruptions) following at noon, 4pm and 9pm; during the rest of the year part one starts at 8pm, with part two following immediately at 9pm.

Activities

Although there are plenty of attractions in and around Reykjavík to keep even the most demanding visitor occupied for several days, it's easy access to some exceptional **adventure activities** that really makes the Icelandic capital such an appealing and unusual destination. **Whale watching** is available aboard boats which sail from the harbour right in the city centre; **snowmobile tours,** although not possible in the immediate vicinity of the capital, depart regularly from Reykjavík for several of the country's southeastern glaciers, and **horseriding** astride Iceland's very own breed of horse, the Íslandshest, a short, stocky creature renowned for its unusual gait, is already inordinately popular.

The **swimming pool** is to the Icelanders what the pub is to the British or the coffee shop to Americans. This is the place to come when in Reykjavík to meet people, catch up on the local gossip and to relax in divine geothermally heated waters. The locals loll around in the pools for hours, as there is no time limit on how long you can stay in the pool. Entrance fees are around 220kr; the cost is kept low by subsidies from the Icelandic taxpayer.

Although Reykjavík is surrounded by superb **hiking** terrain, much of it is difficult to reach without your own transport. However, two excellent areas, both accessible by bus, lie within easy striking distance of the capital. Hengill, south of Reykjavík on the Ringroad towards Selfoss, offers the best hiking opportunities around Reykjavík, whereas the slopes of Mount Esja, between Reykjavík and Akranes, offer steep climbs and superb views of the Greater Reykjavík region.

Lastly, there are also several opportunites for **skiing** at Bláfjöll, Skálafell and Hamragill, all of which are suitable for varying levels of expertise, from beginner upwards.

Whale watching

Operated by Destination Iceland (☎591 1020, ⓦwww.dice.is), **whale watching tours** leave daily (April–Sept 9am & 1pm, plus 5pm in July & Aug; 4000kr) from Ægisgarður, the main jetty in Reykjavík harbour, between Geirsgata and Mýrargata, sailing for Faxaflói bay north of Reykjavík onboard a highspeed catamaran. Although a little shorter in duration (2.5–3hr) when compared to other similar tours operating from Ólafsvík on the Snæfellsnes peninsula and Húsavík up on the north coast, this tour not only offers exceptional value for money but also a chance to see birdlife at close quarters since the vessel calls at Lundey, renowned for its large population of puffins. A similar three-hour tour (April–Oct daily 9am & 1pm, plus 5pm May–Aug; 4200kr) onboard the former trawler *Moby Dick* also operates from the harbour, boasting extremely high rates of whale sightings; if, on the off-chance you're unlucky, they'll book you onto another trip free of charge. On both tours you're most likely to encounter minke whales, orcas, humpbacks and dolphins, although, occasionally, blue, fin and sei whales also put in an appearance.

Snowmobiling

Destination Iceland (see p.83) are also the people to contact for year-round **snowmobile tours,** though sadly they're not in everybody's price range. For a steep 20,900kr, you buy nine hours of sheer exhilaration on the Langjökull glacier south of Húsafell (see p.165) plus a tour round some of western Iceland's other attractions. Although the price is high, if you're intent on seeing this part of the country without your own transport it might be worth splashing out and paying up. **Departures** are at 8am on Tuesday, Friday and Sunday from Reykjavík; you'll head first for Hvalfjörður fjord before cutting inland to the Deildartunguhver hot spring (see p.165) and the Hraunfossar waterfalls (see p.167). From here the tour takes the Kaldidalur interior route (see p.168) towards the glacier, where you transfer to snowmobile – or to dog sled (same price) for a tour to the top of the icesheet. On from here you call at Þingvellir (see p.107) before returning to Reykjavík.

Horse riding

Horse riding is an altogether less expensive option with several companies offering tours of anything from one hour to one day. The most established operator is Íshestar (☎555 7000, ⓦwww.ishestar.is), based in Hafnarfjörður at Sörlaskeið 26. Their tours operate all year round and range from a three-hour excursion around the local lavafields (daily 10am & 2pm; 4200kr) to a nine-hour trip out to Geysir and Gullfoss (May–Oct 10am; 8500kr). Alternatively, the Reykjavík based Thyrill-Víðidalur (☎567 3370, ⓦwww.islandia .is/thyrill), at Hraunbær 2, run a one-hour tour through the Rauðhólar crater area (daily 9am & 2pm; 3500kr); a three-hour tour to Heiðmörk (same times; 5500kr), as well as a longer full-day ride out to the Reynisvatnsheiði moors (daily 9am; 8200kr).

Swimming

The abundance of natural hot water around the capital means there's a good choice of **swimming pools**, which are always at a comfortably warm 29°C, often with hot pots at 39–43°C. **Opening hours** during April to September are generally from 6.30am until around 10pm Monday to Friday, and from 8am or so until 6 or 7pm Saturday and Sunday, while outside these months they may open an hour later and close an hour earlier than this. Remember you must shower without a swimming costume before entering the pools and thoroughly wash the areas of your body marked on the signs by the showers – because pool water in Iceland doesn't contain large amounts of chlorine to kill germs as is common in most other countries. The best three city-centre pools are: Laugardalslaug (☎553 4039), on Sundlaugavegur and adjacent to the youth hostel (see p.61), Iceland's largest outdoor swimming complex, complete with fifty-metre pool, four hot pots, a jacuzzi, steam room, waterslide and masseuse; Sundhöllin (☎551 4059), on Barónsstígur and close to Hallgrímskirkja, with an indoor 25-metre pool, two outdoor hot pots, plus single-sex nude sunbathing on outdoor terraces (*svalir*); and the recently modernised Vesturbæjarlaug (☎561 5004), on Hofsvallagata, with an outdoor 25-metre pool plus three hot pots, a sauna, steam bath and solarium. Swimming costumes can be hired for a small charge at all three.

Hiking

Set in an area of lush vegetation, hot springs (harnessed by the Reykjavík District Heating Company to provide central heating for the capital) and volcanic activity, **Hengill** (803m) has around 125km of well-marked hiking trails, all detailed on free **maps** available at the tourist information centre in Reykjavík (see p.54). Hengill mountain, which dominates the area, is in fact a volcanic ridge (*gill* is an old Viking word that still exists in northern English dialects meaning cleft or ravine) that has erupted several times in the past, and the surrounding area is made up of numerous lavafields, craters, hot springs and bubbling mud pools – it's therefore vital to follow marked paths that have been carefully laid out. To get here, take the 8.30am (June to mid-Sept) long-distance **bus** to Selfoss and ask the driver to let you off at the bottom of the Hveradala hill at Kolviðarhóll, from where you can start hiking, choosing a route that fits your time available and physical ability. To return to the capital, head back for the Ringroad and catch the 4pm bus coming back from Selfoss.

Proudly standing guard over Reykjavík, **Mount Esja** is a familiar sight to anyone who's spent even a few hours in the capital. At 909m, the mountain appears to change colour – from light purple to deep blue, from light grey to golden – depending on the prevailing weather conditions and the light that reflects on the basalt rock and palagonite minerals which make up the mountain, although locals say it depends on her mood. Several hiking trails wind their way around the mountain – once again, a detailed **itinerary** is available from the tourist office – but it's best to start out at Mógilsá where the Icelandic state forestry station has its base. From here an easy path leads up the mountain towards the rocky higher stretches.

Skiing

Although **skiing** is possible in the Reykjavík area, there's so little daylight during the winter period that the amount of time you can actually spend skiing in the day is severely limited. For winter **bus** times to all of the ski areas below, call ☎591 1020.

Thirty minutes by car or bus outside the capital there are three winter downhill skiing areas. The best of the bunch is **Bláfjöll** (Blue Mountains), 20km away with five ski areas of varying difficulty. For cross-country skiing there are tracks of 3–10km, with night skiing available on a five-kilometre route. Get here by taking the Ringroad east until you see a sign for Bláfjöll – turn right onto Route 417 and follow the signs to the mountains.

Skálafell lies to the northeast of Reykjavík and, once again, has beginner, intermediate and advanced hills though it isn't as extensive as Bláfjöll. Incidentally, if you're a fan of chairlifts, you'll find Iceland's longest here at 1500m. Excellent cross-country skiing is also available. From the capital take the Ringroad north until you see a sign for Þingvellir, turn right onto Route 36 and continue until you see a sign for Skálafell, finally turn left into the ski area.

Heading east on the Ringroad for around twenty minutes until just beyond the turn for Route 39 – don't take this road but continue one minute beyond it and turn into the ski area marked on the left – brings you to the **Hamragill** skiing area with its seven ski lifts. Pistes of varying degrees of difficulty are available here, as are some decent cross-country routes.

Listings

Airlines Iceland Express, Suðurlandsbraut 24 ☎550 0600, ⓦwww.icelandexpress.com; Flugfélag Íslands, Reykjavík city airport ☎570 3030, ⓦwww.airiceland.is; Icelandair switchboard ☎505 0300, departure and arrival information ☎505 0500, international ticket sales ☎505 0100, ⓦwww.icelandair.com.

Alcohol stores Austurstræti 10a Mon–Thurs 11am–6pm, Fri 11am–7pm, Sat 11am–2pm, ☎562 6511.

Banks and exchange Búnaðarbanki Íslands, Austurstræti 5, ☎525 6000; Íslandsbanki, Lækjargata 12, ☎560 8600; Landsbanki Íslands, Austurstræti 11, ☎560 6000.

Bookshops Bóksala Stúdenta, Hringbraut, ☎570 0777; Eymundsson, Austurstræti 18, ☎511 1130; Mál og Menning, Laugavegur 18, ☎515 2500, both Eymundsson and Mál og Menning sell English-language books and videos on Iceland, Icelandic–English dictionaries and foreign newspapers.

Camping and outdoors equipment Nanoq-kringlan shopping centre ☎575 5100. All the gear you're likely to need for venturing into the Icelandic outdoors, from tents to clothing, fishing gear and bikes.

Car rental ALP, Vatnsmýrarvegur 10, ☎562 6060; Avis, Knarrarvogur 2, ☎591 4000; Bílahöllin, Bíldshöfði 5, ☎587 1390; Bílaleigan Geysir, Dugguvogur 10, ☎568 8888; Hasso-Ísland, Álfaskeið 115, ☎555 3330; Hertz, Flugvallabraut, ☎505 0600.

Dentist For the duty dentist call ☎575 0505. English spoken.

Embassies and consulates Canada, Túngata 14, ☎533 5550; UK, Laufásvegur 31, ☎550 5100; USA, Laufásvegur 21, ☎562 9100.

Emergencies Fire, ambulance and police ☎112.

Ferries Norræna travel agency, Stangarhyl 3a (☎591 9000, ⓦwww.smyril-line.fo), for the Smyril Line ferry from Seyðisfjörður to Tórshavn (Faroe Islands), Lerwick (Shetland Islands), Bergen (Norway) and Hanstholm (Denmark); Viðey island from Sundahöfn (☎568 1010).

Internet BSÍ bus terminal, Vatnsmýrarvegur 10; Ráðhúskaffi, Reykjavík City Hall; Reykjavík travel service, Lækjargata 2; Reykjavík city library (Borgarbókasafn Reykjavíkur), Tryggvagata 15.

Laundry Þvottahúsið Emla, Barónsstígur 3, ☎552 7499.

Lost property Police headquarters, Hverfisgata 113–115, ☎569 9016.

News in English BBC World Service is relayed live to Reykjavík on FM 90.9, though the signal is weak. There is also an English-language news summary on Teletext page 130 on the state Icelandic TV channel, Sjónvarpið.

Pharmacies Lyfja, Lágmúli 5 (8am–midnight; ☎533 2300); Lyfja, Laugavegur 16, ☎552 4045.

Police Tryggvagata 19, ☎569 9000.

Post office Pósthússtræti 5, ☎580 1000; Mon–Fri 9am–4.30pm.

Travel agents Destination Iceland, Vatnsmýrarvegur 10, ☎591 1020 for bus excursions and activity tours; Norræna, Stangarhyl 3a, ☎591 9000, for the Smyril Line ferry from Seyðisfjörður; Útivist, Laugavegur 178, ☎562 1000, for excursions and plane tickets.

Around Reykjavík: Hafnarfjörður and the islands

Home to three out of every five Icelanders, **Greater Reykjavík** is composed of the neighbouring municipalities of Seltjarnarnes, northwest of the city centre, Mosfellsbær to the northeast, and, in the southwest, Hafnarfjörður, Garðabær and Kópavogur, the last three of which are passed through by the road into the city centre from Keflavík airport.

Comprising row upon row of neat, tidy suburban dwellings of dormitory overspill for Reykjavík, all but **Hafnarfjörður** hold little of interest to the visitor. During the past twenty or thirty years several of these places, in particular Kópavogur and Garðabær, have grown enormously, sending shivers down the spines of city planners and politicians in Reykjavík who admit to fighting a losing battle to stem the flow of people from the villages and towns in the rest of the country, and new tax breaks and other incentives are constantly being dreamed up to prevent population overload – and ever-rising prices – in Reykjavík. Whether these measures succeed in the long term remains to be seen.

Lying just offshore from Reykjavík, the islands of **Viðey** and **Akurey** both make excellent destinations for a short boat trip; the former is renowned for its good restaurant and enjoyable walking trails whilst the latter is the place to head for if you're interested in bird watching, particularly puffins, which crowd onto the island's steep cliff faces to dig their nesting burrows. Viðey is accessible by ferry from the Sundahöfn harbour north of Laugardalur; boats to Akurey leave from Reykjavík harbour.

Hafnarfjörður

Stealing the limelight from its neighbours thanks to its dramatic setting amid an extensive lavafield, **Hafnarfjörður**, with a population of around 19,000 and just 10km from the capital, is as big as the centre of Reykjavík, although it's not as likeable. However, there are several good reasons to make the twenty-five minute bus ride out here, the main ones being to sample some real Viking food at the town's Viking village, **Fjörukráin**, and to learn more about the Icelanders' obsession with elves, dwarves and other spiritual beings – Hafnarfjörður is renowned across the country as the home to the greatest concentration of **huldufólk** ("hidden people").

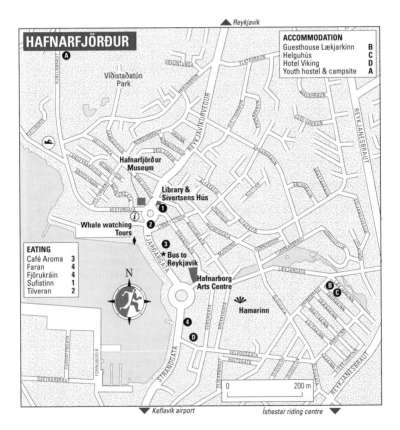

The town's prosperity stems from its superbly sheltered harbour (Hafnarfjörður meaning "the harbour fjord") – 7000 years ago the volcano Búrfell (see p.121), around 5km east of the centre, erupted, spewing lava out along the northern side of the fjord that is now home to Hafnarfjörður, creating a protective wall. At the beginning of the fifteenth century the village became a strategic centre for trade with England, which was then just starting up, and the harbour was often full of English boats profiting from the then rich fishing grounds offshore. Seventy-five years later, a dispute broke out between the English and newly arrived German fishermen who challenged, and won, the right to operate out of the burgeoning town. Their victory, however, was shortlived, since Hafnarfjörður fell under the trade monopoly of the Danes in 1602, which lasted until 1787, when the place fell into obscurity. Today, however, the place is known for its inhabitants, called *hafnies*, the unfortunate subjects of many an Icelandic joke – it's said, for example, that local children take ladders when they start at high school, which their parents also use to go shopping with if they hear that prices have gone up. Needless to say, Icelandic humour can be an acquired taste.

Arrival, information and accommodation

From Lækjartorg and Hlemmur in Reykjavík city centre, **bus** #140 runs to Hafnarfjörður (every 20min Mon–Fri, every 30min Sat & Sun), passing the **tourist information office** (mid-May to mid-Sept Mon–Fri 9am–6pm, Sat & Sun 9am–2pm; rest of the year Mon–Fri 1–4pm; ☏565 0661, Ⓦwww.lava.is), at Vesturgata 8, and terminating outside the Fjörður shopping centre, halfway along Fjarðargata.

There's a decent outdoor **swimming pool** at Hringbraut 77 (☏565 3080) and an indoor pool at Herjólfsgata 10 (☏555 0088). If you've come to Hafnarfjörður to go **horse riding** (see "Activities", p.84), you'll find Íshestar (☏555 7000, Ⓦwww.ishestar.is), at Sörlaskeið 26, southeast of the town centre along Kaldárselsvegur. Try the **library** (Mon–Thurs 10am–7pm, Fri 11am–7pm, plus Oct–Apr Sat 11am–3pm; ☏585 5690), opposite the tourist office at Strandgata 1, and the youth hostel (see below) for **Internet access**.

There's little reason to stay overnight in Hafnarfjörður, given that Reykjavík is so close, but should you wish to extend your visit here you'll find the **youth hostel**, *Hraunbyrgi* (☏565 0900, Ⓦwww.hraunbuar.is/hostel; 1900kr), located north of the centre in Víðistaðatún park on Flókagata, where there's also a **campsite** (June–Aug) with hot and cold running water. East of the centre on Lækjarkinn there are two **guesthouses** virtually next door to each other and with nothing to choose between them: *Guesthouse Lækjarkinn* (☏565 5132, Ⓔolgunn@simnet.is; ➋) is at no.2, whereas *Helguhús* (☏555 2842, Ⓦwww .helguhus.is; ➋) is a little further on at no. 8. Both have a handful of rooms, with shared facilities including a kitchen. Upmarket **hotel** accommodation is available at the *Viking Hótel* (☏565 1213, Ⓦwww.fjorukrain.is; ➒) at Strandgata 55 where all 29 rooms have private facilities and a Viking feel to the décor with lots of wooden flourishes and Gothic prints hanging on the walls.

The Town

The **harbour** is the best place to start your wanderings. Home port for many of Iceland's ocean-going trawlers, it's interesting enough just watching the bustle as fishermen land their catches, wash down their vessels and mend their nets. This is also the departure point for the town's **whale watching tours** aboard the *Húni II*, a splendid oak-built former fishing boat (May–Sept daily 10am; 3000kr; ☏894 1388 or ☏868 2886, Ⓦwww.islandia.is/huni), which last between three and four hours and generally manage to spot the odd minke whale, dolphin or porpoise; it's unusual though that the larger humpback whale is seen since it only rarely visits the bay off Hafnarfjörður.

From the harbour, it's a five-minute walk south along Fjarðargata to the roundabout to find the arts centre of **Hafnarborg** (Wed–Mon 11am–5pm; 300kr, free Mon) at Strandgata 34. In a fit of generosity the building was donated to the town by a local chemist and his wife in 1983 and today exhibits work by local Icelandic artists as well as doubling as a concert venue – it's worth a quick look, but you're more likely to satisfy your artistic appetite in Reykjavík. Walking south from here, crossing the roundabout into what is now Strandgata, will take you towards the curious steeply roofed wooden structure called **Fjörukráin**, set back from the seafront at no.55. Although a bit of a tourist trap, this hotel and restaurant is a good place to sample some pretty authentic **Viking food** (see p.90).

From *Fjörukráin*, retrace your steps to the roundabout and follow Strandgata back towards the town centre. This is Hafnarfjörður's diminutive main shopping street, though don't expect the stores here to come close to the selection in Reykjavík – although the capital is only just down the road, this is provincial Iceland. Instead, the interest here lies in the fact that the street of Strandgata and neighbouring Austurgata are, according to Icelandic folklore, home to Hafnarfjörður's population of **hidden people** – elves, dwarves and other spirits who live in entire families between the rocks that are dotted around the town centre. Apparently elves are only visible to those with second sight, though a majority of Icelanders are quite prepared to admit they believe in them. In fact, an alarming number of new roads constructed across the country have been subject to minor detours around large rocks after workers attempted to move the boulders only to find that their diggers and earth movers broke down time and again in the process. Should you be keen to try out your second sight, **tours** (mid-June to mid-Aug daily 10am & 2pm; 1800kr; ☎565 0661) lasting an hour and led by the inimitable local clairvoyant Erla Stefánsdóttir, weave their way through Hafnarfjörður visiting the homes of the *huldufólk*.

A stone's throw from the northern end of Strandgata, one block to the north of the harbour at Vesturgata 8, is **Hafnarfjörður museum** (June–Aug daily 1–5pm; Sept–May Sat & Sun 1–5pm; 300kr), housed in a wooden warehouse dating from the late 1800s. Inside is a passable if somewhat dull portrayal of Hafnarfjörður's life and times. Next door, across the main Reykjavíkurvegur at Vesturgata 6, stands **Sívertsens-Hús**, the town's oldest building, dated to 1803 and once the residence of local trader, boat builder and man about town Bjarni Sívertsen, today home to a folk museum (same times). The interior is stuffed with dreary how-we-used-to-live paraphernalia from the nineteenth century.

More rewarding than Hafnarfjörður's slight attempt at culture are the views from **Hamarinn** cliffs – retrace your steps along the harbour front along Strandgata to the roundabout just before *Fjörukráin*, where you should turn left into Lækjargata, then head east along this road and take the footpath up the hill to the wall of lava you'll see; this leads to the viewpoint. The protected wooded natural area up here offers good views out over the harbour and the surrounding countryside and is a pleasant place to have a picnic when the weather's good. Incidentally, the ugly red- and white-striped towers you can see from here, which dominate the surrounding flat landscape of lavafields, belong to the vast aluminium smelter at Straumsvík, which imports its raw materials from Australia and uses local geothermal power to produce the metal.

Eating

Unusually for provincial Iceland, **eating** throws up more than two opportunities, but by far the best option is the Viking-theme restaurant-cum-hotel, *Fjörukráin*, at Strandgata 55 (see also p.89). This is the place in Iceland to sample traditional **Viking food**, the best time to visit being during the old Icelandic month of Þorri (from the Fri between Jan 19 & 25 until late Feb) when the hotel's *Fjörugarðinn* restaurant hosts nightly Viking banquets known as *þorrablót* (3800kr), offering the dubious delight of sampling traditional foods – rotten shark, singed sheep's head, pickled rams' testicles, squashed flat and eaten as a topping to an open sandwich – washed down with generous quantities of the potent Icelandic schnapps, *Black Death*. Should this fail to tempt you, you could always try their regular Viking feast (4900kr), which is served year round and comprises a half-litre of beer, some *Black Death* and three courses of herring, dried hardfish and shark. Next door, *Fjaran* is altogether less touristy, with an atmosphere similar to a British country pub, replete with a beamed ceiling and brass plates hanging on the walls. Here they serve up delicious, if expensive, fresh fare such as baked salmon and grilled chicken for 2500–3000kr per head, plus bottles of wine from a whopping 3650kr. If your conscience allows, there's also fried dolphin with onion potatoes and redcurrant sauce for 2200kr; the owners claim the dolphins are caught accidentally in fishing nets.

Alternatively, there's *Tilveran* at Linnetstígur 1, the town's most popular restaurant with locals, renowned for its tasty fish dishes: panfried catfish in an orange and ginger sauce is just 1050kr at lunchtime, otherwise count on 2100kr for fish dishes in the evenings. The respectable *Súfistinn*, at Strandgata 9, serves up sandwiches and snacks as well as some excellent cakes at reasonable prices – reckon on 500–800kr for something light. Close by at Vesturgata 4, the old-fashioned, wooden-beamed *A Hansen* has delicious seafood as well as lamb and meat dishes, though you're looking over 2000kr. For a good **café**, head for the light and airy *Café Aroma* upstairs in the *Fjörður* shopping centre on Fjarðargata enjoying an unsurpassed view through giant floor to ceiling windows out over the harbour. Here pasta dishes go for around 1390kr, beer is 550kr and the wicked chocolate cheesecake an indulgent 490kr. Just down the escalator from *Aroma* is the *vínbúð* (**alchohol store**; Mon–Thurs 11am–6pm, Fri 11am–7pm, Sat 11am–4pm; ☎565 2222).

Viðey

In the Kollafjörður inlet, a nature reserve immediately north of the Laugardalur area of Reykjavík, lies **Viðey** (Wood Island – though it's no longer forested), an island with a rich historical background. Actually the top of a now extinct volcano and measuring barely 1.7 square kilometres, the land here was first claimed by Reykjavík's original settler, **Ingólfur Arnarson** as part of his estate. Archeological studies have shown that Viðey was inhabited during the tenth century and that a church was located here sometime in the twelfth century, but it was for the Augustinian monastery, consecrated here in 1225, that Viðey is better known. However, the island's monks fled when, in 1539, representatives of the Danish king proclaimed Viðey property of the Lutheran royal crown. Barely eleven years later, in 1550, Iceland's last Catholic bishop, **Jón Arason**, regained possession of the island through an armed campaign, restored the monastery and built a fort here to defend the island from his Lutheran enemies. Little did that help, however, and in the same year, Arason was beheaded and the Reformation, taking place across mainland Europe, began in Iceland.

Two centuries of peace ensued and in 1751 Viðey was given to the royal treasurer and sheriff, **Skúli Magnússon**, with the Rococo-style **Viðeyjarstofa**, Iceland's first stone building, being built as his residence four years later. In 1817, the island passed into the ownership of the President of the High Court, **Magnús Stephensen**, who brought Iceland's only printing press to Viðey, furthering the tiny place's claim as the country's main centre of culture – a reputation that spread from the establishment of the island's Augustinian monastery. Following several more changes of ownership, the City of Reykjavík finally bought the island in 1983.

Viðey practicalities

Viðey is easily accessible from Sundahöfn harbour, northeast of Laugardalur, reached by buses #4 from Lækjartorg (see p.55) and #14 from Hlemmur (see p.55) in the city centre. From the harbour, the **ferry** (late May to mid–Sept Mon–Fri 1pm, 2pm & 3pm, Sat & Sun also 4pm & 5pm; plus Fri, Sat & Sun 7pm, 7.30pm & 8pm for the restaurant; ☎581 1010) takes just seven minutes.

A short walk up the path from the jetty where the ferry deposits you is **Viðeyjarstofa**, Skúli Magnússon's residence, the oldest stone building in the country and now functioning as an expensive but excellent **restaurant** (☎568 1045), where booking is recommended. Designed in simple Rococo style by the architect who worked on the Amalienborg royal palace in Copenhagen, the outer walls are made of basalt and sandstone whilst the interior is of Danish brick and timber. Standing next to the restaurant is a **church**, consecrated in 1774, the second oldest in Iceland, and worth a glance inside for its original interior furnishings and Skúli's grave beneath the altar. Walk east of here to the site of the old fort, **Virkið,** of which nothing now remains, to see the Skúli Magnússon **monument** (he died here in 1794) and **Danadys** (Danes' Grave), the final resting place for a number of Danish citizens who lived on the island over the centuries.

Other than these few attractions there's little to do on Viðey other than enjoy the spectacular views of the mainland and take a stroll on one of the many **paths** that lead around the island. From Viðeyjarstofa, a road heads beyond the island's schoolhouse to the easternmost point, from where a path takes over, following the south coast back towards the ferry jetty, skirting a protected area (closed May & June) that's home to thousands of nesting birds. Alternatively, from the easternmost point, a track leads back along the north coast past the restaurant and out to the northwestern part of the island, Vesturey, a peninsula connected to the main island by the small isthmus, Eiði. The greatest **coastal rescue** Iceland has ever seen took place off the island's westernmost point in October 1944 after the Canadian destroyer *HMCS Skeena*, with over two hundred men onboard, ran aground in heavy seas and blizzard conditions. Although fifteen crew members perished, the remainder were rescued by a team of Icelanders led by Einar Sigurðsson who was later awarded the MBE for his courage and guidance. Whilst in the western part of the island keep an eye out, too, for the **Áfangar**, an alfresco display by artist Richard Serra, consisting of numerous basalt columns arranged in ring formation.

Akurey

West of Viðey is **Akurey**, a tiny steep-sided islet renowned for its **puffin colony**, one of only two near the capital (the other one is Lundey, north of Viðey). The staggeringly large population of birds comes in at around 30,000 (the total Icelandic puffin population is put at ten million and the average bird lives for around twenty-five years). Although it's only possible to see the island as part of a boat cruise and it's not possible to go ashore, it's still a truly remarkable experience. From the boat you'll have a great view of the cliffs and grassy slopes which make up the island's sides, and the burrows where the puffins live. The smell of guano here is also very strong. The birds remain on the island until late August when they head out to sea for a period of approximately eight months.

Tours depart daily from Reykjavík harbour (*not* Sundahöfn; mid-May to late Aug 10.30am & 4.45pm; 2000kr; ☎581 1010) and last an hour. The boats circle the island several times to give you a good chance to see the puffins up close, clinging to the cliff tops and diving into the sea in search of food. Bookings are necessary and can also be made at the tourist office on Aðalstræti (see p.54).

Travel details

Buses

The bus details given below are relevant for May to September; for winter times, visit ⓦ www.dice.is.

Reykjavík to: Akranes (5 daily; 50min); Akureyri (daily; 6hr); Blönduós (daily; 4hr); Blue Lagoon (6 daily; 40min); Borgarnes (4 daily; 1hr10min); Búðardalur (5 weekly; 4hr); Brú (daily; 2hr); Gullfoss/Geysir (daily; 2hr30min); Höfn (daily; 8hr); Hólmavík via Brú (3 weekly; 6hr30min); Ísafjörður via Brú and Hólmavík (3 weekly; 11hr); Ólafsvík (daily; 3hr); Sauðárkrókur (daily; 5hr30min); Siglufjörður (3 weekly; 7hr); Skaftafell (daily; 6hr); Stykkishólmur (daily; 2hr30min); Þingvellir (daily; 50min); Þorlákshöfn (daily; 1hr).

Flights
Reykjavík to: Akureyri (7 daily; 50min); Bíldudalur (daily; 40min); Egilsstaðir (2 daily; 1hr); Gjögur (2 weekly; 50min); Höfn (1 daily; 1hr); Ísafjörður (2 daily; 40min); Sauðárkrókur (1 daily; 45min); Westman Islands (2 daily; 30min).

Ferries
Reykjavík to: Viðey (late May to mid–Sept Mon–Fri 2 daily, Sat & Sun 5 daily; 7min).

Southwestern Iceland

2

SOUTHWESTERN ICELAND

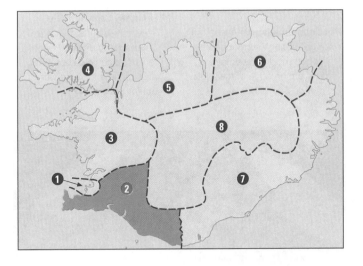

CHAPTER 2 # Highlights

* **Blue Lagoon** Soak outdoors in the steaming waters of Iceland's most trumpeted thermal spa, set amongst the Reykjanes Peninsula's barren lava flows. **See p.97**

* **The Golden Circle** Circuit three of the country's most famous sights – the rift valley at Þingvellir, Geysir's spurting pools, and Gullfoss, the Golden Falls – on a day-trip from the capital. **See p.103**

* **Landmannalaugar** Camp out at hot springs surrounded by rugged rhyolite mountains, right on the edge of Iceland's Interior. **See p.122**

* **Laugavegur** Follow this four-day hiking trail between Landmannalaugar and Þórsmörk, through some exceptional scenery. **See p.124**

* **Þórsmörk** This beautifully wooded highland valley, surrounded by glaciers, is a great spot to camp, hike, or just party away the long summer days. **See p.133**

* **Heimaey** Largest of the Westman Islands, this is a great spot to unwind, witness recent volcanic catastrophe, and become intimate with puffins. **See p.142**

Southwestern Iceland

Spread either side of Reykjavík, **southwestern Iceland** extends barely 200km from end to end, but nowhere else are Iceland's key elements of history and the land so visibly intertwined, and it's a pivotal region for both Icelanders and tour-group itineraries alike. Here you'll see where Iceland's original parliament was founded over a thousand years ago, sites that saw the violence of saga-age dramas played out, and where the country's earliest churches became seats of power and learning. Culture aside, if you're expecting the scenery this close to Reykjavík to be tame, think again: the southwest contains some of Iceland's most iconic – and frequently explosive – landscapes, compelling viewing whether used as a simple backdrop to a day's drive, or as an excuse to spend a week trekking cross-country.

The region splits into four well-defined areas. Southwest of Reykjavík, bleak, semi-vegetated lava fields characterise the **Reykjanes Peninsula**, though the famous **Blue Lagoon** adds a splash of colour, while there's good whale-watching potential out from **Keflavík**, a service town for the nearby US airbase and adjacent international airport. Due east of Reykjavík, a clutch of essential historical and geological features – including the original parliament site at **Þingvellir**, **Geysir**'s hot water spouts, and **Gullfoss**' rainbow-tinged cataract – are strung out around the **Golden Circle**, an easy route tackled by just about every visitor to the country. Then there's the central south, a broad stretch of grassy river plains further southeast again, whose inland features the blasted landscape surrounding the volcano **Hekla**, and hot springs at **Landmannalaugar**; while back on its coast the rolling farmland of **Njál's Saga** country is dotted with landmarks from this famous tale. Further east, there's beautiful scenery around the glaciated highland valley of **Þórsmörk**, along with some spectacular waterfalls down near the highway, which runs out of the region via the coastal hamlet of **Vík**. Offshore, a short ferry ride or flight from the mainland brings you to **Heimaey**, the small, intimate core of the **Westman islands**, alive with birdlife and further recent proof of Iceland's unstable vulcanology.

The southwest enjoys good access: most **roads** – with the exception of a few on the Reykjanes Peninsula, around Hekla, and those to Landmannalaugar and Þórsmörk – are surfaced and generally accessible year-round. **Buses** ply the Golden Circle and coastal Ringroad to Vík throughout the year, with Landmannalaugar and Þórsmörk connected over the summer; services around the Reykjanes Peninsula are more restricted, though you can easily get to the Blue Lagoon or Keflavík. The **climate** here is relatively mild, despite being the wettest, windiest part of the country, prone to fog along the coast and potentially heavy snowfalls through the year on higher ground.

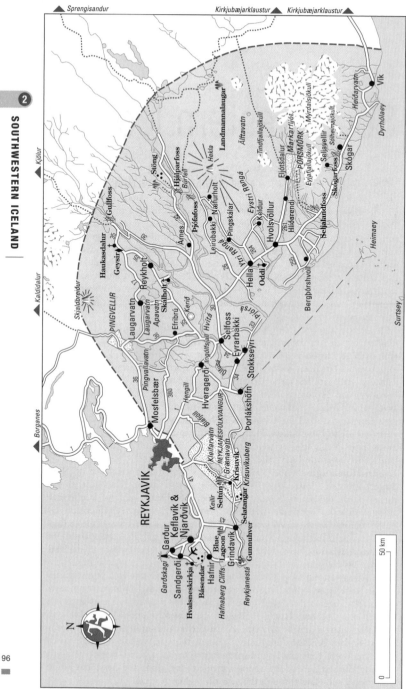

▲ Sprengisandur   Kirkjubæjarklaustur ▲ Kirkjubæjarklaustur ▲

▲ Kjölur

▲ Kaldidalur

▲ Borganes

Sprengisandur

Skjaldbreiður

ÞINGVELLIR

Laugarvatn
Laugarvatn
Apavatn

Efribrú

Þingvallavatn

Gullfoss

Haukasdalur
Geysir
Reykholt

Skálholt
Kerið

Stöng
Hjálparfoss
Búrfell
Þjófafoss
Árnes

Hekla
Næfurholt
Þingskálar
Leirubakki

Landmannalaugar

Álftavatn

Eystri Rangá

Keldur
Hvolsvöllur
Hildarendi

Fljótsdalur
ÞÓRSMÖRK
Markarfljót
Tindfjallajökull
Eyjafjallajökull

Mýrdalsjökull

Seljavellir
Sólheimajökull
Skógar

Heiðarvatn

Dyrhólaey

Vík

Selfoss
Eyrarbakki
Stokkseyri

Ölfusá
Þjórsá
Ytri Rangá
Hella
Oddi

Bergþórshvoll

Seljalandsfoss
Skógafoss

Heimaey

Surtsey

Hveragerði
Ingólfsfjall
Hvítá

Hengill

Mosfellsbær

Bláfjöll

Þorlákshöfn

REYKJAVÍK

REYKJANESFÓLKVANGUR
Kleifarvatn
Grænavatn
Krýsuvík
Krýsuvíkurberg

Keilir
Seltún
Selatangar

Garður
Keflavík &
Njarðvík
Blue
Lagoon
Grindavík
Gunnuhver

Garðskagi
Sandgerði
Hvalsneskirkja
Básendar
Hafnir
Hafnaberg Cliffs
Reykjanestá

50 km

N

The Reykjanes Peninsula

The **Reykjanes Peninsula**, Iceland's southwestern extremity, provides most visitors with their first look at the country, as they exit **Keflavík**'s international airport and take Route 41 east towards Reykjavík. Unfortunately, local vistas are unremittingly barren – rough, contoured piles of lava and distant peaks, the rocks only coloured by a light dusting of lichen and mosses – and, lured by grander prospects elsewhere, most people leave Reykjanes behind without a second thought. But if you've a few hours to fill in – while waiting for a flight, perhaps – the peninsula is conveniently close to the capital and has plenty to offer: there's the **Blue Lagoon**, Iceland's most renowned spa; Keflavík is a departure point for summer **whale-watching** trips; and there's a wild, rocky coastline with associated birdlife and lonely ruins – not to mention a museum at **Grindavík** to that great Icelandic icon, the cod.

The peninsula is covered in **hiking trails**, taking anything from a few minutes to several days to complete. There's a tourist **map** of Reykjanes with all the trails marked (available at information outlets in Reykjavík and Keflavík), which is too simple for serious navigation but works well enough with Landmælingar Íslands' *Suðurland* 1:250,000. Be prepared to carry plenty of **water** (there are very few sources anywhere on the peninsula), and note that there's almost no soft ground to pitch a tent over.

The Reykjavík–Keflavík highway (Route 41) is surfaced, as is the road south off this to the Blue Lagoon and Grindavík (Route 43), and much of the coastal stretch between Keflavík and Grindavík. Other roads are mostly gravel, and can be rough going at times. **Buses** run daily all year from Reyjavík to Keflavík and the airport, and from Reyjavík to Blue Lagoon and Grindavík; and the region is also covered on numerous **tours** from the capital – see Reykjavík "Listings" (p.186) or contact Iceland Excursions (℡540 1313, ⓦwww .icelandexcursions.is).

The Blue Lagoon and Keflavík

Heading west from the capital, the straight, fast forty-kilometre-long Reykjavík–Keflavík highway is the busiest road in Iceland. After the satellite suburb of Hafnarfjörður (p.87) drops away, you're confronted with the peninsula's bald vistas: ranges frame the horizon, with the flat, petrified lava flow of **Þránsskjaldarhraun** in between, blistered with solidified burst gas bubbles and resembling the top of a badly baked cake. **Keilir**, the distant conical mountain rising over it all, can be accessed by turning south off the highway approximately 11km west of Hafnarfjörður onto a rough gravel road (you can also hike here from the south through Móhálsadalur; see p.103). Some 8km along, a four-wheel-drive track climbs a bank and heads towards the mountain, though you'll still have to walk the final 4km or so across a twisted lava plain. The ascent is easier than it appears, and, for some reason, there's a book to sign at the 379-metre-high summit. Otherwise, stay on the highway until you reach the amply signed intersection 8km short of Keflavík, where Route 43 heads down to the Blue Lagoon and Grindavík (for more of which, see p.101).

The Blue Lagoon

Known in Icelandic as Bláa lónið, the **Blue Lagoon** (April, May & Sept daily 10am–9pm; June–Aug daily 9am–10pm; Oct–March daily 11am–8pm; 980kr) is Iceland's most trumpeted bathing spot. Popular enough with Icelanders, it's worth the trip if you've not yet had an outdoor hot-pot experience – especially on cold days, when thick fog swirls over the warm, milky-blue water while your hair, dampened by vapour, freezes solid. On the down side, it's expensive and too shallow to swim in comfortably, though the spa's fine white silt is said to cure skin disorders.

Blue Lagoon is actually artificial, set in the middle of a flat expanse of black lava blocks and filled by outflow from the nearby **Svartsengi thermal power station**, whose glowing lights and organic loops of silver piping are sadly no longer within sight of the waters. Svartsengi taps into steam vents fed by sea water seeping down into subterranean hot pots, and by the time it emerges at Blue Lagoon it has cooled to a comfortable 38°C. There are decoratively positioned caves and arches, a sauna, and the famous silvery-grey **silt** – Icelanders scoop handfuls off the bottom and smear it all over their bodies, and the shop sells beauty products made from this stuff. Whatever the effects on your skin, hair takes a real battering from the lagoon's enriched mineral content; rub conditioner in as protection before bathing.

There are several daily **buses** here year-round from Grindavík and Reykjavík, and a limited summer service from Keflavík between June and September. The **café** at the spa has sandwiches, ice cream and drinks, and there's also a reasonable **restaurant** – both are expensive, however. If you're after local **accommodation**, the friendly, single-storey *Northern Light Inn* (☎426 8650, ⓦwww.northernlightinn.is; ❻) is right by the power station and offers guests free airport transfers.

Keflavík

Stretching for 5km along the seafront, **KEFLAVÍK** and its adjoining satellite **Njarðvík** – collectively known as Reykjanesbær – between them form the Reykjanes Peninsula's biggest centre, with a population of around 11,000. Keflavík was a trading port as far back as the sixteenth century, but it was World War II that established the town's current status, when US defence forces stationed here took advantage of the peninsula's lava flats and built an **airstrip** west of town. At the war's end, US attempts to make this refuelling and supply base permanent proved unpopular with Icelanders and were abandoned, but following Iceland's joining of **NATO** in 1949 – an event that sparked a riot in Reykjavík – the US pressured Iceland into agreeing to the idea. A new airbase opened in 1951, and Keflavík flourished alongside as a service centre, busy through the Cold War era but in its aftermath, like the base itself, slightly at a loss. In 2003, the US government went so far as to suggest closing the base down and removing the four F15/F16 fighter jets based here, which would have left the country defenceless and – rather more importantly – made around 2000 workers in Keflavík redundant. The plan was abandoned, but it demonstrated how fears over job losses now outweigh former ambivalence about the US–NATO presence.

Aside from the odd fighter jet screeching overhead, the effects of all this are implied rather than seen, and Keflavík remains ordinary and functional – not really a stopover of choice unless you want to catch an early flight from the international airport (see p.53), just 5km west, or hook up with a **whale-watching tour** aboard the *Moby Dick* (☎421 7777, ⓦwww.dolphin.is) or

Sjóskoðun (☎321 2660). These leave mid-April to mid-September, with June through to August as the most likely time to spot minke whales, porpoise and dolphin; if you're exceptionally lucky, blue whales or orca may show. Tours last around three hours, cost 2800kr, and you'll need warm clothing. Both companies can also collect or deliver to the airport.

Practicalities

There's little to clearly distinguish easterly Njarðvík from Keflavík, excepting that Njarðvík is more residential. The main road branches off the highway as Njarðarbraut before running for a couple of kilometres west through Keflavík as Hafnargata and fizzling out at the **harbour**. The SBK **bus station** is here, with year-round services to the airport, Reykjavík, and Blue Lagoon, and offering summer **tours** all over the peninsula. Your accommodation can arrange an airport bus pickup, or you can call a **taxi** (☎421 4141, or 421 1515). Most services are in Keflavík on Hafnargata, including **tourist information** (Mon–Fri 10am–7pm, Sat 10am–4pm) and **internet** access (both housed inside the library behind the *Flug Hotel*), as are all **banks**; while the **post office** and Samkaup **supermarket** are further east on Njarðarbraut.

The Reykjanesbær **campsite** (☎ & ℱ421 1460; 350kr per person plus 300kr per tent) is behind the supermarket on Njarðarbraut, with phones, showers, toilets, plus a small dining room. Off Njarðarbraut's eastern end, just as you enter town, Njarðvík's IYHA **youth hostel** (☎421 8889, ⓦwww.fithostel.is; sleeping bag 1900kr) at Fitjabraut 6A has a dreary blocky exterior, but is warm and well equipped; it's easily missed, however – look for the blue triangular logo. Another budget option with shared bathrooms and **self-catering** facilities is *B&B Guesthouse* (☎421 8989, ℮bbguesthouse@simnet.is; ❸), three streets back from Hafnargata at Hringbraut 92. There's more upmarket **hotel** accommodation in Keflavík around the intersection of Hafnargata and Vatnsnesvegur, at either *Flug Hótel* (☎421 5222, ⓦwww.icehotel.is; ❼) or the adjacent *Hótel Keflavík* (☎420 7000, ⓦwww.hotelkeflavik.is; ❽), who run a lower-key **guesthouse** opposite (same tel; ❹); both are modern transit hotels.

Keflavík's **places to eat** are all west of the *Flug Hótel* on Hafnargata, and include the culturally confused *Paddy's Irish Bar & Pizzeria*, though the best food is at the long-established *Raïn* – they've got pizzas, fish dishes and salads (the grilled-chicken salad is very tasty) – and it's also a comfortable place for a drink.

Garður and Sandgerði

In fair weather, the peninsula west of Keflavík is an easy place to spend a couple of hours trolling around in a car. **GARÐUR** is the first place to aim for, a tiny, scattered community just 7km from town, with a small **museum** (May–Sept daily 1–5pm; 350kr) of fishing memorabilia and farm gear. A grassed-over ridge marks the remains of an old wall, apparently the original eleventh-century estate boundary; the discovery of nine Viking graves found south of here in the 1850s supports the theory. Later associations can be found at the nineteenth-century **Útskálakirkja**, a church dedicated to Iceland's only saint, **Þorlákur Þórhallsson**, bishop at Skálholt in 1178–93 (see p.111). Reykjanes' northwestern tip, **Garðskagi**, is marked by two lighthouses; the older, red-striped affair is right on the seafront and was once used to monitor bird migrations. Its base is a sheltered spot to look seawards – with a pair of binoculars you can spot seals, eider ducks, turnstones, gannets and assorted wading birds.

Heading south of here for another 6km brings you to **SANDGERÐI**, a small fishing village with a busy harbour and another lighthouse. At the harbour, **Fraeðasetrið Nature Centre** (Mon–Fri 9am–noon & 1–5pm, Sat 1–5pm; 350kr) is a research centre investigating newly discovered invertebrate marine creatures found off Reykjanes, but there's also a display of larger stuffed animals and, for enthusiasts, extensive files on local botany and geology to sort through. Pick of the exhibits is a huge walrus in the lobby; these are unknown from this area, though they appear on the town coat of arms. *Vitinn* **restaurant**, at the harbour entrance, has good seafood and lamb dishes.

A final 7km south past a huge **arctic tern colony**, another church, and a grouping of abandoned, century-old stone sheep-pens opposite *Bali* (Washtub) farm, brings you to the end of the road at the orange **Stafnes** lighthouse; views from here take in heavy surf and distant airport buildings. There's a half-day walking trail south along the coast from Stafnes to Hafnir (see below), which after about 1km passes the site of **Básendar**, the Reykjanes Peninsula's largest trading town until it was totally destroyed by an overnight storm in January 1799 – killing just one person. Very little remains besides nondescript rubble.

Southern Reykjanes: from Hafnir to Krýsuvík

The road to southern Reykjanes splits off the Reykjavík–Keflavík highway a little before Keflavík, running for 35km past prime **bird-watching** sites, a scattering of historic and geological sites around **Reykjanestá**, and winding up at the historic fishing settlement of **Grindavík**. From here, a rougher 21km track continues east through characteristically dire lava plains and loose shale hills to **Krýsuvík**, with more coastal scenery, an abandoned fishing camp, and some inland hiking potential on the way. **Buses** only run as far as Grindavík, so you'll need your own transport to see the rest.

The first stop is 10km along at **HAFNIR**, another speck of a settlement based around a harbour and old wooden church, by which is a large, rusting anchor, a memento from the 1870 wreck of the schooner *Jamestown*. Hafnir's harbour is pretty inactive nowadays, but the adjacent former fish-processing factory has been painted lilac and green and converted into the **Sæfiskasafnið** (May–Sept daily 2–4pm; 300kr), an aquarium and halibut farm with display tanks full of local fish and crustaceans.

There's a bit more of interest south of Hafnir, where the road crosses a positively lunar landscape strewn with virtually unvegetated lava rubble – probably through a combination of salt spray and porous soil, which sees rainwater drain straight into the earth. For a closer look, **cairns** (locally known as "priests", because they point the way but never go there themselves) around 5km from Hafnir mark the start of the relatively easy fifteen-kilometre **Prestsastígur walking trail** southeast to Grindavík, and also a shorter trail west from a roadside parking bay 2km further on to some avian real estate on the coastal **Hafnaberg cliffs**. This latter route takes about forty-five tiring minutes over sandy slopes – beware of aggressive, ground-nesting greater skuas – past two large volcanic "blisters", and finally ends on top of forty-metre-high cliffs. From spring through to autumn, these are home to tens of thousands of nesting kittiwakes and fulmars, along with a dusting of shags and black guillemots, all of which you'll hear (and smell) well before you crawl up to look over for a peek – loose soil and strong winds make standing up near the edge extremely dangerous.

Reykjanestá

Ten kilometres south of Hafnir, **Reykjanestá** is the Reykjanes Peninsula's southwestern extremity, the seascapes here embellished by the white tower of **Reykjanesviti**, one of the area's more interesting lighthouses. To reach it, turn off the main road at the steaming salt-making plant – the only building along the way, but unmistakable anyway – and keep going until you're under Reykjanesviti around 2km later. Standing some way from the sea atop a knoll, it replaced Iceland's first lighthouse, which for seventeen years stood on high cliffs overlooking the stormy surf until an earthquake knocked it down in 1896.

About 100m further on is a parking area beside the cliff where the lighthouse originally stood; it's an easy walk up the grassy back to enjoy views across the ocean to **Eldey**, a tall platform of rock rising straight out of the sea 15km to the southwest. This is Europe's biggest gannet colony, and has the sad distinction of being where the last known pair of **great auks** (and their single egg) were destroyed on June 3, 1844. These flightless sea birds looked like giant razorbills and were common right across the north Atlantic until being hunted into extinction for their meat and oil; for the whole sorry tale, read Jeremy Gaskell's *Who Killed the Great Auk* (see "Contexts", p.356). From the mainland at least, it's hard to believe that a flightless bird ever roosted on Eldey's sheer cliffs, but the back of the island has more accessible niches.

Back on land, a bumpy circuit back to the main road takes you to another patch of greenery at **Gunnuhver thermal springs**, a small area of bubbling, muddy pools into which an eighteenth-century witch was dragged by a magic rope after she'd killed off her landlord. As always at hot springs, stay on the boardwalks and take care.

Grindavík

GRINDAVÍK is a sizeable town for this part of the country, a well-serviced fishing port of two thousand souls 14km east of Reykjanestá, where coastal roads and Route 43 (via the Blue Lagoon) from the Reykjavík–Keflavík highway meet. Like Keflavík, Grindavík has a long history as a trading centre and was important enough to be raided by pirates looking for slaves and plunder in 1627; unlike Keflavík, however, its harbour remains busy and is now given over to a sizeable fishing fleet, whose catches are processed at a factory here.

All this has spawned Saltfisksetur Íslands, the **Icelandic Saltfish Museum** (daily 11am–6pm; 500kr), down near the harbour on Hafnargata, whose motto "Lífið er saltfiskur" – "Life is saltfish" – kicks off a fine display of models, videos, dioramas and life-sized photos, all laced with the pervasive aroma of **cod**. It's no exaggeration to say that modern Iceland was built on the back of this fish: the country's original coat of arms, ratified by the Alþing in 1593, was a golden cod, filleted, crowned on a red field. Fishing started off slowly as a seasonal adjunct to farming, however, the catch preserved as wind-dried **stockfish** until better methods became available when salt began to be imported in bulk during the nineteenth century. This point coincided with the first large, ocean-going vessels being used in Iceland, increasing catches six-fold and sparking a new industry that undermined Iceland's traditional agricultural economy by drawing people off the land to swell coastal settlements. Today, saltfish accounts for sixty percent of Iceland's annual exports, the fish ending up mostly in Spain, West Africa, and South America. One strange void in the display is any mention of the "Cod Wars" between Iceland and Britain during the 1970s (see Contexts, p.345), in which Grindavík was – given its history – presumably involved.

Fish aside, the town is also strategically placed at the intersection of many of the Reykjanes Peninsula's **walking trails**, which start right at the town's boundaries. Local trails include a three-kilometre track heading north off Route 43 to the obvious pinnacle of **Þorbjarnfell** (231m); another good walk follows the coast east from town for 3km to the apex of **Festarfjall** (202m), the remains of a volcano core and splashed with purple, potash-rich rocks. If you'd rather go **horse riding** on these trails, contact Víkhestar (☎426 8303, ⓦwww.vikhestar.is) to arrange time in the saddle.

Practicalities

Grindavík is arranged on the low slopes around its harbour. Route 43 drops south into town as Víkurbraut, where **buses** from Reykjavík via the Blue Lagoon (daily throughout the year), and Keflavík (daily in summer) pull in at a **shopping complex** with supermarket and bank. Ránargata heads 250m down to the harbour from here, and halfway along you cross the intersection with Hafnargata: turn right onto Hafnargata and the Saltfish Museum is just on the left; or turn left for the **fish factory**. There's **accommodation** in town either at the **campground** behind the shopping complex, or, if you want a roof over your head, at *Fiskanes* (☎897 6388, 426 8481, ⓔeikil@isl.is; dorm bed 1000kr, sleeping-bag accommodation 1400kr, made-up bed 2000kr), opposite the fish factory at Hafnargata 17 – as this is primarily a boarding house for factory workers, booking is essential. For **food**, *Vörr*, facing the museum on Hafnargata, is a down-to-earth diner patronised by factory workers, with fish-oriented lunchtime specials and a lively evening bar.

Selatangar, Reykjanesfólkvangur, and Krísuvík

The road east from Grindavík winds over the back of Festarfjall's volcanic core and then twists down again to run parallel to the coast along the base of a rugged, boulder-strewn range. About 12km along, a marked track heads 1.7km south to end at a parking area above a small shingle and sand beach. Have a good look at the distinctive **lava flow** immediately west – you can see how the front hardened into a wall as it hit the water and then piled up with the weight of the lava behind it – before following a **walking track** east, defined by rocks and driftwood. This brings you, in about ten minutes, to the remains of **Selatangar**, a seasonal fishing settlement last used in the 1880s and comprising lava-block dwellings perched above the sea, ranging from buildings the size and shape of a hollow cairn through to large, walled-in caves. There's far more here than you realize at first, but poke around and you'll soon find a score or more sites, some almost completely intact, others just foundations – look for carefully made walls, and neatly framed window and door lintels. No roofs have survived; these may well have been constructed from driftwood (plenty washes up here) or weatherproofed cloth. With near constant wind howling in from the south, rapidly bringing in and dispersing fog with little warning, Selatangar can be quite spooky – some say that there's even a resident ghost – and it doesn't take much imagination to conjure up what life was like here when the place was last occupied.

Back on the main road and not far past the Selatangar track, a minor road twists northwards up a ridge. Just over the other side is the broad and unexpectedly fertile **Móhálsadalur**, a valley extending 14km northeast through the centre of **Reykjanesfólkvangur**, a three-hundred-square-kilometre nature reserve; there's good camping here (but no facilities), and a set of hiking tracks running north to Keilir (see p.97).

If you don't follow this road, it's another 9km from the Selatangar junction to **Krísuvík**, a region farmed since Settlement times, though today the site is basically just a wooden chapel the size of a large dog kennel. Shortly before you reach the church, there's a rough track 6km south to the coast at **Krísuvíkurberg**, for which you might need four-wheel-drive or at least high clearance. Krísuvíkurberg is a long, curved, vertical cliff topped by a crust of green grass (an unusual sight for this part of the coast), packed solid all summer long with nesting **birds**: the cliffs are kittiwake grand central, and the turf is riddled with puffin burrows. The east end is topped by a triangulation point, with wonderful seascapes from the red scoria headland behind.

Krísuvík also marks an intersection, with one road heading 54km east to Hverargerði (see p.114), and the other running 3km north past **Grænavatn**, a pale-green crater lake, to the **Seltún hot springs**. This was the site of a moderately impressive geyser until it exploded in 1999, leaving a large, steaming grey pond, but boardwalks climb up to where hot water and steam continue to bubble out of the hills above. Beyond Seltún, the road skirts the western shore of **Kleifarvatn**, a five-kilometre-long lake filling the upper reaches of the Krísuvík valley, for the final 20km run north back to Route 41 at Hafnarfjörður.

The Golden Circle

The name **Golden Circle** might be a tourist-industry tag, but it's also apt, as this broad circuit east from Reykjavík covers many of Iceland's best-known features and touches on the root of much of its history. The key area is **Þingvellir**, whose dramatic rift valley and associated lake mark the area where the Icelandic state sprang into being in Viking times. East from here on the banks of the Hvítá is the religious centre of **Skálholt**, while following the river northeast takes you past **Geysir**, the original hot blowhole that has lent its name to similar vents worldwide, to **Gullfoss'** powerful twin cataracts. Visitors – local and foreign – flock to the main sights, mostly on hurried day-trips or weekend camping excursions; if this sounds discouraging, stay a little longer or explore a little wider and you'll soon escape the crowds.

Making your own way around, either head northeast from Reykjavík along Route 36 straight to Þingvellir, or take the Ringroad southeast via Hveragerði to Selfoss (pp.114–116), from where separate roads run up to Þingvellir and the Geysir–Gullfoss area. **Buses** from Reykjavík run daily through the summer, either direct to Þingvellir, or via Reykholt and Geysir to Gullfoss.

Another way to cover the highlights, either out of season or if you're pushed for time, is to take a **Golden Circle tour**, which leave daily from the Hotel

Loftleiðir in Reykjavík (see p.55). These cost from 4000kr, last up to seven hours, and are best booked a day in advance (most accommodation and tourist information centres in Reykjavík can do this). With English-speaking guides providing commentary, the tour crams in hothouses at Hveragerði (see p.114), the church at Skálholt, assorted craters, Gullfoss, Geysir and, unless there's been serious snow, Þingvellir. It's an ambitious schedule for a single day and necessarily superficial, though many people also find that a disproportionate amount of time is given to stopovers at the numerous gift shops and cafés that line the way. If you're planning on tackling the **Kjölur route** at any stage (p.331), it's probably not worth bothering with a Golden Circle tour, as you'll stop off at Gulfoss and Geysir along the way.

Þingvellir and around

The region northeast of Reykjavík is scarred by one of the world's great geological boundaries, a **rift valley** marking where the North American and Eurasian continental plates are physically tearing apart. It was in this monumental landmark that Iceland's clan chieftains, or **goðar**, first gathered in the tenth century to formalize their laws and forge a national identity for themselves (see box, p.106). Although this rift stretches right across Iceland, nowhere else is it so expansively evident – a four-kilometre-wide, forty-metre-deep slash in the landscape, sided in basalt columns and extending for 16km from Iceland's largest lake, **Þingvallavatn**, to the low, rounded cone of the **Skjaldbreiður** volcano in the northeast. Þingvellir itself – the plains where the chieftains met at the southwestern end of the rift – has been protected since 1930 as a national park.

The main **road** here is Route 36, which runs northeast of Reykjavík to Þingvellir (an often dangerously icy section in winter) and then south to Selfoss and the Ringroad, with the Rekjavík stretch covered from late May until September by daily **buses**. Þingvellir also marks the southern terminus of the Kaldidalur route through the Interior (see p.168). Once here, you can organise **horse riding** with Ferðhestar (☎894 7200, ⓦwww.travelhorse.is), who offer year-round day-trips (7500kr), and late-night summer excursions to see Þingvellir under the long dusk light (5500kr), and there are plenty of **hiking** trails around the scenery, along with a couple of **accommodation** options.

Þingvellir National Park

Þingvellir National Park encompasses the flat moors at the southern end of the rift valley, with boundaries reaching 6km north from Þingvallavatn to the foothills of **Ármannsfell** – said to be the abode of the region's mythical guardian, Ármann Dalmannsson – and around the same distance east towards the solitary massif of **Hrafnabjörg**. The main focus is, of course, Þingvellir itself, a surprisingly small area at the southwestern corner of the park where the narrow **Öxará** – the Axe River – flows down to the lake shore past a **church** and other historic monuments, all hemmed in on the west by the two-kilometre-long **Almannagjá**, the region's most impressive rift wall.

Buses deliver to the park **visitor centre** (☎482 2660, ⓕ3635; daily May–Sept) on Route 36 around 2km north of the church, just where the road descends into the rift. They have a phone, showers, café, sell maps and post weather reports, and issue **camping permits** (500kr) for the park – the

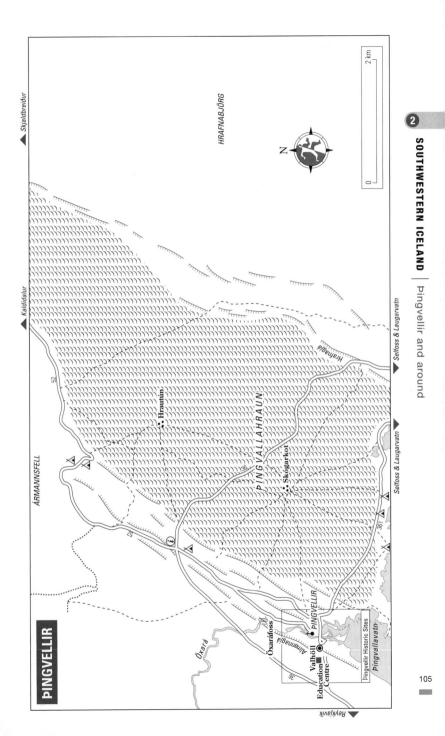

PINGVELLIR

Skjaldbreiður

HRAFNABJÖRG

N

0   2 km

Kaldidalur

Selfoss & Laugarvatn

Selfoss & Laugarvatn

ÁRMANNSFELL

Hrafnagjá

52

Hraun

ÞINGVALLAHRAUN

361

36

Skógarkot

25

1

36

Öxará

Öxaráfoss

Almannagjá

Valhöll

Education Centre

ÞINGVELLIR

Þingvellir Historic Sites

Þingvallavatn

Reykjavík

The Alþing at Þingvellir

With laws shall our land be built up, but with lawlessness laid waste.

Njál's Saga

By the beginning of the tenth century, Iceland's 36 regional chieftains were already meeting at local **assemblies** to sort out disputes, but as the country became more established, they recognized the need for some form of overall government. With this in mind, Norwegian law was adapted and the first **Alþing**, or General Assembly, was held in the rift valley north of Þingvallavatn in 930 AD, at a place which became known as **Þingvellir**, the Assembly Plains. Though the Alþing's power declined through the ages, Þingvellir remained the seat of Iceland's government for the next eight centuries.

The Alþing was held for two weeks every summer, and attendance for chieftains was mandatory. In fact, almost everyone who could attend did so, setting up their tented camps – **buðs** – and coming to watch the courts in action or settle disputes, pick up on gossip, trade, compete at sports, and generally socialize. The whole event was co-ordinated by the **lawspeaker**, while the laws themselves were legislated by the **Law Council**, and dispensed at four regional courts, along with a fifth **supreme court**. Strangely, however, none of these authorities had the power to enforce their verdicts, beyond bringing pressure to bear through public opinion. The adoption of **Christianity** as Iceland's official religion in 1000 AD was one of the Alþing's major successes, but if litigants refused to accept a court's decision, they had to seek satisfaction privately. Njál's Saga (see pp.126–127) contains a vivid account of one such event, when a battle between two feuding clans and their allies broke out at the Alþing itself around 1011 AD; while Hrafnkel's Saga (p.300) shows how people manipulated processes at the Alþing, and could, if they wanted, ignore court verdicts.

This lack of real authority undermined the Alþing's effectiveness, creating a power vacuum in Iceland that ultimately saw Norway and then Denmark assume control of the country. By the late thirteenth century the Alþing was losing its importance, with the lawspeaker's position abolished and the courts stripped of all legislative power. They had rather more ability to act on their judgements though, and from the mid-sixteenth century public **executions** – unknown before – were carried out at Þingvellir. Eventually, while still meeting for a few days every year, the Alþing became a minor affair, and the last assembly was held at Þingvellir in 1798, replaced after 1800 by a national court and parliament at Reykjavík.

A century later, however, and Þingvellir had become the focus of the **nationalist movement**, with large crowds witnessing various independence debates here – the Danish king even attended Iceland's millennial celebrations at Þingvellir in 1874. It remained a symbol of national identity through the twentieth century, peaking when half the country turned up at Þingvellir to hear the **declaration of independence** from Denmark and the formation of the Icelandic Republic on June 17, 1944. Surprisingly few, however, attended ceremonies here in July 2000 to mark a thousand years of Icelandic Christianity – though maybe this was due more to the advent of television than lack of interest in Þingvellir's associations.

---

nearest campground is just south. Back near the church, there's formal **accommodation** at the lakeside *Hótel Valhöll* (☎486 1777, ⓦ www.hotelthingvellir.is; ⑤), a slightly gloomy, 1930s affair imposingly placed below Almannagjá's walls. There are three other exposed basic **campsites** east of here, along a quiet, one-kilometre strip of lake shore between Vatnskot and Öfugsnáði bays; and a couple more for hikers 3km north of the information centre, beyond the park border at the base of Ármannsfell. Park rules protect all plants, animals and natural formations, and prohibit open fires, off-road driving and camping outside designated sites. Finally, you can join free hour-long **tours** of the locality that leave from the church at 10am and 3pm daily through summer.

Þingvellir

It's hard to overstate the historical importance of **Þingvellir**, though there are very few specific monuments to see, and to capture the spirit of the place you need to familiarize yourself with the buildings and natural formations around which events were played. Coming from Reykjavík, there's a great **lookout** point just where Route 36 grazes the top of Almannagjá, on the very edge of the **North American continental plate**: the Alþing site is directly below, with the church and red-roofed hotel separated by the Öxará which flows south to the lake. Looking northeast up the rift, a flagpole rises in front of where vertical basalt columns topped by rope lava cleave away from the rift wall, while in the distance, Ármannsfell and Hrafnabjörg frame the valley, fist-like and solid. Permanence is an illusion, however – the rift is widening by 1.5cm further each year as the continental plates drift apart. As they move, the valley floor sinks, on average, a couple of millimetres anually, though in 1789 it fell half a metre in just ten days after an earthquake. Away in the distance, Skjaldbreiður's apparently low summit is easily overlooked, though at 1060m it's actually one of the highest peaks in view. Once you've taken in the landscape, duck into the **Educational Centre** here, which has interactive videos outlining Þingvellir's history.

From the lookout, a hundred-metre track descends into Almannagjá and down to the **flagpole**, which marks the presumed site of Lögberg, the rock where important speeches were made and the lawspeaker recited Iceland's laws to the masses below. Its exact location is obscure, the victim of subsidence and plain forgetfulness, but this is the spot used during twenti-eth-century assemblies. Continuing along Almannagjá, a plaque and traces of walls outline the remains of an eighteenth-century **búð**, one of the temporary roofed camps raised by participants during assemblies. They seemed to shrink through the ages; the sagas suggest that *búðs* were large enough to accommodate entire clans, though storekeepers and traders presumably kept smaller establishments. But nobody really knows: of the thirty or so *búð* sites located in the area, only two are thought to predate the thirteenth century.

Beyond here, the Öxará cascades over Almannagjá as the twenty-metre-high **Öxarárfoss**, flows down along the gorge for 150m then breaks through the wall in a brief tumble down onto plains, and so past the church and into the lake. Rift walls near Öxarárfoss are clearly layered, marking falls of ash from at least twenty separate volcanic eruptions, though river rocks themselves are barely worn, suggesting that the Öxará's path is fairly new. This supports oral accounts of the river's diversion into the rift around 1000 AD to provide water for the sizeable chunk of Iceland's population who descended at each Alþing. After Danish laws were enforced in the sixteenth century, **pools** near the second falls were used to drown women convicted of witchcraft or sexual offences (men were beheaded for the same crimes), though the idea of a death penalty was repugnant to Icelanders and few such executions were carried out. During the Christian millennial celebrations in July 2000, a wreath was laid here in atonement for those who were executed before capital punishment was abolished in the late eighteenth century.

Moving down into the valley, cross over the Öxará and follow the road back towards the church. East of here is the splintered wall forming **Flosagjá**, a deep fissure whose southern end has been flooded by underground springs creating

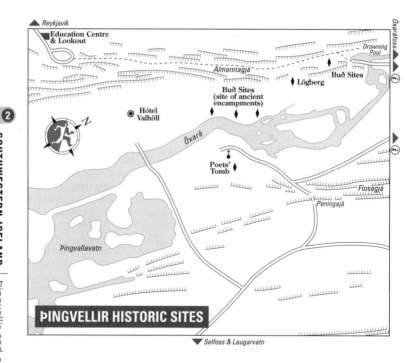

Reykjavík

Education Centre & Lookout

Almannagjá

Buð Sites (site of ancient encampments)

Hótel Valhöll

Öxará

Poets' Tomb

Þingvallavatn

Öxaráfoss

Drowning Pool

Buð Sites

Lögberg

Flosagjá

Peningajá

ÞINGVELLIR HISTORIC SITES

Selfoss & Laugarvatn

Peningagjá, an exceedingly clear, deep wishing pool; coins glint silver and electric blue at the bottom. A little further on is the **church**, the site of which was apparently in use – possibly as a giant *buð* – before the Norwegian king Ólafur Haraldsson supplied timber for the first church building in 1018. The current white and blue structure, from 1859, is misleadingly small and unpretentious, as by the eighteenth century Þingvellir church was wealthy, owning a huge swathe of farmland stretching right up the valley. A raised area behind is reserved for the tombs of outstanding Icelanders; at present the only two incumbents are the patriotic poets **Einar Benediktsson** and **Jónas Hallgrímsson**; the latter also inspired the nineteenth-century independence movement and drew great inspiration from Þingvellir. Former farm buildings next door are now a school and home to the church warden, who doubles as the national park manager, and the marshlands in front were once possibly an island where duels at the Alþing were fought, before the practice was banned in the thirteenth century.

Around Þingvellir

Þingvellir's valley is covered in the overgrown nine-thousand-year-old lavafield **Þingvallahraun**, product of the up-valley Skjaldbreiður (Shield-broad). Though now extinct, this was the first **shield volcano** ever to be classified, a type that spews out high-volume fluid lava in a steady rather than violent eruption, leaving wide, flattened cones. The valley is beautiful in summer and early autumn, carpeted in patchy pine plantations, dwarf birch forest and heathland plants, with the national park covered in a web of marked walking and riding **trails** – note that some of these cross minor rifts and gorges, which might be dangerously concealed if there has been any snow. To venture further, or climb any of the mountains, you'll need at least basic orienteering skills and the Landmælingar Islands *Þingvellir* 1:25,000 **map**.

Of the **marked trails**, the easiest lead east of Þingvellir's church or north from Þingvallavatn's shore, converging 2km on at **Skógarkot**, a sheep farm abandoned in the 1930s – paths from Þingvellir are best, as they cross a couple of interesting rifts and avoid most of the boggy ground you'll find on the other routes. The long-beaked birds zigzagging away in panic at your approach, or flying high to drop earthwards with a strange drumming noise, are **snipe**, or *hrossagaukur* in Icelandic (horse-cuckoo). Skógarkot's ruined but strongly constructed **stone buildings** occupy a grassy hillock roughly halfway across the valley, not a high position but still elevated enough for you to take in a panorama of distant peaks and rift walls, and feel dwarfed by the scale of the Þingvallahraun flow. From here you could either continue north to another farm site at **Hrauntún**, and then turn west for the main campsite (another 4km in all); or walk a couple more kilometres across the valley to where Route 36 climbs the eastern rift wall – and onto the Eurasian continental plate – at **Hrafnagjá**, Raven's Rift.

Of the **mountains**, Ármannsfell (765m) is the easiest to climb, though it's still a full-day, eight-kilometre return hike to the summit from the campsite on its southern slopes; there's snow up here until the middle of the year. Hrafnbjörg is not really climbable, but you could hike out here from the main campsite, circuit the base, and return in a very full day – it's about an eighteen-kilometre round-trip, only negotiable by taking the road, or marked trails via Skógarkot, to Hrafnagjá before striking northeast cross-country. For Skjaldbreiður, you're looking at a two- to three-day hike to the rim of the three-hundred-metre-wide crater, and need advice on the route from the information centre or one of Iceland's walking clubs (see p.41) before setting out.

Þingvallavatn

Immediately south of Þingvellir, **Þingvallavatn** formed nine thousand years ago when fresh lava blocked off the outflow of springs rising in a basin, back-filling it with water to form a fourteen-kilometre-long lake, Iceland's largest. Although no great scenic wonder, Þingvallavatn and its sole outflow, the **Sog** river, are surrounded by alternately rugged hills and undulating moorland, good for both hiking and bird-watching, while the lake is dotted with three tiny volcanic islands and, on rare windless days, forms a perfect blue mirror to the sky. Three surprisingly non-intrusive **hydroelectric stations** at the head of the Sog provide power for the region, while healthy stocks of char and a dwindling trout population keep the fly population down and anglers happy – winter fishing is especially popular, when holes have to be cut through the ice. In summer, you can get **fishing permits** through Þingvellir's visitors' centre or *Hótel Valhöll*.

You can circuit Þingvallavatn in your own transport along a gravel road which runs around the south side of the lake between both prongs of Route 36. **Lake cruises** (℡854 7664, ℻482 3610) lasting from forty minutes to a couple of hours depart Sat & Sun 11am, 2pm and 5pm from June until October; cruises leave from *Skálabrekka* farm, about 5km south of the Þingvellir visitor centre just off Route 36.

Around the lake

From Þingvellir's visitor centre, you head 10km back towards Reykjavík on Route 36 before turning off for the 12km run down Þingvallavatn's western shore and then inland to Nesjavallavirkjun, the **Nesjavellir Thermal Power Station** (guided tours June–Aug Mon–Sat 9am–noon & 1–6pm; free), which steams away at the base of jagged, rough fells. Nesjavallavirkjun supplies Reykjavík with hot water from superheated sources 2km underground, while roadside overflows attract wildfowl in cold weather; nearby low wooden buildings at *Hótel Nesbúð* (T482 3415, Wwww.nesbud.iss; sleeping-bag accommodation 1100kr, ❶) provide **accommodation**, hot tubs, and a good **restaurant**, with a range of marked **walking tracks** into the hills from here lasting between an hour and – if you want to hike all the way to Hveragerði – a day or more.

Heading east from the power station, you reach the lake again at **Hagavík**, a tiny bay fringed in black shingle, then leave it once more and pass the signed access track to **Olfusvatnsvík** (a 2.5km walk), a marshy bay with camping potential at the start of the signed, seventeen-kilometre hiking trail south to Hveragerði (see p.114). Cross another stretch of moorland and you'll find yourself above **Úlfljótsvatn**, Þingvallavatn's southernmost bay, where a huge cross on the hillside hovers over a tiny lakeside church. Just beyond here is a bridge across the Sog to **Írafossstöð hydro station**, lowest of the three – the other two are invisible from the road – and then you rejoin Route 36 at the few houses comprising **Syðribrú**: turn south to follow the Sog to Selfoss, or north to head back towards Þingvellir. A curved basalt gorge by the roadside after here is the Sog's original exit from Þingvallavatn, now used to regulate outflow through the power stations. Construction of the uppermost hydro station here in 1937 uncovered a Settlement-era burial mound enclosing two skeletons, various weapons, and a boat, now in the National Museum in Reykjavík.

Skálholt, Geysir, and Gullfoss

One way or another, a tangle of roads east of Þingvellir follow the marshy swards of the Hvítá basin up past the religious centre of **Skálholt**, before converging some 60km later at Iceland's two most famous sights: the erupting hot pools at **Geysir**, and **Gullfoss**' thundering falls, 7km beyond. It's beautiful countryside, fertile, flat, framed by distant hills and – if you've spent any time in Iceland's rougher areas – startling green in summer, thanks to one of Iceland's longest rivers, the **Hvítá**. This starts around 140km northeast at Hvítarvatn, an isolated lake below Langjökull on the Interior Kjölur route (see p.331), and flows swiftly to Gullfoss, where it drops into the plains between here and Selfoss, joins the Sog, and runs the last few kilometres to the sea as the Ölfusá.

Coming directly **from Þingvellir**, you follow Route 365 to lakeside hot springs at **LAUGARVATN**, home to the National School for Sports and their excellent swimming pool (Mon–Fri 10am–9pm, Sat & Sun 10am–6pm; 250kr) – there's **accommodation** here at the IYHA hostel *Dalsel* on the main road (T486 1215, Wwww.simnet.is/framus; dorm bed 2000kr) and a summer-only *Edda* hotel overlooking the lake (T448 4810, Wwww.hoteledda.is; sleeping bag 2000kr, ❹). From here it's a straight run east on routes 37 and 35 to Geysir and then Gullfoss, though it's a bit of a detour on back roads to reach Skálholt, unless you leave it for your return journey after Gulfoss.

Coming **from Reykjavík**, turn off the Ringroad just west of Selfoss (p.116) and follow Route 35 northeast past the sights; this is the trail followed by

Golden Circle and **public buses,** which run year-round, and also by summer buses continuing past Gullfoss along the Kjöllur route to Akureyri (see p.241). Coming this way, you pass **Kerið crater** after about 15km, probably created three thousand years ago by a sudden gas explosion through the ground, leaving a neat, conical hill whose crater is 70m deep and the same distance across. The bottom is flooded and used for farming fish, and there's an easy, fifteen-minute path around the red, gravelly rim, with a view northwest to the similar **Seyðishólar** crater.

Skálholt and Reykholt

The region of small lakes and streams north of the middle Hvítá is known as **Biskupstungur,** the Bishop's Tongue, a name which probably originated after the foundation of the church at **SKÁLHOLT,** which lies off Route 35 around 40km from Selfoss. It's easy to overdose on churches in Iceland, but Skálholt's definitely warrants a stop: seat of a bishopric as early as 1056 AD, the huge wooden **cathedral** later established here grew wealthy on land revenues. A **school** was also established – Iceland's first – and by the early thirteenth century there were two hundred people living here, making it the country's largest settlement. Surviving numerous reconstructions and the Reformation, Skálholt became, along with Hólar in northern Iceland, a major seat of learning, and lasted until the region was hit by a catastrophic earthquake in the late eighteenth century. The bishop subsequently shifted to Reykjavík, and Skálholt was largely abandoned, though a chapel was maintained until the church and school were restored and reconsecrated in 1963.

Today, the church is elegantly underplayed, plainly decked out and unusual only for its size. Inside, a mitre over the door identifies Skálholt as a bishopric; there's a nicely proportioned wooden ceiling, abstract stained-glass windows, and a tapestry-like **mosaic** of Christ behind the altar. Reconstruction work in the 1950s also uncovered a thirteenth-century stone **sarcophagus** belonging to Bishop Páll Jónsson, a charismatic churchman who added a tower and sumptuous decorations to the original building: a wooden crook carved with a dragon's head was found with his remains, and the sarcophagus itself is on view here in the summer. Out in front, a twinned rock **sculpture** represents Christianity and Paganism, while a rough-cut stone monument, 100m away, commemorates Iceland's last Catholic bishop, Jón Arason. Arason was actually bishop at Hólar in the north, but rode south in 1550 and captured Skálholt in an attempt to prevent the Danish king from forcing Lutheranism on the country; after a brief struggle he was taken and beheaded by the king's men.

You can **stay** year-round at Skálholt's school (☎486 8870, ⓔskoli@ skalholt.is; sleeping bag 1350kr, ❷), or it's a further 7km up Route 35 to the steaming hillside vents that pin **REYKHOLT** down, like Hveragerði (p.114) as one of the southwest's greenhouse villages. The roadside **fuel station** incorporates a store, café, bus stop, and bank, and is also where to arrange **camping.** From here, it's an uneventful 20km to the Geysir–Gullfoss area.

Geysir

Visible from miles away as a pall of steam rising above the plains, **GEYSIR'**s hot springs bubble out over a grassy slope at the foot of **Bjarnfell,** studded with circular pools atop grey, mineral-streaked mounds. The area has been active for thousands of years, but the springs' positions have periodically shifted as geological seams crack open or close down, and the current vents are believed to have appeared following a thirteenth-century earthquake. Just what makes geysers erupt is subject to speculation: some theorists favour gaseous subterranean burps; others believe that cooler surface water forms a "lid", trapping superheated fluid below until enough pressure builds up to burst through as an eruption. What nobody doubts is just how hot the springs are: underground temperatures reach 125°C, and even surface water is only just off boiling point – under no circumstances should you wander off marked paths (some vents are covered by a paper-thin crust), step anywhere without looking first, or put any part of your body in the springs or their outlets.

The deep, clear blue pool of **Geysir** – the Gusher – is, of course, what everyone comes to see, and in its heyday was certainly impressive, regularly spitting its load seventy metres skywards. Sadly, it hasn't erupted naturally since the 1960s, though it used to be triggered for important visitors by dumping forty kilos of soap powder into it, which somehow sparked activity. Today, you'll have to be content with the antics of nearby **Strokkur**, the Churn, which fires off a thirty-metre-high spout every few minutes. A split second before it explodes, Strokkur's pool surface forms a distinct dome, through which the rising waters tear. Lesser spouts in the vicinity include **Blesi**'s inactive twin pools, one clear and colourless, the other opaque blue; the unpredictably tempered **Fata**; and **Litli Geysir**, which does little but slosh around from time to time.

Aside from Geysir, you can also climb well-worn **tracks** to the summit of Bjarnarfell (727m) for views down on Geysir's surrounds, though it's a miserable proposition in bad weather. Another option is to follow the signposted, three-kilometre-long gravel vehicle track up **Haukadalur** – Hawk Valley – from Geysir to a forestry reserve and church. In saga times Haukadalur was an important holding, another famous educational centre that was eventually incorporated into Skálholt's lands. Extensive felling and ensuing erosion put paid to the estate, which was in a sorry condition when turned into a reserve in the 1930s. Since then, the hillsides here have been planted thickly with green pine trees, and thousands of new saplings spread down the valley, coloured in spring by wildflowers. Have a quick look at the nineteenth-century **church** too, whose brass door-ring is said to have belonged to the friendly giant **Bergþór**, who asked to be buried here.

Practicalities

The Geysir thermal area, along with a **roadhouse** and various services, is right by the roadside, 60km from Selfoss and a bit less than that from Þingvellir. All Golden Circle tours and public **buses** stop here for at least an hour, long enough to catch an eruption and get fed, but not to ascend Bjarnfell or get out to Haukadalur. Moving on, there are daily buses all through the year on to Gullfoss, and back to Selfoss and Reykjavík.

There's good-value **accommodation** either at *Hótel Geysir* (℡486 8915, ⓦwww.geysircentre.is; studio flats with bathroom and kitchen ❹), or at the hostel-style *Geysir Guesthouse/Haukadalur III* (℡486 8733, ℻872 1573, ⓔagustath@visit.is; sleeping bag 1400kr, made-up bed 1800kr), which tends to get booked out in advance. For **food**, the roadhouse's café is overpriced and mediocre; you'll get a better deal at the hotel restaurant, even if you're only after a bowl of soup and coffee. Note that there's no store at Geysir, and you'll need to bring supplies if you're self-catering.

Gullfoss

About 6km up the road from Geysir on the Hvítá river, **Gullfoss** – Golden Falls – can hardly fail to impress, whether in full flood during the spring thaw or frozen and almost still in the depths of winter. Although most people bypass it unknowingly on the bus, the approach road over moorland follows the top of a two-kilometre-long canyon sided in organ-pipe basalt columns, into which Gullfoss drops in a pair of broad cataracts: the first steps out ten metres in full view, then the river bends a sharp ninety degrees and falls a further twenty metres into the gorge's spray-filled shadow. Paths along the edge are dangerous when icy, but at other times they allow you to get thoroughly soaked while viewing spray rainbows above the drop.

The falls are a nature reserve, formed after **Sigríður Tómasdóttir**, daughter of the owner of the estate that incorporated Gullfoss, who fought first her father and then the government to stop a hydroelectric dam being built here in the 1920s. Permission to build the dam was granted, but, fanned by Sigríður, public feeling ran so strongly against the project that construction never started. The land was later sold to Einar Guðmundsson of nearby **Brattholt farm**, who donated it to the Icelandic Nature Conservation Council in 1976.

There's a gift shop and **café** at the top of the gorge above the falls, and **accommodation** between March and October 3km down the road at *Brattholt* (Ⓣ486 8979, Ⓔbrattholtii@islandia.is; tents 450kr, dorms 1550kr, ❷). Gullfoss marks the end of the Golden Circle, though the Kjölur route continues northeast across the Interior from here (p.331), covered by summer buses.

The Central South

East of Reykjavík on the Ringroad, the hothouse town of **Hveragerði** and nearby transit hub **Selfoss** are the gateway to Iceland's **central south**, a swathe of fertile plains watered by the Hvítá, Rangá, and **Þjórsá** – Iceland's longest river at 230km – and the clutch of bulky glaciers to its west. The inland here cowers beneath **Hekla**, the destructive volcano whose antics have put paid to regional farming at least twice in recorded history, with tracks past the mountain leading to hot springs and brightly coloured hills at **Landmannalaugar**, right on the edge of Iceland's rugged Interior. Meanwhile, the Ringroad crosses the grassy swards that formed the setting for much of **Njál's Saga** (see box on pp.126–127), Iceland's great medieval epic, beyond which loom the **Eyjarfjallajökull** and **Mýrdalsjökull** ice caps, offering superlative scenery around their wooded edges at **Þórsmörk**. With Mýrdalsjökull squeezing down on an ever-narrowing shore, the Ringroad reaches Iceland's southernmost point near the pleasant coastal village of **Vík**, an area famed for its black sand beaches, eroded cliffs, and birdlife.

The region is one of the best places in the country to get out and about, especially considering how accessible it all is from Reykjavík: if you enjoy camping and hiking, Landmannalaugar and Þórsmörk are worth a trip to Iceland in their own right, as is the four-day **Laugavegur hiking trail** between the two. If you're not that serious, consider less demanding tracks over the hills above Hveragerði, or the coastal paths in the vicinity of Vík. For regional **horse treks**, contact Eldhestar at Vellir, about 2km southeast of Hveragerði (Ⓣ480 4800, Ⓦwww.eldhestar.is), who offer anything from one hour to two weeks in the saddle. As far as transport goes, the Ringroad is the central south's main artery, running for some 200km through the region via all the main towns, and plied by year-round **buses**. In summer, there are also daily services to Landmannalaugar and Þórsmörk, which are about the only two destinations here that you shouldn't try to reach in a conventional vehicle.

Hveragerði

Following the Ringroad southeast from Reykjavík, you cross various flat, lichen-covered lava flows for 45km before the road twists down off the ranges to the coastal plains and the glowing hothouses of **HVERAGERÐI**, a cluster of low buildings on the Vármá (Warm River), nestled beneath steaming fell slopes. Sitting on the edge of a geothermal area, which extends north under the mountains and right up to Þingvellir, a wool mill and hydroelectric dam were already established here when, for the first time in Iceland, subterranean heat was harnessed to grow vegetables in the 1920s. Today, this has spawned a Horticultural College, a clinic specializing in hot-mud cures for arthritis, and scores of hothouses, from small backyard setups to giant commercial affairs, artificially lit to aid the propagation of fruit, vegetables, and exotic plants. That said, there's not a huge amount to see in Hveragerði itself, though some fine **hiking** hereabouts might encourage a stopover.

The most obvious thing to do in Hveragerði is to head for a **hothouse**, and a couple of minutes' walk east off main street Breiðamörk down Austurmörk brings you to Eden, the darling of Golden Circle bus tours. A pricey gift shop, garden centre and café rolled into one, coffee, ornamental figs, bougainvillea, palms, cactus, heliconias and much trumpeted **bananas** (which are not exported in bulk, as often reported), bask in a tropical warmth, stolidly defying the outdoor temperatures. Another 100m up Breiðamörk, Blómaborg is a smaller affair, aimed more at Reykjavík residents seeking colourful house plants, and you can also tour the **Horticultural College** (call in advance for times ☏480 4300; Mon–Fri 500kr, Sat 700kr), over the river to the north of town, where the whole hothouse process was pioneered.

West from here on parallel Hveramörk and overlooked by Hveragerði's rather ordinary modern **church**, thermal outflows have been turned into a **hot springs park** (450kr; irregular hours), complete with bubbling pools and miniature geyser. To see the real thing follow Breiðamörk for about 1km out of town to **Grýla**, a small hot spout named after a child-devouring troll – it usually erupts every few minutes. The other place to spend some time is at Hveragerði's excellent **pool** (250kr) just north of the centre and over the river on Reykjamörk.

Practicalities

A small, quiet mesh of streets, Hveragerði is laid out either side of the main drag **Breiðamörk**, which runs north off the highway, past the compact town centre, and out into the countryside and the start of hiking trails. The South Iceland **information centre** (☏483 4601, ℻483 4604; Mon-Fri 9am–5pm, Sat & Sun 10am–2pm) is about 200m along, just off Breiðamörk on the right, and has brochures, **maps**, and **internet** (100kr), hands out sound advice and can make tour bookings. A **supermarket**, **bank** (with ATM), and **post office** lie another 100m up Breiðamork, grouped around the open square that serves as the **bus stop** – services along the Ringroad, and to Þorlákshöfn, the port for the Westman Islands' ferry (p.140), call in here.

For **accommodation**, Hveragerði's **campsite** (☎483 4601, ℻483 4604; 400kr) is east of the centre on Reykjamörk; it has toilets and showers but is a bit basic. Next to the bus stop, the hospitable *Hótel Ljósbrá* and adjoined IYHA **hostel** *Ból* (☎483 4198, ⓦ www.hotelljosbra.is; sleeping bag 2150kr, ❹) are self-catering and offer sleeping-bag space through to double rooms with private bath. A few minutes' walk west on Frumskógar, the recently renovated *Frumskógar Guesthouse* (☎896 2780, ⓦ www.frumskogar .is; ❸, studios ❺) has cosy doubles in the main building and self-contained studio flats with spas; about 200m north of town up Breiðamörk, *Frost and Fire* (☎483 4959, ⓦ www.frostandfire.is; ❹) is a modern guesthouse overlooking the river. Otherwise, there's the upmarket business venue, *Hótel Örk*, just off the highway on Breiðamörk (☎483 4700, ℻483 4775; ❼), whose facilities include a casino and nightclub. Pick of the local **farmstays** is *Núpa*, 3km south of town (☎846 9286, ⓦ www.nupar.is; 2–6 person cabins 6500–9000kr).

You can get coffee and cakes at the **bakery** on Breiðamörk, with a *Pizza 67* next to the information centre. If you're self-catering, take advantage of Hveragerði's glut of vegetables (tasting none the worse for their hothouse origins), and hunt out rectangular loaves of dense, dark, *hverabrauð*, rye bread baked in underground ovens (for more of which, see p.274) at the bakery or supermarket.

Hveragerði hikes

Hengill, the steamy heights above Hveragerði, is covered in trails and hot springs, hillsides stained by volcanic salts, heathland plants, and, in fine weather, inspiring views coastwards. A range of day-return tracks allow a good sniff around, though with more time it's feasible to push right on up to Þingvallavatn lake (see p.109). *Gönguleiðir á Hengilssvæðinu* is a good **map** of the area, available at the IYHA hostel and information centre, with all trails and distances marked; on the ground, many routes are staked out with coloured pegs. As always, carry a compass and come prepared for bad weather. There are few huts and no stores or official campsites along the way, though you could set up a tent more or less anywhere.

For an easy four-hour circuit – or to tackle longer trails to Þingvallavatn – follow Breiðamörk north out of town for about forty minutes to a **bridged stream** at the base of the fells, from where a pegged trail heads uphill. Crossing the muddy top, you descend green boggy slopes into **Reykjadalir**, Steam Valley, named after the hot stream that runs through the middle. You need to wade across this at any convenient point – there's a shallow ford – and then follow the far bank at the base of the forbidding rubble slopes of **Molddalahnúkar**, past a number of hot spots belching vapour and sulphur – stay on the path. At the head of the valley, 3km from the bridge, the stream bends west, with **Ölkelduhnúkur's** solid platform straight ahead: on the slope to the east, **Dalasel hut** (bunks and pit toilet) marks the start of a 13km trail northeast to Úlfljótsvatn at Þingvallavatn (p.109); while the main trail follows the stream west along **Klambragil**, another steamy valley. There's a short climb and then the path circuits 2km around the back of Ölkelduhnúkur, where it divides again, two trails heading northeast either side of a series of high ridges for 12km to Þingvallavatn at Ölfusvatnsvík (p.110), the other continuing around Ölkelduhnúkur to Dalasel (around 1.5km), from where you can retrace your steps back down Reykjadalir to Hveragerði.

Selfoss and around

Some 15km east of Hveragerði, the Ringroad passes the junction of routes north towards Þingvellir and the Geysir–Gullfoss area (see p.110), before crossing a suspension bridge over the fast-flowing Ölfusá and running into the unassuming town of **SELFOSS**. Caught between the looming bulk of **Ingólfsfjall** to the north and flat grasslands running to the horizon in all other directions, it's been the centre of Iceland's **dairy industry** since the 1930s and with a population of 4000 is easily the southwest's largest settlement. Although there's little to Selfoss besides its history, good facilities and a crossroads position on the southwest's main roads combine to make the town a useful base, especially for visiting the nearby coastal fishing villages of **Stokkseyri** and **Eyrarbakki** – the latter of which was a staging post for the Viking discovery of North America.

The original English-engineered **suspension bridge** itself, built in 1891, is the reason Selfoss ever came into existence. Before then, roads through the region ran to a point further south, on the Ölfusá estuary, where traffic was ferried across. Rough waters made these ferry crossings hazardous however, and when the bridge was opened it became an immediate success, a focus for the new stores and homes that gradually coalesced into the country's first inland town, drawing trade away from the older coastal settlements. The bridge also gave Selfoss the distinction of being the cause of the country's first **strike**, sparked not over wages but the fact that its builders were supplied with only salmon to eat. The current bridge – which is just about the only two-lane span in the whole of southern Iceland – dates from 1945, built after the original collapsed when two milk trucks crossed it simultaneously. Equally distinctive is Selfoss's modern riverside **church**, just south of the bridge on the same side as the town, whose standard black-tiles-and-whitewash exterior compliments a beautifully elongated bell tower and steeply peaked roof. Inside, exposed wooden rafters and murals based on decorative medieval designs are handsome touches.

For a look at the countryside around Selfoss, cross back over the bridge and head north up Route 35, which squeezes between Ölfusá and **Ingólfsfjall**'s eastern side. This flat-topped mountain is a sandwich of lava and assorted detritus formed by sub-glacial volcanic activity, and a trail ascends to the 551m **summit** (two strenuous hours) from *Alviðra* farm, 5km north of Selfoss. Ingólfsfjall is named after Iceland's first official settler, **Ingólfur**, who wintered here in the early 870s before moving on to settle at Reykjavík (for more on which, see Contexts, p.338). Today, a scattering of summer houses are planted – somewhat alarmingly – on Ingólfsfjall's unstable, boulder-strewn lower slopes.

The view further along Route 35 takes in the sharp-lined confluence of the clear, glacier-fed Hvítá river system and the darker **Sog** river, which drains Þingvallavatn lake to the north, to form the Ölfusá – which, in its turn, flows the final 10km to the sea. The two-kilometre-broad wedge of land immediately north of their confluence is a private reserve known as **Þrastaskógur**, the Thrush Forest, which covers a six-thousand-year-old lava field in a low stand of birch and pine woodland. There are several good, easy **walking tracks** around the reserve from the entrance on Route 35, just by the bridge on the north bank of the Sog, around 9km from Selfoss; and you can also **camp** here (see below).

Practicalities

Coming over the bridge from Hveragerði, the first thing you encounter is a **roundabout**: from here, Eyravegur heads south towards the coast; while the

Ringroad bears east for a kilometre through Selfoss as Austurvegur. The **bus station** is at the Esso fuel station on Austurvegur at the eastern exit of town, staging post for services along the Ringroad, and also a partially coastal run daily to Reykjavík via Stokkseyri, Eyrarbakki, and Þorlákshöfn (p.148). **Tourist information** (June 1–Sept 15, Mon–Fri 10am-7pm, Sat 11am-2pm; T482 2422, F482 3599) is in the library, near the roundabout on Austurvegur, which also has **Internet** access (100kr). Austurvegur is also where to find the **banks** (all have ATMs) and **post office**. The local **liquor store** is tucked behind the bus station at Vallholt 19; there's a large **shopping centre**, which includes a well-supplied supermarket, opposite the tourist information office; and a branch of cut-price *Bónus* supermarket on the roundabout.

Accommodation options include the excellent **campsite** and *Gesthús Selfossi* (T482 3585, Wwww.gesthus.is; camping 500kr, sleeping bag 2000kr, ④) on Engjavegur, two blocks south of parallel Austurvegur, with showers, kitchen facilities, and self-contained cabins. You can also camp about 9km up Route 35 in the woods at Þrastaskógur (1000kr per tent), where there are barbecues, picnic tables and a toilet block with cold water. Otherwise, there are further guesthouse-style lodgings at *Heimagisting* (T482 1471; ③), at Heiðmörk 2a, a small lane north off Austurvegur at the eastern edge of town; and above the *Menam* Thai restaurant (T482 4099, Wwww.menam.is; ③), just off the roundabout on Eyravegur. Also on the roundabout, *Hótel Selfoss* (T482 2500, F482 2524, Www.icehotels.is; ⑦) fills the town's upmarket niche.

Selfoss boasts some unexpectedly good **places to eat**. *Kaffi-krús*, opposite the library on Austurvegur, is open from 10am until midnight for coffee and excellent cakes in candlelit ambience, and *Menam* (see above) restaurant's authentic Thai cuisine is a gem – treat yourself to chicken and green beans in coconut milk for little more than the price of a pizza. There's also *Stekihús* in a former cowshed on Tryggvagata, a road south off Austurvegur just east of the library, which serves up a good lunchtime buffet and an evening menu featuring steak, duck, and salmon.

Stokkseyri

South of Selfoss, Route 34 runs straight to the coast across the **Flói**, a ten-kilometre stretch of land so flat that halfway across you can see both your starting point and destination. Within sight of the sea you reach an intersection; turn eastwards and it's a couple of kilometres to **STOKKSEYRI**, a village of a few houses, a fish factory, a supermarket and a fuel station congregating around a church behind a protective storm wall. Over the wall is a windswept, vestigial and unattended **harbour** – though even in its heyday in the 1900s it must have been tough to launch a boat here – and, oddly, a little yellow sand beach nestled amongst black, weed-strewn rocks. It's not obvious today, but Stokkseyri was once a busy fishing port whose most famous resident was **Thurídur Einarsdottír**, an early nineteenth-century woman who worked on commercial fishing boats for most of her life and was a fleet foreman for 25 years. The idea of women going to sea wasn't too unusual at the time, but Thurídur was also renowned for successfully defending, in court, her then-illegal preference for wearing men's clothing. A couple of old turf-and-stone buildings lurk nearby – one is right beside the church.

One of the best reasons to visit Stokkseyri is to splash out for an evening meal at *Fjöruborðið* **lobster restaurant** (T483 1550, bookings essential), just behind the storm wall near the beach, which is a trendy place with Reykjavík's elite –

count on spending at least 3000kr per head. There's **no accommodation** in Stokkseyri, but at least one **bus** daily from Selfoss, which continues on to Eyrarbakki, Þorlákshöfn and Reykjavík.

Eyrarbakki

Four kilometres west from Stokkseyri and just past the intersection, **EYRAR-BAKKI** is a larger version of its neighbour, and has a greater claim to fame: local boy **Bjarni Herjólfsson** sailed from here in 985 aiming for Greenland, lost his way in a storm, and became the first European to set eyes on **North America** – though, displaying an incredible lack of curiosity, he failed to land. After reaching Greenland, he told his story and sold his ship to Leif Eiriksson, who retraced Bjarni's route, made landfall, and named the place "**Vinland**" after his foster-father reported finding grape vines. Two versions of the tale – and subsequent abortive attempts to settle Vinland – are recounted in *Greenlanders' Saga* and *Eirik the Red's Saga*, usually coupled together as the *Vinland Sagas* (see "Books", p.357).

Until the early twentieth century, Eyrarbakki's **harbour** was considered one of the best in southern Iceland, though it's difficult to understand why: there's no shelter from the elements and boats were traditionally launched by dragging and pushing them through the surf into deeper water where they could be rowed out. Nonetheless, fishing and a proximity to the Ölfusá estuary ferry ensured Eyrarbakki's success as a trading centre until the Selfoss bridge was completed; thereafter, decline was compounded when the town's harbour was rendered redundant by a more effective, man-made effort west across the Ölfusá at Þorlákshöfn, and the town's fish factory finally closed in the 1990s. Today, the hamlet's main employer would seem to be the local **jail**, one of Iceland's largest.

Despite this downturn of fortune, Eyrarbakki is an attractive place with a core of early twentieth-century houses, many of which have been bought up and restored by city folk as weekend retreats. Two older survivors are the timber-sided **church**, and nearby **Húsið**, a Norwegian wooden kit-home dating back to 1765 which, along with adjacent buildings, now serves as a **museum** (June–Aug daily 1–6pm; 450kr). Aside from a random assortment of Eyrarbakki's historical flotsam, a couple of rooms have been refurbished in period style, and there's a partial reconstruction of the once pivotal town store, whose proprietor – Guðlaugur Pálsson – served customers from 1917 until 1989. Your ticket includes entry into the **Maritime Museum** (same hours) across the lawn behind, whose centrepiece is a wooden fishing boat of the kind used until the 1930s. It must have taken some courage to go to sea in these broad, open, low-sided vessels, let alone fish from one; sails were used, though boats were classified not by the shape of the sails or overall length, but by the number of oars used to row them – and hence the size of the crew. A few photos and weather-beaten oilskins complete the display. Outside, climb the **storm wall** for a look seawards at what fishermen were up against as they set off or returned – a difficult entry over a rocky shore.

Eyrarbakki sports the small, self-catering **guesthouse** *Hjá Ása* (☎483 1120, or 854 1136; ❸), for which bookings are essential, and the *Rauða húsið* **café-restaurant**, which was changing hands at the time of writing but had a grill-oriented menu. The only facilities in town are a small fuel station; **buses** are the same as for Stokkseyri. There's a good drive westwards towards Þorlákshöfn and Reykjavík via a causeway over the Ölfusá's improbably broad estuary, which takes in heathland, coastal flats, vegetated lava flows and a series of brackish marshland pools, all ideal for **bird-watching** – swans, geese, snipe and godwit are all common.

Þjórsárdalur, Hekla, and Landmannalaugar

Upstream along the Þjórsá east of Selfoss, there's a rare surviving relic of Viking settlement in **Þjórsárdalur**, a once fertile valley laid waste over nine hundred years ago by a particularly violent eruption of **Hekla**, which lies over the river to the southeast. The volcano last let rip in 2000, and the whole region remains patently active, with Iceland's highest concentration of **hot springs** east again from Hekla around **Landmannalaugar**. While Hekla's immediate vicinity is a predictable carpet of rubbly lava fields in various degrees of vegetation, Landmannalaugar – with its bathable springs surrounded by a landscape oozing rugged grandeur – makes a great target, and sits at the northern end of **Laugavegur**, a wonderful hiking trail to Þórsmörk. It's worth noting that cross-country routes on from Landmannalaugar include the **Sprengisandur** (F26) to Mývatn (p.265) and **Fjallabak** to Kirkjubærklaustur and Skaftafell (p.315), making it a good staging post for wider travels. Between April and November you can also get a good introduction to **white water rafting** on the Þjórsá with Arctic Rafting (☎487 5557, ⓦwww.arcticrafting.is), who charge 5900kr for around two hours on the river.

Route 30/32 to Þjórsárdalur, and Route 26 to Hekla and Landmannalaugar, are both accessed off the Ringroad east of Selfoss; see p.122 and p.123 for details. **Buses** run past Hekla to Landmannalaugar through the summer; there is no public transport to Þjórsárdalur. While there are a good few kilometres of gravel roads, Þjórsárdalur and the area around Hekla are accessible to normal vehicles in good weather, though the track from Hekla to Landmannalaugar is really for four-wheel-drives only. Take everything you'll need with you, as there are few shops or supplies in the region.

Þjórsárdalur

Around 15km out of Selfoss, Route 30 branches northeast off the Ringroad to follow the west bank of the Þjórsá, mutating along the way into the 32 at the one-horse hamlet of **ARNES**, where there's a fuel station, small café-store, and IYHA **hostel** (☎486 6048, ⓔbergleif@centrum.is; camping 450kr, sleeping bag 1850kr; ❸) with campsite, kitchen, and pool. Past here, there are excellent views from a roadside ridge at **Hagafell** straight across the Þjórsá to Hekla.

Forty-five kilometres from Selfoss, **Þjórsárdalur** – the Bull River valley – sits north of the road, flanked by grey and orange gravel slopes and framed at its eastern end by the flat tops of **Skeljafell** and larger **Búrfell**. The valley is floored with an eight-thousand-year-old lava flow, and subsequent thick falls of ash from Hekla have regularly wiped out vegetation, making Þjórsárdalur an awesomely sterile place. On the valley's western side, there's an unsurfaced, seven-kilometre signed track up to bathable **hot springs** near the abandoned farm of Reykholt, or, just south of the main road, a brief detour to **Hjálparfoss**, a parallel pair of short, foaming falls 100m south of the main road. They drop into a round pool, surrounded by thin basalt columns that both spray in all directions and lie piled up like woodstacks; it would be a fine spot to swim if there wasn't a second, rougher cataract draining the pool towards a

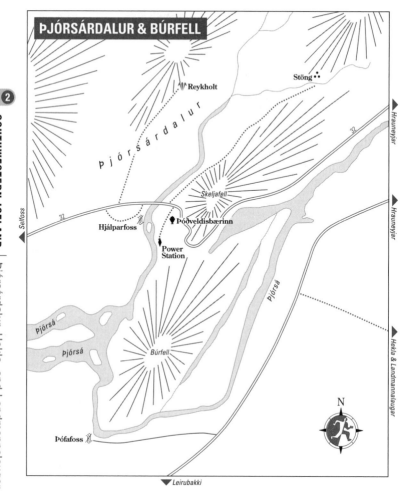

power station below Búrfell. Grassy banks do make Hjálparfoss a good place to picnic, however, and there are **harlequin ducks** around in early summer.

On Þjórsárdalur's eastern side, the signposted Route 327 heads another 7km up to the remains of **Stöng**; it's a rough and then muddy drive, but even without four-wheel-drive you should be able to get within sight of the red-roofed shelter-shed protecting the site. Set on a small stream below the dark slopes of Stangarfjall, Stöng was the home of a chieftain named **Gaukur Trándilsson** until Hekla erupted in 1104, the first time since Settlement, smothering all of Þjórsárdalur under ash and pumice. Stöng was excavated in 1939 and illustrates a typical **Viking homestead**: a longhouse formed the main hall, with a second, smaller hall and two attached outhouses serving as women's quarters, washroom and pens, all built from stone and timber and sided with turf. Neatly built stone foundations, central fireplace and post supports all give a good outline of the original buildings, but it's the stark setting – distant orange and green-streaked valley walls, and patches of pasture clinging on along the stream – which really impresses.

For a more complete picture of how Stöng once appeared, return to Route 32 and take the surfaced turning south marked "Búrfellsstöð", roughly opposite the Stöng junction and immediately below Búrfell. This descends 100m down to the power station, but before this follow signs left to **Þóðveldisbærinn** (June to early Sept daily 10am–noon & 1–6pm; 300kr), a reconstructed period homestead based on archeological evidence provided by Stöng and other sites, roofed with turf and authentically decked out in hand-cut timber, flagstones, and woollen furnishings.

Búrfell and beyond

Past Þjórsádalur, Route 32 winds up between Búrfell and Skeljafell; from the saddle there's a four-wheel-drive track right up to the **transmitter tower** on Búrfell's flattened summit (699m); you can walk it in an hour and, if the weather's unusually good, you won't get a better glimpse of Hekla – just 12km southeast over the river.

Continuing along the Þórsá, you pass a network of dams and spillways, part of an extensive **hydroelectric project**. It's best viewed from a bridge 10km further along the road, from where you can look back towards Búrfell, or north to where the river explodes out from below another power station into the tight confines of a gorge. Once over the bridge, it's a couple of kilometres to Route 26, where you can turn south to trails around Hekla (see below), or north towards Hrauneyjar farm, first stop on the **Sprengisandur** route (see p.330).

Hekla

Believed to be the literal entrance to hell in medieval times – a fact that left the mountain unclimbed until daring students Eggert Olafsson and Bjarni Palsson scrambled up in 1750 – **Hekla** is Iceland's second-most-active volcano, with at least eighteen eruptions known to have occurred in the last thousand years. Oriented northeast, the mountain forms a forty-kilometre-long, snow-covered oval ridge cresting at around 1500m; it should be visible for miles around, but a heavy smudge of cloud usually obscures the peak and gives Hekla – Hooded – its name.

Though several thousand years old, Hekla's **earliest recorded eruption** was the one that buried Stöng in 1104 (see opposite), and it has been active, on and off, ever since. The mountain tends to fire up with little warning, spraying out clouds of fluorine-rich **tephra** ash, which blankets the landscape, poisons groundwater, and kills fish and livestock. Lava follows the ash, welling up at various points along a fissure that splits Hekla's crest lengthways for 5km; during the notorious 1768 eruption – before which the mountain had been dormant for seventy years – flows covered over 65 square kilometres. Eruptions often subside relatively quickly, most of the action occurring within the first few days and followed by months of grumbling – the anguished voices of tormented souls, according to legend. Stöng was by no means the only farm to have been abandoned following such an event – the same eruption is believed to have wiped out twenty similar homesteads – and there are only two working farms around the volcano today.

Hekla has erupted every ten years since 1970, the **most recent eruption** occurring on the evening of February 26, 2000. It wasn't much by the mountain's standards – a plume of ash and steam reaching upwards for 15km and a few days' worth of lava spilling east – but it was notable in that most of Reykjavík descended on the area to watch, only to be trapped on Hekla's slopes by a sudden snowfall. This triggered the largest emergency operation in Icelandic history, with over a thousand people having to be rescued – fortunately, the lava went the other way.

If you want to **climb Hekla**, get in touch with Ferðafélag Íslands, the Icelandic Hiking Association (see Basics, p.41), who can advise about routes and organise a "night time"group ascent on June 21 (the longest and lightest day of the year); or you can arrange a **snowcat** all the way to the top in winter with Toppferðir (☎864 5530, ⓦwww.mmedia.is/toppbrenna). Mountain Taxis (ⓦwww.mountain-taxi.com) also make a **four-wheel-drive** circuit of Hekla for 18,000kr.

Around the mountain

About 30km east of Selfoss along the Ringroad, via a single-lane suspension bridge over the Þjórsá, you reach a lone fuel station, marking where Route 26 points northeast towards Hekla and the track to Landmannalaugar. Both Landmannalaugar and Sprengisandur **buses** pass through the region in summer via the Ringroad town of Hella (p.126).

Those after a local base should pull in 30km along Route 26 on Hekla's western edge at *Leirubakki* farm (☎487 6591, ⓦwww.leirubakki.is; camping 650kr, sleeping-bag accommodation 1800kr, dorm bed 2500kr, ❸), which can supply fuel, meals by arrangement, outside hot tubs, **horses**, and year-round **accommodation** in a self-catering guesthouse. Past *Leirubakki*, you immediately find yourself in a wilderness between the Þórsá river and Hekla's western slopes, the ground covered in tiny pieces of lightweight yellow pumice that are collected hereabouts for export. After about 5km there's a road towards the mountain itself and **Næfurholt farm**, one of the area's few functioning survivors – though it actually had to be moved after one eruption – then a roadside ridge blocks in Hekla's foothills while the Búrfell mesa springs up ahead of you, looking from this position like the perfect setting for an impregnable fortress. Wheel ruts and guide posts heading off-road towards Búrfell at this point can be followed for 4km to **Þófafoss**, where the river bends right under Búrfell's southern tip in a wide, low waterfall, a friendly splash of blue in a monochrome landscape.

Route 26 continues northeast, passing another waterfall called **Tröllkonuhlaup**, the Troll Woman's Leap, named after one of these unpleasant creatures crossed the river in a single bound while chasing a farmer. Bearing east off this road from here is Route F225, the four-wheel-drive-only track to Landmannalaugar; Route 26 continues to parallel the river for 15km up to the junction with Route 32 and the roads to Búrfell and Þjórsárdalur (p.119), or northeast towards Sprengisandur (p.330).

Landmannalaugar and Laugavegur

Thirty kilometres due east of Hekla, **Landmannalaugar** is an astonishing place, a **hot springs** area set in a flat gravel plain between a glacial river and the front of fifteenth-century lava flow, all hemmed in by sharp-peaked obsidian and rhyolite mountains, brightly streaked in orange, grey, and green. Despite its proximity to Hekla, the area has provided summer pasture for sheep since medieval times, and was once a stage on the **Fjallabak Nyrðri** route (see box on p.131), which ran as an alternative way to the coast if flooding from Katla had closed the preferred southern trails. Today Landmannalaugar is a popular destination in its own right, both for the springs and numerous local **hiking tracks** – not to mention being at the start of the exceptional four-day **Laugavegur trail** down to Þórsmörk.

The main **road to Landmannalaugar** is the four-wheel-drive F225, which turns east off Route 26 just past Tröllkonuhlaup (p.122) via thirty-year-old black ash and lava deposits on Hekla's northern flanks, crosses a couple of rivers and intermittent oases of grassland, and finally reaches a major **ford** immediately west of Landmannalaugar. **Buses** from Reykjavík and Selfoss run here daily between mid-June and mid-September; in July and August these also continue southeast via the **Fjallabak nyrðra** route to Kirkjubærklaustur and Skaftafell (see box on p.131), and northeast via the Sprengisandur route to Mývatn (see p.265) – both stop for at least a couple of hours, giving you time for a soak in the springs and a quick walk. In good conditions skilled drivers *might* be able to nurse a conventional vehicle to the ford at Landmannalaugar, the passengers then hitching a ride across with something more sturdy, but you're not advised to try.

Landmannalaugar's **accommodation** is run by Ferðafélag Íslands, the Icelandic Hiking Association (☎568 2533, ✉fi@fi.is), and you'll either be staying in their well-equipped, self-catering **hut** (July–Aug; sleeping bag only, 1700kr), or **camping** (600kr) beside it; book bunk space in the hut as far in advance as possible, although there are often last-minute cancellations. If camping, be aware that **weather** here can be atrocious, with incredibly strong winds – ominously, the campsite has bins full of rocks for weighting down tent edges. The **ranger's office** is at the hut, where you can buy **maps** of the hiking trails. **Toilets and showers** are in a big, separate block. Campers are not meant to use the hut's kitchen, so bring cooking gear along – though there is, incredibly, the small *Fjallafang* **café** in a converted bus (July & Aug 11.30am–8pm), selling beverages, sandwiches and burgers. To organise **horse treks** in the region, contact Hraunhestar (☎854 7735).

Around Landmannalaugar

Your first stop at Landmannalaugar has to be the celebrated **hot springs**, which are in a patch of green at the end of a boardwalk up against the lava front. A scalding stream emerges from underneath the lava and merges with a cold flow; you simply wade up the latter to where they mix, find a spot where the temperature is just right, and sit down up to your neck. You have to keep shifting every time a fellow bather moves, which alters the water currents and temperature, but you couldn't ask for a better place to unwind.

For a couple of easy **hikes**, either head south from the campsite for 2km down **Brandsgil**, a tight, colourful canyon full of shallow streamlets; or west past the hut and up onto the **Laugahraun** lava field, following the first couple of kilometres of the Laugavegur trail. You end up on a ridge overlooking the flow, near a concentration of steam vents at **Brennisteinsalda**, from where you can circuit back to the campsite via **Grænagil**, a small gully.

On a clear day you really should ascend **Bláhnúkur** (945m), the large, bald peak to the south. There's a reasonable trail up the northeast face from the campsite, but for a three-hour circuit, cross the Laugahraun lava field as above, but from Brennisteinsalda, head towards Bláhnúkur's west side, wading the small stream at the mountain's base, and cast around for the trail up (several small tracks from here join it – just take any of them uphill). This looks very

Laugavegur, the fifty-five-kilometre hiking trail between Landmannalaugar and Þórsmörk, is the best of its kind in Iceland, with easy walking and magnificent scenery. Huts with campsites are laid out at roughly fourteen-kilometre intervals, splitting Laugavegur comfortably into **four stages**: six days is an ideal time to spend on the trip, allowing four for the trail and a day at either end, though you could hike the trail in just two days.

The trail is open throughout July and August, when **buses** run daily from Reykjavík to the end points at Landmannalaugar and Þórsmörk. Ferðafélag Íslands' **huts** (☏568 2533, ⓔfi@fi.is) sleep up to 70 people, cost around 1700kr a night for sleeping-bag space, have toilets, kitchens and usually showers, and need to be booked well in advance; if booking through an agent, make sure you get a **receipt** to show to hut wardens, who are out of contact with Ferðafélag Íslands for days at a time. **Campsites** at the huts cost 600kr, with access to toilets and showers, but not kitchens. Bring everything with you, including food and sleeping bags (you can get water at the huts) and, if camping, a tent, stove and cooking gear.

Weather varies between fair and foul, with gale-force winds a speciality of the region; you need full waterproof gear, warm clothing, solid hiking boots, and some old trainers or surf boots for fording the several frigid **rivers**. The trail is well pegged, but carry Lanmælingar Íslands' *Þórsmörk-Landmannalaugar* **map** and a compass. Although the overall **gradients** are the same whichever end you begin, in practice it's easier from the north, where you spend a whole day gradually reaching the trail's apex (around 1120m) between Hrafntinnusker and Álftvatn, instead of doing it in one short, brutal ascent from the south.

The trail

The 12km stretch between Landmannalaugar and the first hut at Hrafntinnusker is mostly up. You leave Landmannalaugar via Brennisteinsalda onto the muddy moorland atop the plateau, surrounded by stark, wild hills. About two-thirds of the way along is **Stórihver thermal area**, a steaming gully and rare patch of grass, beyond which there's a scramble onto a higher **snowfield** which peaks at **Söðull**, the ridge above the huge volcanic crater of **Hrafntinnusker**. "Hrafntin" means **obsidian**, and just about all rocks in the area are made of this black volcanic glass. The Hrafntinnusker **hut** has no shower; the campsite here is on scree and very exposed. The tightly folded ridges due west conceal Iceland's densest concentration of **hot springs**, with a pegged walking track (about 40min each way) out to where one set rises under the stratified edge of a glacier, hollowing out 5m-high **ice caves** – these are best earlier on in the season, before their roofs have collapsed. You can also hike due south from the caves for about thirty minutes to two hot pools about 200m apart – one a boiling cauldron, the other gushing steam – though there is no trail.

It's a further 12km from Harfntinnusker to the second hut at Álftavatn. The first stage continues the plateau scenery across snowfields to a rocky outcrop just

steep from below, but after the first section on loose, ash-like scree it's not too bad, though you wouldn't want to be coming down this way. Around forty minutes should see you on the summit enjoying staggering 360 degree views; all around are multicoloured hills, with the campsite edged by moss-covered lava. Off to the northeast is **Tungnaá**, a sprawling area of lakes and intertwined streams at the source of the Skaftá, which empties into the sea near Kirkjubærklaustur. For the descent, simply follow the main path down the northeast face to the campsite.

west of **Háskerðingur**, whose sharp, snow-clad peak makes a good two-hour detour – though views northwest from the outcrop, over worn rhyolite hills, patches of steam from scattered vents, and Laufafell's distinctive black mass, are just as good. The plateau's edge at **Jökultungur** is not much further on, revealing a blast of colour below which is a bit of a shock after the highland's muted tones: Álftavatn sits in a vivid green glacial valley, lined with sharp ridges and abrupt pyramidal hills, with Mýrdalsjökull's outlying glaciers visible to the south. The subsequent **descent** into the valley is steep but not difficult, and ends with you having to wade a small stream before the trail flattens out near the **two huts** (one owned by Útivist; ☏ 562 1000, ⓦ www.utivist.is) and campground on the lakeshore at **Álftavatn**. After getting settled in, hike around Álftavatn's west side and follow the valley for 5km down to **Torfahlaup**, a narrow canyon near where the **Markarfljót river** flows roughly between the green flanks of Stóra-Grænfjall and Illasúla, two steep-sided peaks.

The next stage to Botnar-Emstrur is 16km. Around 5km east from Álftavatn via a couple more streams, **Hvanngil** is a sheltered valley with a privately run **hut and campground** (1600kr/600kr) with showers and toilet; after here you cross a bridge over **Kaldaklofskvísl**, and have to wade the substantial but fairly shallow **Bláfjallakvísl**. The scenery beyond opens up into a grey-brown gravel **desert**, fringed by the surreally green hills and Mýrdalsjökull's ice cap, as you follow a four-wheel-drive track southwest. Part-way across the desert, there's another bridge over the **Innri-Emstruá**, where this chocolate-brown glacial river hammers over a short waterfall with such force that it sends geyser-like spurts skywards. Then it's back across the gravel, up and over various hillocks, until you find yourself descending bleak slopes to the **hut** at **Botnar-Emstrur**, whose campground is in a small, surprisingly lush gully. Otherwise, the immediate scenery appears barren, though there's a short walk west to **Markarfljótsgljúfur**, a narrow, 180m-deep gorge on the Markarfljót, and superlative views of **Entujökull**, the nearest of Mýrdalsjökull's glaciers, from clifftops around 3km southeast of the hut.

The final 15km southwest to Þórsmörk is perhaps the least interesting section of the journey, though there's initially another good view of the glacier, just before the path crosses the Emstruá over a narrow bridge. This is followed by a climb onto a gravelly heath, with the Markafljót flowing through a series of deep canyons to the west – easy enough to investigate, though out of sight of the path. As you follow the ever-widening valley, you'll start to encounter a few shrubs before crossing a further bridge over the **Ljósá** and descending to the gravel beds of the **Þröngá**, the deepest river you have to ford on the trail – don't attempt it if it's more than thigh deep. Once across you immediately enter birch and juniper **woodland** marking Þórsmörk's boundary at **Hamraskógar**: shady, carpeted in thick grass, and with colourful flowers everywhere. From here, it's a final 2km into Þórsmörk to the huts at either Húsadalur or Skagfjörðsskáli – for more on which, see p.135.

Njál's Saga country

Heading southeast from the Þórsá on the Ringroad, the first thing you'll notice are disproportionate numbers of four-wheel-drives towing boxes, and a wide, rolling expanse of pasture, positively reeking of **horse** – this is one of Iceland's premier horse-breeding areas, with *Oddhóll*, the country's biggest stud farm, near the small town of **Hella**. The countryside between here and the distant slopes of **Eyjafjallajökull** to the east comprises the plains of the

Njal's saga

There was a man called Mörm Fiddle . . .
Such is the innocuous beginning of **Njál's Saga**, Iceland's great tale of Viking-age clan warfare. The longest saga of them all, Njál's Saga was written in the thirteenth century, three hundred years after the events it portrays, and owes more to oral tradition than historical sources – though later records and archeology tend to confirm the story's factual basis (dates below are mostly estimates, however).

The tale centres on the life of **Njál Þorgeirsson** and his family, who are casually ensnared in a minor issue that somehow escalates into a frightful, fifty-year blood feud. Bound by their own personalities, fate, and sense of honour, nobody is able to stop the bloodshed, which ends only after the original characters – and many of their descendants – have been killed. But there's far more to Njál's Saga than its violence, and the tale paints a vivid picture of Iceland at what was, in some ways, an idyllic time: the power of the Alþing at Þingvellir was at its peak, Christianity was overpowering paganism, and the country's settlers lived by their own efforts on farming and freebooting.

The tale splits into three uneven parts, beginning in the late tenth century at a point where the fate of several participants is already intertwined. Gifted with foresight and generally respected by all, Njál himself is often a background figure, mediating and advising rather than confronting or fighting, but his sons play a far more active role, especially the proud and ferocious **Skarp-héðinn**. Njál's best friend is the heroic **Gunnar Hámundarson** of Hlíðarendi, whose superb martial skills and physical prowess never get in the way of his generosity or sense of justice. Balancing this nobility is the malevolent **Mörð Valgarðsson**, a second cousin of Gunnar's who grows up hating him for his intrinsic goodness and spends the saga's first third plotting his downfall.

Around 970 Gunnar goes against Njál's advice and marries "Thief-eyed" **Hallgerð**, a thorny character who, amongst other things, provokes a violent feud with Njál's household. Njál and Gunnar manage to remain firm friends, but Njál's sons are drawn into the fray by the murder of their foster-father **Þórð**, and the cycle of payback killings begins, quickly spiralling out beyond the two immediate families. Mörð sees his chance, and manipulates various disreputable characters into picking fights with Gunnar, who emerges undefeated yet increasingly worn down from each confrontation. At last, Gunnar is ambushed by **Þorgeir Otkelsson**, whose father he

---

two-pronged **Rangá** river system, famed for its **salmon** and the setting for much of the action of Njál's Saga (see box above), though parts of this tale were played out right across southern Iceland. With the highway towns of Hella or **Hvolsvöllur** as a base, getting out to a handful of the saga sites is straightforward enough in your own vehicle, even if you do find more in the way of associations rather than concrete remains when you arrive. Ringroad **buses** pass through Hella and Hvolsvöllur year-round, with summer services stopping at Hvolsvöllur en route to Þórsmörk and the Fjallabak route.

Hella and around

HELLA, a service centre of 600 inhabitants where the highway crosses the narrow flow of the **Ytri-Rangá** – also known as the Hólsá, the western branch of the river Rang – grew through the twentieth century to serve **Rangárvallahreppur**, the fertile farming district beyond Hekla's southwestern extremities. Though hosting the annual Landsmót **National Horse Show**, in late June, Hella is really just somewhere to pause before heading on,

killed earlier as a result of Mörð's scheming; he kills Þorgeir too, but is outlawed for it and banished from Iceland at the Alþing in 990. Torn between his respect for the law and love of his country, Gunnar finds himself unable to leave, and is hunted down to Hlíðarendi by a posse led by Mörð and the upstanding chieftain Gizur the White. When Gunnar's bowstring snaps during the siege, Hallgerð spitefully refuses to give him two locks of her hair to restring the weapon: "To each their own way of earning fame," says Gunnar, in one of the most quoted lines from any saga, and is cut down.

After an interlude describing Iceland's **conversion to Christianity** in 1000, the violence sparked by Hallgerð thirty years earlier resurfaces when Njál's sons kill her distant relative, the arrogant Þráin Sigfússon, for his part in Þórð's death. Attempting to placate Þráin's family, Njál adopts his son **Höskuld** and buys him a priesthood, and for a while all seems well. But over the next decade resentment at this favouritism eats away at Njál's sons, and, encouraged by Mörð – who, now that Gunnar is dead, has shifted his vindictive attentions to Njál – they kill Höskuld one sunny morning. Höskuld's influential father-in-law **Flósi of Svínafell** agrees initially to a cash settlement for the murder, but Njál inadvertently offends him at the Alþing in 1011: confrontation is inevitable and the eighty-year-old Njál, bowing to fate, retreats with his sons to his homestead **Bergþórshvoll**. Flósi and his men torch the building, killing all but Njal's son-in-law **Kári**, who escapes through the burning roof and runs into the night, his clothes ablaze.

Public opinion against the burning of Njál runs so high that Kári is able to remain free, though a hunted man, and at the following year's Alþing he confronts Flósi and his allies – now known as the **Burners**. Mörð stirs up trouble again and a pitched battle breaks out; in the aftermath, all but Kári accept the Alþing's conditions for peace, which banish Flósi and the Burners from Iceland until tempers have cooled. For his part, Kári swears vengeance, and swiftly tracks down and kills a group of Burners before fleeing the country himself. For the next few years, the action follows Kári's peregrinations around northern Europe after his enemies, before he makes a pilgrimage to seek absolution from the Pope. Returning to Iceland, Kári's ship is wrecked at Ingólfshöfði off the southeast coast; walking inland through a blizzard he finds sanctuary at Svínafell and becomes reconciled with Flósi, bringing Njál's Saga to an end.

either to historic sites nearby, or Hekla, clearly visible 50km to the northeast (see p.121).

The town focusses on a shopping centre on the highway, from where Þrúðavegur runs back along the river. **Buses** – both Ringroad services and those heading to Landmannalaugar – pull in here, where there's also an **information centre** (☎487 5165, ℱ487 5365; Mon–Fri 8.30am–12.30pm & 1.30–5.30pm, Sat & Sun 8.30am-1.30pm), fuel station, supermarket and bank with ATM. Hella's primary source of **accommodation** is behind the fuel station on Þrúðavegur at *Gistihúsið Mosfell* (☎487 5828, ℱ487 5004; camping 500kr, sleeping bag 2900kr, doubles without bathroom ❷, with bathroom ❹), who also hire out bicycles; though a good self-catering option is *Gitiheimilið Brenna* (☎864 5531, ⓦwww.mmedia.is/toppbrenna; ❷), 500m back along the riverbank in a bright pink corrugated iron building, who run winter **snowcat** ascents of Hekla (see p.121). Also on Þrúðavegur, *Krisján X* **restaurant** is good for grills and staples.

The nearest place to organize a **horse** is at *Arbakki* farm (☎487 5041, ⓦwww.vortex.is/arbakki), about 5km north of town on the west bank of the river. If you fancy **salmon fishing** on the Rangá, you need to base yourself 8km east down the Ringroad at the *Hótel Rangá* (📞478 5700, 🌐www .icehotel.is; ❼), a four-star establishment where – if you contact them well in advance – you can arrange licenses to cast along the Eystri-Rangá, the river's eastern branch.

Þingskallar and Keldur

Just east of Hella, Route 264 heads north off the main highway back towards Hekla. Seven kilometres along at an airstrip, Route 268 and the Ytri-Rangá branch up to the road on which *Leirubakki* farm sits, on Hekla's western slopes at Næfurholt – a forty-kilometre journey in all, mostly on gravel tracks. About halfway there, **Þingskallar farm** was a medieval assembly site, and traces of around thirty *buðs*, temporary encampments similar to those at Þingvellir (see p.104), have been found in the fields here.

Stay on Route 264 past the airstrip, and 20km east of Hella is the pretty farm of **Keldur** (June–Sept daily 10am–noon & 1–6pm), named after the "cold springs" that seep out from under a grassed-over lava flow to form a sizeable stream winding off across the plains. Keldur is mentioned in Njál's Saga (see box on pp.126–127) as the home of **Ingjald Höskuldsson**, uncle of Njál's illegitimate son. Initially siding with Flósi, as Njál's kinsman Ingjald refused to take part in the burning and defected to Kári's side. Although there's a modern farm at Keldur, an older string of a half-dozen **turf-covered halls** date back almost to saga times – part of the central one here was built in the thirteenth century and is Iceland's only extant example of a stave-built hall from this period. There's also a fifty-metre, block-lined **tunnel** running over to an ensemble of stalls, stable and a barn; estimates date this to the eleventh century. Take a moment to register Keldur's location, right on the steep front of one of Hekla's flows: the few stone walls defining the fields below were built to limit ash drifts and erosion following periodic eruptions.

While you're in the area, ask at Keldur for directions to **Gunnarsstein**, a boulder where Gunnar and his allies were ambushed by a group led by local horseman **Starkað of Þríhyrningur**. The battle that followed contains some of Njál's Saga's most savage imagery; when it was over, Gunnar and his brothers had killed fourteen of their attackers, but at the cost of Gunnar's brother **Hjört** (whose name means "heart"). The tale describes Hjört's burial here afterwards, and in the mid-nineteenth century a mound at the site was indeed found to contain a skeleton and a bracelet engraved with two hearts.

Oddi

Not mentioned in Njál's Saga, though of a similar vintage, **ODDI**'s couple of houses and prominent, red-roofed **church**, all set on the only hill for miles around, are 5km southwest down the highway from Hella and then the same distance directly south along Route 266. Though you'd hardly credit it today, Oddi was once famous, when the French-educated **Sæmundur Sigfússon** became priest here in 1078 and established an ecclesiastical school, whose later alumni included thirteenth-century law speaker, historian and diplomat Snorri Sturluson, and St Þorlákur Þórhallsson. Sæmundur himself is the subject of several legends, including one in which the devil – disguised as a seal – offered to carry him back to Iceland from France so that Sæmundur could apply for the post at Oddi. When they were within sight of the shore, the resourceful Sæmundur brained the devil with a psalter, swam to safety, and got the job. Less to his credit, he's also held responsible for causing Hekla's 1104 eruption by tossing a keepsake from a jilted lover – who turned out to be a witch – into the volcano. Built in 1924, the current church is pretty plain, though it has thirteenth-century relics squirrelled away, and a nice modern organ.

Hvolsvöllur

Eleven kilometres southwest down the highway from Hella you reach the broad, open mouth of the **Markarfljót valley**, along which the intricately tangled shallow river flows westwards out from the Mýrdalsjökull and Eyjafjallajökull caps. Right on the western edge is the Ringroad town of **HVOLSVÖLLUR**, a few short streets labouring under an unattractive transmitter tower, marking where Route 261 diverges east off down the valley to Fljótsdalur and the Fjallabak route (see p.131). It's a good place to get to grips with Njál's Saga country; you're close to the settings for some of the most important scenes in the tale, and Hvolsvöllur itself – or rather the farm, *Völlur*, 5km north – was the homestead of Mörð Fiddle, with whom Njál's Saga opens. Mörð's daughter **Unn** was both Gunnar's cousin, and mother to the tale's arch-villain, Mörð Valgardsson. On a purely practical note, the town is also the last place to stock up on provisions before heading eastwards to **hiking** grounds at Flótsdalur or Þórsmörk.

Hvolsvöllur's only attraction is the **Saga Centre** (☏487 8781, ⓕ487 8782, ⓦwww.islandia.is/~njala; June–Aug daily 9am–5pm; 500kr), just off the highway down Route 261. The bulk of this is a thorough museum, with models of Viking houses and ships; maps, dioramas and paintings showing the location of local sites and the extent of Viking travels across the northern hemisphere; and replica clothes and artefacts. There's also a Viking-style **Eating Hall** here, complete with wooden beams and horsehide rugs, venue for Friday night "saga feasts" – a couple of fun hours' worth of food and storytelling, with the staff dressed up in period costume (bookings essential; 5000kr).

Practicalities

Most of Hvolsvöllur is laid out along a hundred-metre strip of the highway, just where Route 261 kinks east. **Buses** along the Ringroad, and also to Þórsmörk and along the Fjallabak route, stop at the easterly Hlíðarendi **fuel station**; the town's services – bank, post office and supermarket – are all nearby. Hvolsvöllur's **campground** is next to the fuel station, with two **places to stay**, both down Route 261: the slightly faded *Hótel Hvolsvöllur* (☏487 8187, ⓕ487 8391, ⓦwww.hotelhvolsvollur.is; sleeping bag 2000kr, double without bathroom ❸, with bathroom ❻), about 50m along; and 200m further on at the popular *Ásgarður* guesthouse's cabins or dormitories (☏487 5750, ⓕ487 5752, ⓔasgard@simnet.is; sleeping-bag accommodation 1900kr, ❸) – they also have outdoor hot tubs. **Places to eat** are limited to the hotel's restaurant, the fuel station's café, or a small pizza place just up from the Saga Centre.

Bergþórshvoll

South of Hvollsvöllur, follow Route 255 coastwards for 20km off the highway and across the flat, waterlogged countryside to **Bergþórshvoll**, where Njál's homestead sat a thousand years ago. Today, a modern house occupies the low crest 1km from the sea, and there's no visible trace of the original hall, which was besieged by Flósi and his hundred-strong Burners in the autumn of 1011. The two sides (Njál's party consisting of about thirty of his family and servants) met face to face in the open, but, urged by the old man, the defenders retreated into the house, and Flósi – certain that Njál's sons would kill him if they escaped – ordered the building to be set alight. After women, children, and servants were allowed to leave, Njál, his wife, and sons burned to death; only "lucky" Kári managed to break out. In support of the story, charred remains found here during twentieth century excavations have been carbon-dated to the saga period.

❷ The Markarfljót valley: Hlíðarendi and Fljótsdalur

It's a beautiful thirty-kilometre run east along Route 261 from Hvolsvöllur up **Fljótshlíð**, the flat-bottomed, heavily farmed northern border of the Markarfljót valley, with the saga site of **Hlíðarendi** and beautiful valley setting at **Fljótsdalur** to draw you out this way – it's also the approach road to the **Fjallabak route** around the back of the southern glaciers, covered by summer **buses** from Reykjavík. Ahead loom Eyjafjallajökull's black sided, ice-capped heights, while on a clear day the view south extends all the way to the sea; in summer, streams and ponds draining the wetlands in between are alive with birds – especially black-tailed godwits, with their vivid orange and black plumage.

Hlíðarendi

The road follows the base of a long line of green hills heading up the valley, whose slopes contrast strongly with the starker-toned mountains opposite. About 15km from Hvolsvöllur there's **accommodation** at *Smáratún* farm (☎ 487 8471, ✉ smaratun@simnet.is; sleeping-bag accommodation 1650kr, ❸), and a few kilometres further, a side road climbs steeply up to where a red-roofed **church** and handful of farm buildings command a splendid view of the area. This is **Hlíðarendi**, home to Njál's great friend Gunnar, the most exemplary of all saga characters; unfortunately, however, his fine character always tended to inspire envy rather than admiration. When Gunnar found that his wife **Hallgerð** had encouraged a slave to steal food from the prosperous farmer Otkel, he fatefully slapped her – hence Hallgerð's refusal to help him later on (see box on pp.126–127) – and offered Otkel repayment. Otkel's malicious friend Skamkel, however, advised him against accepting, starting the long sequence of blood-letting that led to Gunnar being declared an outlaw. But on the way to the coast to leave Iceland, Gunnar's horse stumbled and he looked back to Hlíðarendi across fields of newly cut hay, and knew he could never leave his homeland – and so, returning to Hlíðarendi, met his end.

Though there are a couple of turf outhouses behind Hlíðarendi's church, nothing besides the scenery remains from the saga period – though, as Gunnar felt, this can be ample reward (at least on a sunny day). Look on the plains below for **Stóra-Dímon**, an isolated rocky platform called **Rauðuskriður** in the saga, where Njál's sons Skarp-héðinn and Helgi ambushed Þráin Sigfússon, who had participated in the murder of their foster-father. Þráin spotted them but Skarp-héðinn slid over the frozen river and killed Þráin before he had time to put on his armour, setting in motion events which were to lead directly to the burning of Njál.

Fljótsdalur and Fjallabaksleið

East of Hlíðarendi, the hills grow steeper as the valley narrows, with a frill of small, ribbon-like waterfalls dropping down to the roadside. A track pointing south past Stóra-Dímon to the Ringroad marks the start of the gravel, and then you're running alongside the Markarfljót river-system's continually shifting

The Fjallabak routes

Fjallabaksleið comprises the area covering the old traffic routes which ran, quite literally, *fjallabak*, "behind the mountains" – or rather, north of the ice-caps. There were two recognised tracks: the northern **Fjallabak Nyrðra** from Landmannalaugar (see p.122) to Kirkjubæklaustur; and southern **Syðri Fjallabaksleið** from Fljótsdalur, which skirted around Mýrdalsjökull's northern edge via Álftavatn (now on the Laugavegur hiking trail; see p.124) and down to Vík. The southern route from was always considered the easiest, though occasionally closed by outflows from Katla, the restless volcano underneath Mýrdalsjökull. Today, the two trails converge at **Hólaskjól**, a hut northeast of Mýrdalsjökull on the F208, and run down to the Ringroad near Kirkjubæklaustur (see p.322); the highlight of either lies just north of Hólaskjól at **Eldgjá**, a 40km-long volcanic canyon up to 200m deep.

    Buses from Reykjavík along Fjallabak Nyrðra via Landmannalaugar, Eldgjá, Hólaskjól, Kirkjubæklaustur and Skafafell depart daily from mid-June until late August. Syðri Fjallabaksleið buses depart Reykjavík daily between mid-July and late August, via Hvollsvöllur and Fljótsdalur to Álftavatn and Hólaskjól, where you can connect with further buses heading northwest to Landmannalaugar, or southeast to Kirkjubæklaustur and Skaftafell.

maze of flat, intertwined streams up **Fljótsdalur**, a valley caught between the steep, glaciated slopes of Tindafjall to the north and Eyjafjöll to the south. Ten kilometres from Hlíðarendi and 27km from Hvolsvöllur, where the road crosses a ford and becomes a four-wheel-drive track, the basic, self-catering Fljótsdalur **youth hostel** (☎487 8498 or 487 8497; sleeping-bag accommodation 1750kr) occupies a renovated turf house, open from mid-April to mid-October – you'll definitely need to book in advance. Fljótsdalur forms the southern boundary of **Fjallabaksleið** (see box above), and there are any number of **hikes** to attempt in the area – Þórsmörk itself (see below) is only 15km east, though very hard to reach directly given the intervening rivers – the most ambitious of which would be up Tindafjall to its ice cap, **Tindfjallajökull** (1462m), via a series of mountain huts.

Skógar and Þórsmörk

Southeast across the Markarfljót's sprawl, the highway finds itself pinched between the coast and Eyjafjöll, the mountainous platform for the **Eyjafjallajökull** glacier. Though dwarfed by its big sister Mýrdalsjökull immediately to the east, Eyjafjallajökull's 1666m apex is southwestern Iceland's highest point, and the mountain has stamped its personality on the area: an active volcano smoulders away below the ice, which enjoyed major eruptions in the seventeenth and nineteenth centuries and whose sub-glacial melting in 1967 sent a rock- and gravel-laden flash flood – a *jökulhlaup* – west down the Markarfljót.

    Back on the coast, melt from Eyjafjallajökull's fringes has created a string of roadside **waterfalls** around the settlement of **Skógar**; while in the highlands north of Eyjafjallajökull, streams feeding into the Markarfljót flow through beautiful valleys at **Þórsmörk**, whose steep, wooded slopes and dark mountains are capped by encircling glaciers. Skógar is on the Ringroad and served by **buses** through the year, while you can reach Þórsmörk either on summer buses traversing the 249/F249 west of Skógar, or on a popular **hiking trail** which ascends from Skógar via a broad pass between Eyjafjallajökull and Mýrdalsjökull.

Seljalandfoss and Seljavellir

Right at Eyjafjöll's western tip, **Route 249** heads north off the highway and around the back of the mountain to Þórsmörk, becoming the four-wheel-drive-only F249 in the process. Just a few hundred metres along is **Seljalandfoss**, a narrow but powerful waterfall that drops straight off the fellside into a shallow pool; paths run behind the curtain – you'll get soaked but the noise of the falls is impressively magnified – and over to a couple of smaller falls (one of which is almost enclosed by the cliff-face), the meadow in between thick with a summer crop of cottongrass, kingcups, and angelica. There's also a **campsite** with a turf-covered shower block just further on at *Hamragarðar* farm (☎487 8952; 550kr). If you're heading up to Þórsmörk, the last **place to stay** is 7km up the road from the highway at *Stóra Mörk III* (☎487 8903, ℱ487 8901; self-catering; sleeping bag 1750kr; ❸), a **farm** that featured in Njál's Saga as the property of Ketil Sigfússon, a decent man who had the awkward task of being both Njál's son-in-law and brother to Þráin, killed by Njál's sons at nearby Stóra-Dímon (p.130).

Back on the Ringroad past the 249 junction, layered, rough cliffs rise back from the roadside, with plenty more waterfalls cascading over the edges. Twenty kilometres along, the hills suddenly recede, allowing views inland right up to the glacier, and a gravel road heads 3km north up the valley to further farm-stay **camping** at *Seljavellir* (☎487 8810; 550kr) – call in advance and they'll collect you from the highway. This is an excellent spot, with an outdoor **pool** and hot tub to relax in, and some wild **hiking** along the glowering valley and, via hot springs and yet more waterfalls just below the snowline, up onto Eyjafjallajökull itself.

Skógar and the Þórsmörk trail

A further 7km past the Seljavellir road, **SKÓGAR** is an insubstantial, scattered collection of buildings set back off the highway beside Skógarfoss, the biggest of the local **waterfalls** and worth a look even if you've otherwise had enough of these things. Other reasons to stop are the entertaining museum, or the rewarding two-day hiking **trail to Þórsmörk** up over inter-glacial passes.

Skógar was settled by the twelfth century, and you'll find a detailed record of the region's farming and fishing communities at Skógar's **folk museum** (June–Aug 9am–7pm, May & Sept 10am–5pm; 600kr), up against the hills to the east. Impromptu guided tours or folk-singing sessions organized by local character and curator Þórður Tómasson are one of the museum's highlights, but even if he doesn't appear the exhibits themselves are interesting enough. Various types of traditional stone and turf farm buildings have been relocated to an adjacent field, while inside the main building, the centrepiece is a ten-metre-long, heavy wooden **fishing boat** from 1855, tough enough to survive being dragged regularly over miles of sand and gravel to be launched. Along with associated fishing gear aranged around the walls, look for the wooden moulds used to cast fish-shaped hook weights – a design considered to be lucky. Contemporary agricultural and domestic items flesh out the rest of the display, though there are a few older items too, most notably a Viking **jade cloak pin**, an edition of Iceland's first printed **bible**, dated to 1544, and a fourteenth-century fragment from the Book of David written in Icelandic on vellum. Ask to be shown (it's easy to overlook otherwise) the **brass ring** found hundreds of years ago, said to have once adorned a chest of gold hidden behind Skógarfoss by the Viking settler **Þrasi** – legend has it he argued with his children and didn't want them to inherit his wealth.

Skógarfoss falls themselves, at 62m high, are justifiably famous, looking good from a distance and nothing short of huge, powerful and dramatic close up as they drop straight off the plateau – stand on the flat gravel river bed in front of the rainbow-tinged plunge pool, and the rest of the world vanishes into the soaking white mists and noise. A steep but otherwise easy **track** climbs to the top, putting you eye-to-eye with fulmars as they sit on nests or wheel through the spray, beyond which a muddy trail heads upstream to a much smaller but violent cataract and brilliant views coastwards and up across mossy moorland towards the distant glacier cap. If you're properly prepared, you can follow the river in this direction right up to Þórsmörk – see box on p.134.

Practicalities

The kilometre-long Skógar road runs north off the highway, passing a side-road left to the falls, before coming to a T-junction: the grey, box-like building ahead of you is Skógar's **school**; turn right, and it's 250m to the museum. There's a **bank** (no ATM) on the falls' road, but no other services; the nearest **store** is some 30km east in Vík.

Skógar's **information centre** (June 1-Aug 31; ☎487 8843) is right next to the **campground** (with toilets and shower; 500kr), a big, flat, grassy area in front of the falls. **Accommodation** comprises the summer-only *Hótel Edda* (☎444 4830, ☎487 8858; sleeping bag 1100kr, dorm 2000kr) at the school; while along the falls road you'll find hot-tubs and upmarket ambiance at the small *Hótel Skógar* (☎487 8988, ✉hotelskogar@simnet.is; ❻), and more functional amenities at the *Fossbuð* (☎487 8841, ☎487 8821; sleeping bag 1500kr), another summer-only option with self-catering facilities. For **eating**, the *Edda* puts on an expensive evening buffet (2300kr), while the *Fossbuð* has a decent fast-food café.

Þórsmörk

Hidden from the rest of the world by encircling glaciers and mountain wilderness, **Þórsmörk** – Thor's Wood – covers a ten-kilometre-long series of highland valleys north of Eyjafjallajökull, watered by a host of multistreamed glacial rivers that flow west off Mýrdalsjökull's heights and down into the Markarfljót. Green-sloped, covered in dwarf willow, birch, and wildflowers, with icy peaks rising above, this is one of Iceland's most beautiful spots, a forestry reserve since 1921 and, through the summer months, a magnet for everyone from hard-core hikers coming to tackle the numerous trails, to equally energetic partygoers here to unwind in a bucolic setting. For those on a saga quest, Þórsmörk also features indirectly in the latter part of Njál's Saga as the homeland of the boastful comic character Björn, who, despite his innate cowardice, proves a useful ally to Kári in his vengeance against the Burners.

Aside from hiking **trails from Skógar or Landmannalaugur** (see pp.134 & 124), there's only one **road to Þórsmörk**, the thirty-kilometre Route 249/F249 off the Ringroad between Hvolsvöllur and Skógar at Seljalandsfoss (see p.132). The last half of this is a bumpy, high-clearance, four-wheel-drive-only route, and can be quite an adventure in itself, following the south side of the Markarfljót before turning east across a handful of broad glacial rivers – which can be impassable in bad conditions – and reaching the Þórsmörk area. From June 1 until September 15 there's a **daily bus** from Reykjavík's BSÍ

The Skógar–Þórsmörk trail

The **Þórsmörk trail** (20km) from Skógar, over the Fimmvörðuháls pass between Eyjafallajökull and Mýrdalsjökull, and down the other side to Þórsmörk, is, for its scenery (at least in good weather) and relatively easy grade, a thoroughly enjoyable walk. The first 12km to the pass makes a good day-return hike from Skógar, while most people heading on to Þórsmörk spread the trip over two days, overnighting at one of the two mountain **huts** en route run by Útivist (bookings essential; ☎562 1000, ⓦwww.utivist.is). It's also perfectly feasible to do the whole Skogar–Þórsmörk stretch in one day if you're reasonably fit and start early enough. The trail is passable only in summer, and even then you should come prepared for possible rain and snow, poor visibility and cold; the track is well defined but it's advisable to take a compass and Landmælingar Íslands' *þórsmörk-Landmannalaugur* **map**. If you don't want to walk alone, both Útivist and Ferðafélag Íslands (see p.41, in Basics) organise **hikes** along the route most weekends from mid-June to late August – June 21 is especially popular, when you'll find hundreds of people making the trek through the mid-summer "night".

The trail starts by taking the track up Skógarfoss, then simply follows the river uphill for the next 8km or so, over a muddy, shaly **heath** carpeted by thick patches of moss and plants – wild thyme, with its tiny purple flowers and pungent scent, is abundant. There are many, many small **waterfalls** along the way, each of them unique: some twist through incredibly contorted gorges, others drop in a single narrow sheet, bore tunnels through obstructive rocks, or rush smoothly over broad, rocky beds. Around 8km along you cross a **bridge** and leave most of the vegetation behind for a dark, rocky plain flanked by the smooth contours of Eyjafallajökull to the west and and easterly Mýrdalsjökull. It's another hour from here, following marker poles across gravel and snow fields, to the red-roofed *Balduinsskali*, the small and rather squalid **first hut** (pit toilet; 1000kr), though almost everybody seems to push on for another forty minutes to the far better appointed **second hut**, *Fimmvörðuskáli* (1700kr), near the route's highest point on the **Fimmvörðuháls pass** (1043m).

If you have the necessary gear and experience on ice, both glaciers are within easy reach from here; if not, your options are to return to Skógar or continue past a lake and on through the pass over snowfields – in clear weather, there are excellent views of the mountains further north during this section. A short, steep stretch beyond (with a chain to help you along) descends via easier gradients to Goðaland and Básar (see pp.135–136), at Þórsmörk's eastern end, then it's another few kilometres west along the valley to the rest of Þórsmörk's attractions – allow six hours in total from Fimmvörðuskáli. For more about Þórsmörk itself, see below.

terminal via Hvolsvöllur; the Útivist and Ferðafélag Íslands walking clubs (see p.41 for details) also organize **guided hikes** here every weekend in summer, with less frequent excursions year-round – including over New Year.

Accommodation is at designated campsites (around 600kr), or using your own sleeping bags in hiking huts, which need to be booked in advance. Most huts have communal kitchens, with showers a couple of hundred kronur extra, though you'll need to provide food – the closest places to buy **supplies** are Hvolsvöllur and Vík. Ideally you'll enjoy sunny weather, but come armed for wet, cold conditions, and carry Landmælingar Íslands' *Þórsmörk-Landmannalaugur* **map**, along with Ferðafélag Íslands's brochure of Þórsmörk's hiking trails, if you plan to do any serious exploration – only a few routes are described below, and marker posts are a rarity. For a totally different take on the area, you can also **raft** the upper Markarfljót and Emstruá rivers, arranged in advance with Tindfjöll (☎487 5557, www.tindfjoll.is) or

Arctic Rafting (℡ 487 5557, ⓦ www.arcticrafting.is) – trips plus a barbeque cost from 9400kr.

In Þórsmörk

Þórsmörk is laid out west–east along the seven-kilometre-long **Krossá river valley** and its offshoots, with the area north of the river generally referred to as Þórsmörk proper, and the area south of the river as **Goðaland**. Walking trails are everywhere, and there's a four-wheel-drive road right up the valley past the three huts and various campsites.

The F249 terminates at the **bus stop** and knot of cabins comprising **Húsadalur**, set at Þórsmörk's western border where the broad river plain ends at a wall of low peaks. Arrange bus tickets and local **accommodation** (℡ 852 5506) at the bus-stop **café**: there's a campsite, family-sized cabins, an unpleasantly drab prefab block with sleeping-bag accommodation, and more pleasant wooden bunkhouses with kitchens. The scenery here is pretty bland, however, and it's better to follow walking tracks east for twenty minutes, past a former outlaw's hideout at Snorraríki cave, into Þórsmörk itself at Ferðafélag Ísland's **Skagfjörðsskáli hut** and campsite (bookings on ℡ 568 2533; 1700kr) – they also have a tiny **store** selling chocolate, biscuits, soap, and soft drinks. This is beautifully located at river level underneath fang-like **Valahnúkur**; you can sit

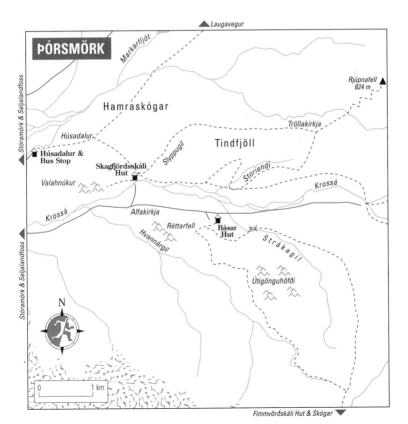

on the porch and watch vehicles coming to grief on the river crossings (the hut has a photo collection of four-wheel-drive disasters), or make a stiff, twenty-minute ascent of Valahnúkur to see the whole of Þórsmörk laid out beneath you: the flat riverbeds with their interlaced streams between black hills buffed in green, all rising eastwards to where the valley is terminated by Mýrdalsjökull's blue-white glaciers.

Of the many possible walks north of the Krossá, one of the most satisfying begins at **Slyppugil**, a narrow, wooded gully cutting through a jagged ridge known as **Tindfjoll**, some 500m east of Valahnúkur along the river – there's a further campsite here and a very basic, tiny IYHA-owned **hut** (ⓦwww .hostel.is). Follow the stream up the valley, which gradually widens and curves eastwards, opening up at the top for a long view out over streams and a grim, black-ash canyon to **Rjúpnafell**'s double-tipped cone. Heading towards it, the path weaves along Tindfjoll's steep, landslip-prone north face to the solitary spire of **Tröllakirkja**, before emerging onto open heath at Tindfjoll's eastern end: way to the north, you can see the pinky-brown spike of ýmír protruding from Tindfjallajökull, while the steep, zig-zag path up to Rjúpnafell's 824-metre summit is about an hour away to the east. Alternatively, you can descend back into the valley down Tindfjoll's southern slopes via **Stóriendi**; the path is intermittently pegged and often seems to be leading off the edge, but always reappears, with some fantastic views of Þórsmörk's eastern end along the way. You end up down in the valley, approximately 2km from your starting point; the entire circuit takes around four hours.

To explore south of the river at **Goðaland**, cross using the pedestrian bridge and base yourself 2km east of Valahnúkur at Útivist's **Básar hut** (bookings on ☎562 1000; 1700kr) and campground at the start of the trail over Fimmvörðuháls to Skógar (see box on p.134). With Eyjafjallajökull looming above, the landscape here is more extreme than across the river, and the hiking is generally harder: one excellent route takes you a short way up **Hvannárgil**, the valley diagonally opposite Valahnúkur, where you'll have to cast around to find the faint trail heading up the back of **Réttarfell**, a blocky, isolated peak. As you climb the trail suddenly becomes clear, and you can follow the heights all the way southeast to Útigönguhöfði (805m) – a full day's return hike from Básar.

From Mýrdalsjökull to Vík

The country's fourth-largest ice cap, **Mýrdalsjökull** blocks off and protects southwestern Iceland from the scouring effects of the glacial deserts – **sandurs** – further east, though it's also responsible for creating the extensive strips of black, basaltic sand fringing the 30km of coastline between Skógar and **Vík**. Like neighbouring Eyjafjallajökull, Mýrdalsjökull harbours a powerful volcano, 1300-metre **Katla**, which last erupted in 1918 and is worryingly over-due for another blast – they occur once every seventy years on average, and a recent spate of **earthquakes** in the region might be heralding future activity. Katla's *jökulhlaups* (volcanically induced flash floods; see p.348 for more about these) have extended the coastline and devastated the area's farms a dozen or more times since Settlement, and the possibility of an imminent eruption is taken very seriously.

Moving down the coast, the mountains supporting Mýrdalsjökull – and occa-sional outlying glaciers, such as **Sólheimajökull** – intrude further and further towards the sea, finally reaching it around Iceland's southernmost tip, **Dyrhólaey**, where they form impressively sculpted cliffs, home to innumerable seabirds. Past Dyrhólaey, the sleepy village of Vík has more birds and some easy walks, and also marks the beginning of the long cross-desert run into southeastern Iceland. Ringroad **buses** can get you to Vík, though you'll need your own transport elsewhere.

Sólheimajökull and Dyrhólaey

Not far east of Skógar, the Ringroad crosses the shallow, foul-smelling Jökulsá Fulilækur, a glacial river whose sulphurous scent points to origins beneath the ice surrounding Katla. Look upstream from the roadside and you'll see the apparently insignificant, narrow ice tongue of **Sólheimajökull**, one of Mýrdalsjökull's outrunners; a track heads up the broad river valley for 5km to the front of the glacier, but you'll need a four-wheel-drive vehicle or at least high clearance for the abundant boggy patches along the way. Close up, Sólheimajökull is steep-faced, blackened with melted-out grit, and heavily streaked in crevasses, and is worth a look if you haven't seen this sort of thing before – though don't walk out onto it, as the front is unstable. You can, however, arrange a ride on a **snowmobile** with Arcanum (☎487 1500, ⓦwww.arcanum.is; 7200kr) from their hut higher up on the glacier's edge at **Sólheimskáli**, which is about 5km further east down the Ringroad and then 10km north along the four-wheel-drive F222 – call ahead if you need a pickup from the highway.

Dyrhólaey

Around 12km down the Ringroad from Jökulsa Fulilækur, an unsurfaced, bumpy Route 218 slides 5km coastwards past a handful of farms and then over a causeway to where the country reaches its southernmost extremes at **Dyrhólaey**. A set of rugged cliffs rising over a long expanse of black sand, Dyrhólaey is a beautiful place just to watch the sea on a sunny day, though it's also a noted **seabird reserve**, with every cliffside crevice occupied from April until the winter sets in, white streaks of guano a sign of tenancy. Stumpy, ubiquitous fulmars – gull-like but related to albatrosses – chatter nervously at you from their half-burrow roosts, or soar in on narrow wings for a closer look; out at sea, rafts of eider duck bob in the waves, while razorbills, guillemots and puffins, bills full of fish, dodge scavenging brown skuas on their way homewards.

Once over the causeway, bear left at the junction and you'll find yourself on a rocky shelf above the sea with the swell hammering into the low cliffs at your feet; there's a surprisingly sheltered bay around to one side, though, where a dense matting of tussocky grass holding the clifftop together is riddled with **puffin burrows** – sit still for long enough and you can get some good photos.

If you bear right at the junction, the road rises steeply to end at a dumpy, orange-topped **lighthouse** on the grassy hill above. From here you can see Iceland's southernmost headland, a narrow face of rock pierced by a large **arch**, said to be large enough for a sailboat to pass through. You can walk out to a cairn here, for views west of black sand beaches stretching up towards Skógar; to the east, the weather-sculpted rocks off Vík stand out clearly, though the town itself is hidden behind round-backed **Reynisfjall**, a ridge that divides the southwest's fertile farmland from the bleak expanses of sand beyond. It also blocks the weather: it's not unusual for it to be snowing one side, and bright and sunny on the other.

Vík

Despite averaging the highest rainfall in Iceland, **VÍK** – known more fully as Vík-í-Mýrdal – is a pleasant coastal village of 300 souls nestling on the toe of Reynisfjall's steep eastern slopes, a last haven before taking on the deadening horizons of the **Mýrdalssandur** beyond, the desert laid down by Katla's overflows. The only coastal village in Iceland without a harbour, Vík got going as a trading station in the late nineteenth century and today serves a few farms and the tourist traffic, with a **wool factory** and outlet that's making a name for itself with some innovative designs – it's the last building heading east on the Ringroad.

Vík's older quarter is south of the highway along the hundred-metre-long main street of Víkurbraut – though the only sight as such is **Brydebúð**, the original nineteenth-century store. This was actually built in 1831 on the Westman Islands (p.140) and relocated here in 1895; amongst other things, it houses a small **museum** of photographs (summer 11am–9pm). A short road and walking track continues along Reynisfjall's lower slopes to a black beach opposite three tall, offshore spires known as **Reynisdrangar**, the Troll Rocks, said to be petrified trolls caught by the sun as they were trying to drag a boat ashore. The headland above is a huge, stratified bird colony: lower down are kittiwakes, with puffins nesting on the steep middle slopes, and fulmar occupying the rocky cliffs near the top; the sky is full of evening activity as birds return from a day's fishing. The flat foreshore above the beach east of here is also a nesting ground for thousands of arctic terns – don't approach as you'll be mercilessly dive-bombed by every bird you disturb. If the weather is fine, the trail **up Reynisfjall** from the highway also makes for a good hour's climb, ending by the weather station on a muddy hill top, with views east of Vatnajökull's mighty ice cap floating above the desert haze.

Practicalities

Vík is laid out either side of a two-hundred-metre stretch of the Ringroad, with Víkurbraut heading south as you come down the hill from Skógar, and another road more or less opposite leading up to the **church**. **Buses** heading either way along the Ringroad pull in on the eastern edge of town at a **fuel station-road-house**; there's **tourist information** (℡487 1395, ⓦwww.vik.is; 15 June-1 Sept 11am-9pm) available from the old store Brydebúð on Víkurbraut. There's a well-stocked **supermarket** on Víkurbraut – again, the roadhouse has some basics if this is closed – with the village's **bank** (with ATM) and **post office** out on the highway. Your accommodation should be able to set up **tours**, such as guided bird-watching hikes or snowmobiling on Mýrdalsjökull; while Dyrhólaeyjarferðir (℡487 8500, ⓦwww.dyrholaey.com) explore Dyrhólaey and the adjacent coastline by boat and amphibious vehicle.

The **campsite** (℡487 1345) with showers, a large shelter shed, and cooking facilities, is opposite the fuel station. Top of Vík's **places to stay** is the new IYHA hostel (℡487 1106, ⓕ487 1303; sleeping bag 1750kr), which has cornered the market in views from its rise near the church; runner up is the characterful *Hótel Lundi* at Vikurbraut 26 (℡487 1212, ⓦwww.hotelpuffin.is; sleeping bag 1800kr, ❹) – the inn-like main house has the better rooms, while cheaper board is in an older, tin-sided building with self-catering facilities. Worthy alternatives are *Gistihús Arsalir*, a big, homely guesthouse on the hillside as you descend to Vík (℡487 1400; sleeping-bag accommodation 1700kr, ❸); the lower-budget *Gistihús Katrinar*, on the highway near the bank (℡487 1186; sleeping bag 1700kr, ❸); and modern *Hótel Edda* (℡487 1480; ❺) near the campsite – unusually for an *Edda*, they have no budget accommodation.

Brydebúð has a good, unnamed café-**restaurant** (Mon–Sat roughly 11am–8pm), with good trout, coffee, and cakes; the only alternatives are the burgers and sandwiches from the roadhouse (daily 9am–9pm). **Leaving**, the highway east of Vík is highlighted by two alarming orange warning signs, alerting you to the possibility of a Katla eruption and the dangers of sandstorms in Mýrdalssandur. If you're crossing under your own steam, take any sandstorm warnings seriously and note that it's over 70km to the next town, Kirkjubæjarklaustur (see p.322).

Vestmannaeyjar

Vestmannaeyjar – the **Westman Islands** – are an archipelago of fifteen or so scattered, mostly minuscule volcanic islands around 10km off the coast south of Hvolsvöllur. The only inhabited one in the group, **Heimaey**, is an easy trip from the mainland, and there are two immediate draws: **Eldfell** volcano, still steaming from its 1973 eruption, an event that doubled the width of the island and almost swallowed Heimaey town; and the legendary birdlife, especially the large **puffin** population (see box opposite). Heimaey is small enough to explore thoroughly in a short time, and you might get to know some of the people too, who form a self-contained community that sees itself as quite distinct from the mainland, and talk about "going over to Iceland", as if it were another country. Heimaey aside, the other Westmans are difficult to land on and so only infrequently visited by bird or egg collectors, but you may be very lucky and score a trip around **Surtsey**, the group's southernmost outpost and newest island, which sprang from beneath the waves during the 1960s.

Geological babies at only 12,000 years old overall, the Westman Islands were inhabited some time before the mainland was officially colonized in the ninth century by Ingólfur Arnarson and his foster-brother Hjörleifur Hróðmarsson. The brothers had brought British slaves with them who, coming from the lands at the west of the Viking world, were known as **Westmen**; Hjörleifur's revolted, killing him and fleeing to these islands – hence the name – where they were tracked down and slaughtered by a vengeful Ingólfur. Over the succeeding centuries Heimaey became permanently settled by fisher-farmers, but was generally outside the mainstream of Icelandic history until **Algerian pirates** raided on July 16, 1627, killing or enslaving half the population of five hundred. It took some time to get over this disaster, but by the twentieth century mechanization and the country's economic shift from farming to fishing saw Heimaey becoming a prosperous little haven, well positioned for taking advantage of what are still the North Atlantic's richest cod and haddock grounds.

Fresh problems lay ahead, however. The submarine eruption that formed Surtsey turned out to be the prelude to events a decade later on January 23, 1973, when a two-kilometre-long volcanic fissure suddenly opened up eastern Heimaey below the long-extinct cone of **Helgafell**. Within 24 hours the entire island had been evacuated and the new volcano Eldfell was gushing lava in violent spasms; houses were buried beneath the flow, set afire by lava bombs, or simply collapsed under the weight of accompanying ash. Worse still, the lava threatened to block the harbour mouth until halted by the novel method of pumping sea water onto the front of the flow. When the eruption ceased in June, Heimaey was two square kilometres bigger, had a new mountain, and, amazingly, a better harbour – the entrance is narrower now, but more effectively shielded from prevailing easterly winds. Only one person was killed during the eruption, but 1700 islanders never returned – around 4500 people live here today – and the disruption to the fishing industry contributed to Iceland's runaway inflation during the late 1970s.

Getting to Vestmannaeyjar

Heimaey is connected to the mainland by year-round ferries and flights. The *Herjólfur* car and passenger **ferry** (bookings & timetables on ☎481 2800, ⓦwww.herjolfur.is; 1700kr each way) departs daily at noon from **Þorlákshöfn**, a small town 20km south of Hveragerði, comprising a port and a sprawl of relief housing for islanders evacuated from Heimaey in 1973. **Buses** from Reykjavík's main bus terminal (700kr) connect with all ferries, and bus-ferry combined tickets are available; Þorlákshöfn's **ferry terminal** is left off the main road as you enter town, where you can buy tickets if you haven't done so already – you need to arrive at least thirty minutes before departure. An onboard cinema and café make the *Herjólfur* as comfortable as possible, though

---

Icelandic puffins

Puffins – *lundi* in Icelandic – belong to the auk family, which includes razorbills and guillemots (murres), and are basically the northern hemisphere's equivalent of penguins. They are, without doubt, the most charismatic of the auks, plump little birds with an upright build and pied plumage, all set off by bright orange feet and a ridiculous, sail-shaped bill striped yellow and red. This comical livery is compounded by an aeronautic ineptitude: their method of landing seems to consist simply of putting out their feet and stopping flying – bad enough to watch on water, but painful to see them bounce and skid on land. Puffins also seem to get victimized by just about every other seabird species: when feeding young, they fly back from fishing with their catch carried crosswise in the beak like a moustache, a clear signal for gulls, skuas and even razorbills to chase them, hoping they'll drop their chick's meal.

Each April, around six million puffins arrive to **breed** in Iceland from unknown wintering grounds, a sizeable chunk of which home in on Heimaey, excavating nesting burrows in huge, dense colonies on the island's grassy cliffs – surrounding seas are rich in herring fry, on which puffins raise their young. Watching a colony involves a bit of sensory overload at first, and it takes a while before you can sort through the confusion and concentrate on details: pairs excavating and cleaning up burrows with foot and bill, preening each other, or just sunning themselves on the grass, and the adults' desperate flights back from their fishing grounds. The fledgeling puffins, or **pufflings** – who lack the adults' colourful bill – apparently stay in the burrow until, one night in August, all the adult birds depart Heimaey at the same time, and hunger draws the pufflings out for their first flight. Many then become confused by the town's bright lights and fly, dazzled, into buildings; local cats get fat on this easy prey, but residents round up birds and release them.

Westman Islanders also eat puffins, collecting eggs and netting up to a quarter of a million birds annually as food – all hunters are licensed, and great care is taken to catch only non-breeding birds. The **meat** is dark and rich, and often tangy from being smoked; if you want a taste, several of Heimaey's restaurants offer it during the summer, or you may be able to buy birds more cheaply in the town's super-markets.

141

the crossing (2hr 45min) can be notoriously rough. Flugfélag Vestmannaeyja (☎481 3255, ⓦwww.eyjaflug.is; from 3900kr each way) operate **flights** from Reykjavík, Selfoss, Hella, and Bakki, a tiny coastal airstrip off the Ringroad south of Hvolsvöllur from where the journey takes just six minutes.

Many of Vestmannaeyjar's other islands sport shelter huts, but as their sheer cliffs emphasize, actually landing on them is beyond the scope of casual tourism. **Surtsey** – 20km to Heimaey's southwest – is the only one that you might get a close look at, and even that's unlikely; see the box on p.148.

If you can choose, pick a sunny couple of days between May and September for your visit, which will give you time for walks, intimate contact with puffins and thirty other breeding bird species, plus the chance to see whales and seals. If you want to party, join in the August Bank Holiday Weekend **Þjóðhátíð**, a festival to commemorate Iceland's first steps towards full independence in 1874, which involves bands, fireworks, a huge bonfire and three days of hard drinking with thousands of other revellers. As to the Westmans' **weather**, temperatures are amongst the mildest in Iceland, but things can get extremely blustery – the country's highest windspeed, 220km an hour, was recorded here.

Heimaey

By far the largest of the Westman Islands, **Heimaey** – Home Island – is only around 6km in length and, except along the east and north coasts, is pretty flat and grassy. At its broad top end you'll find **Heimaey town** and the harbour faced by a narrow peninsula of sheer-sided cliffs; east of here, buildings are hemmed in by Eldfell, the fractionally higher slopes of Helgafell, and the rough, grey-brown solidified lavafield, **Kirkjubæjarhraun**, under which a third of the original town vanished in 1973. Moving south down Heimaey, you pass the cross-shaped airstrip, beyond which the island tapers to a narrow isthmus, over which the rounded hummock of **Stórahöfði** rises as an end point – one of the best places on the island to watch birds.

Heimaey town

Heimaey town is an attractive but quiet place, and its attractions are low-key. The **aquarium and natural history museum**, south of the ferry terminal on Heiðarvegur (May–Aug daily 11am–5pm; Sept–April Sat & Sun 3–5pm; 450kr), sports cases of rocks and stuffed animals, and more entertaining tanks of live marine fauna. Up the road on the corner with Vestmannabraut, Heimaey's **cinema** hosts the summertime **Volcanic Film Show** in English (daily June 15–Aug 20; 600kr), an hour-long account of the eruption and snippets about life in the islands – when they run, the evening show is best as there's a question-and-answer session afterwards. A few minutes away down Hásteinsvegur, there's also a **Folk Museum** at the library (June to mid-Sept 11am–5pm daily; 400kr), whose extensive collection dates from the Algerian invasion onwards, padded out with cases of stamps and coins.

Down at the **harbour**, you'll find a tightly packed fleet of fishing boats and several warehouses processing their catches, yards piled with kilometres of black and green fishing nets being examined and repaired. Around 500m east along Strandvegur, the road crosses the edge of the 1973 flow and passes a neat square of lava-block walls forming **Skansinn fort**, first built by the English in the thirteenth century but revived in 1630 after the pirate raid to house Iceland's first and only army. This wasn't the sole occasion that pirates took

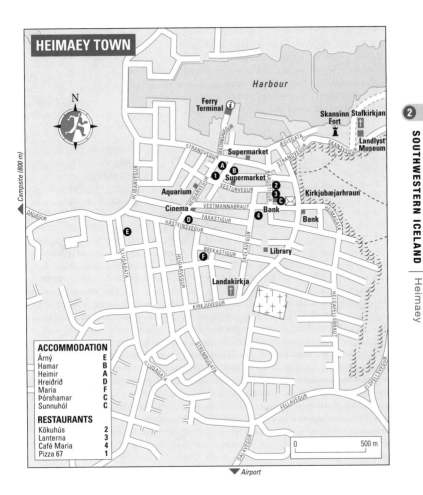

HEIMAEY TOWN

N

Campsite (800 m)

Harbour

Ferry
Terminal (i)

Skansinn Stafkirkjan
Fort

Landlyst
Museum

STRANDVEGUR

Supermarket

ÆGISGATA

SKANSVEGUR

STRANDVEGUR

A
1 B
Supermarket

BÁRUSTÍGUR

HEIDARVEGUR

VESTURVEGUR

Aquarium

2
3

Kirkjubæjarhraun

HILDARVEGUR

DALVEGUR

Cinema

VESTMANNABRAUT

Bank

HEIMAGATA

D FAXASTÍGUR

4

Bank

HÁSTEINSVEGUR

E

SKÓLAVEGUR

BREKASTÍGUR

Library

HEIDARVEGUR

F

Landakirkja

HELGAFELLSBRAUT

ILLUGAGATA

KIRKJUVEGUR

ACCOMMODATION
Árný   E
Hamar   B
Heimir   A
Hreiðrið   D
Maria   F
Þórshamar   C
Sunnuhól   C

RESTAURANTS
Kökuhús   2
Lanterna   3
Café Maria   4
Pizza 67   1

STRANBUGATA

ILLUGAGATA

DALAVEGUR

FELLAVEGUR

ELDFELLSVEGUR

0   500 m

▼ Airport

advantage of the Westmans' isolation: a sixteenth-century rover named Gentleman John once stole Heimaey's church bell. Just across from Skansinn, **Landlyst** (June to mid-Sept daily 11am–5pm; 400kr) was Iceland's first maternity hospital, though aside from the nineteenth-century building, the exhibition is a bit dry; while the extraordinary **Stafkirkjan** is a Viking-era-style wooden church with a steep, black shingle roof, consecrated in 2000 to celebrate a thousand years of Christianity in Iceland. The building faces the presumed site of the country's first purpose-built church (rather than a converted pagan shrine), raised by Gissur the White a few years before he championed the new faith at the Alþing in 1000 AD.

Back near the harbour off Strandvegur, you can follow first Kirkjuvegur and then Heimagata below the two-storey-high, steeply sloping **Kirkjubæjarhraun lava flow** that swallowed up the eastern end of town. There used to be several half-crushed houses emerging from the embankment along here, but these have been cleared and now there's just one very weatherbeaten shed in the rubble off Heimagata.

For a final idea of just what Heimaey's population went through in 1973, head south to black roofed **Landakirkja** on Kirkjuvegur, the island's main church. Enter the cemetery opposite through its arched, wrought-iron gates and on the left you'll find the grave of Theódóra Jónsdóttir, whose two-metre-high memorial is topped by a statuette of an angel, missing a hand. Ash buried this to the angel's thighs; it took Heimaey's residents over a year after the erup-tion to dig their town out of the black drifts.

Practicalities

Inevitably clustered around its harbour, Heimaey's small centre is split by the south-running main street **Heiðarvegur**, with most services and attractions in the streets east of here between the harbour and Hásteinsvegur.

The **airport** is a couple of kilometres south of town; a bus or taxi will be waiting. At the harbour you'll find the **ferry terminal**, with departures each morning back to the mainland, and **tourist information office** (Mon–Fri 8am–5pm, Sat 10am-4pm, Sun 1–5pm; ☎481 3555) housed in the same build-ing. Both **banks** – one at the corner of Kirkjuvegur and Vestmannabraut, the other on Bárústigur – have ATMs and handle foreign exchange. For **payphones** try either the post office on Vestmannabraut, the town's fuel stations, or the cinema – which also has the town's only public **toilet**. There are three **super-markets**: Vöruval, which looks like a domed tent, on Vesturvegur (daily 8am–7pm); the slightly better-stocked Kronan two streets over on Strandvegur (noon–7pm); and 11-11 (10 am–11pm) on Áshamar, not far from the campsite. The state **alcohol** shop is next door to Kronan on Stranvegur.

Heimaey's **campground** (700kr) is expensive, and spectacularly located 1km west of town at Herjólfsdalur (see below), where you'll be lulled to sleep by the mutterings of thousands of fulmars roosting above you; it has showers, toilets, laundry and shelter shed for cooking. If you're here for the August fes-tivities, come a few days early to find a pitch. You need to book all other **accommodation** in advance – in winter, places may be closed, and in summer, full. The most central guesthouse is *Hreiðrið*, at the corner of Faxastígur and Heiðarvegur (☎481 1045, ℗481 1414; sleeping bag 1700kr, ❷), a friendly place with half a dozen beds, able to organize everything you'd want to do on Heimaey; guests get a discount for the Volcanic Film Show. Other similar options include the drab but very convenient *Heimir* (☎481 2929, ℗481 2912; ❷) near the harbour on Heiðarvegur; the long-established *Árný*, a few minutes' walk east of the centre at Illugagata 7 (☎ & ℗481 2082; sleeping bag 1700kr, ❸); and *Maria*, nearby at Brekastígur 37 (☎481 2744, ℗481 2745; sleeping bag 2500kr, ❸). Heimaey's only hotel is the plush *Þórshamar*, on Vestmannabraut 28 (☎481 2900, ℮thorshamar@simnet.is; ❺), who also operate the nearby self-catering guesthouses *Sunnuhól* (sleeping bag 2200kr) and *Hamar* (❹).

Heimaey has plenty of **places to eat**. For coffee and cake, try the excellent *Kökuhús* bakery on Bárústigur; fast food is available at *Pizza 67* on Heiðarvegur. *Café Maria*, on Vestmannabraut and Skólavegur, is a cosy upmar-ket café-restaurant, serving relatively expensive though big portions – try their excellent grilled monkfish, lamb, or savoury crepes. For a different atmosphere, the mid-range *Lanterna*'s incongruous Greek taverna style surroundings are highly recommended, as is the menu, which covers everything from puffin, cod and mussels, to grills and salads.

Around the island

Heimaey's compact spread of lava and volcanoes – including a still-steaming

Eldfell – some stiff cliff hikes around the north peninsula or easier trails down south, and abundant bird life, need a day or two to do them justice, but try and allow extra time to return to favourite spots. It's possible to **walk** everywhere along tracks and roads, though in summer Viking Tours (☎488 4884, Ⓦwww.boattours.is) also organise **bus and boat tours** around the island.

Heimaklettur, Eldfell and Helgafell
Steps from Heimagata take you up on top of the 1973 **lava flow**, though it's

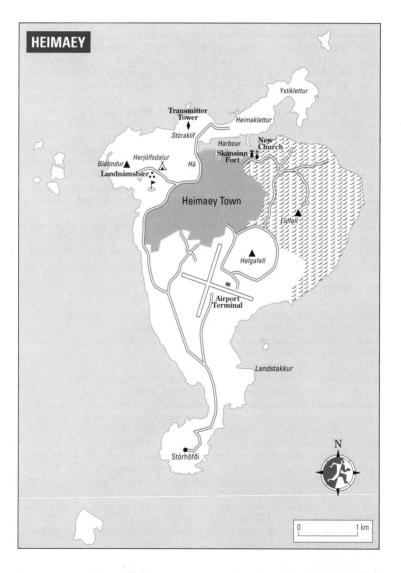

HEIMAEY

Ystiklettur

Transmitter Tower

Heimaklettur

Stóraklif

Harbour

New Church

Skansinn Fort

Blátindur▲ Herjólfsdalur Há

Landnámsbær

Heimaey Town

Eldfell▲

Helgafell

Airport Terminal

Landstakkur

Stórhöfði

N

0   1 km

hard to imagine this huge mass of sharp-sided, weirdly shaped rubble moving at all, let alone flowing. Newly placed signs map out the original street plan 16m underfoot, while engraved headstones and collections of little stones painted with windows and doors mark where somebody's home lies buried.

Heading northeast, you cross the road and end up at a lookout opposite yellow **Heimaklettur cliffs**, a good first spot to spy on seabirds: and it's pure chaos, the rocks packed to critical mass with various types of **guillemots**. If you're wondering how they manage to nest successfully on such incredibly narrow ledges, the secret is in the almost conical shape of their eggs, designed to roll in a circle around their tips, rather than in a straight line over the edge. Red marker poles lead around the coast from here across ankle-twisting debris, with quick asides down to shingle beaches or deeper into the flow; half an hour will see you rejoin the road a short distance from Eldfell's north face.

Both Eldfell and Helgafell are close to town and not too steep: you won't need much time or energy to climb them on any one of a dozen or more tracks. **Eldfell** is easiest, with any one of a number of tracks up the volcano's east or north slopes bringing you to the 205-metre-high rim in about ten minutes. One of the first things islanders did on returning in 1973 was to start turfing Eldfell's slopes to cover up and stabilize the ash; aerial seed drops during the 1990s also helped, and today about half the cone is well grassed – enough to make it hard to believe that what you're climbing on is so young. Eldfell's top is capped in red-grey scree and lava bombs, with views from the narrow rim of the other Westman islands and the mainland's entire southwest coast and crisp ice caps. The soil is still steaming up here – in fact, a metre down it's over 500°C – and there are further hot patches inside the steep-walled crater, which the sure-footed can slip and slide down into from the top, and then exit through a gash in the north wall and onto the road.

Immediately southwest of Eldfell, **Helgafell** looks similar but is a bit taller (226m) and some 5000 years older. The north and southwest faces present the swiftest routes to the summit, which was used as a lookout post during Heimaey's pirate period; today the crater is almost filled in, a shallow, sterile depression.

The north peninsula

Heimaey's **north peninsula** is the wildest part of the whole island, a four-kilometre string of sheer-sided cliffs and hills that includes the island's apex. Be aware that some of the tracks described below are potentially very dangerous, and to tackle them you need to be confident on narrow trails with hundred-metre drops either side.

Start a kilometre west of town by the campsite and golf course at **Herjólfsdalur**, a dramatically scaled bowl formed from a long-dead, partially collapsed volcano. Setting for the August festival, there are also the remains of **Landnámsbær** to examine, Iceland's oldest known settlement. While only traces of foundations remain, the type of buildings they recall is typically Norse, marking a longhouse, kitchen area, pigsty and outhouses; carbon-dating places parts of Landnámsbær in the seventh century, though Icelandic historical records say that the farm was founded two hundred years later. Either way, it was abandoned around 1100, perhaps due to overgrazing on the island. The easy hike up the slopes behind looks much steeper than it actually proves to be, and views from the top take in the peninsula rising precipitously from a wild seascape and Landnámsbær's outline picked out by the early morning sun. The peak to the west is **Blátindur** (273m), its base circled by a slippery path; east is a tricky, if not almost impossible goat-track along the peninsula to **Há**, and taking this is not recommended.

For an easier ascent of Há, return to the western side of the harbour on Hliðarvegur, where there's a rope dangling down the rocks for practising **sprengur**, the traditional cliff-climbing method on Heimaey, used by young men collecting puffins and bird eggs; free beginners' sessions are held here in July (ask at the tourist information for when to turn up). Walk up the grassy hillside behind and you're on Há, from where you can peer down into Herjólfsdalur, or walk north along the rim to opposite the transmitter tower atop **Stórakliff**. Climbing this latter peak is exhausting work; the track again begins down below on the western side of the harbour, ascending first on steps, then scree, then ropes, and finally, a chain – presumably, transmitter maintenance crews are airlifted in.

The peninsula's northeastern heights are far harder propositions, though you can reach the start on the north side of the harbour easily enough. First is **Heimaklettur**, requiring a rough scramble to reach the Westman Islands' highest point of 283m. Beyond is Ystiklettur, regularly visited by puffin collectors but best not attempted without local knowledge and help – make enquiries at the tourist office or *Hreiðrið* guesthouse (see p.144).

Heimaey's coastal trails

Due to the airstrip running over the eastern cliffs, it's not possible to circuit Heimaey completely, though that still leaves you with a decent 12km of **coastal trails** to follow. In summer you'll definitely see plenty of **birds**: wheatear, snipe and golden plovers love the island's grassy slopes; ringed plovers, redshanks and purple sandpipers pick over the shoreline for edibles; while skuas, eiders, gannets and auks patrol the seas. And if you've come to Heimaey hoping to see puffins, you'll be able to get within spitting distance of several million of them.

A clear 6km trail heads down the west coast from the golf course, a pleasant couple of hours following the crumbly cliff tops south to Stórhöfði. Initially there's plenty of bald basalt overlaid by later lava flows, which clearly poured over the edge and into the sea, then the path rises almost imperceptibly over spongy grass until, halfway along, you suddenly realize that you're fairly high up above the water. After crossing several fencelines, you run down to sea level

Surtsey

Surtsey's history proves that Heimaey is by no means the only island in the group to bear volcanic scars. In the late nineteenth century, **Hellisey** unexpectedly popped out of the waves about 5km off Heimaey's southern tip, the first in a series of underwater eruptions that continued at odd intervals for the next few decades. Then, on November 14, 1963, a colossal explosion, accompanied by towering plumes of steam and ash, heralded Surtsey's birth: within a week, there was a volcano rising 70m out of the sea. April 1964 saw lava appear for the first time; and when the eruption finished three years later, what was suddenly the Westmans' second-largest island covered almost three square kilometres. Erosion has since shrunk it by half, but Surtsey remains of great interest to scientists, who are using it as a model to study how islands are colonised by plants and animals. Unexpectedly, they found that larger plants were the first to become established; previous theories had suggested grasses were first needed to hold the soil together.

As it's a special reserve, **landing on Surtsey** is prohibited unless you're part of a scientific team. Your only chance of a trip over is with Viking (see p.145), who make four- to six-hour circuits from Heimaey – you'll get a good look but they don't land – once or twice each summer, if they get enough people interested and the weather's suitable.

again past frames for preparing that Icelandic delicacy *harðfiskur*, dried fish; you'll get an idea of how windy things get here from the huge bags of rocks weighting the frames down. The little beach beyond is good for ducks and waders, then it's a steep, short climb up **Stórhöfði** itself, site of a radio tower and sizeable **puffin colony**, and also an excellent place to scan the seas for whales and gannets, the latter nesting on the sheer-sided islets to the southwest.

From Stórhöfði, carry on up Heimaey's **east coast** to a steeper, rockier and weedier beach, often with some serious surf – this side of the island catches the prevailing winds – and occasional **seals** dodging in and out of the swell. Tidal pools and a couple of interesting caves might slow you down for a while – if you can get to them – otherwise climb the messy scree behind up onto a ridge and follow this north until it reaches a fenceline. A stile here gives access to the high, stumpy **Landstakkur** peninsula, complete with another puffin colony and scenic views. Continuing up the coast, you stay high above the sea with a dramatic drop into the deep blue on one side, and a gentle, grassy backslope on the other. Another stiff stretch uphill and you're at a **beacon** above the airstrip, from where you'll have to cut west across country to the road and so back up to town.

Travel details

Buses

Blue Lagoon to: Grindavík (2 daily; 10min); Hafnarfjörður (5 daily; 30min) Keflavík (June–Aug 2 daily; 15min); Reykjavík (5 daily; 45min).

Geysir* to: Gullfoss (daily; 10min); Hveragerði (daily; 1hr 50min); Laugarvatn (daily; 1hr 20min); Reykholt (daily; 5min); Reykjavík (daily; 2hr 30min); Selfoss (daily; 1hr 30min).

Grindavík to: Blue Lagoon (2 daily; 10min); Hafnarfjörður (2 daily; 35min); Reykjavík (2 daily; 55min).

Hella to: Höfn (1 daily-3 weekly; 5hr 15min); Hveragerði (daily; 55min); Hvolsvöllur (daily; 20min); Kirkjubæjarklaustur (1 daily-3 weekly; 2hr 45min); Reykjavík (daily; 1hr 40min); Selfoss (daily; 35min); Skógar (daily; 1hr 5min); Vík (daily; 1hr 35min).

Hveragerði to: Eyrarbakki (2 daily; 1hr); Geysir* (daily; 1hr 35min); Gullfoss* (daily; 1hr 45min); Hella (daily; 55min); Höfn (1 daily-3 weekly; 6hr 20min); Hvolsvöllur (daily; 1hr 25min); Kirkjubæjarklaustur (1 daily-3 weekly; 3hr 50min); Laugarvatn* (2 daily; 1hr 20min); Reykholt* (daily; 1hr 35min); Reykjavík (daily; 40min); Selfoss (daily; 30min); Skógar (daily; 2hr 10min); Vík (daily; 2hr 40min).

Hvolsvöllur to: Hella (daily; 20min); Höfn (1 daily-3 weekly; 4hr 55min); Hveragerði (daily; 1hr 25min); Kirkjubæjarklaustur (1 daily-3 weekly; 2hr 25min); Reykjavík (daily; 1hr 50min); Selfoss (daily; 1hr); Skógar (daily; 45min); Vík (daily; 1hr 15min).

Keflavík to: Blue Lagoon (Jun–Aug 2 daily; 15min); Hafnarfjörður (5 daily; 45min); Reykjavík (5 daily; 1hr).

Selfoss to: Eyrarbakki (2 daily; 25min); Geysir* (daily; 1hr 30min); Gullfoss* (daily; 1hr 40min); Hella (daily; 35min); Höfn (1 daily-3 weekly; 5hr 50min); Hveragerði (daily; 30min); Hvolsvöllur (daily; 1hr); Kirkjubæjarklaustur (1 daily-3 weekly; 3hr 20min); Laugarvatn* (daily; 1hr); Reykjavík (daily; 1hr); Skógar (daily; 1hr 40min); Stokkseyri (2 daily; 15min); Þorlákshöfn (2 daily; 1hr); Vík (daily; 2hr 10min).

Skógar to: Hella (daily; 1hr 5min); Höfn (1 daily-3 weekly; 4hr 10min); Hveragerði (daily; 2hr 10min); Hvolsvöllur (daily; 45min); Kirkjubæjarklaustur (1 daily-3 weekly; 1hr 40min); Reykjavík (daily; 2hr 40min); Selfoss (daily; 1hr 40min); Vík (daily; 30min).

Vík to: Hella (daily; 1hr 35min); Höfn (1 daily-3 weekly; 3hr 40min); Hveragerði (daily; 2hr 40min); Hvolsvöllur (daily; 1hr 15min); Kirkjubæjarklaustur (1 daily-3 weekly; 1hr 10min); Reykjavík (daily; 3hr 15min); Selfoss (daily; 2hr 10min); Skógar (daily; 30min).

Þingvellir* to: Reykjavík (late May–September, daily; 50min).

*June-September only

Planes

Heimaey (on demand) to: Bakki (6min); Hella (15min); Reykjavík (30min); Selfoss (20min)

Ferries

Heimaey to Þorlákshöfn: daily; 2hr 45min.
Þorlákshöfn to Heimaey: daily; 2hr 45min.

The west coast

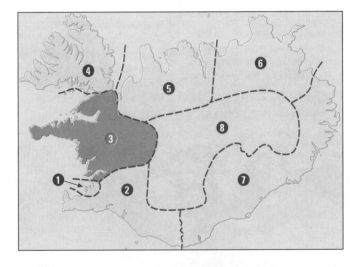

CHAPTER 3 # Highlights

✳ **Flatey, Breiðafjörður** A night spent in the guesthouse on this idyllic farming island is the perfect escape from the beaten track. **See p.179**

✳ **Deildatunguhver hot spring, Reykholt** Witness the power of Iceland's geothermal activity at the country's biggest natural hot spring. **See p.165**

✳ **Hraunfossar cascades, Húsafell** Iceland's most unusual waterfalls, where subterranean aquamarine water tumbles lazily over moss-dressed rocks. **See p.167**

✳ **Kaldidalur valley** An excellent taster of Iceland's remote landscapes of glaciers and grey sand deserts. **See p.168**

✳ **Eiríksstaðir, Haukadalur valley** Stand on the spot from which the Vikings set out to discover Greenland and North America. **See p.170**

✳ **Hiking up Snæfellsjökull** A rare chance to get up close to one of Iceland's glaciers. **See p.183**

✳ **Big whale-watching, Ólafsvík** The best chance in Iceland to spot the magnificent blue whale is to be had on tours from the tip of the Snæfellsnes peninsula. **See p.176**

The west coast

The panorama of the bay of Faxa Fiord is magnificent – with a width of fifty miles from horn to horn, the one running down into a rocky ridge of pumice, the other towering to the height of five thousand feet in a pyramid of eternal snow, while round the intervening semicircle crowd the peaks of a hundred noble mountains.

Letters from High Latitudes, Lord Dufferin

Reykjavík and the Reykjanes peninsula together form the southern edge of **Faxaflói**, the sweeping bay that dominates Iceland's west coast and any journey north of the capital – the Ringroad clings to its shores as far as the small commercial centre of Borgarnes before striking off inland on its way towards Brú and the north coast. Although the scenery is not Iceland's most dramatic, it provides visitors travelling around the country in a clockwise direction with their first taste of small-town Iceland and as such makes a satisfying introduction to the rest of the country. If you can it's a good idea to break your journey at one of the small towns hereabouts to get a feel for what rural Iceland really is all about – in summer the views of flower meadows dotted with isolated farms sheltering at the foot of cloud-topped mountains are picture-postcard pretty. Travelling north, the first town you come to, the disappointing, ugly **Akranes**, with its concrete factory and fish-processing plants, is best passed over in favour of nearby **Borgarnes**, a small commercial centre that also makes a good jumping off point for the historical riches of **Reykholt**, Iceland's largest hot spring, Deildatungahver, and the excellent hiking around Húsafell.

The "pyramid of eternal snow" to which Dufferin, who sailed his yacht *Foam* to Iceland in 1856, was referring is the glacier, **Snæfellsjökull**, which sits majestically on top of a dormant volcano at the tip of Snæfellsnes, a long arm of volcanic and mountainous land jutting out into the sea and the highlight of any trip up the west coast. Divided by a jagged mountain ridge, the peninsula not only marks the northern edge of Faxaflói bay but also the southern reaches of the more sheltered **Breiðafjörður**, with its hundreds of islands and skerries, over which lie the table mountains of the West Fjords. On a clear day the snowcap is clearly visible across the water from both Reykjavík and the West Fjords. The best whale watching in Iceland can be experienced off the western point of Snæfellsnes aboard catamarans sailing from the fishing village of **Ólafsvík** – this is undoubtedly the best place to come to see the biggest mammal on Earth, the blue whale, regularly spotted off shore as well as the more common humpback whale. From **Arnarstapi** on the peninsula's southern coast it's possible to take a snowmobile up onto the glacier for some of the most exhilarating driving – and vistas – you'll ever experience. Of all the west coast's towns and villages, only **Stykkishólmur** on the northern coast of Snæfellsnes with its wooden houses and its vibrant harbour busy with

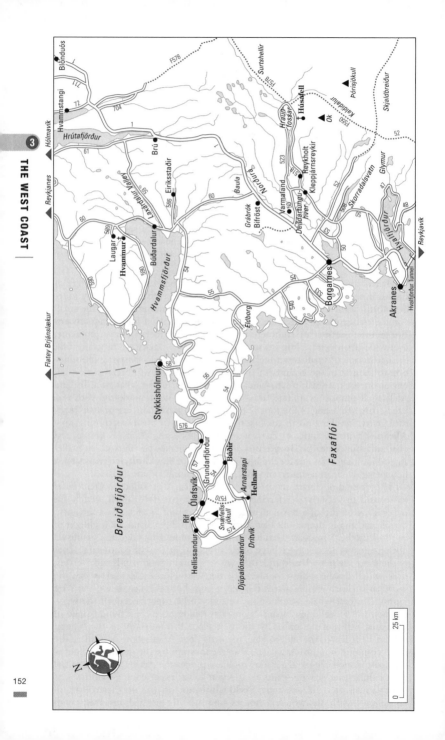

chugging fishing vessels is immediately appealing, and it is the only town on the peninsula worth an overnight stay. Occupying a sheltered spot in the neck of land which links the West Fjords with the rest of the country, **Laugar** in Sælingsdalur with its hot springs is a good place to break the long journey from Reykjavík to the West Fjords as well as offering a few cultural diversions. For splendid isolation there can be few better places than **Búðir** on the southern coast of Snæfellsnes – a wide sandy bay, home only to a charming hotel complete with creaking floorboards and ocean views.

What the west coast may lack in scenic splendour, it makes up for in historical and cultural significance – landscapes here are steeped in the drama and tragedy of the sagas. Close to **Búðardalur**, to the north of Snæfellsnes, Haukadalur valley was the starting point for **Viking** expansion westwards which took explorers first to Greenland and later to the shores of North America as heroically recounted in the **Saga of Eirík the Red**. The farm at **Eiríksstaðir** was once home to the eponymous hero and his wife, who together pioneered the settlement of Greenland having been outlawed from Iceland. It's also thought that **Leifur Eiríksson**, the first European to set foot in North America, was born on a farm that has now been expertly reconstructed on the original site. Although the farm is remote and difficult to reach without your own transport, it's worth making the effort to get here since there are few places in Iceland where historical events are more tangible – standing beside the turf-rooved farmstead overlooking the barren expanses of the valley westwards out to sea it's easy to see what inspired the early Icelanders to take to the ocean to search for lands anew. Equally rich in history is the tiny village of **Reykholt**, just forty-five minutes outside Borgarnes, and home to arguably the most famous and influential man who lived during the age of the sagas, **Snorri Sturluson** (see box, p.164). Here you can still see the outdoor warm pool where the great man bathed and received visitors. More saga history can be found in Laxárdalur valley, northeast of Búðardalur, where characters from the **Laxdæla Saga** (see box, p.172) lived out their feud-torn lives.

Getting around the west coast

The west coast is one of the easiest areas in Iceland to explore by public transport. From the ESSO station forecourt in **Borgarnes**, the transport hub for the entire west coast, five different bus routes depart south to Akranes and Reykjavík, east to Reykholt, west to Snæfellsnes, and north to Búðardalur and the southern West Fjords, as well as continuing along the Ringroad to Brú and all points north. In fact, three stick to Route 1 on their way to their final destinations (Akureyri, Siglufjörður and Hólmavík), with several daily departures between Borgarnes and Brú. The tiny settlement of **Brú** is also a strategic interchange point for passengers travelling between the West Fjords and destinations along the north coast such as Akureyri.

Two services operate between Reykjavík and **Snæfellsnes**; one travels along the south coast of the peninsula along Route 54 via Búðir to Ólafsvík and Hellisandur, whereas the other bears right onto Route 56 (shortly after the farm Gröf) to head for the north coast and Stykkishólmur and Grundarfjörður. Unfortunately there is no public transport around the tip of the peninsula, but it is possible to connect at **Búðir** crossroads with an excursion bus round the glacier in summer. This service operates twice daily (June–Aug Mon–Fri) from Ólafsvík and travels first in a clockwise direction via Búðir, Arnastapi and Hellissandur before performing an anti-clockwise circuit via the same villages back to Ólafsvík. Connections exist in both directions at Búðir crossroads for passengers travelling to and from Reykjavík on the scheduled bus.

Travel up the west coast also offers three alternative ways of reaching the West Fjords. One option is to take the bus the entire way from Reykjavík to Ísafjörður via Brú and Hólmavík. The other is to take the bus to Stykkishólmur, and connect there to the ferry, Baldur, across Breiðafjörður to Brjánslækur from where another bus leaves for Ísafjörður (see box, p.178 and "Travel Details", p.221, for details). A third but more limiting option is the bus from Reykjavík to Reykhólar via Búðardalur and Laugar. This service may be regular but there are no onward connections at all from Reykhólar.

Akranes and around

Once beyond Reykjavík and its adjacent overspill town, Mosfellsbær, the Ringroad makes its way round the towering form of Mount Esja towards industrial Akranes, one of the most economically vibrant towns in Iceland. Until recently, to reach the town, the national artery was forced to weave its way around Hvalfjörður, or Whale Fjord, the biggest in southwest Iceland, named after the large number of whales seen here ever since the time of the Settlement. More recently, during World War II, the fjord's deep anchorages made it one of the most important bases in the North Atlantic, when British and American naval vessels were stationed here, providing a port and safe haven for supply ships travelling between Europe and North America. Today though, the fjord is no longer the obstacle to travel it once was, and an impressive **tunnel**, opened in 1998, dramatically improved communications. Nearly 6km in length, of which around 4km lie below the seabed, it slices through the mouth of the fjord, a massive engineering project by Icelandic standards that took just over two years to complete. Blasting through the basalt bedrock began simultaneously on both shores of the fjord in 1996 amid commercial concerns from the people of Akranes that the shorter distance to the capital (49km through the tunnel compared with a massive 108km round the fjord) would kill off their local shops and services – fortunately their fears have proved unfounded. Twenty-four hour **toll booths** are in place at both ends currently charging a hefty 1000kr per car, which, although expensive, is well worth it to save a tedious detour.

Just beyond the exit from the tunnel, Route 51 strikes off west from the Ringroad for **AKRANES**, the west coast's biggest town and home to 5600 people and one of the few places outside Reykjavík experiencing population growth. Although you'd never guess by wandering around the modern streets today, Akranes traces its history all the way back to 880 AD when, according to the Book of Settlement, Landnámabók, the area was first settled by two Irish brothers, Þormóður and Ketill Bresason, most probably monks. Over the following centuries the tiny village grew into a successful agricultural settlement as the town's name, literally "field promontory", indicates – corn was grown on the fertile land around Mount Akrafjall. However, around the middle of the seventeeth century, one of Iceland's leading bishops, Brynjólfur Sveinsson from the Skálholt bishopric, stationed a number of his fishing boats in Akranes and unwittingly gave birth to the country's first fishing village. The town never looked back and today fishing and fish processing account for roughly half of the town's economy.

Although fish processing, ship maintenance, cement making and the production of ferro-silicon for export are the four mainstays of the local economy, smaller firms, including banks and insurance companies, are also based here, lending the town a busy, commercial air. However, Akranes is best known for its **sporting** prowess – the local football team, Íþróttabandalag Akraness, have been national champions nineteen times – and its two sports halls, swimming pools and soccer stadium are of a correspondingly high standard. Despite this, gritty Akranes is hard to like, entirely without architectural charm and a terribly cold spot even in summer as the icy winds straight off the sea howl round street corners, sending the hardiest locals scurrying for cover. However, it's a good base from which to explore the heights of **Mount Akrafjall**, which dominates the easterly skyline and where there's some decent hiking to be had, or, when the sun is shining, the long sandy beach, **Langisandur**, a fifteen-minute walk from the town centre. Before leaving town, however, there's a chance to get to grips with the history of the **Cod Wars** and to see the actual cutters used to slice through British trawler nets in the 1972 and 1975 disputes, housed in the **Akranes Museum Centre**, the town's one cultural grace.

Hvalfjörður and whaling

At the head of **Hvalfjörður**, the disused open-air **whaling** station is a poignant reminder of Iceland's days as a whaling nation and of the key role Hvalfjörður played. In fact, until the late 1980s, tourist buses from Reykjavík would even wiggle their way round the fjord to allow visitors to watch the grisly spectacle of a whale being sliced up alfresco.

Commercial whaling out of Hvalfjörður began in 1948 and continued right up until the summer of 1989, the end of a four year period that the Icelandic government termed "scientific research whaling". During this period, specially equipped ships (four of which now stand idle in Reykjavík harbour) harpooned fin, sei and sperm whales in the deep waters off the west coast of Iceland and towed them back to the Hvalfjörður whaling station. Minke whales were also caught from ordinary fishing boats. In latter years, however, there was immense international opposition to the slaughter from various quarters, not least a boycott of Icelandic seafood instigated by Greenpeace, and direct action, when a Canadian craft sank two Icelandic whaling vessels and destroyed the whaling station here in November 1986.

With its economy declining as a result of the boycott, Iceland withdrew from the International Whaling Commission in 1992, claiming the organisation set up to manage whaling had become one devoted solely to preventing all hunts. As an island nation, the Icelanders passionately believe in the right to harvest all living marine resources, and opinion polls consistently show a vast majority of the population, generally around eighty percent, in favour of resumption. Indeed, every year the contentious issue resurfaces, with the owner of the remaining four whaling ships claiming he could have the vessels ready for service within a matter of weeks. Matters came to a head in March 1999 when, after much debate, the Icelandic parliament voted by a huge majority to resume whaling and called on the government to begin preparations. However, since Iceland's most important markets for fish are in Britain, France, Germany and the United States, where opposition to whaling is strongest, ministers are treading carefully – and slowly – painfully aware that a country where three-quarters of all exports are fish related simply cannot risk another boycott. In October 2002 Iceland was finally readmitted to the IWC following lengthy and heated debate over whether a country should be permitted to join whilst still objecting to the international moratorium on whaling. The move was a first step towards the resumption of Icelandic commercial whaling within the jurisdiction of the Commission, and in August 2003, amid ongoing concerns and in the face of international outcry, the country started hunting minke whales for the first time in 14 years, albeit, the government claimed, for scientific purposes.

Arrival, information and accommodation

All **buses** arrive at the Skútan filling station (☎ 431 2061) at the western end of Þjóðbraut, from where it's a left turn into Skagabraut (also known as Sleipnisvegur) and a ten-minute walk to the main street, Kirkjubraut, and the diminutive Akratorg square. Annoyingly, the **tourist information office** (mid-May to mid-Sept daily 10am-6pm; rest of the year Mon-Fri 1pm-6pm; ☎ 431 5566, ⓦ www.akranes.is) is in the opposite direction, out at the Museum Centre, a twenty-minute walk from the bus terminal along Garðabraut, right into Innesvegur, then left up Víkurbraut followed by a dogleg into the unnamed road signed for the musuem. Here you can get practical information from the friendly staff about Akranes, as well as leaflets on hiking routes up Mount Akrafjall.

The town's one and only **hotel** is back in town at Kirkjubraut 11 – the *Hótel Barbró* (☎ 431 4240, ⓦ www.barbro.is; ❹), a plain and simple place whose décor is outdated and overly flowery but which does have perfectly decent en-suite doubles (❸ with shared facilities) and sleeping-bag accommodation (2500kr). Breakfast is included in the price. To get to Akranes's oceanside **campsite** (May–Sept; ☎ 431 5100) from the town centre, walk northeast up Kirkjubraut for five–ten minutes to the junction with Kalmansbraut (actually the beginning of Route 509 out of town towards Borgarnes) to the small bay, Kalmansvík.

The Town

Although there are no sights as such in Akranes, sooner or later you'll come across the concrete buildings of the Haraldur Böðvarsson **fish-processing factory**, one of Iceland's largest, which completely dominate the **harbour** area, emblazoned with the name of their founder in bold red letters. Close by, the **shipyard** of Þorgeir og Ellert is at the cutting edge of not only Icelandic but also world technology in fishing-trawler production. However, it's the founding of the **Icelandic National Cement Works** (Sementverksmiðjan) in 1958 that really gets locals excited, an environmentally friendly plant close to the harbour at Mánabraut, which uses crushed shells from the sea bed rather than lime as raw material; mercifully, the cement works are closed to visitors.

Once you've exhaused the handful of streets in the centre of town, take a stroll up to the town's engaging **Museum Centre** (May–Sept daily 10am–6pm; Sept–April Mon–Fri 1am–6pm; 700kr; ⓦ www.museum.is) off Garðagrund, home to four different museums containing everything from information on the Akranes football team to samples of quartz stone. The granite stone in front of the site inscribed in Gaelic and Icelandic commemorates the Irish role in Akranes's history and was given to the town by Ireland in 1974 to mark 1100 years of settlement in Iceland. Close by, also in front of the centre, the twin-masted cutter *Sigurfari*, built on the River Humber in Britain in 1885, carries the honour of working as the last sailing ship in the Icelandic fleet before being sold to the Faroe Islands where, remarkably, it fished until 1970. Although it's possible to board the ship via a wooden walkway, it's easier to gain an impression of how agile and speedy it was by walking around the hull in its dry grassy moorings. Your first port of call should be the **Akranes folk musem** located in the building between the granite stone and the cutter. The most interesting exhibits are the hook-shaped cutters that were used to sever the nets of British trawlers during the Cod Wars of 1972 and 1975. Though quite ordinary to look at, they proved devastatingly effective when dragged across British trawler wires by the Icelandic coastguard, who also made use of the naval gun alongside, orginally made in Portsmouth.

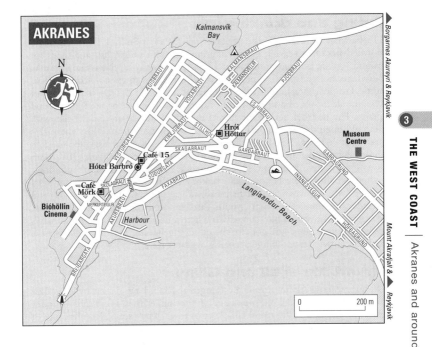

The low-roofed white building called Safnaskálinn is home to the centre's three other museums: the Icelandic sports museum, the mineral museum and the newly opened national land survey of Iceland (all open same times and with same entrance ticket). Although the **Mineral Museum** with its mind-numbing displays of carbonates, zeolites and other Icelandic stones will delay you no more than a couple of minutes, it's worth devoting more attention to the adjacent **Sports Museum**. Amongst its dizzying collections of cups, medals and shoes owned by famous (at least in Iceland) sportsmen and women, it boasts everything there is to know about one Vilhjálmur Einarsson, who, at the Melbourne Olympics in 1956, managed an astonishing 16.7m in the triple jump – you'll feel instant respect when you see the footprints marked on the museum floor that plot the exact distance of this feat, still an Icelandic record today. The **Land Survey Museum**, stuffed to the gills with maps and charts of this geologically pockmarked country, is a must for anyone interested in Iceland's peculiar geography – the expert staff are ready to answer any question you might have on matters cartographical.

The best **swimming pool** (Mon-Fri 6.45am-9pm, Sat & Sun 9am-6pm; ☎433 1100) and sports centre in town are found off Garðabraut at Jaðarsbakkar; the modern changing rooms at the swimming pool contain a steam room, whereas outdoors there's a pool and four hot pots. Behind the sports centre complex lies the one kilometre long stretch of sandy beach known as **Langisandur** – a must in Akranes when the sun is shining, since the southern aspect of the shore will do wonders for your tan. Bear in mind, though, that although the water can look tempting on a sunny day it fails the big-toe test by a long way; it's barely 5°C warm at the height of summer.

Eating and drinking

The best bet for **eating** is the popular *Hrói Höttur* at Stillholt 23, essentially a glorified **pizzeria** serving good-value burgers from 660kr, fish and chips for around 1000kr, and decent pizzas for 1250kr; a takeaway service is also available. Beer here though is more expensive than elsewhere in town at 490kr for a 33cl bottle. For finer fare, head for the **restaurant** inside *Hótel Barbró* at Kirkjubraut 11 – the décor may be maroon and of questionable taste but the food is good quality. The best bet here is the fish of the day, generally around 1295kr with salad, although there's also beef steak for 1380kr, burgers from 700kr and pizzas starting at 1135kr; a half-litre of beer costs 500kr. *Café 15*, at Kirkjubraut 15, is a good lunchtime choice for soups, **sandwiches** and **cakes**, with a TV room downstairs where you can sit and ponder Icelandic television's offerings. Otherwise, there's the Harðarbakarí **bakery** at Kirkjubraut 54, with the usual range of white loaves, Icelandic flatbread and cakes. Come Thursday, Friday and Saturday evenings, the town's youth can be found drinking at *Café Mörk*, Skólabraut 14, a stylish **bar**-cum-disco where a beer costs 500kr. On Thursdays it's beer night when a litre goes for the quite unbelievable price of 700kr; snacks such as sandwiches and burgers are also available for around 900kr.

Mount Akrafjall and Glymur

On approaching Akranes from the Ringroad you'll have driven by **Akrafjall** mountain, which, at 643m, is not only 200m higher than Reykjavík's Mount Esja, but also dominates the skyline east of town. The mountain offers one of the best panoramas in the west of Iceland, with spectacular **views** not only of Akranes but also, on a clear day, of Reykjavík. On a sunny day you'll find most of the town out here either climbing the flat-topped mountain or picnicking in the lush meadows at its foot – during summer you'll also find copious numbers of **seabirds**, especially kittiwakes, nesting on the mountain's craggy sides. Of the mountain's two peaks, the southern one, **Háihnúkur** (555m) is easiest to climb thanks to a well-defined **path** leading to the summit from the car park below. The northern peak, Geirmundartindur, measures 643m, split from the other by a river valley, Berjadalur, through which most of the town's water supply flows. For details of the various ascents ask at Akranes's tourist office (see p.156) for their free map, *Uppgönguleiðir á Akrafjall.*

From the mountain, Route 47 winds its way east around the northern shore of Hvalfjörður towards Iceland's highest waterfall, **Glymur**. The falls drop nearly 200m from the boggy ground to the west of **Hvalvatn** lake, but it can be difficult to find a vantage point from where to see the spectacle at its best. A rough **track** leads up through Botnsdalur valley at the head of Hvalfjörður towards the falls – allow about an hour from the road. Incidentally, according to Icelandic folklore, a mythical creature, half-man, half-whale, which once terrified locals from its home in the dark waters of Hvalfjörður, was tricked into swimming out of the fjord, up the river and the Glymur falls, before dying in the waters of Hvalvatn – where, oddly, whale bones have been found.

Borgarnes and around

On leaving Akranes the Ringroad covers a lonely and exposed 38km before reaching **BORGARNES**, the principal town of the Borgarfjörður region, which not only enjoys a spectacular setting on a narrow neck of land which reaches out into the eponymous fjord but also has excellent views inland to the glaciers of Eiríksjökull and Langjökull. The stretch of road from Akranes, particularly around Hafnarfjall, on the southern approach to Borgarnes, is one of the most hazardous in the entire country – facing westwards, it takes the full brunt of violent storms which drive in from the Atlantic and not surprisingly closes frequently during the winter months, as cars have been overturned here by the brute force of the wind. In summer things are not quite so severe but it is still an extremely windy spot.

Unlike most other coastal settlements, Borgarnes isn't dependent on fishing – powerful tidal currents in the fjord have put paid to that – but is primarily a service centre for the surrounding dairy farmers who rely on the town's slaughterhouse and good roads for their livelihoods. However, the town's main claim to fame and your attention is its historical association with Skallagrímur Kveldúlfsson, father of **Egill Skallagrímsson**. A ninth-century pirate, thug and poet, Egill was the hero of *Egill's Saga* and is commemorated here by a statue of himself carrying his drowned son, Böðvar, who's buried alongside his grandfather in the town. Indeed, as you wander around town, you'll come across plenty of streets named after characters from the saga: Skallagrímsgata, Kveldúlfsgata, Böðvarsgata and Egilsgata to name but a few.

Arrival and information

All **buses** from Akranes and Reykjavík cross the long and exposed bridge over Borgarfjörður before pulling into Borgarnes. In the terminal building here there's a branch of Búnaðarbanki Íslands **bank** (Mon–Fri 9.15am–4pm), complete with ATM, a small **supermarket** and a postbox. For details of onward buses, see the box on p.161.

The regional **tourist office** (June–Aug Mon–Fri 9am–7pm, Sat & Sun 9am–3pm; Sept–May Mon–Fri 9am–5pm, Sat & Sun 8am–noon; ☎437 2214, ⓦwww.west.is) is located in the banana-shaped building, Hyrnan, next to the filling station. Here you can not only glean masses of information from the staff about the west of Iceland but also buy maps and books about the region. Most other services are to be found in the adjacent Hyrnutorg shopping complex which contains a larger supermarket, another ATM, a **pharmacy** (Mon–Thurs 9am–6pm, Fri 9am–9pm, Sat 10am–2pm; ☎437 1168) as well as the *vínbúð* **liquor store** (Mon–Thurs 11am–6pm, Fri 11am–7pm, Sat 11am–2pm). The library, upstairs from the museum at Bjarnarbraut 4–6, has free **Internet access**.

Accommodation

There's just one **hotel** actually in town, the plain *Hótel Borgarnes* (☎437 1119, ⓕ437 1443, ⓔhotelbo@centrum.is; ⑨) dating from 1891 at Egilsgata 12–14, a ten-minute walk from the bus terminal down Borgarbraut, then right into Egilsgata; choose one of the neutrally decorated and quiet en-suite doubles in the most recently renovated part of the hotel (to the right as you enter) to avoid being affronted by garish 1950s and 1980s décor. Alternatively, across the fjord and a twenty-five-minute walk over the bridge back towards Akranes, in a stunning setting at the foot of Hafnarfjall, the *Mótel Venus* (☎437 2345, ⓕ437 2344, ⓔmotel@centrum.is; sleeping-bag accommodation 1450kr, ❸), at Hafnarskógur, has simple, comfortable doubles for around half the price, albeit with shared facilities; all buses pass the motel. For cheaper **farmhouse** accommodation, it's hard to beat the working farm, *Bjarg* (☎ & ⓕ437 1925, ⓔbjarg@simnet.is; sleeping-bag accommodation 1600kr, ❶), a twenty-minute walk north of town following Borgarbraut all the way; here, the smells and sights will give you a real taste of Icelandic country life, as well as a healthy appetite for their traditional cooking. Although the **youth hostel**, *Hamar* (mid-May to mid-Sept; ☎437 1663, ℻437 2063, ✉gb@aknet.is; 1900kr, breakfast 800kr extra), is inconveniently situated a good hour's walk north of Borgarnes, it sits right on the Ringroad and is therefore reachable by bus, and the gabled farmhouse that houses the hostel is charming. The **campsite** (☎437 2214) is back in town on Borgarbraut, just behind the ESSO station.

The Town

Home to barely 1800 people, Borgarnes is not a big place. Indeed, if it has a town centre it's the area around **Brúartorg** square and the ESSO station that merits the title, though like so many other provincial Icelandic towns, the handful of suburban streets here can easily be seen in an hour or so. From the bus station at the filling station, it's a short walk down the main drag, Borgarbraut, containing the town's main shops and services, to Borgarnes's main attraction, **Skallagrímsgarður**, a small but pleasant park at the junction with Skallagrímsgata. By the entrance on the left is the **burial mound** of one of Iceland's earliest settlers, **Skallagrímur Kveldúlfsson**, complete with horse, weapons and various other Viking accoutrements. Originally just plain Grímur, he obtained the first part of his name, Skalla ("bald"), because he lost all his hair at an early age. Skallagrímur's son, **Egill**, is portrayed on the accompanying monument carrying home the body of his own son, Böðvar. According to the saga, Egill's son fell to his death in the Hvítá river during a severe storm and was laid to rest here, next to his grandfather. Distraught, Egill fell into a deep depression and vowed to neither eat nor drink until the day he died. However, his daughter-in-law tricked him into sipping a cup of milk and persuaded him to write a poem in memory of his beloved son. Egill soon became so involved in his composition that he forgot his vow to die; his work, *Sonatorrek*, is remembered by a statue by Ásmundur Sveinsson in nearby Borg á Mýrum (see p.161).

Continue down Borgarbraut, turning left at the post office into Sæunnargata, and you'll soon come to **Safnahús Borgarfjarðar** (June–Aug daily 1–6pm, other times by arrangement in advance; ☎430 7200, ⓦwww.safnahus.is; 400kr), the regional **museum** at Bjarnarbraut 4–6 with its pedestrian and somewhat tedious displays of local art, natural history and folk exhibits. Inside there's a tired collection of every Icelandic bird you can think of – including a dazed-looking gannet suspended upside down from a stone pillar – as well as equally uninspiring how-we-used-to-live paraphernalia such as a rickety spinning wheel and an old cash register. Much better, though, is the worthwhile exhibition on Icelandic woodland, which offers an insight into why there are so few trees in Iceland by highlighting the interaction between man and tree over the centuries. However, if none of the exhibits appeal, head instead for the excellent open-air **swimming pool** and sports centre (Mon–Fri 7am–10pm, Sat & Sun 9am–6pm; ☎437 1444) on Þorsteinsgata, a continuation of Skallagrímsgata, situated right by the water's edge with great views of the fjord and the surrounding hills; there are also a couple of hot pots here, a waterslide, a steam room and a sauna.

Eating and drinking

The best-value **place to eat** is *Hyrnan*, inside the service building attached to the filling station. Popular with truckers and holidaying Icelanders, it serves up

Moving on from Borganes

Oddly, for such a small place, **buses** out of Borganes leave from several different places. Those from the *Hotel Borganes* and the Esso filling station on Brúartorg square go to Reykjavík, Reykholt, Akranes, Snæfellsnes, Búðardalur and Reykhólar in the West Fjords; buses from the adjacent Shell station go to Hólmavík, where there are connections with Ísafjörður; while those from the Esso station go only to Akureyri and Siglufjörður. For **timetables**, ask at the tourist office, the *Hótel Borgarnes* or the *Hyrnan* restaurant. Buy **tickets** on board.

main dishes such as fish and chips with salad for 1390kr as well as pizzas at 990kr, open sandwiches 690kr and soup 480kr; coffee is 170kr whilst a beer is a whopping 680kr. Alternatively, try the tatty Filipino-run *Matstofan*, Brákarbraut 3, beyond the museum, that dishes up burgers and pizzas, and which will save a walk back to the main square if you're staying at the hotel. For a more upmaket dining experience, the restaurant inside *Hótel Borgarnes* itself (see p.159) is hard to beat – their pan-fried puffin breast in blueberry sauce for 2650kr, or garlic fried fillet of lamb with pepper sauce at 2950kr, may be expensive but they are certainly mouthwatering. For evening **drinking**, if you don't fancy the quiet hotel bar (beer 600kr) with its extensive wine list (bottles from 3000kr), try the cheaper *Matstofan* or make sure you stock up during the day at the *vínbúð*.

Borg á Mýrum

Another site mentioned in the sagas, the farm of **Borg á Mýrum**, just a couple of kilometres north of Borgarnes on Route 54, is easily reached by buses to the Snæfellsnes peninsula. First settled by **Skallagrímur Kveldúlfsson**, this spot is, to Icelanders at least, of double historical significance because of its association with one of Iceland's greatest writers, Snorri Sturluson (see p.164). The fact that all that remains today is the *borg*, or large rock, after which Skallagrímur's original farm was named, seems to matter little to the misty-eyed home-grown tourists who make the visit here. That said, you're unlikely to find crowds of visitors as most stay no more than ten minutes or so before

Egill's Saga

Although there's no concrete evidence, historians generally believe that **Egill's Saga** was most likely written by Iceland's greatest thirteenth-century writer and politician, **Snorri Sturluson**. It tells of the Viking age adventures of **Egill Skallagrímsson** (c910–990) on his many seaborne forays, first to Norway and then later to England. Key to the story is Egill's conflict with King **Eric Bloodaxe** of Norway (c895–954), son of Harald Fairhair. Following in his father's footsteps, Egill decides to challenge the growing central power of the Norwegian crown and manages to humiliate King Eric publicly, kill his son and survive an attempt by Queen Gunnhildur to poison him – all in one night. Having lost the respect of his subjects and accordingly been shamed out of Norway, King Eric takes up residence across the North Sea in Viking Jórvík (York) only to receive an unexpected visitor – Egill has been shipwrecked on the Yorkshire coast and soon stands to face with Eric and Gunnhildur again. Although condemned to death, he composes a poem in praise of King Eric and is spared. According to the saga, Egill returned to Borg in Iceland in 957 and lived out his final years in Mosfell just outside Reykjavík.

moving on, because the original farmhouse is long gone and there's precious little to see here today other than a small white church, the *borg* itself and a sculpture by Ásmundur Sveinsson entitled *Sonatorrek* (*The Great Loss of my Sons*) in memory of the moving poem written by Egill mourning the death of his sons, Böðvar and Gunnar.

Like so many of Iceland's historical sites, archeological remains are thin on the ground, so you'll have to arm yourself with the facts and let your imagination do the rest. Skallagrímur ended up here very much by chance after falling foul of his king, Harald Fairhair of Norway. Together with his father, Kveldúlfur (Evening Wolf – so named because he grew tired and irritable in the evenings), he fled the wrath of King Harald and set sail westwards for Iceland. However, during the lengthy and stormy voyage, Kveldúlfur fell ill and ordered that, on his death, his coffin be tossed overboard and his grieving family settle wherever it washed up. Following his father's instruction, Skallagrímur first set foot in Iceland in an area rich in bogs, forests and salmon rivers, at Borg á Mýrum (Rock in the Bogs), where he raised his family, naming the surrounding area, accordingly, Borgarfjörður (Rocky Fjord). The family struggle against the Norwegian king continued when Skallagrímur's son, **Egill**, who also lived at Borg, returned to Norway to do battle with his arch enemy, Eric Bloodaxe (see box, p.161).

The third great man to live at Borg was **Snorri Sturluson**. At the age of nineteen Snorri married the only daughter of Father Bersi the Wealthy, of Borg, and moved to the farm following his father-in-law's death in 1202 to run the estate as his heir. However, his marriage was not a happy one and just four or five years later, around 1206, he decided to move inland to Reykholt, leaving his wife behind.

Reykholt and around

The cultural highlight of any trip up the west coast, **REYKHOLT** is immediately appealing. Not only does this little hamlet set in the wide open spaces of the fertile Reykholtsdalur valley enjoy a stunning setting amid dusky mountains and the sleepy meanders of the Reykjadalsá river, but it also contains much more tangible memorials to **Snorri Sturluson**. The excellent museum here is is by far and away the best place to get to grips with Iceland's rich and, at times, downright confusing history of saga events, characters and writing. However, don't view a trip here as simply a way of mugging up on Icelandic history. Reykholt is also a fantastic place to fetch up for a couple of days to enjoy the pastoral delights, solitude and fairly reliable weather of the west coast at its best.

The hamlet itself now consists of little more than a few geothermally heated greenhouses and a church. At the foot of the hillock on which the former school stands, Snorri's pool, the **Snorralaug**, provides a rare visual example of a piece of medieval Iceland and is even mentioned in the *Landnámabók* (*Book of Settlements*) and the *Sturlunga Saga*. A four-metre-wide geothermally heated pool ringed with stones, it's believed this is where Snorri would bathe and receive visitors, and next to it are the restored remains of the **tunnel** thought to have led to the cellar of Snorri's farmhouse, where he was assassinated in 1241 (see box on p.164). The pool is fed by an ancient stone aqueduct from the nearby hot spring, Skrifla. Back up the steps from the pool, the Snorri **statue** which graces the front of the former school was presented to Iceland

Snorri Sturluson

Born at the farm of Hvammur (see p.171) near Búðardalur in 1179, **Snorri Sturluson** was descended from some of the greatest figures in early Icelandic history; on his father's side were influential chieftains, on his mother's, amongst others, the warrior poet Egill Skallagrímsson. At the age of two he was fostered and taken to one of Iceland's leading cultural centres, Oddi (see p.128), where, over the years, he became acquainted not only with historical writing but also the court of Norway – a relationship that would eventually lead to his death. In 1206, following his marriage to a wealthy heiress, he moved to Reykholt and consolidated his grip on power by becoming a chieftain, legislator and respected historian and writer; he also developed a distinct taste for promiscuity, fathering three children to women other than his long-suffering first wife, Herdís.

Snorri Sturluson is the most celebrated figure in Icelandic literature, producing first his *Edda* then *Egill's Saga* and *Heimskringla*, which from its geographical detail shows that Snorri spent several years living in Norway. During this period he developed a close bond of allegiance to the Norwegian earl who reigned alongside the teenage king, Hákon. However, following a civil war in Norway, which resulted in the earl's death, the Norwegian king declared Snorri a traitor to him and ordered one of his followers, Gissur Þorvaldsson, to bring the writer back to Norway – dead or alive. On the dark night of September 23, 1241, seventy armed men led by Gissur burst into Snorri's farmhouse in Reykholt sending him fleeing from his bed unarmed and defenceless, down into the cellar. Five of the thugs pursued Snorri, and there, they hacked Iceland's most distinguished man of letters to death.

by Norway's King Olaf shortly after independence in 1947. It's a clear reminder of the continuing wrangle between the two Nordic nations over Snorri's origins; the Norwegians strongly maintain that Snorri is theirs and claim he was born in Norway. Although the Icelanders have gratefully accepted over three million Norwegian kroner to help set up the Snorri exhibition hall, the new library and Snorri research centre attached to the village church (see below), suspicions remain that the Norwegians haven't yet renounced their claims on Snorri.

The Town

Although Reykholt grew up around the old church, which today stands marooned between the village hotel and the former school, it's the new, snow-white **church**, with its steep V-shaped roof, which is the centrepoint today. Underneath the church, the **Heimskringla museum** (June–Aug daily 10am–6pm; Sept–May open on request, ☎435 1490, ⓦ www.reykholt.is; 400kr) is a good place to get to grips with Snorri and his writings. Run by the mustachioed village priest, Geir Waage, and his wife Dagný Emilsdóttir, the critically acclaimed museum has more information on Snorri than you can shake a stick at and much on Reykholt's role as a centre of culture and learning over the centuries in the history of Iceland. The large prints of the sagas hung on the walls will give you an idea of what the documents actually looked like if you failed to see examples in the Culture House in Reykjavík. Geir is known throughout Iceland for his outspoken views on all things Snorri and has even done battle with the Icelandic government over the taxation of the Snorri estate, quoting a medieval document penned by the great man himself as his defence. Indeed, following meticulous research, Geir even claims that the handwriting contained on one of the museum prints is actually Snorri's –

make sure to see it before you leave. The church itself, with its specially designed acoustic walls, is used to host the Reykholt Music Festival (☎435 1490, ⓦ www.vortex.is/festival/reykholt; 2000kr per concert) during the last weekend in July when visiting singers and musicians gather here for a series of classical music concerts open to the public – look out for details posted around the village.

Practicalities

Getting here from Borgarnes is a straightforward affair – a daily **bus** (except Sat) covers the 18km along Route 527 in about an hour; on Friday and Sunday there's also a direct service from Reykjavík. Arriving from the north of Iceland, connections can be made at Borgarnes but generally require an overnight stay, since the Reykholt bus currently leaves at 9.15am. Services arrive at and depart from the ESSO filling station at the eastern end of the village, where there's also a small **shop** (daily 10am–10pm) which sells most basics, including food.

Originally built as a boarding school in 1931, friendly *Hótel Reykholt* (☎435 1260, ⓦ www.reykholt.is; sleeping-bag accommodation 1675kr, ❸) with fantastic views of the Okjökull and Eiríksjökull glaciers is a wonderfully peaceful **place to stay** right at the centre of the tiny village; Snorri had his farmhouse next to where the hotel now stands. Of the eighty or so rooms here, around a quarter have now been modernized to provide en-suite facilities; however, until work is complete, there will still be a variety of rooms available including the cheapest former student accommodation with shared facilities (❶), plain but perfectly adequate; breakfast is an extra 875kr, though there are self-catering facilities available. The adjoining **restaurant** serves the dish of the day for 1190kr, but beer here is expensive at 600kr.

Deildartunguhver

Whilst in the Reykholt area, it's well worth checking out the biggest **hot spring** in Europe, **Deildartunguhver**. Drawing on the geothermal reserves that lie all around Reykholtsdalur valley, and pumping out a staggering 180 litres of 97C°-water a second, the billowing clouds of steam created by this mighty fissure are truly impressive, reaching up high into the cool air – in fact it's water from here that runs via two specially constructed pipelines to heat the towns of Borgarnes and Akranes, 34km and 64km away, respectively. As in so many other geothermal areas around Iceland, water from the spring is also used to speed up the growth of plants and vegetables by heating up the surrounding greenhouses, and during the summer local farmers often set up stalls here to sell their produce to passing visitors. The spring is located by the side of Route 50, just north of the hamlet of Kleppjárnsreykir, 1km after the right turn for Route 518 to Reykholt. From the car park, a footpath leads to the spring; although the spring is safe to visit, it's wise not to get too close to the open pools of bubbling boiling water and clouds of steam to avoid the risk of burns – the water can, and does, splash over the protective fence in front. Incidentally, should you be short of ideas for your postcards home, the area around the spring is the only place in Iceland where the unusual variety of hard fern, *blechnum spicant*, is found.

Húsafell and around

The main draw of **HÚSAFELL** (ⓦ www.husafell.is), a favourite activity centre for holidaying Icelanders, 25km east of Reykholt, amid birchwoods and a geothermal area where many Reykjavíkers own summer cottages, is the vast lavafield, **Hallmundarhraun** (named after a local cave-dwelling giant who features in *Grettis Saga*). However, the area also offers some excellent **hiking** with trails leading off into the **Húsafellsskógur** forest and, more adventurously, up to the **Eiríksjökull** and **Okjökull** glaciers. The village itself consists of little more than a **church**, originally built in 1170 but today dating only from 1905, and a hundred or so private summer cottages, mostly owned by the trade unions (whose employees use these cottages in rotation) and individual families. There are also a number of **campsites** (all contactable on ☏435 1550), a **service centre** with a food store and filling station, and a fantastic geothermally heated outdoor **swimming pool** (☏435 1552) offering great views of the surrounding hills and glaciers. For information on cottages to rent (☏435 1550, ☏435 1551; 5-berth for 32,500–37,500kr) ask at the store or call in advance. There are six **rooms** for rent in an old farmhouse, the *Gamli bærinn* (3,500–5,000kr; ☏435 1325); sleeping bag accommodation is also available here for 1,700kr.

Annoyingly, there is no **public transport** from Reykholt to Húsafell – the only way to get here by public bus is to take the once daily Kaldidalur service (see box, p.168) and alight in the village.

Hallmundarhraun lavafield

From the centre of Húsafell, Route 518 heads northeast to **Kalmanstunga** farm from where Interior Route F578, Arnarvatnsvegur, leads to the edge of Hallmundarhraun (14km from Húsafell), thought to have been formed at the time of the Settlement when magma poured out from underneath the northwestern edge of the Langjökull and entered the Hvitá river. Just beyond the eastern edge of **Strútur** mountain (939m) a rough track leads into the lavafield, incidentally, named after the giant Hallmundur of *Grettis Saga*. You can walk on the lava, but it is hard going and requires tough-soled shoes; take care not to twist an ankle. Left off this track is **Surtshellir**, a 1970-metre-long cavern thought to have been a hideout of the eighteenth-century outlaw Eyvindur á Fjöllum and his friends. Exercise extreme caution if you decide to go inside as the uneven floor and darkness can prove disorientating, so you'll need to bring a torch with you. Nearby **Stefánshellir**, part of the same cave network, is also worth a quick look but is essentially more of the same – together these caves measure a whopping 3.5km. The F578 is passable for all cars as far as the caves, after which point it deteriorates as it heads for the Arnarvatnhæðir hills where it swings to the northwest to join up with Route 704 and eventually the Ringroad near Hvammstangi; the total distance of this interior route from Kalamanstunga to Núpsárbrú bridge in Austurárdal valley (Route 704) is 42km.

Back at Kalmanstunga farm, follow the road left towards **Fljótstunga** and take the rough track 1km southeast of the farm to reach one of the biggest lava caves in the world, **Víðgelmir**. Full of stalagmites, stalactites and strangely shaped icicles, this cave is 1585m long and has an impressive volume of 148,000 cubic metres though it may only be entered with a guide (contactable on ☏435 1198). A number of Viking age artefacts dating to before 1000 A.D. have been found inside, including a fireplace with ashes, remains of crushed bones, a skin pouch and, most impressively, stone pearls from a neckalce. **Accommodation** is available here at *Fljótstunga* in farmhouse rooms (❸), as sleeping-bag accommodation (1900kr) and in three small cabins (3500–8000kr). All are bookable on ☏435 1198, ☏435 1498, ⓦwww .fljotstunga.is.

Hraunfossar and Barnafoss

Six kilometres west of Húsafell on Route 518 and reached on the Kaldidalur bus from Reykjavík (see box, p.168), the waterfalls of **Hraunfossar** and **Barnafoss** are two of the most well-known natural features in Iceland. Although both are on the Hvítá, it's Hraunfossar (Lava Falls) that make for the best photographs: however, don't expect thundering torrents of white water – the falls here are gentle cascades of bright, turquoise water, emerging from under the moss-covered lava to tumble down a series of rock steps into the river. From here, a track leads upstream to Barnafoss (Children's Falls), so called because it was here that two children fell to their deaths when crossing the narrow stone arch that once spanned the river linking the districts of Hálsasveit and Hvítársíða; a footbridge now spans the falls affording an excellent view of the ravine here.

Okjökull and Eiríksjökull glaciers

One of Iceland's smaller glaciers, **Okjökull** is perfect for a **day hike** from Húsafell. At a height of 1141m, the glacier sits in a dolerite shield volcano and is easily reached from Húsafell by first following the western edge of the Bæjargil ravine up to the Drangsteinabrún ridge. Cross to the eastern side of the small ponds which lie south of the ridge and continue straight up to Ok. On a clear day the **views** from here are truly spectacular – west you can see to the coastline and the town of Borgarnes, inland there are sweeping vistas of the Interior. Allow five or six hours and take enough food and drink to last for a day.

Eiríksjökull (1675m) is the highest mountain in western Iceland and the long **hike** here should only be undertaken by seasoned walkers. Before setting out, get detailed information from the service centre in Húsafell, where you can also get helpful **maps**; the following description, however, should help you trace your route along them. Head along the hard, dry grass of the northern slope of Strútur mountain, northeast of Kalmanstunga farm, from where there are difficult trails east across Hallmundarhraun to Hvítárdrög at the foot of the glacier. Begin the climb itself by hiking up the prominent ravine on the western edge of the glacier, remembering your route to help your descent – it can be very disorientating up here. Beyond the ravine, the going gets considerably easier but watch out for crevasses. Allow a full day and bear in mind that sun-melt can make the hike a lot harder.

Langjökull

Just 20km southeast of Húsafell, but not readily accessible on foot to the inde-pependent traveller due to its isolated location on the western edges of the Interior, **Langjökull** is nevertheless a popular destination for people who want to experience riding across a glacier. At 950 square kilometres, Langjökull (Long Glacier) is Iceland's second-largest glacier, resembling a narrow pro-truding finger wedged between the Hallmundarhraun lavafield and the F35 Kjölur Interior route (see box on p.331). From June to August are daily (not Wed & Sat) **snowmobile** tours onto the glacier operated from Reykjavík by Destination Iceland, at Vatnsmýrarvegur 10, Reykjavík (☏591 1020, Ⓦwww.dice.is; 9hr costs 20,900kr; on Mon & Thurs a shorter 6hr tour runs, costing 16,500kr), who also provide all necessary protective clothing, includ-ing helmets and boots, plus transfer to and from the capital. Skis are also avail-able for rent for anyone who fancies being towed up onto the glacier before making their own way back down. On a clear day, the views out over the ice cap are simply breathtaking, but if it's foggy or raining don't be tempted to

The Kaldidalur interior route

From Húsafell, Route F550 (Kaldadalsvegur) winds its way south through the haunting beauty of the **Kaldidalur** valley on its way to the Hallbjarnavörður pass and the junction with Route 52 at Brunnar, a distance of 40km. If you're short of time but want a taste of the barren expanses of the Icelandic Interior, this is a good option, remember, though, that the route doesn't generally open until the middle of June. Not only will you come face to face with the four **glaciers**, Eiríksjökull, Okjökull Langjökull (see p.167) and Þórisjökull, a small oval-shaped ice cap rising to a height of 1350m at the southwestern edge of Langjökull and formerly part of it, but you'll pass through a vast grey **desert** where ferocious sandstorms can appear in seconds transforming what was once a clear vista of majestic ice caps and volcanic sands into an impenetrable cloud of grit and dirt. As the neck of land carrying the road narrows to pass between the Ok and Þórisjökull glaciers, the route climbs and rides along the straight Langihyrggur ridge affording spectacular views of Þórisjökull opposite.

In July and August a daily **bus** leaves Reykjavík at 8am for Kaldidalur and Húsafell, continuing from Húsafell at 3.15pm towards Hraunfossar, Reykholt and Borgarnes before returning to Reykjavík. Note this bus only runs in an anti-clockwise direction, meaning there is public transport from Húsafell to Reykholt but not vice versa. It's possible to break your journey at any point en route and to pick up the same bus either the next day or a couple of days later. However, because the bus only operates north through Kaldidalur (in an anti-clockwise circle from Reykjavík), it's not possible to travel from Húsafell into the valley. The only way to do this would be to try to **hitch** a lift – your chances, however, are not likely to be high because of the low amount of tourist traffic which uses this road.

make the trip, despite what the party guides may tell you – you'll see absolutely nothing. The snowmobiles can also be booked at the service centre building in Húsafell (℡435 1550).

North along the Ringroad: Varmaland and Bifröst

Between Borgarnes and Brú, a distance of 85km, there is little to detain you. However, if you fancy a spot of **hiking** amid lavafields or lush river valleys or scaling a couple of extinct **volcanic craters** before hitting the north coast, there are a couple of diversions close to the Ringroad worthy of your attention. The first is the village of **VARMALAND**, a small and uneventful place popular with holidaying Icelanders northwest of Reykholt. **Buses** from Reykholt to Borgarnes (but not vice versa) pass through the village, whilst coming in the opposite direction from Borgarnes, you simply take a Ringroad bus to Baulan, from where it's an easy five-kilometre walk east along Route 50 then north along the 527. Admittedly, other than its geothermally heated **swimming pool** (℡435 1480) and the market-gardening centre, Laugaland, where mushroom production began in Iceland, there's little to the place but it does offer a decent **day hike** from here to Bifröst of around 13km. The route follows the course upstream of one of the country's best salmon rivers: the Norðurá. Originating high on the moors of Holtavörðuheiði south of Brú, the river flows southwest to meet up with western Iceland's biggest river, the glacial Hvítá, at the head of Borgarfjörður where it finally empties into the sea. This hike is an excellent way to see off-the-beaten-track Iceland: crystal-clear waterfalls, isolated farms and craggy hilltops surrounded by a carpet of summer wildflowers and rich springy grassland. From Varmaland head north along Route 527 to Einifell farm where the road downgrades into a jeep track as it heads to a T-junction west of Höll farm. From here head west around the foot of Hallarmúli hill (260m) towards the Laxfoss **waterfalls** in the Norðurá. Continue past the abandoned farm,Veiðilækur, on to the farmstead at Svartagil and the Glanni **waterfalls**. Here you pick up Route 528 and fork left, crossing the Norðurá and Bjarnardalsá rivers, over the Grábrókarhraun **lavafield** (see below) to join the Ringroad a kilometre or so east of Bifröst.

Accommodation in Varmaland is limited to the predictably named *Gistiheimilið Varmaland* (mid-June to early Aug only, ☎430 1516, ⓕ430 1501, ⓔkof@ismennt.is), which has unadorned rooms (❸) and sleeping bag accommodation (1650kr) and the **campsite** (☎430 1545), a five-minute walk from the guesthouse and pool.

Bifröst

Alternatively you could head straight for minuscule **BIFRÖST**, nothing more than a filling station and a hotel, conveniently situated on the Ringroad and a twenty-five-minute bus ride from Borgarnes. Although a mere dot on the map and of little interest in itself, Bifröst's attractions are all close at hand: a couple of kilometres south of the village, spread either side of the Ringroad, the **Grábrókarhraun** lavafield was formed 3000 years ago when lava spewed from three craters on the north side of the main road, Grábrók, Grábrókafell and a third cone that has now been dug up to provide gravel for road building. Over the centuries, various mosses, heathers and shrubs have quite remarkably managed to get a foothold on many parts of the lava. Otherwise, the forested shores of **Hreðavatn**, 1km southwest of Bifröst, make for a pleasant stroll and a picnic if the weather's playing along; there's also trout fishing here. Look out for plant fossils in the rocks around the lake. Northeast of the village, the **Grábrók** crater can be ascended by means of a marked trail, as can the **Baula** rhyolite mountain (934m), 11km from Bifröst and reached along Route 60 or by **buses** heading for Búðardalur if you don't fancy walking from the Ringroad; although the sides of this cone-shaped mountain are steep and scree-covered there are no particular obstacles to the ascent and once at the summit there's a small shelter made of rocks.

Accommodation is restricted to *Fosshótel Bifröst* (June to late-Aug; ☎433 3090, ⓦwww.fosshotel.is; ❻, ❹ with shared facilities) which also serves **meals**. There's also a **filling station** here. From the forecourt, **buses** continue north to Brú from where they head for Hólmavík (change here for Ísafjörður) in the West Fjords or east towards Akureyri. Limited services also leave for Búðardalur and Reykhólar via Route 60.

Búðardalur and around

North of the Snæfellsnes peninsula lies the wide and sheltered **Hvammsfjörður**, protected from the open sea at its mouth by dozens of small islands. The uninspiring village of **Búðardalur**, at the head of the fjord, although the main service centre for the surrounding hamlets, is best passed over in favour of the rich historical sites close by. From Búðardalur Route 59 runs coast to coast to Hrútafjörður passing through **Laxárdalur**: this is saga country and it was in this valley that one of the best known Viking romances, the **Laxdæla Saga**, was played out. South of here, **Eiríksstaðir**, in Haukadalur, was home to **Eirík the Red**, discoverer of Greenland, and the birthplace of his son, **Leifur**, who went on to discover North America. Although there's plenty of historical significance in this corner of the country, the towns and settlements listed below can be difficult to reach on public transport – although buses do run to Búðardalur, there's no service through Laxárdalur or to Eiríksstaðir.

Búðardalur

Reached by bus from Reykjavík and Borgarnes, **BÚÐARDALUR**, home to just 260 people, provides banking, postal and retail services to the surrounding rural districts. It's an unkempt place, consisting of little more than a collection of a dozen or so suburban streets. In fact, the only reason to break your journey here is to visit nearby Eiríksstaðir. The **tourist information office** (June–Aug Mon–Sat 10am–6pm, Sun midday–6pm; ☎434 1410, ⓦ www.dalir.is), located next door to the village **filling station** and **supermarket** at Vesturbraut 12C, can also help out with information about the local sights. Should you wish to stay in the village, in order to visit Eiríksstaðir or Laxárdalur, there's **guesthouse** accommodation with shared facilities available at *Bjarg*, Dalbraut 2 (☎434 1644, ⓦ www.aknet.is/bjarg; ❸) and a **campsite** (☎434 1132) near the junction of the main Vesturbraut with Miðbraut, opposite the filling station. For food, head for the restaurant in the *Bjarg* or the basic *Dalakjör* restaurant (set lunch menus are around 1000kr) at the filling station at Vesturbraut 10.

Eiríksstaðir

The country which is called Greenland was discovered and settled from Iceland. Eirík the Red was the name of a man from Breiðafjörður who went out there and took possession of land in the place which has since been called Eiríksfjörður. He named the country Greenland and said it would make people want to go there if the country had a good name.

Extract from *Book of the Icelanders* by Ari the Learned (1067–1148).

Twenty kilometres southeast of Búðardalur and reached by Route 586 (8km from the junction with Route 60) into Haukadalur valley, the former farm of **Eiríksstaðir** (June–Aug daily 9am–6pm; 500kr) is one of the most historically significant locations in Iceland. This was the starting point for all westward expansion by the Vikings, first to Greenland and later to the shores of North America. Following a couple of earlier failed archaeological digs, a third attempt was made between 1997 and 2000 to excavate this site, which experts believe to be the most likely home of Eiríkur Þorvaldsson, better known as **Eirík the Red** and father of **Leifur**, who became the first European to set foot in North America (see box on p.173). During the dig archeologists found the remnants of a fifty-square-metre hall dated to 890–980 AD, and, although no timber was unearthed, they did come across doorways, clearly marked out with stone pavings. It's believed that Eiríkur moved here from Drangar in Hornstrandir after marrying Þjóðhildur whose parents already lived at nearby Vatn in Haukadalur. However, he was an unruly man, and, after getting into a row and murdering several of his neighbours, he was driven out of the valley having lived there barely ten to twenty years. Eiríkur then set up home on Suðurey (part of Brokey) and Öxney, two islands east of Stykkishólmur in Breiðafjörður, where he once again fell out with his neighbours who outlawed him from the islands – it was then, with a ship full of friends, that he set sail, charting a course south of Snæfellsnes, for new land and adventure.

An evocative reconstruction of Eiríkur's original **longhouse** now stands in front of the ruins and is a must for anyone interested in the Viking period –

turf walls 12m long by 4m wide huddled around a dirt floor and support a roof made of rafters covered over with twigs atop a layer of turf. **Guides**, evocatively dressed as Vikings, expertly bring the period to life and will also point out the significant features of the ruins. To the untrained eye they can be hard to find (they're located immediately behind the small statue of Leifur; from the statue take the gravel path to the right up the hillside heading towards the waterfall).

The only option for **accommodation** is the comfortable farmhouse at *Stóra-Vatnshorn* (☎434 1342, Ⓦwww.islandia.is/~storavatnshorn), adjacent to Eiríksstaðir, which has single and double rooms (❷) as well as sleeping-bag accommodation for 1500kr; breakfast is 700kr and traditional home cooking is also available. There are fantastic views out over the Haukadalsá river to the summit of Jörfahnúkur (557m) from here – the peace and tranquility of Haukadalur certainly make a night here preferable to one in Búðardalur.

Laxárdalur

The tragedy renowned as one of the great masterpieces of medieval literature, the **Laxdæla Saga** (see box, p.172), unfolded in **Laxárdalur**, the valley northeast of Búðardalur and traversed by Route 59. Although there are few remains of the homes of the characters of the tale, the rolling green landscapes are reminiscent of the most romantic scenes in the epic, and the mere mention to an Icelander of virtually any local place name will conjure up images of forsaken love.

Five kilometres out of Búðardalur just to the north of Route 59 lies the farm of **Hjarðarholt**, established by Ólafur the Peacock and later taken over by his son, Kjartan. In the saga, Ólafur moves his livestock from **Goddastaðir**, now a couple of kilometres to the northeast off Route 587, to Hjarðarholt and asks a local chieftain, Höskuldur, to watch the procession from his own farm. The first of Ólafur's animals were arriving at Hjarðarholt while the last were still leaving Goddastaðir – a visual demonstration of wealth which can still be appreciated today by standing at Hjarðarholt and looking at the distant hillside to the northeast. Incidentally, Höskuldur lived next door to Ólafur at **Höskuldsstaðir**, directly located on Route 59 and still inhabited today. Route 59 continues east over the lake-studded moors of Laxárdalsheiði to the fjord of Hrútafjörður from where Route 61 heads north to Hólmavík in the West Fjords and south to the tiny settlement of Brú (see p.228).

Hvammur and Laugar

The other branch of Ólafur the Peacock's feud-torn family lived a little further north in the valleys which run down to **HVAMMUR**. Located 2km off Route 60, beside Route 590 (take the track leading inland just after the farm, Skerðingsstaðir), this is one of Iceland's oldest settlements and was first occupied by Auður Djúpúðga (Auður the Deepminded) around the year 895, the only woman recorded in the Book of Settlements. Firm but compassionate, she was the matriarch of a leading family in the saga age, though confusingly, the *Laxdæla Saga* refers to her as Unnuras – as taking land on her own account. Auður, the daughter of Ketill Suðureyjajarl (Earl of the Hebrides) and married to King Ólafur Hvíti of Dublin, first came to Iceland with her children and grandchildren around 890 after one of her sons, Þorsteinn, died in battle in Scotland, bringing with her a large number of Scots and Irish. The land settled by Auður was long occupied by her descendants, one of whom was Þorfinn Karlsefni, who explored America for three years in an attempt to establish a Viking settlement. There's a small memorial to Auður at Hvammur, erected by

The Laxdæla Saga

The Laxdæla Saga has three main characters – the tall, blonde and heroic **Kjartan**; the beautiful **Gudrun Osvífsdóttir**; and Kjartan's cousin **Bolli**, who lurks in the background to complete a classic love triangle. It takes thirty or so chapters before the three figures are centre stage, but before they have met, a wise man predicts that Gudrun will have four husbands. Later that day, seeing Kjartan and Bolli swimming together he predicts that one day Bolli will stand over the dead Kjartan, and be killed for his deeds; and thus the inescapable template for the characters' lives is set out to the reader.

Gudrun is married to her first husband against her will and divorces him after two years. She then marries Thord, who incurs the enmity of a family of sorcerers and is drowned as a result. Gudrun then meets Kjartan, and they become close, but Kjartan decides to seek his fortune abroad, and asks Gudrun to wait three years for him, but she refuses.

While in Norway, Kjartan is held hostage, but still finds time to have an affair with the beautiful princess Ingibjorg. Bolli, who has been with his cousin during his courtship and on Viking expeditions, now returns to Iceland and tells Gudrun that Kjartan intends to settle in Norway, whereupon Gudrun's family persuade her to marry Bolli. Kjartan subsequently returns and marries another woman, Hrefna, giving her a priceless headdress as a wedding gift, a gift actually bestowed on him by Ingibjorg, who had told him to give it to Gudrun as a wedding present.

There is no love lost between the two neighbouring households, and things only worsen when the headdress is stolen. In revenge, Kjartan lays siege to Gudrun and Bolli and humiliates them by not letting them go to the lavatory for three days. Eventually, Gudrun goads Bolli and his brothers to try to kill Kjartan – Bolli is reluctant but eventually joins the fight, dealing a death blow to a barely injured but exhausted Kjartan, who gives himself to be killed by Bolli and dies in his arms. Gudrun gloats over his death but Bolli is inconsolable. Kjartan's brothers avenge him by eventually killing Bolli – Gudrun is pregnant at the time, and one of the killers wipes his sword on her dress.

Eventually Gudrun gives birth to a son whom she names Bolli, after his father. She decides she won't marry again until her husband is avenged, and makes a promise to Thorgils Holluson that she will marry no other man in the land than him if he kills her husband's murderer. This he does, at which point Gudrun reveals she is betrothed to another, Thorkel Eyjolfsson, who is abroad. She does indeed marry Thorkel, but he drowns, after which Gudrun becomes a nun. She dies a hermit at Helgafell (see p.178) but before she dies, her son Bolli asks her which man in her life she loved the most, to which she replies "I was worst to him I loved the most" – one of the best-known lines of saga literature.

the University Women of Iceland. She was the first in a long line of prominent Icelanders to live here, the most famous being **Snorri Sturluson** (see p.164), who was born here in 1179; a memorial in his honour stands in the churchyard. **Árni Magnússon**, whose greatest achievement was to persuade Denmark to return many of the sagas to Iceland, was also born and raised here.

Nearby **LAUGUR**, in Sælingsdalur valley on Route 589, just 2km off the main Route 60, was the birthplace of Guðrún Ósvifsdóttir and remains of the old baths where she had frequent meetings with Kjartan can still be seen at Laugar farm; follow the signs to it along Route 589. This valley is also where her husband Bolli was ambushed and murdered by Kjartan's brothers. In Guðrún's day, the geothermal springs here were an important landmark for travellers on the long journey to and from the West Fjords. Inside the school is

The Vikings, Greenland and North America

Although Icelanders don't like to admit it, **Eirík the Red** and his father were actually Norwegian. According to the Book of Settlements, *Landnámabók*, they left Norway to settle in the Hornstrandir region of the West Fjords where they lived until Eirík's father died. Eirík then moved south to Breiðafjörður where he met his wife and set up home with her at Eiríkstadir, in Haukadalur, and fathered his first child, Leifur. From here the couple moved to the island of Öxney at the mouth of Hvammsfjörður, but Eirík committed several murders and was declared an outlaw. Forced out of the country, he sailed far and wide to the west, eventually discovering land in 985 and, according to the sagas, promptly named it **Greenland**, "because it would encourage people to go there if the land had a good name".

He settled at Brattahlíð in a fjord he named after himself, Eiríksfjörður, near present day Narsarsuaq. No doubt inspired by his father, Leifur set out to the west from his new home, Greenland, first reaching barren, rocky land that he named Helluland (Baffin Island), from where he continued south to an area of flat woodland he named Markland (Labrador), in 1000 AD. After another two days at sea he reached more land, where, the sagas have us believe, grapes grew in abundance. Leifur named this land **Vínland**, which experts believe could mean "Wineland". However, since two days' sailing from Labrador would only take him as far south as current day New England, not exactly known for its wines, speculation remains as to where Viking Vínland is.

a small **folk museum** (mid-June to Aug daily 3–7pm; 300kr) with the usual displays on local history.

Today the springs feed a wonderful outdoor **swimming pool** and small steam room (T434 1465) which forms part of the *Edda Laugar* **hotel** (June to mid-Sept ; T434 1265, Www.hoteledda.is; ❸-❹), itself housed in the school; as a result the rooms are somewhat spartan and share facilities; sleeping bag accommodation in a classroom is also available for 1100kr; 1500kr in a room sharing facilities. The **campsite** is adjacent to the hotel. The hotel **restaurant** serves good fish and lamb dishes from 1600kr and provides breakfast. **Buses** to Reykhólar, in the West Fjords (see p.216), call at Laugar (1 daily Tues & Thurs, 2 daily Fri & Sun). From here Route 60 continues north to the bridge over Gilsfjörður, marking the start of the West Fjords. Halfway between Laugar and the fjord, the road follows the course of the Svínadalsá river through Svínadalur, which contains the gorge where Kjartan was ambushed and murdered.

The Snæfellsnes Peninsula

From Borgarnes, Route 54 branches off west past Borg á Mýrum (see p.161) through the sparsely populated **Mýrar** district, a region of low-lying plains and bogs with a few small lakes, heading for the southern coast of the **Snæfellsnes Peninsula**, a rugged yet beautiful arm of the Icelandic west coast that juts out into the Atlantic between Faxaflói bay and Breiðafjörður. The north and south coasts are divided one from the other by a string of majestic mountains which run down the spine of the peninsula and culminate in the magnificent **Snæfellsjökull**, a glacier at the land's westernmost point. Towns here are mostly confined to the north coast, where harbours are good and plentiful, and it's from picturesque **Stykkishólmur**, far and away the best place to base

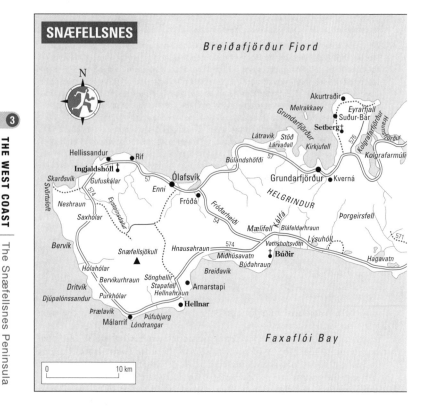

SNÆFELLSNES

Breiðafjörður Fjord

N

Akurtraðir
Melrakkaey   Eyrarfjall
Grundarfjörður   Suður-Bár
Setberg
Látravik   Stöð
Lárvaðal   Kirkjufell   Kolgrafarfjörður
Hellissandur   Rif   Búlandshöfði   Kolgrafarmúli
Ingjaldshöll   57
Skarðsvík   Ólafsvík   Grundarfjörður   Kverná
Gufuskálar   57   Enni   HELGRINDUR
Svörtuloft   574   Fróðá   Þorgeirsfell
Neshraun   Eysteinsdalur   Fróðárheiði   54
Saxhólar   Mælifell   Bláfeldarhraun   571
Bervík   Lýsuhóll
Snæfellsjökull   Hnausahraun   574   Vatnsholtsvötn
Hólahólar   Miðhúsavatn   Búðir   Hagavatn
Bervíkurhraun   Sönghellir   Búðahraun
Dritvík   Stapafell   Breiðavík
Djúpalónssandur   Þúrkhólar   Hellnahraun   Arnarstapi
Prælavík   Hellnar
Málarrif   Púfubjarg
Lóndrangar

Faxaflói Bay

0   10 km

yourself on the peninsula, that boat trips can be made across to the peaceful island haven of **Flatey**. From here a road runs west round the tip of the peninsula via **Ólafsvík** where regular **whale-watching tours** leave daily during the short summer months. If you're keen to head straight for the glacier, it's possible to head west along the less rugged and more sandy south coast to **Arnarstapi** where **snowmobile tours** of Snæfellsjökull can be arranged. Remember though that it's the south coast which more often than not bears the brunt of the moisture-laden low pressure systems that sweep in from the Atlantic, emptying their load here rather than over the mountains on the north coast.

Stykkishólmur and around

The first town of note on the north coast, whether you're approaching on Route 54 from Búðardalur or on Route 56 through Dökkólfsdalur valley from the south, is picturesque **STYKKISHÓLMUR**, with its brightly coloured harbourside buildings. The largest and most enjoyable town on Snæfellsnes with a population of 1230 people, today the place is renowned for its halibut and scallops landed from the waters of Breiðafjörður, which borders the northern coast of the peninsula and is technically more a sea bay than a fjord, full of skerries and rocky islets. However, during the days of the sagas, the ancient

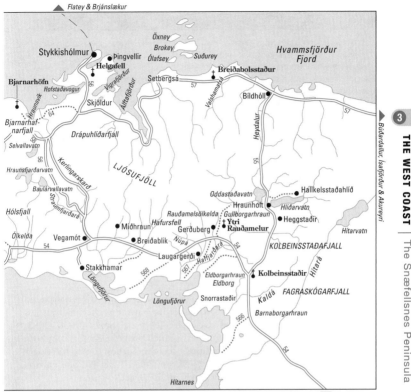

Stykkishólmur
Þingvellir
Helgafell
Bjarnarhöfn
Hofstaðavogur
Skjöldur
Bjarnarhaf-narfjall
Selvallavatn
Drápuhlíðarfjall
Hraunsfjarðarvatn
Baulárvallavatn
Hólsfjall
Ölkelda
Vegamót
Stakkhamar

Öxney
Brokey
Ólafsey
Suðurey
Setbergsá
Breiðabólsstaður
Bildhóll
Heydalur

Hvammsfjörður Fjord

LJÓSUFJÖLL

Oddastaðavatn
Hraunholt
Hallkelsstaðahlíð
Hlíðarvatn
Rauðamelsölkelda
Gullborgarhraun
Heggstaðir
Hafursfell
Gerðuberg
Ytri Rauðamelur
Hítarvatn
Miðhraun
Breiðablik
Núpá
Laugargerði
Hafljarðará
KOLBEINSSTAÐAFJALL
Eldborgarhraun
Eldborg
Kolbeinsstaðir
FAGRASKÓGARFJALL
Löngufjörur
Snorrastaðir
Kaldá
Barnaborgarhraun
Hítarnes

parliament site, **Þingvöllur**, just to the south of the town was regularly attended and the mountain which marks the entrance to the town, **Helgafell**, became the final resting place for saga heroine Guðrún Ósvifsdóttir – both are easily accessible.

Arrival, information and accommodation

Arriving by **bus**, you'll be deposited at the entrance to town by the **filling station** at Aðalgata 25, which also functions as the town's bus station. From there it's a ten-minute walk along Aðalgata to the harbour, where the **ferry** goes to and from Brjánslækur and Flatey (see box on p.178). On the way you'll pass the excellent outdoor **swimming pool** with three hotpots and a sports complex (☎438 1150) at the corner of Borgarbraut. The **tourist information office** (June–Aug daily 10am–6pm; ☎438 1750, ⓦwww.stykkisholmur.is) is a little further into town inside Egilshús, Aðalgata 2, and dishes out information about the town and surrounding area. **Internet** facilities are available at the library (Mon & Thurs 1–7pm all year, plus Fri Sept–May; ☎438 1281) at Bókhlöðuhöfði, near the youth hostel (see p.176).

For **hotel** accommodation, the choice is limited to the box-like and totally charmless rooms at *Hotel Stykkishólmur* (☎430 2100, ⓕ430 2101, ⓔhotelstykkisholmur@simnet.is; ⑤), beyond the swimming pool at the top of

Big whale-watching

Whale-watching tours from Ólafsvík on the Særún and Brimrun, two catamarans operated by Sæferðir (also known as Seatours in English; ☏438 1450, ⓦwww .saeferdir.is; 7950k) depart one to two times daily (generally 10am & 4pm) from June to mid-August and last from four to eight hours, depending on weather and the number of whales there are to spot. The boat leaves from the western side of the harbour, near the tourist office, and follows the shoreline towards the open ocean, where there's a chance of seeing **killer whales** and **bottlenose dolphins**; once the boat is out on the open sea **blue whales** and **humpback whales** are common. Humpbacks are spotted very close to the boat, breaching the surface of the water, or "spy-hopping", the technical term for poking their head out of the water and having a look around. Much, much larger than the humpback, the blue whale is the largest mammal on earth weighing 120,000kg (the equivalent of 2000 people standing on one spot) and is as long as two coaches. Less frequently, **minke whales**, long-finned **pilot whales** and **fin whales** are also spotted.

Bring waterproof clothing, a thick woollen hat and gloves – and plenty of camera film. Light snacks and hot drinks are available from the café on board. You can simply pay as you board but to be sure of a seat it's wise to book in advance with Sæferðir, at Smiðjustígur 3 in Stykkishólmur, or at the tourist office in Ólafsvík (see p.182).

Borgarbraut. From its hill-top location, the hotel certainly has unsurpassed views of the islands and skerries of Breiðafjörður but the service, sadly, is less inspirational. The **youth hostel** *Sjónarhóll* (May to Sept; ☏438 1095, ⓦwww.hostel.is; 1550kr) at Höfðagata 1, is a much better bet in terms of both price and warmth of welcome. **Guesthouse** accommodation can be had down the road at Höfðagata 11 at *Heimagisting Maríu* (☏438 1258; ❸). The **campsite** (☏438 1150) is next to the sports field, off Aðalgata.

The Town

Little more than one long straight main street, **Aðalgata**, which leads to the harbour, it was here that the first settler in the region, Þórólfur Mostraskegg, found his high-seat pillars; in true Viking seafaring fashion he'd thrown them overboard vowing to settle wherever they washed up. He named the *nes*, or promontory, after the god of thunder, Þór, hence the name Þórsnes, Þór's promontory. It wasn't until the beginning of the nineteenth century that things really got moving in Stykkishólmur, though, when a man by the name of Árni Thorlacius (1802–1891) inherited the town's trading rights from his father. In 1832, he set about building **Norska húsið** (Norwegian House; June–Aug daily 11am–5pm; 300kr) at Hafnargata 5, with coarsely hewn timber from Norway, as was the tradition in the nineteenth century – Iceland then, as now, had little timber of its own with which to build. Today the building is still the most impressive in the town. It houses a district **museum** that attempts a potted history of Stykkishólmur; look out for the old black-and-white photographs of Árni and his wife, Anna, with whom he had eleven children, on the second floor which has been reconstructed as their living room. Rather curiously, Icelanders remember Árni not so much for his commercial success in drawing the town into the modern age but for his weather reports from 1845, which have continued uninterrupted to this day. If you want more of Árni, you'll find a triangular concrete and steel structure that serves as a **monument** to him and his wife on Sæbraut at the harbour entrance.

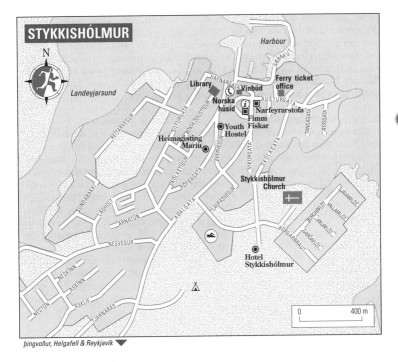

STYKKISHÓLMUR

Harbour

N

Landeyjarsund

Library
Norska
húsid
Heimagisting
Mariu
Youth
Hostel

Vínbúd

Ferry ticket
office
Narfeyrarstofa
Fimm
Fiskar

Stykkishólmur
Church

Hotel
Stykkishólmur

0   400 m

þingvollur, Helgafell & Reykjavík

Whilst down at the harbour it's worth strolling past the Sæferðir shipping office (see below) and continuing around the harbour on Sæbraut to the set of steps which leads up to **Súgandisey**, the rocky island which protects the town from the ravages of the open waters of Breiðafjörður. From the bright orange lighthouse that sits amid tussocky grass at the highest point of the island, there are unsurpassed picture-postcard-perfect **views** of the multi-coloured houses of Stykkishólmur and of Helgafell in the distance. When the wind is not roaring in from the Atlantic (rare), Súgandisey makes a wonderful place for a picnic; there is a wooden bench halfway up the steps to the island, built into the cliff face, which offers some protection from the wind.

The only other sight is the space-age looking **church** (Mon–Fri 10am–5pm; free), a ten-minute walk from the harbour up on a rocky hill off Borgarbraut overlooking the town and with good views on a clear day out towards the waters of Breiðafjörður. Although construction began in 1975, the church wasn't consecrated until fifteen years later; its design includes a vast white ladder-like bell tower rearing up over the doorway and its semicircular domed rear roof. The interior is equally unusual, with hundreds of light bulbs suspended from the ceiling providing the lighting. **Music recitals** (generally classical) are held here every Sunday (mid-June to end Aug; 1000–1500kr), usually at 5pm.

What Stykkishólmur lacks in terms of sights, it more than makes up for with its excellent two hour long **nature watching tours** (May–Sept daily; 3600kr) operated from the harbour by Sæferðir, Smiðjustígur 3 (☎438 1450, ⒲www.saeferdir.is) out to the dozens of tiny islands northeast of Stykkishólmur, where you'll see plenty of species including puffins, eider ducks, kittiwakes, cormorants, and, if you're lucky, the white tailed eagle. During the tour the crew fish for shellfish using a small drag net and everyone onboard gets a chance to taste the contents. The boat passes close to the small and now uninhabited **Öxney** island, east of Stykkishólmur, where Eirík the Red, discoverer of Greenland, and his son, Leifur Eiríksson, who went on to discover North America, lived for several years. Sæferðir also run **whale-watching tours** from nearby Ólafsvík (see box, p.176).

Eating and drinking

For **eating** head straight away to the excellent *Narfeyrarstofa* at Aðalgata 3, a cosy place with red painted walls and square white-framed windows that give the impression of eating in a doll's house; take a table upstairs (no-smoking) where you can later relax in sumptuous leather armchairs under the steep V-shaped roof. The menu here is equally inspired: scallops with garlic and a gorgonzola sauce (1990kr); fillet of sole with camembert and shrimps (1890kr); or tasty solid burgers with salad (790kr). A bottle of wine here is 2900kr. Otherwise you're looking at *Finn Fiskar* across the way at Aðalgata 4, which serves up pizzas (900kr), burgers (from 700kr) as well as more substantial fish dishes such as grilled monkfish with banana (1900kr) – all similar in price to *Narfeyrarstofa* but without the atmosphere. Don't be tempted to eat at the stuffy restaurant inside *Hotel Stykkishólmur*, which is expense-account material. Sandwiches can also be found at the filling station/bus terminal on Aðalgata. The state **liquor store**, *vínbúð* (Mon–Thurs 11am–6pm, Fri 11am–7pm), is at Hafnargata 7, adjacent to Norska húsið.

Þingvöllur and Helgafell

A couple of kilometres south of Stykkishólmur, a small track leads off Route 58 to the east and running parallel with the Nesvogur inlet leads to the old parliament site of **Þingvöllur**, at the mouth of the Nesvogur inlet and right on the water's edge. This became a meeting place for the surrounding area following the death of Þórólfur Mostraskegg. During his lifetime the parliament was on Þórsnes, and, indeed, it was here that Eirík the Red was outlawed following a spate of murders (see box, p.173). A few ruins can still be seen, including a sacrificial site that served as the altar to the god Þór. The site is located at the end of the track from Route 58.

Moving on from Stykkishólmur

Taking the Baldur ferry from Stykkishólmur harbour across Breiðafjörður **to Brjánslækur** (3hr; 1650kr) in the West Fjords, via the island of Flatey (1hr 45min; 1220kr) can save a lengthy and time-consuming drive. Sailings are twice daily from June to August (9am & 4pm) and once daily for the rest of the year on Tuesday, Wednesday, Friday and Saturday at 10am, and at 1pm on Sunday, Monday and Thursday from Stykkishólmur harbour. For more information call ☏438 1450 or check out ⊛www.saeferdir.is.

By taking the 9am ferry, it's possible to continue by bus (June–Aug Mon, Wed & Sat only) from Brjánslækur **to Patreksfjörður** (see p.212) and the **Látrabjarg bird cliffs** (see p.213); the return journey is possible on the same days, using the 7.30pm sailing from Brjánslækur to Stykkishólmur.

From Stykkishólmur, daily buses also run south all year **to Reykjavík** via **Vegamót** and **Borgarnes** and west **to Grundarfjörður** (Mon 8.15am, Fri & Sun 6.20pm) by changing at Vegamót, it's possible to continue along the south coast **to Búðir** then back over to the north coast **to Ólafsvík** and **Hellissandur** (see p.182).

From Þingvöllur, the small mountain you can see to the southwest (though reached via a different route), conspicuous on the flat plain is **Helgafell** (73m), or Holy Mountain, regarded in pagan times as sacred, when early settlers here believed it was an entrance to Valhalla, into which they would go after their deaths. A monastery moved here from the island of Flatey, and stood at the foot of the mountain from 1184 until the Reformation.

It's possible to climb the mountain: the path on the west side is easy enough, but the eastern descent is steep and rocky and you have to pick your way carefully. The ascent is worth making though: at the top there are ruins of a tiny thirteenth-century **chapel**, Tótt, and striking **views** over the islands of Breiðafjörður and to the mountains of the West Fjords. Guðrún Ósvifsdóttir, heroine of *Laxdæla Saga*, spent the last years of her life at the farm at the southern foot of Helgafell and, over 900 years on, people still decorate her grave with wild flowers – it's in the simple churchyard marked by a headstone. Even today, local myth has it that anyone climbing from her grave to the chapel remains on top of the mountain will be granted three wishes, on the condition that they climb in silence and the wishes are pure-hearted, kept totally secret and made whilst standing beside the remains facing east. **To get to Helgafell** it's a four-kilometre walk out of town on Route 58, past the airstrip and beyond the Nesvogur inlet, to the second turn on the left. All **buses** in and out of Stykkishólmur pass this junction.

Services to and from Reykjavík sadly no longer pass through the narrow **Kerlingarskarð** mountain pass off Route 56, south of Stykkishólmur, following the building of a new road to the west. However, this enigmatic loop road is named after an old female troll who, local legend has it, was caught by the sun and turned to stone whilst on her way home from a good night's fishing. Locals say she can still be seen with her line of trout over her shoulder on a ridge of the Kerlingarfjall mountain, opposite Hafrafell, at the northern end of the pass. Stories are also rife of drivers experiencing the eerie presence of an extra passenger in their cars as they drive through the pass.

Flatey

The largest of the Breiðafjörður islands, **FLATEY** is a tranquil haven of two dozen or so restored wooden cottages set amid fields of bright yellow buttercups. If you like the idea of having nothing to do all day but stroll through undisturbed meadows whilst taking in magnificent vistas of the west fjord mountains and Snæfellsjökull, then dining by evening on succulent cod caught the same afternoon, this is the place to come. The weather is most dependable in August, but remember if you're coming here out of season the island will be virtually deserted, since most of the houses are only occupied in summer by Reykjavík cityslickers; just four people spend the winter on Flatey.

Although today low key in the extreme, Flatey was once one of Iceland's leading cultural centres, and in 1172 a **monastery** was founded on the island's highest point, a little behind where the present-day church stands, though there's nothing left of it today. The island was also once home to the **Flateyjarbók**, a collection of illuminated medieval manuscripts written on 113 calfskins. Although the book was written at Víðidalstunga, in northern Iceland around 1387, it turned up here and remained in the possession of a local farmer's family until they gave it to the Bishop of Skálholt, who in turn sent it by royal request to King Frederik III of Denmark in 1659. The Flateyjarbók finally returned to Iceland in 1971 and is today housed in the Árni Magnússon institute in Reykjavík (see p.69).

The island

From the ferry jetty it's a ten-minute walk down the rough track that passes as the island's one and only road to the **old village**, a restored collection of painted houses nestling around a tiny **harbour**. It's from here that the island's sheep are painstakingly bundled into boats and taken to surrounding islands for summer grazing – quite a sight if you're around to witness it.

Past the harbour the track bears right, turns into a well-trodden path and climbs a little to the diminutive **Lundaberg** cliffs where you'll find plenty of **black guillemot**, **kittiwakes**, **fulmars** and **puffins** from April onwards, when the birds first start to arrive; half of all the 37 different species of bird that breed in Iceland are found on the islands of Breiðafjörður. Beyond the hill, the path continues towards the eastern part of the island, which has been declared a **nature reserve**, marked by the odd sign or two and closed to the public during the breeding season (May 15–July 20); the birds migrate south in late August or early September. It's possible, though, to pass round the edge of the reserve, following the marked wooden posts, to the island's south coast where you'll be bombarded by arctic tern who show no mercy for man nor beast – even the island's sheep are subject to regular divebombing raids. If you don't mind this (keeping still seems to deter the birds a little), there are some secluded pebbly coves here, home to the odd wrecked fishing boat, with excellent views on a clear day across to Snæfellsjökull. From the shoreline, the path continues up past the campsite (see below) up to the **church** with its dramatic roof and wall paintings of island life – and puffins — by the Catalan painter **Baltasar**. Quite the entrepreneur, whilst visiting the island in the 1960s he suggested painting the church in return for free accommodation; his picture behind the altar shows Christ, unconventionally wearing a traditional Icelandic woolly sweater, standing alongside two local sheep farmers. After much hard work, the yellow building behind the church has been restored to its former glory and proudly claims the title of the oldest and smallest library in Iceland, established in 1864.

Practicalities

For details of the ferry from Stykkishólmur, see the box on p.178. Right by the harbour's edge is the island's only **guesthouse**, *Vogur* (℡438 1413, Ⓔvogurflatey@simnet.is; sleeping bag accommodation 2500kr, ❸), a rickety old wooden house dating from 1885 that was once used to accommodate priests sent to serve on Flatey. There are only four rooms here, so it's wise to book in advance. A steep staircase leads to the two top rooms, right under the eaves, one of which has superb views out over Breiðafjörður. Be sparing with water here since the guesthouse has access to the only clean well on the island; you'll often see people dropping in to fill up their buckets. The restaurant also functions as a small **café** during the day, serving up good home-made cakes and lunches. By evening, you can sample fresh fish landed just a matter of hours earlier for around 1500kr, or alternatively, after the end of the breeding season in mid-July flambéed puffin is on the menu for 2300kr. At lunchtime there's soup for 550kr or pasta salad at 850kr. The **campsite** is in a field behind Krákuvör farm, on the main track to the main harbour, and looks out over the sea. The island **post office** (Mon–Fri midday–1.30pm) is between the farm and the ferry jetty.

Berserkjahraun and Grundarfjörður

From Stykkishólmur, one daily bus (2 buses Fri & Sun) heads west along Route 57 to Grundarfjörður. Just after the junction with Route 56 the road veers round the 4000-year-old **Berserkjahraun lavafield** named after the two **Berserkers** who cleared a route through it in 982 AD. Berserkers, periodically mentioned in the sagas, were formidable warriors, able to go into a trance that made them impervious to wounds; much valued as fighters they were given a wide berth socially, since they were considered to be very dangerous. Local man Víga-Styr persuaded the two to undertake this odd task because he had to take a circuitous route round the lava every time he wanted to visit his brother's farm. However, he later killed them after one fell in love with his daughter. Look carefully and you'll see the path, known as Beserkjagata, which is still visible in the lava; beside it is the men's burial mound.

Once across the small bridge over Hraunsfjörður, the road soon comes to **GRUNDARFJÖRÐUR**, dominated by the neighbouring **Kirkjufell** mountain. Established in 1786 by the Danish king as one of six commercial centres in Iceland, the place exerted a strong influence on the west coast; in the early 1800s, for example, traders could only operate in the region if they had a branch in Grundarfjörður. From 1800–60, French fishermen also profited from the excellent harbour here and used the town as a base, owning the church, hospital and shipping operations. When they left, they dismantled their buildings and even exhumed their dead, shipping the bodies back to France. Today the village and its 850 inhabitants depend on their position as the commercial centre of western Iceland, and the local freezing plant, for prosperity. Although Grundarfjörður isn't bursting with attractions, it is an excellent place to get the lowdown on village life in Iceland; locals Johanna and Shelagh run **guided walks** around the place, explaining how life in rural Iceland is changing and offering a first-hand insight into everything from the local fish factory to the village church; contact them at Detours, Hlíðarvegur 15 (☎562 6533, ⓔdetours@grundarfjordur.com).

Practicalities

The **tourist information office** (ⓦwww.grundarfjordur.is) is located in the *Eyrbyggja* centre at Grundargata. For **Internet** access head for the **library** (☎430 8570) at Grundargata 16. The local **swimming pool** (☎438 6964) boasting an outdoor pool, two hotpots and sauna is located at the southern end of Borgarbraut.

Accommodation can be found at the functional *Hótel Framnes* (☎438 6893, ⓦwww.hotel-framnes.is; ❹), Nesvegur 6–8, or better at the excellent new **youth hostel** (mid-May to mid-Sept ☎562 6533, ⓦwww.hostel.is) at Hlíðarvegur 15, complete with cosy rooms and two kitchens. The **campsite** (☎438 6813) is 1km east of the village at the farm located by the Kverná river. For top-notch **eating and drinking** check out the homely *Krákan*, Sæból 13 (signed from the main road); with its heavy wooden tables draped in crocheted white tablecloths, this place really is a home from home, renowned as much for its excellent fresh fish (everything from catfish to halibut; 1800kr) and tasty homemade lobster soup (950kr), as its gregarious hosts, Halla and Finni. As you step through the door look out for the wooden carving, on the piano, of the

Moving on from Grundarfjörður

Moving on from Grundarfjörður **by bus** to Ólafsvík involves backtracking to Stykkishólmur in order to pick up a service to Vegamót on the south coast, from where there are limited connections back north to Ólafsvík (see Moving on from Stykkishólmur, p.178, for details of connections).

naked man with cigarette in mouth, bottle of beer in hand carrying a pizza – it's Finni. The other option, *Kaffi 59*, Grundargata 59, is the place to come for pizzas, burgers and light snacks. If you want to buy **alcohol**, you'll have to time things carefully since the *vínbúð* at Hrannarstígur 3 has ludicrously short opening hours (Mon–Thurs 5–6pm, Fri 4–6pm; ☎438 6994).

Ólafsvík

ÓLAFSVÍK is not only the most productive fishing town on Snæfellsnes, it is Iceland's oldest established trading town, granted its charter in 1687. Squeezed between the sea and the towering Enni (415m), it's a quiet working fishing village whose population goes about its daily business seemingly unmoved by the groups of travellers who turn up here in search of Ólafsvík's main attraction, the chance of spotting **whales**, including the biggest mammal on earth, the mighty blue whale (see box, p.176). The town is also one of several places to use as a base for climbing Snæfellsjökull, the nearby glacier (see box opposite).

Other than whales, Ólafsvík's only other sight is the **Gamla Pakkhúsið** on Ólafsbraut, a solid-looking timber warehouse built in 1841 by the town's leading trading firm who, naturally, dealt in fish. Today it houses a **folk museum** (late May to Aug daily 9am–7pm; 300kr), which has a few good black-and-white photographs of the town and the obligatory exhibitions about fishing. The **church** on Kirkjutún is worth a quick look for its three-legged detached bell tower and its sharply pointed spire.

Practicalities

A once-daily bus (2 daily Fri & Sun) runs all year round from Reykjavík and Borgarnes to Ólafsvík. The **tourist office** (late May to Aug daily 9am–7pm; ☎436 1543, ⓦwww.snb.is/pakkhus) is in the Gamla Pakkhúsið, on Ólafsbraut. There's little choice when it comes to **accommodation**: the *Hótel Ólafsvík* (☎436 1650, ⓔhotelo@simnet.is; ❻), with small but passable rooms with shared bath at Ólafsbraut 20, and the not dissimilar but much cheaper *Guesthouse Ólafsvík* (☎436 1300, ⓕ436 1302; ❸) opposite at Ólafsbraut 19. The campsite (☎436 6900) with showers and hot and cold running water is on Dalbraut, about 1km east of the town centre, beside the Hvalsá river.

Sadly, a meal in Ólafsvík is not going to be the culinary highlight of any trip to Iceland. The most tasteful place for something filling is the **restaurant** inside the *Hótel Ólafsvík*, where the dish of the day (usually fish) goes for around 1650kr but there are also burgers and sandwiches. Across the road, in the cheap restaurant attached to the *Guesthouse Ólafsvík*, things are altogether more basic, not to mention drab: panfried fish (990kr), lam steek (1490kr), plus pizzas from 990kr, as well as more sandwiches and burgers (690kr). The *vínbúð* (Mon–Thurs 2–6pm, Fri 10am–6pm; ☎436 1226) is at Mýrarholt 12. The indoor **swimming pool** (☎436 1199) is at Ennisbraut 9.

Rif and Hellissandur

From Ólafsvík, Route 574 continues west past a dramatic beach of black volcanic sand, Harðikambur, on its way towards the minuscule fishing hamlet of **Rif**, which, with a population of just 150 souls, is really nothing more than a well-protected harbour and a few fish-processing plants, and its marginally bigger neighbour **HELLISSANDUR**, 2km further on. Known locally as just Sandur, the latter of these two places is the westernmost settlement on Snæfellsnes and home to most of the fishermen from nearby Rif. There's very

> Enter the Snæfellsjökull crater, which is kissed by Scatari's shadow before the first of July, adventurous traveller, and thou wilt descend to the centre of the Earth.
>
> *Journey to the Centre of the Earth*, Jules Verne

Made world famous in the nineteenth century by Jules Verne's *Journey to the Centre of the Earth*, **Snæfellsjökull** stands guard at the very tip of the peninsula to which it gave its name (**Snæfell** means "Snow Mountain"; Snæfellsnes means "Snow Mountain Peninsula"). It is from here that Verne's hero, the German geologist Professor Lidenbrock of Hamburg, descends into a crater in the dormant volcano under the glacier and embarks upon a fantastic subterranean journey accompanied by his nephew and Icelandic guide with the very un-Icelandic name of Hans. The Professor has managed to decipher a document written in runic script that leads him to believe that this is the way to the centre of the earth; rather inexplicably he finally emerges on the volcanic Mediterranean island of Stromboli. This remote part of Iceland has long been associated with supernatural forces and mystery, and stories like this only strengthen this belief. In recent years the glacier even became a point of pilgrimage for New Age travellers who, to the bemusement of locals, consider the area one of the world's great power centres, though they're not much in evidence today.

Experienced hikers have a choice of three **ascents** of the 1446-metre-high, three-peaked glacier, which incidentally sits on a dormant volcano marked by a large crater, one kilometre in diameter, with cliff walls 200m high; three eruptions have occurred under the glacier in the past 10,000 years, the last around 250 AD. **Maps** and **information** about the routes can be found at the tourist offices in Ólafsvík and Arnarstapi.

The easiest is via Route F570 **from Ólafsvík**, which begins just 1km east of the town's campsite and runs through Gerðubergsdalur valley up to the glacier's eastern edge then via the narrow Jökulháls pass down to Arnarstapi on the south coast. Although this road is passable by four-wheel-drive vehicles, it's often blocked by snow, even in the height of summer. Take extreme care once on the ice for hidden crevasses; picks and crampons may be needed; allow three to four hours to reach the glacier and another two to descend to Arnarstapi. This approach is also possible **from Arnarstapi** (see p.186), also via the F570, leading first past the eastern flank of Stapafell (526m) and winding its way up to the glacier; allow at least five hours to reach the ice. This is the route taken by the **snowmobile tours** from Arnarstapi.

The third and longest ascent of the glacier begins **from Hellissandur** (see opposite); take Route 574 west out of town to its junction with the unnumbered road that follows the course of the Móðulækur river up through Eysteinsdalur valley to the glacier – note that on some maps this road is not marked. From the road's end a walking path continues up to the glacier's highest point, Jökulþúfur (1446m) atop three crags on the crater rim, from where another track leads down the ice cap's eastern flank to join up with mountain road F570.

little to do in Hellissandur other than to pay a quick visit to the two old **fishermen's cottages**, complete with turf rooves, which make up the Maritime Museum, **Sjómannagarður** (June–Aug daily except Wed, 9am–midday & 1–6pm; 300kr) beside the main road, Útnesvegur. In the larger of the two buildings is the oldest rowing boat in Iceland, dating from 1826. Otherwise, Hellissandur makes a good base from which to explore the various **hikes** around western Snæfellsnes (see box).

Practicalities

A daily **bus** (2 daily Fri & Sun) runs from Reykjavík via the south coast of Snæfellsnes and Ólafsvík to Rif and Hellissandur. For details of travelling by bus from Hellissandur to Arnarstapi, see p.153. The town's few facilities include a branch of *Landsbankinn* **bank** at Klettsbúð 4, a **swimming pool** (T 436 6710), at the junction of Klettsbúð and Skólabraut, and a **filling station** adjacent to the hotel (see below).

For **accommodation** there's the brand spanking new *Hótel Edda Hellissandur* (mid-May to Sept; T 430 8600, W www.hoteledda.is; ●) parallel to the main road at Klettsbúð 9, which also has sleeping bag accommodation in classrooms for 1100kr or in a room with shared facilities for 1500kr. Alternatively the **campsite** is on the eastern edge of the village by the main road, Útnesvegur, beautifully set by an open meadow. The seafront

Hiking around western Snæfellsnes

Hellissandur makes a good base for exploring the foot of the Snæfellsjökull and the surrounding **lavafields**. A recommended day hike of around 20km leads from the village to Eysteinsdalur valley; take the unmarked secondary road between the campsite and the maritime museum that leads towards the glacier. After around 1km the road becomes a hiking path which strikes out across the **Prestahraun** lavafield, joining up after 4km with the un-numbered road that runs up through the valley. Here, on the south side of the road, a signed path leads up to the hill, **Rauðhóll**, to a red scoria crater. An impressive rift in the lava can also be seen to the east of the hill. Continue another 1km along the road towards the glacier and you'll come to a signposted path to the south of the road, which leads to the prominent basalt spur, **Klukka**, and a beautiful waterfall, **Klukkufoss**, where the Móðulækur river flows through a narrow canyon lined with basalt columns. Back on the main road and another 1km towards the glacier, a path to the north of the road leads to the **Blágil** ravine, where the Ljósulækir glacial river thunders through the narrow rugged gorge. To return to Hellissandur, retrace your steps along the main road, beyond the turn for the waterfall, to the hiking path that heads out to the north across the **Væjuhraun** lavafield for Rif. From here, simply head west along the coastal road to Hellissandur. Maps of these routes should be available from the tourist office in Ólafsvík (see p.182) and at the hotel in Hellissandur (see above).

Another recommended day hike (18km) leads first to the sandy bay, **Skarðsvík**, walled in by cliffs and crags on its northern and western edges. The lava above the cliffs is overgrown with moss and can be a good place to see rare plants. Excellent **fishing** can be had in the bay's protected waters and it's therefore a favourite spot for local boats. To get here, follow Route 574 west out of Hellissandur to its junction with the unnumbered road signed for Skarðsvík; it's at this point that the main road swings inland, heading for the glacier and the turn for Eysteinsdalur valley. Just 2km west of Skarðsvík the road terminates at the peninsula's westernmost point, **Önd-verðarnes**, a dramatic and weatherbeaten spot marked only by a lonely lighthouse and a stone well which legend has it is linked to three springs: one of fresh water, one of sea water and one of wine. The promontory is a favourite destination for basking **seals**, who favour the pebbly beach here. South of the cape the **Svörtuloft** cliffs are worth a visit; swarming with **seabirds** in summer, the cliffs provided a major source of eggs and birds for the tables of local villagers until the 1950s, when living standards began to rise. The free-standing crag in the sea here, **Skálasnagi**, was once connected to the mainland by a natural stone bridge until it fell victim to the pounding of Atlantic breakers in 1973. From the cliffs, a path heads east, inland through the **Neshraun** lavafield to an area of small hillocks known as **Neshólar** before emerging at Skarðsvík.

pizza and seafood **restaurant** at Hellisbraut 10, *Svörtuloft*, is the best bet for food.

Dritvík, Djúpalónssandur and Lóndrangar

On leaving Hellissandur, the horizon is dominated by the huge mast that transmits the 189kHz long-wave signal for Icelandic national radio, anchored down by wire cables against the brute force of Atlantic storms. Beyond this last sign of civilisation the landscape becomes increasingly desolate and the road surface more and more potholed – there's nothing but wilderness between here and **Dritvík** bay, 24km southwest of Hellissandur, first along Route 574 then down the 572 signed for Dritvík and Djúpalónssandur. Once home to sixty fishing boats and accordingly one of the most prolific fishing villages on the peninsula, today the bay is uninhabited, and centuries of fishing tradition would have been completely lost if it were not for the continuing presence today of four mighty lifting **stones** at nearby **Djúpalónssandur beach**, a short stroll south from the bay, all with individual names: the largest, *fullsterkur* (full strength) weighs in at 155kg, next comes *hálfsterkur* (half strength) at 140kg, then *hálf-drættingur* (weakling) 49kg and finally *amlóði* (useless) weighing just 23kg. Any fisherman worth his salt had to be able to lift at least the latter two onto a ledge of rock at hip height to prove his strength. The smallest stone is now broken – perhaps after one too many attempts by weakling tourists.

The lofty rock pillars, **Lóndrangar**, are just 5km southeast of the Djúpalón lagoon and easily reached from Route 574 on the unnumbered road signed "Malarrif". The taller of the two is 75m high and known locally as the "Christian pillar", with its smaller neighbour called the "heathen pillar" although nobody seems to know why; both are remnants of a basalt cinder cone. Although there's no public transport here, it is possible to get here on the Snæfellsnes **excursion tour** to and from Ólafsvík (see p.153).

Hellnar

Just like its western neighbour of Dritvík, the tiny settlement of **HELLNAR** was once one of the peninsula's most prosperous fishing communities. However, the village is better known as the birthplace of one of medieval Iceland's greatest explorers and travellers, **Guðríður Þorbjarnardóttir**, the wife of Þorfinnur Karlsefni. Together they attempted to settle in Viking Vínland in 1004, and, indeed, Guðríður gave birth to the first white child to be born in America, Snorri Þorfinnsson. She eventually settled at Glaumbær, near Sauðárkrókur, where a statue in her memory stands in the churchyard. Today though, Hellnar consists of nothing more than a couple of farm buildings and the odd holiday cottage either side of a steep, dead-end road that winds its way down to a picturesque hoof-shaped **harbour** and a tiny pebbly **beach** where the occasional fishing boat is moored. To the left of the harbour, the sea cave, **Baðstofa**, is known for its rich birdlife as well as its unusual light shades and hues caused by the swell of the sea.

The old salting house, dating from 1937, still stands on the harbourside, its walls now housing a charming **café**, the *Fjöruhúsið* (late May to late Sept daily noon–7pm; ☎435 6844), which serves up home-made cakes and great espresso, as well as some excellent fish soup of an evening when the arty interior lighting is provided by a dozen light bulbs suspended on long wire flexes. If the weather's poor, sit inside and savour the uninterrupted views of the Atlantic through the café's small square windows; in fine weather you can sit on the wooden terrace outside, which overlooks the harbour and the boulder-strewn bay.

Arnarstapi

From the cave at Hellnar, an easy **path** (2.5km) leads east along the cliff tops to nearby **ARNARSTAPI**, at the foot of Stapafell (526m). The village itself comprises a few holiday cottages and a **harbour**, reached by following the road through the village down to the sea – but beware of the large number of arctic tern that gather here during summer and take pleasure in divebombing unsuspecting intruders. On entering the village look out too for the large stone **monument** to the pagan-age figure Barður Snæfellsás, who, according to local legend still lives in Snæfellsjökull and protects the area from evil.

The village is the starting point for hikes and jeep drives up to Snæfellsjökull via Route F570 (see box, p.183), but is better known for its **snowmobiling** excursions across the glacier. One-hour trips depart from here and go up onto the icecap (5200kr per person for two sharing one snowmobile, 6400kr for your own machine). Speeding along the ice top is an exhilarating experience, and the views of the glacier and the coastline are quite simply breathtaking when the weather is good – but don't be tempted to head onto the ice if it's raining because you'll see nothing. If speed isn't your thing, a slower snowcat, a sort of open-top truck on caterpillar tracks, also carries groups of twenty or so across the ice (3500kr). Buses leave from the tourist information office (see below) every two hours between 9am and 7pm (daily May to Sept; other times on request) for the glacier where, once on its snout, you transfer to snowmobile. With your own transport it's possible to begin the tour there; from Arnarstapi, head east on Route 574 to the junction with mountain road F570, from where the snowmobile tours are signed. Although this road can be extremely bumpy, even small cars can use it.

Practicalities

Although there's no public transport to and from Arnarstapi it is possible to get here by **excursion bus** (June–Aug) from Ólafsvík and Hellissandur. From Arnarstapi, the bus leaves at 1.30pm for Hellissandur and Ólafsvík and at 4.40pm for Búðir and Ólafsvík; take the later bus and change at Búðir for Reykjavík. What little life there is in the village is centred on the red-walled, turf-rooved cottage, *Snjófell* (☎ 435 6783, ⓦ www.snjofell.is), by the car park off the main road, which acts as the **tourist information office** and a booking centre for the one and only choice of **accommodation**, the yellow-walled *Arnarfell* next door. There are just fifteen rooms (❷) here offering cosy farmhouse-style accommodation; alternatively there's sleeping-bag accommodation (from 1400kr); cooking facilities are also available; breakfast is 750kr. Bikes are also available for rent here at 1200kr per day. The campsite (☎435 6783 or ☎854 5150) is close by. Although the restaurant inside the Snjófell complex is the only place to eat, it does offer a decent menu, with some good fish dishes.

Búðir and Lýsuhóll

Nineteen kilometres east of Arnarstapi, and served by all buses from Reykjavík, **BÚÐIR** is a romantic, windswept location, a former fishing village at the head of the sweeping expanse of white sand that backs the bay here, Búðavík. The settlement, like so many others in this part of the country, was abandoned in the early nineteenth century and today consists of nothing more than a hotel and a church, both situated just a stone's throw from the ocean. Surrounded by the **Búðahraun lavafield**, rumoured to be home to countless leprechauns, and enjoying unsurpassed views out over the foam-capped waves of the Atlantic, the tiny **church**, which dates from 1703, pitch-black and with three white-framed windows, cuts an evocative image when viewed from the adjoining graveyard with the majestic Snæfellsnes mountain range as a backdrop. Look out too for the unusual wall, made of lava and topped with turf, that surrounds the churchyard.

The enchanting *Hótel Búðir* (☎ 435 6700, ⓦ www.budir.is; ❼), located in a timber building dating from 1836, was once a favourite haunt of Iceland's Nobel-prize winning author, Halldór Laxness, who would come here to write in a room where he had a view of the majestic Snæfellsjökull glacier. Following a recent renovation work has been underway to restore the hotel to its former glory. **Rooms** here, although a little small, enjoy a view either of the lavafield or of the sandy bay.

Five kilometres east of Búðir and reached on Route 54, the dot on the map that is **LÝSUHÓLL** is one of the few places on the peninsula with its own source of geothermal mineral water. The spring provides natural hot bubbling water for the outdoor **swimming pool** (☎ 435 6730) and hot pots which are open daily from mid-June to late August (10am–10pm) and offers fantastic views of the surrounding mountains. For a place to stay there are **cabins** (☎ 435 6716, ⓔ lysuholl@islandia.is; ❸) and a **campsite**, both on the same site as the swimming pool. The farmhouse here has a small **restaurant** which is good for snacks such as soup and home-made bread. All **buses** to and from Reykjavík call here.

East along Route 54 to Borgarnes

From Lýsuhóll, **Route 54** continues east crossing the powerful Straumfjarðará river flowing down from Seljafell before reaching the lonely Löngufjörur bay. From here (opposite the turn for Route 567) an unnumbered road signed for "Rauðamelur" and "Gerðuberg" heads inland to the **Gerðuberg basalt columns**, the longest (around 2km) in Iceland. This escarpment of grey basalt rising to a height of around 50m resembles a shattered cliff face with piles of scree and broken rock lying at its base. From here Route 54 continues east (it's a further 35km to Borg á Mýrum) around the **Eldborgarhraun** lavafield and, as the road swings east for Borgarnes, you get a view of the oval-shaped crater, **Eldborg**, sitting conspicuously amid the flat expanse of the lava. To the east of Eldborg, **Fagraskógarfjall** mountain was the haunt of Grettir of *Grettir's Saga*: "a savage and dreadful place" according to William Morris, who was here in 1871 – though these days it seems much more green and peaceful. North of here, along Route 55, the caves of **Gullborgarhraun** lavafield are a maze of intricate passageways containing coloured stalagmites and stalactites. It's advisable though to seek local advice before exploring them. Once again, **buses** to and from Reykjavík on Route 54 pass these attractions.

Travel details

Buses

The bus details given below are relevant for May to September; for winter times, visit ⓦ www.bsi.is.

Akranes to: Bifröst (daily; 1hr); Borgarnes (4 daily; 1hr); Búðardalur (4 weekly; 2hr 15min); Búðir (daily; 2hr); Grundarfjörður (daily; 2hr 45min); Hellissandur (daily; 3hr); Ólafsvík (daily; 2hr 45min); Reykjavík (5 daily; 1hr); Stykkishólmur (daily; 2hr)

Bifröst to: Akranes (daily; 1hr); Borgarnes (daily; 30min); Reykjavík (daily; 1hr 40min)

Borgarnes to: Akranes (4 daily, 1hr); Bifröst (daily; 30min); Búðardalur (5 weekly; 1hr 30min); Búðir (daily; 1hr 15min); Grundarfjörður (daily; 2hr); Hellissandur (daily; 1hr 45min); Ólafsvík (daily; 1hr 30min); Reykjavík (4 daily; 1hr); Stykkishólmur (daily; 1hr 15min)

Búðardalur to: Akranes (5 weekly; 2hr 15min); Borgarnes (5 weekly; 1hr 30min); Reykjavík (5 weekly; 2hr 45min)

Búðir to: Akranes (daily; 2hr); Borgarnes (daily; 1hr 15min); Hellissandur (daily; 30min); Ólafsvík (daily, 15min); Reykjavík (daily; 2hr 30min)

Grundarfjörður to: Akranes (daily; 2hr 45min); Borgarnes (daily; 2hr); Reykjavík (daily; 2hr 15min); Stykkishólmur (daily; 45min)

Hellissandur to: Akranes (daily; 2hr 30min); Borgarnes (daily; 1hr 45min); Búðir (daily; 30min);

Ólafsvík (daily; 15min); Reykjavík (daily; 3hr)

Ólafsvík to: Akranes (daily; 2hr 45min); Borgarnes (daily; 1hr 30min); Búðir (daily; 15min); Reykjavík (daily; 2hr 45min)

Reykholt to: Borgarnes (daily; 45min); Reykjavík (2 weekly; 1hr 45min)

Stykkishólmur to: Akranes (daily; 2hr); Borgarnes (daily; 1hr 15min); Grundarfjörður (daily; 45min); Reykjavík (daily; 2hr 30min)

Ferries

The ferry details given below are relevant for May to September; for winter times, check the relevant entries in the guide.

Flatey to: Stykkishólmur (2 daily; 1hr 45min)

Stykkishólmur to: Flatey (2 daily; 1hr 45min)

The West Fjords

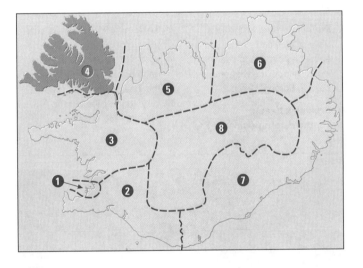

CHAPTER 4 # Highlights

* **Hiking in Hornstrandir**
Experience nature in the raw in
this remote and unspoilt
national park of lush valleys
and rocky plateaux on the very
edge of Europe. See p.201

* **Dynjandi, Arnarfjörður**
Meaning "The Thundering
One", this mighty triangular-
shaped waterfall is West
Fjords nature at its most pow-
erful. See p.210

* **Puffin spotting, Látrabjarg**
Seek out Iceland's most
endearing bird along this vertig-
inous cliffface, the westernmost
point in Europe. See p.213

* **Breiðavík beach,
southwestern peninsula** The
white sands and aquamarine
water of this idyllic bay make
the perfect place to chill out
and work on your tan –
weather permitting.
See p.214

* **Hótel Djúpavík, Strandir
coast** Enjoy a relaxing stay at
this remote retreat, one of
Iceland's friendliest hotels, in
the former herring capital of
the West Fjords. See p.220

* **Swimming in Krossneslaug
pool, Norðurfjörður** Cast off
your clothes and soak in the
geothermally heated waters of
this beachside pool on the
very edge of the North
Atlantic. See p.221

The West Fjords

Attached to the mainland by a narrow isthmus of land barely 10km wide, the **West Fjords** are one of the most breathtakingly beautiful and least-visited corners of Iceland. This peninsula of 8600 square kilometres, stretching out into the icy waters of the Denmark Strait, with its dramatic fjords cutting deep into its heart, is the result of intense glaciation. Everything here is extreme – from the table mountains that dominate the landscape, plunging precipitously into the Atlantic, to the ferocious storms that have gnawed the coastline into countless craggy inlets. Life up here, on the edge of the Arctic Circle, is tough – even in summer, temperatures seldom rise above 10°C, and drifting pack ice is never far from the north coast.

Since flat land is at a premium in this rugged part of the country, towns and villages have grown up on the narrow strip of lowland that separates the mountains from the fjords. Geologically all but cut off from the outside world, the people of the West Fjords have historically turned to the sea for their livelihood, and today the majority of the 7900 people who still live here are financially dependent on **fishing** and its related industries. However, the traditional way of life is changing, and the effects of rural depopulation are being felt in every village as outlying farms are abandoned and dozens of young people choose the bright lights of Reykjavík over a precarious and uncertain future on the very edge of Europe.

The unforgiving geography of the West Fjords makes travel here difficult and convoluted. Many roads are surfaced with gravel, and they're always potholed and often circuitous. **Route 61**, for example, wiggles its way exasperatingly round no fewer than seven deeply indented fjords en route to the regional capital, **Ísafjörður**. Benefiting from a spectacular setting on a narrow spit of land jutting out into **Ísafjarðardjúp**, the town makes an excellent base from which to explore this 75-kilometre-long arm of the Denmark Strait at the heart of the West Fjords, plus **Drangajökull**, the only glacier in the region, and the outstanding natural beauty of the uninhabited **Hornstrandir** peninsula, which offers some of the wildest and most rewarding hiking in Iceland. From Ísafjörður, Route 60 weaves its way over mountain tops, round several fjords and past a handful of tiny fishing villages on its way to the ferry port of **Brjánslækur**, from where a daily boat leaves the West Fjords for Flatey and Snæfellsnes. A brooding, lonely peninsula reaches out into the Atlantic from this point, terminating at **Látrabjarg**, Europe's most westerly point, and one of the world's greatest bird cliffs, with large numbers of puffins, razorbills and other seabirds and **Breiðavík**, one of Iceland's most stunning beaches with mile upon mile of deserted golden sand. Nearby **Patreksfjörður**, the second town of the West Fjords, is the only place in the region with a population big enough for life to go on independently of Ísafjörður. Meanwhile, on the other side of

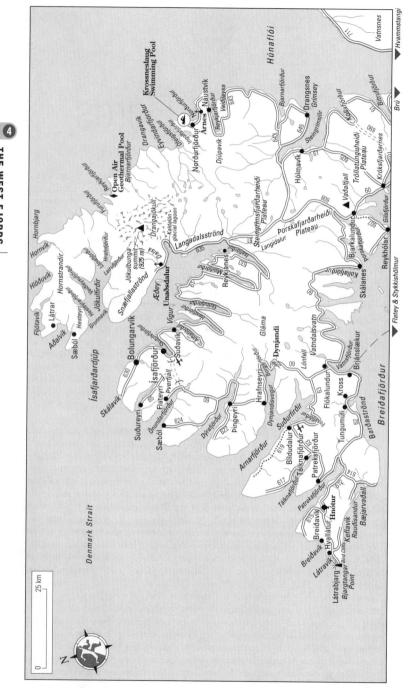

Krossneslaug
Swimming Pool

Open Air
Geothermal Pool

Hvammstangi ▶

Brú ▶

Flatey & Stykkishólmur ▶

Denmark Strait

25 km

0

the West Fjords, the eastern Strandir coast, which stretches north from the busy fishing village of **Hólmavík**, is hard to beat for splendid isolation, its few villages hardly visited by tourists, and with some of the most dramatic, forbidding landscapes this corner of the country has to offer, particularly around the former herring port of **Djúpavík**.

As for **getting around the West Fjords**, from June to August it's possible to travel across the region by **long-distance bus**. From Ísafjörður, services run on Tuesday, Friday and Sunday morning via Súðavík (30min), Ísafjarðardjúp (3hr) and the Steingrímsfjarðarheiði plateau to Hólmavík (5hr), from where onward connections can be made to Reykjavík and, by changing again at Staðarskáli (about 3km east of Brú), to Akureyri. An afternoon service runs back to Ísafjörður from Hólmavík on the same days. On Monday, Wednesday and Saturday mornings, a bus leaves Ísafjörður for Þingeyri, Hrafnseyri, Brjánslækur, Patreksfjörður, Breiðavík and Látrabjarg, a total journey of six hours. The bus waits at the cliffs for 1hr20min before returning via the same route; ferry connections to and from Flatey and Snæfellsnes exist at Brjánslækur.

Local buses operate several times daily all year round between Ísafjörður and Bolungarvík and Flateyri. From September to May, two buses daily follow the route between from Tálknafjörður to Patreksfjörður, then back to Tálknafjörður before continuing to Bíldudalur and its airport. On Friday only, a service runs in both directions between Brú, Hólmavík and Drangsnes.

Ísafjörður

With a population of just over 2900, **ÍSAFJÖRÐUR** is by far and away the largest settlement in the West Fjords and is where most travellers choose to base themselves when exploring the region, not least because this is the only place from which to reach the Hornstrandir peninsula by boat, a major goal for many visitors. All administration for the area is centred here too, and there's also a significant **fishing industry**. It's hard to imagine a much more dramatic location; built on the L-shaped sandspit, **Eyri**, which stretches out into the narrow waters of **Skutulsfjörður** fjord and provides exceptionally good shelter for the ocean-going fishing vessels, the town is surrounded by towering mountains on three sides and by the open waters of **Ísafjarðardjúp** on the fourth. During the long winter months, locals are forced to battle against the elements to keep open the tiny airport, which very often provides the only point of contact between the entire region and the rest of the country. Should you be able to arrive in Ísafjörður by plane, however, you'll be treated to an unforgettable experience as you bank steeply around the fjord, then skim past the sheer mountainside of Kirkjubólshlíð before dropping onto the landing strip. In fact, during the darkest months of the year (Dec & Jan), the sheer height of the mountains either side of the fjord prevents the low winter sun from shining directly onto the town for a number of weeks, and the sun's reappearance over the mountain tops at the end of January is celebrated with **sólarkaffi**, "sun coffee" (in fact just normal coffee) and pancakes on January 25.

According to the *Landnámabók*, a Viking by the name of **Helgi Hrolfsson** was the first person to settle in Skutulsfjörður and build his farm there during the ninth century. However, although the sandspit was inhabited from the time of the Settlement, it took several centuries for Eyri at Skutulsfjörður, as Ísafjörður was then called, to emerge as one of the country's main commercial centres, an enviable status due to the establishment of a trading post on the spit by foreign merchants during the late sixteenth century. It was also around this time that the town's most notorious resident, **Jón Magnússon**, a fundamentalist priest, ordered two men on a neighbouring farm to be burned at the stake for sorcery, a practice that was reputed to be widespread in the West Fjords at the time. Finally, in 1786, with the winding-up of the Danish trade monopoly, the town was granted municipal status and became one of Iceland's six official trading posts. Just over a hundred years later, Eyri finally received city status and celebrated by changing its name to the present Ísafjörður, meaning Ice fjord.

Today Ísafjörður is a quiet and likeable place where you'd be wise to make the most of the shops, restaurants and bars on offer before venturing out into the wilds beyond such as the Hornstrandir peninsula or one of the much smaller West Fjords villages. There's very little of note, though, in the town – Ísafjörður's pleasures are more to be found in strolling through its streets and watching the fishermen at work in the harbour rather than in tourist sights. The **West Fjords Maritime Museum**, though, one of the very few museums in the region, is worth visiting for an insight into the extreme conditions that past generations have lived under here. That it's located in one of the country's oldest timber buildings, dating from the harsh days of the trade monopoly with Denmark, is unusual in itself, when you consider that the climate here is so severe that anything made out of wood doesn't normally last long at all.

Arrival, information and accommodation

Long distance buses, which are operated by Stjörnubílar (℡456 3518, Ⓦwww.stjornubilar.is), stop outside the **tourist information office** at Aðalstræti 7 (June–Aug Mon–Fri 8am–6pm, Sat & Sun 10am–3pm, Sept–May Mon–Fri noon–5.30pm; ℡456 5121, Ⓦwww.vestferdir.is). Buses also stop in the western part of town outside the hotel, *Torfnes* (see below), on Skutulsfjarðarbraut. Passenger **ferries** to and from the Hornstrandir peninsula arrive at Sundahöfn harbour, at the eastern end of Mjósund, which leads down to the harbour from the tourist office. The **airport**, 7km out of town, is on a narrow stretch of land on the eastern edge of the fjord; an bus into Ísafjörður, continuing to Bolungarvík, meets all flights; taxis (800kr) are also available.

You'll find most of Ísafjörður's shops and services in and around the town's main square, Silfurtorg, including the bookshop, Penninn, which is handy for camera accessories and carries a couple of books in English on the West Fjords. The **post office** is at Aðalstræti 18; while from Silfurtorg, Hafnarstræti pushes north to the town's main **supermarket**, Samkaup. **Internet** terminals can be found inside the smoke and alcohol-free café *Gamla Apótekið* (daily 2–11.30pm), Hafnarstræti 18, as well as at the **library** (Mon–Fri 2–7pm, Sat till 5pm), which is beside the church (see p.196). The **cinema**, at Norðurvegur 1, generally has several showings a week. The indoor **swimming pool**, at Austurvegur 9, also has a small **sauna** for men on Monday, Wednesday, Friday and Saturday and for women on Tuesday, Thursday and Sunday.

Accommodation

The only **hotel** in town that's open year-round is *Hótel Ísafjörður* (℡456 4111, Ⓦwww.hotelisafjordur.is; ❻), centrally located on Silfurtorg, just off the main street, Hafnarstræti. Don't be put off by the grey concrete exterior, inside the doubles are comfortable, if somewhat plain, are well insulated against the biting wind, and breakfast is included. A considerably cheaper alternative is the summer-only *Torfnes* (June–Aug; ℡456 4485, Ⓦwww.hotelisafjordur.is; ❹;

sleeping-bag accommodation from 1100kr), set in a boarding school in the western part of town on Skutulsfjarðarbraut, where rooms comprise nothing more than a bed and a washbasin; breakfast costs 850kr extra. The **campsite** (June to mid-Aug; ☎456 4485; 550kr per tent) is behind the *Torfnes*.

Ísafjörður also several **guesthouses**: the friendly *Gistiheimili Áslaugar* (☎456 3868, Ⓦwww.randburg.com/is/aslaug.html; sleeping-bag accommodation from 1800kr, ❷) at Austurvegur 7 is the best, whose owner can tell you all you ever wanted to know about Ísafjörður. The plain but comfortable rooms with shared facilities here are located in a basement, though all have windows; there's also access to a kitchen. Breakfast (900kr extra) is served in the elegant *Faktorshús* opposite (see p.197; note this is not the same one as the museum), which dates from 1788. Alternatively, there are two other establishments facing each other a couple of blocks away on Mánagata: the two-star *Gamla Gistihúsið* (☎456 4146, Ⓦwww.gistihus.is; sleeping bag accommodation 1800kr; breakfast 800kr extra; ❷) at no.5 is slightly more upmarket than *Auður Ásberg* at no.6 (☎456 4263, Ⓔeyrin@simnet.is; sleeping bag accommodation 1800kr, ❷), although there's no great difference between the two.

The Town

Although there are no specific sights in Ísafjörður, it's a pleasant enough place to stroll round for a couple of hours. It's most logical to start your wanderings in what passes as the town's main square, **Silfurtorg**, in reality little more than the location of the blocklike *Hótel Ísafjörður* (see p.194) ringed by a couple of concrete flowerbeds, itself the point where the two roads, Hafnarstræti and Aðalstræti, meet. Opposite the hotel and a couple of shops beyond the bakery, it's worth having a quick look in at **Gallerí Slunkaríki** (Thurs–Sun 4–6pm; free), which exhibits local art work. If you're lucky enough to find it open, there's the possibility of buying some of the paintings on display.

Things liven up marginally on Suðurgata as it heads westwards towards the town's only tourist sight: **Neðstikaupstaður**, comprising four of Iceland's oldest buildings, all timber structures dating from the late eighteenth century, located on Suðurtangi. One, the carefully restored **Turnhús**, with its unusual roof tower, was constructed in Denmark before being moved to Iceland in 1784, where it was used as a warehouse and fish salting house. As the tallest structure in Ísafjörður, it also served as a lookout from where returning fishing boats were spotted – livelihoods depended on being first to the dockside when the boats came in, it being paramount that the fish were processed as quickly as possible. The Turnhús now houses the **West Fjords Maritime Museum** (late June to late Aug Mon–Fri 11am–5pm, May and June Sat & Sun 1–5pm, July to late Aug Sat & Sun 10am–5pm; 300kr). Inside, fishing paraphernalia and old black-and-white photographs give a good idea of what life used to be like during the early twentieth century; look out for those depicting the thousands of fish that would be laid out to dry and salted in the open air; in later years, ice cut from the fjord was used to preserve them instead. One photo, from the winter of 1918, was taken when plummeting temperatures and ferocious storms ushered in one of the severest winters for decades, when sheets of ice crept up the fjord, choking up the harbour and freezing the entire fishing fleet – bar one boat – into the ice.

Of the remaining buildings on the museum site, the **Krambuð**, immediately to the right of the museum, is the oldest dating from 1757. Used as a store-house until the early 1900s, it was then converted into a private residence. The **Faktorshús** from 1765, to the left of the museum, was once home to the site's

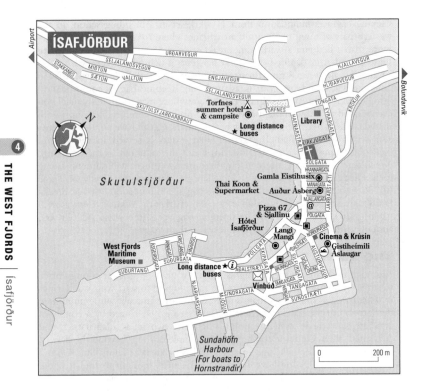

trading manager though is now home, somewhat curiously, to the chief librarian at Ísafjörður library. The fourth building, the **Tjöruhús** dates to 1781 and was once used as a warehouse for the store. Today an agreeable café (same times as museum) serving up delicious waffles and coffee occupies the heavy wooden interior and makes a splendid place to ponder Ísafjörður's past times. Only Tjöruhús and the Turnhús are open to the public.

From the museum, retrace your steps north along Suðurgata turning right into Njarðarsund and then left into Sindragata, to reach the oldest part of town, just north of the harbour. Here, the brightly painted timber houses on **Tangagata** (a continuation of Sindragata) and **Silfurgata**, which leads from Tangagata back towards the hotel, are particularly beautiful with their mountain backdrop. Now back in the main square, Hafnarstræti leads north to Ísafjörður's highly unusual **church**, at the junction with Sólgata, resembling a folding concertina. Built to replace the former timber church that burned down in 1987, this architectural monster of peach-coloured pebbledash comprises four column-like wedges that seemingly collapse into one another beneath a brilliant metal roof. The source of much local controversy ever since its inception, to add insult to injury during its construction thirty graves were unceremoniously cemented over to make way for it; a plaque bearing the names of those buried there now stands beside the statue of Christ inside the unadorned interior. Beside the church, in the tussocky field in front of the library, stands a **sculpture** of two burly Ísafjörður fishermen hauling in a net full of cod, a reminder of the town's dependence on the sea; the poignant inscription reads simply "in honour of those who disappeared, for luck for those who still put out to sea".

Opposite, the diminutive well-tended **town park** sandwiched between Torfnes and Seljalandsvegur, is remarkable for the arching form of the white-painted whale bone marking the entrance. Dedicated to two local characters, Jón Jónsson and Karlinna Jóhannesdóttir, who painstakingly tended and encouraged all greenery in this remote town on the edge of the Arctic for several decades, the park is a pleasant place to sit and admire the soaring fjord-sides surrounded by angelica and flowering pansies – ultimately, a pure West Fjords experience.

Eating and drinking

The liveliest, though not the best, **restaurant** in town is *Pizza 67*, at Hafnarstræti 12, which serves up pizzas and fish dishes from 1300kr, chicken and lamb creations from 1700kr until 10pm (until 3am Fri & Sat). A much better bet though is the excellent *Thai Koon* café-cum-restaurant inside the building opposite which houses the *Samkaup* supermarket on Hafnarstræti; here genuinely tasty chicken, pork and beef dishes accompanied by either rice or noodles cost 790kr or 990kr depending on the size of the portion you want; beer is 500kr. The finest food in town, however, is to be had at the restaurant inside *Hótel Ísafjörður* although the chances are you'll be dining alone if you come here, as the high prices deter most locals; reckon on 2000kr per person for roast catfish or 2200kr for grilled chicken breast; the evening set tourist-menu, featuring fish of one kind or another, is 2100kr. The lunchtime fish set menu is 1250kr.

The best **café** in town is the elegant *Faktorshús* adjacent to *Gistiheimili Áslauga*, at Austurvegur 7; this grand old wooden structure complete with creaking floorboards, handsome dressers and delicate floral wall coverings once was home to the local *faktor* (trading manager of the town); it serves light snacks, cakes, coffee and beer. Otherwise, for other light bites, including crêpes, try the altogether more modern *Langi Mangi* at Aðalstræti 22, or the **bakery**, *Gamla Bakaríið*, at Aðalstræti 24, if you fancy a coffee and a sandwich. There are two **pubs** in town: the aptly named *Krúsin* (Fri & Sat) at Norðurvegur 1 attracts a slightly older crowd with its 60s and 70s tunes, whereas *Sjallinn*, next door to Pizza 67 on Hafnarstræti, is the place to go to meet young Ísafjörðers who gather nightly to expensively quench their thirst (a beer is 650kr). Alternatively, the **vínbúð** (Mon–Thurs 11am–6pm, Fri 11am–7pm, Sat 11am–2pm), is at Aðalstræti 20.

Around Ísafjörður: Bolungarvík and Skálavík

Fifteen kilometres northwest of Ísafjörður along Route 61, the fishing village of **BOLUNGARVÍK**, at the mouth of Ísafjarðardjúp, suffers from one of the most exposed locations in the country. Not only does it receive some of the foulest weather in Iceland, but its position at the foot of three mountains, two of which are close to 700m high, means it's also susceptible to avalanches and landslides, and a large section of Route 61 is protected from rock and snow-falls by sturdy metal nets suspended between posts at the roadside.

Although Bolungarvík is one of the larger settlements in the West Fjords, with a population of around 950, it's a workaday place with little to entertain visitors. However, it is worth making the twenty-minute trip from Ísafjörður to visit the open-air **Ósvör Maritime Museum** (May to mid-Sept daily 10am–5pm; 200kr) at the entrance to town, just before the bridge. The tiny, turf-rooved huts here, with their thick stone lower walls, are reconstructions of structures that were once used to house fishing-boat crews, a salting house and a rack for drying fish, and give a good idea of how cramped conditions were in the early twentieth century. The museum also has a six-oared rowing boat from the 1940s, built to a traditional local design on display. The landing stage, beyond the huts, was used when the weather conditions were too severe for boats to land in more exposed Bolungarvík itself.

The town's only other attraction, the **Natural History Museum** (Mon–Fri 9am–5pm, plus mid-June to mid-Aug Sat & Sun 1–5pm; ⓦ www.nave.is /nattgr.htm; 300kr), is a ten-minute walk from the maritime museum following the main road into town, Þuríðarbraut, across the Hólsá river, and straight on into the main street, Aðalstræti. From here, turn right into Vitastígur and you'll see the museum at no.3 down by the harbour. Inside there's an excellent collection of stuffed birds – everything from a wigeon to a pink flamingo which oddly turned up out of the blue in eastern Iceland – you name it, they've got it stuffed. The prize exhibit though is the three year old male polar bear (minus penis which was immediately claimed by the phallological museum in Reykjavík) found floating on spring pack ice off Hornstrandir a couple of years ago. The bear's death (it was snared by local fishermen who spotted him drifting, exhausted, on the ice), most likely caused by hanging over the side of a fishing boat, needless to say, came in for much public criticism. The museum is also a good place to buy decent postcards, which you can send from the nearby post office at Aðalstræti 14.

Bolungarvík practicalities

A local **bus** arrives and departs from the post office on Aðalstræti three times daily Monday to Friday for Ísafjörður and its airport. The town's only **guesthouse**, in the same building as the Natural History Museum, is *Finnabær* (☎456 7254, ⓔellijoh@simnet.is; sleeping-bag accommodation 1500kr, ❶), Vitastígur 1, a simple affair inside what looks like a small office complex. Rooms are small and plain but cheap, while breakfast is 700kr extra. The **campsite** is at Höfðastígur 1, next to a **swimming pool** and the Hólsá river, where Route 61 from Ísafjörður enters town. Eating is restricted to the greasy spoon **café** *Veitingahúsið Finnabær*, on Vitastígur, where fresh fish and other simple dishes can be had from 1000kr, though service here is slow and impolite.

Skálavík

From the western edge of Bolungarvík, Þjóðólfsvegur continues 12km northwest through the uninhabited Hlíðardalur valley until it reaches the exposed **Skálavík** bay, which takes regular batterings from Atlantic storms as they sweep in mercilessly from the northwest. Although Skálavík is today uninhabited bar a couple of summer houses owned by brave souls who don't seem to mind the weather, at the end of the nineteenth century around one hundred people were living here, ekeing out an existence from the surrounding barren land. Given the village's vulnerable location between the Deild and Öskubakur mountains, avalances were always a particular hazard and claimed several lives; perhaps not surprisingly therefore, the last farmer gave up his struggle to keep the village alive in 1964 and left.

There's no public transport to Skálavík but it is possible to **walk** from Bolungarvík in around two hours – simply follow Þjóðólfsvegur all the way.

The bay offers a real chance to commune with nature and a night spent camping here, battling against the weather, is certainly a memorable experience; bring all the supplies you'll need. There's also some good **hiking** around here; one good route (7km) begins at the western edge of the bay and leads west along the shore round Öskubakar to the lonely lighthouse in Keflavík bay, before the Göltur headland. From here, another track (5km) heads inland through the valleys of Norðdalur and Bakkadalur back to Skálavík and the beginning of the track back to Bolungarvík. A detailed map of these routes is included in the hiking **leaflet** *Gönguleiðir í nágrenni Bolungarvíkur*, available free from the tourist office in Ísafjörður (see p.194) and from the museum in Bolungarvík (see above).

Around Ísafjarðardjúp

The largest and most breathtaking of all the West Fjords, the seventy-five kilometre-long **Ísafjarðardjúp** stretches all the way from the mountains around Bolungarvík at its mouth to the shores of Ísafjörður fjord, the most easterly of the nine smaller fjords that make up the southern coastline of this extended arm of the Denmark Strait. Approaching from the southeast, descending from the Steingrímsfjarðarheiði plateau on the newly asphalted Road 61, the views of Ísafjarðardjúp are spectacular – remote, uninhabited forbidding fjordlands as far as the eye can see, which form this northwestern corner of Iceland. In fact, from the head of Ísafjörður fjord to the regional capital there's just one village along a very lonely road stretching around two hundred kilometres. Look across the waters of the bay and, on the northern shoreline, you'll see the sheer, snow-capped mountains of **Langadalsströnd** and **Snæfjallaströnd**, themselves divided by the glacial lagoon, **Kaldalón**, which is fed by meltwater from the only glacier in the West Fjords, **Drangajökull**. Until just a couple of decades ago these coasts were dotted with isolated farms making an uncertain living from sheep farming and growing the odd crop, today though most have been deserted, reminders of how difficult life was up here. In addition to working the land, many farmers also eked out an existence as fishermen on Ísafjarðardjúp, where whitefish was once so abundant. Today though, the bay is better known for the rich shrimping grounds found at its mouth, as the whitefish have moved further out to sea.

Súðavík and Reykjanes

Twenty kilometres southeast of Ísafjörður, Route 61 passes through sleepy **SÚÐAVÍK**, the one and only settlement on the southern shoreline of Ísafjarðardjúp. This tiny fishing village, with a population of barely two hundred, is your last chance to stock up with essentials before the start of the circuitous negotiation of fjords involved in leaving Ísafjörður. There's very little of note in the village, consisting solely of the main road lined on each side by a few brightly coloured suburban homes, other than the simple wooden **church**, now next to the main road at the Ísafjörður end of the village but once located in the deserted settlement of Hesteyri (see p.201) across the water on Hornstrandir – when Hesteyri was abandoned in 1952 it was decided that the old church should be dismantled and brought to Súðavík, where several families chose to begin their new lives. The church became a centre for prayer in January 1995, when fourteen people were killed and many homes destroyed by an avalanche that crashed onto the village from the precipitous slopes of

Súðavíkurhlíd, the steep mountain that bears down on the village. If you need to stay overnight, there's a **campsite** (no tel) next to a **swimming pool**, at Nesvegur 3, or there are rooms available at *Sumarbyggð* **guesthouse** (☎456 4986, ⓔsumarbyggd@sudavik.is; sleeping-bag accommodation only, 1700kr), which also has a kitchen for guests' use. For snacks and burgers, head for the *Víkurbúðin* **café** at the filling station on the main road where there's also a **bank** and **post office** (Mon–Fri 9.15am–4pm).

Reykjanes

As Route 61 leaves Súðavík and begins its course around the Álftafjörður fjord it passes the remains of the Norwegian whaling station that provided employment for the village in the early 1900s. The next 150km, as you twist around the fjords, are remarkable only for their dullness – this section is one of the most infuriating in the entirety of the West Fjords, as you'll often drive up to 50km around one of the five fjords that punctuate the road to the foot of Steingrímsfjarðarheiði, only to make two or three kilometres of actual headway. With your own transport – and the will to navigate yet another fjord – you can detour northwest off Route 61 onto Route 633, about 100km from Súdavik, and go northeast to the tiny settlement of **REYKJANES**, set on a geothermal area located on a spit of land between the diminutive fjord of Reykjafjörður and much bigger Ísafjörður, and looking out onto the open waters of Ísafjarðardjúp. Virtually the only building here is a hotel, the functional *Hótel Reykjanes* (☎456 4844, ⓦwww.rnes.is, sleeping bag accommodation 1800kr, ❸), where breakfast costs an extra 850kr. Although there's very little to do here, it's an excellent place for a swim in the naturally heated **outdoor pool** (daily 8am–11pm) and **sauna** in the village, after or ahead of the long drive to Ísafjörður. Back on Route 61, at the mouth of Ísafjörður, the road then swings right to climb up to the Steingrímsfjarðarheiði plateau; a couple of kilometres after this sharp turn up, Road 635 turns left to head for Kaldalón.

Kaldalón glacial lagoon, Drangajökull and Unaðsdalur

The southeastern shore of Ísafjarðardjúp, **Langadalsströnd**, is named after Langidalur (Long Valley), which climbs into the hills immediately east of the mouth of Ísafjörður fjord. Just 3km east of there, Route 635 branches north off Route 61 at a bridge over Bæjardalsá river, passing lush green fields and a few scattered farms as it heads north along the shore to the **Kaldalón glacial lagoon**, an exceedingly bumpy thirty-minute drive from the junction in your own transport – there's no public transport on this section of road.

Approaching the lagoon, a U-shaped inlet from Ísafjarðardjúp between the cliffs of Snæfjallaströnd to the west and Langadalsströnd to the east, you spot the trail of brown, muddy meltwater that has come down from the glacier of **Drangajökull** as it merges into the saltwater of the bay. From the parking area by the low hills at the head of the lagoon it's possible to walk up to the snout of the glacier along a trail, marked by cairns, in roughly ninety minutes; from the car park head east, following the low hills, to the track leading along the eastern side of the valley up to the glacier. Keep to the eastern side of the cairns and you'll find the going easier, although there are still boulders, stones and streams to negotiate. Note that you shouldn't underestimate the time it'll take to walk to the glacier – the clear air makes the ice appear much closer than it actually is. If you spot the unmarked path leading up the western edge of the snout, past Drangajökull's highest point, **Jökulbunga**

(925m) before descending into Furufjörður on the eastern shore of Hornstrandir, don't be tempted to follow it – it's strictly for experienced mountaineers only.

From Kaldalón, Route 635 crosses the glacial river, Mórillá, before continuing northwest for another fifteen minutes (drive) to the farming settlement of **UNAÐSDALUR** where there's a small **church** right on the shoreline. From here the now uninhabited mountainous coastline of Snæfjallaströnd stretches to the northwest – although it's hard to imagine, this entire coast was once inhabited as far as the cliffs at Bjarnarnúpur, which look across to Bolungarvík on the opposite side of the bay. However, in 1995 the last family, perhaps unsurprisingly, upped sticks and left this remote, chilly coast – not even in the warmest summer does the snow melt from the mountains here – abandoning Snæfjallaströnd to the elements alone.

Hornstrandir

Once you've seen the remote snow-covered hills and cliffs of the Snæfjallaströnd coastline, you'll have an idea of what lies immediately north, on Iceland's very last corner of inhospitable terrain. A claw-shaped peninsula of land bordered by the Jökulfirðir fjords to the south and the Greenland Sea to the north, and attached to the rest of the West Fjords by a narrow neck of land just 6km wide, the coastline of **Hornstrandir** is the most magnificent the country has to offer. The rugged cliffs, precipitous mountainsides and sandy bays backed by meadows of wildflowers make up this official nature reserve on the very edge of the Arctic Circle, and hiking here is an exhilarating experience; it's quite common to walk for an entire day without seeing another person. The highlight of any trip to Hornstrandir is a visit to the majestic **Hornbjarg cliff** (533m) at the eastern end of Hornvík bay and the highest point on the peninsula. The cliff is home to one of the country's greatest **bird colonies** and its many ledges are stuffed full with fulmars, guillemots, kittiwakes, puffins and razorbills. Elsewhere, where farmed sheep once devoured everything edible, there is now wild, lush vegetation of unexpected beauty and the wildlife is free to roam – the Arctic fox makes regular appearances – while offshore, seals and whales can be spotted.

Life for settlers on Hornstrandir has always been extreme. For starters, the summer is appreciably shorter than elsewhere in the West Fjords and, bar a geothermal spring in remote **Reykjafjörður**, there's no natural hot-water source, no waterfall to generate electricity, no natural harbour, and no road or airstrip. In fact, the fertile valleys and inlets throughout this uninhabited wilderness are littered with traces of derelict buildings where hardy farmers and fishermen once eked out an existence here battling against the inhospitable climate. However, the peninsula's two main settlements, **Aðalvík** and **Hesteyri**, are now almost completely deserted, their abandonment marking the end of yet another Icelandic community. Founded in around 1894, Hesteyri depended entirely on a Norwegian whaling station – remains of which can still be seen today at the head of Hesteyrarfjörður fjord – until a drastic decline in stocks led to the station being taken over for the processing of herring. At this time, around eighty people lived permanently in Hesteyri, with another hundred temporarily resident at the factory, but a fall in herring stocks led to the closure of the factory in 1940. One by one, farmers and fishermen left, and in 1952 the last families abandoned both Hesteyri

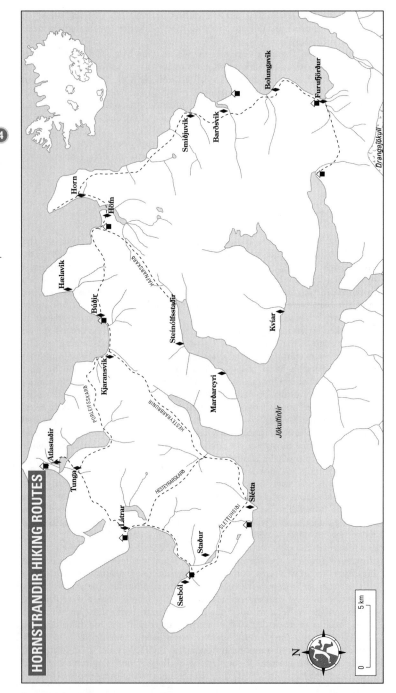

HORNSTRANDIR HIKING ROUTES

Ísafjarðardjúp

Drangajökull

Furufjörður

Bolungavík

Barðsvík

Smiðjuvík

Horn

Höfn

Hælavík

Búðir

Kjaransvík

Aðalstaðir

Tunga

Látrar

Sæból

Staður

Slétta

Steinólfsstaðir

Marðareyri

Kviar

Jökulfirðir

HAFNARSKARÐ

ÞÓRLEIFSSKARÐ

HESTEYRARBRÚNIR

HESTEYRARSKARÐ

SLÉTTUHEÐI

N

0   5 km

and neighbouring Aðalvík. Incidentally, the closing shots of the Icelandic film *Children of Nature* (*Börn Náttúrunnar*), by Friðrik Þór Friðriksson, were filmed on the mountains of Straumnesfjall, which form the northern wall of Aðalvík bay.

Today Hesteyri consists of nothing more than a handful of abandoned cottages, disintegrating skeletons of concrete and timber clothed with bits of corrugated iron, broken stone and blocks of turf, with just one or two being renovated by families whose roots lie here. The only functioning building is *Læknishúsið* (☎456 7138 or ☎456 3879), the former doctor's house, on the western side of the Hesteyrará river, which offers sleeping-bag **accommodation** (2000kr) from late June to late August, with cooking facilities available.

Practicalities

Since there are no roads to or within this area, **approaches to Hornstrandir** are either by passenger ferry or on foot. Of the **ferry** companies, Hornstrandir EFH (☎456 5690; ⓦwww.hornstrandir.is) sail to Hornvík (early June to early Aug Mon 10am, plus early July to early Aug Wed 10am; 4500kr); Aðalvík (June–Aug Mon & Tues 10am, also Thurs 6pm mid-June to mid-Aug; 3000kr); Hesteyri (early June to early Aug Mon 6pm; 3000kr) and to the emergency hut at the head of Hrafnfjörður (June–Aug Sat 9am; 5000kr), which is useful if you're walking to and from Norðurfjörður on the Strandir coast (see p.220). Routes and times change slightly from year to year but the above pattern generally holds; check their website or ask at the tourist office in Ísafjörður for the latest details when planning a trip. **Sjóferðir** (☎456 5111, ⓦwww.sjoferdir.is) also operate from Ísafjörður to Hesteyri (late June to mid-Aug Wed, Fri & Sun 2pm; 2900kr) and Hrafnfjörður (late June to mid-Aug Mon & Thurs 9am; 3100kr). Bookings for all services can also be made at the tourist office in Ísafjörður.

On foot, the main approaches are from Unaðsdalur (see p.201), where a good path heads north for Leirufjörður following the Dalsá on its way up out of the village. From Leirufjörður it's possible to cross the tidal flats and head towards the mouth of Hrafnsfjörður and on to Hornvík in around four days. Take extra care when crossing the Leirufjörður at low tide, however, because the flats are composed of glacial waste washed down from Drangajökull and can be particularly soggy. Alternatively a much longer and more demanding route leads from Ófeigsfjörður, northwest of Norðurfjörður, the last main settlement on the Strandir coast (see p.220). The path follows the coast north to Drangavík, Reykjafjörður (where there's an open air geothermally heated swimming pool) and Furufjörður, from where it's possible to cut west into Hrafnsfjörður or continue north to Hornvík; for this, you should allow at least a week.

Unfortunately the **weather** in this part of the country, on the edge of the Greenland Sea, is especially unpredictable. Deep snow often lies on the ground until July and snow showers are not uncommon even in July and August. Fog, too, can be a particular problem. It's essential therefore to bring the following **equipment**: a sturdy tent and warm sleeping bag, waterproof clothing and boots, more food than you'll need in case of unforseen delays (there are no facilities anywhere on the peninsula), a compass and the 1:100 000 **hiking map**, *Göngukort yfir Hornstrandir*, produced by Landmælingar Íslands. Although many routes are marked on the map as clearly defined, this is often not the case in reality; in poor weather conditions it can be all too easy to lose the path, so

An excellent way to see the best of Hornstrandir is to do the demanding **three-day hike** from Hornvík to Aðalvík. By taking a boat to Hornvík (see p.203) it's possible to walk west in time to catch a boat back to Ísafjörður from Hesteyri or Aðalvík. See pp.203–204 for advice on safety and the weather in this part of the country.

Day one: from Hornvík to Hlöðuvík
Once ashore there's the option of heading east along the beach at Hornvík, wading across the Hafnarós estuary and climbing up to Hornbjarg to see the birds. Alternatively, head west along the beach and look for the path that leads up from the sand to take you round the headland into Hælavík bay. From here, a well-trodden path heads up the western edge of an unnamed stream heading for the narrow pass in the mountains, which gives access down to neighbouring Hlöðuvík via a rockfield (where the cairns marking the path disappear at times). The steep descent into the bay offers spectacular views. Reckon on around four and a half hours for this stretch.

Day two: from Hlöðuvík to Hesteyri
Head west along the beach at Hlöðuvík and wade across the river that cuts the beach in two. Continue along the beach around Álfsfell, before turning south inland following the cairns which mark the indistinct path to the mountain pass of Kjaransvíkurskarð (426m); the last part of the ascent is rather rocky. From here the going is considerably easier as the path leads southeast to a mountain plateau, which follows the shoreline of Hesteyrarfjörður fjord. Note that none of the streams that cross the plateau are bridged and even in July there are still large snowfields on the plateau. At the western edge of the plateau, the path descends the valley wall into Hesteyri; this descent can be difficult if the wall is still covered in snow. This stretch will take you about seven hours in total.

Day three: from Hesteyri to Aðalvík
Cross the chilly waters of Hesteyrará river to *Læknishúsið*. From here, a good path – actually the old road that led west to now abandoned Slettá – leads up the hill following the course of the river. At the top, the trail strikes out across an extensive rockfield, which can be hard going in parts; even in July, there is a lot of snow left up here. Follow the cairns through the rock field until the track descends into sandy Aðalvík; the bottom of this path is rather boggy. Cross the shallow river to reach the beach and the tiny settlement of Látrar, at the eastern edge of the bay, or Sæból at the western edge, both surrounded by snowy mountains on all sides. If you're walking in reverse, note that the path to Hesteyri can be found by crossing the river and heading for the single house on the river bank. From here head up the hill to the right of the house to reach the rockfield plateau to Hesteyri. Either way, this leg should take around four hours to complete.

make sure that you can use a compass properly before setting out. Remember, too, that in June and July it doesn't get dark here, which means you can extend your time hiking if needed. Incidentally, mobile **phones** do not work in Hornstrandir, but there are landline phones for use in emergencies in the orange shelters dotted around the coast and marked on the map. Take extra care if you're crossing **tidal flats**, such as at Leirufjörður (see p.203), or rounding headlands at low tide, as the going can often be very boggy. There are no footbridges in Hornstrandir, so bring an old pair of running shoes to cross rivers and streams – and be prepared to grit your teeth against the bitingly cold water.

From Ísafjörður to the southwestern peninsula

Passing through some of the most dramatic scenery the West Fjords have to offer, **Route 60** is the access route for the southern and western sections of this region. It's predominantly a mountain road, winding through narrow passes and deep-green valleys as often as it rounds the heads of fjords. Public buses operate from June to August (see p.193 for details of winter services) through the handful of tiny villages which mark the way between Ísafjörður and the tip of the southwestern peninsula, the **Látrabjarg** bird cliffs (see p.213) and the outstanding golden strands at **Breiðavík**. Yet despite this being the main road to the south and west, providing the only access to and from Ísafjörður that avoids the Ísafjarðardjúp fjord system, once you're south of the villages of **Flateyri** and **Þingeyri**, small sleepy fishing settlements where you'll be lucky to see anybody in the one main street which runs through each place, it's actually little more than an unsurfaced and badly potholed dirt track, where driving requires slow speeds, much gear changing and even more patience. Things look up, though, after the hair-raising descent into minute **Hrafnseyri**, the birthplace of **Jón Sigurðsson**, the man who led Iceland towards independence during the late nineteenth century. The small museum dedicated to him here details the man's life and is a great place to be on Independence Day (June 17) when there's much singing, dancing and celebration of this fiercely proud nation's achievements. Beyond here, look out for the most impressive waterfall in the West Fjords, **Dynjandi**, at the head of the eponymously named fjord, a favourite rest break for the bus from Ísafjörður on its long journey to and from Látrabjarg. One of the main entrance points into the West Fjords lies due south of here, the **ferry** terminal at **Brjánslækur**, from where the *Baldur* sails to the island of Flatey (see p.179) and on to Stykkishólmur (see p.174) on the Snæfellsnes peninsula – an unusual choice for a regional departure and arrival point, since there is no settlement here at all.

Beginning on the southwestern edge of Ísafjörður, the road immediately enters a tunnel to bypass Þverfjall (752m), and after 2km, the tunnel divides in two; the right-hand turn, Route 65, leads to **SUÐUREYRI**, a dreary workaday fishing village distinguished only by its outdoor **swimming pool** (℡456 6121), which has the edge over Ísafjörður's indoor pool. The main tunnel, Route 60, continues for another 4km before emerging into Önundarfjörður fjord where there's a junction with Road 64 to **Flateyri**.

From June to August, a **long-distance bus** service goes from Ísafjörður to Brjánslækur (3hr), departing at 9am on Monday, Wednesday and Saturday and stopping along the way at most (not Flateyri) settlements in between; it then continues on to Látrabjarg, at the end of the southwestern peninsula itself (see p.213), returning late afternoon via the same route, connecting with the evening ferry from Brjánslækur to Snæfellsnes.

Flateyri and around

The small fishing village of **FLATEYRI**, just 22km west of Ísafjörður, reached from Route 60 via Route 64, which heads northwest to the village as it leaves the tunnel, is known across the country for its **avalanche** problems, and the colossal **earth dams** separated by 15m high walls on the lower slopes of the ominpresent mountains are man-made barriers against the snowfalls which occur here every year. A memorial stone next to the church, at the entrance to the village, bears the names of the twenty people who died in the most recent devastating avalanche in October, 1995. The tragedy was a painful loss for this closely knit community where the total population is barely over three hundred, not least because the frozen ground and heavy snow prevented the bodies from being buried in the village cemetery; instead, they had to be kept in the morgue in Ísafjörður until the ground thawed and they could be buried in Reykjavík. Extensive rebuilding was necessary after the accident, including the erection of avalanche defences which now effectively channel all snow-slides into the sea. From the filling station at the entrance to the village, a short walking path (10min) leads up to a **viewpoint** on the mountainside giving a superb panorama, not only of Flateyri and Önundarfjörður fjord, but down into the lifesaving earth dams.

Founded as a trading centre in 1792, the village was once a base for shark and whale hunting. Today, however, it's thanks to the fish-processing factory, one of the largest in Iceland, that the village has finally shaken off its dependence on Ísafjörður, where until recently all financial and shipping services needed in the village were to be found. In fact, Flateyri prides itself on the fact that all major services can be found in the village despite it being so small. However, it's not a good idea to get stuck here since there's very little to do other than marvel at the avalanche defences and the open vistas of the surrounding fjord and mountains that tower over Flateyri.

Flateyri practicalities

Local **buses** operate all year (2–3 daily Mon–Fri) from Ísafjörður and the **post office** (Mon–Fri 9.15am–4pm) in Flateyri at Ránargata 1. In summer, the long-distance bus from Ísafjörður to Brjánslækur and Látrabjarg doesn't call at Flateyri (see p.205) but can be caught at the junction of Routes 64 and 60.

Flateyri has one **guesthouse**, the *Brynjukot* (☎456 7762, ✉jens@snerpa.is; ❸), at Ránargata 6, with self-catering facilities though no en-suite rooms. The **campsite** (☎456 7807), with toilets and running water, is behind the filling station at the entrance to the village. The **swimming pool** (☎456 7738) is in Tjarnargata, close to the mountains, west of the church. For eating and drinking there's the bright and airy *Vagninn* **restaurant**, its wall painted vibrant reds and yellows, at Hafnarstræti 19, run by a charming South African and her Icelandic husband, which serves up burgers with fries and salad (980kr), pizzas (1300kr) and steamed halibut with soup (1500kr), beer here is 600kr, whilst a bottle of wine is around 2700kr.

Ingjaldssandur and Sæból

One of the most beautiful beaches in the West Fjords, **Ingjaldssandur** (the settlement here is known as **Sæból**, the name used on most maps) is located at the mouth of Önundarfjörður, across the water from Flateyri at the tip of the mountainous finger of land that separates the fjord from its southern neighbour, Dyrafjörður. Bordered to the west and east by tall, craggy mountains and backed by lush green fields, the beach's grassy foreshore is an idyllic place from which to watch the huge Atlantic breakers crash onto the sand and pebbles below. In summer this is a good place to spot arctic tern and various species of waders; oystercatchers are particularly common here.

Ingjaldssandur is only accessible with your own transport and entails a circuitous drive of 44km from Flateyri, heading south on Route 64, then rejoining Route 60 and heading for Þingeyri before Route 624 forks off to the west and eventually heads north back towards Önundarfjörður; although the road is in poor condition it is accessible to non-four-wheel-drive vehicles. The farm, *Hraun* (☎456 7767, though no English is spoken), located right on the beach and the only building here, offers sleeping-bag **accommodation** and cooking facilities for 1500kr; for splendid isolation, it's hard to beat.

Þingeyri

Although one of the oldest settlements in the West Fjords, **ÞINGEYRI**, 48km southwest of Ísafjörður along Road 60, is also one of the dullest. The village takes its name from the ancient *þing* (assembly) mentioned in *Gísla Saga*, the singularly unimpressive ruins, nothing more than a couple of grassy mounds, can be seen behind the church in the centre of the village. Over the centuries Þingeyri developed into a significant fishing centre thanks to its sheltered location near the head of Dyrafjörður, and even attracted the interest of the French who applied, unsuccessfully, to establish a base here to service their fishing vessels operating in the region.

Today life is centred on the one main street, **Aðalstræti** but there's little of interest in Þingeyri itself beyond a stroll down to the harbour to see the fishing boats landing their catch; better instead, head up Sandafell (367m), which stands guard behind the village. This is a favourite place for locals to watch the sun go down as it offers fantastic views out over the fjord and of the mountain ridge, topped by the highest peak in the West Fjords, Kaldbakur (998m), which separates Dyrafjörður from the much larger and multi-fingered Arnarfjörður to the south. Although steep, Sandafell can be climbed from the village – several clear paths lead up the mountainside. Alternatively, a four-wheel-drive track there heads southwest off Route 60 just 1km after climbing up out of Þingeyri heading for Hrafnseyri.

Practicalities

Aðalstræti is where what few services the village offers – a **bank**-cum-**post office** (9.15am-4pm) and a few shops – are located. If you have to stay here, *Gistiheimilið Vera* (☎456 8232 and ☎891 6832; ❷) at Hlíðargata 22 has simple **rooms** without shower and toilet, or sleeping-bag accommodation for 2000kr. Breakfast is not available but cooking facilities are. The **campsite** (☎456 8225; 550kr per tent), with washing facilities, is located next to the modern **swimming pool** (☎456 8375) at the western end of the village. **Eating out** is limited to the evening-only *Tóki Munkur* pizzeria (pizzas from 1200kr, beer 600kr), at Hafnarstræti 1, and the snack bar at the ESSO filling station on the main road, which also functions as the terminus for **buses** on the Ísafjörður–Látrabjarg run (see p.193).

Hrafnseyri

The seventeen-kilometre drive south from Þingeyri to minuscule Hrafnseyri is one of the most hair-raising sections of Route 60. Climbing all the while to squeeze through a narrow pass between mountains over 700m high, the road then makes a heart-stopping descent into Hrafnseyri on the shores of **Arnarfjörður**; when viewed from the village, the road appears to cling precariously to a vertical wall of rock. Named after the fjord's first settler, Örn (meaning "eagle", *arnar* being its genitive case), who lasted just one winter here, and 30km long and up to ten kilometres wide, Arnarfjörður forks at its head to form four smaller fjords, Suðurfirðir, to the southwest and Borgarfjörður and Dynjandisvogur inlet to the northeast. It's widely, and quite rightly, regarded by locals as the most picturesque of all the West Fjords, enclosed by towering mountains.

HRAFNSEYRI itself, consisting of a tiny church, a museum and a solitary petrol pump – which is where the summer-only Ísafjörður–Látrabjarg bus service stops, see p.193 – is one of only two settlements on Arnarfjörður (the other is Bíldudalur, 79km away). It was named after **Hrafn Sveinbjarnarson**, who died here in 1213, one of Iceland's earliest doctors; he trained in Europe before returning home to practise. A memorial stone next to the church here commemorates his life and the grass mound nearby is thought to be the site of his boathouse. This tiny settlement, though, is of much greater historical significance to Icelanders since it was here that **Jón Sigurðsson** (see box below) was born, the man who won independence for Iceland in the nineteenth century. The excellent adjoining **museum** (mid-June to Aug daily 10am–8pm; Sept to mid-June by arrangement with the curator, who lives next door; ☏456 8260, ⓦwww.hrafnseyri; 300kr) records his life, mostly with photographs, some of his letters and contemporary drawings. Particularly evocative is the painting of the meeting of 1851, which Jón Sigurðsson and a number of Icelandic MPs held with representatives of the Danish state in the Grammar School, Menntaskólinn, in Reykjavík, and which helped pave the way for Icelandic independence. The friendly curator, Sigurður, will gladly translate some of the information inside the museum and will also tickle the ivories on the church piano and crank out a song from your home country if you tell him where you're from (he's even produced a CD, on sale for 2000kr). Jón Sigurðsson himself was born in the restored turf farmhouse, opened on request by the curator, with three gabled roofs, next to the church. At the rear of the building, his bedroom, containing the original desk from his office in Copenhagen, has been kept in its original state and offers an insight into the ascetic life of one of Iceland's most revered figures.

The best time to be in Hrafnseyri is **Icelandic National Day** (June 17), when a special mass is held in the church and prominent Icelanders from across the country travel to the village to remember their most distinguished

Jón Sigurðsson

To Icelanders, **Jón Sigurðsson** (1811–69) is what Winston Churchill is to the British and George Washington to the Americans. This is the man who, through his tremendous skills of diplomacy, achieved independence from the Danes, who had almost bankrupted Iceland during the time of the Trade Monopoly. Born in Hrafnseyri in 1811, Jón spent the first twenty-two years of his life in his native West Fjords, and after completing the entry examination for university study, he left for Copenhagen where he chose history and political science among his subjects. Although a committed student, he never graduated from the university, opting instead to dedicate his life to the Árni Magnússon Institute, then a powerful symbol of the struggle for recognition against the Danes; this institute fought a long battle to have many of Iceland's most treasured medieval manuscripts, kept in Copenhagen by the Danish authorities, returned home. However, it wasn't until 1841 that Jón Sigurðsson began his political activities, publishing a magazine in which he put forward historical arguments for Iceland's right to independence. A prolific writer about Icelandic history, politics and economics, he was later elected to the Icelandic parliament, which regained its powers as a consultative body in 1843 thanks to his agitation. Further reforms followed as a direct consequence of his influence, including the right to free trade in 1854, and eventually, twenty years later, a constitution making Iceland self-governing in home affairs, though Jón didn't live to see Iceland become a sovereign state under the Danish crown on December 1, 1918. Iceland gained full independence from Denmark on June 17, 1944, the anniversary of his birth.

champion of freedom. Although it's a serious occasion there's a mood of optimism and good humour in the air, with plenty of singing and celebration.

Dynjandi

Twenty kilometres east of Hrafnseyri, at the point where Route 60 weaves around the northeastern corner of Arnarfjörður, the most impressive waterfall in the West Fjords, **Dynjandi**, plunges over a hundred-metre-high cliff top into the fjord at Dynjandisvogur inlet, forming a triangular cascade roughly 30m wide at its top spreading to over 60m at its bottom. Below the main waterfall a series of five smaller chutes carries the waters of the Dynjandisá to the sea. With your own transport, it's possible to reach the head of the falls – continue south along Route 60 for around 5km, and once the road has climbed up onto the Dynjandisheiði plateau, you'll see the Dynjandisá river, which crosses the road; walk west from here, following the course of the river to the falls.

All buses between Ísafjörður and Brjánslækur (see p.193) make a ten-minute stop at the falls, where there are also a simple **campsite**, toilets and running water. If, however, you choose to stay here bear in mind that the waterfall is incredibly noisy – *dynjandi* means "the thundering one".

Flókalundur and Brjánslækur

South of Dynjandisheiði, Route 60 continues through an extensive rocky highland plateau, passing the turn-off onto Route 63 for Bíldudalur (see opposite) beside Lónfell (725m), before it finally descends towards the road junction that is the setting for civilization at **FLÓKALUNDUR**. Consisting of a hotel, restaurant and a petrol pump, there's little to note here other than the fact that the Viking **Flóki Vilgerðarson**, who named Iceland, once spent a winter here. He climbed Lónfell, only to be dismayed by the icebergs floating in the fjord and named the land "Ísland", as the inscription on the monument in front of the functional but expensive **hotel** *Flókalundur* (☎456 2011, Ⓦwww .flokalundur.is; ❹), overlooking Vatnsfjörður, reminds modern day Icelanders. The hotel **restaurant** is nothing special, but it does serve up decent if pricey food and makes for a good break on the long journey in and out of the West Fjords. The free **campsite** on the same site is run by the hotel and has running water and toilet facilities. All buses between Ísafjörður and Látrabjarg pass through here in summer.

Barely 7km west of Flókalundur, Route 62 leads to **BRJÁNSLÆKUR**, essentially just the ferry jetty for crossings on board the *Baldur* to Flatey and Stykkishólmur. Other than the **snack-bar**-cum-**ticket office** in the small wooden building on the main road by the jetty, and a free **campsite** with washing facilities (☎456 2011), there are no facilities here. The summer-only long-distance **bus** from Ísafjörður and Látrabjarg (see p.193) is timed to connect with the ferry in both directions.

The southwestern peninsula

From its mountain-top junction with Route 60 by Lónfell, Route 63 descends towards the small fjord Trostansfjörður, one of the four baby fjords which make up the **Suðurfirðir**, the southern fjords, forming the southwestern corner of **Arnarfjörður**. This section of the road is in very poor condition and features some alarmingly large potholes and ruts. Unusually for the West Fjords, three fishing villages are found within close proximity to one another here – barely 30km separates the uneventful port of **Bíldudalur** from its neighbours, identical **Tálknafjörður**, and the larger **Patreksfjörður**, a commercial centre for the surrounding farms and smaller villages. However, it's the **Látrabjarg** cliffs, 60km beyond Patreksfjörður to the west, that draw most visitors to this last peninsula of rugged land. Here, in summer, thousands upon thousands of **seabirds** including guillemots, kittiwakes and puffins nest in the cliff's nooks and crannies making for one of the most spectacular sights anywhere in the region – what's more, the cliffs are easily accessible from nearby **Breiðavík**, an idyllic bay of aquamarine water backed by white sand and dusky mountains.

Other than local buses, from June to August, the long-distance bus from Ísafjörður (see p.193) continues on from the Brjánslækur ferry jetty to Patreksfjörður (4hr 10min), Breiðavík (5hr 35min) and Látravík (5hr 45min), arriving at Látrabjarg at 2.10pm. It returns to Ísafjörður at 3.30pm via the same route.

Bíldudalur and around

A thriving fishing port processing vast amounts of local shrimp, there's little to see or do in **BÍLDUDALUR**, a workaday village of just two hundred and fifty people at the foot of Bíldudalsfjall mountain on the southern shores of Arnarfjörður. However, the airport, just 7km south of the village at the mouth of Fossfjörður, has made Bíldudalur a gateway to the southwestern peninsula of the West Fjords with its regular connections with Reykjavík, cutting out the need for the long and tiring journey up hill and down dale from Ísafjörður. The village's only attraction is the curious Memories of Melodies (Tónlistarsafn) **music museum** (June–Aug daily 2–6pm, at other times simply knock on the door; 400kr) at Tjarnarbraut 5. Cobbled together by Bíldudalur's most famous son, singer Jón Kristján Ólafsson, this rambling collection of old 33s and other Icelandic music memorabilia from the 1940–60s, whilst certainly a worthy tribute exhibition to Iceland's past musical greats, is unlikely to grab the attention of foreign visitors since the featured singers and groups were, mercifully, never big abroad.

Bíldudalur practicalities

Daily **buses** operate all year round between here and Tálknafjörður and Patreksfjörður (see p.212) from outside the **post office** and **bank** (Mon–Fri 11.30–4pm) in the main street, as well as to the **airport** (information on ☎456 2151) to connect with the once-daily flight to and from Reykjavík, operated by Icebird.

Bíldudalur has just one **guesthouse**, *Við Hafnina* (☎456 2328, ⊜bfjalli@snerpa.is; ❸, breakfast is an extra 700kr), a grey pebble-dashed building, true to its name, down by the harbour on Hafnarbraut which, in fact, is much more comfortable inside than its dreary appearance would first suggest. For the **campsite** head for the sports field on the southern edge of the village. The one and only restaurant, *Vegamót*, located on the main road at Tjarnarbraut 2, once again close to the harbour, serves up pizzas (from 1250kr) and burgers (600kr) as well as decent fish and lamb dishes for around 2000kr; there's also beer here for 550kr. The nameless **café** attached to the guesthouse also serves up light meals and snacks during the day.

Around Bíldudalur

What Bíldudalur lacks in attractions it more than makes up for with stunning scenery; an excellent fifteen-kilometre **hike** (4–5hr) up the Fossdalur valley to the tiny settlement of **Tungumuli** on the Barðaströnd coast (Route 62) begins at Foss farm, 6km south of the airport at the head of Fossfjörður, following the route taken by local postmen in the late 1800s. From the western side of the farm, the track leads up through Fossdalur towards the small lake, Mjósund, beyond which the route forks. Keep right and take the path over the Fossheiði plateau, which has fantastic views over the surrounding rocky countryside, until it descends through Arnbylisdalur valley on the western edge of Tungumúlafjall mountain, to Tungumuli. A couple of kilometres east of here along Route 62 brings you to the equally small settlement of **Kross**, where there's **accommodation** at *Gistiheimilið Bjarkarholt* (☎456 2025; sleeping-bag accommodation 1500kr, ❷, breakfast is an extra 700kr). It's actually possible to hike directly to Kross by following the left fork just beyond Mjósund, then climbing through the Geilingadalur and Mórudalur valleys. Both routes are shown in the hiking leaflet, *Gönguleiðir á Barðaströnd*, available from tourist offices and some accommodation establishments. From Kross and Tungumuli, the bus (June–Aug) to Látrabjarg departs at around 12.15pm on Monday, Wednesday and Saturday, plus there's one going in the opposite direction to Ísafjörður, via the ferry jetty at Brjánslækur, at about 6.30pm.

Tálknafjörður

Although marginally bigger than neighbouring Bíldudalur, 19km to the east along Routes 617 and 63, there is little that makes **TÁLKNAFJÖRÐUR** any more appealing. Though a prosperous village with a population of around three hundred and twenty-five, this place on the eastern shore of the narrow fjord of the same name, is dreary and devoid of attractions, with tourism on the decline due to the closure of its outdoor activities centre. There's no reason at all now to stop here other than to enjoy a dip in the superb open-air **swimming pool** (☎456 2639), complete with hot pots with fantastic views over the surrounding mountains. There are also a couple of natural alfresco hotspots fed by water from a nearby spring just behind the church on the western outskirts of the village; ask for precise directions from the guesthouses listed below before setting out.

Practicalities

Buses run all year round between here and Patreksfjörður and Bíldudalur, going via the airport at the latter place. There are a couple of **guesthouses**: the *Gistiheimilið Skrúðhamrar* (☎456 2604, ✉hopid@centrum.is; ❷), Strandgata 20; and the *Gistiheimilið Hamraborg* (☎456 2514, ⓕ456 2794; sleeping-bag accommodation 1500kr, ❷), a little further down the main road, which has simple doubles but breakfast costs an extra 600kr; the old couple who run the place don't speak any English. The **campsite** (☎456 2639) is in the centre of the village next to the swimming pool.

Of an evening, locals gravitate towards the *Posthús* **café** and **bar** at the corner of Lækjargata and Strandgata where a beer costs 550kr and light meals such as pizzas (1350kr) are available. At the *Hópið*, the bar and restaurant at the western end of the main road, a dish of freshly caught fish costs around 1200kr. For snacks, soft drinks and other provisions, head for the Mettubúd shop and **filling station** on the main street.

Patreksfjörður

Located on the shores of the southernmost of all the West Fjords, **PATREKSFJÖRÐUR** bears not only the name of the eponymous fjord but also that of **Saint Patrick**, a bishop from the Scottish islands who acted as spiritual adviser to one of the region's first settlers, Örlygur Hrappson. Today with a population of 715, the village is large enough to exist independently of Ísafjörður, 172km away, and is the only place in the West Fjords, outside the regional capital, to boast more than the odd shop and restaurant. Over the years, this tiny village has won a reputation for pioneering excellence; trawler fishing in Iceland began here, a particular style of saltfish now popular in Mediterranean markets was developed here; somewhat less notably, the town also dispatched the only Icelandic vessel ever to hunt seal in the Arctic.

Little entrepreneurial spirit is visible in Patreksfjörður today and, although a refreshing change from the other smaller villages to the north, the place is best seen as a stop-off en route to Breiðavík and Látrabjarg. Built on two sandspits, Geirseyri and Vatnseyri, the village simply comprises a main road in and out of the town, Strandgata, which runs along the shoreside to the harbour. Several side streets branch off Strandgata's western end – one of which, Eyrargata, has an excellent open-air **swimming pool** (☎434 2044) on it – while the main shopping street, Aðalstræti, runs parallel to it.

Practicalities

Buses run all year round between here, Tálknafjörður, and Bíldudalur and its airport. From June to August services also go every Monday, Wednesday and Saturday to Látrabjarg (1.10pm) and Ísafjörður via the Brjánslækur ferry (6pm); they depart from the ESSO filling station on Strandgata. The **post office** (Mon–Fri 9am–4.30pm) is at Bjarkagata 10. For cash withdrawals there's an **ATM** inside the small food store at Aðalstræti 89, attached to *Rabbabarinn* (see below).

Both **accommodation** options are located in the eastern part of town: the guesthouse *Stekkaból* (June–Aug; ☎456 1675, ✉stekkabol@snerpa.is; sleeping bag accommodation 1600kr, ❸, breakfast 700kr extra), is at Stekkar 19, behind the church off Aðalstræti; while the altogether better-value *Erla* (☎456 1227, 🖷456 1209; ❷, sleeping bag accommodation 1500kr, breakfast included) is just a few doors down at Brunnar 14, heading east from the church.

For **eating**, the best choice is *Þorpið* up on Aðalstræti, an airy modern place with excellent views out over the fjord and bad local art on the walls inside – the deep fried catfish with salad and fries is just 1090kr at lunchtime; otherwise there's lamb chops for 1550kr, soups at 600kr or burgers from 750kr. The only other option is smoky *Rabbabarinn* bar, at Aðalstræti 89 inside the blue and white building called Albína, on the eastern edge of the village, where there's occasional live music; it's also possible to eat here in the day though the menu is virtually identical to that of *Þorpið*. It stays open until 3am at weekends. Patrekfjörður also boasts the only **vínbúð** alcohol shop in the entire West Fjords outside of Ísafjörður (Mon–Thurs 1–6pm, Fri 10am–6pm; ☎456 1177), at Þórsgata 10, down by the harbour.

Látrabjarg and around

The cliffs of **Látrabjarg**, 59km southwest of Patreksfjörður along Route 612, rank as the highlight of any trip to the remote southwestern peninsula of the West Fjords. Extending for 14km, from the lighthouse marking the end of Route 612 and also the westernmost point in Europe, **Bjargtangar**, to the small inlet of Keflavík to the east, they rise up to 441m above the churning sea below. A footpath leads along the cliff tops, with excellent views of some of the one thousand or so seabirds that come here to nest on the countless ledges below. For centuries, locals would abseil down the cliffs to collect their eggs and trap the birds for food – it's estimated that around 35,000 birds were caught here every year until the late 1950s – and, occasionally, they still do.

Although the **guillemot** is the most common bird at Látrabjarg, it's the thousands of **puffins** that most people come here to see. The high ground of the cliff tops is riddled with their burrows, often up to 2m in length, since they nest in locations well away from the pounding surf, ideally surrounded by lush grass and thick soil. They return to the same burrows they occupied the year before, almost always during the third week of April, where they remain until August or September. The cliffs are also home to the largest colony of **razor-bills** in the world, as well as to thousands of other screeching breeds of seabird including **cormorants, fulmars** and **kittiwakes**; the din from the thousands upon thousands of birds here can be quite overpowering, as can the stench from the piles of guano on the cliff face.

Incidentally, one of Iceland's most daring sea-rescue operations occurred here in December 1947, when farmers from Hvallátur set out to rescue the crew of a British trawler, the *Dhoon*, which had been wrecked off the rocky shoreline during a severe snow storm. After sliding down the ice-covered cliffs by rope, the Icelanders pulled the sailors to safety using a rescue line they fired across to the stricken vessel – although it took two separate attempts to hoist all the men up the treacherous cliff face from where they were taken by horseback to nearby farms to recover. A year later, a film crew arrived in Hvallátur to make a documentary about the accident, in which several locals were to reenact the rescue – however, while they were filming, another British trawler, *Sargon*, became stranded in nearby Patreksfjörður fjord, giving the film makers a chance to catch a drama on film for real.

The best place to stay near Látrabjarg is the wonderfully located *Gistiheimilið Breiðavík* (T456 1575, ⓔbreidavi@li.is; ➋, sleeping bag accommodation is 1800kr, breakfast 700kr extra), 12km to the northeast and right on the sandy shores of the remote and idyllic **Breiðavík** bay, enclosed by hills to the west and east but with open views out over white sand to the aquamarine waters of the Atlantic to the west. When the weather is good (anything from light drizzle to menacing grey cloud) this exquisite **beach**, without a doubt one of Iceland's finest, is irresistible. It's when the sun shines that the sands are seen to their best advantage though: kilometres of empty, unsullied white strands, punctuated solely by trickling mountain streams finally reaching the ocean, flocks of squawking seabirds and the odd piece of white-washed driftwood, which can provide welcome shelter from the wind if you're intent on catching the rays. A former boys' reform school is now a weatherbeaten, friendly **guesthouse**, where the home cooking is legendary (fish costs 1500kr, beer is 600kr, and wine costs from 2500kr a bottle; breakfast is an extra 900kr). An even remoter option involves informal **camping** at **Brunnar** on the white sands of Látravík bay, beyond Hvallátur, where there's a farmhouse that's home to just two people, immediately to the south of Breiðavík and reached on Route 612; other than fresh water from the stream that flows into the bay from the mountains at the western end of the bay, remember that there are no facilities here at all and no habitation other than the farmhouse.

From June to August, the long-distance **bus service** from Ísafjörður to Látrabjarg (see p.193) arrives here around 1.55pm. It returns to Ísafjörður at 3.45pm via the same route.

Rauðisandur beach and the Hnjótur folk museum

The cliff-top path at Látrabjarg continues east, rounding Keflavík bay and finally descending to the serene red-orange sands at **Rauðisandur** bay after around 20km, where a couple of farming families still live. The lush, open fields that slowly give way to the vast expanse of sand that forms this part of the shore of Breiðafjörður have been cultivated for centuries, and today flocks of hardy sheep wander from field to shore in search of patches of grass. North of the **Bæjarvaðall** lagoon, which marks the eastern end of the sands, Route 614 leads down to Rauðisandur from the head of Patreksfjörður fjord, east of the tiny airstrip at **Sandoddi**, which until a couple of years ago, unbelievably for such an isolated location, had regular flights to Reykjavík.

At the mouth of Patreksfjörður, opposite the identically named village of Patreksfjörður (see p.212), the **Hnjótur folk museum** (mid-May to mid-Sept daily 10am–6pm; 500kr), on Route 612 and served by all **buses** to Látrabjarg from Ísafjörður (see p.193), has a poignant semi-circular stone monument dedicated to the sailors who lost their lives off the treacherous shores of the south-western peninsula during the early twentieth century – all bar one were from the British ports of Grimsby and Hull. Inside the museum, there are two short **films** worth catching. The first, on the ground floor, features the rescue of the *Sargon* (see opposite); the second, on the upper floor, is a late-1980s documentary on the then 74-year-old Gísli Gíslason, a hermit who lived all of his 79 years in remote Selárdalur at the mouth of Arnarfjörður fjord and only once ventured to his nearest village, Bíldudalur. Even Icelanders found his bleating speech virtually incomprehensible on the few occasions he spoke and there was general disbelief that such an existence was still possible. Otherwise the museum contains a jumble of assorted nostalgic paraphernalia, the prize exhibits being two rusting old planes: an Aeroflot biplane that landed in Iceland after running out of fuel, having been turned back to Russia from the US, where it was refused permission to land; and an American DC3 that served at the American NATO base at Keflavík and took part in the evacuation of Heimaey during the eruption of 1973. Neither can fly, the former due to wear and tear from the prevailing climatic conditions, the latter, more obviously, due to a lack of wings. Outside the museum is a replica of a Viking longship, presented to Iceland by Norway to mark 1100 years of settlement. Close by, the *Mummi*, the country's oldest steam-powered fishing boat, is also worth a cursory glance.

The south coast: Bjarkalundur and Reykhólar

The south coast of the West Fjords is all but uninhabited. As Route 60 rounds the head of Vatnsfjörður fjord east of Flókalundur, 6km northeast of the Brjánslækur ferry jetty, it's well over a hundred kilometres before civilization reappears at **Bjarkalundur**, itself little more than a hotel and a filling station. Although still dramatic, the mountains along this stretch of road are less rugged and angular than those along the northern and western coasts. The coastline is dominated by small bays separated by high bluffs, and wide areas of heavily vegetated flatland that gently slope down to the shores of Breiðafjörður. In fact the only village of any significance along this stretch of road is geothermal **Reykhólar**, one of the few settlements in the West Fjords to have its own source of naturally heated water and, although there's little to do here, it's a good place to break the long journey in or out of the region with an invigorating dip in the first-rate outdoor pool. East of here, the dot on the map that is **Króksfjarðarnes** serves as a road junction: from here routes head across Gilsfjörður fjord to Reykjavík and via the desolate Tröllatunguheiði plateau (Road 605; 41km) to Hólmavík (62km from Reykhólar).

If you have your own transport, another good place to break the long journey towards Gilsfjörður, the southwestern entry and exit point from the West Fjords, is at **Vatnsdalsvatn** nature reserve, a couple of kilometres east of Flókalundur, where an easy **hiking trail** (8km, 2–3hr) begins at the eastern side of the bridge over the lake and leads through along the eastern shore, known for its rich birdlife and a favourite nesting spot for the dramatically coloured harlequin duck, and the red-throated and great northern diver. Don't attempt to cross the Vatnsdalsá at the head of the lake in order to return down the western shore, since the river is very wide and fast flowing; instead, retrace your steps.

Bjarkalundur

Hiking is just about all there is to do at the small service centre of **BJARKALUNDUR**, 126km east of Flókalundur, nothing more than a restaurant and a modern and uninspiring **hotel** bearing the same name (☎434 7762, ⓦwww.bjarkalundur.is; sleeping-bag accommodation 2000kr, breakfast 950kr extra, ❸), where they have clean but plain doubles. The **campsite** at the hotel charges 1000kr per tent and has new toilet and shower facilities. Roughly 1km east of the hotel a four-wheel-drive track marks the beginning of a **trail** (7km) leading to the twin peaks of **Vaðalfjöll**, an extinct volcano whose outer layers have eroded away, leaving just a bare chimney from where there are fantastic views out over the fjords and islands of Breiðafjörður. To return to Bjarkalundur, head southwest from the mountains to the old road that leads down to Kinnarstaðir farm, from where it's a couple of kilometres east along Route 60 to the hotel. **Buses** run all year on Tuesday and Sunday (1 daily) from Bjarkalundur to Reykhólar (see below) and Reykjavík. There is no public transport, however, between Bjarkalundur and Brjánslækur.

Reykhólar

From Bjarkalundur, buses continue 15km south on Route 607 to **REYKHÓLAR**, a small farming settlement home to just 120 people at the head of the Reykjanes peninsula with attractive views out over Breiðafjörður. Although Reykhólar's history can be traced back to the time of the Sagas, there's little reminder today of the village's wealthy past, when it was considered to have some of the best farmland in all of Iceland; the village once made a handsome profit from selling the wheat grown on the 300 or so offshore islands hereabouts and the surrounding areas on the mainland. It is one of the few places in the West Fjords to have a ready supply of geothermal energy, which today has been harnessed and provides the village with its main source of activity – the ugly Þörungaverksmiðja algae plant, located a couple of kilometres south of the village, that extracts minerals from seaweed to make toothpaste, soap and handcream. There's little to do in the village except enjoy a relaxing dip in the warm waters of the outdoor geothermally heated **swimming pool** (☎434 7738), which also has two hot pots.

Practicalities

The **tourist information office** (mid-June to mid-Aug daily 10am–noon and 2–6pm; ☎434 7830), located in the former community centre between the guesthouse (see p.217) and the filling station, is friendly enough, though understandably has few suggestions on how to fill your time in this remote corner of the country. **Buses** to and from Reykjavík operate all year round on Tuesday and Sunday, but remember that there is no connection west or east of Reykhólar; to continue by bus from here you have to backtrack all the way south to Bifröst and then continue north again on a service to Brú – don't get stuck here. Should this happen, the only **accommodation** in the village is the pleasant guesthouse, *Álftaland* (☎434 7878, ✉alftaland@hotmail.com; ❸), set on the one and only main road, Hellisbraut, at the entrance to Reykhólar. The **campsite** can be found at the opposite end of the village next to the swimming pool; it costs 600kr to pitch a tent, and there are toilets, running water and showers. **Food** is available at the Arnhóll store at the ESSO filling station, which also serves as the bus terminal.

Gilsfjörður, Króksfjarðarnes and approaches to Hólmavík

From Bjarkalundur, Route 60 heads southeast to **Gilsfjörður**, the narrow fjord that slices into the narrow neck of land connecting the West Fjords to the rest of Iceland, from where it's a drive of 258km south to Reykjavík via Búðardalur (see p.170). A new bridge across the mouth of the fjord makes this journey a little shorter than it would otherwise be.

From the tiny farming settlement of **KRÓKSFJARÐARNES**, halfway between Bjarkalundur and Gilsfjörður, Route 605 heads northeast over the mountains and the austere Tröllatunguheiði plateau to Steingrímsfjörður, from where Route 61 continues to Hólmavík. Although the road has been recently improved and is passable for all cars, there are still some alarmingly large potholes and a steep climb and descent either side of the plateau. Alternatively, it's also possible to reach Hólmavík from Bjarkalundur by taking the atrociously poor Route 608 from the head of Þorskafjörður, 4km west of Bjarkalundur, over the Þorskafjarðarheiði plateau, to meet Route 61 up on the bleak Steingrímsfjarðarheiði highland plateau marked only by rock ridges and a few small lakes, then following it southeast.

Hólmavík and the Strandir coast

From Brú in the south to Norðurfjörður in the north, the lonely 220km of the **Strandir coast** form one of the least-visited corners of Iceland, and if you're looking to really get off the beaten track, this is the place to come. The coastline is dominated by the vast Steingrímsfjörður, roughly two-thirds of the way up the coast, which provides superb shelter to the main settlement in the region, **Hólmavík**, a busy shrimp fishing village and an excellent base from which to explore the surrounding wilderness. South of here, the countryside is characterized by low hills and rolling farmland, set either side of Route 61, which links Hólmavík with Brú (see p.228) – a strategic transport junction for buses to the region at the head of the narrow Hrútafjörður fjord, marking the easternmost reaches of the West Fjords. North of Steingrímsfjörður, the land is much more rugged in nature, with snow-capped mountains and deeply indented fjords, reminiscent of the dramatic scenery around Ísafjörður.

There are very few services along this stretch of coast, and public transport expires at Drangsnes on the eastern shores of Steingrímsfjörður. With your own transport it's possible to continue north to some of the country's most isolated communities, dependent on fishing and sheep farming for their existence;

remember, though, that **Route 643** north of Bjarnarfjörður is in poor condition – and that it closes during the first snows of the autumn and isn't cleared until late spring. However, it's worth making every effort to drive this earth road to really experience the wild and pioneering spirit of Iceland, notably at **Djúpavík**, a former herring fishing village, now all but abandoned, and home to one of the West Fjords' most welcoming hotels. Beyond here, the road battles on north towards Iceland's most remote airport, **Gjögur**, handy for reaching this forgotten corner of the country, and finally **Norðurfjörður**, where it finally expires, marking the jumping-off point for ambitious overland treks north towards the uninhabited wilds of Hornstrandir (see p.201 for walking route).

Hólmavík and around

A thriving fishing village on the southern shore of Steingrímsfjörður with a population of around 380, **HÓLMAVÍK** was granted municipal status in 1890 but only really began to grow during the twentieth century. Today life is centred around the natural harbour at the northern edge of the village, home to around a dozen fishing boats and the shrimp-processing plant, Hólmadrangur Rækjuvinnsla, that potent symbol of economic independence in rural Iceland, of which locals are justifiably proud. The village economy is dependent on the shrimps the local boats catch – inshore in the fjords in winter, deep-sea shrimping in summer. Hólmavík also functions as a service centre for the surrounding sheep farms and boasts a large supermarket, two banks, a post office (Mon–Fri 9am–4.30pm) and the West Fjords' most offbeat exhibition, the **Museum of Sorcery and Witchcraft** (Galdrasýning á Ströndum; June–Aug daily 10am–6pm; Ⓦwww.vestfirdir.is/galdrasyning; 500kr), located in the turf-rooved building behind the shrimp plant at Höfðagata 8–10. An English commentary available on CD will guide you through the various exhibits which recount the occurrence of witchcraft and sorcery in this part of the country during the seventeenth century. The Strandir region, always one of Iceland's most remote, seems to have hung onto Viking superstitions longer than elsewhere, and even today is reputed as the home of cunning. During the late 1600s, twenty men and one woman were burnt at the stake in the West Fjords for sorcery, which included the practice of wearing *nábrók* ("necropants"), a supernatural means of getting rich quick; having gained the permission of a living man to dig up his body after death, the sorcerer would skin the body from the waist down and step into the skin, which would become one with his own. On placing a coin in the dead man's scrotum, the coin would continually draw money from other living people. A copy of a pair is on display in the museum, alongside other items such as a tree trunk with shackles and birch twigs for whipping offenders.

Other than the museum, there are no sights to speak of, though sooner or later you'll undoubtedly come across the oldest building in the village, **Riishús**, on the main street, Hafnarbraut, which runs parallel to the fjord. Built by and named after a local merchant, Richard Peter Riis, the two-storey wooden structure dates from 1897 and now is home to the one and only restaurant in town (see p.219).

Practicalities

Buses link Hólmavík with Reykjavík and Akureyri; from June to Aug there's one bus daily at 9am on Tuesday, Friday and Sunday to Brú where you change; during the rest of the year it's best to check with BSÍ (☎591 1020,

@www.bsi.is) in Reykjavík on how services are running. Services call at the ESSO filling station at the entrance to the village. The **tourist information office** (June-Aug daily 10am-6pm; @451 3510; during the rest of the year @451 3403) is located at the entrance to the village, opposite the supermarket and the filling station and also has **Internet** access (150kr for 30min).

Accommodation is available at the wonderfully located, nameless guest-house (@451 3136, @ 451 3413; sleeping-bag accommodation 1700kr, @), up on a hill at Borgabraut 4 and overlooking the harbour and the snow-covered mountains on the opposite side of the fjord; from the tourist office, follow the main road into town and you'll find Borgabraut running parallel with the northern end of Hafnarbraut. Self-catering facilities and TV are available on both the ground and upper floor; breakfast is not served here and the old couple who run the place don't speak English. The **campsite** is located at the entrance to the village next to the tourist office and charges 500kr per person; showers and toilets are available in the building housing the tourist office.

Eating is best enjoyed at the trendy *Café Riis* at Hafnarbraut 39, whose interior is full of black-and-white photographs of Holmavík's fishing past; fish of the day costs 1500kr, while pan-fried trout with almonds and prawns is 1650kr and their tasty pan-fried puffin breast in blueberry sauce is exceptionally good value at 1650kr. During the day, this place serves up delicious cakes, muffins and brownies for 300–400kr. For cheap eats such as burgers and sandwiches, there's a small snack-bar inside the filling station.

Laugarhóll and Drangsnes

The hamlet of **LAUGARHÓLL**, 30km northeast of Hólmavík and reached by taking Route 61 north to the head of Steingrímsfjörður from where Road 643 heads east, consists of little more than a couple of farms grouped around a source of geothermal water, which feeds an **outdoor pool** and natural **hotpot**, and a **hotel**, the Laugarhóll (@451 3380, @mattimat@mail.mi.is; sleeping-bag accommodation from 1900kr, breakfast 800kr, @). Although the rooms are rather drab, the hotel is a great place to stay to enjoy the slow pace of life in rural Iceland and an early morning swim in the pool, taking in the inspiring views of the gentle Hólsfjall mountains, which form a serene backdrop to the place; there is no swimming pool in Hólmavík. Laugarhóll is accessible only with your own transport.

A **hiking trail** leads from the hotel, first going east along Route 643 towards Norðurfjörður before heading up towards the mountains following the eastern bank of the Hallá, beyond the small Goðafoss waterfall, for Þverarvatn lake. The path then descends towards Laugarhóll following the Þverá river; ask at the hotel for the **hiking guide**, *Gönguleiðir í Strandasyslu*, or pick it up from the tourist office in Hólmavík (see above).

A once-weekly **bus** (ask at the tourist office in Hólmavík for exact details) terminates in **DRANGSNES**, a tiny fishing village home to barely one hundred people overlooking the inaccessible island of Grímsey, the second largest puffin colony in the world, in the mouth of Steingrímsfjörður. According to ancient legend, Grímsey was formed when three night trolls tried to separate the West Fjords from the rest of Iceland by digging a channel from Húnaflói bay all the way to Breiðafjörður. As the sun rose, the trolls in the west ran east but were turned to stone in Kollafjörður, whereas the troll in the north jumped over Streingrímsfjörður, landing on a rocky peninsula where she had left her ox. In anger she threw down her shovel, breaking off part of the cliff, and creating Grímsey. Locals maintain she, too, was turned to stone, and indeed, a tall rockstack known as **Kerling** (The Old Woman), stands down by the harbour in Grímsey looking out at her island and her ox, just off Grímsey's northern promontory.

The village itself consists of a **campsite** with full facilities, one petrol pump, one shop, a dozen or so houses and three **hotpots** on the seafront opposite the church (note the signs requiring all bathers to shower beforehand at the campsite). For **accommodation** there's a farm, Bær III (☎451 3241, fax 451 3274; sleeping bag accommodation 1700kr, ❷, breakfast is 800kr), 2km to the north of the village and right on the shore, with excellent views out over Húnaflói.

Djúpavík and Norðurfjörður

Very few visitors to Iceland venture north of Drangsnes because of the complete lack of public transport, but for those who do there's a chance to explore a remote corner of Europe, where towering rock buttresses plunge precipitously into the icy sea and where the coastline is strewn with vast expanses of driftwood that originated on the other side of the Arctic Ocean, in Russian Siberia. Tourist facilities in this part of the country are virtually non-existent but if you want to experience the raw side to Iceland – and an area of outstanding beauty – this is the place to head for.

DJÚPAVÍK, a village close to the head of the shadowy Reykjarfjörður fjord, is dominated by the huge carcass of its old **herring factory** and the rusting hull of the 100 year old former passenger and cargo ship *Suðurland*, another victim of the West Fjords weather. Opened in 1935, the factory produced salted herring until 1955, when the company went bankrupt following a disastrous collapse in fish catches. When production was at its height in the mid-1940s, several hundred people lived in this remote outpost, women salting the herring, men turning the remains into animal meal and oil. Today though, due to the enormous costs involved in demolishing the factory, which was once the largest concrete structure in Europe, its hollow shell still dominates the tiny hamlet, reminiscent of a Hollywood film set. Despite the evident failure of the herring adventure, there's an endearing air to diminutive Djúpavík, consisting of just seven houses, a petrol pump and one of Iceland's most charming **hotels**, *Hótel Djúpavík* (☎451 4037, ⓦwww.djupavik.com; sleeping-bag accommodation 1700kr, ❷, breakfast 850kr extra, dinner around 1400kr), a former hostel for the women who worked on the dockside and in the herring factory. This remote retreat has rooms (all with shared facilities) at the front overlooking the fjord (dolphins are sometimes spotted from the hotel), whereas those at the rear have views of Háafell (791m), which bears down on the tiny hamlet. In a separate building there are also a number of simple rooms (sleeping bag accommodation 2000kr) that share a kitchen. Since there's no bus service to Djúpavík, the only way other than driving of reaching the hotel is by plane to Gjögur; during the winter months the hotel will pick you up from the airport by snowmobile if the weather demands, otherwise more conventionally by car, for around 1000kr. The hotel now owns the herring plant and runs **tours** (June–Aug daily 2pm) inside which include access to Sögusýning Djúpavíkur (Historical Exhibition of Djúpavík; 500kr) containing evocative black-and-white photographs from the herring years.

Norðurfjörður

Eighteen kilometres northwest of Djúpavík, **NORÐURFJÖRÐUR** is one of Iceland's last places. Occupying a stunning position amid fertile farmland at the head of the fjord of the same name, which opens out into Trékyllisvík bay, the village is dominated by the mountain Krossnesfjall (646m) to the east and rarely receives any visitors. The best place to stay here is the friendly **youth hostel** (☎451 4017, Ⓦwww.fi.is; 1200kr), also known as *Valgeirsstaðir*, and adjoining tiny **campsite** (600kr; shared facilities with the hostel) at the head of the fjord. On the northern shore of the fjord by the harbour there's a small **food store** selling a limited range of fruit and vegetables, a petrol pump and the unimpressive **guesthouse** *Norðurfjörður* (☎451 4060, Ⓔarneshreppur @simnet.is; sleeping bag accommodation 1600kr). One of the country's most dramatically situated swimming pools, **Krossneslaug**, is just 4km northeast of the village, north of the farm at Krossnes. Here, natural springs provide a continuous source of hot water to feed the open-air pool down on the pebble beach, whose walls are barely a couple of metres from the icy waters of the Atlantic; a swim here is one of the most memorable experiences Iceland has to offer.

Six kilometres south of Norðurfjörður, a **hiking trail** leads from the farm at Árnes in Trékyllisvík bay via the Göngumannaskarð pass across the Reykjanes peninsula to Naustavík bay, on the northern shores of Reykjafjörður. Details of this hike are included in the hiking guide *Gönguleiðir í Strandasyslu*, available from the tourist office in Hólmavík (see p.219) and the hotel in Djúpavík (see opposite).

Travel details

Buses

Bíldudalur to: Patreksfjörður (1 daily; 1hr); Tálknafjörður (1 daily; 30min).
Brjánslækur to: Ísafjörður (3 weekly; 6hr); Látrabjarg (3 weekly; 3hr).
Flateyri to: Ísafjörður (2–3 daily Mon–Fri; 20min.
Hólmavík to: Drangsnes (1 weekly; 1hr); Ísafjörður (3 weekly; 4hr 15min); Reykjavík (3 weekly; 4hr).
Ísafjörður to: Bolungarvík (3 daily Mon–Fri, 20min); Brjánslækur (3 weekly; 3hr); Flateyri (2–3 daily Mon–Fri; 20min); Hólmavík (3 weekly; 6hr); Hrafnseyri (3 weekly; 2hr); Látrabjarg (3 weekly; 6hr); Patreksfjörður (3 weekly; 4hr 10min); Reykjavík (3 weekly; 10hr 15min); Þingeyri (3 weekly; 1hr 30min).
Látrabjarg to: Brjánslækur (3 weekly; 3hr); Ísafjörður (3 weekly; 6hr).

Patreksfjörður to: Brjánslækur (3 weekly; 50min); Ísafjörður (3 weekly; 4hr); Tálknafjörður (1 daily; 30min).
Tálknafjörður to: Bíldudalur (1 daily; 30min); Patreksfjörður (1 daily; 30min).
Þingeyri to: Brjánslækur (3 weekly; 1hr 30min); Ísafjörður (3 weekly; 1hr 30min); Látrabjarg (3 weekly; 4hr 30min).

Ferries

Brjánslækur to: Flatey (2 daily; 1hr 15); Stykkishólmur (2 daily; 3hr).

Flights

Bíldudalur to: Reykjavík (1 daily; 50min).
Gjögur to: Reykjavík (2 weekly; 50min).
Ísafjörsur to: Reykjavík (2 daily; 40min).

Northwest Iceland

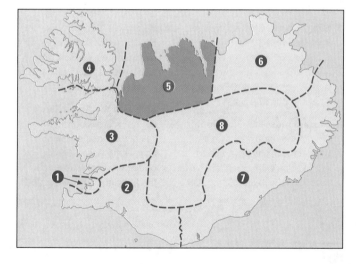

CHAPTER 5 # Highlights

✳ **Þingeyrakirkja, Þingeyrar**
One of Iceland's most spectacular church interiors,
Þingeyrar's church boasts an
intricate wooden pulpit from
the late 1600s. See p.230

✳ **Skagi peninsula,
Skagafjörður** Witness the austere beauty of one of Iceland's
most exposed coastlines and
gain instant respect for the
hardy people who live here.
See p.231

✳ **Swimming in Grettislaug pool,
Reykjaströnd** Follow in the
footsteps of saga hero Grettir
and bathe in this geothermally
heated hotpot on the shores of
Skagafjörður. See p.234

✳ **Herring museum, Siglufjörður**
One of the northwest's best
museums, this is the place to
get to grips with Icelanders'
fascination with fish. See p.238

✳ **Ptarmigan spotting, Hrísey** In
summer dozens of these little
birds waddle through Hrísey's
main village with their offspring
in tow. See p.251

✳ **Botanical Garden, Akureyri**
Seemingly defying the northerly
latitude, this delightful garden
is awash with colour during the
short summer months containing an example of virtually
every Icelandic flower, shrub
and moss. See p.246

✳ **Hiking in Í Fjörðum** Hike
through uninhabited valleys
and mountain passes, all
within easy striking distance of
Akureyri. See p.254

✳ **Crossing the Arctic Circle,
Grímsey** Crossing the magic
line gives a real sense of
achievement, and Grímsey is
one of the best places to see
the Midnight Sun. See p.256

Northwest Iceland

ompared with the neighbouring West Fjords, the scenery of
Northwest Iceland is much gentler and less forbidding – undulating
meadows dotted with isolated barns and farmhouses are the norm
here, rather than twisting fjords, though there are still plenty of impressive mountains to provide a satisfying backdrop to the whole coastline.
However, what makes this section of the country stand out is the location of
two of Iceland's great historical sites, the first of which, **Þingeyrar**, is roughly
an hour's drive east of Brú, where Route 61 from Hólmavík meets the
Ringroad, past the wildlife rich Vatnsnes peninsula. This site was once the
location for an ancient assembly and monastery where monks compiled some
of Iceland's most outstanding pieces of medieval literature. As the Ringroad
heads northeast of Þingeyrar on its way to Akureyri, it passes through some of
Iceland's most sparsely populated areas and **Blönduós**, an unprepossessing
service centre for the surrounding farms and hamlets. The village is, though,
the starting point for a worthwhile trip round the **Skagi** peninsula along
Route 745, one of the northwest's most enchanting stretches of wilderness
coastline and barren moorland. The best place to break the long journey along
the north coast is the likeable, if unpronounceable, **Sauðárkrókur**, enlivened
by stunning sea views out over **Skagafjörður** fjord and **Drangey** island, once
home to saga hero Grettir, who bathed here in the nearby natural hot pool
named after him. Close by, just half an hour's drive away, is the north's
second great site, **Hólar í Hjaltadal**, which functioned as the ecumenical and
educational centre of the north of the country between the twelfth century
and the Reformation. Hard to get to, but worth the sidestep from Route 1
via the Icelandic emigration centre at **Hofsós** telling the story of the
Icelanders who began new lives in North America, is the fishing village of
Siglufjörður. Hemmed in on three sides by sheer rock walls, the village more
than repays the effort of getting there and is especially worth a visit if you've
not managed to make it to the West Fjords since the surrounding scenery is,
unusually for the north coast, almost identical.

Slicing deep into the coastline of this part of northern Iceland, **Eyjafjörður**,
or Island Fjord, is named after the island of **Hrísey** at its mouth, renowned for
its rich birdlife. Bordered by flat-topped perpetually snow covered mountains,
Eyjafjörður is the country's longest fjord and has for centuries been **Akureyri**'s
window on the world as ships sailed its length to deliver their goods to the
largest market in northern Iceland. Today, though, fisheries have taken over as
the town's economic mainstay, profiting from the rich fishing grounds found
offshore. With a population of 15,000 the largest town in Iceland outside the
Reykjavík area, not only does Akureyri boast a stunning setting at the head of

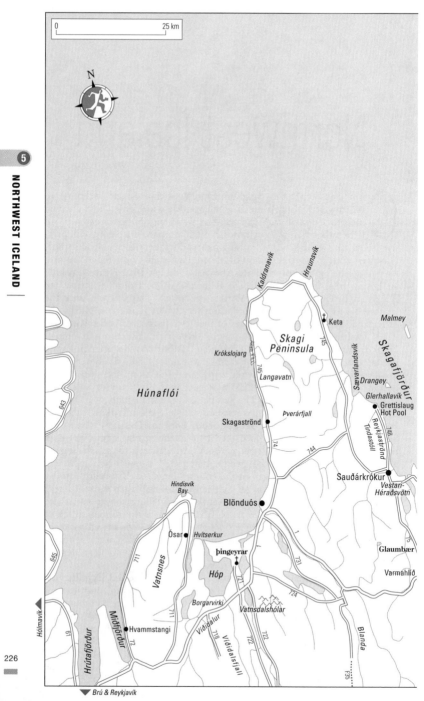

0   25 km

N

Kaldranavík

Hraunsvík

† Keta

Malmey

Skagi
Peninsula

Krókslojarg

745

Sævarlandsvík

Skagafjörður

Langavatn

Drangey

Glerhallavík

Grettislaug
Hot Pool

Húnaflói

Þverárfjall

Skagaströnd

Reykjaströnd

Tindastóll

748

643

74

744

Sauðárkrókur

Vestari-
Héraðsvötn

Hindisvík
Bay

Blönduós

Glaumbær

Ósar

Hvítserkur

Varmahlíð

711

Þingeyrar

645

Vatnsnes

Hóp

721

731

Borgarvirki

Vatnsdalshólar

724

Hvammstangi

711

Víðidalur

Víðidalsfjall

718

722

722

Blanda

712

61

Hrútafjörður

Miðfjörður

Hólmavík ◀

735

▼ Brú & Reykjavík

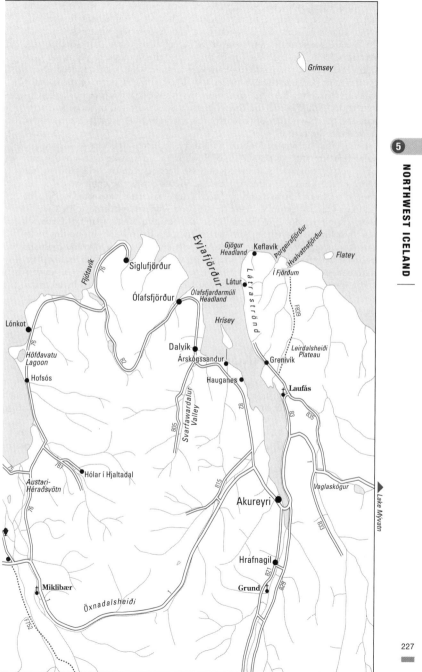

Grímsey

Flútavík

Siglufjörður

Eyjafjörður

Gjögur
Headland

Keflavík

Þorgeirsfjörður

Hvalvatnsfjörður

Flatey

Ólafsfjörður

Ólafsfjarðarmúli
Headland

Látur

Í Fjörðum

Lónkot

Hrísey

L á t r a s t r ö n d

Höfðavatu
Lagoon

Dalvík

Árskógssandur

Leirdalsheiði
Plateau

Grenivík

Hofsós

Hauganes

Laufás

Svarfaðardalur
Valley

Hólar í Hjaltadal

Austari-
Héraðsvötn

Vaglaskógur

Akureyri

▶ Lake Mývatn

Hrafnagil

Miklibær

Grund

Öxnadalsheiði

the fjord, Eyjafjörður, but it's also blessed with some of the warmest and most stable weather anywhere in the country, a perfect complement to the long white nights of summer. Between June and August temperatures can reach 20°C hereabouts, really quite warm for somewhere just 100km south of the **Arctic Circle**, much to the joy of the locals who're quick to point out how sunny Akureyri is compared to windswept and rainy Reykjavík. Indeed, there's great rivalry between the two places and although the "Capital of the North", as Akureyri is often known, can't compete with Reykjavík's eclectic bar, restaurant and nightlife scene, the town's pleasant streets are full of shops and services, and the raw beauty of the surrounding countryside is barely a ten-minute drive from the centre.

The fishing villages of **Dalvík**, with ferry connections across to Hrísey, and **Ólafsfjörður**, close to the mouth of Eyjafjörður, both make excellent day trips once you've exhaused Akureyri; Route 82 between the two villages hugs the shore of the fjord and offers spectacular **views** across the chilly water to the rugged peaks of **Látraströnd**, the fjord's northeastern tip, deserted during the middle of the last century, where there's good wilderness **hiking** to be had. Just forty kilometres north of the mainland, the beautiful Arctic island of **Grímsey** is a must for anyone visiting this part of the country; on the ground this rocky island, bisected by the Arctic Circle, is a springy carpet of moor and grassland bursting with flowering plants whilst aloft the skies are alive with around sixty different species of screeching birds, many of which consider you an unwelcome intruder to their territory; if you haven't yet been attacked by an Arctic tern, you will be here – they even divebomb visitors as they board the plane back to the mainland.

From Brú to Akureyri

The stretch of the Ringroad between Brú and Akureyri is, unfortunately, one of its least interesting. A grinding distance of 230km, many travellers see it as an area to be covered quickly in order to reach Akureyri. However, it can be worth breaking the journey at one or two places en route, and indeed, if you're travelling between the West Fjords and Akureyri, sooner or later you'll wind up at the road junction, **BRÚ** (Bridge), 85km from Borgarnes on the west coast and 38km from Hvammstangi, to the northeast, the nearest settlements of any size. Brú began life in the 1950s as a telephone exchange and post office and today lives down to its name, comprising little more than a bridge over the Hrútafjarðará, which flows into Hrútafjörður fjord, itself part of the much greater Húnaflói bay. Today the post office has been downgraded to a postbox and the only other signs of life here belong to the ESSO filling station (with an ATM), busy with travellers taking a snack break at the *Veitingaskálinn* **restaurant** inside or waiting for an onward bus connection. East of Brú the Ringroad hugs the shores of Hrútafjörður before turning sharply inland towards the next fjord along this stretch of coastline, the minuscule **Miðfjörður**. Beyond here, however, things liven up considerably with the possibility of rounding the Vatnsnes peninsula, where there's a good chance of seeing seals, and, further along the Ringroad, of heading for the north's great historical sites of Þingeyrar and Hólar í Hjaltadal, or taking in small town Iceland in Sauðárkrókur or Siglufjörður.

Hvammstangi and the Vatnsnes peninsula

The eastern shore of Midfjörður fjord is the setting for the only town in the area, **HVAMMSTANGI**, although "town" is something of a misnomer since barely 590 people live here. Just 6km north of the Ringroad, and reached by smaller Route 72 (buses will pull in here on request), the place survives on shrimp fishing, and a couple of brightly coloured fishing vessels are often moored in the tiny harbour, right by the one and only main road which cuts through the handful of suburban houses that pass as the town centre. Should you end up needing a **place to stay** here, the *Hanna Siggu* guesthouse, at Garðavegur 26 (☎451 2407, ⓦwww.simnet.is/gistihus; sleeping bag accommodation 1600kr, ❶), has plain and uninspiring rooms overlooking the fjord; you might be able to persuade the owner to provide dinner but don't count on it.

From Hvammstangi, you'll need your own transport to follow Route 711 as it heads northeast around the **Vatnsnes** peninsula, a wild and uninhabited finger of land on the eastern side of Húnaflói known for its superb views out over the bay towards the needle-sharp peaks of the Strandir coast in the West Fjords (see p.217). While ascending tiers of craggy, inaccessible hills form the spine of the peninsula, the land closer to the shore is surprisingly green and is given over to grazing land for horses; you'll also spot flocks of **greylag geese**. At **Hindisvík**, at the head of the promontory, there's a **seal**-breeding ground, where many of the creatures and their young can be seen lolling idly on the low rocks during June and July. Around the headland, on the more sheltered eastern side of Vatnsnes, the fifteen-metre-high high rock formation, **Hvítserkur**, is a striking landmark. Sculpted by the tremendous force of the sea, this craggy rock, just off the coast, looks like a forbidding prehistoric monster rearing up from the waves; definitely worth a quick stop. Opposite, the friendly **youth hostel** *Ósar* (☎ and ⓕ 451 2678, ⓔ osar@simnet.is; 1600kr per person, bed linen 500kr extra), set on a farm, is worth seeking out for its peaceful surroundings and undisturbed views of mountains and ocean across to the rugged coastline of the Skagi peninusula, which marks the eastern edge of Húnaflói bay. If you call ahead, the owners of the youth hostel will pick you up from the Ringroad or from Hvammstangi.

Þingeyrar

As it heads southwards down the eastern shore of Vatnsnes, Route 711 rejoins the Ringroad in **Víðidalur**, one of the area's most populated valleys and dotted with some beautifully located farms, most notably **Auðunarstaðir** (between the junctions of Routes 711 and 716 with the Ringroad), named after the evidently well-endowed settler Auðun Skökull (Horse's Phallus), to whom the British royal family can trace its family line. The breathtaking backdrop of the brown and green hues of Víðidalsfjall mountain (993m) forms the eastern side of the valley through which one of the northwest's best salmon rivers, the lengthy Víðidalsá, flows from its source at Stórisandur in the Interior.

However, it's not for the scenery that this part of the country is best known, since it's also the location of the ancient site of **Þingeyrar**, which lies just 6km north of the Ringroad along Route 721. If you don't have your own transport, it's a straightforward walk, despite the distance. This was originally the site of a **legislative assembly** during the Icelandic Commonwealth (see "Contexts", p.338), and the first Bishop of Hólar, Jón Ögmundarson, pledged to build a church and an associated farm here if God were to relieve a severe local famine. When the land began to regain its productivity, and the bishop took things one step further and established Iceland's first monastery, Þingeyraklaustur, here in 1133, which remained in existence up until the Reformation in 1550. The monks went on to copy and transcribe some of the country's most outstanding pieces of medieval literature, and it was on this spot that many of the sagas were first written down for posterity.

There's nothing left of the monastery, but a superb nineteenth-century church, **Þingeyrakirkja**, now stands adjacent to where the monks once lived and worked. Constructed of large blocks of basalt, brought here on sledges dragged across the nearby frozen lagoon of Hóp, the church was the first building on the site to be made of stone – all previous structures had been of turf – and it brought much admiration from local worthies. Although its grey mass is indeed an impressive sight, clearly visible from miles around, it's the interior that really makes a trip here worthwhile, with its stark white walls setting off the blue ceiling, painted with 1000 golden stars, and simple green pews. The wooden pulpit dates from 1696 and is thought to come from Denmark or Holland, whereas the altarpiece, inset with religious figures made of alabaster, dates from the fifteenth century and was originally made in the English town of Nottingham for the monastery here. The wooden figures of Christ and the twelve apostles lining the balcony were made in 1983 to replace the original figures from Germany that once stood here – the originals are in the National Museum in Reykjavík (see p.66). The building is often locked, so check with the tourist office in Blönduós (see below) about entry or call in to the horse farm, Þingeyrar, next to the church where keys are kept.

Blönduós

Clustered around the turn-off to Route 721 for Þingeyrar, the extensive area of small hillocks known as **Vatnsdalshólar** is leftover debris from a massive landslide from the Vatnsdalsfjall mountains west of the Hóp lagoon. These conical shaped hills cover a total area of around four square kilometres and are so numerous that they have become one of Iceland's three "uncountables": the other two are the islands of Breiðafjörður and the lakes of Arnarvatnsheiði moors near Húsafell. One of the hillocks, Þrístapar, has gone down in history as the location for Iceland's last beheading, when a couple were executed on it in 1830 for a double murder.

From the Vatnsdalshólar, it's a further 19km along the Ringroad to **BLÖNDUÓS** (84km from Brú), the focal point of Húnaflói bay, with a huge modern hospital and its modern, multicoloured houses grouped on either side of one of Iceland's longest rivers, the glacial Blanda. Without a good harbour the town is merely a service centre for the locality, pasteurising milk from the surrounding farms, although forestry reasearch on the island of Hrútey near the campsite (see opposite) does play some part in the local economy. The centre, consisiting of a handful of uneventful suburban streets and the odd shop, straddles both banks of the river, accessed from the Ringroad by the roads of Blöndubyggð on the southern side and Húnabraut on the northern shore.

Although there's really little reason to break a journey here, if you do, you'll spot the town's astonishingly ugly concrete **church**, right on the edge of the Ringroad opposite the tourist office. Designed to resemble a volcanic crater, the church sits atop a small hill overlooking the town and its charmless grey walls therefore dominate almost any view of Blönduós. The interior is equally austere, with unadorned walls of concrete producing superb acoustics and weaving certain spell over any visitor – if the church is locked ask at the tourist office for the key.

If you're keen to get out onto the waters of Húnaflói, renowned for its rich variery of wildlife, Blönduós is the place to do it: **seal** and **birdwatching**

tours (☎452 4520 or 864 4823, ⓦwww.islandia.is/selir, 3500kr) lasting around two hours leave twice daily (10am & 9pm) from the harbour between mid-June and mid-August. Generally, the boat, *Kópur HU*, sails north towards Skagaströnd before returning via the island of Eyjarey offering plentiful opportunities to spot puffins, eider ducks, seals and, if you're lucky, whales as well. Otherwise, the only other thing to detain you – and frankly it's not going to be the highlight of your trip to Iceland – is the unpronounceable **Heimilisiðnaðarsafnið**, the Museum Of Handicrafts (late June to late Aug daily 2–5pm; ☎452 4067; 300kr) at Árbraut 7, reached by walking along Húnabraut towards the sea, then turning left into Árbraut and continuing to its end. The collection here was assembled by Halldóra Bjarnardóttir, one of the country's leading women's rights campaigners. Part of Halldóra's platform was the elevation of domestic crafts like knitting and weaving to the status of art – an aim, however, that seems hard to justify when looking at the exhibits. Halldóra also happens to be one of the longest-lived Icelanders ever known – 108 years old when she died in 1981.

Blönduós practicalities

All **buses** from Reykjavík via Borgarnes and Brú to Akureyri stop at the ESSO **filling station**. The indoor **pool** (June–Aug Mon–Fri 8am–9pm, Sat & Sun 9am–5pm; Sept–May Tues–Thurs 3-8pm, Sat 10am-4pm; ☎452 4451), with its outdoor hotpot, can be found off Húnabraut down from the church. The **tourist information office** (early June to late Aug daily 9am–9pm, closed noon-1pm; ☎452 4520, ⓦwww.northwest.is) is on the northern side of the river on the main street, just over the bridge, by the **campsite** at Brautarhvammur. If you fancy renting out a cabin head for the seven wooden ones, *Glaðheimar* (☎452 4403, ⓦwww.gladheimar.is; 4100–9300kr) next to the tourist office and overlooking the river; each sleeps up to eight, is complete with kitchen and shower and most also have their own outdoor Jacuzzi on the terrace. Alternatively, there's the comfortable *Glaðheimar* **guesthouse** at Blöndubyggð 10 (same ☎452 4403, ⓦwww.gladheimar.is; ❸) with its riverside views down by the harbour, well-equipped kitchen, wooden floors and IKEA-style furnishings, though the fake velvet bedspreads and wall art featuring naked female nymphs draped in green silk may not be to everyone's taste. The only other choice is the characterless *Hótel Blanda* (☎452 4126, ⓦwww.lax-a.is; ❺), on the southern side of the river at Aðalgata 6, which has very average rooms.

    Eating options in Blönduós are poor, though the best choice is the homely *Við Árbakkann* café-bar, at the corner of Húnabraut and Holtabraut, which serves up tasty toasted sandwiches (400kr), soups and salads (550kr) or good value smoked salmon (980kr); coffee here is 200kr, a beer is 550kr. Otherwise you're left with the greasy burgers, chips and pizzas from the ESSO filling station, opposite the tourist office, or the run-of-the-mill fish dishes at the *Hótel Blanda*. The **vínbúð** (Mon–Thurs 11am–6pm, Fri 11am–7pm, Sat 11am–2pm; Sept–May Mon–Thurs 1–6pm, Fri 11am–7pm, Sat closed; ☎452 4501) is at Aðalgata 8, next to the *Hótel Blanda*.

The Skagi peninsula

Barely a kilometre or so outside Blönduós, where the Ringroad swings sharply inland to follow the course of Langidalur valley towards Varmahlíð, Route 74 (no public transport beyond Skagaströnd) strikes off north for the **Skagi peninsula**, a tooth-shaped chunk of land that forms the eastern side of

Húnaflói bay. After 23km the road comes to the peninsula's only centre of habitation (barely 610 people live here), **SKAGASTRÖND**, a terribly ugly place dominated by a hulking fish factory down by the harbour and the brooding heights of the **Spákonufellsborg** (646m) mountain which bears down on the settlement from across the main road. Although trading began here centuries ago, there's precious little to show for it since most buildings today date from the tasteless expansion of the 1940s herring boom. There's no real reason to tarry, and it's a much better idea to press on to the unspoilt nature of the peninsula beyond, unless you're looking for fuel at the ESSO **filling station** at the entrance to the village or a bite **to eat** at the log cabin *Kántrýbær*, that most curious of Icelandic establishments – an imitation country-and-western restaurant serving up steaks, burgers and fries – next door on Hólanesvegur.

From Skagaströnd, Route 745 begins its circuit of the **Skagi peninsula**, a lonely uninhabited landscape of desolate rocky moorland studded with numerous tarns and tussocky grassland. Here and there a few fields have been cleared of rocks for cultivation, though the true story of the peninsula's decline is told through the abandoned farms that bear silent witness to man's final surrender to the unforgiving forces of nature. This finger of land is one of the best places in Iceland to experience nature in the raw: turn off your car engine, stand outside and listen to the eerie silence, disturbed only by the cries of thousands of seabirds, the crashing of the waves on this exposed shoreline and the howl of the Arctic wind.

Although the attraction of the peninsula is primarily its barren landscapes, it's worth stopping for a closer look at one or two points of interest along the way. On the western shore, roughly 15km north of Skagaströnd, the ten-kilometre-long cliffs at **Króksbjarg** and the glittering **waterfall** where the Fossá river tumbles down the clifface into the sea make a worthwhile first stop. Curiously, the make up of the base of the cliffs – a 15m thick layer of clay topped with 8m of sandstone – has reversed the magnetic polarisation of this part of the coastline. Beyond Króksbjarg, the road passes several deserted farms before reaching the sweeping bay of **Kaldranavík**, at the tip of the peninsula, one of the best places for truly magnificient ocean vistas. Having weaved past the remote farm of Hraun on the northeastern extremity of the peninsula, the road finally veers south following the coastline of **Skagafjörður** fjord for the rugged sheer sea cliff (signed from the road) **Ketubjörg**, actually the remains of an old volcano, and the accompanying rock pillar, **Kerling**, just off the shore to the northeast. From here it's an uneventful and easy drive on towards Sauðárkrókur, routing to the west of the Tindastóll mountains (989m) and the turn for Route 748 to Grettislaug pool (see p.234).

Sauðárkrókur

Although difficult to get around by public transport, the area around Skagafjörður, east of the Skagi peninsula and Blönduós, is worth exploring for a few days. The best base for this is **SAUÐÁRKRÓKUR**, the second-largest town on the northern Icelandic coast, with a population of 2610 and immediately likeable since there are signs of life in the streets on summer evenings, unlike the town's diminutive neighbours. Although the town centre takes no longer than an hour or so to see, it's boat trips to the nearby island of **Drangey** and a dip in **Grettislaug hot pool**, both known from *Grettis Saga*, that make the place unmissable. Equally engaging is the historic turf-rooved farmstead of

Glaumbær, where the first Viking to be born in America lies buried, south of town, handily close to **Varmahlíð**, northern Iceland's leading outdoor activities centre specialising in **whitewater rafting**.

Arrival, information and accommodation

Although the town is 23km north of the Ringroad, getting to Sauðárkrókur is a straightforward affair. **Buses** operate all year between Varmahlíð (daily connections from here at 10.45am when coming from Akureyri and at 1.20pm arriving from Reykjavík) and Sauðárkrókur, using the Haraldar Júlíussonar filling station, at Aðalgata 22, as a terminus. As for **driving**, although it's a tempting shortcut check first before attempting Route 744 to Blönduós up over Þverárfjall mountain, since it's a summer-only road whose summit can close with even the lightest snowfall. Instead, take the Ringroad southeast to Varmahlíð, from where Route 75 heads north to Sauðárkrókur. The **tourist information office** (June–Aug daily 8am–10pm; ☎453 6717) operates from inside the *Fosshótel Áning* (see below) at Skagfirðingabraut 21. For **Internet** access try the **library** inside the Safnahúsið building in Faxatorg square, opposite the *Shell* station, on Skagfirðingabraut.

Curiously, for such an off-the-beaten-track provincial town, Sauðárkrókur boasts one of the best (haunted) **hotels** in Iceland, the *Hótel Tindastóll* (☎453 5002, ⓦwww.hoteltindastoll.com; ❻). This elegant listed timber building dating to 1820 oozes old-fashioned charm at every turn during World War II – one room was the temporary residence of Marlene Dietrich, who entertained the British troops stationed in the area. Dietrich stayed in the *Guðríður Þorbjarnardóttir* suite, which is reputed to be haunted, often smelling of cigar smoke although it's a no-smoking room. Each of the ten low-ceilinged rooms has original wooden floors, beams and an Internet point for laptop connection; out of season, prices fall to ❺. There's even a copy of Grettislaug (see p.234) at the back of the hotel.

Less extravagant is the *Mikligarður* **guesthouse**, opposite the church, at Kirkjutorg 3 (☎453 6880, ⓕ453 6441, ⓔ gisti@krokur.is; ❹), a pretty little blue house with a white balcony, with small but perfectly adequate rooms and sleeping bag accommodation for just 2000kr. The *Fosshótel Áning* (☎453 6717, ⓦwww.fosshotel.is; ❹ with shared facilities, ❻ with bath), opposite the hospital at Skagfirðingabraut 21, swings into operation between June and August in the local boarding school, renting out its numerous box-like rooms. The **campsite** (☎453 8860) is on Skagfirðingabraut, next to the swimming pool, at the southern end of the town.

The Town

Occupying a triangle of suburban streets bordered by fjordside Strandvegur, Hegrabraut and Skagfirðingabraut, Sauðárkrókur's brightly painted houses and wide open spaces, with views of the bustling harbour on the edge of its centre, lend a pioneering edge to the town. Although there are few sights to speak of, wandering around the streets is a pleasant enough way to pass an hour or two – there's no set route to take, but sooner or later you'll wind up on the main street, **Aðalgata**, which is home to shops, restaurants and accommodation. Here, **Sauðárkrókskirkja**, an impressive wooden church from 1892 standing amid an area of residential homes and commercial premises, is worth a look for its fourteen highly unusual stained-glass windows. The futuristic patterns on the centre panes portray a variety of scenes from the Crucifixion to the Holy Trinity – although to the untrained eye, they're perhaps not immediately obvious. Nearby, at Aðalgata 16B, the Sauðárkrókur **folk museum** (June–Aug daily 2–6pm; other times by arrangement on ☎453 6870, ⊛www.krokur.is /glaumb; 400kr) containing a private collection of old sewing machines, chests of drawers and the like, is only worth a peek on a very rainy day.

Much better is to stroll down Aðalgata (which becomes Eyrarvegur), past the **harbour**, to the vast collection of **dried fish racks** just beyond where the stench can be quite overpowering. Here row upon row of wooden frames have been erected and draped in several hundred thousand fish heads and bodies – all awaiting export to various African countries where wind-dried Icelandic fish is considered a delicacy.

Drangey and Grettislaug

It's from the harbour off Eyrarvegur that **boat trips** operated by Fagranes-Drangey Tours (May–Aug daily at 10am; 5hr; 4000kr; ☎453 6503, bookings necessary; min 6 passengers) go to the steep-sided, flat-topped island of **Drangey**, which resembles an arrow pointing north. This is undoubtedly one of the best tours in northern Iceland and a must if you're anywhere in the vicinity of Sauðarkrókur for its unbeatable combination of birdlife and history, although it's not one for the faint-hearted given the steep climb required once ashore and several dizzying drops. Indeed, although the island is now a bird sanctuary where kittiwakes, puffins and guillemots can be seen in abundance, it was once the hideout of Grettir the Strong, or **Grettir Ásmundarson**, the courageous but savage outlaw of *Grettis Saga* (see p.357), who stayed here for three years with his brother Illugi, living off the birds and their eggs. For fresh water the men depended on a spring virtually hidden under a steep rock over-hang on the island's southern cliff. Even today, the only way to reach the source is to clamber hand over hand down a knotted rope, trying not to look down at the 500m sheer drop beneath.

From the boat moorings a narrow winding path streaks steeply up the island's rocky cliffs to the grassy meadow at the summit of this 180m high plug of palagonite rock. Incidentally, the deep hollow in the turf here, where the bedrock shows through, is where Grettir once lived, with a lookout to the west. The island's northern summit is accessible only by climbing a rusty ladder, erected by local bird hunters, which overhangs an area of crumbling rock — definitely not one to attempt if you're afraid of heights.

The stretch of bitterly cold sea between the island and the Reykjaströnd coastline opposite is known as **Grettir's Swim**, which the outlaw reputedly swam across to fetch the glowing embers he'd spotted on the mainland after his own fire has gone out; its 7.5km are still sometimes swum for sport despite the water temperature in summer barely rising above 9°C. However, if the bawdy humour of the sagas is anything to go by, this feat certainly takes its toll, even on Viking superheros; according to *Grettis Saga* two young women, find-ing Grettir lying naked on the ground numb after his swim through the freez-ing waters, declare "he is certainly big enough in the chest but it seems very odd how small he is farther down. That part of him isn't up to the rest of him"; to which Grettir retorts "the wench has complained that my penis is small and the boastful slut may well be right. But a small one can grow and I'm still a young man, so wait until I get into action, my lass". Indeed, to revive himself after the swim, Grettir jumped into the **hot pool** at the now abandoned farm Reykir, which is reached along the very bumpy twenty-kilometre Route 748 from the harbour in Sauðárkrókur; take extreme care if you're driving, as it is all but washed away in parts. At its end, walk down to the sea and the black rocky beach towards the two turf shacks; the pool, which ever since has borne his name, **Grettislaug**, is to the left, although stone slabs now act as seats and the area around it has been paved with blocks of basalt. As Grettir did, you can cast off your clothes, step into the hot water and steam to your heart's content, admiring the twenty-kilometre-long, snow-splashed mountainface of Tindastóll (989m) on one side, the open ocean and views of Drangey on the other – a quintessentially Icelandic experience.

At low tide only it's possible to reach the enchanting **Glerhallavík** bay from Grettislaug: from the pool, walk along the beach around the foot of Tindastóll to the bay, where the sight of thousands and thousands of shining quartz stones on the beach, buffed by the pounding surf, is quite breathtaking. Note that it's forbidden to remove them from the bay.

Eating and drinking

Sauðárkrókur's few **places to eat and drink** are all located in the centre of town along Aðalgata. *Kaffi Krókur* at Aðalgata 16 is a good place to meet the locals over a beer (600kr) and sample good Icelandic and international cuisine, with chicken fajitas and baked salmon for 2200kr, pasta dishes from 1350kr and burgers from 910kr. Opposite, at Aðalgata 15, the bright blue wooden building houses the *Ólafshús* restaurant, which also serves fish but at much more reasonable prices – haddock with vegetables is 920kr whereas a generous starter of marinated sea bass (the house speciality) with salad is 1060kr. For a drink and a dance, most young people gravitate towards the *Sportbar*, Aðalgata 7; the dancefloor is upstairs and they have occasional live music. Alternatively buy your own at the *vínbúð* at Smáragrund 2 (Mon–Thurs 11am–6pm, Fri 11am–7pm Sat 11am–2pm; ☎453 5990).

Glaumbær and Varmahlíð

Just 18km south of Sauðárkrókur, Route 75 passes an immaculately maintained eighteenth-century farm, **Glaumbær** (June to late-Sept daily 9am–6pm; ⓦwww.krokur.is/glaumb; 400kr). A private home until 1947, the farm consists of a row of wood-fronted turf-walled and turf-rooved dwellings dating from 1750 to 1879, and is a powerful reminder of the impoverished lifestyle many people led in Iceland during the eighteenth and nineteenth centuries. The adjacent timber building houses the Skagafjörður **folk museum** (same hours and ticket) and displays a collection of rustic implements once used on the farm, from spinning-wheels to brightly painted clothes' chests. Not only does the farm demonstrate centuries-old Icelandic building techniques, but it's also where **Snorri Þorfinsson**, the first American born of European parents (in 1003) is buried; Snorri came to Iceland with his parents and lived out his life on the farm here. A simple statue of Snorri and his mother, **Guðríður Þorbjarnardóttir** (see Hellnar, p.185), by sculptor Ásmundur Sveinsson stands in the graveyard next to the church. All buses heading to Sauðárkrókur (see p.232) call here – or it's an easy two-hour walk (8km) from the Ringroad and the minuscule settlement of **VARMAHLÍÐ**, home to just 130 people, which has grown up around a hot spring over the past couple of decades. Although the village, dotted around the junction of Routes 1 and 75, is of little inherent interest itself, it sees a steady throughflow of visitors since it is the location of one of Iceland's best activity centres specializing in **whitewater rafting**. Established in 1992, *Ævintýraferðir* (☎453 8383, ⓦwww.rafting.is) operate a whole variety of rafting tours (2–3 daily May–Sept) of varying degrees of difficulty on the nearby rivers, Blanda, Vestari Jökulsá and Austari Jökulsá – their office is west of the centre, 150m off the Ringroad near the junction with Route 752. Trips last four to five hours on the Vestari Jökulsá (the easiest tour and suitable for anyone over 12; 4900kr) to two days of serious rapid shooting on the Austari Jökulsá, beginning high in the mountains of the Interior, which requires some previous experience and is only available to people in good physical shape over the age of eighteen (38,000kr).

Practicalities

If you want to stay in Varmahlíð either before or after a tour, **accommodation** is limited to the charmless *Hotel Varmahlíð* (☎453 8170, ⓕ453 8870, ⓔvarmah@krokur.is; ❺), the **campsite** (☎453 8320) off the road towards Akureyri, or the much better-value *Lauftún* (☎453 8133; ❶), a simple private farm that also has sleeping bag accommodation for 1500kr, a kilometre or so east of Varmahlíð on the Ringroad, just beyond the bridge over the Húseyjarkvísl river. **Eating** opportunities come down to the hotel restaurant or self-catering from the supermarket Kaupfélag Skagfirðinga at the central road junction. The **swimming pool** (☎453 8824) is up on Norðurbrún above the hotel. All Ringroad **buses** between Reykjavík and Akureyri call at Varmahlíð.

Eastern Skagafjörður

The region's greatest historical site lies within easy striking distance of Sauðárkrókur: **Hólar í Hjaltadal**, roughly a thirty-minute drive east along Routes 75 and 76 over the watery expanses of Vestari-Héraðsvötn and Austari-Héraðsvötn at the head of **Skagafjörður** (buses to Siglufjörður pass within 15km), was northern Iceland's ecumenical and educational centre until the Reformation. Today, this tranquil place in the foothills of Hjaltadalur valley consists solely of a redstone cathedral and an agricultural college, a remote and peaceful spot that's worth seeking out – particularly if you fancy **hiking**, since a trail leads from here over to Dalvík (see p.249). Beyond Hólar, Route 76 leads north to **Hofsós**, another diminutive settlement, best known as a study centre for North Americans of Icelandic origin keen to trace their roots, and beyond to **Lónkot**, an ideal choice of accommodation if you want to spend the night out in the wilds – and sample some truly inspiring local cuisine.

Hólar í Hjaltadal

On the eastern side of Skagafjörður, reached on Route 76 as it heads towards Siglufjörður, then another 15km inland on Route 767, the hamlet of **HÓLAR Í HJALTADAL** (ⓦwww.holar.is), or simply Hólar, was very much the cultural capital of the north from the twelfth until the eighteenth century – monks studied here, manuscripts were transcribed and Catholicism flourished until the Reformation. Now home to just sixty-odd people most of whom work at the agricultural college – this and the cathedral are the only buildings remaining – it was the site of the country's first printing press in 1530, set up by Iceland's last Catholic bishop, Jón Arason (who was beheaded twenty years later at Skálholt for his resistance to the spread of the Reformation from the south). A church has stood on this spot since his day, but the present **cathedral** (to enter, ask in the college next door), the successor of earlier religious buildings here, was built in 1759–63 in late Baroque style, using local red sandstone from the mountain Hólabyrða, and is the second-oldest stone building in the country. Inside, the fifteenth-century alabaster altarpiece over the cathedral's south door is similar in design to that in the church at Þingeyrar (see p.229), and was likewise made in Nottingham, England. The main altarpiece, with its ornate carvings of Biblical figures originated in Germany around 1500 and was given to the cathedral by its most famous bishop, whose memory is honoured in the adjacent bell tower: a mosaic of tiny tiles, by Icelandic artist **Erró**, marks a small chapel and headstone, under which the bishop's bones are buried.

There is no public transport to and from Hólar but, with determination, it is possible to walk here from the junction with Route 1. Alternatively, a long-distance hiking path leads here from Dalvík (see p.249). The agricultural college operates as a summer-only **hotel** (June–Aug; ☎453 6333, ⓔtourist @holar.is; 3000kr per person). A limited number of rooms is also available at other times of the year but must be booked in advance. There's a swimming pool and hot pot attached. The **campsite** (400kr per person) is located behind the main building. The school's **restaurant** (2–8pm) serves up a changing range of dishes, often including locally reared Arctic char.

From Hofsós to Siglufjörður

Thirty-six kilometres from Sauðárkrókur, **HOFSÓS** is a tiny, non-descript village on the eastern shores of Skagafjörður, consisting of one street and a tiny harbour, with a population of around two hundred. It's primarily a base for the hundreds of Americans and Canadians of Icelandic descent who come here to visit the Vesturfarasetrið, or **Icelandic Emigration Center** (June to early Sept daily 11am–6pm; other times by arrangement; 400kr; ☎453 7935, ⓦwww.hofsos.is), tracing their roots through the center's genealogy and information service, located in the adjacent building, Frændgarður. Beautifully set on the seafront by the harbour, it makes for an interesting visit whther you have Icelandic blood in you or not, with displays and exhibitions tracing the history of the Icelanders who emigrated west over the sea, some of which are on show in the nearby building, Konungsverslunarhúsið.

Beside the centre, the single wooden **Pakkhúsið** (mid-June to mid-Sept daily 11am–6pm; donation of 200kr) is preserved under the supervision of the National Museum of Iceland as a fine example of a traditional warehouse, built from coarsely hewn timber planks imported from Denmark. Today this hulk of a building, with its sharply pointed roof, is covered in black tar to protect it from the worst of the weather, making the tiny square windows with their white frames all the more striking. Dating from 1772, it was used to store goods for local Danish merchants – it's thought that trading began from Hofsós as early as the sixteenth century. Inside is a cheesy collection of various bird-trapping devices: everything from rafts to snare unsuspecting birds out in Skagafjörður, to nooses made out of stallion's hair – there are also a couple of stuffed puffins, presumably duped by one or other of these techniques.

Up the hill from the emigration center and the warehouse, the *Sunnuberg* (☎453 7434 and ☎453 7935, ⓔvestur@krokur.is; ❸, breakfast 700kr extra) at Suðurbraut 8 has rooms with sea views, although the extremely pink walls may not be to all tastes. **Eating** is best at the *Sigtún*, next to the *Sunnuberg*, where haddock or trout will cost you 1500kr, a burger is 700kr and a beer 650kr; there's outdoor seating in summer, with pleasant views out over Skagafjörður. Alternatively there's the small café, *Sólvík*, opposite the warehouse with a delightful wooden terrace with sea views, serving snacks and sandwiches. However, for truly inspirational local cuisine it's worth pushing on to the **restaurant** and **guesthouse** of *Lónkot* (June-Aug ☎453 7432, ⓦwww.lonkot.is), 12km further north beyond the Höfðavatn lagoon and opposite the now abandoned island of **Malmey**, where, according to legend, neither mice nor horses will thrive, and a married couple may live no longer than twenty years if the wife is not to disappear never to be seen again. Run by a brother and sister team, *Lónkot* specialises in cuisine using only the finest local ingredients, for example, pan-fried breast of Skagafjörður guillemot in blueberry sauce (1500kr). Accommodation here comes in various forms: double rooms with simple kitchenettes located in a converted barn or larger appartments where beds are found in curtained-off ship-style cabins. Before leaving make sure to clamber up the small tower, right by the fjord side, that holds a small seating area – the perfect place to stare out to sea, drink in hand.

Siglufjörður

The highlight of any trip along this stretch of northern coastline is undoubtedly the remote fishing village of **SIGLUFJÖRÐUR** (Ⓦ www.siglo.is), 61km east of Hofsós, an enjoyable end-of-the-road sort of place that also makes an excellent base from which to hike across the surrounding mountains. Clinging precariously to the foot of steep mountain walls which enclose an isolated narrow fjord on the very edge of Iceland, Siglufjörður is the country's most northerly town, as good a place as any to take stock of just where you've reached: the **Arctic Circle** is barely 40km away and you're as far north as Canada's Baffin Island and central Alaska. Winters here can be particularly severe and the mountain road, Route 82, which links Siglufjörður with its eastern neighbour of Ólafsfjörður, rarely opens before late April. Despite its extreme location, it's worth making every effort to get here from Hofsós on the winding, switchback road along the shore of the northernmost reaches of the Atlantic Ocean, culminating in an unpleasantly dark and narrow single-lane tunnel of 830m which cuts through the mountain Strákar (678m) to gain access to Siglufjörður fjord. Things though are set to improve in the next few years once work starts in 2005 on two proposed **tunnels** that will slice through into neighbouring Héðinsfjörður to the east and then again into Ólafsfjörður, radically shortening the whopping 200km journey to Akureyri today which backtracks via Varmahlíð.

From 1900 to 1970, Siglufjörður was the **herring** capital of the North Atlantic, when hundreds of fishing boats would crowd into the tiny fjord to unload their catches onto the rickety piers that once stretched out from the quayside, where herring girls, as they were known, would gut and salt them – during a good season, casual labour and the number of fishermen (who were, in the early part of the century at any rate, primarily Norwegian) could swell the town's population threefold to over 10,000. Their story is brought to life in film, photographs and exhibits at the Síldarminjasafnið **herring era museum** (late June to mid-Aug daily 10–6pm, rest of the year daily 1–5pm; Ⓦ www.siglo.is/herring; 400kr), at Snorragata 15, an old salting station that housed around fifty herring girls – you can still see graffiti, daubed in nail varnish, on the walls of the second-floor room where they once slept, alongside faded black-and-white photographs of heart-throb Cary Grant. The new grey building adjacent to the main museum has been authentically designed to show exactly what a 1930s herring factory actually looked like.

Today, Siglufjörður's heyday is long gone and the place is considerably quieter with a population of just 1500 people. It's a pleasant place, consisting of a handful of parallel streets with unkempt multi-coloured homes grouped around the main street, **Túngata**, which turns into **Snorragata** as it approaches the **harbour**, busy with the goings-on of a low-key port, with fishermen mending their nets in the shipyard and fish hanging out to dry – the town still produces kippers (smoked herring) from a factory down by the harbour. Once you've seen the herring museum there's some excellent **hiking** to be had along the trails that lead up out of the fjord (see box below).

Practicalities

Accommodation in Siglufjörður throws up precisely two options. *Gistiheimilið Hvanneyri* (T and F 467 1378; ❸), Aðalgata 10, is a monument to bad taste: plastic flowers, garish floral drapes and multi-coloured swirls of paint daubed over the staircase. Rooms here all share facilities and are a little on the small side, though there is a well-equipped kitchen for self-caterers available. Otherwise, it's just the **campsite** on Snorragata, south of town beyond the harbour.

When it comes to **eating** things are not much better: food supplies, including locally produced kippers, *Egils síld*, are available at the Strax supermarket at Suðurgata 2-4, or, alternatively, housed in a former cinema at Aðalgata 30, *Bíó Café* is the only restaurant in town. More pizzeria than café, this place serves up really tasty pizzas for around 1050kr, all named after recent blockbuster cinema hits, burgers for 550–850kr and lamb cutlets at 1400kr. It's also a good place to try local **herring** – a plate of three or four varieties with dark bread and salad is 750kr. It's also the town's favourite **drinking** spot and, when the trawlers are in, it's full of rowdy sailors; beer here is 500kr. The other bar in town is *Allinn Sportbar* on Þormóðsgata, serving beer until 1am (3am on Fri & Sat) and has large screens showing football matches. Other facilities in Siglufjörður are limited although there is a **vínbúð** (Mon–Thurs 1–6pm, Fri 11am–7pm; T 467 1262) at Eyrargata 25, and a **library** with **Internet** access at Gránugata 24 with restricted opening hours (Tues, Wed & Fri 2–5.30pm, Thu till 6pm). The **swimming pool** (T 467 1352) is located at the entrance to the town at Hvanneyrarbraut 52. **Buses** stop at the *Olís* filling station at the junction of Aðalgata and Tjarnargata.

> ### Hiking around Siglufjörsur
>
> Several excellent day **hikes** can easily be undertaken from Siglufjörður. The trails described below are shown on the hiking **map** of Siglufjörður available at the Síldarminjasafnið herring era museum (see opposite), and you can check out details in advance at www.siglo.is/en.
>
> The best of the shorter routes (5–7hr), forming a clockwise circle around the town, begins at the southern edge of Siglufjörður, where the road veers left around the head of the fjord. Follow the walking path up **Eyrafjall**, heading towards the Dalaskarð pass, then over the mountain tops and up **Hafnarfjall**, from where there's an excellent view over the fjord, the surrounding peaks and even Grímsey. From here it's an easy climb up **Hafnarhyrna** (687m), the highest point on Hafnarfjall and the starting point for the easy descent towards the bowl-shaped hollow of **Hvanneyrarskál**, a well-known lovers' haunt during the herring boom. From this hollow, a road leads back down into town.
>
> A second, longer trail (10–14hr) begins beyond the disused airport on the eastern side of the fjord (follow the main road through the village to get there) and leads southeast up the valley of **Kálfsdalur**, which begins just above the lighthouse beyond the airport, past **Kálfsvatn** lake, over the **Kálfsskarð** pass (450m) before descending into Nesdalur valley on the other side of the ridge. The trail then leads north through the valley to the coast and the deserted farm, **Reyðará**. From the farm, the trail leads west along the steep slopes of Nesnúpur (595m) passing a lighthouse and several abandoned huts, built by the American military during World War II as a radar station. Once back on the eastern side of the fjord the path trail continues along the shoreline towards the airport and Siglufjörður.

Akureyri

According to *Landnámabók*, the first Viking ships sailed into Eyjafjörður fjord, its mouth barely 40km south of the Arctic Circle, around 890, fifteen years after the Settlement began. The first intrepid pioneers to set foot in the hitherto uninhabited north, **Helgi Magri** (Helgi the Lean) and Þórunn Hyrna, made landfall at Kristnes, 9km south of where **AKUREYRI** presently stands, believing that Þór had guided them into Eyjafjörður. Their faith seems, however, to be been in a state of confusion since they curiously chose to bestow an unqualified Christian name (Christ's Point) on their new home. Although little more is known about this early period of Akureyri's history, it is thought that Helgi suffered from a nutritional disease he developed as a child in the Hebrides, where he lived with his Irish mother and Swedish father before coming to Iceland. Several centuries would then pass before mention of what is now Akureyri was made, its name "the cornfield on the sand spit" a clear indication of its current location, the land promontory where **Laxdalshús**, the oldest building in town dating from 1795 and now a private home, currently stands at Hafnarstræti 11. In 1602, however, Akureyri became a trading post with the establishment of a commercial monopoly which gave the Danish merchants of Helsingør the exclusive right to trade with Iceland. Curiously though, the traders were not permitted to take up permanent residence in the town, forced instead to leave for Denmark after closing their stores in the autumn. It wasn't until 1787 that this punitive monopoly was lifted and Akureyri became one of six towns in Iceland to be granted municipal status, despite the fact that its population then numbered little more than a dozen and most trade remained firmly in the hands of Danish merchants and their families. However, it was to the sea and its sheltered harbour, today located right in the heart of the town between **Drottningarbraut** and **Strandgata**, that Akureyri looked for renewed prosperity. Indeed, from then on the town prospered, and in the late nineteenth century one of Iceland's first cooperatives, **KEA**, was established here, going on to play a key role in the economy. Iceland's only **university** outside Reykjavík was established here in 1987 giving the town a much needed youthful boost.

Today, the transport hub and commercial centre of the whole of northern Iceland is divided into two distinct areas: the town centre, harbour and commercial district north of **Hafnarstræti**, the main street, and the suburban areas to its south, where the distinctive **Akureyrarkirkja** church, **museums** and the superb **botanical gardens** can all be found. As far as entertainment goes, the town is a decent enough place to relax in for a day or two, with an excellent open-air swimming pool and enough cafés and restaurants to keep you well fed and watered. That most un-Icelandic thing, the **forest**, makes a welcome appearance just south of Akureyri in the form of **Kjarnaskógur**, easily accessible on foot from the town centre and a popular destination for locals at weekends who come here to walk the many trails that crisscross the forest and to picnic. If you're doing much touring, you're almost certain to find yourself in town sooner or later, as it makes an excellent base from which to explore nearby Lake Mývatn and the Jökulsárgljúfur National Park (both covered in Chapter Six; see p.265 & p.281).

Getting to Akureyri from Siglufjörður involves a long and winding drive along Route 82. However, this route is often closed due to bad weather, and the only other way to reach Akureyri is to backtrack on Route 76 towards Hofsós (see p.237) until you reach the Ringroad again, a tiring 192km drive. From this junction, Route 1 makes the steep ascent up to the high moorland

KEA

Spend any time in and around Akureyri and you can't fail to notice the ubiquitous **KEA** logo, plastered on hotels, fishing boats and even Kaffibrensla Akureyrar, the town's coffee-roasting plant. It's said locally that KEA, the Kaupfélag Eyfirðinga Akureyri (Cooperative Society of Eyjafjörður and Akureyri), owns everything except the church and, whilst that's not strictly true, KEA does have fingers in many pies. Established in June 1886 by local farmers keen to win a better price for the live export of their sheep to England, ten years later the society opened its first co-op store and never looked back. Still with headquarters on the main street in Akureyri, KEA now owns shares in virtually any local business you choose to mention, concentrating on the food and merchandise sectors.

of Öxnadalsheiði, where, legend states, many of the victims of the Sturlung Age battles are buried, close to the road at Miklibær. There are countless stories of the ghosts of lost travellers haunting the pass and in winter it's one of the first in the country to become blocked. The government subsidises the highest farm here, ensuring not only that it keeps going but also that help is available for anyone stranded. Bus travellers, though, will have to make do with glancing through the window since services along this stretch of road don't stop.

Arrival and information

The **airport** is stunningly located on a spit of land in the middle of the fjord, a couple of kilometres south of town, from where it's possible to walk into the centre following the highway, Drottningarbraut, northwards as it runs parallel to the fjord, in around thirty minutes; alternatively, taxis (800kr) are available outside the terminal building. The airport is served by domestic flights from Reykjavík, Grímsey, Vopnafjörður and Þórshöfn. The only international year round link is the twice-weekly service from Copenhagen with Air Greenland. **Long-distance buses** terminate in the station at the southern end of Hafnarstræti, the main street, which is pedestrianized north of its junction with Kaupvangsstræti, from where it leads towards the diminutive main square, Ráðhústorg.

The friendly **tourist information office** (June–Aug Mon–Fri 7.30am–7pm, Sat & Sun 8am–5pm; Sept–May Mon–Fri 8am–5pm; ☎462 7733, ⓦwww.eyjafjordur.is) is in the bus station, and has seemingly endless supplies of maps, brochures and good advice. The pedestrianized **Hafnarstræti** is the main shopping street and runs to Akureyri's main square, **Ráðhústorg**. From Ráðhústorg's northwestern corner, Brekkugata leads up to the **library** (Mon–Fri 10am–7pm, plus late Sept to mid-June Sat 10am–3pm), a veritable haven on rainy afternoons with numerous books in English about Iceland; there's also **Internet** access here.

Accommodation

There's no shortage of **accommodation** in Akureyri and there's no need to book in advance, even in summer, unless you wish to stay at the cheapest place in town, the excellent and well-appointed **youth hostel** (☎462 3657, ⓦwww.simnet.is/storholt1; ❸) at Stórholt 1, an easy twenty- to thirty-minute walk north of the main square along Glerágata (Route 1 from Reykjavík), opposite the ESSO filling station and, unusually for Iceland, surrounded by trees. Rooms here sleep up to four people, and there are two kitchens and a

TV room; doubles with private facilities are 6200kr, a room for four costs 2500kr per person, while sleeping-bag accommodation is 2100kr per person (1650kr for HI members). The **campsite** (mid-June to Aug; ☎462 3379) is at Þórunnarstræti, next to the university; get here by walking up Kaupvangsstræti, past the swimming pool on Þingvallastræti, and turning left at the crossroads. Shower and toilet facilities are on the other side of Þórunnarstræti in the school building.

Three of Akureyri's four **hotels** are on the same road, virtually next door to each other and just a five-minute walk from the town centre; as in Reykjavík, **guesthouses** charge pretty much the same prices as each other for rooms of similar standards. Breakfast is usually included in the price for hotels but not guesthouses. If you're planning to base yourself in Akureyri and want room to spread out in, it's worth considering renting an **apartment**.

Ás Hafnarstræti 77 ☎461 2249, ℉461 3810. Conveniently situated opposite the bus station; a few of the five rooms in this guesthouse have views out over the fjord, as well as access to kitchen facilities. Don't be tempted to take a room in the sister guesthouse of the same name on Skipagata because the traffic noise there is unbearable. Sleeping-bag accommodation 3000kr. **❶**

Brekkusel Byggðavegur 97 ☎461 2660, ℮guesthouse@isl.is. A pleasant suburban guesthouse, handy for the town swimming pool, with its own garden and outdoor hot pot. The clean rooms are simple in style, though the omnipresent pink colour scheme is rather intrusive. Breakfast is extra. Sleeping-bag accommodation 4400kr for two people per double. **❸**

Gula Villan Brekkugata 8 (all year) & Þingvallastræti 14 (June–Aug only) ☎461 2860, ℮gulavillan@nett.is. A total of nineteen identical rooms in two guesthouses, all with shared facilities, kitchen and TV. Breakfast (800kr) is only at Þingvallastræti 14. Sleeping-bag accommodation 4400kr per double room. **❸**

Harpa Hafnarstræti 83–85 ☎460 2000, ⓦwww.hotelkea.is. Not quite as upmarket as its neighbour, the *Kea*, but correspondingly a little cheaper. Sharing the same reception and breakfast room as the *Kea*, you get the best of both worlds: comfortable communal surroundings and virtually the same room – all you lack is a minibar and a hairdryer. **❻**

Hótel Íbúðir Geislagata 10 ☎462 2300 or mobile ☎892 9838, ⓦwww.hotelibudir.is. Pleasant two- to four-room apartments with sitting room and kitchen, usefully located within two minutes' walk of Ráðhústorg. Depending on size **❻**–**❼**. There are also a number of regular undistinguished

double and single rooms here; with or without private facilities for **❸**–**❹**.

Hótel Norðurland Geislagata 7 ☎462 2600, ⓦwww.hotelkea.is. A good location for this KEA owned hotel, within easy striking distance of the main square, though the en-suite rooms are rather dreary. Breakfast is included. **❻**

Kea Hafnarstræti 87–89 ☎460 2000, ⓦwww.hotelkea.is. The largest and most expensive hotel in Akureyri with modern, comfortable en-suite rooms kitted out with satellite TV and a minibar, though the feel is old-fashioned and sterile and the place is crying out for a makeover. Rooms at the front have good views of the town, however. There's a free Internet terminal in reception for guests' use. **❼**

mhotel Hafnarstræti 67 ☎462 5600, ⓦwww.mhotel.is. Located in a black-and-white painted house virtually opposite the bus station, this newly renovated hotel is Nordic chic to a T. Plain, tasteful rooms with minimalist décor and wooden floors, all with private facilities and some with good views out over the fjord, though they are somewhat small for the price. **❻**

Sólgarðar Brekkugata 6 ☎461 1133, ℮solgarda @binet.is. Four highly agreeable, bright and spacious rooms with TV and access to a kitchen, just one minute from the main square. Breakfast is 700kr extra. Sleeping-bag accommodation 2000kr. **❸**

Súlur Þórunnarstræti 93 ☎461 1160, ℮sulur@islandia.is. Summer-only (June–Aug) rooms in a guesthouse, with self-catering facilities available, in a guesthouse near the campsite and the botanical garden, a fifteen-minute walk from the centre. Breakfast is 800kr; sleeping-bag accommodation 4400kr per double room. **❸**

The Town: north of Kaupvangsstræti

North of Kaupvangsstræti, the pedestrianized **Hafnarstræti**, the main shopping street, runs to Akureyri's main square, **Ráðhústorg**. This modest street, no

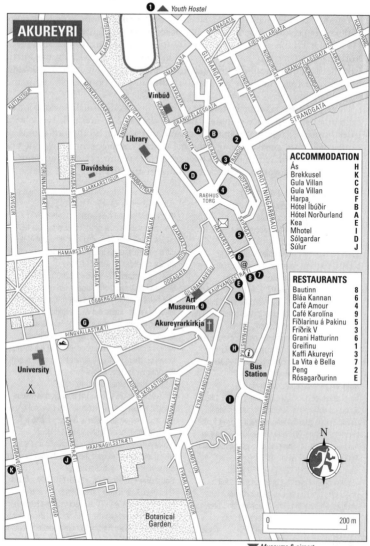

AKUREYRI

Youth Hostel

Vínbúð

Library

Davíðshús

RÁÐHÚS
TORG

Art
Museum

Akureyrarkirkja

University

Bus
Station

Botanical
Garden

N

0   200 m

Museums & airport

ACCOMMODATION

Ás	H
Brekkusel	K
Gula Villan	C
Gula Villan	G
Harpa	F
Hótel Íbúðir	B
Hótel Norðurland	A
Kea	E
Mhotel	I
Sólgardar	D
Súlur	J

RESTAURANTS

Bautinn	8
Bláa Kannan	6
Café Amour	4
Café Karolína	9
Fiðlarinu á Þakinu	5
Friðrik V	3
Grani Hatturinn	6
Greifinu	1
Kaffi Akureyri	3
La Vita è Bella	7
Peng	2
Rósagarðurinn	E

more than 150m in length, and its parallel neighbour to the east, **Skipagata**, together contain virtually all the shops and services that the town has to offer and it's within this rectangle that you'll spend much of your time.

From Ráðhústorg itself, a couple of diversions are within easy striking distance. Head northwest up to the library, then south onto Oddeyrargata, take the first right into Krabbastígur and finally turn left into Bjarkastígur to reach the austere building at no. 6 known informally as **Davíðshús** (June–Aug Mon–Sat 4–5.30pm; 300kr), the former home of one of Iceland's most famous poets, novelists and playwrights, Davíð Stefánsson. Born in 1895 to the north of Akureyri, he published his first anthology of poems at the age of 24 and went on to write verse and novels that were often critical of the state. It was only after his death in 1964 that Davíð was finally taken into Icelanders' hearts and is now regarded as one of the country's greatest writers. Inside, in addition to his numerous books that adorn the walls, are many of his personal effects, including his piano and writing desk as he left them.

From the top of Bjarkarstígur, the long, straight Helgamagrastræti, named after Helgi Magri, the first settler in the Eyjafjörður region, leads south to Þingvallastræti and the town's excellent and newly refurbished outdoor **swimming pool**, which has two large pools, several hot pots, a steam room and a **sauna** (women only Tues & Thurs; men only Wed & Fri), and is an absolute treat when the sun is shining. Head east down Þingvallastræti and you'll come to the uninspiring **Akureyri Art Museum** at Kaupvangsstræti 24 (Listasafnið á Akureyri; Tues–Sun 1–6pm; ⓦ www.listasafn.akureyri.is; 350kr). Inside is a collection of works by local artists as well as a number of studios alongside, known as Listagilið, where workshops are occasionally held.

It's worth venturing east of the commercial centre of town to explore the harbourside, best reached along the main road, Drottningarbraut, running parallel to Skipagata. Although the small southern **harbour**, Akureyrarhöfn, is close to the junction of Drottningarbraut and Kaupvangstræti, it's really along Strandgata, which runs along the harbour's northern edge, that the industrial face of Akureyri becomes more prominent. The shipyard and freighter terminal here make up the largest commercial port outside Reykjavík, a bustling part of town where the clanking of cranes accompanies the seemingly endless unloading and loading of ocean-going vessels at the dockside. In summer it's not uncommon for cruise liners to be moored in the fjord opposite the docks here, awaiting the return of passengers who have been whisked ashore by a flotilla of small boats.

The Town: south of Kaupvangsstræti

Although Akureyri is far from ostentatious, you can't miss the dramatic **Akureyrarkirkja** (daily 10am–noon & 2–4pm; ⓦ www.akirkja.is), whose twin towers loom over the town, perched on a hill up a flight of steps from the junction of Hafnarstræti and Kaupvangsstræti. Comparisons with Hallgrímskirkja in Reykjavík (see p.71) are unavoidable, especially since both were designed by the same architect, Guðjón Samúelsson, and not only tower over neighbouring buildings but are modelled on basalt columns. Inside, there are some dazzling stained-glass windows, the central panes of which are originally from the old Coventry cathedral in Britain – removed, with remarkable foresight, at the start of World War II before it was demolished during bombing raids, and sold to an Icelandic dealer who came across them in an antiques shop in London. The church's other stained-glass windows depict scenes from Icelandic history and legends.

A pathway leads round the church to **Sigurhæðir**, at Eyrarlandsvegur 3 (The House of Verbal Arts; June to Aug daily 1.30–3.30pm; 300kr), the former home of **Matthías Jochumsson** (1835-1920), the distinguished poet and author of the stirring Icelandic national anthem. Now a museum containing a small and unexceptional collection of his furnishings and a few portraits, the house was built in 1902 and was his home until his death in 1920. Unless you have a burning desire to immerse yourself in obscure Icelandic poetry, however, it's better to walk right on by, passing close to the university specialising, amongst other things, in degrees in fisheries, and head instead for the glorious **Botanical Gardens** (Lystigarður; June–Sept Mon–Fri 8am–10pm, Sat & Sun 9am–10pm; free), at the end of Eyrarlandsvegur. Established in 1912 by Margrethe Schiöth, a Danish woman who lived in Akureyri, the gardens are a rich display of plant life enclosed by that Icelandic rarity, fully grown trees. Besides virtually every Icelandic species, there's an astonishing number of sub-tropical plants from South America and Africa – seemingly defying nature by existing at all in these high latitudes, the annual mean temperature for Akureyri being barely 3.4°C. In summer, when the fragance of hundreds of flowers hangs in the air, the gardens, with undisturbed views out over the fjord, are a real haven of peace and tranquility. Incidentally, the dozens of kids you'll see around the gardens, and indeed the rest of Akureyri, are there on behalf of the town council, keeping the place tidy and earning a little pocket money in the process.

Below the gardens is the oldest part of Akureyri, and many of its wooden buildings, including several along Aðalstræti, to the southeast, have been preserved and turned into museums. The first, however, is the least interesting: the **Good Templars Museum**, or Friðbjarnarhús (July & Aug Sat & Sun 2–5pm; free), at no. 46, where the Icelandic Good Templars Order was founded in 1884 – an occasion recorded inside with singularly uninteresting documents and photos. The museum is named after a local book merchant, Friðbjörn Steinsson, who once lived here.

Further on, at Aðalstræti 54, the black wooden house with white window frames is **Nonnahús** (Jón Sveinsson Memorial Museum; June to Aug daily 10am–5pm; ⓦ www.nonni.is; 350kr, 550kr for combined entry with Akureyri museum); the childhood home of Jón Sveinsson – Nonni is the diminutive form of Jón in Icelandic – the Jesuit priest and author of the *Nonni* children's books. Based on his experiences of growing up in northern Iceland, the stories are little known to English-speaking audiences but are inordinately popular in German-speaking countries – most were written in German – and are translated into around forty other languages. Nonni lived here until he was twelve, when, following his father's death, he moved first to Denmark, where he converted to Catholicism, then moved again to France and then, in 1914, to Austria, where he wrote his first book, before settling in Germany. Inside the house illustrations from his stories decorate the walls and numerous translations of his dozen books are displayed. Dating from 1850, the house itself is one of the oldest in the town and still has its original furniture, giving a good indication of the living conditions at the time of construction; note the low ceilings and narrow doorways, which were designed to keep the heat in. Incidentally, when Nonni lived here the fjord stretched right up to his front door – all the area east of the house, where the main road now runs, is reclaimed land.

A few strides on is the **Akureyri Museum** (June to mid-Sept daily 11am–5pm, rest of the year Sun 2–4pm; 400kr) at Aðalstræti 58, set back a little from the street behind a well-tended garden. The upper floor of the museum has a good assortment of farming and fishing items from Akureyri and Eyjafjörður's past, plus a spectacular wooden pulpit from 1768, which once proudly stood in the church at nearby Kaupangur, hand-painted in subtle greens and blues and bedecked with painted flowers by local Jón Hallgrímsson. However, it's the skeleton of a middle-aged woman with a horse, found in separate graves at nearby Dalvík, that really impresses. Dating from around the year 1000, this woman was one of the first settlers in the Eyjafjörður region. Downstairs, an exhibition detailing how the town has developed from the 1700s to the present day contains a glorious jumble of household items including a mangle, cashtill and even a sleigh on skis.

Kjarnaskógur

Not content with the trees that line most of Akureyri's streets, locals have now planted an entire forest on former farmland roughly an hour's walk south of the town, the first stage in a much more ambitious plan to encircle Akureyri with forest. **Kjarnaskógur**, easily reached by walking south from the museums along Drottningarbraut out past the airport, is a favourite recreational spot at weekends and on summer evenings, when the air is heavy with the scent of pine. Although birch and larch predominate, there are over fifty species of shrubs and trees here, some of which have grown to over 12m in height, quite a feat for a country where trees rarely reach little more than waist height – witness the long-standing Icelandic joke about what to do when you get lost in an Icelandic forest (answer: you stand up). Within the forest there are easy walking paths complete with picnic sites, a jogging track for the more energetic that doubles as a skiing trail in winter, plus a children's play area. Camping is not permitted here.

Eating, drinking and nightlife

Unless you're arrived directly from Reykjavík, you'll feel quite dizzy at the wide choice of eateries in Akureyri. Thanks to the town's small university and its role as a commercial centre for the entire north of the country, there's now a fair choice of **cafés** and **restaurants** – even the odd **bar** or two. In short, indulge yourself before moving on.

Cafés and restaurants

Bautinn Hafnarstræti 92. Always busy and popular with locals as well as visitors, this is essentially a cheap and cheerful dine-and-dash type place. Although the menu does extend to a couple of meat and fish dishes (around 1500kr), it's not going to be the culinary highlight of any visit to Akureyri and is best used for a quick burger and chips (950kr).

Bláa Kannan Hafnarstræti 96. No-smoking café in an old wooden building on the main street, good for a cup of coffee or a bite to eat during the day, and popular with local shoppers.

Café Karólína Kaupvangsstræti 23. Akureyri's most stylish café, with works of art hanging from the walls, popular with budding artists and trendy students. Known for its wide selection of coffees and delicious cakes. Also serves open sandwiches for 600kr.

Fiðlarinn á Þakinu Skipagata 14. Top-notch restaurant overlooking the harbour and the fjord serving expensive but delicious fish from 2400kr and lamb from 3700kr. However, if you've looking to treat yourself, you'll do better at *Friðrik V* for price and atmosphere.

Friðrik V Strandgata 7. Quite simply the best restaurant in Akureyri, run by the ebullient Friðrik who trained at *Hótel Holt* in Reykjavík and London's *River Café*. The inventive Mediterranean cuisine here is quite extraordinary and always scrumptious. In terms of price, quality and atmos-

phere nowhere else in town even comes close. The menu changes frequently, but the flavours are generally Italian or Spanish; count on 2500–3500kr per main dish. Alternatively, try the four-course gourmet menu (5950kr) and allow Friðrik to personally create your dinner.

Greifinn Glerárgata 20. Close to the youth hostel, this pizza and pasta joint is worth seeking out for its lively atmosphere; it's the most popular restaurant with locals and is usually busy. Although prices are similar to those of *La Vita è Bella* in town, there's a more extensive menu including salads. Reckon around 1400kr for a large pizza.

Kaffi Akureyri Strandgata 7. More bar than café, with a wooden interior touched off by a parquet floor and window blinds. A spacious place popular of an evening for a drink or a coffee, with occasional live music at weekends.

La Vita è Bella Hafnarstræti 92. The most authentic Italian restaurant in town, with pizzas at 1350kr, calzone 1080kr and pasta dishes from 1500kr. However, the meat here is expensive (lamb from 3000kr, beef from 3500kr) and not worth the extra expense.

Peng Strandgata 13. Akureyri's only Chinese restaurant close to the bourbside, serving up reasonable if not overly authentic dishes. The weekday lunch buffet for 1150kr is extremely good value; otherwise a two course set evening meal is 2090kr. Vegetarian options available.

Rósagarðurinn Hafnarstræti 87–89 inside Hótel Kea. A good choice for excellent fish, 2290kr, or lamb, 3400kr, though the sombre interior and lack of other diners is offputting. Frankly, if you're going to spend upwards of 3000kr there are other places more worthy of your cash.

Bars and nightlife

Café Amour Ráðhústorg 7. This place quite fancies itself, all Nordic minimalist, leather chairs and wooden floors undeniably creating a laidback, trendy atmosphere popular with Akureyri's young things who congregate here from early evening onwards.
Góði Dátinn Geislagata 14. Dance club where you'll find virtually every young person in Akureyri

on Thursday to Sunday evenings grooving to the latest tunes or to live music. Beer in the club is more expensive than in the basement bar, *Sjallinn* (see below).
Græni Hatturinn Hafnarstræti 96. A popular, evenings-only British-style pub in the basement of the *Bláa Kannan* (see p.247), and good for a beer (around 600kr).
Odd Vitinn Strandgata 53. A lively harbourside pub, particularly popular at weekends for its entertaining karaoke events; great for a drink before a night out.
Sjallinn Geislagata 14. Great basement bar inside the *Góði Dátinn* club complex (see above) serving the cheapest beer in Akureyri, around 450kr.

Listings

Airlines Flugfélag Íslands, at the airport ☎460 7000, ⓦwww.airiceland.is
Alcohol store Hólabraut 16. Mon–Thurs 11am–6pm, Fri 11am–7pm, Sat 11am–4pm ☎462 1655.
Bookshops Penning Bókval, Hafnarstræti 91–93, is good for maps and guidebooks. For second-hand English paperbacks, try Fornbókabúðin Fróði, Kaupvangsstræti 19.
Car rental ALP, Glerárgata 36, ☎462 3400; Hertz, Akureyri airport, ☎461 1005.
Cinemas Nýja Bíó, Strandgata 2 ☎461 4666; Borgarbíó, Holarbraut 12 ☎462 3500.
Emergencies ☎112.
Hospital The hospital on Eyrarlandsvegur has a 24hr accident-and-emergency ward ☎463 0100.
Internet Akureyri Centrum, Hafnarstræti 94 (daily

10am–9pm; 300kr per 15min, 750kr per hour); and at the library (see p.242).
Laundry Þvottahúsið Höfði, Hafnarstræti 34, ☎462 2580.
Library Brekkugata 17 ☎462 4141.
Pharmacy Apótekarinn, Hafnarstræti 95.
Police Þórunnarstræti 138, ☎112.
Post office Skipagata 10 Mon–Fri 9am–4.40pm, ☎460 2600.
Supermarket Strax, Byggðavegur 98, close to the campsite.
Swimming pool Þingvallastræti 21 ☎461 4455
Taxi BSO ☎461 1010.
Travel agent Nonni Travel, Brekkugata 5, ☎461 1841, ⓦwww.nonnitravel.is; agent for Air Greenland flights to Copenhagen.
Woollen goods The Viking, Hafnarstræti 104; Fold-Anna, Hafnarstræti 85.

Western Eyjafjörður

Running up Eyjafjörður's western flank from Akureyri, Route 82 affords stunning views over icy waters to the glacier-formed mountains which serve as a protective wall all around the fjord. If you have time, it's well worth making the trip from Akureyri to see not only the mountains but also the rich farmland hereabouts, which is heavily grazed during the summer by cattle and sheep. The long hours of daylight in this part of Iceland, coupled with mild temperatures, make excellent growing conditions for various crops, and the small white dots you'll see in the fields are barrel-shaped bundles of hay, neatly packaged in white plastic, to provide the animals with much needed food during the long months of winter. The highlight of any trip up the fjord is the island of **Hrísey**, noted for its hundreds of wild ptarmigan, found near the mouth of Eyjafjörður and overlooked by the fishing village of **Dalvík**, itself the starting point for some excellent hiking. Nearby the village of **Hauganes** is the place to make for if you facy a spot of whale watching whilst in the north. Beyond here, a dark tunnel slices through the exposed headland, Ólafsfjarðarheiði, to reach the isolated village of **Ólafsfjörður**, although with few attractions itself, it does have splendid end-of-the-world feeling about it thanks to its location overlooking the northern reaches of the Atlantic Ocean.

Dalvík and around

DALVÍK, a nondescript fishing village 42km north of Akureyri with just 1400 inhabitants, enjoys a superbly sheltered location on the western shores of Eyjafjörður overlooking the island of Hrísey (see p.251). Paradoxically though, its poor natural harbour hampered the growth of the fishing industry here until a new harbour was built in 1939 to remedy matters, today used as the departure point for the ferry to Grímsey. A major shipbuilding and fish-curing centre early in the twentieth century, today Dalvík has lost its buzz, and its quiet **harbour** front, lined by the main road, **Hafnarbraut**, stands guard over the familiar cluster of uniformly shaped modern homes that are so prevalent in the country's smaller communities. Dalvík's lack of older buildings is due to the devastating **earthquake** of 1934, measuring 7.2 on the Richter Scale, which demolished half the structures in the village and caused serious damage to the ones that did survive – two thousand people lost their homes.

The village is really only visited by people en route to Hrísey, but should you find yourself with time to kill whilst waiting for the ferry from nearby Árskógssandur take a quick look inside the folklore museum, **Byggðasafnið Hvoll** (June–Aug daily 11am–6pm; ☎466 1497; 400kr), one block behind the harbour at Karlsrauðatorg 7; you'll easily spot the building as it's painted bright red. The museum is divided into four small sections, and it's the collection of photographs and personal belongings of Iceland's tallest man, Jóhann Kristinn Pétursson, born in nearby Svarfaðardalur valley in 1913, that catches the eye. Measuring a whopping 2.34 metres in height (7 feet 7 inches), Jóhann the Giant, as he was known locally, spent most of his life performing in circuses in Europe and America before retiring to Dalvík, where he died in 1984. The museum also contains a collection of birds' eggs, several species of stuffed seabirds and a stuffed polar bear.

The excellent outdoor **swimming pool** (☎466 3233), with its mountain backdrop, also has a couple of hotpots and a mixed steam room; it's on Svarfaðarbraut, which runs roughly parallel with Hafnarbraut.

Practicalities

For information on the three-times weekly **ferry** to and from Grímsey call ☎466 1444 or go to ⓦwww.samskip.is; see also p.258 for times. For online tourist **information**, check out ⓦwww.dalvik.is. The **library** is located in the basement of the town hall (*ráðhús*) at the corner of Kirkjubraut and Goðabraut and has **Internet** access.

The best **place to stay**, the friendly *Árgerði* guesthouse (☎466 3326, ⓦwww.islandia.is/argerdi; ❸) is a fifteen-minute walk south of Dalvík along Route 82 towards Akureyri, in the Svarfaðardalur valley. Beautifully set beside a nature reserve, next to a small river that tumbles down from the mountain tops behind the guesthouse, all eight rooms here are tastefully appointed with plain carpets and light-coloured walls and offer serene views of the surrounding hills. Otherwise, rooms are available at the **guesthouse** at Stórhóltsvegur 6 (☎466 3088; kr). The **campsite** (☎466 3233; free) next door is administered by the swimming pool.

There are two **places to eat** in Dalvík, with little to choose between them. First up is the *Kaffi Sogn*, opposite the town hall at Goðabraut 3, open for lunch and dinner (closed Mon afternoon & Sun), which serves pizzas, fish and other light dishes for around 1000kr. The *Axið* bakery, meanwhile, further west along the main road at Hafnarbraut 5, with a pleasant outside terrace overlooking the harbour, has simple sandwiches, light snacks and coffee. The **vínbúð** (June–Aug Mon–Thurs 11am–6pm, Fri 11am–7pm, Sat 11am–2pm; Sept–May Mon–Thurs 1–6pm, Fri 11am–7pm; ☎466 3430) is on the main road, Hafnarbraut 7.

Hauganes

The minuscule fishing village of **Hauganes**, 14km south of Dalvík, is the place to make for if you fancy **whale watching** in Eyjafjörður. Between late June and August the wooden fishing boat *Níels Jónsson* (☎867 0000 & 852

Hikes around Dalvík

Surrounded by magnificent mountain peaks readily accessed through the gentle **Svarfaðardalur valley**, which begins at the *Árgerði* guesthouse (see p.249) a short distance south of the town, Dalvík has scenery that makes it one of the best places around Eyjafjörður for hiking. The summer **weather** in this part of the country is often quite stable, making for good walking conditions. Although the valley is popular with locals in summer and autumn for its blueberries and crowberries, which grow in abundance, it's the **whortleberry** that dominates and, after the few short but generally sunny summer months, the bushes turn purple, filling the entire valley with burning colour. Further up the valley, as the land rises, scrub and dwarf birch trees are seen in abundance.

The best **long-distance hike**, lasting two to three or four days, leads over the Heljardalsheiði plateau from Dalvík to the episcopal seat at **Hólar í Hjaltadal** (see p.236). From the *Árgerði*, two roads lead up through Svarfaðardalsá valley as they follow the river: Route 807 heads up the southern side, whereas Route 805 hugs the northern bank (no public transport along either). Both meet after roughly 10km at the foot of the wedge-shaped **Stóll**, a mountain dividing the valley in two, though note that the northern road Route 805 is in better condition and is a few kilometres shorter. From here, Route 805 continues another 10km southwest past a couple of farms before petering out, at which point it becomes a track and heads up over the flat-topped mountains of the Tröllskagi peninsula, which separates Eyjafjörður from its western neighbour, Skagafjörður, heading for Hólar, passing through some of Iceland's best mountain scenery. It should take two or three days to reach this point, but you'll need another half-day to reach the main road, Route 76 (see below), itself reached along Route 767 from here. From Route 76, evening buses head off to Siglufjörður every Monday, Wednesday and Friday from June to September, while during the same months on Tuesday and Thursday mornings, plus Sunday afternoons, there are services to Reykjavík.

North of the Svarfaðardalur valley, a shorter **day hike** (around 20km in total) leads from Dalvík to nearby Ólafsfjörður via the old road named Drangaleið, once used by locals to reach their northern neighbour. Since the path crosses the Drangar ridge, which is very steep, it's not recommended for anyone who suffers from vertigo. The trail starts a couple of kilometres north of Dalvík, reached by heading north along Route 82 north from town to just south of the now deserted farm, Karlsá, at the foot of the Karlsá, where it flows into Eyjafjörður. Follow the river up through the Karlsárdalur valley towards the steep mountain ridge of Drangar (964m), which you'll see in front of you. From here, the track heads east over the ridge to the Burstarbrekkudalur valley, then descends into Ólafsfjörður. A bus (Mon–Fri all year) returns from Ólafsfjörður at 4.45pm to Dalvík and Akureyri.

2606) sails north from the harbour here to complete a circuit around Hrísey (3–3.5hr; 3200kr), which normally produces sightings of whales; Eyjafjörður is frequently visited by minke whales, porpoises and dolphins, less often by killer whales and humpbacks. Advance booking is necessary for these tours on either of the above telephone numbers or via the tourist office in Akureyri. **Buses** between Akureyri and Dalvík pass within 2.5km of Hauganes; from the junction with Route 82, it's a straightforward walk to the village along Route 809.

Hrísey

No trip to the north coast of Iceland is complete without seeing the hundreds of **ptarmigan** on **HRÍSEY**, a flat, teardrop-shaped island at the mouth of Eyjafjörður, reached by ferry from Árskógssandur, about 10km southeast of Dalvík. Although the country's second-largest island (Heimaey in the Westman Islands is the biggest; see p.142), at 7.5km long and 2.5km wide, it's home to barely two hundred people. However, it's also the habitat for more ptarmigan than anywhere else in Iceland, since here they're protected by law and there are no natural predators – such as mink or foxes – on the island. As a result, the birds are very tame and roam the entire island, and you'll spot them in the picturesque village here, laying their eggs in people's gardens or, particularly in August after the breeding season, strolling down the main street with a string of fluffy chicks in tow.

The island's history, however, is more tied to fish than birds and its population peaked at 340 in the mid-twentieth century, when fishing boats from across the country landed their catches in the tiny harbour, making it the second-largest herring port on the north coast, after Siglufjörður. Since then things have declined, and in 1999 the main source of employment, the fish-processing factory down at the harbour that once provided the British supermarkets with fresh North Atlantic fish, closed with the loss of dozens of redundancies, and over thirty people left the island to look for work in Akureyri and Reykjavík. Today, it's the Icelandic National Quarantine Centre, established in 1974 so that stocks of Galloway cattle could be imported from Scotland, that keeps many islanders in employment. Vegetation is particularly lush in summer, since all animals on the island were slaughtered for health reasons when the **quarantine centre** opened. **Reafforestation** has also begun in a couple of areas, in an attempt to protect the thin layer of soil atop the basalt rock of which Hrísey is formed from further erosion.

Hrísey **village** is tiny, consisting of two or three parallel streets perched on a small hill above the walled **harbour**. Brightly painted houses, unfortunately all of them modern and block-like, look out over the fjord and the handful of small boats that bob up and down in the tiny port. Otherwise, there's a minuscule outdoor **swimming pool** (☎466 3012) on the main street, Norðurvegur, at the eastern end of the village; at just 12.5m in length, it's heated by geothermal water from Hrísey's very own borehole on the west coast. Even though the village can easily be walked around in 10min there's a map down on the harbourside.

Once you've explored the village, there's some wonderful walking to be had along tracks that head around the southeastern corner of the island; all three (colour-coded green, 2.3km; yellow, 4.5km and red, 5km) begin just ten minutes from the village near the island's southernmost tip, beyond the couple of colourful private summer cottages that look out over the fjord. The green route traces a circular route up to the hills of Háaborð, dropping towards Beinalág and returning to the village; the red path heads further north along the coast whereas the yellow route follows essentially the same routing though further inland; both routes turn south again at the Borgarbrík cliffs. Unfortunately for visitors, Hrísey also has the largest breeding colony of arctic tern in Europe (see box), which means you'll pretty much need hard hats if you get too close to their nesting sites; it's also a good place to spot **golden plover** and **eider ducks**, who have a significant breeding colony in the northern part of Hrísey which is out of bounds to visitors.

Practicalities

A **ferry** shuttles between Árskógssandur on the mainland (where there's a three times daily bus connection Mon–Fri with Akureyri, Dalvík and Ólafsfjörður) and Hrísey every hour from 9.30am to 11.30pm from mid-June to mid-August, and every two hours from 9.30am to 9.30pm during the rest of the year (a 15min trip; ☎462 7733; 600kr return).

The island's only **guesthouse**, Brekka (☎466 1751, ☻466 3051, ⓔbrekkahrisey@isl.is; sleeping bag accommodation 1800kr, ❷), a wooden building painted bright yellow up on the hill behind the harbour at Brekkugata 5, has just three doubles with shared facilities, but if those are full the owners will endeavour to find a room in a private house somewhere in the village. Lunch here, in the restaurant overlooking the sea and the jagged mountains of the western shore of Eyjafjörður, is truly excellent; try the smoked rainbow trout with garlic butter and baked potato (1950kr) or chicken breast filled with mushrooms, cheese and sundried tomatoes (2350kr); there's also burgers (1250kr), toasted sandwiches (650kr) and pizzas (850kr). The **campsite** is located beside the swimming pool on Norðurvegur. The only other facilities are a **grocery** store, Þorpið, at Sjávargata 2, which also has coffee and light meals, and a bank with a cash machine on Skólavegur.

Ólafsfjörður

From Dalvík, Route 82 winds its way north for 17km to the fishing village of **ÓLAFSFJÖRÐUR** (ⓦwww.olafsfjordur.is), clinging all the way to the steep slopes of the mountains that plunge into the steely waters of Eyjafjörður, and with superb views of the snowy peaks of the uninhabited Látraströnd coastline on the opposite shore. On a clear day it's easily possible to spot the island of Grímsey (see p.256), northeast of the fjord's mouth, bisected by the **Arctic Circle**. The village is connected to Akureyri by means of a single lane, claustrophobic, 3.4-kilometre tunnel through the Ólafsfjarðarmúli headland, which divides Eyjafjörður from its smaller cousin, Ólafsfjörður, which gives the settlement its name. On emerging into daylight and turning the corner into Ólafsfjörður, it's not hard to see why the tunnel was necessary – this really is the end of the road, an isolated fishing village walled in by sheer mountains.

Surviving the arctic tern

In June and July Hrísey is a favourite destination for the **arctic tern**, the pluckiest of all the island's birds, who, should you come too close to its young, will readily dive bomb you from on high, delivering a sharp blow to the back of your head with its pointed beak. Protect yourself by carrying a stick above your head – the birds will then strike this, as the highest point, instead of screeching towards your tender scalp. Incidentally, the Icelandic name for the arctic tern, kría, is an aptly onomatopoeic word for the sound the bird makes as it comes on for the attack.

Although the drive to Ólafsfjörður and its setting are breathtaking, the village, unfortunately, isn't: this is an unattractive, workaday place of just a thousand people, set behind the working **harbour** (four trawlers are based here) on Sjávargata, one block northeast of the main road, **Aðalgata**. There's little here to detain you other than the taxidermist's dream, the well-stocked **natural history museum** (Náttúrugripasafn) at Aðalgata 14 (June–Aug Tues–Sun 2–5pm; Sept–May by arrangement with Sparisjóður bank, in the same building; 300kr), containing the usual suspects – everything from a ringed seal to a stuffed polar bear shot by a local fisherman off Grímsey as he saw it approaching his boat while balancing precariously on a piece of pack ice. With over one hundred and forty bird species stuffed for posterity, you'll at least learn the names of some of the living birds you'll see in the wild; pick up the free museum catalogue for the English translations.

Practicalities

Buses to Ólafsfjörður arrive at the only **hotel** in the village, the drab *Brimnes Hótel* (☎466 2400, ⑩www.brimnes.is; ④), at Bylgjubyggð 2. Doubles here are cramped and so plainly furnished they resemble a school dorm rather than an expensive hotel. Much better are the eight Finnish-built log **cabins** (four with kitchen, all with shower and bathroom), overlooking the lake opposite the hotel, where a room costs 8500kr, or, for groups of three or more, ⑤ buys the entire (small) cabin, ⑥ a large one. The hotel **restaurant** serves tasty fish meals, as well as hamburgers and pizzas. The tasteful café and restaurant, *Glaumbær*, at Ægisgata 10, two blocks west of Aðalgata and right next to the harbour, is popular with local fishermen and the best bet for decent food – pizzas for 1340kr, burgers 650kr, haddock 1350kr – and a beer for 550kr. Alternatively, there's a small **supermarket**, Úrval, at the corner of Strandgata and Aðalgata, next to the harbour. The **swimming pool** and the **campsite** are together, just off Hornbrekkuvegur, which heads south from Aðalgata.

Route 82 to Siglufjörður

If you're thinking of moving on to Siglufjörður from Ólafsfjörður along **Route 82**, which continues southwest from the village, be aware that it's essentially a poor, unsurfaced, summer-only track, which closes with even the lightest of snowfalls; out of season, ask at the hotel about its condition, and if in doubt, don't risk it. When the road is open though, it is one of the most beautiful drives in the north of Iceland, snaking gracefully through the valley behind Ólafsfjörður, passing one abandoned farm after another; no other trip affords a more intriguing insight into the hardships endured by the handful of farming families who once eked out a living on the rocky soils of northern Iceland. Look on the map and you'll see entire groups of farm names in brackets (signifying they are now empty), abandoned by their owners when life became untenable: Hóll, Grund, Lundur, Húnstaðir and Gil to name but a few. As the road weaves its way between barren outcrops of rock and alongside a succession of frost-shattered sheer mountainsides towards its summit high on the flat-tops of **Tröllaskagi**, the utter remoteness of this all but forgotten corner of the country soon becomes apparent; this is northern exposure at its extreme. The descent is no less spectacular, the road clinging to the sides of **Hreppsendasúlur** mountain (1052m) all the way down to **Stífluvatn** lake and past another clutch of disused farms towards the relative civilisation of **Fljótavík** bay, midway between Hofsós and Siglufjörður on Route 76.

Eastern Eyjafjörður

The eastern shore of Eyjafjörður offers something quite rare in Iceland – remote, uninhabited wilderness that is relatively easily accessible from a major town. North of the small village of **Grenivík**, now the only centre of population on the eastern side of the fjord, the perpetually snow-capped **Látraströnd** coastline is made up of some of the most rugged mountains in the north of Iceland, including the peak of **Kaldbakur** (1167m), which dominates any view of the eastern shore. Excellent and challenging **hiking** routes lead through the wilderness to now abandoned farms which, until World War II, made up some of the country's most remote and desolate communities, where life was a constant struggle against the elements in this area of unforgiving Arctic fjordland, known here as Í Fjörðum. The region's other attraction, however, is not nearly so remote: the unusual five-gabled turf farmhouse and church at **Laufás**, 10km south of Grenivík and close to the Ringroad.

Laufás

Although there's no public transport going all the way to **Laufás** (mid-May to mid-Sept daily 10am–6pm; 400kr), a superb example of a nineteenth-century turf farmhouse, 30km northeast of Akureyri, it's worth making the effort to get here. Dating from 1866, the building is timber fronted and has five gabled rooves, all made of turf, giving the impression that it's composed of several separate cottages all joined under one roof. The most remarkable feature, however, is the fabulous herringbone arrangement of turf pieces used to make up part of the front wall. Don't miss the unusual carved eider duck that sits on one

---

Hiking from Grenivík to Gjögur

A circular four- to five-day **hike** leads from Grenivík via the Látraströnd coast to the Gjögur headland, guarding the eastern entrance to Eyjafjörður, east through the coastal Í Fjörðum region to Hvalvatnsfjörður and the beginning of Route F839, which then returns towards Grenivík.

From Grenivík, follow the unnumbered road northwest from the village to the now deserted farm, **Svínarnes**, where the road ends and a track continues along the Látraströnd shoreline, passing several more abandoned farms, including **Látrar**, which has been empty since 1942. The path then swings inland through the **Uxaskarð pass** (in order to avoid the Gjögur headland) and drops down through Keflavíkurdalur to reach the shore at **Keflavík**, one of Iceland's remotest locations, a now deserted farm that was regularly cut off from the rest of the country for weeks and months in the wintertime. At the beginning of the eighteenth century, people on the farm here were taken ill and died one by one as the harsh winter weather set in – all except for an eleven-year-old girl, who remained alone here for ten weeks until people from the nearest farmstead finally managed to dig their way through the heavy snowdrifts to rescue her. Passing Þorgeirsfjörður, the path heads southwest for the next fjord, Hvalvatnsfjörður, and the beginning of the mountain road back over the hills up to the Leirdalsheiði plateau and finally down into Grenivík; there can often be snow along this route until the middle of July.

On certain dates in July it's possible to do this tour in the opposite direction as part of an **organized tour**; for a cost of 33,500kr, the trip includes transport to Hvalvatnsfjörður and back from Svínarnes, breakfast and dinner – and most importantly horses to carry all your equipment. Contact Jón at the snack bar in Grenivík (see p.235) or call ☎463 3236, ℻ 463 3258; for **information** in Icelandic, visit www.vip.is/fjordungar.

of the gable ends, serving as a reminder of the local nesting area belonging to the property; the eider down once brought the owners a considerable income. Inside, sadly, is the usual array of mind-numbing how-we-used-to-live paraphernalia, showing household and farm life from the days when the house was used as a manor farm and a parsonage for the next door **church**, which itself dates from 1865 and contains a pulpit with wood carvings from 1698; the local priest shared the building with his labourers.

From Akureyri, **buses** to Lake Mývatn and Egilsstaðir run along the Ringroad to the junction with Route 83, from where you could either walk or hitch the final 11km to the farm.

Grenivík

Ten kilometres northwest of Laufás, **GRENIVÍK** is a modern fjordside village, which only began life in 1910. Although improvements to the tiny **harbour**, around which the village is situated, brought about a slight increase in trade and thus population, there are still only around 260 people who call the place home. It's principal use is as a starting and finishing point for **hikes** along the fjord to **Látraströnd** and the **Í Fjörðum** region of the north coast (see box opposite), although there is a snack bar in the centre of the village, at Túngata 3, and a **swimming pool** (☎463 3159) next to the school. For **accommodation**, rooms are available to rent at *Miðgarðar*, at Miðgarður 4 (☎463 3223, ✉giljard@simnet.is; sleeping-bag accommodation 1500kr, ❸), where breakfast is an extra 800kr. Simple fish meals are also available in the small **restaurant** here. The **campsite** is next to the swimming pool beside the village school.

South from Akureyri: Eyjafjarðardalur valley

South of Akureyri, beyond the head of Eyjafjörður, the tongue-twisting **Eyjafjarðardalur** (pronounced ay-ya-farther-darler) is the wide fertile floodplain surrounding the Eyjafjarðará river, which flows down the valley from its source near Nýjarbæjarafrétt, up in the country's Interior. An extensive range of crops are grown, and the animals that graze the valley produce twenty percent of Iceland's milk. The farms throughout the valley do good business from the rich soil too, with most of Iceland's potatoes grown here, and in good years the country is virtually self-sufficient in this crop. However, bad weather can – and all too often does – wipe out entire harvests. The further inland the valley stretches, the wider it becomes, before getting lost in the foothills of the vast highland plateau generally known as Hálendið that forms the uninhabited centre of the country. It's here that the **F821 mountain road** begins, as it heads towards the Sprengisandur area of the Interior (see p.330). If you don't have your own transport, note that **highland tours** arranged through a travel agent in Reykjavík (see p.86) provide the only form of transport to the Eyjafjörður valley from Akureyri.

The drive around the wide Eyjafjarðardalur valley (Routes 821 and 829 run either side of the Eyjafjarðará, meeting up 8km south of Grund, see p.256) offers a chance to escape the mountains that box in so many Icelandic villages and to enjoy wide open vistas of rolling farmland and undisturbed views of the **midnight sun**; the upper reaches of the valley are one of the most enjoyable spots from which to watch the sun dip to the horizon over some of Iceland's greenest countryside, then skim the North Atlantic before rising again towards the east. There are few specific sights – instead, make a trip here to stay on a farm or to enjoy the open countryside around the valley's only real settlement, **HRAFNAGIL**, a mere dot on the map some 12km along Route 821 that runs up the western side of the valley. Home to barely 95 inhabitants, during the time of the Settlement the area around the hamlet was once a chieftain's estate and, later, the residence of Iceland's last Catholic bishop, Jón Arason, although there's nothing today, unfortunately, to attest to the place's historical significance. Five kilometres further south along the same road, the apparently Byzantine-inspired church in the hamlet of **GRUND**, with its onion-shaped dome and Romanesque mini-spires, is one of the most unusual in Iceland; designed by a local farmer to serve the entire valley, it broke with tradition by being built on a north–south, not east–west, axis. If the church is locked, you'll find the key at the neighbouring farmhouse.

By far and away the best place to stay in the valley is the good *Öngulsstaðir III* **farmstay** (☎463 1380, ⓕ 463 1390, ⓔongulsstadir@ongulsstadir.is; ❸), whose friendly owners will make you feel at home. The pleasant rooms, simply decorated and en suite, are located in the former cow sheds, whereas the main building, where breakfast (830kr) is served up, is a converted barn. Get here by taking Route 829 (signposted to "Laugaland") up the eastern side of the valley. For **hotel** accommodation there's the *Vin* in Hrafnagil (☎463 1400 or ☎463 1333; sleeping-bag accommodation 1200–1800kr, ❸), where breakfast is an extra 750kr.

Grímsey

Forty kilometres north of the mainland, the five-square-kilometre chunk of craggy basalt that defiantly rears up out of the Atlantic is the island of **Grímsey**, straddled by the **Arctic Circle**, where Iceland ends and the Arctic begins. First settled by the Viking **Vestfjarða-Grímur Sigurðsson**, and named after him ("Grímsey" means Grímur's Island), the island supports one tiny settlement, scruffy **Sandvík**, on the southwest coast. Although many come here to cross that magical geographical line (you get a cheesy certificate as proof from the one member of staff who runs the airstrip), it's for the island's amazing birdlife that most people visit. Sixty or more species, including **puffins, razorbills** and **guillemots**, are resident on the island for all or most of the year, found predominantly around the cliffs on the northern and eastern shores, where the din is cacophonous; of these, thirty-six species nest on the island. Take special care when walking around the island since you're likely to be attacked by **arctic tern**, in particular, who will stop at nothing to protect their eggs (see box on p.252).

There's just one road on Grímsey, which runs the length of the west coast from the lighthouse at its southernmost point, Flesjar, through the village to the airport at Básar – a total length of 3km. Landing here in one of the light aircraft that link the island with Akureyri can be quite an experience, as planes are often forced to buzz over the runway on the initial approach to clear the hundreds of potentially dangerous birds that gather on it before coming in a second time to land. Taking off is no less hazardous – although one of the island's few cars is sometimes driven up and down the runway to achieve the same result.

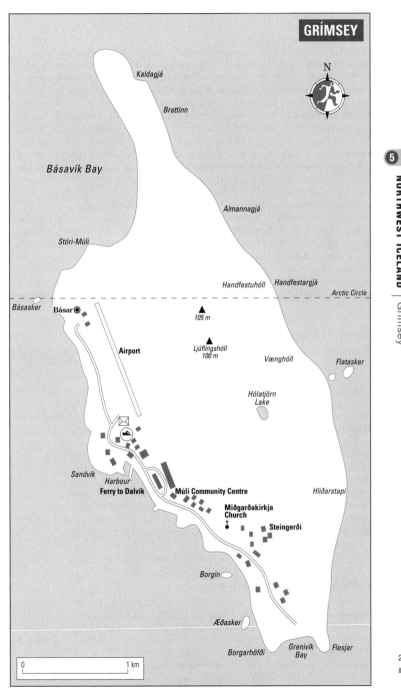

GRÍMSEY

N

Kaldagjá

Brattinn

Básavík Bay

Almannagjá

Stóri-Múli

Handfestuhóll   Handfestargjá

Arctic Circle

Básasker   Básar ◉

▲
105 m

Airport   ▲
Ljúflingshóll
100 m   Vænghóll   Flatasker

Hólatjörn
Lake

Sandvík

Harbour
Ferry to Dalvík   Múli Community Centre   Hlíðarstapi

Miðgarðakirkja
Church
✝   Steingerði

Borgin

Æðasker

Borgarhöfði   Grenivík
Bay   Flesjar

0   1 km

Sandvík

SANDVÍK is essentially nothing more than a dozen or so houses grouped around a harbour, which is where the ferry from Dalvík docks. Southeast of the harbour, the road leads to the community centre, **Múli**, where every year on November 11, the birthday of the island's benefactor, nineteenth-century American chess champion **Daniel Willard Fiske** is celebrated with coffee and cakes. A prominent journalist during the nineteenth century, and a leading scholar on things Icelandic, Fiske left the islanders US$12,000 upon his death and gave instruction for a school and library to be built. Oddly, Fiske had never once set foot on Grímsey, but it seems the islanders' reputation as the greatest **chess** players in the whole of Iceland (chess was introduced to Grímsey by the Vikings) furthered his own love of the game; he even donated eleven marble chess sets to the island. The last remaining set can be seen, alongside Fiske's portrait, in the library inside Múli, which stands on the original site of the school he financed. Sadly, hardly anyone plays chess on the island today.

A few steps beyond the community centre, the whitewashed walls of the village **church** cut a sharp image against the heavy skies. It seems to be thanks to one former priest that this isolated community still exists: in 1793, Grímsey came close to being abandoned when a plague swept through the island causing the deaths of many strong and able-bodied men. The six who didn't succumb sailed to the mainland to seek help, but were all drowned when their boat capsized, leaving the priest the only able-bodied man on the island to fulfil his duties.

Around the island

Setting out from the airport it's possible to **walk round the island** following the path, across the runway. Thereafter, however, it's wise to use the cliff tops as a guide, as the track soon gets lost amid the many springy tussocks that mark this part of the island, as it heads up the hillside to the east coast, by far the most dramatic aspect of the island; here sheer cliffs plunge down into the foam and the roaring waves of the Arctic Ocean. The promontory you can see from here, **Eyjarfótur**, stretching out to the north, is a good place to watch the birds since it affords views out over the sea and back over the low fields around the guesthouse and airport where so many species congregate. However, there is no area of the island devoid of birds and simply walking around Grímsey, be it on the cliffs or in the village, will bring you into contact with various varieties of seabirds. Heading south from the headland following the shoreline, the path climbs a little as it goes over **Handfestuhóll** from where you can see the rock fissures, **Almannagjá** and **Handfestargjá**, in the cliff face. Beyond the small islet, **Flatasker**, the coast swings southwest heading for the lighthouse at Grímsey's southeastern point, **Flesjar**. From here the road continues along the west coast into the village and back to the harbour.

Island practicalities

Arriving on Grímsey by either air or sea will bring you to the west coast; the **airport** and the **harbour** are barely five minutes walk from each other, at the northwestern edge of Sandvík. Most people choose to take one of the **flights** to the island from Akureyri (3 weekly) for the sake of convenience and speed – the trip takes around twenty-five minutes, compared with a total journey time by bus and ferry of four and a quarter hours. However, when the **ferry** runs (3500kr return, 4000kr including bus connection from Akureyri) the little island is often busy – though not overcrowded – with day-trippers. The connecting bus leaves Akureyri on Mon, Wed & Fri at 7.30am for Dalvík, from where the ferry sails at 8am (9.30am on Mon); it returns on the same days from Grímsey at 4pm, arriving in Dalvík at 7.30pm; a bus then continues to Akureyri, arriving at 8pm.

To really appreciate Grímsey's charms you need to stay overnight – simple accommodation is available at the superbly located *Básar* **guesthouse** (T467 3103, F461 1030, Eljosbud@nett.is; sleeping bag accommodation 1700kr, ❷), whose front door opens out onto the tiny airport runway, whilst the rear of the house has a balcony overlooking the sea. Breakfast is an extra 800kr and, in fact, the guesthouse is the only place to get cooked **food** on the island, too: lunch is 1200kr and dinner 1900kr – both consisting of delicious fresh fish. **Camping** is permitted anywhere on the island away from the village. The indoor **swimming pool** (T467 3155) is located in the grey building at the eastern end of the runway but it's often closed in summer. Back in the harbour, there's a small cooperative **supermarket** that closes any time between 5pm and 6pm.

Travel details

Buses

The bus details given below are relevant for May to September; for winter times, visit @www.bsi.is.

Akureyri to: Árskógssandur (2 daily; 35min); Blönduós (daily; 2hr); Brú (daily; 4hr); Dalvík (2 daily; 45min); Egilsstaðir (daily; 5hr); Hólmavík (3 weekly; 6hr 30min); Húsavík (4 daily; 1hr 10min); Ísafjörður (3 weekly; 11hr); Mývatn (4 daily; 1hr 45min); Ólafsfjörður (2 daily; 1hr 30min); Reykjavík (daily; 6hr).

Árskógssandur to: Akureyri (2 daily; 35min); Dalvik (2 daily; 10min).

Blönduós to: Akureyri (daily; 2hr); Hofsós (3 weekly; 2hr); Reykjavík (3 weekly; 4hr); Sauðárkrókur (3 weekly; 1hr 15min); Siglufjörður (3 weekly; 3hr).

Brú to: Akureyri (daily; 4hr); Blönduós (daily; 1hr 45min); Hofsós (3 weekly; 3hr 30min); Hólmavík (3 weekly; 2hr 30min); Ísafjörður (3 weekly; 7hr); Reykjavík (2 daily; 2hr); Sauðárkrókur (3 weekly; 2hr 45min); Siglufjörður (3 weekly; 4hr 30min).

Dalvík to: Akureyri (2 daily; 45min); Árskógssandur (2 daily; 10min); Ólafsfjörður (2 daily; 45min).

Hofsós to: Blönduós (3 weekly; 2hr); Brú (3 weekly; 3hr 30min); Reykjavík (3 weekly; 5hr 30min); Sauðárkrókur (3 weekly; 45min); Siglufjörður (3 weekly; 1hr).

Ólafsfjörður to: Akureyri (2 daily; 1hr 30min); Árskógssandur (2 daily; 1hr); Dalvík (2 daily; 45min).

Sauðárkrókur to: Blönduós (3 weekly; 1hr 15min); Brú (3 weekly; 2hr 30min); Hofsós (3 weekly; 45min); Reykjavík (3 weekly; 5hr); Siglufjörður (3 weekly; 1hr 45min).

Siglufjörður to: Blönduós (3 weekly; 3hr); Brú (3 weekly; 4hr 30min); Hofsós (3 weekly; 1hr); Reykjavík (3 weekly; 6hr 30min); Sauðárkrókur (3 weekly; 1hr 45min).

Ferries

Árskógssandur to: Hrísey (hourly May–Aug, every two hours Sept–April; 15min).
Dalvík to: Grímsey (2 weekly; 3hr 15min).

Flights

Akureyri to: Egilsstaðir (3 weekly; 45min); Grímsey (3 weekly; 25min); Ísafjörður (4 weekly; 1hr); Reykjavík (7 daily; 50min); Vopnafjörður (6 weekly; 45min); Þórshöfn (5 weekly; 40min).

Mývatn and the
northeast

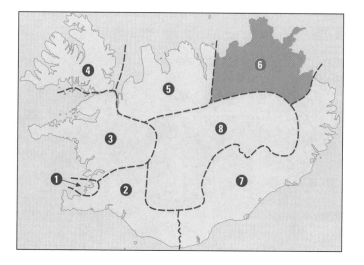

CHAPTER 6

Highlights

✳ **Lake Mývatn** Clock up the birdlife and explore surrounding craters, hot mud pools, and an underground bakery. See p.265

✳ **Krafla & Leirhnjúkur** Spend a morning hiking around this volcano crater and rugged lava flow, still steaming after an eruption in the 1980s. See p.275

✳ **Húsavík** Iceland's premier whale-watching venue, where you're almost guaranteed sightings through the summer. See p.277

✳ **Jökulsárgljúfur** Superb camping and hiking amongst heath and weird rock formations at this deep river gorge and National Park. See p.281

✳ **Ásbergi** Huge horseshoe-shaped cliff face, reputedly a hoofprint made by the Norse god Oðinn's eight-legged horse. See p.282

✳ **Dettifoss** Europe's most powerful waterfall is spectacular at the start of summer, as glacial melt upstream turns the river into a furious brown torrent. See p.284

6

Mývatn and the northeast

Northeast Iceland forms a thinly populated, open expanse between Akureyri and the Eastfjords, the western half of which is dominated by the lava-covered Ódáxahraun plateau, which slopes gently from the Interior to the sea, drained by glacial rivers and underground springs. Tourists, along with most of Iceland's wildfowl population, flock to **Mývatn**, an attractive lake just over an hour's drive from Akureyri, whose surrounds are thick with hot springs and volcanic formations – many of them still visibly active. North of here, the pleasant town of **Húsavík** offers summer **whale-watching** excursions, and is just a short jaunt from **Jökulsárgljúfur**, a broad canyon cut into the wilderness by one of the region's glacial rivers, which thunders through a series of gorges and waterfalls – a superb place to spend a few days hiking or camping.

The eastern half of the region has far less obvious attractions; indeed, the only real access to this mix of mountains, lava desert, and boggy lowlands is along the coastal road between Húsavík and **Vopnafjörður**. However, it's a great place for purposeless travel, bringing you close to some wild countryside, breezy coastal walks, and small, isolated communities – plus the chance to reach the mainland's northernmost tip, which lies fractionally outside the Arctic Circle.

The northeast's **main roads** are the Ringroad (Route 1), which crosses east from Akureyri to Mývatn and then heads out of the region to Egilsstaðir; and Route 85, which mostly follows the coast via Húsavík and Jökulsárgljúfur to Vopnafjörður, before cutting inland and down to the Ringroad. **Buses** cover both routes in peak season – roughly June through to September – though at other times services are limited or non-existent; there are also **tours** of the regional highlights, primarily out of Mývatn. If taking your own transport, note that as there are few fuel stations between towns it's best to top up the tank whenever you can. The main roads are sound, though not always surfaced and sometimes closed at short notice by snow. Minor roads in the area, while not necessarily needing four-wheel-drives, may only be open for a month or two in summer, so you'll need to find out their condition by asking other visitors or by contacting local information centres before tackling them.

Away from Mývatn and Húsavík, services are thinly spread, though most settlements have at least a bank, a supermarket and somewhere to stay; elsewhere,

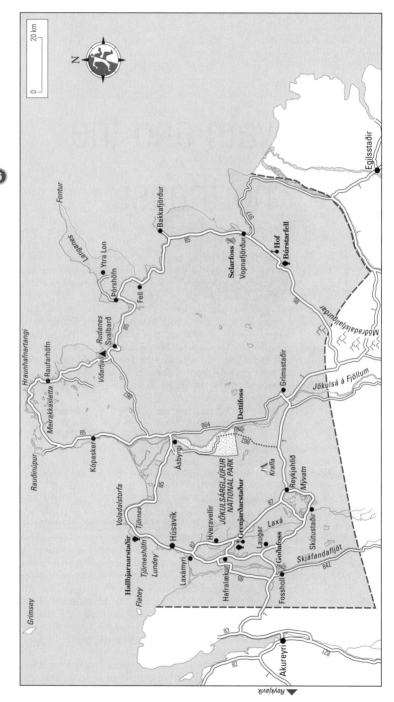

Egilsstaðir

Bakkafjörður

85

Selárfoss

Vopnafjörður

Hof
Bústarfell

Fontur

Langanes

Ytra Lón

Þórshöfn

Fell

Rudanes
Svalbarð

85

Móðrudalsöræfi

98

Hraunhafnartangi

Raufarhöfn

Viðarfjall

Grímsstaðir

Melrakkaslétta

85

Jökulsá á Fjöllum

Dettifoss

Rauðinúpur

Kópasker

864

Ásbyrgi

296

Krafla

JÖKULSÁRGLJÚFUR
NATIONAL PARK

Reykjahlíð
Mývatn

Voladalstorfa

Tjörnes

Húsavík

Hveravellir

87

Grenjaðarstaður

Laxá

Skútustaðir

Hallbjarnarstaðir

Tjörneshöfn

Lundey

Laxámýri

87

Laugar

Goðafoss

Skjáfandafljót

Flatey

Hafralækur

58

Fosshóll

842

Grímsey

83

128

Akureyri

82

N

20 km

0

Reykjavík

there are farmstays, a few hostels, and limitless camping opportunities. The northeast's **weather** is much drier and often sunnier than southern Iceland's – and this far north it barely gets dark for three months of the year – though winters are bitterly cold, with heavy snowfalls throughout.

Mývatn and around

Around 100km east of Akureyri on Route 1, **Mývatn**'s placid, shallow spread of water belies its status as one of the country's most touristed locations. Admittedly, Mývatn has had its detractors ever since the Middle Ages – when the lake and its steaming surrounds were fearfully dismissed as a pool of the devil's piss – though now it's the summertime swarms of tiny black **flies** (Mývatn means "Midge Lake") that are most likely to get up your nose. While visitors seek sanctuary behind gauze netting, the flies and their larvae provide an abundant food source for both fish and the hundreds of thousands of **wildfowl**, which descend on the lake each year to raise their young. All of Iceland's duck species breed either here or close by on the **Laxá**, Mývatn's fast-flowing, salmon-rich outlet, and one – **Barrow's goldeneye** – nests nowhere else in Europe.

There's plenty more to hold your attention beyond the birds and bugs. Covering over 36 square kilometres, Mývatn sits on the western side of a major tectonic fault, eruptions along which not only created the lake itself by damming local springs, but also the collection of hulking, flat-topped mountains away to the southeast, and the cones, craters and oddly contorted lava which surround the lakeshore. Due east of Mývatn, the land is still smoking and bubbling away at **Bjarnarflag** and **Hverarönd**'s mud pits, though the region's hottest spot lies northeast in the highlands around **Krafla** and **Leirhnjúkur**, where explosively violent fissures were fully active just twenty years ago.

Most people base themselves on the northern side of the lake at **Reykjahlíð**, Mývatn's small service centre, where you'll find most of the region's facilities, with a few alternatives dotted elsewhere around the shore – especially at southerly **Skútustaðir**. A good **road** circuits Mývatn, with tracks and footpaths elsewhere; and there are several **bus tours** offered in season. You could easily spend a week picking over the region, though three days is enough time to take in the main sights – some people even day-trip from Reykjavík by plane.

Mývatn looks its best in summer, but can get very crowded then, when beds are in short supply and it's a toss-up to decide whether there are more tourists, insects, or ducks. As for the flies: a few bite, but most just buzz irritatingly around your face – keep them off by buying a hat with attached netting. Alternatively, hit a few good days in late spring and, while you'll miss out on some of the bird life, there are no flies, you'll have the place to yourself and could also indulge in **cross-country skiing** to reach some of the sights. If you do this, however, remember that tour operators spend the off-season working elsewhere, and facilities will be limited.

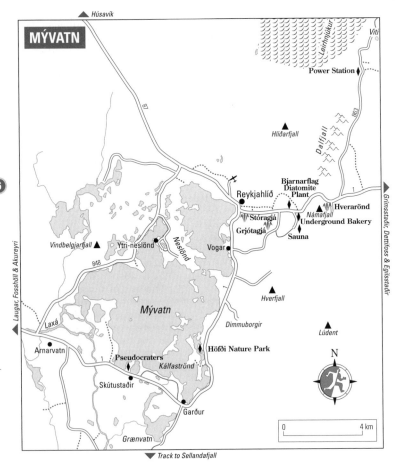

MÝVATN

Húsavík

Power Station

Hliðarfjall

Viti

Dalfjall

Bjarnarflag
Diatomite
Plant

Reykjahlíð

Stóragjá

Grjótagjá

Námafjall
Underground Bakery

Hveraönd

Sauna

Grímsstaðir, Dettifoss & Egilsstaðir

Vindbelgjarfjall

Ytri-neslönd

Neslönd

Vogar

Hverfjall

Mývatn

Dimmuborgir

Lúdent

Laxá

Arnarvatn

Pseudocraters

Kálfaströnd

Höfði Nature Park

N

Skútustaðir

Garður

0   4 km

Grænvatn

Track to Sellandafjall

Laugar, Fosshöll & Akureyri

Getting to Mývatn

In season, you can reach Reykjahlíð, Mývatn's main service centre, by daily
buses from Akureyri (mid-May to end Sept), Egilsstaðir (June–Aug), and
Húsavík (late June to Aug); less regular services from Egilsstaðir begin in mid-
May and continue to the end of September. Also in summer only, you can get
here by bus direct from Reykjavík via the remote Sprengisandur route (see
p.330). SBA buses in Akureyri (see p.288) run **day trips** to Mývatn and Krafla
in summer, and less regular **winter tours**, when you get to see the lake and
surrounds under snow. Otherwise, there are no buses to Mývatn from anywhere between October and mid-May.

Coming in from Akureyri, it's worth stopping about 40km along at tiny
FOSSHÓLL, where the ice-blue Skálfandáfljöt (which originates way down
south at Vatnajökull) tears through horseshoe-shaped basalt canyons in a pair of
cataracts. The largest of these, **Goðafoss** (God's Waterfall), is where Þorgeir –
the lawspeaker who decided that Christianity should be Iceland's official religion at the historic Alþing in 1000 – destroyed his pagan statues by pushing

6

MÝVATN AND THE NORTHEAST | Mývatn and around

266

Mývatn's ducks

In summer, plentiful food and nesting space make Mývatn the best place to see **wild ducks** in northern Europe and, armed with a pair of binoculars and a little patience, you should be able to clock up eighteen species during your stay. Their favourite **nesting area** is in spongy heathland on the northwest side of the lake (given the country's often treeless environment, all Icelandic ducks are ground-nesting), though better places to spy on them include Mývatn's southeastern corner (especially good for Barrow's goldeneye); the Laxá outflow on the western side of the lake (for harlequin ducks); and even the shore at Reykjahlíð (anything). Female ducks tend to be drably coloured, to blend in with vegetation while incubating their eggs, and unless otherwise stated, the following descriptions are of breeding males.

Several types of duck at Mývatn have a black head, and black-and-white body (females with a brown or russet head and grey elsewhere). The most celebrated is the locally abundant – though otherwise rare – **Barrow's goldeneye**, easily identified by a characteristic white comma-shaped patch between the manic golden eye and bill. They live here year-round, and their courtship displays start in late April: males stretch their necks out towards a potential partner until their beak touches the water, then flick their heads backwards; females respond in a similar manner. Keep an eye open too for their cute, black-and-white-striped chicks. Barrow's goldeneye are most likely to be confused with either the similar-looking **tufted duck** or **scaup**, though neither share its "comma" – tufted ducks also have a droopy back-swept crest, while the scaup has a grey, not white, back.

Mývatn's other speciality is the **harlequin duck**, which sports unmistakable chestnut, white and blue plumage, though as indicated by its Icelandic name – *straumönd*, stream duck – is less likely to be seen on the lake than bobbing in and out of rough water on the Laxá. In fact, adult harlequins prefer the sea and spend as little time inland as possible, arriving to nest in late April and moving on by mid-July. Other marine ducks spending their summers at Mývatn include the **scoter**, a uniquely all-black diving duck, which in Iceland breeds only at Mývatn, and the **long-tailed** or **old squaw**, another strikingly patterned bird with a summer plumage including a black neck and crown and very long, pointed tail (the similar **pintail** has a white throat, though so does the long-tail in winter).

One species largely absent from the lake is the **eider**, which nests mostly up along the Laxá – both sexes have wedge-shaped bills and a distinctive low posture in the water; the two-tone males have subtle pastel pink and green touches on their chests and napes. The eider's bulky build comes into its own at sea, where the birds gather into huge "rafts" and calmly ride out heavy swells, as unsinkable as a fleet of lifeboats. They pad their nests with special down, and it's this which is commercially collected (after the ducks have moved on) for stuffing cushions, sleeping bags, and the like – a small but profitable business in Iceland.

Otherwise, you'll be fairly familiar with most of Mývatn's ducks, which are primarily freshwater species. Some of the more plentiful include the **mallard**; the red-headed **pochard**; the long-beaked **merganser** and **goosander**, and the wide-beaked **shoveler**; **wigeon**, with their coppery heads and vertical blond streak between the eyes; the uniformly nondescript **gadwall**; and **teals**, who sport a glossy red head and green eyepatch.

---

them over the falls. It's a beautiful spot, and if you decide to stay you'll find that Fosshóll itself comprises a roadhouse, a café-restaurant, and **guesthouse** (℡464 3108, Ⓕ464 3318; sleeping-bag 1600kr, beds 2500kr), which also has space for campers. Beyond Fosshóll, the other place to pause before Mývatn is 10km further on at **LAUGAR**, a small town with a fuel station, bank, and a school where *Fosshótel* run summer accommodation (☎464 6300, Ⓦwww.fosshotel.is; sleeping-bag 2300kr). From here, it's another 45km to Reykjahlíð along Route 1, via alternative accommodation at **Skútustaðir** (see p.272) at the south end of the lake.

Reykjahlíð and the lake

Given the number of visitors who invade each summer, **REYKJAHLÍÐ** is surprisingly insubstantial – just a thin handful of services and a couple of residential streets up at Mývatn's northeastern corner, where Route 1 from Akureyri and Egilsstaðir and the Húsavík road converge. Marking the western edge of things, Reykjahlíð's **church** is worth a look, less for the neat white structure itself than the **lava flows** either side. These date to August 1729, when erupting fissures 10km northeast at Leirhnjúkur (see p.275) rounded off a prolonged spell of activity. Fast-flowing lava descended from the hills and covered three nearby farms, but was mysteriously deflected around the low-lying church – some say by the cemetery wall, others (in keeping with similar cases elsewhere in Iceland) by prayer. A carving on the pulpit depicts the church of the time under threat, and check out the lava too: there are some good stretches of rope-lava pavements, and plenty of fissures caused by escaping gases. Other than this, Reykjahlíð's main attraction is its **swimming pool** (daily 9am–10pm; 250kr), shallow but long and with the usual complement of hotpots.

On a cold day you'll see steam rising from small cracks in the ground all around Reykjahlíð, and for a closer look walk just southeast of the Húsavík-Route 1 intersection, where you'll find **Stóragjá**, the most accessible of Mývatn's sunken hot springs, hidden in amongst the rough scrub and lava. A ladder and rope reach down into the two-metre-wide cleft from ground level, and it was a popular bathing hole until it cooled during the 1990s, allowing harmful algae to invade. Some people do still swim here, but at the risk of getting any cuts or grazes infected – best stick to the swimming pool.

The lake shore around Reykjahlíð is flat and good for **bird-watching**, with a few pairs of rare **slavonian grebes** – sleek diving birds with yellow tufts behind the ears – nesting each year; take the short track to the water from opposite the *Reynihlíð* hotel and you should find them. There's also a fair chance of spotting **red-necked phalaropes**, small waders with pointy beaks and a distinctive red stripe, which perform "pirouettes" on the water; this creates a whirlpool which sucks up bottom-dwelling bugs on which the birds feed. The northeast bit of Mývatn is also the only place that you don't need a boat to go **fishing** on the lake, though you will require a permit (see "Practicalities" for more on this and gear rental); stocks of trout and arctic char are generally good, though for salmon you're better off on the Laxá (see p.273). Several people in Reykjahlíð have smoke houses for curing fish – there's one at the *Eldá* guesthouse – which you can buy direct or through the store; in the absence of timber they use dried sheep-dung for smoking, and the results are somewhat coarser than wood-smoked fish. Ash from the process is also used to preserve duck eggs by simply burying them in it for several months, turning the yolks green and the albumen a clear, smoky brown – they sound revolting but actually have a pleasantly mild, alkaline flavour.

Tours from Reykjahlíð cover various sights around Mývatn, and can also get you northeast to Jökulsárgljúfur, and south to the Askja caldera and Kverkfjöll. Most operate only from around June until September, and need to be booked a day or so in advance. Note that the Krafla area is served by a **bus** from Reykjahlíð and Skútustaðir (see p.272), which then continues to Dettifoss (see p.284); and that an easy walking (or off-road bike) trail runs from Reykjahlíð to Dimmuborgir (p.271), making coach tours of these regions redundant.

The *Eldá* guesthouse (see below) offers a range of guided **hikes** – most covering 20km – around Mývatn and Krafla, as well as organising **horse riding**. Their main bus tour is out to **Lofthellir Ice Caves** (Tues, Thurs, Sat; 6000kr), frozen lava caverns discovered in 1989 and impossible to locate without local knowledge. Further afield, *Eldá* also run a trip to **Dettifoss** and **Ásbergi** at Jökulsárgljúfur (6500kr; see p.281); while Mývatn Tours (☎464 4196, ⊛www.isholf.is/myvatntours) head south across the Interior's lava fields to **Askja** (7500kr; see p.333) – both operate as lengthy day trips, though you can arrange with them in advance to go out one day and return another. There's also a three-day expedition departing on Mondays from mid-July until mid-August to ice caves and glacier traverses at **Kverkfjöll** (17,900kr; see p.334). Groups of three or more people can set up four-wheel-drive tours to the Krafla area and Dettifoss (6–8hr; 9000kr) or Askja (8–10hr; 10,000kr) with Highland Expedition Tours (☎464 3940; ⊛www.fjallasyn.is).

For **scenic flights**, Mýflug Air (☎464 4400, 🖷464 4401, ⊛www.myflug.is) out of Reykjalíð can take you for a spin over Mývatn and Krafla, or out to Askja and Dettifoss – trips last from twenty minutes to two hours and cost 4500–20,000kr.

Practicalities

Reykjahlíð is strung out along 500m of road on Mývatn's northeastern shore. The main focus is a new, well-stocked STRAX **supermarket** and **fuel station** (daily: summer 9am–9pm; winter 11am–4pm) at the eastern side of "town"; there's a **tourist information** counter inside at the supermarket (same hours; ☎464 4390, Ⓔinfomyvatn@myv.is) along with showers and toilets. Immediately behind you'll find a **post office** and **bank** (Mon–Fri 9am–4pm), with an ATM; and further back, beyond a clutch of houses, is the **swimming pool**. About 250m west along the shore, past several places to stay, is the church, behind which is Reykjahlíð's **airstrip**. SBA **buses** pull up near the church at the *Reynihlíð* hotel's forecourt (consequently, Reykjahlíð is often confusingly marked "Reynihlíð" on bus timetables). There are **payphones** outside the post office, at the *Eldá* guesthouse, and at *Hlíð*; ever enterprising, the *Eldá* guesthouse has also installed **Internet**, open to all (250kr for 30min).

Most accommodation can book **transport and tours** – or, again, head to the *Eldá* guesthouse, who also rent out mountain bikes (1500kr a day), horses (1300kr an hour), or boats with fishing tackle and permits (1500kr a day). See the box above for more on tours.

For **food**, make sure you try some smoked fish, along with *hverabrauð* – bread baked in the underground ovens east at Bjarnaflag (see p.274) – both of which are available through the supermarket and a stall outside *Hótel Reynihlíð*. At the time of writing, Reykjahlíð's **places to eat** were limited to the *Gamli Bærinn* (daily 10am–midnight), a cosy café-bar in a converted farmhouse next to *Hótel Reynihlíð* – packed solid around noon when tour buses pass through – with a good but pricey selection of sandwiches, cooked meals, cakes, coffee, and beer. There was also talk of resurrecting the fast food joint next to the supermarket, which will presumably be less upmarket in outlook.

Accommodation

Accommodation is very tourist-season oriented. Prices are high at peak times, falling heavily in winter – if establishments even bother to open. In summer, the main source of **sleeping-bag accommodation** is *Hlíð*, though it's more widely available off-season; if all of Reykjahlíð is full, there's further accommodation in Skútustaðir (see p.272). Reykjahlíð's two **campsites** are at *Eldá* and *Hlíð*, with other options around the lake at Vogar (below) and Skútustaðir – camping elsewhere is prohibited.

Birkihraun II Birkihraun Street ☎464 4285. Recently renovated guesthouse about two lanes behind the post office. Dorm beds 2100kr, ❸

Eldá ☎464 4220, ⓦwww.elda.is. Friendly, family-run business utilizing several places around Reykjahlíð; check in at main house, more or less opposite the supermarket. Lakeshore campsite (including use of showers and kitchen), or singles and doubles. Camping 625kr, ❸

Hlíð Off the airstrip road behind the church ☎464 4103, ⓦwww.simnet.is/hlid. Good budget option with nice views over lake, town, and distant mountains. Very spacious campsite with a laundry, bathrooms, hot-tubs and kitchen; a roomy, self-catering bunkhouse favoured by tour groups with

around twenty four-person dorms, plus a large kitchen and dining area; and self-catering, four-person cabins. Camping 600kr, sleeping bag 1800kr, made-up bed 2800kr.

Reykjahlíð On the lakeshore between the supermarket and church ☎464 4142, ⓦwww .reykjahlid@islandia.is. Well-organized, low-key hotel overlooking the lake, whose pleasantly laconic owner and relaxed furnishings make it feel more like a guesthouse. Self-catering or b&b. ❺

Reynihlíð Next to the church ☎464 4170, ⓦwww.reynihlid.is. A modern, upmarket motel-like affair with well-furnished rooms. ❼

The lakeshore

Moving clockwise around Mývatn from Rekjahlíð, you follow Route 1 down around the lake via the hamlets of **Vogar** and **Skútustaðir** to where the Laxá drains westwards, then cross the river and take a minor road up the west shore and back to town. This circuit is about 35km long in itself, but there are several places to make fairly extensive detours away from the lake, principally **Grótagjá** hot springs; the rough lavafield at **Dimmuborgir** and **Hverfjall** cone, east of the lake; and **Vindbelgjar** peak, on Mývatn's northwestern side. Aside from the highly visible wildfowl, keep your eyes peeled for ptarmigan, arctic foxes and maybe even gyrfalcons. Also note that erosion is a serious problem at many popular sites and that you should stick to marked paths where you find them.

As there are few tour options available at present, you really need your own **vehicle** – either a car, or bicycle – to circuit the lake; with a car, you can fit the main sights into a long day. You can of course **walk** (many of Mývatn's residents spend Good Friday circuiting the lake on foot in memory of Christ's walk to Golgotha), and should at least tackle the well-marked, eight-kilometre **trail** that links Reykjahlíð with highlights at Grótagjá, Hverfell and Dimmuborgir. There are also some harder routes to distant formations south and east of the lake, for which you'll need patience for crossing lava and a copy of the *Landmælingar Íslands* Mývatn 1:50,000 map – the tourist information office or *Eldá* might have these, otherwise Akureyri's bookshops are the nearest source.

Vogar and Grótagjá

Heading south from Reykjahlíð, you pass sheep pens built of lava blocks, and the first small stands of **birch** that appear in patches all down the eastern lakeshore. Big chunks of lava by the roadside also mark the edge of a vast expanse of volcanic detritus – once out of the woods you'll realize how extensive this is.

Only about 2km from Reykjahlíð, **VOGAR** is a handful of farms offering comfortable beds and **camping** (☎464 4399, ℻464 4341; camping 550kr, sleeping bag 2100kr, doubles including breakfast ❸); there's no store, but you can take a seat in the *Cowshed Café* (8am–10pm in summer), snack on *hverabrauð* and smoked trout, drink coffee or beer, and even watch the cows being milked (7.30am & 5pm). From here, it's another couple of kilometres northeast along a gravel road to **Grótagjá**, the best-known of Mývatn's flooded fissures. From the outside, the lava is heaped up in a long, 5m-high ridge; entering through a crack, you find yourself in a low-ceilinged tunnel harbouring a couple of clear blue, steaming pools (one for men, one for women), lit by daylight through the entrance. The drawback is that unless you're here in winter – when the women's pool is just about bearable for a quick immersion (take care on the rough rocks) – Grótagjá is a bit too hot to get into at 48°C, though it is cooling down each year. There are more comfortable hot pools elsewhere at Mývatn, however, and if you're lucky locals may show you their favourites – some are superb in winter, when you have to climb down into the ice into them.

Hverfjall and Lúdent

Around 3km southeast of Vogar, **Hverfjall** is Mývatn's most easily identified landmark, looking just how a volcano should: broad, conical and strewn with black rubble and rocks, it's a classic **tephra cone**, made of consolidated ash and pumice. At 2500 years old, Hverfjall is also a bit younger than the lake, and its rim (400m) presents a satisfying, straightforward climb from the end of the access road (1.5km) off the highway. Two hours is ample time for a slow ascent and circuit of the kilometre-wide caldera, which is a great way to orient yourself: immediately west lie the lake's flat blue waters, its scattering of islands and convoluted shore; views north take in the town, steaming thermal areas, and the plateau harbouring Krafla (despite the distance, you can usually hear steam vents on the mountain roaring away); southeast lurks Lúdent, beyond which lava stretches out to the distant string of impressively solid rhyolitic table-top formations of Búrfel, Heilagsdalsfjall and Bláfjall. Give yourself an extra hour if you plan to climb down in to Hverfjall's flat-floored crater, where previous visitors have left giant yellow graffiti by scraping away the dark topsoil – don't add to their destructive mess.

If you enjoyed Hverfjall, it's worth trekking the additional 5km out to see **Lúdent**'s similar formations (if you're driving, you'll need a four-wheel-drive for the soft black sand along the way). The track curls around Hverfjall's south side and then bears southeast, rising to cross a line of rough-edged, overgrown volcanic blisters and miniature outlying craters on the abrupt western edge of the Mývatn fault. A further kilometre across the rift and you're on top of the iron-rich, red gravel slopes of Lúdent's main crater; the rim lacks Hverfjall's symmetry, being partially collapsed and invaded by several secondary cones – the one directly north is almost as wide as Lúdent, and slightly higher at 490m. Look back the way you've come and there's a superb line of sight right along the rift wall. It's possible to carefully circuit Lúdent's crater, but – properly equipped for navigation and a camp-out – you'll get more by following the rift south for 7km from here to Seljahjallagil; see "Grænavatn" on p.272 for more on this.

Dimmuborgir

Back on the lake road a kilometre or so south of the Hverfjall junction, another access road east brings you to **Dimmuborgir** after 1500m, a collection of weird, crumbled and contorted lava towers set amongst the birch scrub. This was once a **lava lake**, whose crust had solidified by the time its containing wall collapsed, allowing the liquid underneath to drain out but leaving the crust as a broken-up mess behind. Taller formations may have been where steam erupted through the deep pool of molten rock, cooling it enough to form surface-high columns which were left standing on their own once the lava drained away. All this aside, you could easily spend a couple of hours on Dimmuborgir's marked paths, examining the rocks' unexpected and indescribable shapes; none of the forms is very tall but every inch is differently textured, all finished in tiny twists and spires. A moon-shaped hole in a wall at **Gatklettur** beautifully frames Hverfjall to the northeast; otherwise Dimmuborgir's highlight is the lava cave known as **Kirkja**, the Church, about half an hour east from the entrance – what looks like a giant burst bubble of lava, into which around twenty people could comfortably squeeze.

Höfði, Kálfaströnd, and around Grænvatn

A couple of kilometres south past Dimmuborgir on the lake road, the private nature park **Höfði** marks the first specific lakeside stop. Stack-like formations and tiny islets in the crystal-clear waters here attract birds in some numbers, while the flower-strewn birch woodland along the shore offers good cover for watching them. A local speciality is the **great northern diver** (known as "loon" in the US), which nests here; with luck you'll see the less common red-throated variety too, along with countless Barrow's goldeneyes – this area is their main hangout. Across the inlet at Höfði, **Kálfaströnd** is a long peninsula with similar appeal; get here by taking the next turning after Höfði, then walking around the shoreline from the farm area.

Rounding Mývatn's southeastern corner, you pass where the lake's **springs** well up below the waters, though this is invisible except in winter, when their warmth stops the surface from freezing. A kilometre further on, the tiny hamlet of **GARDUR** marks a two-kilometre road south to **Grænvatn**, both a farm and much smaller satellite lake of Mývatn. The lake isn't that interesting, but the farmhouse is, roofed in turf and sided in timber and basalt blocks; built in the late nineteenth century and now one of the oldest buildings in the region, it's still lived in.

The farm also marks the start of some serious cross-lavafield hikes. The easiest follows a rough vehicle track for 15km south to **Sellandafjall's** steep slopes – the northwest corner is the best place to try an ascent. Alternatively, take the track for about a third of the way, then follow the edge of the lava approximately southeast for 4km to the impressive gorge **Gyðuhnjúksgil**. Another option is to head 10km southeast from Grænavatn across the lava to Bláfjall's wild escarpments, north of which are a couple of steep-sided canyons – one, **Seljahjallagil**, is strikingly faced in hexagonal columns – though there's an easier route here from Lúdent. Don't attempt any of these hikes without at least the Landmælingar Íslands Mývatn 1:50,000 map and orientation skills; carry all the water you'll need; and give yourself at least two days for a return trip to any one of them – the lava is rough and very slow going. Away from the lakeside area, you can camp anywhere you're lucky enough to find a suitable spot to pitch a tent.

Skútustaðir

Three kilometres west of Gardur, **SKÚTUSTAÐIR** is an alternative base to Reykjahlíð, a small knot of buildings right by the lake comprising a **church**, a store with basic supplies, a café and fuel pump, plus several places to stay. Running most of these amenities is the comfy *Hótel Mývatn* (☎464 4164, ⓦwww.myvatn.is; ➐), which also rents out bikes; diagonally opposite, its more modern rival *Hótel Gígur* (☎464 4455, ⓦwww.keahotels.is; ➐) has better views. The budget bracket is served by the *Skútustaðir* guesthouse, next to *Hótel Mývatn*, who have self-catering rooms and also run the lakeshore **campsite** (☎464 4212; camping 550kr, sleeping bag 1400kr, ➍); and the *Skjólbrekka* community hall's summertime sleeping-bag accommodation (no cooking facilities; ☎464 4202; 1400kr). If you're after **smoked fish**, the smoke house Reykhusíð Skútustoðum, on the road in front of the church, sells salmon, char and trout at around 1800kr per kilo.

Whether or not you stay the night, Skútustaðir's **pseudocraters**, on the lakeshore right in front of the hamlet, warrant a close look. Looking like bonsai volcanoes, pseudocraters are created when lava pours over marshland, boiling the water beneath, which bursts through the solidifying crust to form a cone. They tend to occur in clutches around the lake shore, though most of Mývatn's islands are also pseudocraters, including the largest, **Geitey** – a mere 30m high. There are about a dozen closely packed together at Skútustaðir, known as **skútustaðagígar**, and it takes about an hour to walk from the campsite around the collection of grassy hillocks, following paths and boardwalks.

The west shore: the Laxá, Vindbelgjarfjall and Neslönd

Another 4km west from Skútustaðir the Laxá drains quickly out of Mývatn through a collection of low, marshy islands and starts its journey northwest towards the sea at Húsavík. Route 1 continues west towards Fosshól and Akureyri, but for the western side of the lake, turn over the **bridge** here onto Route 848. Immediately across the Laxá there's a rough parking area, from where a walking track follows the river's rapids upstream for about 1km – before they head seawards in late June, you'll almost certainly see big groups of **harlequin ducks** here, along with geese, phalaropes and whooper swans.

Past here, the lake circuit continues north for 12km along Mývatn's western shore, passing small, black-sand beaches where the Icelandic National Parks set up canvas bird-watching **hides** in summer. Beyond rises the unmistakably tall **Vindbelgjarfjall** (529m), whose access track leaves the main road at a sharp bend just before Vagnbrekka farm – don't attempt driving this in anything less than high-clearance four-wheel-drive. On foot, it takes about twenty minutes along this track to reach an obscure path up the back of the mountain, marked with white pegs; if you find yourself in a seriously boggy patch, you've gone too far. Once through lowland heather and scrubby thickets, it's scree all the way around the top – quite slippery and steep – but the scramble to the cairn marking the summit only takes around thirty minutes, from where there are dramatic **views** of the mountain's steep east face and over the lake.

Past the mountain, the main road clips more **pseudocraters** – less visited and more tightly packed than Skútustaðir's – before passing a track eastwards into **Neslönd**, a marshy, scrubby bird-breeding area. Access is restricted to the track in summer, though you can see plenty of birds on nearby ponds, including divers and grebes. At the end of the road is **Ytri-Neslönd farm**, whose late owner amassed a truly extraordinary collection of stuffed birds covering just about every species that it's possible to see in Iceland. The future of this place is uncertain, though you might be able to arrange a visit through regional tour operators – but don't turn up here unannounced. Past the Neslönd turning, it's another 8km back to Reykjahlíð.

Bjarnarflag, Krafla, Leirhnjúkur and around

While Mývatn's immediate surrounds appear fairly stable, the plateau rising just outside town at **Bjarnarflag** and extending northeast is anything but serene, the barren, pock-marked landscape pouring out lively quantities of steam and – when the mood takes it – lava. Even so, this being Iceland you can see not only how destructive such events have been, but also how their energy has been harnessed by the local community – not only are there two thermal power stations in the area, but locals have set up an unusual **bakery** to make use of the abundant free heat. Off the Ringroad past **Hverarönd**'s bubbling mud pools, a detour north along a sealed track brings you to Mývatn's most active region on the slopes of the **Krafla volcano**: the mountain itself is abundantly active, as are neighbouring plains at **Leirhnjúkur**, still dangerously hot after a particularly violent session during the 1980s.

From late June until September there's a daily **bus to Krafla** via these sights from Skútustaðir and Reykjahlíð (which then continues on to Dettifoss; see p.284). There's also a marked, though tiring, 12km **hiking track** direct from Reykjahlíð to Krafla. With your own vehicle, follow Route 1 east to Bjarnarflag (3km from Reykjahlíð) and Hverarönd (6km), and then turn north to the Krafla area (13km).

Bjarnarflag to Hverarönd

Only 3km from Reykjahlíð, **Bjarnarflag** is a thermal zone on the lower slopes of Dalfjall, a long faulted ridge pushed up by subterranean pressures that runs northeast to Krafla itself. Bjarnarflag has a small geothermal power station – Iceland's first, built in 1969 – in front of which a blue-white pond passes for the local version of Reykjavík's Blue Lagoon. Beside here, the **Kísilidjan diatomite plant** processes the silica-rich shells of single-celled organisms whose massed remains form a five- to ten-metre-deep layer of sludge on the bottom of Mývatn; the resulting powder is used in various products from water filters to toothpaste. **Dredging** the lake for the raw material worries conservationists, though locals insist that it creates deeper, cooler water in which fish thrive in summer – and the plant is a major employer outside the tourist season. Note the substantial **wall** behind Kísilidjan, designed to deflect future outflows from the Krafla area above.

Across from Kísilidjan on the south side of the highway, a brickworks makes a good landmark for locating Bjarnarflag's **underground bakery**. This sounds much more technical that it really is; the "bakery" is simply a few small pits dug into the superheated, steaming soil between the road and brickworks, each covered with weighted dustbin lids or sheets of scrap metal. Rye dough is mixed with yeast and molasses in a cardboard milk carton and left underground for a day, where it transforms into neat, rectangular loaves of heavy **hverabrauð** – "steam bread" – which is especially delicious eaten hot with butter. This isn't the only such bakery in Iceland, but it is one of the largest; what isn't made for private consumption is sold through various outlets in

Reykjahlíð. People sometimes cook other things in here too – such as the Icelandic speciality of boiled sheep's head – so prepare for a shock if you lift lids for a look (though residents would rather you left their ovens alone).

If, on a cold afternoon, you also wish you had a steamy pit to crawl into, follow the track up and over the ridge behind the brickworks to a small, wood and fibreglass **sauna**. Though there's a sign outside warning that use is at your own risk, your biggest worry is probably going to be the shock of having to hose the sweat off yourself afterwards with frigid water – but this may well be the point.

Námafjall and Hverarönd

Immediately east of Bjarnaflag, the road twists up and over Dalfjall; on the way, look for a big split in the ridges north, marking the line of the Mývatn rift. The high point south of the road's crest is **Námafjall**, streaked in grey gypsum and yellow **sulphur deposits** – these were once mined and exported for use in gunpowder – and there's an easy twenty-minute track to follow through soft mud to the summit's stony outcrop. The whole Mývatn area is spread below; in particular, look for Hrossaberg to the southwest, a large exploded vent with ragged edges simmering quietly away between here and Hverfjall.

The road meanwhile descends Námafjall's eastern face, and at the base you'll find **Hverarönd**, a large field of **solfataras**, evil-smelling, blue-grey belching mud pools. These are caused by groundwater percolating downwards for over a kilometre to magma levels; heating then forces it back to the surface, where it exits through the sticky red soil at 200°C. It's essential to follow boardwalks and guide ropes here; every year someone leaves them and sinks knee-deep into the scalding pools. These, however, are docile compared with the accompanying **steam vents**, where rocks, gravel and earth have been burst upwards like a bubble to form waist-high, perforated mounds through which vapour screams out ferociously.

Krafla, Viti and Leirhnjúkur

Up in the hills north of Hverarönd, the area around the Krafla volcano has been intermittently erupting for the last three thousand years and shows no signs of cooling down yet. **Krafla** itself (818m) was last active in the 1720s during a period known as the **Mývatn Fires**, which began when the west side of Krafla exploded in 1724, forming a new crater named **Viti** (Hell); earthquakes over the next five years opened up a series of volcanic fissures west of Krafla at **Leirhnjúkur**, producing the lava flows which so nearly destroyed Reykjahlíð's church. More recently, a similar spate of earthquakes between 1977 and 1984 re-opened the fissures running north from Leirhnjúkur in what came to be called the **Krafla Fires**, and it's this mass of still-steaming lava rubble that is the main draw today.

A marked **hiking trail** connects Reykjahlíð with Leirhnjúkur, while the vehicle access road runs north of Route 1 beyond Hverarönd, passing right under piping from **Leirbotn power station** on the way. By harnessing steam vents in the area it was hoped to achieve a 60 megawatt output, but – aside from construction of the plant unfortunately coinciding with the Krafla Fires – one of the boreholes exploded during drilling to form an artificial crater (dryly known as Sjálfskapar Viti, "Homemade Hell"). For years the station ran at half capacity, though newly opened bores have put things back on track; these are what you can hear (and see) roaring away like jet engines up on Krafla's flanks.

After Leirbotn, the road heads steeply uphill to a plateau; at the top, continue straight ahead for 500m to Viti, or turn left for short walking tracks to Leirhnjúkur. **Viti** is a deep, surprisingly attractive crater, sided in steep brown gravel slopes and flooded with aquamarine-coloured water; a slippery track runs around the rim through atmospheric low cloud and plenty of real steam hissing out of bulging vents. **Leirhnjúkur**, on the other hand, is compellingly grotesque, and a testament to the lasting power of molten rock: twenty years on, and the ground here remains, in places, too hot to touch. Tracks from the parking area cross older, vegetated lava before climbing onto the generally darker, rougher new material, splotches of red or purple marking iron and potash deposits, white or yellow patches indicating live steam vents to be avoided – not least for their intensely unpleasant smell. Pegs mark out relatively safe trails around the field, between giant, solidified bubbles, smooth lava pavements, and impossibly cracked, split and twisted mounds. From the high points you can look north towards where the main area of activity was during the 1980s at **Gjástykki**, a black, steaming swathe between light green hills. As usual, apply common sense to any explorations and, in winter – when you'll have to bring your own gear along and ski out here – avoid shallow depressions in the snow, indicating warm areas beneath.

The northeast

Just a brief drive from either Akureyri or Mývatn, **Húsavík** is northeast Iceland's largest town, and the start of the 290-kilometre run eastwards around the coast on Route 85 to **Vopnafjörður**, through a barren, underpopulated countryside (most people left in the late nineteenth century following the volcanic activity at Askja). The regional highlights are **whale watching** out from Húsavík itself, and the gorges, waterfalls and hiking at **Jökulsárgljúfur National Park**, while elsewhere the scattering of small fishing towns and understated landscape of moorland and small beaches have their own quiet appeal. Don't forget that you're almost inside the **Arctic Circle** here, and summer nights are virtually non-existent, the sun just dipping below the horizon at midnight – conversely, winter days are only a couple of hours long. From mid-June until the end of August, **buses** run daily from Mývatn, Akureyri and Húsavík to Jökulsárgljúfur; for Route 85 along the northeast coast, there's a year-round service via Húsavík as far as the town of Þórshöfn.

To Húsavík

Coming **from Akureyri**, Húsavík is a straightforward 90km or so northeast along Route 85; coming **from Mývatn**, the quickest way is by following Route 87 for 55km northwest from Reykjahlíð. Either way, the journey ends up by following the Laxá and its tributaries, with a chance to detour along the way to **Grenjaðarstaður**, around 35km from Mývatn, where a nineteenth-century church and block of turf-roofed farmhouses are well insulated from the icy prevailing winds. Now a **museum** (June–Aug 10am–6pm; 350kr), the estate was founded in medieval times, when it counted as one of the best holdings in all Iceland – a contemporary altar cloth from the original church is now in the Paris Louvre. A couple of kilometres south, the small **Laxárstöðar hydro station** is a monument to environmental terrorism: plans to expand the project by building a new dam had to be shelved after locals, resisting the flooding of their homes, blew up the construction site in 1970.

North of here, Route 85 touches the edge of the prehistoric **Aðaldalshraun lava flow**, which runs almost all the way on up to the coast; if you haven't yet had enough of lava rubble, exploded bubbles and pseudocraters, both *Þinghúsið Hraunbær* (☎464 3695, ✉thinghus@li.is; self-catering, meals by arrangement; ❸), or *Hafralækur* (☎464 3561, ✆464 3461; self-catering, sleeping bag 2500kr, ❸), are fine places to pull up and spend the day exploring. Back on Route 87, **Hveravellir** is a spread of steam-heated greenhouses growing and selling house plants and vegetables; on the roadside here, *Heiðarbær* (☎464 3903, ✉hrivri@mmedia.is; camping 550kr, sleeping bag 2000kr) has summertime accommodation and a good swimming pool. Both routes join up north of these places and run up to Húsavík in around 20km.

Húsavík and around

Approaching **HÚSAVÍK** from the south, you come over a crest and see the town sitting below Húsavíkurfjall on a rare dip in the otherwise high coastline, the blue-green bay out front patched by cloud shadows and a couple of islands. This attractive setting was the site of one of the earliest recorded settlements in Icelandic history, after the ninth-century Swedish rover **Garðar Svavarsson** wintered here while making the first circumnavigation of the country; the shelters he built gave Húsavík (House Bay) its name. It's also said that two of his slaves decamped during his stay and afterwards established a farm, though later historians – looking for nobler lineages than this – tend to overlook the possibility that they were the mainland's first permanent residents.

The area's economy focused on sheep-farming until hit by the nationwide **depression** of the late nineteenth century – caused in part by the 1875 eruption of Viti in the Askja caldera (see p.333) – when those that could switched to fishing, or emigrated to Canada or the US. The remaining farmers, who felt exploited by trade monopolies, formed **Kaupfélag Þingeyinga**, a cooperative that bypassed middlemen and traded directly with merchants from Newcastle in England, an enterprise successful enough to survive right until 2000. Nowadays, Húsavík has reinvented itself as one of the best places in Iceland to go **whale-watching**; so dependent now is the town on this summer income that when commercial whaling resumed in Iceland in 2003, the town hall flew its flag at half mast – nobody here wants to be associated with the whaling industry, nor are whales hunted out of Húsavík. Other than heading to sea for a couple of hours, there isn't a huge amount to do here, though the town and adjacent coast make a pleasant place to stock up before tackling the northeast's rather less well-supplied stretches.

Arrival, information and accommodation

Húsavík is small, with almost all services, including **banks** (with ATMs), STRAX supermarket, and the **post office**, within a short walk of the church and harbour along main-street Garðarsbraut. **Buses** stop outside the church, with services running year-round as far as Akureyri and Þórshöfn, and mid-May to September to Ásbergi and Dettifoss in Jökulsárgljúfur National Park (p.281).

The **tourist information** office (☎464 2520; daily 9am–5pm) is just inside the supermarket, 50m north of the church on Garðarsbraut, and is good at locating inexpensive lodgings. **Internet** is available at the library for 5kr per minute.

Húsavík's **swimming pool** (8am–8pm, 250kr) is on the main road north about 200m up from the harbour, opposite the sports field. **Horses** can be hired through *Saltvík* farm, about 5km south of town on the Akureyri road (☎847 9515, ⓦwww.saltvik.7p.com); they offer anything from riding lessons for beginners to a nine-day Sprengisandur traverse. For **car hire**, try Bílaleiga Húsavíkur (☎464 2500, ⓕ464 1236), and for mainland **tours**, contact Highland Expedition (☎464 3940, ⓦwww.fjallasyn.is), who can take you on four-wheel-drive explorations of Mývatn, Askja, or Dettifoss.

Accommodation

If you're stuck, the tourist information counter know of otherwise unadvertised rooms in **private homes**; the usual deal is sleeping-bag accommodation with or without breakfast. Húsavík's fine **campsite** (☎845 0705) is about 300m up the road from the church on the northern edge of town (a flat rate of 750kr per night, irrespective of how long you stay), with toilets, laundry, a cooking area and sheds for sheltering from inclement weather.

Whale watching at Húsavík

The whale-watching industry in Húsavík got going in the 1990s, after whalers hit by a 1989 moratorium realized that there was still good money to be made by taking tourists out to find the creatures. Though the Icelandic government allowed hunting to resume for "scientific purposes" in 2003, whale stocks remain high, and if you put to sea in summer off Húsavík the chances of seeing at least one species are good. Dolphins, porpoises and medium-sized **minke** whales are seen more frequently, with much larger **humpback** whales runners-up; these are identified by lengthy flippers and their habit of "breaching" – making spectacular, crashing leaps out of the water. Similar-looking **fin whales** are the next most likely candidates, with rarer sightings of colossal **blue whales**; **orca**, or killer whales; and square-headed **sperm** whales. For some reason, only males of the last species are found in Iceland.

Cruises generally head directly across the bay from Húsavík – this can be rough in a northerly wind – where you'll come across puffins and other sea birds fishing; the whales obviously move around a lot but boat crews are expert at locating them. Most of the time you'll see little more than an animal's back, fluke or tail breaking the surface in the middle distance, and perhaps jets of water vapour as they breathe; if you're lucky, whales swim right under the boats, lie on their sides looking up at you, or breach. And you might, of course, see nothing at all – though as tour operators advertise sighting rates, you can check before booking whether much has been seen recently.

Whale-watching **cruises** run at least daily from mid-May through to mid-September (including some evening trips), and last around three hours; it's best to buy **tickets** in advance. Húsavík's two operators are Hvalaferðir (☎464 2551, ⓦwww.hvalaferdir.is), who operate out of the *Salka* restaurant (see p.280) and charge 3300kr; and the award-winning North Sailing Húsavík (☎464 2350, ⓦwww.nordursigling.is), who are based in the *Gamli Baukur* restaurant (see p.280) and charge 3800kr. Both use a range of converted, enclosed wooden whaling boats seating around 40 people (though you spend most of the time outside on deck), and provide essential full waterproof gear, hot drinks and biscuits; differences between the two companies are in the price, and in North Sailing being favoured by large tour groups. Bring binoculars and some warm clothing.

Árból 100m south of the church at the corner of Garðarsbraut and Ásgarðsvegur ☎ 464 2220, ⒻⓍ 464 1463, ⓦ www.simnet.is/arbol. Friendly guesthouse in an early twentieth-century wooden building, with bright rooms and helpful management. Advance booking recommended. Sleeping bag 1500kr, ❹

Aðalbjörg Birgisdottir Baldaursbrekku 20, the second road seawards uphill from the pool ☎ 464 1005, Ⓔ mariam@simnet.is. Sleeping bag accommodation in a retired couple's house, with use of a spotless kitchen; they don't speak much English. 1800kr.

Fosshótel Húsavík A couple of streets back from the harbour at Ketilsbraut 22 ☎ 464 1220, ⒻⓍ 464 2161, ⓦ www.fosshotel.is. Gloomy but still welcoming pile, with cosy rooms and, out of season, relatively good-value budget rates. ❼

Kaldbaks-kot 3km south of Húsavík on the main road ☎ 464 1503, ⓦ www.cottages.is. Self-contained pine cabins with TV, kitchen and bathroom on a rise overlooking the sea and town; can arrange horse riding and fishing. Fourth and seventh nights free, and a good deal for a group. Cabins for 4–8 people 8900–11,900kr a night.

The Town

Backed by a newer residential area, Húsavík's small core of early twentieth-century corrugated-iron and weatherboard businesses cluster around the church and harbour, which face each other across the main street, Garðarsbraut. The **church** is an elaborate wooden structure, with complex eaves and a green painted roof, while the harbour is a good place to see marine ducks, especially long-tailed (old squaw) and eider – both extremely common all along the coast in spring. Views west across wide **Skjálfandi bay** take in the heights of the peninsula opposite, inhabited until its extraordinarily mountainous terrain prevented roads and power being supplied in the early 1960s, after which its scattered farms were abandoned. Look north up the coast and you may be able to spot **Lundey**, a small, uninhabited flat-topped island famed for its puffins.

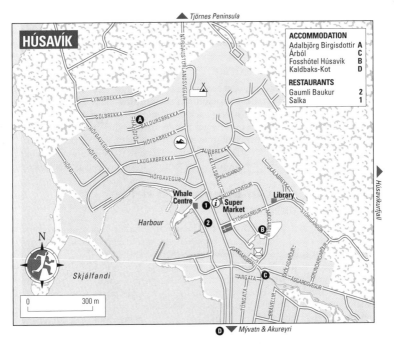

Also at the harbour is Húsavík's excellent **whale centre** (May & Sept daily 10am–5pm June, July, Aug daily 9am–9pm; ⓦ www.icewhale.is; 400kr), sited in an old fish-freezing plant. Inside, an informative assemblage of models, photos, relics, and even skeletons unnervingly suspended above you – all taken from beached or drowned whales – along with a couple of continually playing videos, all fill you in on cetacean biology and the history of whaling in Iceland. Pick of the exhibits are pieces of tremendously hairy baleen plates, with which filter-feeding species strain their nourishing plankton diet like slurping soup through a moustache.

Walk up past the church for 150m along Stóragarður, and Húsavík's library is just on your left, housing an informative local **museum** (daily June-Sept 10am-6pm; 400kr); turn up when they're quiet and the curator may give you a personal tour. Amongst the usual domestic and farmhouse memorabilia, there are bits of medieval weapons found near the town, reconstructions of a Viking longboat, and the wooden room in which Húsavík's cooperative was founded. Glass cases house stuffed representatives of Iceland's indigenous fauna, including a hapless polar bear, killed in 1969 after drifting over from Greenland on an ice floe – an event that the staff here are not proud of.

Past the library, the road runs out of town to the lower slopes of **Húsavíkurfjall**, where a belt of trees marks the entrance to winter **ski slopes**. Out of season, it's about an hour's climb to the hill-top transmitter tower, with further views down on the town and gently steaming fells to the north – locals have private hot tubs up there, fed by underground hot springs.

On a bright day, the coast around Húsavík offers some good, easy **walks** and a chance to rack up your bird-watching tallies. The kilometre-long beach immediately south from the harbour is a fine place to start, or you can head 10km south to **Laxámyri homestead** at the junction of the Akureyri and Reykjahlíð roads. A gravel track here leads out to the mouth of the Laxá at Ærvík, a small, flat bay of black volcanic sand. The river itself ends with a steep, turbulent flurry – attractive both to salmon and to harlequin ducks – before spilling onto the beach for the final few hundred metres to the sea.

Eating and drinking

The **supermarket** itself has a decent range of meat, fish, fruit and vegetables even in winter; and booze is available from the **vínbúð** about 200m south of the harbour and a couple of streets back on Túngata. If you don't fancy fuel-station burgers, try either of Húsavík's two harbourside **restaurants**: the *Gaumli Baukur*, a wood-panelled, mid-range place with top marks going to their pan-fried haddock (1950kr) and juicy lobster tails (2500kr); or *Salka*, next to the whale centre, which has similar fare but more of a café-bar atmosphere.

The Tjörnes peninsula and on to Jökulsárgljúfur

North of Húsavík, the **Tjörnes peninsula** is a rather broad, stubby mass whose roller-coaster roads are cut by numerous small rivers. A few kilometres from town in this direction there's a roadside monument to the locally born patriotic poet **Einar Benediktsson**, one of the key figures of Iceland's early twentieth-century nationalist movement. Past here, now 5km from town, the headlands drop to low **beaches**, reached along vehicle tracks from the road, where you should find the usual melange of **seabirds**, including purple sand-pipers, puffins, black guillemots and gannets; in spring, look out for divers (loons) heading to Mývatn. Walking along the beach, it's also not unusual to find yourself being followed offshore by **seals**.

Moving on, the cliffs soon return and 10km from Húsavík there's another track off the main road marked **Tjörneshöfn**, which descends steeply to a tiny boatshed and harbour looking straight out to Lundey. A shingle beach stretches in both directions below the cliffs, though a small river to the north may stop you heading that way; south there's also seaweed and pleistocene-period **fossil shells** in the headland's layered, vertical faces. These are mostly bivalves, and if you want to see more of them there's a fossil **museum** 2km up the road at **Hallbjarnarstaðir** (☎464 1968; daily in summer 9am–8pm; 350kr).

Tjörnes' northern tip is a further 7km past the museum; park your car when you see the transmitter tower and follow the cliff-top footpath past a far-from-fragrant puffin colony to **Voladalstorfa**, a lighthouse from where it's possible to pick out a very remote Grímsey to the northwest, and **Mánárayjar**, a couple of closer volcanic islets that haven't experienced any stirrings for over a century. From here, the main road rounds the peninsula – at which point you can see northeast over the bay to Kópasker (p.284) – and continues 40km east across the **Bakkahlaup**, a complex of shallow lakes at the Jökulsá á Fjöllum delta, to Ásbergi and the northern end of Jökulsárgljúfur National Park.

Jökulsárgljúfur National Park

Cutting into the northeast's rocky inland plains some 60km east of Húsavík, **Jökulsárgljúfur National Park** encloses a thirty-five-kilometre-long stretch of the middle reaches of the **Jökulsá á Fjöllum**, Iceland's second-longest river. Originating almost 200km south at Vatnajökull, for much of its journey through the park the river flows through the mighty **Jökulsárgljúfur**, a canyon which is 120m deep and 500m wide in places, forming several exceptional waterfalls and an endless array of rock formations. There are two key sights: the **Ásbergi** canyon, a huge, horsesheoe-shaped rockface located in the north of park; and and **Dettifoss**, Europe's most powerful waterfall, at the park's southern boundary. In between, the silt-laden river cuts its way between stark grey gorge walls, though all this is set against an unusually fertile backdrop: over half of the country's **native plant** species are found here, and in summer the heathland above the gorge is lush and splashed pink and white with flowers – except in a couple of places, however, trees are rare.

Park practicalities

With three or four days to spare, the park can be thoroughly investigated on foot along marked **hiking tracks**, the longest of which follows the west side of the gorge for 35km between Ásbergi and Dettifoss. If you're pushed for time, two **roads** run between Ásbergi and Dettifoss, and then continue south to Route 1 east of Mývatn – note, however, that these are unsealed and may be closed by bad weather even in summer, and you should seek advice before using them. The 862/F862 runs down the west side of the gorge, and is usually open for only a couple of months each year; the Ásbergi-Dettifoss section can be OK, if rough, but the stretch south from Dettifoss to Route 1 is four-wheel-drive-only. The east side of the gorge is covered by Route 864, which is generally fine all the way from Ásbergi, past Dettifoss, and down to Route 1.

Between late June and the end of August, two **bus routes** cover the park: one from Akureyri via Húsavík and Ásbergi to Dettifoss; and one from Mývatn via Grímsstaðir (see below) to Dettifoss; both travel down the eastern side of the gorge on Route 864, and their schedules overlap so that it is possible to complete the whole journey in one go.

Within the national park, the sole **accommodation** is by **camping** at one of the three designated sites (600kr per person), which get notoriously busy in summer – camping elsewhere is prohibited. The only other options are outside the park: either 7km west of Ásbergi at *Lundur* (☎465 2247, 🖷465 2246; camping 530kr, sleeping bag 1800kr, beds 2750kr), with a pool and restaurant; or 20km south of Dettifoss at the southern end of Route 864, just before the Ringroad, at either *Grímstunga I* farm (☎464 4294; breakfast by arrangement; sleeping bag 1800kr, made-up beds 3000kr); or next door at *Grímsstaðir* (☎464 4292; camping 400kr, sleeping bag 1700kr) – note that, despite its prominence on maps, Grímsstaðir is not a town and that there are no stores here.

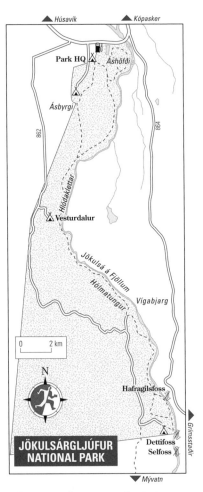

Bring along all **supplies**: the nearest shops are wherever you've just come from, though there's a small **store** at the roadhouse just outside the park at Ásbergi (see below). The best **map** of Jökulsárgljúfur is the inexpensive national park brochure available from the park headquarters. Local **weather** is quite cool, though rain is probably the worst you'll experience from July through to September.

Ásbergi and the park

Coming from Húsavík along Route 85, there's little sign in the otherwise bare landscape of the natural wonders just south of the road. Look for the **roadhouse** (daily 9am–10pm), which sells fuel, fast food, and a pretty good range of bread, cheese, veg, camping gas, and other essentials; just before you reach it, a track heads south to Ásbergi. A short way down here you'll find a golf course and the **park headquarters** (June 1–Sept 15 Mon–Thurs 8am–10pm, Fri & Sat 9am–11pm), where you can pick up a **map**, find out when the next **bus** is due, and organise **camping**. The two local options are either right next to the headquarters, where the facilities include a laundry, barbeque, tables, and shelter (showers are an extra 100kr); or the overflow area about 5km down the road near Ásbergi itself.

At this end of the park the gorge is very broad and not immediately evident, the river having shifted course long ago leaving a flat grassland between low walls. One of these rises behind the park headquarters as **Eyjar**, a long, flat-topped island of rock which can be scaled easily enough from its northern end, giving a good view of this rather open region of the park. Better though, is **Ásbergi**, where the road dead-ends at a pond fringed in birch and pine woods beyond which rises a vertical, ninety-metre-high ampitheatre of dark rock patched in orange lichens and home to a colony of gurgling fulmars. Legend has it that this is the hoofprint of the Norse god Óðinn's eight-legged steed **Sleipnir**, though geologists believe that the canyon was carved by a series of titanic *jökulhlaups* that flooded out from underneath Vatnajökull. Just avoid it in the late afternoon, when the sun catches the cliffs: it looks great, but half of Iceland descends to watch. The view from the top is spectacular too, though inaccessible from here – you need to follow the Dettifoss trail (see below).

Ásbergi to Dettifoss

It takes around two days to walk the largely easy route **from Ásbergi to Dettifoss** (35km), with an overnight stop along the way at **Vesturdalur** (11-14km from Ásbergi depending on route) – though you'll see plenty even if you just make a return day-trip to Vesturdalur. The easiest way to pick up the trail is to head past the roadhouse and turn immediately south down the *Ás* farm road; about 50m along you'll see a wooden signpost and pegs by the roadside which mark the way. Alternatively, cross from the park headquarters below the golf course to where you'll find a **rope** hanging over an 8m ledge, and pull yourself up to the same path. Either way, follow the trail along the clifftop and you soon exit the tight birch scrub onto an open heathland; about an hour from camp will find you looking north from the rounded rocks atop of Ásbergi.

There are two trails to Vesturdalur from here; one short-cuts south (8.5km) but for a fuller view of the gorge, take the longer track (11.5km). This crosses east over the heath for a couple of kilometres – look out for plovers, redshanks, godwits, ravens and **short-eared owls** – suddenly bringing you to the brink of the gorge, where jutting rocks offer a good perch for looking down at the grey river rushing smoothly across a shingle bed. The trail now follows the gorge south, crossing intermittent sections of green heath and dark basalt, joining up with the short-cut from Ásbergi and then entering a brief, slow section of ashy sand. Once through this, a side track makes the short climb to **Rauðhólar**, the remains of a scoria cone whose vivid red, yellow, and black gravel is a shock after the recently monochrome backdrop. Past here you descend to **Hjóðaklettar**, where the noise of the river – which funnels violently through a constriction at this point – is distorted by hexagonal-collumned hollows in huge, shattered cliffs. There are some weird formations to poke around in here, and it's one of the few places on the hike where you're almost at river level. The path then crosses Route 862, with the **Vesturdalur campsite** (toilets and fresh water) about a kilometre away, sited by a pleasant, if sometimes boggy, meadow.

Over the next 8km, the trail moves above the river and then down to the marshy **Hólmatungur**, where underground springs pool up to create three short rivers which flow quickly into the Jökulsá through some thick vegetation. The trail crosses the largest of these tributaries, the Hólmá, on a bridge just above where it tumbles into the main river. Upstream from here on the Jökulsá's east bank, the prominent face of **Vígabjarg** marks where the formerly mighty Vígarbjargfoss ripped through a narrow gorge, before a change in the river's course dried it to a trickle sixty years ago. From here it's another 8km to the twenty-seven-metre-high **Hafragilsfoss**, an aesthetically pleasing set of falls whose path through a row of volcanic craters has exposed more springs, which mix their clear waters with the Jökulsá's muddier glacial flood (there's a particularly good view of Hafragilsfoss off Route 864, on the eastern side of the gorge).

A final tricky couple of kilometres of scrambling brings you to the park's southern limits at **Dettifoss**, where the dirty white, violent river rips across a twisted basalt bed before dropping 45m with enough force to send the spray hundreds of metres skywards. Again, the best – and closest – vantages are actually from the eastern side of the river. On the western side, Route 862 meets the end of the hiking trail, where there's a **basic campground** (no amenities) for hikers wanting to overnight here. After Dettifoss, it's worth carrying on a further kilometre upstream to **Selfoss**, where a diagonal fault across the river has created a long, but only ten-metre-high, cascade.

The northeast coast

After Ásbergi, Route 85 continues around the northeast coast past a string of small communities – **Kópasker**, **Raufarhöfn**, **Þórshöfn** and **Vopnafjörður** – relying on fish-processing, rather than catches themselves, for their main industry. There are a couple of historical echoes here, but mostly it's the landscapes which are memorable: the flat, marshy **Melrakkaslétta** which lies just outside the Arctic Circle; the fells and dales of the foggy **Langanes Peninsula**; and a score of little black sand and shingle beaches strewn with huge piles of driftwood and disproportionate numbers of **whale strandings**. These were once something of a windfall for local landowners (the term *hvalreki*, literally "whale wreck", implies "jackpot" and is used nowadays for lottery winnings), providing meat, oil, bone and various tradeable bits, such as sperm-whale teeth. In saga times, people would actually fight for possession of these riches, but today a whale stranding is a bit of a burden, as the law demands that the landowner is responsible for disposing of the carcass – not an easy matter in the case of a thirty-ton sperm whale. In summer, the region is also infested with **nesting birds** (you'll see orange warning signs asking you to slow down as you pass key nesting grounds), the well-camouflaged, fluffy chicks guarded by overprotective parents – this can make getting out of the car something of an ordeal at times, as you risk being dive-bombed by terns and plovers. Otherwise, there's good **camping** potential along much of the coast, with plenty of soft grass. **Buses** go as far as Þórshöfn; while Vopnafjörður marks the end of the coastal road, and routes divide here westwards back to Mývatn, or southeast to Egilsstaðir and the Eastfjords.

Kópasker

From the Ásbergi junction it's another 40km north to the port of **KÓPASKER**, first following the edge of the Jökulsá's broad delta where fish are farmed in large round ponds, then the gravelly Öxafjörður coast. The village looks small on approach, but is actually tiny, with an outlying church marking a short side-road off the highway into the town's simple square of streets beside the harbour. The church is next to a Settlement-era **assembly site**, giving Kópasker a surprisingly venerable historical anchor, and a new **slaughterhouse** has brought relative prosperity, but otherwise the town is best known for suffering a severe force-eight earthquake in January 1976, thanks to activity at Krafla (see p.275). Kópasker has just enough room for a school with sculptures made from local rocks decorating its lawn, a **bank** (Mon–Fri 1–4pm), **post office**, **supermarket**, **fuel station**, a **campsite** just as you enter town (with a tiny attached **café**), and a **youth hostel** (☎465 2314, ℻467 2314; sleeping-bag accommodation 1350kr, ❸) – they're open all year but you'd be wise to give them advance notice of your arrival, especially in winter.

Melrakkaslétta and towards the Arctic Circle

After Kópasker, the road passes through the partially-greened slopes of the low **Leirhafnalfjöll** range, a string of early nineteenth-century cinder cones, and then turns northeast into the empty horizons of the **Melrakkaslétta** tundra, which forms Iceland's northernmost peninsula. It might not look that inspiring, but in its own way the Melrakkaslétta has as much wildlife as Mývatn: a coastline of shingle and sand beaches pulls in plenty of wading birds; while the tundra and an associated mass of small, fragmented lakes attract big nesting colonies of eider ducks and arctic terns, as well as whimbrel and the otherwise rare **grey phalarope**, along with both of Iceland's diver (loon) species. To cap all this, Melrakkaslétta is also visited by large numbers of non-resident birds, including barnacle geese, arctic redpoll and knot, migrating between Europe and Greenland or Canada – they pass through in late April and early May, and return with young in September.

For a quick look at the coast, turn north off Route 85 around 16km from Kópasker, and follow an eight-kilometre track to the abandoned farm Grjótnes, from where a footpath follows gannet-infested cliffs for 3km to the flat-topped, sheer-sided headland of **Rauðinúpur**. Meanwhile, the main road brushes the shore between some long lagoons; climb the small fise here and you can look south along the geological fault that runs all the way down to Mývatn. Shortly afterwards, the square-sided **Þórgeirsdys lighthouse** lifts out of the horizon, marking **Hraunhafnartangi**, the mainland's northern extremity – a mere 2.5km outside the **Arctic Circle**. Leave the road when you reach a small bridge, and walk the final kilometre across the moorland (though in summer, nesting birds make this virtually impossible without a helmet), past the lighthouse and cairn, and up onto the loosely piled stone sea wall to see the grey-blue Arctic Ocean pounding the far side.

Raufarhöfn

Iceland's northernmost town, **RAUFARHÖFN** sits on the Melrakkaslétta's eastern coast some 55km from Kópasker and 10km past Hraunhafnartangi. In the 1960s Raufarhöfn was at the core of Iceland's herring industry, and the town's salting plant processed more herring than anywhere else in the country, providing seasonal work that attracted a floating population of thousands. Times have changed, however: the 1990s saw the town's prosperity ebb away as demand for herring dried up and the plant shifted to hiring Polish workers to freeze and export Russian cod to the US; even this doesn't seemed to have helped and at last reports the factory was about to close – along with most of Raufarhöfn's services.

The main road runs straight through town, with the turning to the **harbour** and church on the northern side. On this road by the harbour you'll find the good-value *Hótel Norðurljós* (☎465 1233, ℻465 1383, ℰept@vortex.is; sleeping bag 1800kr, ❹), with a **campsite** on Raufarhöfn's south exit by the swimming pool. In between is a **store**, with the only **restaurant** in town at the hotel; don't count on being able to buy **fuel**. The harbour and grassy headland at the end of the church road are good places to admire seascapes from, and the hotel owners give advice on good bird-watching spots and rent out **kayaks** (2000kr a day, including all safety gear) to explore Melrakkaslétta's lakes.

Rauðanes, Þórshöfn and the Langanes peninsula

Out of Raufarhöfn, it's 65km to Þórshöfn ascending high, rocky heathland as the road heads inland and south. Around halfway there's a glimpse of the coast before rounding the knife-edge scree atop **Viðarfjall**, then it's down to ground level again around **Svalbarð** – historians reckon the farm here is one of Iceland's oldest, though the modern, nondescript buildings give no visual evidence of this. Just north on the coast from here, **Rauðanes** is a particularly attractive headland where an easy 7km marked **footpath** takes you to tall, layered cliffs, caves, a couple of beaches, plenty of surf and birdlife (there used to be a huge puffin colony here too, but they were cleared out by feral minks) – it's a great spot to stretch your legs for few hours. On a good day, views from the road beyond reach out to Gunnolfsvíkurfjall, a ridge of hills at the southeastern end of the goose-necked **Langanes peninsula** – which juts out to the northeast for 35km along the divide between the Arctic Ocean and warmer North Atlantic, and so is frequently fog-bound in a fine, wet mist – and the higher Heljardalsfjöll (931m) to the south, whose summit just brushes the clouds.

ÞÓRSHÖFN is a compact, busy little place with terminally pot-holed roads at the base of the Langanes peninsula, and marks the limit of local **buses**, which head back west along Route 85 to Húsavík and Akureyri year round (Mon–Fri at 1pm). The town is just somewhere to stock up, but Langanes offers some good hiking across grassy fells and moorland out to an uninhabited coast, where – unlike Iceland's more popular outdoor venues – you won't have to share the experience with hordes of drunken campers. The road enters Þórshöfn from the south, and runs for 250m past a church, grassy **campground** (free, with toilets and sink – head to the pool for a shower), **bank**, **post office** and **fuel station** (which has the last fuel for at least 80km), to an intersection. Turn right here, and the road heads uphill to the **supermarket**, and a modern **pool** and sports centre (Mon-Fri 8am-7pm, Sat & Sun 10am-4pm, 250kr); turn left for *Hafnarbarinn*, the town's only bar and a pizza-oriented **restaurant**, though the fuel station dishes up the usual staples. **Accommodation** is either at the green-painted *Lyngholt* guesthouse just before the pool (☎468 1238, ℰkarenrut@simnet.is; ❷), or the small and slightly better *Hótel Jorvík* diagonally opposite the pool (☎468 1400, ℻468 1399, jorvik@netfang.com; sleeping bag 1800kr, ❷), which offers meals, self-catering accommodation, and a fantastic view over the sea.

To bypass town and stay on the coastal road, turn right at the church, but to explore Langanes carry on through town and follow the gravel road 15km northeast to **Ytra Lon farm**, a snug and friendly, self-catering **youth hostel** (☎ & ℻468 1242, ⓦwww.mmedia.is/~ytralon; 1550kr) – it's very small

6

though, so book in advance. Open year-round, this is a working sheep farm (they also collect eider down in season); there's the chance to join in or just observe working life – the annual *rettir*, or sheep round-up, takes place in late September – **fish** local streams for trout, or plan a **hike**. There are a couple of good full-day circuits to be made, though to get to the Fontur lighthouse at Langanes' tip you'll need to camp out overnight; keep your eyes peeled for **gyrfalcons** while you walk.

Bakkafjörður and Vopnafjörður

Heading on from Þórshöfn, Route 85 crosses the base of Langanes, then rejoins the coast and meets the Atlantic for the first time above Finnafjörður, a deep bay with campsite and self-catering **accommodation** at *Fell* farm (☎473 1696, ℮fell@li.is; camping 500kr, ❸), where you can also pick up fishing licences for the short rivers in the area. From here it's a fairly uninterrupted run to **Bakkafjörður** and **Vopnafjörður** – the smallest and largest of the northeastern communities – and routes out of the region.

Forty kilometres from Þórshöfn, **BAKKAFJÖRÐUR** is an isolated cliff-top community of rich, reclusive fishermen, some 5km off the main road. As the region's smallest settlement the village endures much "butt of the world"-type humour, and in truth there's not much here beyond the store and obligatory salting plant – even buying fuel often means a chase around the place after the attendant. Nor is there anywhere to eat or stay, though there's a summer **campground**, and a good day walk over the humpy Digranes headland, and around a rocky coastline to the Svatnes lighthouse.

Vopnafjörður

South of Bakkafjörður, the road cuts inland again and suddenly acquires a sealed surface, the first in a long while. About 25km along, a good side road leads southwest down the **Selá**, to where a small riverside **swimming pool** (free) complete with changing rooms and showers utilizes the northeast coast's only economically viable hot spring. A further kilometre upstream along a jeep track brings you to **Selárfoss**, a five-metre-high tumble of clear, emerald green water – there's a fish ramp beside the falls for the salmon in the river.

It's a final 5km along the main road past Selá, over Nipslón lagoon, to **VOPNAFJÖRÐUR**, a relatively sizeable town arrayed on a steep hillside facing east over a fjord of same name. A predictable place with a large harbour and all the usual services, the region around town featured in several intercon-nected Settlement-era tales of clan feuding known as the **Vopnafjörð sagas** – appropriately enough, Vopnafjörður means "Weapons Fjord". Other claims to fame include a reputation for sunshine, and the fact that the 1988 Miss World, Linda Pétursdóttir, grew up here; the town was also the **emigration point** to the US and Canada for around 2000 impoverished farmers and their families, after their lands to the southwest had been blighted by poisonous fallout from the 1875 eruption of Viti in Askja (see p.275). Canada, which at the time had a "populate or perish" policy, offered subsidised passages for anyone wanting to migrate, and sent ships to take them. Vopnafjörður's **information centre** (☎473 1565), in a restored, corrugated-iron wharehouse next to the fish fac-tory, has a small photo exhibition on the migrants, along with a few stuffed birds.

This slope that Vopnafjörður sits on forms the eastern side of the **Kolbeinstangi peninsula**, the tip of a narrow, mountainous ridge that runs 35km northeast from the Interior's high plateaus, backing the town in rock.

You can follow this right out to the end by taking the road past the hotel and harbour to where it splits; bear left, but leave the track soon after and go cross-country along the stony ridges for 3km to the sea. In the opposite direction, there's a less easy walk to the town's transmitter tower, featuring marshy saddles, rounded stone outcrops and flint-like shards everywhere. The top is extremely barren, with views southwest to Bustarfell (see below) and down off steep cliffs to the broad, black beach south of town – a bit too windswept to justify a trip in its own right – where the remains of a modern shipwreck labour in the shallows.

Vopnafjörður's exposed **campsite** (☎473 1300) is on the top road across from the school, with a **bank** and **post office** one street down near the church, while the **supermarket** and sole central **accommodation** option, *Gistiheimilið Vopnafjörður* (☎473 1840, ⓔ gistiheimalid@vopnafjordur.is; ❸), are one street below again on the harbour road. The nearest **farmstay**, *Gistiheimilið Skjól* (☎473 1332, ⓕ473 1362; sleeping bag 1550kr, ❸), is about 2km south of town on the main road and has a kitchen, laundry, and horses. The *Vopnafjörður's* **restaurant** has an inexpensive, warming range of lamb, fish, chicken, pasta and pizza dishes, and has a takeaway service too – useful if you're camping. Otherwise, the two **fuel stations** – one at either end of town – sell snacks.

From Vopnafjörður to Mývatn and Egilsstaðir

Fuel up before you leave Vopnafjörður; to the south, there's no fuel available for at least 120km on the main road, while northwards the next reliable source is Þórshöfn.

The main road is Route 85 southwest, initially climbing up **Bustarfell**, 18km from town, where there's an open-air **museum** (mid-June to mid-Sept daily 10am–6pm; 400kr) featuring well-preserved, turf-gabled farm buildings, founded in the eighteenth century – worth a look if you haven't seen traditional Icelandic houses before. The heights above are exposed, with sudden snowdrifts possible all through the year, and then the road winds slowly down to join Route 1 some 70km from Vopnafjörður. Turn west here for a 65-kilometre run across desolate lava plains and gravel deserts to Mývatn via Grimsstaðir and the turning to Dettifoss (see p.284); or east for the last 100km to **Egilsstaðir**, with the road crossing the **Möðradalsfjallgurðar** range (800m), the highest pass of its entire circuit, before it descends into the long valley of Jökuldalur and passes the turning coastwards to Húsey. There's also a direct, eighty-kilometre road east from Vopnafjörður to Egilsstaðir, though this is very mountainous and only open in summer; turn off the Burstarfell road just outside town and follow the western side of the fjord up to where the road cuts east across the rugged Hellisheiði, then follow the Jökulsá á Brú south to join Route 1 at the Húsey turning.

Travel details

Buses

Most services below run only from around mid-May until some point in September, with the exception of buses from Akureyri to Húsavík and then along Route 85 to Þórshöfn, which run Mon–Fri year-round. For further details contact SBA in Akureyri (☎462 4442, ⓦ www.sba.is).

Ásbergi to: Dettifoss (daily; 1hr 30min); Húsavík (5 weekly; 45min); Kópasker (5 weekly; 30min); Raufarhöfn (5 weekly; 1hr 30min); Þórshöfn (5 weekly; 2hr 45min).

Dettifoss to: Akureyri (daily; 7hr); Ásbergi (daily; 4hr); Húsavík (daily; 5hr 30min); Reykjahlíd/Mývatn (daily; 1hr 30min).

Húsavík to: Akureyri (5 weekly/5 daily; 1hr 10min); Ásbergi (daily; 1hr 40min); Dettifoss (daily; 3hr 20min); Kópasker (5 weekly; 1hr 25min); Raufarhöfn (5 weekly; 2hr 15min); Reykjahlíd (3 daily; 45min); Þórshöfn (5 weekly; 3hr 30min).

Kópasker to: Akureyri (5 weekly; 3hr 25min); Ásbergi (5 weekly; 30min); Húsavík (5 weekly; 2hr 15min); Raufarhöfn (5 weekly; 50min); Þórshöfn (5 weekly; 1hr 55min).

Raufarhöfn to: Akureyri (5 weekly; 4hr 10min); Ásbyrgi (5 weekly; 1hr 15min); Kópasker (5 weekly; 45min); Þórshöfn (5 weekly; 1hr 15min).

Reykjahlíd (Mývatn) to: Akureyri (5 daily; 2hr 45min); Dettifoss (daily; 1hr 30min); Egilsstaðir (3 weekly/1 daily; 2hr 5min); Goðafoss (5 daily; 40min); Grímsstaðir (3 weekly/1 daily; 30min); Húsavík (3 daily; 45min); Krafla (2 daily; 15 min).

Þórshöfn to: Akureyri (5 weekly; 5hr 10min); Ásbergi (5 weekly; 2hr 15min); Húsavík (5 weekly; 4hr); Kópasker (5 weekly; 1hr 45min); Raufarhöfn (5 weekly; 1hr).

7

The Eastfjords and the southeast

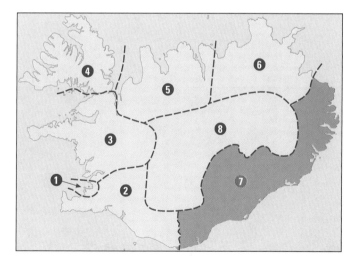

CHAPTER 7

Highlights

* **Borgarfjörður Eystri** The most isolated and picturesque of the Eastfjord towns, surrounded by shattered mountains and stiff walking trails. See p.304

* **Papey** Make a day-trip to this tiny, bird-infested island, with pre-Viking history. See p.310

* **Vatnajökull** Skud across the outrunning glaciers of Europe's largest ice-cap by four-wheel-drive or snowmobile. See p.311

* **Lónsöræfi** Spend a week hiking through wild and remote highlands between the south coast and Snæfell. See p.312

* **Skaftafell** Prime camping and easy walking around this heathland plateau, caught in between two glaciers. See p.319

7

The Eastfjords and the southeast

T he five-hundred-and-fifty-kilometre strip of land and water covering Iceland's Eastfjords and the southeast takes in a quarter of the country's coastal fringe, though the scenery divides into just two distinct regions. About as far as you can possibly get from the urban comforts of Reykjavík and Akureyri, the **Eastfjords** are necessarily self-contained but also unexpectedly well settled, with a population distributed between eastern Iceland's main town of **Egilsstaðir**, and a handful of relatively substantial coastal communities which are dotted at regular intervals along the fjords' convoluted coastline. The area has been farmed since medieval times, but the coastal villages here – each with its own small harbour and fishing fleet – only really took off during the herring boom of the early twentieth century, and a few were even used as Allied naval bases during World War II; today, the port of **Seyðisfjörður** remains important as an alternative entry or departure point for Iceland, via the weekly ferry from Scandinavia. There's a little bit of history to soak up, though the main focus here is the fjords themselves, a mix of brightly coloured cliffs and blue waters, with some relatively easy hiking trails to explore. Southwest of Egilsstaðir, wild highlands of tundra and moorland host substantial reindeer and wildfowl populations, and peak at the solitary heights of **Snæfell**, the core of an extinct volcano – a pristine area presently threatened by the ongoing construction of a controversial hydro-electric plant.

South of the Eastfjords, the landscape becomes more typically bleak and rugged, backed by the icy vastness of **Vatnajökull**, whose sprawling cap and host of outrunning glaciers dominate views west of the town of **Höfn**. With a largely infertile terrain of highland moors and coastal gravel deserts known as **sandurs** to contend with – not to mention a fair share of catastrophic volcanic events – the population centres are few and far between, though you can explore the glacial fringes at the wild **Lónsöræfi reserve**, accessed via Staffafell farm, and at **Skaftafell**, where there are plenty of marked tracks. Further west, the tiny settlement of **Kirkjubæjarklaustur** is the jumping-off point for several trips inland, the best of which touches on one of Iceland's most disastrous eruptions.

Egilsstaðir and Höfn are the regional transport hubs, served by a complement of regular **flights** to Reykjavík and Akureyri, and summertime **buses** travelling the Ringroad. The Eastfjords are less well covered, though everywhere is within

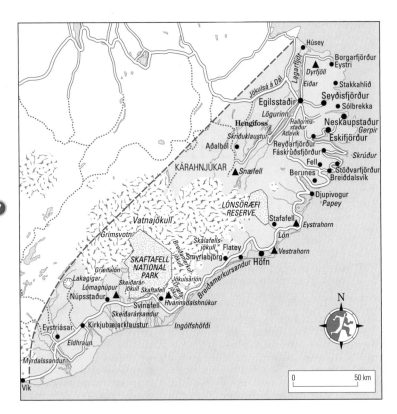

range of local services. Note, though, that between mid-September and mid-May – when Ringroad services terminate at Höfn and Akureyri – there are **no buses** at all to Egilsstaðir. **Weather-wise**, expect cold winters with heavy snowfalls, though the southeast coast tends towards wet conditions, while everywhere east of Vatnajökull seems to have much sunnier weather than the rest of the country – at least when the westerlies are blowing.

Egilsstaðir, Snæfell and the Eastfjords

Far from the flow of things, Egilsstaðir and the Eastfjords form a compact region, whose underrated attractions offer a very different view of Iceland from that presented by the country's more famous sights. Set on Route 1 halfway around the country from Reykjavík, **Egilsstaðir** makes a good base for excursions inland around **Lögurinn**, a narrow, lake-like stretch of river where you'll find some saga history and Iceland's most extensive woodlands; or even for an assault on the highlands around **Snæfell**, eastern Iceland's tallest peak. The Eastfjords themselves provide some wonderfully convoluted coastal scenery – whose headlands host some major seabird colonies – along with an increasingly popular network of **hiking trails** across multi-coloured mountains. Towns along the way are fairly small, however, and the only ones which might prove an essential stop are the international port of **Seyðisfjörður**, where the ferry from Scandinavia docks in summer; and tiny **Djúpivogur**, from where you can make an excellent day-trip to the tiny island of **Papey**.

The regional **airport** at Egilsstaðir is open year-round, but don't forget that buses to Egilsstaðir dry up from mid-September to mid-May. Once here, it's best to have your own transport if possible; Egilsstaðir and the Eastfjord towns are connected by regular **buses**, but you'll have to spend at least a day in each place, waiting for the next service. In winter, only Egilsstaðir is reliably accessible, though you'll find a reasonable amount of accommodation and services open year-round, and tour operators who would love to see the tourist season extended into winter months, if only they had enough visitors.

Egilsstaðir and around

Wherever you've come from, arrival in **EGILSSTAÐIR**, sitting where the roads from Seyðisfjörður, Borgarfjörður Eystri and Reyðarfjörður meet at the Ringroad, is a bit of an anticlimax. Though the area crops up in several historic texts – most famously in **Hrafnkel's Saga** (see p.300) – the town itself dates only to the late 1940s, when a supermarket, a vet, a hospital and a telephone exchange chose to set up shop where roads converged on a narrow strip of moorland between the glacier-fed **Lagarfljót river** and the back of the Eastfjord fells, bringing the first services into this remote corner of the country. Today Egilsstaðir has grown to fill a couple of dozen streets but remains an unadorned service and supply centre, important to the regional economy but containing little in the way of essential viewing.

Egilsstaðir is, however, a major **transportation** hub; the airport has flights to Akureyri and Reykjavík, the port of Seyðisfjörður is nearby, and anyone travelling by bus has to stop here for at least as long as it takes to change services. While the town itself may not slow you down for long, there's a fair amount to hold you in the area for a day or two. Running southwest from Egilsstaðir, the Lagarfljót forms a long lake known as **Lögurinn**, whose eastern shores are famously forested and whose waters are home to a mythical beast somewhat akin to the Loch Ness monster. Continuing southwest beyond the lake, rough roads and hiking tracks wind up to where **Snæfell's** isolated peak – visible on a good day from Egilsstaðir – guards the northeastern edge of the Vatnajökull ice cap, and also roughly marks a wilderness area soon to be dammed and flooded for a power station (see p.302). Meanwhile, heading north from town takes you through boggy, wildflower-strewn heathland to the coast around the mouths of the Lagarfljót and the parallel **Jökulsá á Brú**, a good place to spend a few days fishing, or tracking down wildfowl.

Arrival, information and accommodation

Egilsstaðir sits east off the Ringroad, where main street Fagradalsbraut runs for 150m between a knot of services before transmuting into Norðfjarðarvegur and joining roads to coastal Borgarfjörður (72km), Seyðisfjörður (27km), and Reyðarfjörður (34km). The **airport** and Flúgfelag Íslands airline office (☎471 1210, ⓦwww.airiceland.is) are off the Ringroad a kilometre north of town, with daily services to Reykjavík and Akureyri; a bus to town meets flights in summer. The **bus station** is in town, just off the Ringroad beside the Esso **fuel station**, with departures to Akureyri and Höfn daily from June until September, and several times weekly for around ten days either side of these dates; there are also regular services to the Eastfjord towns (see the relevant town accounts for details). This is also where you'll find the **information office** (June–Aug Mon, Tues, Thurs & Fri 9am–6pm, Wed 9am–8pm, Sat & Sun noon–3pm; ☎471 2320). Some 50m uphill along Norðfjarðarvegur is a **post office** and **payphone**, **bank** (with ATM), and a second fuel station where Tjarnabraut runs north for 250m to the museum, church, pool and residential areas. For **car rental**, try Freyfaxi (☎471 1328) on Norðfjarðarvegur, or Akureyrar Inter Rent (☎892 5700) at the airport. **Tours** are operated by the long-established Tanni Travel, based in the Eastfjord town of Eskifjörður (☎476 1399, ⓔphilip@ismennt.is, ⓦwww.tannitravel.is) – 4WD-trips can be organised around Lögurinn and out to Húsey or Hrafnkelsdalur, or even to Snæfell and the edge of Vatnajökull.

Accommodation

Accommodation fills up fast in summer, particularly mid-week, when the international ferry docks at Seyðisfjörður. The spacious **campsite** is next to the bus station (book through the information office, see above; camping 550kr, beds 1660kr) with showers, kitchen, laundry and potentially boggy tent sites; the other **budget** option is the summer-only *Edda*, across from the pool off Tjarnabraut (☎471 2775, ⓕ471 2776; sleeping-bag accommodation 1100kr, ⑤). Pick of the **hotels** is the very pleasant *Gistihúsið Egilsstöðum* (☎471 1114, ⓦwww.egilsstadir.com; ⑥), 500m west of town on Lögurinn's shore in a converted, solid stone farmhouse with friendly staff and grand views down the lake; otherwise try the smart, Icelandair-run *Hérað*, behind Bónus (☎471 1500, ⓔherad@icehotel.is; ⑦), or the drab but comfortable *Foss-Valaskjálf*, opposite the museum at Skógarlöndum 3 (☎471 1000, ⓦwww.fosshotel.is; with and without shower ④–⑦).

The Town

Egilsstaðir's main distraction is the excellent **Minjasafn Austurlands**, the East Iceland Heritage Museum, a ten-minute walk from the bus station on Tjarnabraut (June–Aug Tues–Sun 11am–5pm, Sept–May Fri 1–5pm; 300kr). Amongst the usual examples of local crafts, there are some less ordinary exhibits dedicated to that old Icelandic pastime of **hunting** – mostly guns and ammunition, but a pair of antique wooden snowshoes also feature (rarely seen elsewhere in Iceland), along with a sixteenth-century sword, whose guard and bone handle are decorated with hunting scenes. The museum's two centrepieces are a complete reconstruction of a **turf farmhouse**, which would have been warm but decidedly cramped if ever filled to its fifteen-bunk capacity; and remains from the **Þórisá Barrow**, a local Viking grave dated to 980 AD, which yielded the skeletons of a forty-year-old male and a horse, along with personal effects which included a wooden bowl and two contemporary

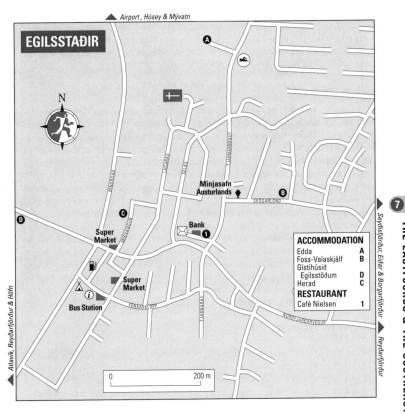

English coins. These were from the reign of Eadwig, the politically inept king of England whose four-year rule saw him lose all authority north of the Thames after nobles ditched him in favour of his brother Edgar, and their presence here throws some light on the extent of trade links and exchanges in the Viking world.

Continue past the museum up Tjarnabraut and you'll pass a modern **church**, whose design dimly echoes volcanic rock formations, and then reach Egilsstaðir's **swimming pool**, somewhere to unwind on a wet day (Mon–Fri 7am–9.30pm, Sat & Sun 10am–7pm; 250kr). In better weather, there's a brief **walk** to be made uphill from the bus station to a rocky outcrop overlooking the town, with long views down the lake towards a distant Snæfell. If you've got your own transport, it's also worth checking out **Fardagafoss**, a small waterfall in a twisting canyon about 5km northeast of town on the lower slopes of the Seyðisfjörður road.

Eating and drinking

Eating wise, the Esso fuel station **café** is inexpensive and well patronized for the usual grills, pizzas, and sandwiches. Up the hill, hidden behind a screen of trees next to the bank, *Café Nielsen* is a cosy **café-restaurant-bar** with a bit of charm – a good place for a beer, snack, or the full "Viking Special" (a smorgasboard of traditional delicacies including smoked lamb, herring, and fermented shark). For **self-catering**, there are two supermarkets, both open until 6pm: Samkaup, behind Esso, is the better stocked of the two and has a good range of road maps; while Bónus, across the road, is cheaper.

Lögurinn

In common with many Icelandic lakes, **Lögurinn**, stretching directly southwest of Egilsstaðir for 30km, fills a glacier-eroded valley. Unusually, however, the valley is fairly well **wooded**, at least along its eastern side. Most people don't get much further than these woods' southern reaches around the bay of **Atlavík**, but a decent road runs right around the lake and elsewhere there's saga lore and medieval remains to take in, along with an impressive waterfall. Deep and green, the lake itself is home to the **Lagarfljótsormur**, a monster of the Scottish Loch Ness and Swedish Storsjön clans, though so elusive that nobody is even very sure what it looks like – a giant snaky form is favoured.

You need only one nice day to appreciate Lögurinn, but if you want to stay longer, **accommodation** is concentrated in the more visited stretch between Egilsstaðir and Atlavík. In your own vehicle, Lögurinn takes an easy few hours to circuit, including time for stops along the way; otherwise you'll have to rely on **tours** from Egilsstaðir (see "Arrival", p.296) or the twice-weekly **bus** to Atlavík. Alternatively, you might pass through en route to Snæfell, as the direct route from Egilsstaðir runs off Lögurinn's southern end.

Down to Atlavík

Iceland's forests were never very extensive in the first place and soon fell to human and grazing pressures after the Settlement. To partially remedy the situation, since the early twentieth century the Icelandic Forestry Commission has put considerable effort into preserving fragmentary pockets of woodland and sponsored replanting programmes around the country, and the eighteen-kilometre stretch along Lögurinn's eastern shore is their showpiece, giving an idea how parts of Iceland might once have looked – and may do so again, given time. The woodland is mostly birch (distinguished by its smooth red or silver bark), though mature plantations of much larger ash, spruce and larch are wildly popular with Icelanders, who are struck by the novelty of seeing vegetation that is taller than they are – visitors from lusher climates may feel that the area, pleasant though it is, doesn't warrant so much excitement.

Start by heading south from Egilsstaðir down the highway, where, 11km along, a blue board by the roadside marks a handful of short trails into **Eyjólfsstaðaskógar**, the smaller and least developed of Lögurinn's two wooded areas – the longest takes about three hours return – with self-catering farm **accommodation** across the road here at *Eyjólfsstaðir* (☎471 2171, ℻471 2071; sleeping-bag accommodation 1350kr, cabin 5500kr). Continuing south, the Ringroad bends east to Breiðdalsvík and the southern fjord towns; bear right to stay on the lake circuit, which passes a layby with good views over the water before entering **Hallormsstaðurskógar**. By now you're 24km from town around **HALLORMSSTAÐUR**, a small group of **summer accommodation** options open roughly from June until late August: first is a lakeshore **campsite** (☎471 1774), while another kilometre on there's a fuel station and small store opposite the 200-metre sideroad to the modern *Fosshótel* (☎471 1705, ℻471 2197; ❼), with the only local **pool** and **restaurant**; and *Hússtjórnarskólans* (☎471 1763, ℻471 2761; sleeping-bag accommodation 2100kr, doubles with or without bath ❸–❺), a nice elderly schoolhouse on the forest fringe. There are marked walking tracks out of the woods and up onto the fellsides here, the longest of which takes around five hours return; *Hússtjórnarskólans* also hires out horses for these trails at around 1500kr per hour.

Back on the lake road, it's 2km past Hallormsstaður to the **forestry office** and **arboretum**, where there's a half-hour stroll around a labelled collection of century-old native and imported tree species, including the country's tallest (a pine), which towers 22m overhead. A couple of kilometres further brings you to a sharp downhill turn to the water's edge at **Atlavík**, a small bay with a half-kilometre-long gravel beach and granite headland, a jetty, and a grassy **campground** (☎471 1774, ✉hallormsstadur@skogur.is) with picnic tables and toilets all fringed by dwarf birch forest – somewhere to spend a few days following walking tracks into the hills, or doing nothing much at all.

Hrafnkelsstaðir and western Lögurinn

Almost immediately after Atlavík, you exit the woods and find yourself well towards Lögurinn's southern end, the slopes above the opposite shore bald and shelved, like very broad steps, along their length. A few kilometres later and the road divides, the better-surfaced stretch heading over Lögurinn via a new bridge, while a gravel road continues straight ahead; stay on this and it's not far to farm buildings at **Hrafnkelsstaðir**, the holding that features in the latter stages of **Hrafnkel's Saga** (see box on p.300), though there's no trace of those times in the current homestead. Press on and you'll come to a second bridge to the lake's western shore; on the far side, turn south for the short run to **Valþjófsstaður**, another historic farm founded by the influential twelfth-century chieftain Þorvarður Þórarinsson. The otherwise unremarkable **church** here, built in 1966, replaced a structure from Þorvarður's time whose original wooden doors, carved with farm scenes, are now in Reykjavík's National Museum – replicas are on the inside of the current doors.

Heading north up the lake, **Skriðuklaustur** was the site of a medieval monastery and now graced by a distinctive stone house built in the 1930s by author **Gunnar Gunnarsson**, whose bronze bust adorns the front lawn and who set several of his early psychological novels in the northeast, before switching his attentions to writing about key events in Icelandic history. Next comes the junction with the F910 up **to Snæfell** (see below), which branches west up the valley wall; by this point the lakeside is very open, with scattered homesteads and stone **rettir pens** set amongst good grazing land. Directly opposite Hrafnkelsstaðir – if you crossed at the first bridge you'll more or less end up here – a good-sized parking bay and notice boards mark the start of an hour-long walking track up to **Hengifoss**, whose 118-metre drop makes it Iceland's third-highest falls. On the way, the lesser **Litlifoss** has wild rock formations of basalt columns, bent in all directions, while Hengifoss itself drops over cliffs layered in distinct black and red bands, composed of compressed ash falling in separate volcanic eruptions. The final 35km back along the lake to Egilsstaðir from Hengifoss is fairly bland, passing a few old turf farmhouses before rejoining the Ringroad just north of town at the hamlet of **Fellabær**.

Around Snæfell and Jökuldalur

The highland southwest of Egilsstaðir is cut by two major rivers originating as melt from glaciers around Vatnajökull, which run 120km northeast to the coast at *Húsey* (see p.303): the **Jökulsá í Fljótsdal**, which feeds the Lagarfljöt; and the **Jökulsá á Brú**, flowing parallel and about 15km further west. **Moorland**

Lögurinn and the lands to the west form the stage for **Hrafnkel's Saga**, a short but very striking story set in the mid-tenth century, before the country had converted to Christianity. Long debated by scholars as to whether it's a straight history or a complex moral tale, it tells of the landowner **Hrafnkel**, a hard-working but headstrong devotee of the pagan fertility god Freyr, who settled what is now known as **Hrafnkelsdalur**, a side-valley off the Jökulsá á Dál some 35km due west of Lögurinn (see pp.301–302). Here he built the farm **Aðalból**, and dedicated a shrine and half his livestock to Freyr – including his favourite stallion, the dark-maned **Freyfaxi**, which he forbade anyone but himself to ride on pain of death.

Inevitably, somebody did. Hard times forced Einar, the son of a neighbouring farmer, to find work as a shepherd with Hrafnkel, who treated him well but warned him not to touch the horse. But one day Einar borrowed Freyfaxi to track down some errant ewes; the sheep were found but, in a seemingly deliberate act, the horse ran back to Aðalból before Einar could clean him. Hrafnkel saw Freyfaxi filthy and exhausted, and, realizing what had happened, felled Einar with his axe.

Though Hrafnkel had never before given compensation in similar circumstances, **Þorbjörn**, Einar's father, demanded redress. Hrafnkel unexpectedly admitted having overreacted and offered a generous settlement that Þorbjörn nevertheless rejected, wanting to set his own terms. Looking for legal help, Þorbjörn enlisted his sharp-witted nephew **Sámur**, who reluctantly took the case to court at the next Alþing at Þingvellir in southwestern Iceland (p.107). But Sámur found that nobody wanted to support a dispute against such a dangerous character as Hrafnkel, until a large party of men from the suitably distant Westfjords offered their services. As Sámur presented his case, his allies crowded around the gathering and Hrafnkel, unable to get close enough to mount a defence, was outlawed.

Disgusted, Hrafnkel returned home where he ignored his sentence, but Sámur and the Westfjorders followed him in secret and descended on his homestead early one morning. Dragged out of bed, Hrafnkel was hung up by his Achilles tendons and told to choose between death or giving his property to Sámur. He took the latter option, leaving Aðalból and moving east over the Lagarfljót to **Hrafnkelsstaðir**, a dilapidated farm that he was forced to buy on credit. Back at Aðalból, Sámur destroyed the shrine to Freyr and drowned Freyfaxi as the unlucky cause of the dispute; hearing about this, Hrafnkel renounced his god.

Over the next six years Hrafnkel laboured hard to build up his new property and, his former arrogance deflated, became a wealthy and respected figure. Meanwhile, Sámur's noble brother **Eyvind** returned from a long overseas trip and landed in the Eastfjords at Reyðarfjörður, where he decided to visit Sámur at Aðalból. Riding past Hrafnkelsstaðir, Eyvind was spotted by one of Hrafnkel's servants who, upset by Eyvind's ostentatious finery, goaded her master into taking revenge against his persecutor's brother. Stung by her rebukes, Hrafnkel and his men cut Eyvind down in a bog and then launched a raid on Aðalból, capturing Sámur and giving him the same choices that Sámur had given him: to die or hand over the farm. Like Hrafnkel, Sámur chose to live and – having vainly tried to reinvolve his friends in the Westfjords – retired unhappily to his former estate. For his part, Hrafnkel retained his power and influence and stayed at Aðalból until his death.

in between terminates at its southern end at the permanently snow-capped, sharply ridged peak of **Snæfell** which, at 1833m, is the highest freestanding mountain in Iceland, formed from the eroded core of a long-extinct stratovolcano. While climbing Snæfell needs experience and equipment, it's not too hard to reach the base, either direct from Egilsstaðir or from the north via **Jökuldalur**, the valley though which the Jökulsá í Fljótsdal flows – coming this way, you pass dramatic canyons and a heathland famous for its natural beauty in the vicinity of the **Kárahnjúkar valley**, which is currently being **dammed** to provide power for an aluminium smelter in the Eastfjords (p.302).

The region is only really accessible through the summer, and you still need to come prepared for wind, rain or snow. Unless you've your own four-wheel-drive you'll have to either take a **tour** (see Egilsstaðir Arrival, p.296), or **hike** in to reach Snæfell, though – thanks to the dam project – there's a reasonable road most of the way to Kárahnjúkar. From Snæfell, seasoned hikers can also continue south **to Lónsöræfi**, skirting around Vatnajökull in a fairly demanding trail that needs experience with glacier traverses but no mountaineering skills – Ferðafélag Íslands and Útivist (see p.41) also organize annual **group hikes** of this route from Egilsstaðir.

Egilsstaðir to Snæfell

The most direct **route to Snæfell** runs 80km southwest from Egilsstaðir via the road around Lögurinn (p.298). There's a vehicle **road** the entire way, but the last half is four-wheel-drive only, and the final sections are very boggy, with several small fords to negotiate. **Accommodation** involves camping out or using huts, which range from basic to well-equipped and should be booked in advance – contact Tanni Travel (see Egilsstaðir Arrival, p.296) or Ferðafélag Íslands (see p.41). All **supplies** need to be brought in with you; hikers also need **maps** – Landmælingar Íslands' *Austurland* 1:250,000 at the very least for Snæfell, and Mál og menning's excellent *Lónsöræfi* 1:100,000 if you're planning to extend your hike to Lónsöræfi.

After leaving Lögurinn's southwestern corner near Skriðuklaustur (p.299), the F910 twists up the valley slopes and on to the top of the fells. Once up here, it's around another 10km to the first shelter hut near **Garðavatn**, one of many small lakes to dot the tundra. The F910 continues southwest for another 25km to wind up below **Laugarfell**'s prominent peak (835m), with a further hut a couple of kilometres east via a small waterfall and **hot springs** near the upper reaches of the Jökulsá í Fljótsdal. Snæfell itself is only 11km southwest as the raven flies but rather more once you start weaving around the outlying peaks and fording rivers along the way: once there, a 30km-long track **circuits Snæfell's base** via three **huts** and **campgrounds**, on the northeast (closest), southeast, and western flanks. The last is run by Ferðafélag Íslands (bookings ☎471 2000 or 853 9098; toilets, water, and showers; 1600kr), and marks the start of the Lónsöræfi hike – for more on which, see the box on p.313.

Jökuldalur and Kárahnjúkar

For a less direct route to Snæfell, the **Jökuldalur** area is accessed south off the Ringroad around 50km northwest of Egilsstaðir. The area was abandoned following the eruption of Askja in 1875 (see p.333), and was never properly resettled, with only a handful of farms remaining.

The most direct road, Route 923, follows Jökuldalur itself, but you can also use routes 901 and then 907, which after about 10km pass **Sænautasel**, a traditional turf farmstead with a summer-only café and **campground** (☎471 1086). Sænautasel was once visited by the great Icelandic novelist **Halldór Laxness**, and recalls the setting of *Independent People*, his Nobel Prize-winning tale of farmers and farm life in northeastern Iceland. Routes 923 and 907 rejoin around 25km from the Ringroad at **Brú** farm (where there's a bathable hot spring), for a final 10km down to *SámurBóndi* **guesthouse** in **Hrafnkelsdalur** (☎471 2788, ⓦ www.simnet.is/samur; meals available; camping 500kr, sleeping-bag accommodation 2000kr, beds 3000kr). This is at the famous **Aðaból farm**, the prize around which Hrafnkel's Saga revolved (p.300) and now a base for exploring the area: they sell fuel and diesel, will collect guests from Egilsstaðir or the Ringroad (for a fee), and run four-wheel-drive **tours** at 3000kr per hour (vehicles seat 11 people) to your choice of destination. Suggestions include Snæfell and Vatnajökull (around 40km south), and **Dimmuglúfur**, a perpendicular-faced canyon around 20km west. **Kárahnjúkar** is 15km southwest, though at this stage visiting the construction site is not encouraged and you might have to make your own way there.

North of Egilsstaðir: Eiðar and Héraðsflói

North of Egilsstaðir, a broad, waterlogged valley contains the last stages of the silt-laden Lagarfljöt and Jökulsá á Brú as they wind their final 50km to the coast at **Héraðsflói**, an equally wide bay. Moors along the way are a prime place to see reindeer in autumn and spring, and birds in summer, while the coast has **seals** all through the year.

The Kárahnjúkar project

Kárahnjúkar, a highland valley located on the headwaters of the Jökulsá á Dal at the northeastern edge of Vatnajökull, is one of Europe's most pristine environments, home to a large reindeer herd and a prime summer nesting site for pink-footed geese. Sadly, the area is threatened by a **hydro power project**, begun in 2003 and due for completion around 2007, which involves building a 190-metre-high **dam** at Kárahnjúkar, creating a seventeen-square-kilometre lake, along with a 630-megawatt power station designed to provide electricity for a forthcoming **aluminium smelter** down on the coast at Reyðarfjörður in the Eastfjords.

The project's backers include the Icelandic government, Landsvirkjun (The National Power Company of Iceland), and the US aluminium company ALCOA, which has promised to buy the end product, thereby helping to pay off the project's cost. It's also a very popular idea in the Eastfjords, where the fishing industry is in the doldrums and employment prospects are few; over 600 people will be needed for the construction site at Kárahnjúkar, with longer-term **jobs** available for staff and workers at the aluminium plant. And in a country that has only one main industry – and whose economy is therefore very sensitive – diversifying into new areas makes sense.

Elsewhere, however, there are few supporters for the scheme. **Environmental** issues aside – witnessed first-hand by the many Icelanders who have now visited this previously unknown area since the project was mooted in 2000 – world aluminium prices have been steadily dwindling in recent years, a situation unlikely to change. Following a negative environmental impact study, the smelter itself has been downsized by around twenty-five percent from the original plans used to promote the project, yet with almost no comparable reduction in scale – and therefore expense – of the hydro power plant. In addition, only half the construction crew at Kárahnjúkar are Icelanders, and the work is being overseen by an Italian company. If nothing else, Icelanders are worried that if the project proves an **economic** failure, the costs will be recouped through higher taxes or electricity prices – something that nobody wants. To get the official line on the story, log on to Ⓦwww.karahnjukar.is; for the environmentalist's viewpoint, check out Ⓦwww.inca.is.

Lastly, concerns have been raised too about the destruction of a part of the nation's **cultural heritage**, with the discovery in 2003 of the long-lost ruins of Reykjarsel, a Viking farm that features in *Hrafnkel's Saga* (see p.300). It stood in the area that's to be flooded, and concerned archeologists are now spending as much time as possible gathering historical evidence from the site before it is submerged and disappears again – this time for good.

Just 12km from town along Route 94 (which eventually runs to Borgarfjörður), a radio mast and scattering of houses along the roadside heralds arrival at the tiny community of **EIÐAR**, which started out as a medieval farm just east of the Lagarfljót before an agricultural college was founded here in 1883. There's good trout fishing in nearby **Eiðavatn**, hiking trails out to fragmented ponds favoured by nesting **red-throated divers** (loons) and, from June until September, accommodation at the *Edda* hotel (☎471 3803, ✉edda@hoteledda.is; sleeping-bag accommodation 1500kr, ❸). During the summer, you can get to Eiðar four times a week from Egilsstaðir on the Borgarfjörður bus (☎472 9805, ✉hlid@centrum.is).

For **Héraðsflói**, follow Route 1 for 20km northwest of Egilsstaðir to the Jökulsá á Brú, from where Route 925 heads 30km coastwards along the east side of the river to a tongue of land between the Jökulsá and Lagarfljót. Covered in wildflowers and grasses, these flat heaths are known as **Hróarstunga**, liberally populated by wading birds, ducks, swans, geese, skuas, and sheep. You'll find all of these at the beautifully isolated working farm and self-catering **IYHA hostel** of *Húsey* (☎471 3010, ⓕ471 3009; sleeping-bag accommodation 1750kr), an excellent place to spend a few days observing an Icelandic farm in action and getting to know the region. The farm breeds horses and rents them by the hour, day, or week, and can set up riding packages including accommodation and meals. Along with netting for salmon and trout, be aware that the farm is one of the last in Iceland to still hunt seals, selling the skins and meat – though they'll point you in the right direction if you want to see them in the wild. Without your own transport, you can reach Húsey by calling them in advance to arrange a pickup from Route 925, then catching a westbound bus to the pickup point from Egilsstaðir.

The Eastfjords

The **Eastfjords** cover a 120-kilometre stretch of eastern Iceland's twisted coastline between Borgarfjörður in the north and southern Berufjörður, with many of the fjords – none of which is particularly large – sporting small villages, mostly given over to fishing. The fjord scenery can be vivid, particularly in summer, with the villages sitting between flat blue sea and steep, steel-grey mountains, their peaks dusted in snow and lower slopes covered in greenery and flowers. Highlights include the northernmost village, **Borgarfjörður Eystri**, which sits surrounded by tall, brightly-coloured fells, over which you can hike south to more central fjords; **Seyðisfjörður**, for its Norwegian-style wooden houses and ferry connection to Scandinavia; and, right at the fjords' southern end near the town of **Djúpivogur**, the seabird-infested island of **Papey** – believed to have been a former retreat for Christian monks.

There isn't a continuous road linking the fjords, so you'll have to backtrack to check out the entire coast: north from Egilsstaðir is the road to Borgarfjörður; east is Seyðisfjörður; and southeast are separate routes to Reyðarfjörður and down around the rest of the region. You can also bypass most of the Eastfjords by taking the Ringroad south from Egilsstaðir, which cuts down through the wonderfully stark **Skríðadalur** and **Breiðdalur** valleys to rejoin the coastal road at Breiðdalsvík. Regular summer **buses** connect Egilsstaðir with all the Eastfjord villages, though not necessarily on a daily basis. Almost everywhere has accommodation, a bank, post office, supermarket and swimming pool, though, as usual, services might be limited outside the main season and it's always worth phoning ahead to check.

Borgarfjörður Eystri

BORGARFJÖRÐUR EYSTRI, also widely known as **Bakkagerði**, is an isolated community of just 120 people, overlooking a wide fjord 70km north-east of Egilsstaðir. Backed by mountains, it's a charming location, steeped in local lore, with some of the Eastfjords' most rewarding hiking trails. Without your own transport, catch the **mail truck** from Egilsstaðir (☎472 9805, ⓔhlid@centrum.is), which makes the journey daily in July, and up to four times a week at other times.

The road from Egilsstaðir runs seawards past Eiðar (p.303), and then cuts east up the flanks of **Geldingafjall** – where there are long vistas west over Héraðsflói's coastal wetlands to distant mountains – before a steep descent on the far side to the coast. Njarðvík, the bay here, is sided in dangerously loose cliffs, a hazard attributed to the malevolent local spirit **Naddi**, who – despite being pushed into the sea by a fourteenth century farmer – remains active, judging by the state of the road: at the time of writing, a protective cross by the roadside with the Latin inscription *Effigiem Christi qui transis pronus honora* ("You who hurry past, honour Christ's image") had just gone over the edge. By now, you're rounding the edge of **Dyrfjöll**, a long rhyolite mountain which rises behind Borgarfjörður, and reach the village itself within a few kilometres.

The village and around

Borgarfjörður sits at the mouth of a ten-kilometre-long valley running south, with Dyrfjöll to the west and steep-sided, colourful fells to the east; a slowly dwindling population just about gets by on fishing and sheep farming. The core of the village is its main **harbour**, where a jetty marks the fish-processing plant and Fuglaskoðunarhús **bird hide** (unrestricted access), overlooking a black shingle beach strewn with seaweed and patrolled by the usual seashore suspects. Across the road, behind the blocky Fjarðarborg school, **Kjarvalsstofa gallery** (daily noon–6pm) displays the works of the late Icelandic painter **Jóhannes Kjarval**, who grew up here and often incorporated local landscapes into his work. About 500m around the harbour from here, the **church** is a standard nineteenth-century wood and corrugated iron affair, with an altar-piece in sunset hues by Kjarval depicting the Sermon on the Mount as delivered atop **Álfaborg**, the rocky hill behind. Álfaborg means "elf-town" and, according to folklore, is home to Iceland's fairy queen.

If you need a further seabird hit, follow the bay road for 5km from town to **Hafnarhólm**, by Borgarfjörður's tiny fishing harbour – worth checking out in its own right to see if any of the bizarre-looking greenland shark (source of the notorious speciality *hákarl* – see p.34) have been landed. The inaccessible head-land beyond is one huge, noisy, high-smelling mess of nesting puffins, fulmars, and kittiwakes, with a couple of **viewing platforms** (summer 10am–7pm) on an adjacent outcrop.

Practicalities

More or less opposite the church, the Álfasteinn rock shop doubles as an **infor-mation centre** (June–Aug daily 10am–6pm, Sept–May Mon–Fri 11am–5pm; ☎472 9977, ⓦwww.alfastein.is) – there's a mineral display here too if you want to know what you're walking over later on. Borgarfjörður has the usual serv-ice trinity of **bank** (with ATM), **fuel station-cum-store** and **post office**, all near the jetty. **Accommodation** is limited to the **campground** between the church and Álfaborg (free, with toilets and showers; ☎472 9999); a summer-only option at *Fjarðarborg* school, next to the Kjarvalsstofa gallery (☎472 9920, ⓔbergrunj@mis.is; sleeping-bag accommodation 1200kr, beds 2500kr); and friendly homestay accommodation through *Borg*, between *Fjarðarborg* and the church (☎472 9870, ⓦwww.austurland.is/borg; sleeping-bag accommodation 1200–1900kr, beds 3000kr). *Fjarðarborg* also runs a **restaurant**, serving light meals and homemade bread; and *Borg* can arrange drop-off/pick ups for hiking trails and four-wheel-drive **tours** for 2500kr an hour.

Seyðisfjörður

Twenty-five kilometres east of Egilsstaðir over a good mountain road, **SEYÐISFJÖRÐUR** is an attractive town set at the base of a long, tight fjord. It has a strong Norwegian heritage: first settled by a tenth-century Norwegian named Bjólf, Seyðisfjörður was established as a herring port a thousand years later by entrepreneurs from Norway, who also imported the town's wooden

Hikes from Borgarfjörður

Borgarfjörður has become quite a hiking haven in recent years, with a good number of **marked trails** around the place. However, the possibility of dense summer fogs and atrocious weather with heavy snow on higher ground make it essential to ensure you're properly equipped, and to seek local advice before setting out. A good **map** showing all the trails is available at Álfasteinn, or you can download it from ⓦwww.alfasteinn.is/gonguleidir.

Prominent behind Borgafjörður, **Dyrfjöll**, the "Door Mountain", gets its name from the huge gap in its sharp-peaked, 1136-metre-high basalt crest. This is another abode of local spirits, this time mischievous imps that emerge around Christmas to tie cows' tails together. A round trip from town would be a major hike, though you could arrange a lift up to the top of the pass at **Geldingafjall** on the Egilsstaðir road, from where there's a marked track around the upper reaches of the mountain, and then down to the end of the valley south of town – a full day's walk.

A good introduction to the area is to hike 4km or so west to the next bay of **Brúnavík**, whose steeply sloping valley was farmed until being abandoned in the 1940s. This is a story typical of the whole northern Eastfjords; as the herring industry fizzled out after World War II, and roads and services began to bypass the region, farms founded in Settlement times were given up as people moved on. There's a small shelter shed here today, and a further rough trail over loose-sided fells to **Breiðavík**, where there's a hiking **hut** and campground with water and toilets (bookings ☎471 2000; 1600kr) and a 7km-long **jeep track** northwest back to town – the round trip via Brúnavík and Breiðavík takes about fourteen hours.

It's also possible to spend a few days hiking **to Seyðisfjörður**, initially following another jeep track south down the valley from Borgarfjörður. One of the highlights is about 10km along where you cross a saddle below **Hvítserkur**, a pink rhyolite mountain, wonderfully streaked with darker bands and stripes. There's another **hut** (same phone and facilities) at the head of the next valley over, whose lush meadows once supported four farms, and remains of a church on the bay here, **Húsavík**. Then it's over a steep hillside to the next fjord, **Loðmundarfjörður**, most of whose population clung on into the 1970s. A partly restored church remains, built in 1891, and you can stay in *Stakkahlíð* **guesthouse** (☎472 1590, ⓔlommi@li.is; meals available; camping 500kr, sleeping-bag accommodation 1500kr, made-up bed 2100kr). Lóðmundarfjörður marks the end of the jeep track, but hikers can follow a rough trail through a pass over **Hjálmárdalsheiði** and then down to Seyðisfjörður.

architecture. During its herring heyday, Seyðisfjörður looked set to become Iceland's largest port, but geography limited expansion. Used as a US naval base during World War II, the town remains an active fishing and processing centre, with a continuing Scandinavian link embodied by the **ferry** *Norrönna*, which calls in every Thursday during summer on its Iceland–Faroes–Norway and Denmark route. The town's summer rhythms follow the ferry schedule and it's generally busy only on Wednesdays, when an afternoon craft **market** is laid on for departing visitors.

Scattered along a kilometre-long crescent of road, Seyðisfjörður gives a good first impression of the country to new arrivals, with its smart, neatly arranged core of older wood and corrugated-iron houses backed by steep fjord walls and greenery. The town is split by the small mouth of the shallow **Fjarðará** as it empties into the fjord – marked by a short bridge – with Bláa kirkjan, the **Blue Church**, and surrounding older buildings to the north; and the ferry terminal and most amenities to the south. The church is one of the nicest examples of Seyðisfjörður's chocolate-box architecture, painted in pastel hues and hosting classical **concerts** on Wednesday evenings in summer. South of the river, Austurvegur runs east along the waterfront, where you'll find a cannon opposite the post office, salvaged from the 1944 wreck of the *El Grillo*, a British oil carrier hit by a German bomb (some of the oil was recently recovered too). Another 250m up along the waterfront takes you past the ferry terminal to Tækniminjasafn, the **East Iceland Technology Museum** (June 15–Aug 31 daily 2–6pm; 350kr), whose collection of historical exhibits is outshone by the imposing museum itself, built in 1894 as east Iceland's first telegraph office.

There are a few **hikes** to be made in the area. One popular walk starts by following the road along the north side of the ford for a couple of kilometres to the **Vestdalsá**, the first real river you'll encounter on the way. Just before you reach it, a trail heads uphill along **Vestadalur**, a valley heading up into the hills to a small lake, Vestdalsvatn, past several pretty waterfalls; allow five hours to make the return hike from town. In the opposite direction, take the coastal track past the Technology Museum for 8km along the south side of the fjord to the site of **Þórarinsstaðir**, a former farm holding where archeologists unearthed the foundations of a church dating from the eleventh century, believed to be the oldest such remains in the country. Not much further on, **Eyrar** is yet another abandoned farm, though here the ruins are far more substantial; it's hard to believe now, but this was once one of the region's busiest settlements. Experienced hikers can spend an extra half-day walking south across mountains from here to the narrow and virtually uninhabited **Mjóifjörður**, the next fjord south, where there's hostel-style accommodation at *Sólbrekka* (℡476 0020 or 476 0007) and a road back towards Egilsstaðir.

Practicalities

Buses connect Egilsstaðir with Seyðisfjörður between June and mid-September only, when there's a twice daily service from Monday to Friday, and an extra Wednesday bus to cope with passengers taking the *Norrönna* the following day. For the **ferry** schedule and facilities, see Basics, p.11.

Seyðisfjörður's main **tourist information** office (Mon–Fri 9am–noon & 1–5pm; ℡472 1551, @www.sfk.is) is at the ferry terminal off Austurvegur, where you can also make ferry bookings (℡472 1111, @www.smyril-line.is) and buy Icelandic bus passes (see Basics, p.25). The **bank** and **post office** are near the terminal on Austurvegur, with a **supermarket** 100m down the road near the bridge.

Accommodation is only likely to be in short supply on ferry days. The campsite (☎472 1551), with showers and toilets, is just north over the river; another 500m in this direction outside town brings you to the *Hafaldan* **youth hostel** (☎472 1410, ⓦwww.simnet.is/hafaldan; 1900kr), a very friendly place with a well-equipped kitchen, warm, wood-panelled rooms, and great views over the fjord. Other options include the *Hótel Snæfell* (☎472 1460, ⓕ472 1570; sleeping-bag accommodation 2000kr, made-up bed 3300kr, ❹), right by the bridge – it's a nice old building, but room prices seem to vary by the day. There's also the heritage-listed *Hótel Aldan*, across from the supermarket (☎472 1277, ⓔhotelaldan@simnet.is; ❻), one of Seyðisfjörður's original Norwegian wooden kit-homes that was being restored at the time of writing.

For food, there's the *Snæfell's* **restaurant**, specializing in fish dishes; the *Kaffi Lára*, opposite the *Hótel Aldan*, for cakes, coffee, and local "El Grillo ale"; and the Skaftfell arts centre, near the ferry terminal on Austurvegur, whose **Internet** café serves light meals.

Fjarðabyggð: Reyðarfjörður, Eskifjörður and Neskaupstaður

The Eastfjords' middle reaches, known as **Fjarðabyggð**, comprise the three relatively large fishing villages of **Reyðarfjörður**, **Eskifjörður** and **Neskaupstaður**, linked by the sixty-kilometre Route 62 from Egilsstaðir. During the summer, there's a **bus** in each direction (Mon–Sat) between Egilsstaðir and Neskaupstaður; at other times call ☎477 1713 or check the timetable at ⓦwww.austfjardaleid.is.

Though there isn't really a huge amount to drag you into the region, Fjarðabyggð has a pleasant character despite being at the centre of a major environmental row. As you travel, you'll see billboards emblazoned with the ALCOA logo: Reyðarfjörður is the proposed site for an **aluminium smelter**, powered by the controversial Kárahnjúkar hydro plant (see p.302), and there's talk of a loading terminal being built at Neskaupstaður to help ship the product out. Consequently, local job prospects look as bright as a piece of aluminium foil, and almost everyone here supports the project – this is not somewhere to start airing negative views about it.

Reyðarfjörður

Around 20km from Egilsstaðir, **REYÐARFJÖRÐUR** is a small port surrounded by imposing, flat-topped mountains either side of town, their faces ground flat by now-vanished glaciers. The town itself is fairly functional, built up as a naval base housing 3000 troops in World War II and now eager for work to start on the aluminium smelter, after the recent closure of its fish factory. The main point of interest here is Stríðsáasafnið, the **Icelandic Wartime Museum** (June 10–Aug 31 daily 1–6pm; 350kr), located back towards the hills off Austurbegur at the end of Heiðarvegur, though the best to be said about this collection of photos and mannequins in period clothes is how well it recreates the dreary dress standards of the time. North of Reyðarfjörður, **Grænafell** isn't particularly high at 581m, but is accessible along a two-hour track that climbs up through a narrow gorge to reveal a broad fjord panorama from the top. Try also to track down the grave of **Völva**, which according to local tales was a supernatural being who watches over the town – the name is applied throughout Nordic countries to a range of benevolent female spirits.

The Norðfjörður road runs through Reyðarfjörður as the town's 700-metre-long main street; the west half is called Búðareyri, and the eastern end

Austurvegur. Most of the town's services are along Búðareyri, including the post office, bank and **bus stop**; there's also a supermarket down towards the water here on Búðargata. At present, **accommodation** is polarised between the **campground** (☏470 9090; 450kr), right on Reyðarfjörður's western boundary; and the small *Fosshótel* next to the post office on Búðareyri (☏474 1600, ℉474 1601; ❼) – the only **restaurant** is at the hotel.

Eskifjörður

Set in its own mini-fjord 18km east of Reyðarfjörður, **ESKIFJÖRÐUR** reeks of fish and revels in fishing, managing to maintain a busy fleet despite the fact that most other Eastfjord towns have fallen on hard times. Road junctions are marked by huge propellers and anchors salvaged from trawlers; the fishing fleet is either clogging up the harbour or out on business between Finland and Ireland; and the town's centre is focused around a huge **fish-freezing plant** whose walls are covered in bright murals and whose director, Elfar Adalsteinsson, is also part of the Icelandic consortium that owns English football club Stoke City. Unsurprisingly, across from the freezing plant you'll also find Sjóminjasafn, the **Maritime Museum** (June 17–Aug 31 daily 1–5pm; 350kr), atmospherically housed in an early nineteenth-century warehouse made of dark, creosoted timber, and full of seafaring memorabilia – a skiff, models of bigger boats, nets, and bits and pieces from the sea. Just down the road, across from the post office, look too for the bronze statue of a kneeling sailor, a general symbol for protection at sea.

Outside of town, 8km up the Norðfjörður road right at the mouth of a tunnel that bores through the mountains and down to Neskaupstaður, there's a small winter **ski slope**, featuring a large wooden hut and chairlift – though there's nowhere to stay and you'll need all your own gear. If you want to stretch your legs, head back a few kilometres towards Reyðarfjörður from Eskifjörður to **Hólmaborgir**, the tall headland that prevents the spring and autumn sun from reaching Eskifjörður. This is actually a nature reserve, and the hour-long walk to the summit is pretty easy, with fine views down on the town from the top.

Though appearing from a distance to be spread out along the fjord shore, Eskifjörður's centre is very compact, with a **post office**, a **bank**, a **bus stop** and **supermarket** within 50m of the freezing plant on Strandgata. Around 200m west along Strandgata is Tanni Travel (☏476 1399, ⓦ www.tannitravel.is), offering tourist **information** and trips to Vatnajökull every Saturday in July and August. For somewhere to stay, the free **campground** is further out again, back towards Reyðarfjörður near the church, while in town your only option is *Hótel Askja* (☏476 1261, ℉476 1561; ❷), a characterful old guesthouse not far up from the post office on Hólsvegur. Food and drink are served up at the *Valhöll* **restaurant** near the museum.

Neskaupstaður

NESKAUPSTAÐUR curls around the northern side of **Norðfjörður** at the end of Route 92, Iceland's easternmost town and the Eastfjords' largest settlement, but again proving a thinly spread one. A two-kilometre road runs, under various names, right along the waterfront, with a core of services and backstreets around halfway along, past which the road eventually runs out. Neskaupstaður may be insubstantial but the setting is splendid, the town backed by tall, avalanche-prone fells and facing a similar view across the fjord; judging by the number of antlers hung over front doors, there's also a healthy reindeer population up in the hills.

Not to be outdone by its neighbours, the town sports two museums, both on main-street Strandgata: the **Museum of Natural History** (June 17–Aug 31 daily 1–5pm; 350kr), which has a rock collection upstairs and various stuffed and mounted fauna downstairs; and what looks like a new **Maritime Museum**, not yet open at the time of writing. Otherwise, Neskaupstaður is probably best seen as the starting point for a difficult **hike** southeast to **Gerpir**, a sheer set of cliffs marking Iceland's easternmost point and famed for their seabird colonies – rocks here are also some of the oldest in the country at 13 million years. You'll need to be completely self-sufficient; contact Tanni Travel in Eskifjörður (see p.308) for more information about the routes and finding a guide.

Most of Neskaupstaður's facilities are near the harbour on Egilsbraut: the **bus stop**, two **banks** and the **supermarket** are here, with the post office two streets back from the bus stop on Þiljuvellir. The free **campground** is a kilometre further on, right at the end of the road; there's a summer-only *Edda* hotel east off Nesgata (T477 1331, E edda@hoteledda.is; sleeping-bag accommodation 1350kr, ❸); and the blue-painted, snug *Hótel Capitano* (T477 1800; ❸), housed in a restored old place in the centre of town on Egilsbraut, which also has an excellent **restaurant**.

The southern fjords

South of Reyðarfjörður the Eastfjords begin to open up, and the mountains – if no lower than before – have room to move into the background, softening the scenery until the fjords themselves fizzle out 160km further on. From Reyðarfjörður, Route 96 follows the coastline via the successively smaller hamlets of **Fáskrúðsfjörður**, **Stöðvarfjörður** and **Breiðdalsvík** – all connected by daily **buses** from Egilsstaðir – where it joins the Ringroad from Egilsstaðir and continues around the coast as Route 1 to the Eastfjords' finale at **Djúpivogur** (on the Egilsstaðir–Höfn bus run). In fair weather, the afternoon trip out from Djúpivogur to **Papey** is one of the Eastfjords' highlights, not to be missed.

Fáskrúðsfjörður

The fifty-kilometre coastal road south of Reyðarfjörður offers some nice seascapes as it passes headlands, the orange **Vattarnes lighthouse** and an assortment of sharp peaks and loose scree slopes flanking the road before it reaches **FÁSKRÚÐSFJÖRÐUR**. This typically quiet, spread-out hamlet was, until the early twentieth century, the seasonal base for **French** fishing fleets from Brittany, who had "discovered" Iceland's rich herring grounds some fifty years earlier. This was no small event: up to 5000 fishermen passed through here in a season, and the French even established stores, a hospital and consulate here, though today the main remnant is a French **cemetery** on the north side of town. There's also an inevitable **museum** on the subject (though its collection of photos isn't worth a special trip), which doubles as a café.

Set back from the sea, Búðavegur is the kilometre-long main street, where you'll find the **bank**, **post office** and **supermarket** all within spitting distance of Fáskrúðsfjörður's main **accommodation** prospect, the wooden *Hótel Bjarg* (T475 1466, E hbjarg@centrum.is; ❸) – the other option is the **campsite**, on the far exit of town. The hotel **restaurant** has a reasonable grill menu and a bar, and *Bjarg* can also get together half-day **boat trips** out to the three small islands of Andey (very flat), Æðey and the high, wind-sharpened Skrúður, famed for its gannet colonies.

Stöðvarfjörður

Another 25km of fjord scenery as you head southwards lands you at **STÖÐVARFJÖRÐUR**, a small spot with diminutive harbour. You'll find big racks of fish drying in the sun on the slopes above town, and if you're here in spring, you're likely to find snow-white ptarmigans wandering fearlessly down the streets, eating ornamental berries in people's front gardens. Everything of note can be found on the through road, Fjarðabraut: on the west side of town, **Gallerí Snærós** displays graphic work and ceramics by local artists; while **Petra Steinasafn** (250kr) is an extraordinary private collection of thousands of rocks and mineral samples from all over the place, accumulated over a life-time of fossicking.

Aside from the **campsite** just back towards Fáskrúðsfjörður, the only **place to stay** is on the hill above town at *Kirkjubær* (T 475 8819, W www.simnet.is /birgiral; 2500kr), a wooden church converted into a comfortable, self-cater-ing lodge sleeping ten; they also hire out fishing gear and boats. The **bus stop** and all other services are huddled together near the Esso fuel station on Fjarðabraut.

Breiðdalsvík

A final 18km south past Stöðvarfjörður and just off the highway overlooking the sea, **BREIÐDALSVÍK** comprises the standard knot of essentials, the friendly *Hótel Bláfell* (T 475 6770, W www.norad.is/blafell; sleeping-bag accommodation 1600kr, ❹), and not much else, though **boat trips** out around the coast after birds and seals with Aki (T 475 6646 or 864 0246; 2000–4000kr depending on duration) come recommended. It also marks where Route 1, which has dropped south from Egilsstaðir and then kinked east, begins its jour-ney south around the coast, so you might need to change **buses** here: local services head back north along the coast to Egilsstaðir, while Ringroad buses follow Route 1, either inland to Egilsstaðir, or south along the coast to Djúpivogur and Höfn.

Djúpivogur and Papey

The coastal road winds a further 26km past some steep basalt cliffs to Berufjörður and *Berunes* **IYHA hostel** (T 478 8988, E berunes@simnet.is; breakfast available; camping 500kr, sleeping-bag accommodation 1750kr, ❸), set on an exposed position facing distant mountains, which float on the hori-zon like icebergs. Ask at the hostel about **hiking** routes in the area – some are quite challenging. Not far up the road, **Gautavík** is where the fiery Norwegian evangelist Þangbrand (see p.339) landed in Iceland in the late tenth century to convert the country to Christianity.

Set slightly off the main road, at the southern tip of Berufjörður, **DJÚPIVOGUR** is the southernmost of the Eastfjord settlements, founded by German traders in 1589, and now a tiny, pretty village surrounding a sheltered harbour where fishing boats cohabit with rafts of eider and long-tailed ducks. On one side of the harbour, the welcoming *Hótel Framtíð* offers **accommoda-tion**, a **bar** and **restaurant**, and even provides **camping** space (T 478 8887, E framtid@simnet.is; camping 500kr, sleeping-bag accommodation 2200kr, doubles with or without bath ❸–❺). Opposite is *Langabúð* (10am–6pm or later), a long wooden building that has variously served as a store, warehouse, slaughterhouse, managers' residence and meeting hall since its construction in 1850, and currently houses a **café**. In between the two is another café and **store**.

The **boat to Papey** (T 478 8119, F 478 8183) departs from the wooden pier near *Langabúð* at 1pm daily in summer, and the four-hour round-trip trip costs

THE EASTFJORDS & THE SOUTHEAST | The Eastfjords

3000kr. It takes about forty minutes to reach the island, slowing down along the way to take in a small shelf of rock favoured by slumbering **seals**. Approaching Papey's green, hummocky form, the boat is further slowed by incredible numbers of swimming seabirds, mostly guillemots, razorbills, and – especially – **puffins**, which flap frantically out of the way or circle overhead in their thousands like a swarm of insects. After landing, you get an hour-long **guided tour** of the two-square-kilometre island, which is mostly flat and somewhat boggy, with a fifty-eight-metre apex topped by a lighthouse, and a few cliffs dropping sharply into the water. According to tradition, it was first settled by monks fleeing the ninth-century Viking expansion – Papey means "Monks' Island" – and excavations here during the early twentieth century uncovered three ancient **wooden crosses**. The island has been sporadically farmed, with a wooden **church** built around 1807 – said to be Iceland's smallest, and chained down against fierce winter winds – and more recent turf and timber farm buildings as evidence, though the only present tenants are the birds and a few sheep. Bring a camera for the puffins; you can get closer to them here than just about anywhere else in Iceland.

The southeast: Vatnajökull

About 50km south of Djúpivogur the fjords finally recede into the background and you enter the altogether different world of **southeastern Iceland**, a coastal band between the Eastfjords and Vík dominated by Europe's largest ice cap, **Vatnajökull**. Covering three thousand square kilometres, almost 150km broad and up to a kilometre thick, Vatnajökull's vast size gradually sinks in as it floats inland for hour after hour as you drive past, its numerous glacier tongues flowing in slow motion from the heights to sea level, grinding out a black gravelly coastline as they go. There are several places to approach this monster, either by hiking up nearby valleys and plateaus, or even by venturing on to the cap itself to ski or ride a snowmobile, though flying is perhaps the only way to absorb Vatnajökull's full immensity: glaring ice sheets shadowed in lilac; pale blue tarns; and grey, needle-sharp *nunataks* – mountain peaks – poking through the ice.

Given Vatnajökull's proximity, Iceland's "mini ice-age" between 1200 and 1900 hit the southeast especially hard – not to mention the devastating **jökulhlaups** (see p.321) that flood out from beneath Vatnajökull's icy skirt from time to time – and it remains a thinly settled area, even though all glaciers here are actually **retreating** as the climate warms once more. Following Route 1 through the region, Vatnajökull's eastern flank is accessed at **Lónsöræfi**, a private reserve managed by **Stafafell farm**, close to the southeast's main town of **Höfn**. Continuing southwest, the ice cap's southern glaciers and adjacent heaths can be explored at **Skaftafell National Park**, after which you cross the **Skeiðarársandur**, a huge glacier-induced wilderness between Vatnajökull and the sea. On the far side and moving away from Vatnajökull, **Kirkjubæjarklaustur** is the only other settlement in the region, near where lava fields and craters at **Lakagígar** stand testament to one of Iceland's most violent volcanic events.

The regional **airport** is at Höfn, with regular flights to Reykjavík. The main road through the region is Route 1, making Höfn, Kirkjubærklaustur, and the rest of the coastal band accessible by **bus** from Reykjavík year-round, and from Egilsstaðir between mid-May and mid-September. From late June until September, an exciting alternative from Reykjavík is to take a bus along the Interior's **Fjallabak route** via Landmannalaugur and Lakagigar to Kirkjubæjarklaustur – see p.322 for more on this. Once here, there are endless **hiking** opportunities, and plenty of **tours** on offer from mid-June until September.

Lón and Höfn

Lón is a glacial river valley whose thirty-kilometre-wide estuary is framed by **Eystrahorn** and **Vestrahorn**, two prominent spikes of granite to the east and west. The central **Jökulsá í Lóni** is a typical glacial flow, its broad gravel bed crisscrossed by intertwined streams that are crystal clear and shallow in winter but flow murky and fast with increased snowmelt in summer. A sandbar across the mouth of bay has silted the estuary up into lagoons – *lón* in Icelandic – with good trout fishing (though the Löni is too small and erratic to suit salmon), thousands of whooper swans nesting on the eastern side below Eystrahorn, and reindeer herds descending from the upper fells in winter. Inland, the heights above the valley are **Lónsöræfi**, the Wilderness of Lón, an area of streams, moor, and fractured rhyolite hills, capped by Vatnajökull's eastern edge – though this is invisible from the main road. It's beautiful **hiking** country, where you could spend a couple of days or more on remote tracks, all incorporated into the private **Lónsöræfi reserve** accessed through **Stafafell** farm. Southwest of Lón, **Höfn** is a transit point and somewhere to dry off and stock up before heading off to attack the score of glaciers further west.

Stafafell and Lónsöræfi

Halfway across Lón and just east of the river, a short road off Route 1 heads inland to **Stafafell farm**, behind which the **Lónsöræfi reserve** stretches back into the mountains. Stafafell has been settled for a long time, and the unassuming **church** here, surrounded by birch trees, was founded a generation after the tenth-century Norwegian missionary **Þangbrand** – armed with a sword, and a crucifix instead of a shield – killed Stafafell's pagan owner in a duel. Þangbrand went on to spread the Christian message across Iceland, surviving attacks by sorcery and a berserker in the process, dividing the country and forcing the Alþing to restore unity by accepting Christianity as the national religion in 1000.

The only buildings besides the church form the farm, an IYHA **hostel** (☎478 1717, ⓦwww.eldhorn.is/stafafell; camping 500kr, sleeping-bag accommodation 1550kr, ❸) with warm 2-4 bed rooms, showers, kitchen, and TV, set just where hills begin to rise off the estuary flats. **Meals** can be arranged, but otherwise bring all your own supplies, as the nearest shops are 20km away in Höfn. The very helpful, slightly eccentric manager can advise and provide guides for **treks** in Lónsöræfi, and also runs horse-riding and four-wheel-drive **tours**. In summer, passing buses will drop off and collect on the highway; in winter, the manager can pick up guests from Höfn with advance warning.

Hiking in Lónsöræfi

Access into Lónsöræfi reserve from Stafafell is either on jeep tracks, or along the dozen or so hiking trails, which cover everything from return walks of a few hours' duration to the week-long trek northeast to Snæfell and Egilsstaðir. However long you're going for, take some warm clothing, food, water, and a tent; weather or navigation errors can see even day-walks accidentally extended. Without a guide, you'll also need Mál og menning's *Lónsöræfi* 1:100,000 **map** and advice from the farm about conditions on the longer routes – the reserve's waterways are all glacier-fed, making for unpredictable flow rates in summer.

A short, easy hike follows the **marker pegs** uphill behind the hostel onto the moor, above but away from the east side of the Jökulsá í Lóni river. It's slightly boggy heathland, with spongy cushions of moss, low birch thickets, and hummocks of gravel; there's a tight grouping of fells looming to the northeast, while the west is more open. Following a general northwest bearing, after a couple of hours you'll find yourself above the shattered, orange and grey rhyolite sides of the **Grákinn valley**; scramble west down the scree and then criss-cross the stream to where the valley appears to dead-end in a wall of dark cliffs. Push through a short canyon and exit to the Jökulsá í Lóni, which you follow southeast downstream along a dull jeep track to the highway and the farm. In all, the walk takes four to five hours; just watch out for where the marker pegs may have fallen over.

If you don't head back through Grákinn, the above route continues – unmarked – into the reserve and most of the other trails; the next **campground** in this direction is around three hours past Grákinn at **Eskifell**, with

Lónsöræfi to Snæfell

The **hiking trail** from Stafafell in Lónsöræfi to Snæfell takes at least four days, with another three to Egilsstaðir – or arrange a pickup from Snæfell with Tanni Travel (see p.308). Factor in a couple of extra days for rest or casual exploration along the way, especially after the lengthy final section to Snæfell. While the hike isn't especially hard, this is a remote area: don't hike alone, and bring everything you'll need with you. There's one short glacier traverse, requiring a little experience; otherwise you just need to be fit. Ferðafélag Íslands, the Iceland Touring Association (see p.41), do this trip every year, should you want to join a **tour**; they also operate many of the **huts** along the way.

Instead of descending into Grákinn (see above), continue northwest along the edge of the fells before crossing westwards over the multi-streamed Jökulsá í Lóni to a hut and campground at **Eskifell**. From here, you follow an ever-tightening gorge, cut by the headwaters of the Lóni, due north to another hut and campground at **Illikambur** (bookings ☏478 1398; water; 1600kr), around 25km from Stafafell, where there's a high concentration of day-walks along side-gorges and up nearby peaks, including a route west up to Rauðhamar for views down onto Öxarfellsjökull, Vatnajökull's easternmost extension.

Back on the main track, around 10km north of Illikambur is **Víðidalur**, an attractive valley with a campground to the south and lakeside hut 2km to the northwest at **Kollumúlvatn** (☏471 2000, or 853 9098; no amenities; 1100kr), where there are further glacial views and trails northwest to a collection of wind-scoured outcrops known as **Tröllakrókar**, "troll spires". The next 17km follows Vatnajökull's north-eastern edge to the **Geldingafell** hut (☏471 2000, or 853 9098; no amenities; 1100kr); from here, the final stage to Snæfell is a lengthy 35km (avoiding unfordable rivers), first westwards over the tip of **Eyjabakkajökull**, then bearing north at Litla-Snæfell to the Ferðafélag Íslands' hut on Snæfell's west side. For more on Snæfell and the route to Egilsstaðir, see p.301.

the famed **Illikambur** area near Vatnajökull's eastern flanks a further 5-6 hours beyond. For details of this hike, which can be continued right through **to Snæfell** outside the reserve, see the box on p.313.

Höfn

Crossing the saddle in Vestrahorn on Route 1 around 15km west of Stafafell, you're suddenly confronted by the first roadside view of Vatnajökull, a hazy white streak on the horizon with more sharply defined glaciers sliding seawards. The steep descent on Vestrahorn's far side lands you more quickly than expected at **HÖFN**, a small town on the tip of a flat peninsula dividing a bay into two. Glaciers descending Vatnajökull make a splendid backdrop – at least on days when the pernicious **fogs** abate – though otherwise Höfn's main function is as a staging post for the southeast, with a bus station, airport, and organised tours onto the ice cap.

The western half of the bay, **Hornafjörður**, offered good landing for vessels in Viking times, and is the reason that Höfn exists at all. The town began life in 1863 as a tiny trading post east at Papafjörður, in Lón, but went into a decline with the advent of modern vessels, whose deep keels prevented them from landing in the shallow bay. Faced with the prospect of having to ride all the way to Reykjavík for supplies, the traders moved shop to deeper anchorage at Hornafjörður, naming the spot Höfn (simply meaning "harbour"); expansion followed the 1950s fishing boom and the establishment of a fish-freezing plant, still the largest local employer. You can come to grips with all this – or just take shelter in wet weather – at Höfn's **museum** Byggðasafn (May 15–Sept 15 daily 1–6pm; free), housed in the original store just up from the bus station on Hafnabraut; look for the red fire-engine exhibit outside. There's also a **Glacier Exhibition** in the gallery near the bank (June-Sept daily 1-6pm, 500kr), whose best feature is film of the 1996 eruption under Grímsvotn and the subsequent *jökulhlaup* flash-flood (p.321).

Practicalities

Most of what you need in Höfn lies along a 700m stretch of main-road **Hafnabraut**, which runs south through the middle of town and down to the harbour. The **bus station** (℡478 1606) is here, with year-round services west along the Ringroad to Skaftafell, Kirkjubæjarklaustur, and through to Reykjavík; and from mid-May to mid-September eastwards via Djúpivogur and Breiðdalsvík to Egilsstaðir. In either direction, buses run daily only between June and September; at other times check with the bus station. The **airport** – known as Hornafjörður on timetables – is 6km west, with daily flights to and from Reykjavík throughout the year; you'll have to hire a taxi from the desk here to reach town.

Höfn's **tourist information office** (summer 9am-8pm; reduced hours at other times; ℡478 1606) is at the bus station, a well-informed place with regional maps, brochures, **Internet** access (2500kr) and a **tour desk** (see p.315). All other services are south down Hafnabraut towards the harbour: two **banks** (with ATMs), two **supermarkets**, the **post office**, and an elderly but good **swimming pool** (250kr).

Accommodation, eating and drinking

Also at the bus station, Höfn's **campsite** (℡478 1000; ℻478 1901; 500kr) has showers, laundry, and plenty of space. The other budget options are the *Nýibær* **IYHA hostel** near the harbour on Hafnabraut (℡478 1736,

ⓔnyibaer@simnet.is; sleeping-bag accommodation 2000kr), and the cosy *Hvammur* guesthouse facing the water nearby (☎478 1503, ⓔhvammur3@simnet.is; sleeping-bag accommodation 2000kr, ❸x). The town's most upmarket option is *Hótel Höfn*, west on Víkurbraut (☎478 1240, ⓦwww.hotelhofn.is; ❻), a comfortable but characterless modern pile open from May to September. For **farmstay** accommodation, *Árnanes*, near the airport (☎478 1550, ⓦwww.arnanes.is; sleeping-bag accommodation 2100kr, doubles with or without bath ❸–❹) has self-contained cabins and rooms in the farmhouse.

For eating, *Kaffi Hornið*, a **café** on the Hafnabraut–Víkurbraut intersection, does fine coffee and huge crepes, pasta, and grills, with similar fare on offer just down Hafnabraut at *Osinn* (*Lighthouse*). East along Víkurbraut, *Vikin* **restaurant** serves up excellent seafood, and there's also a **bar**.

Skálafellsjökull and Skaftafell National Park

It's 125km west along Route 1 from Höfn to **Skaftafell National Park**, with Vatnajökull – or rather, its score of outrunning glaciers – staying with you the whole way, never more than a few kilometres from the roadside. With the clear atmosphere playing tricks with your eyes and making it difficult to judge scale, it's only by the length of time it takes to pass them that you realize how huge these glaciers are, scored and scarred with crevasses and with a light powder of white snow covering the blue-green ice of the glacier tongues themselves.

From Höfn and the road west you can see four of these glaciers at once – from east to west they're Hoffellsjökull, Fláajökull, Heinabergsjökull and **Skálafellsjökull**. This last is the destination of glacier day-trips from Höfn (though if you've a four-wheel-drive you can turn up here yourself), with the 16km, bumpy and steep Route F985 leaving the Ringroad 45km from Höfn and ascending to the snowline at the *Jöklasel* **restaurant**, somewhere to fork out a fortune for a cake and coffee and gaze down to the coast. This is also the departure point for **rides onto the ice** in either an enclosed and sedate snow-cat, or an open-air, speedy two-seater snowmobile (also called a skiddoo). These are certainly not cheap at 8500kr for just over an hour, but it's great fun tearing across a frozen, empty horizon at upwards of 40km an hour. You'll reach the top of Skálafellsjökull and at least get an idea of Vatnajökull's extent;

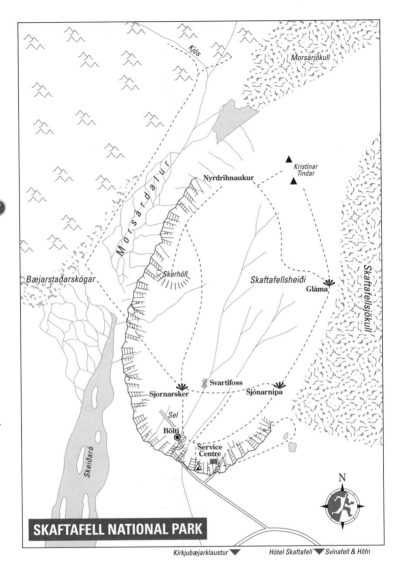

Kirkjubæjarklaustur ▼   Hótel Skaftafell ▼ Svínafell & Höfn

the usual destination is **Brókarbotnstindur**, a sharp-edged *nunatak* with great views west across a deep valley to more tall peaks and ice. Warm clothing, crash helmet, and full instruction are provided (bringing sunglasses is a good idea), but it's best to come a month either side of the main season – in July and August they have over 140 people a day up here. If you need **accommodation** in the area, the motel-like *Smyrlabjörg* (☎ 478 1074, ⓕ 478 2043; sleeping-bag accommodation 2000kr, double with or without bathroom ❹–❺) is at ground level a couple of kilometres west of the F985 junction.

Jökulsárlón, Ingólfshöfði and Svínafell

Southwest of Smyrlabjörg, the road is forced ever closer to the sea by the encroaching glaciers, and after 35km you reach a short bridge spanning the mouth of **Jökulsárlón**, Glacier River Lagoon. This large pool between the nose of **Breiðamerkurjökull** and the sea formed after the glacier began shrinking rapidly in the 1940s, and is chock full of smallish, powder blue icebergs which have split off Breiðamerkurjökull's front and float idly in the lake as if performing some slow ballet, tinted pink by the sub-arctic evening light. All transport stops for a few minutes for a view from the bank, from where you can make thirty–forty minute **boat trips** (1900kr) in fat-bellied craft, or just go for a walk along the shore and soak up the somehow soulful atmosphere – there's a small **café** open in summer.

From here the road continues southwest for another 30km, the coastal strip comprising the black gravel and thin grass glaze of **Breiðamerkursandur**, with the surf breaking on shingle just metres from the road. This provides ideal nesting grounds for **greater skuas**, avian pirates resembling brown, bulky gulls who chase and harass other seabirds until they drop their catches – or simply gang up on weaker birds and kill them. Skuas are best watched from a distance as they take exception to being disturbed while raising their young. At the end of the sandur the road bends sharply northwest at a fuel station and small supermarket, as you round the base of **Öræfajökull**, a glacier covering the Öræfi volcano, whose devastating eruption in 1362 covered the whole region in tephra and caused its abandonment. Öræfi's protruding peak, **Hvannadalshnúkur**, is the highest point in Iceland at 2199m; if you fancy a crack at the summit, contact Öræfaferðir (☏478 2382, Ⓦwww.hofsnes.is) or Mountain Guides (☏894 2959, Ⓦwww.mountainguide.is), who offer a fifteen-hour ascent of Hvannadalshnúkur for the fit and fearless (7500–9900kr), though you don't need previous mountaineering experience.

Ingólfshöfði

Jutting 10km out to sea at this point is the flat prong of **Ingólfshöfði**, said to be where Iceland's first official settler, **Ingólfur Arnarson** (see p.338), made landfall. Tipped by a lighthouse, Ingólfshöfði's soft soil and low cliffs attract summer colonies of puffins, razorbills and guillemots. From June 20 to August 20 you can arrange **tours** out here through *Hofsnes* farm (☏478 2382; 1200kr) just on the Ingólfshöfði turning, and stay in the area at *Littla Hof*, a self-catering **farmstay** 5km up the road (☏478 1670, Ⓔhof@vortex.is; sleeping-bag accommodation 1850kr, ❷) – *Littla Hof*'s nineteenth-century **turf church** was built on the site of a pagan temple.

Svínafell

The final twenty-kilometre run up to Skaftafell crosses the easternmost fringe of Skeiðarársandur (see p.320), a desert of rubble and boulders with the massive spread of Skeiðarárjökull – one of Vatnajökull's largest, most active glaciers – filling the distance but seeming to recede the closer you come. Just short of the national park, and sitting within a few hundred metres of the snout of Svínafellsjökull, modern farmhouses mark out **Svínafell**, once the residence of the **Njál's Saga** character Flosi, who headed the burning of Njál and his family. It was also where Njal's son-in-law Kári, the only one to have survived the burning, finally forgave Flosi in the closing chapters of the tale; see p.126 for the full story.

Skaftafell National Park

Bordered by Öræfajökull to the east and Skeiðarárjökull to the west, **Skaftafell National Park** covers 1700 square kilometres of barren lowland sandurs, highland slopes brimming with wildflowers, sharp mountain ridges and, of course, glaciers. The most accessible part of the park is **Skaftafellsheiði**, a high tongue of moorland protruding from between **Skaftafellsjökull** to the east, and westerly **Morsárjökull**. This is one of Iceland's premier **hiking** venues, with a mass of relatively easy paths of anything from an hour to a full day in length running over the highlands, or along the valleys exposed by the retreating ice.

Park practicalities

Your first port of call is Skaftafell's **Visitor Centre** (May–Sept daily 8am–6pm; ☎478 2288, ⓔskaftafell@mmedia.is), a couple of kilometres north off Route 1 at the foot of Skaftafellsheiði. The **National Park office** here gives accurate advice and sells trail maps, plus there's also a **café** with awful coffee and a **store** selling essentials. The adjacent **campsite** (600kr) is huge with toilets, showers (200kr extra) and laundry; note that camping out in the park itself needs prior permission from the park office. The only alternative **accommodation** close to hiking trails is *Bölti* (☎478 1626, ⓕ478 2426; sleeping-bag accommodation 2000kr), whose six-bunk cabins and tiny turf-roofed kitchen are perched on Skaftafellsheiði's upper front, with beautiful views seawards – it's popular and cheap, so book ahead. The other options are *Hótel Skaftafell* (☎478 1945, ⓕ478 1846; ❻), an ordinary, modern affair on the highway 5km east near *Svínafell*; or *Svínafell* itself (☎478 1765, ⓕ478 1860; camping 550kr, ❸), which also has the area's only **pool** (daily 1–9pm).

Buses along the Ringroad deliver to the Visitor Centre. **Heading on** from Skaftafell, there are buses year-round to Reykjavík or Höfn along Route 1. From late June until early September, you can also reach Reykjavík on daily buses inland via Landmannalaugar (p.122); and from July to September there are return day-trips by bus from Skaftafell, via Kirkjubæjarklaustur, to Lakagígar (p.323). Finally, on your way in or out of the park, check out the twisted girders mounted by the roadside just west of Skaftafell on Route 1 – these were originally part of **Skeidarárbrú**, destroyed in the 1996 Grímsvotn *jökulhlaup* (see p.321).

Skaftafell hikes

Skaftafell's main **hiking trails** are marked and not especially demanding, though you should always take the weather into account – low cloud, rain, and fog can move in quickly – and carry Landmælingar Íslands *Skaftafell* map, which has 1:100,000 and 1:25,000 sheets covering the Skaftafellsheiði area. For a more adventurous take on the area, contact Mountain Guides (☎894 2959, ⓦwww.mountainguide.is), who arrange various introductory **ice-climbing** tours on local glaciers (3000–5000kr for up to 5hr, including equipment).

One of the shortest walks at Skaftafell takes you east of the service centre to the front of **Skaftafellsjökull** itself, an easy thirty minutes through low scrub around the base of yellow cliffs where ravens tumble overhead. The woods end at a pool and stream formed from glacial meltwater, beyond which stretch ice-shattered shingle and the four-metre-high front of the glacier, streaked with mud and grit and surprisingly unattractive. Crevasses, and the generally unstable nature of glacier extremities, make it inadvisable to climb onto the tongue unless you've previous experience.

Most of Skaftafell's trails are up top on **Skaftafellsheiði**, and the following clockwise circuit takes upwards of six hours – though you can easily just walk part of it. From the campground, head 500m west to where the road twists up Skaftafellsheiði's front to end at a parking area, just past the track to *Bölti* guesthouse. Follow signs from here for ten minutes to pretty **Svartifoss**, the Black Falls, named after the dark, underhanging hexagonal columns that the water drops over, which inspired the architecture of Reykjavík's National Theatre. Depending on the track you've taken, you might have to cross below the falls here to the west bank, heading towards **Sjórnarsker**, a stony 310m ridge where the trail to Morsárdalur diverges (see below) – it makes a good general orientation point, as you can see from the coast right up to Vatnajökull from here. Heading due north the path weaves through knee-high birch thickets, silent except for birdcalls, towards **Skerhóll**'s steep front, and then climbs the gently sloping rear of this platform. Next comes a short ascent up to **Nyrðrihnaukur**, a long grassy crest off which you can spy downwards on Morsárdalur's picturesque spread of crumbly grey cliffs, flat valley floor with intertwined streams, and encroaching glaciers.

By now you're about two hours from Svartifoss, right at the foot of **Kristínatindar**, a scree-covered peak rising 1125m to a jagged set of pinnacles. One trail heads eastwards around its south side, but you can also hike on unmarked trails up and over Kristínatindar itself, starting from where the main path curves into a "bowl" between the two main peaks – the ascent is nowhere near as hard as it looks, though tiring enough. You emerge onto an icy saddle, the wind suddenly tearing into your face, with the main peak on your left (difficult in very strong winds) and the minor summit to the right. You want to do this on a good day, when the views are magnificent: the mountain is surrounded on three sides by ice, its wedge-like spine splitting Vatnajökull's outflow into the two glaciers which run either side of it – eastern Skaftafellsjökull is closest, a broad, white ribbon, crinkled and ribbed with the vast pressures squeezing it forward. The trail heads down towards it – you have to cast around to find the steep, indistinct track – landing you at **Gláma**, at the top of the sheer-sided valley filled by Skaftafellsjökull, where the trail meets up with the marked track around Kristínatindar. From here, you simply follow the stony cliff edge for an hour or so south to **Sjónarnípa**, a vantage above the glacier's front, where the path divides to either continue along the edge back to the campsite via birch scrub at **Austurbrekka**, or crosses southwest over the moor to Svartifoss.

Skafatafell's other main track is out to **Morsárdalur**, a ten-kilometre-long, flat-bottomed valley left in Morsárjökull's wake. From Sjórnarsker (see above), the path descends to the flat valley floor, where you have a couple of options: either follow the east side of the valley up to Morsárjökull's noisy front; or cross over to the west side at **Bæjarstaðarskógar**, a small wood of willows and birches, close to a **thermal springs** area – great for soaking feet but a touch too hot for a full immersion. Heading up the valley from here, you bear west in front of the glacier for **Kjós**, a strikingly beautiful canyon of bare, fractured boulders and sharp yellow crests, which peak at 1000m. Again, give yourself at least six hours for the return hike.

Across Skeiðarársandur to Kirkjubæjarklaustur

West of Skaftafell, the highway skirts the massive crescent edge of **Skeiðarárjökull**, the most mobile glacier in Iceland, whose twenty-kilometre-wide front is so vast that it somehow manages to turn its 1000m drop off the top of Vatnajökull into what appears to be a gentle descent. Over the centuries, the scouring action from Skeiðarárjökull and other glaciers running west off Öræfajökull, combined with titanic outflows from the volcanic glacial lakes Grænalón and Grímsvotn, have created **Skeiðarársandur**, and much of the 66km of highway between Skaftafell and the tiny hamlet of **Kirkjubæjarklaustur** is spent scudding over this bleak gravel desert, which stretches 15km south from the road to the sea, and where winds can whip up sandstorms strong enough to strip the paint off your car. Surprisingly, then, Skeiðarársandur is the largest European nesting ground for the greater skua – keep an eye open, too, for **arctic foxes**, which feed on the birds. Near Kirkjubæjarklaustur, you can detour inland to take in the stark gorges and glacial rivers of **Núpsstaðarskógur**, and to **Lakagígar**, the site of Iceland's most destructive volcanic event of historic times.

Under Skeiðarárjökull: Grænalón and Grímsvotn

The complex network of turbulent, ever-shifting glacial rivers flowing out from underneath Skeiðarárjökull were such an obstacle to road-building that it was only with the construction of a series of bridges here in 1975 that the Ringroad around Iceland was completed – prior to which, anyone living to the east had to travel to Reykjavík via inland roads or Akureyri. These bridges – including **Skeidarárbrú**, Iceland's longest – had to be designed to cope with **jökulhlaups**, massive floods that erupt out from under Vatnajökull regularly and carry untold tonnes of boulders, gravel, ice and water before them. One cause of these is **Grænalón**, a lake formed by a short river whose outlet is blocked by the western side of Skeiðararjökull, damming a two-hundred-metre-deep valley; every few years the lake fills enough to float the glacier dam wall and empties.

Far more destructive, however, is **Grímsvotn**, a crater lake above a smouldering volcano buried 400m under Vatnajökull's ice cap. Like Grænalón, Grímsvotn fills and empties every few years, but in October 1996 a force-five earthquake signalled abnormal activity under Vatnajökull and over the next few days the ice cap's surface gradually sagged and collapsed inwards to reveal a six-kilometre-long volcanic vent. For ten days the volcano erupted continuously, blowing steam, ash and smoke 6km into the sky, and melting enough ice to fill Grímsvotn. Then, at 8am on November 5, Grímsvotn suddenly drained out underneath Skeiðarárjökull, sending three billion litres of water spewing across Skeiðarársandur in a five-metre-high wave, sweeping away 7km of road and – despite design precautions – demolishing or badly damaging several bridges, including Skeidarárbrú. Fourteen hours later the flood rate was peaking at 45,000 cubic metres per second, and when the waters subsided a day later, the sandur was dotted with house-sized boulders and chunks of ice ripped off the front of Skeiðarárjökull. Aside from the barren scenery, there's very little evidence for any of this today – the ice has long gone, the boulders have been shifted, and the bridges repaired – though if you're heading to Skaftafell, remains of the original Skeidarárbrú are on display (see p.319).

Núpsstaðarskógur and on to Kirkjubæjarklaustur

Nearing Skeiðarárjökull's western end, the huge red and black outcrop of **Lomagnúpur** gradually rises up out of the scenery, marking the glacier's former limit before it began to retreat a century ago. In doing so, it allowed access to **Núpsstaðarskógur**, a highly scenic valley with sheer cliffs and twisted glacial streams stretching 15km north along the side of the glacier towards Grænalón. You'll need a high-clearance four-wheel-drive to negotiate the fords on the way in, so it's best to line up transport for camping, or join a tour from *Hvoll* or Kirkjubæjarklaustur (see below). Just past the access track and right at the foot of Lomagnúpur, have a quick look at **Núpsstaður**, a neat line of turf-covered buildings including an eighteenth-century stone farmhouse and an older church – the buildings themselves are fairly unremarkable, but the stark location evokes the hardships of farm life in Iceland a century ago. There's summer-only **accommodation** about 5km further west and just off the road at *Hvoll* (℡ 487 4785, Ⓦ www.simnet.is/nupsstadarskogur; sleeping-bag accommodation 1750kr), an IYHA hostel with a kitchen, where you can also pick up day trips to Núpsstaðarskógur.

Past Núpsstaður, the scenery changes quickly as you finally leave Vatnajökull behind, hugging a band of low cliffs inland fronted by rounded hummocks rising over grassland and decayed lavafields, though sandurs still persist to the south. Around 15km along at **Foss**, you can see how the cliffs were pressed down under the weight of now vanished ice, with a thin waterfall falling over the lowest edge above the farm. Across the road, a short walking track from a parking area circuits a pile of twisted hexagonal trachyte known as **Dverghammrar**, the Dwarf Cliffs, whose form indicates rapid and uneven cooling.

Kirkjubæjarklaustur, Lakigígar and around

If it were anywhere else you'd hardly register passing the tiny township of **KIRKJUBÆJARKLAUSTUR**, but as the only place of any size between Höfn and Vík, what few services it harbours are most welcome. The town sits at the foot of an escarpment on the **Skaftá**, whose rather circuitous path originates on the western side of Vatnajökull and is flanked by lavafields from eruptions by Lakagígar in 1783, centred some 75km to the northwest (see opposite). Kirkjubæjarklaustur (whose tongue-twisting name indicates a now-vanished convent; it's often abbreviated to just "Klaustur") has had religious associations since Irish monks set up camp here before the Settlement; a **Benedictine convent** was later established in 1186, though two of its nuns had the misfortune to be burned at the stake for heresy. But it was during the Lakagígar eruptions that the town's church achieved national fame: as lava flows edged into the town, the pastor, **Jón Steingrímsson**, delivered what became known as the "Fire Sermon", and the lava halted. The modern **church**, sided in granite slabs halfway down Kirkjubæjarklaustur's single street, has an unusual facade resembling a ski lodge. It's possible to climb the escarpment behind by means of a chain, and from the top there's a fine view southwest over Landbrot, a collection of a thousand-odd **pseudocraters** (for more on these, see p.348), formed when lava flowed over a lake during another eruption in 950. For a final geological hit, walk a kilometre or so along the road heading north from town, to where you'll find a field paved in a small cross-section of hexagonal basalt "tiles" known as **Kirkjugólf**, or "Church Floor".

Practicalities

Kirkjubæjarklaustur is more or less a single street stretching for 500m west off the highway as it kinks over the river; first comes the **bus stop** and fuel station, then a tiny complex containing a **bank** (with ATM), **post office**, and **supermarket**. Past this complex is the church, with a **tourist information** office (daily June–Sept) opposite, though it's not of great use. Kirkjubæjarklaustur's **campsite** (☎487 4612; 500kr) with toilets and showers, is behind the shopping complex; up past the information office is the Icelandair-run *Hótel Kirkjubæjarklaustur* (☎487 4799, ✉klaustur@icehotel.is; ❼), with budget summer-only lodgings in the school behind (☎487 4838, Ⓕ487 4827; sleeping-bag accommodation 1300kr, ❹), which also houses the town **pool** (250kr). For **meals**, head to *Systrakaffi* at the complex, which has wonderful cakes, light meals, and coffee – the fuel-station café is a poor alternative.

Tours to Núpsstaðarskógur with the English-speaking Hannes Jónsson (☎487 4785, Ⓕ487 4890) leave daily from mid-June until the end of August, and cost 3800kr; buses to Lakagígar run daily from July 1 until the end of August. **Buses** head year-round in both directions along the Ringroad, and also via Landmannalaugar to Reykjavík from late June until early September.

Lakagígar

Reached off the highway along a forty-five-kilometre jeep track some 5km west of Kirkjubæjarklaustur, **Lakagígar** – the Laki Craters – are evidence of the most catastrophic volcanic event in Iceland's recorded history. In June 1783, the earth here split into a twenty-five-kilometre-long **fissure** that, over the next seven months, poured out a continuous thick blanket of poisonous ash and smoke and enough lava to cover 600 square kilometres. So thick were the ash clouds that they reached as far as northern Europe, where they caused poor harvests; in Iceland, however, there were no harvests at all, and livestock dropped dead, poisoned by eating fluorine-tainted grass. Over the next three years Iceland's population plummeted by a quarter – through starvation, earthquakes and an outbreak of smallpox – to just 38,000 people, at which point the Danish government considered evacuating the survivors to Jutland.

A succession of difficult river crossings means that you can only get to Lakagígar on **tours** from Skaftafell or Kirkjubæjarklaustur, which run through July and August, but it's certainly worth the expense to see the succession of low, black craters surrounded by a still sterile landscape, though the flows themselves are largely covered in a carpet of thick, spongy green moss. Pick of the scenery is on the journey in at **Fagrifoss**, the Beautiful Falls, and the view from atop Laki itself (818m), which takes in an incomprehensible expanse of lava.

West to Vík

As you head west out of Kirkjubærjarklaustur, a big orange sign warns of sandstorms and within a few kilometres you've cleared the Landbrot pseudocrater fields and the Lakagígar road and are heading relentlessly over the dismal **Eldhraun** – another of Laki's lava legacies – for the final 60km to Vík and the southwest. It's not an exciting journey: around 23km along you pass Eystriásar farm, which marks the eastern end of the Fjallabak route through the southern Interior via Landmannalaugur (p.122), after which Vík is a brief drive away across the equally eventless Mýrdalssandur.

Travel details

Buses

Buses run along the Ringroad between Reykjavík and Höfn year round; service is daily from June until mid-September, with a restricted service at other times. From mid-May until mid-September, there are also buses between Höfn and Egilsstaðir, and between Egilsstaðir and Akureyri. Between mid-September and mid-May – when Ringroad services terminate at Höfn and Akureyri – there are no buses at all to Egilsstaðir.

Breiðdalsvík to: Djúpivogur (3 weekly/1 daily; 1hr); Egilsstaðir (3 weekly/1 daily; 2hr); Fáskrúðsfjörður (daily; 50min); Höfn (3 weekly/1 daily; 2hr 15min); Stöðvarfjörður (daily; 20min).

Djúpivogur to: Breiðdalsvík (3 weekly/1 daily; 1hr); Egilsstaðir (3 weekly/1 daily; 2hr 20min); Höfn (3 weekly/1 daily; 1hr 15min).

Egilsstaðir to: Akureyri (3 weekly/1 daily; 4hr); Breiðdalsvík (3 weekly/1 daily; 2hr); Djúpivogur (3 weekly/1 daily; 2hr 20min); Eskifjörður (daily; 45min); Fáskrúðsfjörður (daily; 1hr 10min); Höfn (3 weekly/1 daily; 1hr; 3hr 45min); Neskaupstaður (daily; 1hr 10min); Reyðarfjörður (daily; 30min); Seyðisfjörður (3 daily; 25min); Stöðvarfjörður (daily; 1hr 40min).

Eskifjörður to: Egilsstaðir (daily; 45min); Neskaupstaður (2 daily; 25min) Reyðarfjörður (2 daily; 15min).

Fáskrúðsfjörður to: Breiðdalsvík (daily; 50min); Egilsstaðir (daily; 1hr 10min); Stöðvarfjörður (daily; 30min).

Höfn to: Breiðdalsvík (3 weekly/1 daily; 2hr 15min); Djúpivogur (3 weekly/1 daily; 1hr 15min); Egilsstaðir (3 weekly/1 daily; 1hr; 3hr 45min); Jökulsárlón (3 weekly/1 daily; 1hr 30min); Kirkjubæjarklaustur (3 weekly/1 daily; 3hr); Reykjavík (3 weekly/1 daily; 8hr 30min); Selfoss (3 weekly/1 daily; 7hr 30min); Skaftafell (3 weekly/1 daily; 2hr 40min); Skógar (3 weekly/1 daily; 5hr 45min); Vík (3 weekly/1 daily; 3hr 50min).

Kirkjubæjarklaustur to: Höfn (3 weekly/1 daily; 3hr); Jökulsárlón (3 weekly/1 daily; 2hr); Reykjavík (3 weekly/1 daily; 6hr 30min); Selfoss (3 weekly/1 daily; 5hr 30min); Skaftafell (3 weekly/1 daily; 1hr 5min); Skógar (3 weekly/1 daily; 2hr); Vík (3 weekly/1 daily; 1hr 20min).

Neskaupstaður to: Egilsstaðir (daily; 1hr 10min); Eskifjörður (2 daily; 25min); Reyðarfjörður (2 daily; 35min).

Reyðarfjörður to: Egilsstaðir (daily; 30 min); Eskifjörður (2 daily; 15min); Neskaupstaður (2 daily; 35min).

Seyðisfjörður to: Egilsstaðir (3 daily; 25min).

Skaftafell to: Höfn (3 weekly/1 daily; 2hr 40min); Kirkjubærjarklaustur (3 weekly/1 daily; 1hr 5min); Reykjavík (3 weekly/1 daily; 5hr 30min); Selfoss (3 weekly/1 daily; 4hr 30min); Skógar (3 weekly/1 daily; 3hr 50min); Vík (3 weekly/1 daily; 2hr 20min).

Stöðvarfjörður to: Breiðdalsvík (daily; 20min); Egilsstaðir (daily; 1hr 40min); Fáskrúðsfjörður (daily; 30min).

Flights

Egilsstaðir to: Akureyri (daily; 40min); Reykjavík (daily; 1hr).

Höfn to: Reykjavík (daily; 55min).

Ferries

Ferries operate mid-May–mid-September only.
Seyðisfjörður to: Bergen, Norway (weekly; 5 days); Hanstholm, Denmark (weekly, 2 days); Lerwick, Shetland Islands (weekly; 4 days); Tórshafn, Faroe Islands (weekly, 17 hr).

The Interior

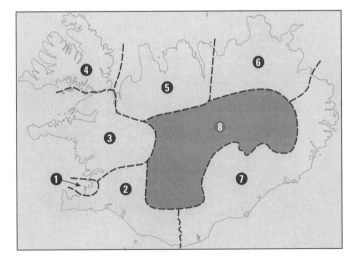

CHAPTER 8

Highlights

* **Sprengisandur** The classic Interior trip, to where outlaws were once banished – an unremittingly bleak and barren desert stretching to a horizon tipped with ice caps. **See p.330**

* **Hveravellir** Unexpected splash of green and a bathable hot spring in the middle of the wilderness, and a great place to break an Interior traverse. **See p.331**

* **Askja** Massive caldera rimmed by rough, snowy peaks, where you can go for a swim in a flooded crater, the remnants of a colossal eruption in 1875. **See p.332**

* **Kverkfjöll** Extremely remote and difficult-to-reach ice caves, hollowed out by hot springs welling up under the northwestern edge of the mighty Vatnajökull ice cap. **See p.334**

The Interior

Stark, desolate and charged with raw beauty, nothing you might see elsewhere in Iceland prepares you for the barren upland plateau (500–900m) that is the **Interior**, Europe's last true wilderness. The strength and unpredictability of the elements here means that the country's heart is a desolate and uninhabited place, with no towns, villages or sights, just cinematic vistas of seemingly infinite plains, glacial rivers and lavafields punctuated only by ice caps, volcanoes and jagged mountains, all reminiscent of lunar landscapes – this is, after all, where the *Apollo* **astronauts** came to train for their moon landing. Sheep are virtually the only living things that manage to survive here, but pasture and vegetation, where they do exist, comprise only scattered clumps of ragged grass, and it's a daunting task for the farmers who venture out into this no-man's-land to round up their livestock every autumn.

Historically, routes through the Interior were forged in Viking times as a shortcut for those making the journey on horseback to the annual law-making sessions at Þingvellir, though the region later provided refuge – if you can call it that – for **outlaws**, who are said to have been pardoned in the unlikely event that they managed to survive here for twenty years. Today, with the advent of the Ringroad and direct flights to Reykjavík from all corners of the country, the need to traverse this area has long gone, and there are **no roads**, just tracks (the main ones are listed on p.329) marked by stakes, and hardly any bridges across the rivers, causing some hairy moments when they are forded. The **weather**, too, is Iceland at its most elemental. Not only can fierce winds whip up the surface layer of loose grit in a matter of seconds, turning a beautiful sunny spell into a blinding haze of sand and dirt, but snow storms are common even in July and August – the summer here is very short indeed, barely a matter of weeks, the winter long and severe, when the tracks are blocked by deep snowdrifts and closed to traffic. Indeed, every year, the Interior claims victims through drownings in the icy rivers, while others perish in snow storms. Occasionally, some simply disappear without trace.

Of all the various tracks, only two **Interior routes** actually cross the whole way between north and south Iceland. The most dramatically barren of these is **Sprengisandur** (F26), which leads from the Þjórsá, east of Selfoss, to the Bárðardalur valley between Akureyri and Lake Mývatn – it's also possible to approach Sprengisandur from Skagafjörður on the F752 and from Akureyri on the F821. The alternative is **Kjölur** (F35), from Gulfoss to the Blöndudalur valley south of Blönduós, which has less dramatic scenery but is the only route on which you can use normal cars. Other routes lead into the Interior but don't offer a complete traverse: there's the western **Kaldidalur** route (F550)

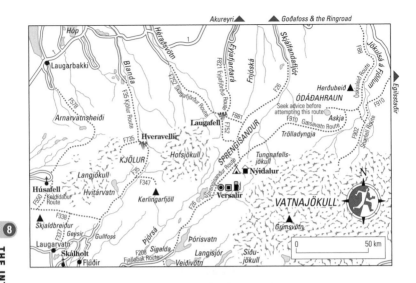

between Borgafjörður and Þingvellir (covered in Chapter 3, p.107); east of Lake Mývatn, the F88 follows the course of the mighty Jökulsá á Fjöllum south to the **Askja caldera**, from where the F902 continues towards **Kverkfjöll**; heading inland from Egilsstaðir, the F910 and F909 wind their way to **Snæfell** and the northeastern flank of Vatnajökull (covered in Chapter 7, p.301); while the two **Fjallabak** routes – Fjallabak nyrðra and Fjallabak syðra – run behind the south coast's ice-caps (both covered in Chapter 2, p.131).

It is possible to get a taste of this utter isolation in safety on **bus tours**, essentially normal bus services but (usually) with a guide, though even then it's a bumpy ride. Should you decide instead to cross the Interior under your own steam, it's essential to be properly prepared before departure; note too that the majority of routes are fully accessible only by **four-wheel-drives**, and that when on them, you should stick to them, as off-road driving is not only illegal, but carries substantial fines and does irreparable damage to the land.

Bus tours

Six **bus tours** penetrate the Interior in summer, most of them originating at the long-distance bus station in Reykjavík (see p.51). A **guide** – or at least recorded commentary – is usually provided, although large parties on the more popular trips tend to make the guides inaccessible. Remember that neither the Full Circle bus nor the Omnibus **passes** (see p.25) are valid for services across the Interior, although they do entitle the holder to a five-percent **discount** off the fares given below. Note that all the trips listed below last a day unless otherwise stated, though it is possible to hop off the buses at any of their stops – there's at least one hut and campsite on each route – and get back on another service the next day.

Buses cross from Reykjavík to Mývatn via **Sprengisandur** daily between mid-July and late August (13,800kr one-way) in two stages, overnighting at Landmannalaugar (p. 000) – no great hardship, though you might have to camp. The more straightforward day-trip between Reykjavík and Akureyri over **Kjölur** runs daily from late June until September (6900kr one-way).

Round-trips to **Askja** leave from Mývatn on Monday, Wednesday and Friday from mid-June to September (7500kr). Lastly, a three-day excursion to **Kverkfjöll** runs out of Mývatn, Akureyri and Húsavík every Monday from early July until mid-Aug, and includes two nights' accommodation and a day's walking on a glacier (17,900kr round trip).

Self-driving, cycling and hiking

Any self-driving, cycling or hiking trip through the Interior must be carefully planned and considered. Never underestimate the extreme conditions, climatic and geological, which you may encounter en route. Remember too that in poor weather, low cloud obscures what precious little there is to see, and one part of cold grey desert looks very much like another. Always wear warm and brightly coloured protective **clothing**, and choose your time of departure carefully, basing it on the latest **weather** forecast from the national newspapers, television or at ⓦ www.vedur.is/english/. Most importantly, check the **condition** of the mountain roads and Interior routes in advance with the Icelandic Highways Department, Vegagerðin (☎ 1777, ⓦ www.vegag.is/indexe.html), although we've given the **official opening times** for routes in the box below, these can vary according to the weather. However you're planning on travelling, read the relevant sections in "Basics" on pp.24–30 and take everything you'll need with you, including a **compass** – at times it can be difficult to determine a route where several sets of car tracks meet.

If you're driving across the Interior, check your **car insurance** policy, as four-wheel-drives aren't usually covered for breakdowns when crossing rivers. **Essential equipment** for drivers to take includes a tow rope, shovel, basic spare parts – and a rudimentary knowledge of how the engine works. It's best to travel in groups of two or more vehicles, and remember to carry plenty of **fuel**, as consumption in low-range gears can be a third more than on well-surfaced roads. Never venture from the marked tracks – the off-road tyre marks you'll see here and there, made by illegal off-roaders, take years to heal and only worsen the country's uphill struggle against soil erosion. Don't expect to find many bridges either – you'll need some previous experience of tackling glacial river crossings before you set out.

The only Interior route that **cyclists and hikers** can tackle unaided is the Kjölur track, since there are no rivers to wade through whilst heavily laden with packs and cycles, and the terrain is less severe. If you are planning on using other routes, you'll have to hitch rides over the more difficult rivers with passing transport, so will probably spend longer on your journey than you intended – making it all the more vital that you carry excess food and water.

Overnight huts and camping

The mainstay of accommodation in the Interior is the network of **overnight huts**, or *sæluhús*, open all year and run by Ferðafélag Íslands, the Touring Club

Interior routes' opening times

Askja/Öskjuleið (F88) June 20	**Kjölur** (F35) June 20
Eyjafjörður (F821) July 20	**Kverkfjöll** (F902) June 20
Fjallabaksleið (F208)	**Skagafjörður** (F752) July 14
Landmannalaugar–Eldgjá July 2	**Sprengisandur** (F26) June 29
Kaldidalur (F550) June 15	

of Iceland (see p.41). Marked on maps of the Interior, the huts are very busy during summer, and it's essential to book them well in advance. Although they differ – the better ones have self-catering facilities and running water – you'll always need to bring your own sleeping bag and all sleeping space is in dorms. The huts are located in two main areas in the Interior: south and east of Langjökull, on and close to the Kjölur route; and north of Vatnajökull around Askja and Kverkfjöll. We've given contact numbers in the guide text; costs are around 1700kr per person per night.

If you're **camping** make sure to take enough tent pegs with you to anchor down your tent since the wind that howls uninterrupted across the Interior plain can be truly ferocious – among seasoned Iceland-travellers, tales of blown-away tents are alarmingly common. **Campsites** (around 650kr), some of which have running water, are at Hveravellir and Hvítárnes, for the Kjölur route; at Nýidalur, for the Sprengisandur route; at Laugafell, for the F752 to Skagafjörður; at Herðubreiðarlindir, Dyngjufjöll (Dreki) and Kverkfjöll, on the Askja and Kverkfjöll routes.

Across Sprengisandur: the F26

Featuring the most desolate terrain found in Iceland, the **Sprengisandur** trip runs from Reykjavík to Mývatn, initially taking the Ringroad to Hella before turning inland and following the course of the Ytri-Rangá river. The Interior section of this route, from Sigalda to Godafoss, covers 244km. On coach trips, you pass within 10km of the foot of Hekla prior to reaching Þjórsárdalur valley and the reconstructed Saga Age farm at Stöng (see p.120) – easily missed unless the guide points its out. You then pass **Þórisvatn**, a lake whose waters find their outlet in the Þjorsá river and feed a hydroelectric power station. After this, the route climbs into the stony highlands between Hofsjökull and the western edge of the mighty Vatnajökull, which mark the beginning of Sprengisandur proper, an incredible journey through mile after mile of grey sand, stones and rocks that have lain untouched for thousands of years. The enduring image is of nothingness: the glaciers and mountains that fringe the desolation seem a long way off.

Glacial rivers are periodically crossed until you reach **Nýidalur**, where the route's sole **campsite** and **hut** (summer only, ☎854 1194) occupies a lonely, cold and windswept spot at 800m, right on the base of Tungnafellsjökull's tiny, isolated ice-cap. The Nýidalur valley leads southeast around the glacier from here towards Vatnajökull, only 20km from camp; while well away to the west below Hofsjökull are the **Þjórsárver** wetlands, breeding ground of many of the world's population of pink-footed geese. This remote spot attracted world attention in 2000 when the government's plans to flood the area to provide hydroelectric power for a new aluminium smelter became widely known outside Iceland. Following sustained pressure from environmentalists – and a petition signed by one in four Icelanders – the plans were shelved.

Three kilometres past Nýidalur comes the turn for the **Gæsvatn route** (F910), which weaves its way over some quite appalling terrain and through an alarming number of rivers, around the north of Vatnajökull, to meet up with the F88 to Askja. Get local advice if you're thinking of taking this route, and only travel in convoy. Otherwise, the F26 continues due north across Sprengisandur to the grey waters of **Fjórdungsvatn**, which marks the turn for the F752 Skagafjörður route, via the **Laugafell** hot springs and overnight hut (☎854 9302), to Varmahlíð and the Ringroad. Then, slowly, the Sprengisandur route gains traces of green, reaching Aldeyjarfoss before descending into the Bárðardalur valley, whose scattered farms seem positively lively after hours spent looking at barren waste. The road down from Bárðardalur hits the Ringroad close to Goðafoss, where coaches turn right for Mývatn. Allow at least eight hours if you're driving this route yourself – which is nothing compared to the week it took for the first car to traverse Sprengisandur in 1933.

Across Kjölur: the F35

Kjölur (also known as Kjalvegur), is the shorter of the two inland routes between north and south Iceland, and the longest known: its discovery is recorded in the *Book of Settlements*. Considered safer than Sprengisandur, though abandoned for a while after the death of a large party in 1780, it qualifies as a highway if any Interior route can claim to be, with buses, coaches, four-wheel-drives and even ordinary family sedans bouncing along it during the summer months. If driving a rental car, however, check with the agency to find out whether your insurance covers you for this journey. This account begins on the north coast and ends in Reykjavík, though it's possible to travel from south to north; from Akureyri, buses follow the Ringroad west before turning off along the course of the Blandaá, passing a hydroelectric power station that's built mostly underground. From the power station to Gullfoss it's a distance of 161km; if driving yourself, allow at least five hours.

You initially pass through an area of moorland and lakes, with ice caps and black-streaked mountains to the south; once into the Interior, the outlook is similar to Sprengisandur – grey sands and stones. For much of its duration, the route follows the line of barbed-wire fencing erected to keep the sheep from the west separate from those in the east and restrict the spread of disease (someone is actually employed to ride back and forth along the fence to check that it hasn't been breached). **Kjölur** itself, the highest point on the route, is a broad rocky pass between the massive icesheets of Langjökull and Hofsjökull. Here the F735 leads the short distance west (around 2km) to a grassy depression in the landscape at **Hveravellir hot springs**, where you'll find a campsite and well-appointed overnight **huts** (☎568 2533) – there's also **fuel** available in July and August. The only bathable **pool** is a small, waist-deep affair next to one of the huts, above which boardwalks head up a calcified slope to where hotter springs, encrusted with sulphur, bubble, belch, and occasionally erupt violently. One of these is named **Eyvindarhver**, after the outlaw Eyvindur (see p.333) who's reputed to have boiled up sheep here for his dinner. In summer, the springs can get busy, so try to time your dip to avoid scheduled daily bus arrivals in the early afternoon – or stay overnight here and have the springs almost to yourself.

South of here the road runs rougher as it passes between **Hofsjökull** to the east, whose ice cap presses down on a black plateau, and easterly Hrútfell, outpost of a more distant **Langjökull**. There was a cricket match up on the ice here in 2003 between the Icelandic national cricket team and an amateur side from the UK – Iceland lost. Around 28km south of the Hveravellir junction, the F347 heads 10km southeast to the tumble of peaks at **Kerlingarfjöll**, where there's a **restaurant** open from mid-June until August. Continuing down the F35, the road runs closer to Langjökull and **Hvítarvatn**, stage on

The **Kjölurvegur** trek is an excellent two- to three-day hike from Hveravellir to the glacial lake of Hvítárvatn, following the original Kjölur route that ran west of the present F35, hugging the slopes of **Langjökull**, punctuated by overnight huts roughly four to six hours' walk apart. From the springs, follow the F735 west towards the glacier and after roughly 14km, at the *Þjófadalir* overnight hut, the jeep track peters out into a walking path as it swings southeast, around the tiny Hrútfell glacier, for another overnight hut at *Þverbrekknamúli*. From here, it's a further straightforward hike of around four to six hours to reach the *Hvítárnes* hut, an idyllic if somewhat lonely place to break the journey – the hut is supposedly haunted by a young woman who lived hereabouts when the area was farmed, though only men who sleep in a certain bed in the hut will see her, apparently. From the hut, it's an easy eight-kilometre walk back to the F35 and the bus to either Reykjavík or Akureyri passing the beautiful **Hvítárvatn** glacial lake, at the foot of Langjökull, on the way.

the Kjölurvegur (see box above) and source of the Hvítá, which flows down to Gullfoss. Heathland surrounding the lakeshore is said to harbour some ninety species of Alpine plant, and you can often see **icebergs**, calved off the front of the Norðurjökull glacier, floating in the serene, pale-blue lake. Once across a substantial **bridge** over the river's headwaters, the road climbs up beside **Bláfell** and then you're suddenly on a plateau with a view extending southwest over green river plains almost to the sea. The road improves too, and it's only a further 25km downhill run from here to Gullfoss, visible in the distance like a puff of smoke. Tours pause briefly at Gullfoss (see p.112) and then Geysir (see p.111) before Laugarvatn (see p.110) and Þingvellir (see p.107) on the way to Reykjavík, which makes this tour an excellent – and cost effective — way of also seeing these Golden Circle attractions.

Herðubreið and Askja: the F88

The crownlike formation of **Herðubreið** has earned it the nickname "Queen of the Icelandic Mountains", and at a height of 1682m, it towers over the surrounding **Ódáðahraun** (Desert of Misdeeds), a featureless lavafield north of Vatnajökull. You can get within a few kilometres of the mountain on the F88 Askja route (Öskjuleið in Icelandic), which leaves the Ringroad not far east of Mývatn and heads south, via Herðubreið, to **Askja**, a vast flooded caldera in the middle of the lavafield.

Marked by wooden posts and tyre tracks weaving off across the usual black gravel plains, the F88 initially follows the west bank of the glacial **Jökulsá á Fjöllum** – which eventually flows north through Jökulsárgljúfur (see p.281) – until reaching **Herðubreiðarlindir**, an oasis of poor grass and hot springs between the river and Herðubreið, where there's a **campsite** and overnight **hut** with kitchen and toilets (☎462 2720). On the edge of the encircling lava, a small stream wells out through a wall of lava blocks that conceal **Eyvindur's cave**, said to have been inhabited by this resourceful outlaw during the harsh winter of 1774–75, during which time he survived on dried horsemeat and the bitter roots of angelica plants, which grow in profusion nearby – he always considered this the worst experience of his entire twenty years on the run (see box opposite). Other sights in the area include the river, which is carving out what will eventually be an impressive gorge around 6km upstream; and **Herðubreið** itself, a brown, snow-streaked cone whose base is about 5km west over the lava – a surprisingly tiring hike over what appears to be flat ground – with a difficult trail to the **summit** from the west side. A third option is a two-day **hike to Askja**: from the hut, follow the path around the mountain until it meets the trail up to the summit, then turn due west, away from the mountain, heading for the shield volcano of **Kollóttadyngja**, where there's an overnight hut *Bræðrafell* (bookings ☎462 7240, ✆ffa@li.is) – allow roughly six hours to cover the 17km here from Herðubreiðarlindir. The route on the second day (20km; 6hr) leads due south from Bræðrafell across the lava to the foot of the Askja volcano and the overnight hut at Drekagil.

Past here, the F88 veers west away from the river towards the black and contorted **Dyngjufjöll** mountains which rim Askja's eastern edge. There's another basic **cabin** and campsite here at **Drekagil** (bookings ☎462 7240, ✆ffa@li.is), a small, rough canyon which you can follow for a short way, then the track continues for a final 8km to a walking track into Askja itself. **Askja** is a partially flooded, eight-kilometre-wide crater formed from a collapsed subterranean magma chamber, source of the prehistoric outflows which drained out over the land and caused the grim and forbidding surrounds. There have been more recent eruptions too: in 1875, a colossal explosion here vapourised two cubic kilometres of rock and blew it northeast with such force that dust and gravel fell on Denmark; land between here and the coast at Vopnafjörður was buried under drifts of yellow pumice up to two metres deep, which poisoned the soil and sterilised the region – some 2000 local farmers emigrated to Canada as a result. The last big outflow of lava here was in the 1960s, and it's over this that you walk up into the caldera and south to the 217-metre-deep lake, **Öskuvatn**, which half-fills Askja. Beside its north shore, **Viti** is a smaller flooded crater marking the site of the 1875 catastrophe, before which, the vent was described by one local traveller as "a complete Devil's cauldron from

---

Eyvindur and Halla

Iceland's most famous **outlaws** were the mid-seventeenth century **Eyvindur** and his harsh-tempered wife, **Halla**. They originally lived in the Westfjords and seem to have just drifted into petty thieving, which eventually became a way of life. They are the only Icelandic outlaws to have managed twenty years on the run, thus earning themselves a pardon; many places around Iceland are named after Eyvindur, showing just how much he had to keep moving.

Abandoning their farm, they set up at Hveravellir, now on the Kjölur route (see p.331), robbing travellers and stealing sheep off nearby properties. Eventually chased on by a vengeful posse, they shifted south to the Þjórsá west of Hekla for a few years – the easiest time of his outlawry, so Eyvindur later said – then to remoter pastures on the Sprengisandur, which hadn't been crossed for many years at this point. Caught after stealing a horse, Eyvindur and Halla were held at Mývatn's church, from where Eyvindur managed to escape by asking to be untied so that he could pray. As luck would have it, a thick fog came down and he was able to hide nearby until people had given up looking for him, thinking him far away. He then stole another horse and rode it south to Herðubreiðarlindir (see opposite), where he somehow survived an appalling winter in a "cave" he built into the lava here. Later on, he met up with Halla again and they drifted around the country, always just managing to evade capture but forced by hunger or pursuit to kill their infant children. Tradition has it that after being pardoned they returned to their farm in the Westfjords, where they died in the late seventeenth century.

which all living things fly; horses quake with mortal fear and can hardly stand when taken to the brink". It's more docile today; you can scramble down its steep sides, dotted with sulphur springs, to bathe in the opaque blue-white waters, which can be a little tepid sometimes but perfect for a quick dip.

From Askja, the F910 wiggles around the northern flank of Vatnajökull to join up with the F26 Sprengisandur route north of Nýidalur (see p.330), but this should only be driven in convoy and after seeking local advice.

Routes to Kverkfjöll

The main track (F905) to the ice-covered Kverkfjöll begins 4km south of **Möðrudalur** – a tiny settlement 8km south of the Ringroad, halfway between Vopnafjörður and Lake Mývatn – crossing undulating gravel and passing the small lake. Twenty kilometres south of Möðrudalur, the route links up with the F910, which leads over the Kreppá, which is bridged, to the junctions with the F902 and F903. The latter leads to the hot springs of **Hvannalindir**, an oasis where eighteenth-century outlaw Eyvindur fashioned a rough shelter using lava blocks around a hollow on the edge of the lavafield. He also built a sheep pen with a covered passageway to the nearby stream, so the animals could drink without being spotted and hence not give away his location. Both can still be found but are well concealed, as Eyvindur intended. Beyond the springs, route F903 joins up with its neighbour to the north, the F902, before reaching **Kverkfjöll** via a maze of ash hills. There's a campsite and an **overnight hut** here (☎853 6236) overlooking the braided streams of the Jökulsá á Fjöllum's upper reaches. Low white clouds hover overhead during the long hard slog up the dormant volcano, which erupted to devastating effect in the fifteenth century, and once at the top these are revealed to be steam issuing from deep fissures in the ice. Nearby sulphur springs, hissing like boiling kettles, prevent ice from forming in their immediate area and the bare yellow earth is in stark contrast to the surroundings. The outstanding views from the glacier take in the entire expanse of Ódáðahraun lavafield, the Dyngjufjöll mountains, Herðubreið mountains, and even the jagged peaks that mark the distant northern coast.

Jökulsá á Fjöllum rises from hot springs under Vatnajökull, and its heat forms an **ice cave**, 5km from the hut. Some daylight penetrates a few metres into the cave, but visibility rapidly diminishes in the thick, damp fog that fills it. The walls and roof are sculpted by constantly dripping water, and the debris embedded in the ice gives a marbled effect. Not far from here the slopes of the glacier are climbable, but they shouldn't be attempted without a guide.

Travel details

Buses

Akureyri to: Reykjavík, via Kjölur (1 daily late June to Sept; 9hr).
Mývatn to: Askja (3 weekly mid-June to Sept; 12hr return); Kverkfjöll (1 weekly early July to mid-Aug; 3 days return); Reykjavík, via Sprengisandur (1 daily July–Aug; 2 days).
Reykjavík to: Akureyri, via Kjölur (1 daily late June to Sept; 9hr); Mývatn, via Sprengisandur (1 daily July–Aug; 2 days).

Contexts

Contexts

Some history 337

Landscape and geology 347

Wildlife and the environment 351

Books and sagas 355

Some history

Iceland is not only one of the more geologically recent places on earth, it was also amongst the last to be colonized. European seafarers may have known that something lay out beyond Scotland as far back as 300 BC, when the historian Pytheas of Marseille wrote about "Ultima Thule" – possibly Iceland – a northern land on the edge of a frozen ocean, where it never became dark in summer.

It wasn't until considerably later, however, that Iceland was regularly visited by outsiders, let alone settled, and it's still unclear who might have been the first to try. Whoever they were, the first arrivals would have found the country much the same as it appears today, but well forested with willow and birch, and with no large animals.

Discovery

Much of the uncertainty in deciding who discovered Iceland, and when it happened, is down to the lack of archeological and written records. **Roman** coins from around 300 AD, found at several sites along Iceland's south coast, provide the earliest evidence of visitors, and suggest that ships from Britain – which was then a Roman colony and just a week's sail away – made landfall here from time to time. These coins could have been brought in at a later date, however, and no other Roman artefacts or camps have been found. Similarly, the age of a **Norse** homestead on Heimaey in the Westman Islands is disputed; archeologists date it to the seventh century, but medieval Icelandic historians – accurate enough in other matters – state that it was founded two hundred years later. It is also believed that by the late eighth century **Irish** monks, having already colonized the Faroes, were visiting Iceland regularly, seeking solitude and, according to contemporary accounts, believing that they had rediscovered Pytheas' Ultima Thule. Oral tradition and place names link them to certain spots around the country – such as Papey, "Monks' Island" in the east – but they left no hard evidence behind them and were driven out over the next century by new invaders, the **Vikings**.

Vikings were Scandinavian adventurers, armed with the fastest ships of the time and forced by politics and a land shortage at home to seek their fortune overseas through war and piracy. They had already exploded into Britain and Ireland in the 790s, which is why Irish monks had sought out Iceland as a more peaceful place to live. Though a few Vikings may have been Christian, the majority believed in the **Norse gods**, the Æsir, which included Óðinn, the creator of mankind; his wild and adventurous hammer-wielding son Þór; and Freyr, the god of fertility and farming. The Æsir themselves were children of the first beings, the Giants, who had also created dwarfs and elves; they lived above the world in Ásgarður, where the great hall Valhalla housed the souls of Champions, men killed in warfare. The Champions awaited Ragnarok, when they would join the Æsir in a final massive battle against the Frost Giants, in which the world would be totally destroyed. Fearsome in battle, honour was everything to the Vikings, and the faintest slur could start a century-long blood feud between families.

According to tradition, the Vikings came across Iceland by accident when a certain mid-ninth-century freebooter named **Naddoddur** lost his way to the

Faroes and landed on the eastern coast of what he called **Snæland**, or Snowland. He didn't stay long, but his reports of this new country were followed up by the Swede **Garðar Svavarsson**, who circumnavigated Iceland in around 860, wintering at modern-day Húsavík in the northeast, where two of his slaves escaped and may have settled. At about the same time, **Flóki Vilgerðarson** left his home in Norway intending to colonize Snæland, which he was led to by following his pet ravens – hence his other name, Hrafna-Flóki, Raven-Flóki. But a hard winter in the northwest killed all his livestock; climbing a mountain he saw a fjord on the other side choked with ice and, frustrated, he renamed the country **Ísland**, Iceland, and returned to Norway.

Settlement

Despite Flóki's experiences, the idea of so much free space proved tempting to two other Norwegians, **Ingólfur Arnarson** and his brother-in-law **Hjörleifur Hróðmarsson**, who had lost their own lands in Norway as compensation for killing the son of a local earl. Around 870 they set sail with their households and possessions for Iceland, intending to settle there permanently. When they came within sight of land, Ingólfur dedicated his wooden **seat-posts** – the cherished symbol of his being head of a household – to his gods and threw them overboard, vowing to found his new home at the spot where they washed up. While his slaves searched for them, Ingólfur spent three years exploring Iceland's southern coast, wintering first at Ingólfshöfði (near Skaftafell), Hjörleifshöfði (just east of Vík), and then at Ingólfsfjall (Selfoss). The posts were duly found in a southwestern bay and there Ingólfur built his homestead in 874, naming the place **Reykjavík** ("Smoky Bay") after the steam rising off nearby hot springs, and becoming Iceland's first official resident.

Although Hjörleifur had meanwhile been murdered by his own Irish slaves, things went well for Ingólfur and this attracted other migrants to Iceland, who spent the next sixty years snapping up vacant land in what has become known as the **Settlement**, or Landnám. These first Icelanders, who were mostly Norwegian, were primarily **farmers**, importing their pagan beliefs along with sheep, horses, and crops such as barley, while also clearing forests to create pasture and provide timber for buildings and ships. While it was available, a man could take as much land as he could light fires around in one day, while a woman could have the area she could lead a heifer around in the same time. Landowners became local **chieftains**, whose religious responsibilities earned them the title of *goðar*, or priests, and who sorted out their differences through negotiations at regional **assemblies** (*Þing*) – or if these failed, by fighting. Conditions must have been very favourable compared to those in Norway, however, as by 930, when the last areas of the country were claimed, an estimated 60,000 people already lived in Iceland – a figure not exceeded until the nineteenth century.

The Commonwealth: 930–1262 AD

By the early tenth century, Iceland was firmly occupied and had begun to see itself as an independent nation in need of national government. The chieftains rejected the idea of a paramount leader, and instead decided, in 930, on a **Commonwealth** governed by a national assembly, or **Alþing**, which came to be held for two weeks every summer at **Þingvellir** in southwestern Iceland. Here laws were recited publicly by a **lawspeaker**, and disputes settled by four regional courts, with a supreme court formed early in the eleventh century. Legal settlement typically involved payment to the injured party or their family; the highest punishment was not death but being declared an **outlaw**, thus being exiled from Iceland. Courts had no power to enforce decisions, however, only make recommendations, and though they held great public authority, in practice their decisions could be ignored – something which was to undermine the Commonwealth in later years.

The first century of the Commonwealth was very much a golden era, however: the country was united, resources were rich, and farming profitable. This was the **Saga Age**, the time when the first generations of Icelanders were carving out great names for themselves in events that passed into oral lore and would only later be written down.

Contact with the outside world continued too, and – in the same way that Iceland itself was discovered – Icelandic seafarers came across their own new worlds. In 980, Eiríkur Þorvaldsson (better known in English as **Eirik the Red**) was outlawed for killing his neighbour and sailed from the Westfjords to follow up earlier reports of land to the northwest. He found a barren, treeless coastline, then returned to Iceland to whip up support for colonizing what he called **Greenland** – a misleading name, chosen deliberately to arouse interest. Enough people were hooked to emigrate along with Eiríkur, and two settlements were founded in Western Greenland which lasted until the sixteenth century. And it was from Greenland that Eiríkur's son **Leif Eiríksson** heard that land had been sighted even further west, and set sail around the year 1000 to discover Baffin Island, Labrador, and "**Vínland**", an as-yet unidentified area of the north American coast. A couple of attempts made by others to colonise these distant lands came to nothing, however, and America was then forgotten about by Europeans until Columbus rediscovered it.

The Coming of Christianity

Meanwhile, the late tenth century had seen Norway convert to **Catholicism** under the fiery king **Ólafur Tryggvason**. Ólafur then sent the missionary **Þangbrand** to evangelize Iceland, where – despite having to physically battle strong resistance from pagan stalwarts – he baptized several influential chieftains. Back in Norway, Þangbrand's unfavourable reports infuriated Ólafur, who was only prevented from executing all Icelanders in the country by the Icelandic chieftain **Gizur the White**, who promised to champion the new religion at home. Gizur mustered his forces and rode to the Alþing in 1000, where civil war was only averted by the lawspeaker **Þorgeir**, who – having made pagan and Christian alike swear to accept his decision – chose Christianity as Iceland's official religion, though pagans were initially allowed to maintain their beliefs in private. Gizur the White's son **Ísleifur** became Iceland's first **bishop** in 1056, and his homestead at **Skálholt** near Þingvellir was made the bishop's seat, with a second, northern diocese founded in 1106 at **Hólar**.

The new religion brought gradual changes with it, notably the introduction in 1097 of **tithes** – property taxes – to fund churches. As their wealth increased, churches founded **monasteries** and **schools**, bringing education and the beginnings of **literature**: Iceland's laws were first written down in 1117; and in 1130 the church commissioned Ari the Learned to compile the **Íslendingabók**, a compendium of the Icelandic people and their lineages. Importantly, Ari wrote not in Latin, the usual language of education and the Church at the time, but in Icelandic, an expression of national identity that was followed by almost all later Icelandic writers.

Collapse of the Commonwealth

Despite these benefits, several factors were beginning to undermine the Alþing's authority. During the twelfth century, for instance, life in Iceland became much tougher. The country's unstable geology made itself felt for the first time with the **eruption** of the volcano Hekla in southern Iceland in 1104, which buried around twenty farms. **Tree felling** had also become so extensive that there was no longer enough timber for ship building; the effects of subsequent **erosion** were compounded by overgrazing and the beginnings of a "**mini ice-age**", which was to last until the late nineteenth century and caused Iceland's glaciers to expand over previously settled areas – all of which reduced available farmland and made the country dependent on **imports**.

Meanwhile, the tithes were dividing Iceland's formerly egalitarian society. With its taxes, the Church became rich and politically powerful, as did chieftains who owned Church lands or had become priests, and so took a share of the tithes. These chieftains formed a new elite group of **aristocrats**, who bought out their poorer neighbours and so concentrated land ownership, wealth, and inherent political power in the hands of just a few clans. At the same time, in 1152 the Icelandic Church came under the jurisdiction of the **Archbishop of Nidaros** in Norway, giving the expansionist Norwegian throne a lever to start pressuring Iceland to accept its authority. Backed by the Archbishop and **Þorlákur Þórhallsson**, bishop at Skálholt from 1179 and later beatified as Iceland's first saint, the Church began to demand freedom from secular laws.

The Alþing's lack of effective power now became clear, as it proved unable to deal with the Church's demands, or the fighting that was breaking out between the six biggest clans as they battled for political supremacy. The period from 1220 is known as the **Sturlung Age** after the most powerful of these clans, led by the historian, lawspeaker and wily politician **Snorri Sturlusson**. Travelling to Norway in 1218, Snorri became a retainer of King Hákon Hákonarson, and returned to Iceland in 1220 to promote Norwegian interests. But his methods were slow, and in 1235 the king sent Snorri's nephew, **Sturla Sighvatsson**, to Iceland to win it over for Norway, by force if necessary. In the ensuing **civil war**, forces led in part by **Gissur Þorvaldsson**, head of the Haukadalur clan, killed Sturla and virtually wiped out the Sturlungs at the battle of **Örlygsstaðir** in 1238. Snorri escaped by being in Norway at the time, but was killed by Gissur after his return.

Amongst this violence, Iceland was also experiencing a literary flowering: Snorri Sturlusson wrote the **Prose Eddas**, containing much of what is known about Norse mythology; his relative Sturla Þordarson compiled the **Book of Settlements Expanded**, accounts of the original landowners and their lives; and it was during this period that the **Sagas** were composed, romanticising the nobler events of the early Commonwealth. Meanwhile the war continued, and by 1246 only two chieftains were left standing: Gissur Þorvaldsson, who held the south of the country; and Sturla's brother **Þordur**, who controlled the north. Rather than fight, they let King Hákon decide who should govern; the king chose Þordur, who ruled Iceland until 1250, sharing power with the two bishops – also Norwegian appointees. In the end, the bishop at Hólar denounced Þordur for putting his own interests before Norway's, and the king replaced him with Gissur who, after a further decade of skirmishes, finally persuaded Icelanders that the only way to obtain lasting peace was by accepting **Norwegian sovereignty**. In 1262, Iceland's chieftains signed the *Gamli sáttmáli* or **Old Treaty**, which allowed Iceland to keep its laws and promised that the Norwegian king would maintain order, in exchange for taxes and replacing the chieftainships with government officials. While the treaty didn't give Norway absolute control of the country, and demanded a return for Icelandic obedience, it marked the beginnings of seven centuries of foreign rule.

Decline, the English Century and the Reformation

With the Alþing discredited by over forty years of conflict, Iceland turned to Norway to help draft a new constitution. The **Jónsbók** of 1280 was the result, a set of laws that were to remain partly in force until the nineteenth century. The country was to be overseen by a **governor**, with twelve regional **sheriffs** acting as local administrators; all officials would be Icelanders, though appointed by Norway. The Alþing would still meet as a national court, retaining some legislative power, but its decisions would have to be approved by the king.

The new system should have brought a much-needed period of stability to Iceland, but it was not always administered as planned – officials often abused their position, leading to several **revolts**, such as when the brutal governor Smiður Andrésson was killed by farmers in 1361. At the same time, the fourteenth century heralded a further succession of **natural disasters**: severe winters wiped out crops and livestock; Hekla became active again; and the volcano under Öræfajökull in the southeast exploded in 1362, covering a third of the country in ash. But most devastating was the **Plague** or Black Death, which had ravaged Europe in the 1350s and arrived in Iceland in 1402, killing half of the population in the following two years. Compared with this, it seems inconsequential that the Danish "lady king" **Margaret** had meanwhile absorbed the Norwegian throne under the **Kalmar Union** of 1397, thereby placing Iceland in Denmark's hands.

The English Century

While all this was going on, the underlying struggles between landowners, the Church and the king were escalating, typified by events during what is known as the **English Century**. At the time there was growing demand in Europe for dried **cod**, which after 1400 became a major Icelandic export, exchanged for linen, wine and grain. **Fishing** – formerly a secondary income – boomed, providing a new source of funds for coastal landowners. Soon English and German vessels were vying for trade with Iceland and even beginning to fish themselves; the English gained the ascendancy after setting up a base on the Westman Islands (where they also indulged in kidnapping and piracy), and managing to get an English bishop – **John Craxton** – appointed to Hólar in the 1420s. Denmark, alarmed at England's rising influence and the taxes it was losing through uncontrolled trade, appointed its own **Jón Gerreksson** as bishop at Skálholt, although this violent man – who had his own military and spent his time levying illegal taxes and harassing his neighbours – ended up being murdered in 1433.

Trying to restore order, Denmark passed laws stopping the Church from raising illegal taxes and banning the English from Iceland. The English response was to kill the Icelandic governor in 1467, so the Danish king encouraged the German trading organization known as the **Hanseatic League** to establish trading bases in the country – a popular move, as the League had better goods than the English and gave better prices. The English returned with cannons, a forceful stance that after 1490 gained them the right to fish Icelandic waters as long as they paid tolls to Denmark. All went well until 1532, when trouble flared between German and English vessels at the trading post at **Grindavík** on the southwestern Reykjanes Peninsula, culminating in the death of the English leader. English involvement in Iceland dropped off sharply after this, leaving Icelandic trade in the hands of Danish and German interests.

The Reformation and its effects

The Church, which by now had complete jurisdiction over Iceland's lands, and profitable stakes in farming and fishing, became even more powerful in 1533 when the two bishops – **Jón Arason** and **Ögmundur Pálsson** – were appointed as joint governors of the country. But outside Iceland, a new Christian view first proposed by the German Martin Luther in 1517 had been gaining ground. **Lutherism** revolted against what was seen as the Catholic Church's growing obsession with material rather than spiritual profits, and encouraged a break with Rome as the head of the Church – a suggestion that European monarchs realized would therefore place the Church's riches and influence in their hands.

During the 1530s, all Scandinavia became Lutheran, and converts were already making headway in Iceland, though threatened with excommunication by the bishops. In 1539, the Danish king **Christian III** ordered the Icelandic governor to appropriate Church lands, which led to the murder of one of his sheriffs and a subsequent military expedition to Iceland to force conversion to Lutherism. This was headed by **Gissur Einarsson**, a former protégé of Ögmundur but covert Lutheran, who replaced Ögmundur as bishop at Skálholt in 1542. A skilful diplomat, he encouraged Lutherism without, by and large, antagonizing Catholics. His appointment left Jón Arason at Hólar as the last Catholic bishop in Scandinavia, and on Gissur's death in 1548, Arason unsuccessfully pushed his own Catholic candidate for Skálholt, an act that got him declared an outlaw. Gathering a band of supporters, Arason marched south and captured Skálholt, but was subsequently defeated and executed along with two of his sons on November 7, 1550, allowing Lutherism to be imposed across the entire country.

The consequences of the Reformation were severe, with the new faith forced on an initially unwilling population, who – in common with many other countries at the time – may have disagreed with Catholic abuses of power but not with Catholicism itself. The Danish king acquired all Church holdings and their revenues, profits from which had previously stayed in Iceland; monasteries were abolished and, deprived of funds, the Church found it hard to sponsor education – though it did manage to publish a translation of the Bible in 1584, the first book printed in Icelandic.

Politically too, the Church was now an instrument of the king, and the Danish crown gained a far more direct hold on the country. Technically, however, Iceland remained an independent state through its treaty with Norway, but in 1661 King **Frederick III** declared his rule absolute over all Danish lands, and the following year sent an armed ambassador to Iceland to make its people swear allegiance. During an assembly at **Bessastaðir**, near Reykjavík, the Alþing's lawspeaker and Skálholt's bishop were forced to submit, removing their final vestiges of authority and handing complete control of the country to the Danish crown.

In the meantime, Iceland's economy – still based on farming and fishing – suffered a severe blow through the **Trade Monopoly** of 1602. This restricted all trade between Iceland and the outside world to a select few Danish merchants, who charged steeply for their goods, while giving poor prices for Icelandic products. By 1700, the monopoly had ruined the country, creating a poor, dispirited population of tenant farmers and landless labourers. Fishing was also on the wane, partly because a shortage of timber meant that Iceland's vessels were basic and small, and easily out-competed by foreign boats. Aside from a fruitless attempt to introduce **reindeer** as livestock, the only concrete action taken to redress trade imbalances was made by the bailiff **Skúli Magnússon**, who in 1752 founded a company at Reykjavík – still just a small farming settlement at the time – to improve agricultural practices and modernize the wool and fishing industries. Though the company was only moderately successful, its warehouses became the core of Reykjavík town, soon to become Iceland's largest settlement and de facto capital.

Unfortunately, a fresh wave of disasters now swept the country, the worst of which was the catastrophic **Laki Eruptions** of 1783–84 in the southeast. Poisonous fallout from Laki wrecked farming over the entire country, and the ensuing **famine** reduced the population to just 38,000. Denmark briefly considered evacuating the survivors to Jutland, but in the end settled for easing the economy by replacing the trade monopoly with a **Free Trade Charter** in 1787, which allowed Iceland to do business with a greater range of Danish merchants. Another effect of the eruptions were accompanying **earthquakes** which knocked over the church at Skálholt and caused subsidence at the Alþing site; the bishopric was moved to Reykjavík, and the Alþing – which by now only met irregularly to discuss minor matters – was finally dissolved.

Nationalism

European political upheavals during the early nineteenth-century Napoleonic Wars had little effect on Iceland, though there was brief excitement in 1809 when opportunistic Danish interpreter **Jörgen Jörgensen** deposed the governor and ran the country for the summer. However, the increasingly liberal political climate that followed the war encouraged **nationalism** throughout Europe and was championed in Iceland by the romantic poet **Jónas Hallgrímsson** and historian **Jón Sigurðsson**, a descendent of Snorri Sturlusson, who pushed for free trade and autonomy from Denmark. Bowing to popular demand, the Danish king reconstituted the Alþing at Reykjavík in 1843, which met every other year and had twenty elected regional members of parliament and six representatives of the king. Jón Sigurðsson was amongst the first members elected.

Even greater changes were on the way, sparked by the French Revolution of 1789, after which Europe's other royal families began to cede real power in order to avoid a similar fate. Following uprisings in Denmark, the **monarchy** there became constitutional in 1848, allowing Jón Sigurðsson to point out that Iceland's 1662 oath of allegiance to the king as an absolute ruler was therefore no longer valid, and that the Old Treaty was now back in force. This didn't make him popular with the king, a situation exacerbated when he led the defeat of a bill at the Alþing, in 1851, that would have legally incorporated Iceland into Denmark. Sigurðsson also managed to have remaining trade restrictions finally lifted four years later, an act which did more than anything else to improve life in Iceland by bringing in modern farm implements and wood for boats at affordable prices, while allowing the profitable export of livestock, wool and fish.

In 1871 Denmark politically **annexed** Iceland, an event that, though not accepted by Icelanders, gave them a favourable **new constitution**. Broadly speaking, this returned full legislative powers to the Alþing and was ratified by King Christian IX himself, while attending celebrations at Þingvellir in 1874 to mark a thousand years since Settlement. Home control of lawmaking saw further benefits to living conditions: the tithe system was abolished; infrastructure improved; schooling was made compulsory; improvements in boats and fishing equipment caused the growth of port towns; and farmers formed the first Icelandic co-operatives to deal directly with foreign suppliers. There followed a sizeable population boom, despite heavy **emigration** to Canada and the US during the late nineteenth century following another spate of harsh weather, the eruption of Víti in the Askja caldera in northeastern Iceland (see p.276), disease and livestock problems.

Home Rule, Union and Independence

The concept of total political autonomy from Denmark grew from ideas planted by Jón Sigurðsson before his death in 1879. By 1900, differences in the way this could be achieved led to the formation of **political parties**, who in 1904 pressured the king into granting Home Rule under the **Home Rule Party** led by **Hannes Hafstein**. Hafstein's decade in office saw the start of trends that were to continue throughout the century: an emerging middle class led a gradual **population shift** from the land to towns, communications picked up with the introduction of telephones in 1906, and new technologies were adopted for farming and fishing, boosting output. Workers also founded the first unions, and women were granted rights to an equal education and allowed to vote.

Hafstein's biggest defeat came in 1908 when the Alþing rejected the **Draft Constitution**, a proposal to make Iceland an independent state under the Danish king. Yet a decade later, a referendum found ninety percent of voters approved of the idea, and in December 1918, Iceland entered into the **Act of Union** with Denmark, where it received recognition as an independent state while still accepting the Danish king as monarch.

World War I itself bypassed Iceland, though during the war the country profited from the high export prices paid for fish, meat, and **wool** (in great demand in Europe for military uniforms). As **World War II** loomed however, Iceland

– dependent on trade with both Britain and Germany – decided to stay neutral, but, after the outbreak of hostilities in 1939, the country's strategic North Atlantic location meant that, neutral or not, it was simply a matter of time before either Germany or Britain invaded. The **British** were first, landing unopposed in May 1940, so gaining a vital supply point for the Allies' North Atlantic operations. The following year **US forces** replaced the British with the approval of the Alþing, on condition that they respected Icelandic sovereignty and left once hostilities were over.

Though fighting never came to Iceland itself, World War II was to trigger the end of foreign rule. When Germany invaded Denmark in 1940 the Alþing decided that, as the king could no longer govern, the Act of Union should be dissolved and therefore that Iceland should declare its full **independence**. The formal ratification took some time, however, as the government was in disarray, with none of the four political parties holding a parliamentary majority. In the end, acting regent **Sveinn Björnsson** founded an apolitical government, which finally proclaimed independence from Denmark on June 17, 1944, with Björnsson elected as the first president of the **Icelandic Republic**.

The Republic: from 1944 to the present

One of the biggest challenges for the new republic came immediately after the war. The US troops departed in 1946 as requested, but as the **Cold War** between the Soviet and Western powers began to take shape Iceland felt uncertain about its lack of defence. With neither the population nor desire to form its own military, in 1949 the Alþing voted that Iceland should instead join the US, Britain and others as part of **NATO**, the North Atlantic Treaty Organisation, and in 1951 agreed to have US forces operate an airforce base at **Keflavík**, using facilities the US had already built during World War II. Though the need for defence was widely accepted, the idea of having foreign influence back in Iceland after having only just got rid of it for the first time in 700 years was not popular; the decision to join NATO caused a **riot** in Reykjavík, and today, with the Cold War long past, the continuing US presence at Keflavík remains a contentious issue.

The country has also had to deal with a rather different defence matter: that of preserving its **fish stocks**, and hence most of its export earnings, in the face of foreign competition. Following skirmishes dating right back to the English Century (see p.341), in 1896 Iceland's **territorial waters** – the area from which it could exclude foreign vessels – had been set as extending three nautical miles from land. As commercial fishing picked up again after World War II, fish stocks through the Atlantic declined, and most countries increased their territorial limits. In 1958, Iceland declared a twelve-mile limit which Britain protested, sending in naval boats to protect its trawlers fishing in these new Icelandic waters in the first act of the **Cod Wars**. These flared on and off for the next thirty years, with Iceland continuing to expand its claims as fish stocks continued to dwindle, and employing its coastguard to cut the cables of any foreign trawlers that were caught poaching. Things came to a head in 1975, when Iceland declared a two-hundred-mile limit around its shores, at which point Britain broke off diplomatic relations and ordered its Navy to ram Icelandic coastguard boats, which happened on several occasions. The situation was only resolved in 1985, when international laws justified Iceland's position by granting the two-hundred-mile limit to all countries involved in the dispute.

Domestically, Iceland has become predominantly urban since 1944, with over half the population of 280,000 living in the Greater Reykjavík area, and just 24,000 remaining on the land as farmers. Standards of living are now equal to any European country – in fact, with little industry and low pollution levels, Icelanders are in some ways better off. Virtually all Icelanders are literate and well educated, and communications are as good as they can be given the natural conditions – the Ringroad around the country was completed in 1974, and Iceland's per-capita usage of **computers** and the Internet is one of the world's highest. New technologies, such as the harnessing of **hydro** and **geothermal energy** for electricity, heating and growing **hothouse** foods, have also been enthusiastically embraced. On the downside, the fact that **fishing** is the single main source of export earnings has made the economy very sensitive, and a reliance on **imports** means that prices are high, with many people needing more than one job in order to make ends meet. The runaway inflation of the 1970s (in part caused by the 1973 eruption of the volcano on Heimaey, which disrupted the season's fishing) has been capped, though at the cost of rising **unemployment** figures – although many Icelanders will tell you that if people don't have jobs in Iceland, it's because they don't want them.

At the beginning of the twenty-first century, three thorny issues dominate the political scene in Iceland: **European Union membership**, the resumption of whaling, and the environment. Following the decision by fellow Nordic nations Sweden and Finland to join the EU in 1995, the question of whether Iceland should follow suit is rarely out of the headlines. At issue is the EU's Common Fisheries Policy, which opponents of membership claim would open up Iceland's territorial waters to other member states and do serious damage to the country's economy, eighty percent of which is dependent on fish and fish-related products. Supporters argue that, as a tiny nation, Icelanders need the international stage offered by the meetings in Brussels that are shaping Europe's future. Public opinion on the issue swings back and forth, monitored closely by politicians of all parties, eager to gain political capital from the mood of the people.

The question of **whaling** is linked to that of EU membership. In 2003, to the despair of environmentalists and the whale-watching industry, Iceland's whaling fleet put to sea for the first time in fifteen years and harvested 36 minke whales for "scientific research", with the meat later sold commercially. Though outwardly defiant of world opinion, the Icelandic government is now carefully assessing whether the resumption of whaling will cause a decline in the volume of tourists visiting the country, and whether the European Commission in Brussels will suggest repeating earlier boycotts of Icelandic fish that sent the economy into freefall.

However, the burning issue for most Icelanders is the protection of their unspoilt **environment**. Despite widespread public condemnation of the project, the government decided in 2003 to proceed with the building of a vast dam in the pristine highland wilderness at **Kárahnjúkar** (see p.302) to provide hydroelectric power for a new US-owned aluminium smelter planned for the East Fjords. And here lies the crux of Iceland's dilemma – how the country's outstanding natural beauty, fierce independence and pride can be protected from the economic and political pressures of a world upon which Iceland is totally dependent for its existence.

Landscape and geology

I celand's lunar landscapes are one of the country's prime attractions, but its apparently ancient façade is in fact an illusion. Geologically, Iceland is very young, with its oldest rocks dating back a mere 14 million years, to a time in the Earth's history when the dinosaurs had long gone and humans were yet to evolve.

The reason that its landscape appears so raw is because Iceland sits on a geological hot spot on the mid-Atlantic ridge, where the **Eurasian** and **American continental plates** are drifting east and west apart from each other. As they do so, Iceland is continually tearing down the middle, allowing **magma** (molten rock from the Earth's core) to well upwards towards the surface. When the surface cracks – in an earthquake, for instance – magma erupts through as a volcano, and when groundwater seeps down to magma levels it boils and returns to the surface as a **thermal spring**, or even a **geyser**.

Almost all such geological activity in Iceland is located over this mid-Atlantic tear, which stretches northeast in a wide band across the country, taking in everything between the Reykjanes Peninsula, the Westman Islands and Mýrdalsjökull in the southwest, and Mývatn and Þórshöfn in the northeast. As this band is where volcanoes are creating all the new land, it's here that you'll find the most recent rocks; conversely, the oldest, most geologically stable parts of the country are around Ísafjörður in the Westfjords and Gerpir cliffs in Iceland's extreme east.

At the same time, Iceland is close enough to the Arctic for its higher mountains and plateaus – most of which are in the south of the country – to have become permanently ice capped, forming extensive **glaciers**. Melt from around their edges contributes to many of Iceland's **rivers**, which are further fed by **underground springs** – also the source of the country's largest **lakes**. Cold, dry **air** formed by sub-zero temperatures over the ice caps is also responsible for some of the weird **atmospheric effects** you'll encounter here, while others have an extraterrestrial origin.

Volcanoes

Though Iceland's volcanoes share a common origin, they form many different types, based on the chemical composition of their magma, which flows out of the volcano as **lava**. Where the lava is very fluid and the eruption is slow and continuous, the lava builds up to form a wide, flattened cone known as a **shield volcano**, a type that takes its name from the Skjaldbreiður (Shield-broad) volcano at Þingvellir. Where an eruption is violent, the lava is thrown out as a fine spray, cooling in mid-air and forming cones of ash or **tephra**, a cover-all name for volcanic ejecta; typical examples of tephra cones are found at Mývatn's Hverfjall, and Eldfell on Heimaey in the Westman Islands. Relatively rare in Iceland, **strato volcanoes** are tall, regular cones built from very long-term lava and tephra accumulations; westerly Snæfellsjökull is a good example, though the country's most consistently active volcano, Hekla, has formed in a similar manner but along a line of craters rather than a single vent.

Crater rows are one of the country's most common volcanic formations, caused when lava erupts at points along a lengthy fissure, such as occurred at Leirhnjukur north of Mývatn in the 1970s, and Lakagigar in southeast Iceland during the 1780s. Both eruptions produced a string of low, multiple cones and large quantities of lava – in Lakagigar's case, flows covered 600 square kilometres. Submarine eruptions also occur off Iceland and are how the Westman Islands originally formed, as demonstrated by the creation of the new island of Surtsey in the 1960s. Looking like mini-volcanoes but actually nothing of the sort, aptly named pseudocraters – like those at Mývatn and Kirkjubæjarklaustur – form when lava flows over damp ground, vapourising the water beneath, which explodes through the soft rock as a giant blister.

Most rocks in Iceland were created in volcanic eruptions, and two common forms are easily identifiable. Basalt forms fluid lava solidifying into dark rock, weathered expanses of which cover the Reykjanes Peninsula and elsewhere. Where basaltic lavas cool rapidly – by flowing into a river or the sea, for instance – they form characteristic hexagonal pillars, with excellent examples at Svartifoss in Skaftafell National Park and Hjálparfoss at Þórsárdalur. In contrast, rhyolite forms a very thick lava, which often builds up into dome-like volcanoes such as Mælifell on the Snæfellsnes Peninsula. Cooled, it normally produces distinctively crumbly, grey, yellow and pink rocks, typified by the peaks of the central Landmannalaugar region, though in some cases rhyolite solidifies into black, glass-like obsidian (best seen at Hrafntinnusker, on the Laugavegur hiking trail). Types of tephra to look for include black or red, gravel-like scoria; solidified lava foam or pumice, which is light enough to float on water; and bombs, spherical or elongated twists of rock formed when semi-congealed lava is thrown high into the air and hardens as it spins – they can be as big as a football but are usually fist-sized.

Aside from their cones and lava fields, volcanoes affect the landscape in other ways. Historically, dense clouds of tephra have destroyed farms and farmland on a number of occasions – such as the twelfth-century eruption of Hekla that buried Stöng in Þórsárdalur, or the 1875 explosion of Viti, at Askja. Volcanic activity under ice caps can also cause catastrophic flash floods known as jökulhlaups, the most recent being at Grímsvotn in 1996. On the other hand, extinct volcano craters often become flooded themselves and form lakes, or maars; one of the biggest is Öskjuvatn in the Askja caldera, but there are also smaller examples at Grænvatn on the Reykjanes Peninsula and Kerið crater near Selfoss.

Thermal springs and geysers

Thermal springs are found all over Iceland, sometimes emerging at ground-level literally as a hot-water spring – such as at Hveragerði – or flooding natural depressions or crevasses to form hot pools, which can be found at Mývatn and Landmannalaugur. In some cases the water emerges from the ground as steam through a vent; where this mixes with clay, boiling mud pits or solfataras are formed, of which the most extensive are those at Hverarönd, east of Mývatn. Natural steam is harnessed in Iceland to drive turbines and generate geothermal power, and also as heating for homes and hothouses.

While **geysers** tap into the same subterranean hot water as thermal springs, nobody is quite sure exactly why they erupt – it's either a gradual buildup of water pressure or a subterranean hiccup. Since the Krísuvík geyser blew itself to pieces in 1999, Iceland's only example of note is at **Geysir**, northeast of Selfoss.

Glaciers, rivers and lakes

Glaciers can be thought of as giant, frozen rivers or waterfalls that move downhill under their own colossal weight. Usually movement is slow – maybe a few centimetres a year – though some can shift a metre or more annually. In Iceland, they're all associated with ice caps, the biggest of which, **Vatnajökull** (which more or less means Glacial Sea), spreads over 150km across the country's southeast. These caps sit atop plateaus, with a few isolated rocky peaks or **nunataks** poking through the ice, off which scores of glaciers descend to lower levels.

Deeper glacial ice is often distinctly blue, caused by the air being squeezed out from between the ice crystals by the weight of the ice above. However, glaciers are also full of debris, either from falls of volcanic ash, or simply from the way they grind down the rocks underneath them into fine gravel or sand. As this dark grit and gravel nears the surface of the glacier it warms up in the sunlight, causing surrounding ice to melt, exposing the gravel and thereby making the front of most Icelandic glaciers appear very "dirty". The debris ultimately is carried away from the glacier by streams or rivers which are also the product of glacial friction, and deposited as desert-like **sandurs**, such as those that occupy much of Iceland's southeastern coastline.

It's also possible to see the effects that the glaciers themselves leave on the landscape, as both ice caps and glaciers were formerly far more extensive than they appear today. During previous ice ages – the last of which ended around 12,000 years ago – much of the country was beneath the ice, but there has been considerable fluctuation in glacier limits even in recorded times, and at present most are **shrinking**. The intricate inlets of the Eastfjords and Westfjords were carved by vanished glaciers, as were the characteristically flat-topped mountains known as **móbergs** southeast of Mývatn. Former glacial valleys – typically broad and rounded – can be seen along the Ringroad southwest of Akureyri; and Iceland's most mobile glacier, Skeiðarárjökull in Skaftafell National Park, has been retreating over the last eighty years leaving raised **morraine** gravel ridges in its wake.

The majority of Iceland's **rivers** are fairly short, glacial-fed affairs, though two of the largest – the **Hvíta** in the southwest, and northeastern **Jökulsá á Fjöllum** – each exceed a respectable 200km in length. Both have quite spectacular stretches where they have carved **canyons** and **waterfalls** out of the landscape: at Gullfoss on the Hvíta; and Dettifoss and Ásbergi along the Jökulsa. Icelandic **lakes** are not especially large and tend to be caused – as with Mývatn or Þingvallavatn – when lava walls dam a spring-fed outflow, causing it to back-flood.

Atmospheric phenomena

One of the strangest features of being in Iceland during the summer is the extremely **long days**. The northernmost part of the mainland is actually just outside the Arctic Circle, and so the sun does set (briefly) even on the longest day of the year, though you can cross over to the little island of Grímsey, whose northern tip is inside the Arctic and so enjoys midnight sun for a few days of the year. Conversely, winter days are correspondingly short, with the sun barely getting above the horizon for three months of the year.

One consequence of Iceland's often cold, dry atmosphere is that – on sunny days at least – it can play serious tricks on your sense of scale. Massive objects such as mountains and glaciers seem to stay the same size, or even shrink, the closer you come to them, and sometimes phantom hills or peaks appear on the horizon. Another effect – best viewed on cold, clear nights – are the **northern lights**, or **Aurora Borealis**, which form huge, shifting sheets of green or red in the winter skies. They're caused by the solar wind bringing electrically charged particles into contact with the Earth's atmosphere, and you'll have to be in luck to catch a really good show – they improve the further north you travel.

Wildlife and the environment

I celand's first settlers found a land whose coastal fringe, compared with today, was relatively well wooded; there were virtually no land mammals, but birdlife and fish stocks were abundant and the volcanic soil was reasonably fertile. Over a thousand years of farming has brought great changes: big trees are a rare sight, fish stocks have plummeted, and introduced mammals have contributed to erosion and other problems, but a growing regard for Iceland's natural heritage is beginning to redress the imbalance, and the country's natural history remains very much alive.

Flora

Though fossils indicate that around 12 million years ago Iceland had stands of maples and other broad-leaved trees, dawn redwood and even giant sequoias, subsequent ice ages had wiped these out long before humans ever landed here. It's likely that the Vikings found woods mostly comprising **dwarf birch** and **willow** that you still see here today. Both can grow up to 10m or so in height, but generally form shrub-like thickets – original forests, however, would have been fairly extensive, reaching from the coast up into highland valleys. Clearances for timber and pasture have reduced Iceland's tree cover to just one percent of the land, though since 1994 over four million trees – including commercial stands of **pine** – have been planted in an attempt to restore levels to pre-settlement estimates.

The most widespread flora – **mosses** and **lichens** – tend to get overlooked, but they cover almost every lava flow and cliff in the country and provide a colourful mosaic of greens, greys and oranges, especially after rain has darkened the surrounding rocks. **Flowering plants** are most obvious in mid-summer, and include the very common, blue vertical spikes of **arctic lupins**, introduced from North America to help reduce erosion; the tiny magenta flowers and spongy green clumps of **arctic river beauty** and **thyme** (which you can also idenity from its smell); fluffy **cottongrass** growing in boggy areas; the cauliflower-shaped, yellow-green flower heads of **angelica**, often covered in flies; blue **harebells**; and yellow **kingcups** and **dandelions**. In early autumn, **berries** are also plentiful, and many people collect them to eat.

Mammals

The **arctic fox**, which feeds almost exclusively on birds, was the only land mammal in Iceland when the first settlers arrived. Common throughout Iceland, they're chubbier than European foxes, with short, rounded ears, bushy tail, and a coat that turns white in winter. **Polar bears** have never flourished here, though every decade one or two float over on ice floes from Greenland (which is probably how foxes first arrived too), only to be shot as a dangerous pest by the first person who sees them.

Domestic animals arrived with the Vikings. The **Icelandic horse** is a unique breed descended from medieval Norwegian stock, as none have been imported since the tenth century. Cattle numbers are fairly low, but **sheep** outnumber the human population by four to one. **Reindeer** were introduced from Norway and Finland in the late seventeenth century for hunting purposes – today they're restricted to eastern Iceland, where they stick to high altitude pasture in summer, descending to coastal areas in winter. Iceland's cold climate has limited the spread of smaller vermin such as **rats** and **mice**, which were unintentionally brought in on boats and only occur around human habitations; escaped **rabbits** have recently established themselves around Reykjavík and on Heimaey, however. **Minks** have also broken out of fur farms and seem to be surviving in the wild, much to the detriment of native birdlife.

Offshore, Iceland has a number of **whale** species. Traditionally, their valuable meat, bones and teeth were most frequently obtained from washed-up corpses, and – as described in *Eyrbyggja Saga* (see p.358) - battles were even fought over the rights to their carcasses. **Commercial whaling** began in the nineteenth century, and resumed after a fifteen-year-long moratorium ended in 2003, though numbers remain high and you've a good chance to see some if you put to sea. Most common are a couple of species of **dolphin** and the five-metre-long **pilot whale**, but there are also substantial numbers of far larger **fin whales**, **sei whales** and **minke whales**, all of which feed by straining plankton from sea water through moustache-like baleen plates inside their mouths. Far less common are **orca** (also known as killer whales), square-headed **sperm whales**, and **blue whales**, which reach 30m in length and are the largest known animal ever to have lived.

Grey and harbour **seals** are found in Iceland, with the biggest numbers seen around the north coast and off the Westman Islands. Both seal species are also hunted, despite being depicted as almost human in Icelandic folktales, appearing as "were-seals" who have human families on land and seal families in the sea. According to these stories, if you walk along a beach and find a seal following you out from shore, it may be looking to see if you're one of its children.

Birds

Iceland has some 300 recorded bird species, of which around 80 breed regularly. The **gyrfalcon**, a large bird of prey with variable grey-white plumage, is a national icon, once appearing on the Icelandic coat of arms and exported for hunting purposes until the nineteenth century. They're not common, but occur throughout mountainous country; rather oddly, in folklore the gyrfalcon is said to be brother to the ptarmigan, its main source of food. Another spectacular bird of prey is the huge **white-tailed sea eagle**, whose numbers have recently rebounded following a low point in the 1980s, when birds took poison baits intended for escaped minks. Around forty pairs breed annually in the Westfjords, though juveniles travel quite widely over the country.

The **ptarmigan** is a plump game bird, plentiful across Iceland wherever there is low scrub or trees. They're well camouflaged, patterned a mottled brown to blend with summer vegetation, and changing – with the exception

Below is a partial list of **Icelandic birds**, with English and Icelandic names (US names are given in brackets where they differ substantially from British usage). You won't have to be an ardent twitcher to clock up most of these, though a couple of less widespread species are also included.

Arctic skua	Kjói	Merlin	Smyrill
Arctic tern	Kría	Oystercatcher	Tjaldur
Barnacle goose	Helsingi	Pink-footed goose	Heiðagæs
Barrow's goldeneye	Húsönd	Pintail	Grafönd
Black guillemot	Teista	Ptarmigan	Rjúpa
Black-headed gull	Hettumáfur	Puffin	Lundi
Black-tailed godwit	Jaðrakan	Purple sandpiper	Sendlingur
Black-throated diver (Loon)	Himbrimi	Raven	Hrafn
		Razorbill	Álka
Brünnich's guillemot (Thick-billed murre)	Stuttnefja	Red-necked (Northern) phalarope	Óðinshani
Cormorant	Dílaskarfur	Red-throated diver	Lómur
Dunlin	Lóuðraell	Redpoll	Auðnutittlingur
Eider	Æðarfugl	Redshank	Stelkur
Fulmar	Fýll	Redwing	Skógarðröstur
Gannet	Súla	Ringed plover	Sandlóa
Golden plover	Heiðlóa	Scaup	Duggönd
Goosander	Gulönd	Scoter	Hrafnsönd
Great auk*	Geirfug	Shag	Toppskarfur
Great skua	Skúmur	Short-eared owl	Brandugla
Greater black-backed gull	Svartbakur	Slavonian grebe	Flórgoði
		Snipe	Hrossagaukur
Guillemot (Murre)	Langvía	Snow bunting	Snjótittlingur
Gyrfalcon	Fálki	Starling	Stari
Harlequin duck	Straumönd	Storm petrel	Stormsvala
Herring gull	Silfurmáfur	Teal	Urtönd
Iceland gull	Bjartmáfur	Tufted duck	Sitúfönd
Kittiwake	Rita	Turnstone	Tildra
Lesser black-backed gull	Sílamáfur	Wheatear	Steindepill
		White wagtail	Maríuerla
Little auk (Dovekie)	Haftyrðill	White-tailed sea eagle	Haförn
Longtail duck (Old squaw)	Hávella	Whooper swan	Álft
Mallard	Stokkönd	Widgeon	Rauðhöfðaönd
Meadow pipit	Ðúfutittlingur	Wren	Músarrindill
Merganser	Toppönd	*Extinct	

of black tail feathers and a red wattle around the eye – to snow-white plumage in winter. Aside from being preyed upon year-round by foxes and gyrfalcons, ptarmigan are also a traditional Christmas food, eaten instead of turkey. Their population goes through boom-and-bust cycles, and in bad years Christmas ptarmigan have to be brought in from Scotland, allowing Icelanders to bemoan the flavour of imported birds.

Other common heathland birds include the **golden plover**, a migrant whose mournful piping is eagerly awaited in Iceland as the harbinger of summer; long-legged **redshank** and **godwit**; and **snipe**, identified by their long beaks, zigzag flight, and strange "buzzing" noise made by two stiffened tail feathers

C

CONTEXTS | Wildlife and the environment

which protrude at right angles to its body. In fields and estuaries you'll see **pink-footed geese**, the most common of Iceland's wildfowl species, with **whooper swans** resident even in downtown Reykjavík. Similarly widespread are **raven**, held by some Icelanders to be highly intelligent, though often associated in tales with portents of doom. Norse mythology describes Óðinn as having two ravens called Huginn (the Thinker) and Muninn (the Rememberer), who report to him on the state of the world; and folklore holds that the congregations of ravens commonly seen in autumn are dividing up Iceland's farms between them, so that each pair will have a home over winter.

Many of Iceland's **ducks** are coastal, though you can see almost all recorded species either on or around Mývatn, a lake in the northeast. **Eider** are probably the most famous Icelandic duck, known for their warm down, but birders will want to clock up **harlequin** and **barrow's goldeneye**, which occur nowhere else in Europe; for more about these species and others, see the box on p.267.

Of all the country's birdlife, however, it's the huge, noisy, teeming **seabird colonies** which really stick in the mind. There are several types of gull – including the uniformly pale **Iceland gull**, and slight, graceful **kittiwake** – but far more common are narrow winged, stumpy **fulmars**, which look gull-like but are actually related to albatrosses. They nest in half-burrows or overhangs on steep slopes and cliffs, and are relatively fearless, often allowing you to approach fairly close – come too near, however, and they spit a foul-smelling oil from their double-chambered beak.

In summer, flat, open places around the coast are utilised by colossal numbers of ground-nesting **arctic terns**, small, white birds with narrow wings, trailing tails, black caps and bright red beaks. It's interesting to watch the activity in a tern colony, but bear in mind that the birds relentlessly attack anything that threatens their eggs or chicks. **Skuas** are heavily built, brown birds with nasty tempers and a piratic lifestyle – they chase and harass weaker sea birds into dropping their catches. Like terns, they also nest on the ground in vast colonies across the southeastern coastal sandurs, and are equally defensive of their territory.

Iceland's equivalent to penguins are the similar-looking **auks**, a family that includes **guillemot** (murre), **razorbill**, and **puffin**. Like penguins, these hunt fish, live in huge seaside colonies, and have black-and-white plumage. Unlike penguins, however, they can also fly. Auks' **beaks** are distinctively specialized: long and pointed in guillemots; mid-length and broad in razorbills; and colourfully striped, sail-shaped in puffins – all aids to their specific fishing techniques. The best place to see puffins is on Heimaey in the Westman Islands – for more on them see p.141 & p.148 – but you'll find other auks anywhere around Iceland where there are suitable nesting cliffs. One exception is the arctic-dwelling **little auk**, or dovekie, now seen only rarely on Grímsey, Iceland's northernmost outpost.

Books and sagas

With a population of barely over a quarter of a million, Iceland boasts more writers per capita than any other country in the world. The long dark winter months are said to to be the reason so many folk put pen to paper, and native-language books on all matters Icelandic can be found in shops across the country. Conversely, as the Icelandic-language market is so small, prices can be inordinately high – specialist publications cost the equivalent of hundreds of dollars, and even a popular-fiction paperback comes in at around 2000kr.

On the other hand, the **sagas** and associated literature have been widely translated into English – Penguin Books, Everyman and Oxford University Press publish a good range of the longer sagas and their own compilations of the shorter tales, some of which are reviewed below (with the publisher of specific compilations indicated in brackets). Icelandic Review also publish a series of collections of folk tales, lesser sagas, and mythologies, available in bookshops across Iceland.

There's an increasing amount of **contemporary fiction** available in English too, though it's not always easy to find outside of Iceland. Foreign books about Iceland remain, unfortunately, remarkably scant, and often lapse into "land of fire and ice"-style clichés.

History and culture

Johannes Brøndsted *The Vikings*. Solid overview of the causes and motivation of the Viking explosion through Europe, focussing mostly on Scandinavia rather than Iceland but giving heaps of details – backed up by archeology - about religion, customs, and daily life.

Jesse Byock *Viking Age Iceland*. A bit academic in character but helpfully fills in background on the environment, politics and peoples of Iceland's "Viking republic".

Terry Lacy *Ring of Seasons*. An interwoven, perceptive and lively account of Iceland's history,

mythology, culture, and daily life, seen through the eyes of a long-term foreign resident.

David Roberts *Iceland Land of the Sagas*. Beautiful glossy pictures by photographer Jon Krakauer accompany the rich text in this coffee-table book of Iceland.

Anna Yates *Leifur Eiríksson and Vínland the Good*. An excellent and readable account of the discovery of North America by Icelandic Vikings. A thorough argument of where exactly Vínland is accompanies debate on why the Norse settlements in North America died out.

Modern fiction

Frans G. Bengtsson *The Long Ships*. Buckle your swash for this lusty novel set in Viking times, as the

irrepressible hero Orm pillages and hacks his way from Scandinavia to Russia and Constantinople and back.

Historically spot-on, and never lets up the good-humoured, rollicking pace.

Guðbergur Bergsson *The Swan*. The story of a young girl sent to a country farm to serve her probation for shoplifting – a characteristic Icelandic sentence. Here she becomes torn between ancient tradition and new attitudes, but by submitting to the inevitable restraints of remote rural life she finds a new kind of freedom.

Einar Már Gudmundsson *Angels of the Universe*. A sad, challenging story of a young man's descent into schizophrenia and the way society treats him, based on the life of the author's brother. Difficult reading at times but never patronising or pointlessly grim – a great work.

Hallgrímur Helgason *101 Reykjavík*. An often side-splittingly funny slant on the undemanding values of an urban existence, centering on the self-inflicted, crisis-ridden life of central Reykjavík resident Hlynur Björn, an introverted, unemployed thirty-year-old living at home with his mother and her girlfriend.

Einar Kárason *Devil's Island*. First in a trilogy of novels set in 1950s Reykjavík, seen through the eyes of an eccentric family housed in an abandoned US army barracks. Lively, satirical, and sharp, it has also been made into a film.

Halldór Laxness *Independent People*. Nobel Prize-winning novel about the toils and troubles of the almost comically stubborn sheep-farmer Bjartur to live free and unbeholden to any man, despite his poverty – only to see his one and only daughter live unbeholden to him. A potentially downbeat tale of have and have-nots, lifted by humorous undercurrents, a lack of bitterness, and real humanity.

Travel and wildlife

W.H. Auden & Louis MacNeice *Letters from Iceland*. Amusing and unorthodox travelogue, the result of a summer journey the young poets undertook through Iceland in 1936. Especially enjoyable are the irreverent comments about local people, politicians and literature.

Sigurður Ægisson *Icelandic Whales*. Slim, pocket-sized guide to the 23 species recorded from Icelandic waters, well illustrated and with entertaining, informative text.

Mark Cawardine *Iceland Nature's Meeting Place*. Plenty of colour photos and maps in this wildlife guide which provides useful information for the amateur naturalist. Advice, too, on where to go to see individual species of birds.

Jeremy Gaskell *Who Killed the Great Auk?* The sad history of this now-extinct species of seabird, the last pair of which were bludgeoned to death off southwestern Iceland by hunters in the mid-nineteenth century.

Mark Kurlansky *Cod*. Entertaining and offbeat account of the cod in history, and a trade in it which reached from Iceland to the US and Spain. A good number of recipes too, if you want to see what all the fuss was about.

Tim Moore *Frost on my Moustache*. Highly enjoyable account of the author's attempts to follow in the footsteps of adventurer Lord Dufferin, who sailed to Iceland in 1856. A critical and well-observed account of the Icelandic nation makes this book a must-read.

Christopher Perrins *Birds of Britain and Europe*. One of many similarly handy field guides covering all the birds you'll see in Iceland. Text and distribution maps are overly Brit-centric but illustrations are excellent.

Sagas and classics

Icelanders will tell you that the greatest of the **sagas** contain everything you need to know about life, and getting acquainted with them certainly reveals something of the culture and history of Iceland. No other ancient literature matches them for their hard-boiled style, laconic but gripping delivery, or their trademark theme of individuals caught in inexorable, often terrible fates.

The word *saga* itself simply means "thing told", and they cover a range of subjects. They were written anonymously between the twelfth and fifteenth centuries, often long after the events they describe; Snorri Sturlusson – the thirteenth-century historian and politician – is the only known **author** of any of the Sagas, with the Heimskringla and Egil's Saga attributed to him. All this leaves scholars to debate whether the Sagas are historically accurate, or historical novels written to extol the virtues of an earlier age. But none of this really matters – what makes the Sagas great is that, even today, they feel immediate and believable.

The most characteristic group of sagas are the so-called "Sagas of Icelanders", which deal mostly with the events of Settlement and the early Commonwealth (around 870-1050). They read like histories, being set in real places (many of which still bear the same name today), and usually begin with a series of genealogies establishing the "historical" origins of the main characters. Some are biographies of individuals, such as in **Egil's Saga** (see p.161) or **Grettir's Saga**. Many tell of long-running feuds, from origin to conclusion; **Njal's Saga** (see p.126) is the greatest of these, but the **Eyrbyggja Saga** and short but impressive **Hrafnkel's Saga** (p.300) are other good examples. There are also a few that focus in on a particular area – most famous is the tragic love-story recounted in **Laxdæla Saga** (see p.172).

Other sagas range widely in theme, from chivalric stories of knights in armour and outright romances (often influenced by contemporary foreign literature, or even Homer), to folklore, lives of the saints and Icelandic bishops, and far more historical works such as the **Vinland Sagas**, the massive saga of the Sturlung age (**Sturlunga saga**), or Snorri Sturlusson's **Heimskringla**, the history of the Norse Kings.

The Saga manuscripts were first recognised for what they were and collected together by just one man, **Arni Magnusson** (1663–1730). As the Icelanders became increasingly poor under Danish rule, many manuscripts could be found stuffing holes in farmhouse walls, and Arni Magnusson made it his mission to save them and take them to Copenhagen for storage. Once there, however, they were nearly all destroyed in a fire, though Arni saved many himself. Following Iceland's independence in 1944, a strong political movement arose to return the manuscripts from Copenhagen and an institute was established to receive them. Such was the political importance attached to these priceless artifacts that some were brought back by gun boat (for more on this, see p.69)

Egil's Saga A powerful and lucid narrative, unmatched for the vivid presence of the central figure, Egil, a mean, mischief-making, murdering poet and grandson of a reputed werewolf, whose last wish in old age is to cause a violent riot at the Alþing by publicly scattering his hoarded cash.

Eirík the Red and other Iceland Sagas Oxford University Press. The tale of one of Iceland's most notorious Viking heros, whose son went on to discover North America, plus some shorter period pieces – *Hrafnkel's* and the *Vopnafjörd* sagas are the most coherent.

Eyrbyggja Saga A strange and often unsettling story, mixing historical events with tales of ghosts, Viking ceremony and family intrigue, whilst mapping out the shadowy life of Snorri Þórgrimsson, who advocated the introduction of Christianity in 1000. Uneven, but with some great set-pieces and character sketches.

Njal's Saga The longest of all the sagas, this is a compelling, visceral account of the schemings and personalities involved in a fifty-year medieval feud, full of bloodshed, pride and falls, and laconic humour.

Laxdæla Saga One of the world's great tragic love stories, following the lives of the families sharing a river valley, and the consequences of Gudrun Osvifsdottir's forced marriage to her lover's best friend.

Robert Kellog & Jane Smiley *The Sagas of Icelanders* Allen Lane-Penguin. Hefty compendium of a dozen key sagas, including *Laxdæla*, *Egil's*, *Hrafnkel's* and the *Vinland Sagas* but strangely omitting that of *Njál*. Comprehensive explanatory text and a few less well-known short

stories flesh out the era – and the tale of Auðun and his bear is a gem.

Sagas of Warrior-Poets Penguin. Being a poet brought respect in Viking times, but poets typically suffered from thorny temperaments, often bringing unhappy fates. The most famous is portrayed in *Egil's Saga*, but this collection of shorter tales also emphasises the poet's lot – the best here is the wonderfully named saga of *Gunnlaug Serpent-tongue*.

Seven Viking Romances Penguin. Unlike the moral, realistic sagas, these contemporary tales stretch belief a bit and have fun along the way, as warriors outwit gods, overcome monsters and vast armies, and get up to all sorts of bawdy mischief. Tellingly, this always happens away from Iceland – and reliable witnesses.

Snorri Sturlusson *King Harald's Saga* Penguin. Part of the *Heimskringla*, recording the turbulent life of King Harald of Norway, felled in battle at Stamford Bridge in Yorkshire, when invading England in 1066, just three weeks before the Battle of Hastings – had he won, English history might have been very different.

Snorri Sturlusson *The Prose Edda*. The *Prose Edda* contain almost all of what is known about Norse mythology, so for the details on everything from the creation of the Æsir, to the events leading to Ragnarok, read this book. The other source of Norse myths is the difficult *Poetic Edda*, an earlier compilation of even older poetry fragments.

The Vinland Sagas Two versions of the Viking discovery of Greenland and North America ("Vinland"), recounted in *Saga of the Greenlanders* and *Eirik the Red's Saga*.

Language

Language

Language 361

Glossary 367

Language

N
otwithstanding the odd change in pronunciation, today's Icelandic is
essentially the same language the Vikings spoke over 1300 years ago.
As a result, it is an oddly archaic language, heavy with declensions,
genders and cases, not to mention Norse peculiarities. Whereas the
other principal members of the North Germanic group of languages,
Danish, Norwegian and Swedish, lost much of their grammar over time,
Icelandic has proudly maintained features that make even the most polyglottal
language student cough and splutter.

It is also one of the most linguistically pure languages in Europe in terms of
vocabulary, and a campaign to rid the language of foreign (mostly English)
words has led to the coining of many new, purely Icelandic words and phrases,
devised by a committee of linguistic experts. Modern inventions especially
have been given names from existing Icelandic words, such as *sími* for telephone (literally "long thread"), and hence *bréfasími* ("letter telephone") for "fax
machine"; *eggjakaka* ("egg cake") for "omelette"; and even *fara á puttanu* ("to
travel on the thumb"), for "to hitchhike". Although there's no Icelandic word
for "interesting" (the closest is *gaman* – "fun"), there's a plethora of words to do
with fish and the sea: *þín þorskur!* ("you cod!") is a term of abuse, whilst "to
give up" is often rendered as *leggja ára í bát*, "to lay one's oars in the boat". If
something isn't up to much, it's *ekki upp á marga fiska* – "not worth many fish".
Rural life has also left its mark on the language: on Friday nights in Reykjavík
you'll find plenty of people who're *sauðdrukkinnn* – "as drunk as a sheep"; the
word for sheep, *fé*, is also the generic term for money. Dogs also speak Icelandic
and can quite clearly be heard to say *voff* (small children will refer to a dog as
a *voffi*) whilst cows on the other hand say *mö*.

Icelandic has also maintained many old names for European cities that were
in use at the time of the Settlement, such as Dyflinni (Dublin), Jórvík (York, in
Britain, hence Nýa Jórvík for New York) and Lundúnir (London).

Anyone learning Icelandic will also have to grapple with a mind blowing use
of grammatical cases for the most straightforward of activities: "to open a
door", for instance, requires the accusative case (*opna dyrnar*) whilst "to close a
door" takes the dative case (*loka dyrunum*). Not only that, but "door" is plural
in Icelandic, as is the word for Christmas, *jólin*, hence *jólin eru í desember*, literally "Christmasses are in December" (as opposed to the English "Christmas is
in December"). Thankfully, there are no dialects anywhere in the country.

Basic grammar

There are 32 **letters** in the Icelandic alphabet. Accented á, é, í, ó, ú and ý count
as separate letters. Letters þ, æ and ö come at the end of the alphabet in that
order. Hence a dictionary entry for mögulegur comes after morgunn.

Verbs come in many classes and are either strong and characterized by a
vowel change (*tek, tók, tekinn*: "take", "took", "taken") or weak (*tala, talaði*:
"speak", "spoke"), without a vowel shift. Verb endings agree with **pronouns**,
which are as follows: *ég* ("I"), *þú* ("you", singular), *hann* ("he"), *hún* ("she"),

það ("it"), við ("we"), þið ("you", plural), þeir ("you", masculine plural), þaer ("you", feminine plural), þau ("you", neuter or mixed gender plural).

Icelandic **nouns** can have one of three genders (masculine, feminine or neuter) and can appear in any one of four different grammatical cases (nominative, accusative, genitive and dative). For example, the masculine word *fjörður*, meaning "a fjord", is *fjörður* in the nominative case, *fjörð* in the accusative case, *fjarðar* in the genitive and *firði* in the dative case. The case of a noun is determined by many factors, including the use of a preceding preposition, for instance, *í Reykjavík* ("in Reykjavík") but *til Reykjavíkur* ("to Reykjavík").

Vowels also have an unnerving ability to shift – for example, *hér er amma* ("here is grandma") but *ég sé ömmu* ("I see grandma"). This even happens with proper names: *þetta er Lada* ("this is a Lada car") but *ég á Lödu* ("I own a Lada"). There is no **indefinite article** in Icelandic with the result that *fjörður* can mean both "fjord" and "a fjord". The **definite article**, as in the other Scandinavian languages, is suffixed to the noun; for example, *maður* means "a man", but *maðurinn* means "the man". The definite article is declined according to the gender and number of the noun.

Adjectives generally precede the noun they qualify and are inflected according to the gender and case gender of the noun. The strong declension is used with indefinite nouns, as in *góður maður* – "a good man". Definite nouns (those with the definite article or other determinatives) require the weak declension, so *góði maðurinn*, "the good man".

Names and numbers

Icelanders take the forename of their father as the first part of their own **surname**, plus the Icelandic word for son (*son*) or daughter (*dóttir*). For example, the son of a man whose forename is Jón will have Jónsson as a surname; a daughter of the same man will have Jónsdóttir as a surname. A family of four in Iceland will therefore have four different surnames, which can certainly throw things into confusion when they travel abroad. When asking someone's surname Icelanders will enquire "hvers son er Kristbjörn?" ("Whose son is Kristbjörn?") for example, to which the reply might be "hann er Egils son" ("He's Egil's son"). Formally or informally, Icelanders are always addressed by their forename and are listed accordingly in the telephone directory. Even the Prime Minister can be found under his forename, Davið; his surname, Oddsson, seems very much an afterthought.

When giving their **addresses**, Icelanders put their street names in the dative case but their town and country in the nominative case. They decline their own names, for instance, *ég tala við Önnu* – "I'm speaking to Anna" (Önnu is the accusative, genitive and dative form of "Anna") and *bókin er eftir Ingibjörgu Sigurðardóttur* – "the book is by Ingibjörg Sigurðardóttir".

When **counting**, the nominative masculine form of the numerals is used, i.e. einn, tveir, þrír, fjórir. However, **street numbers** and the **time** are given in the neuter form. It's a good idea to familiarise yourself with the feminine and neuter forms because they are frequently used in shops and restaurants, since *króna* (plural: krónur) and *þúsund* (thousand: plural þúsundir) are feminine, whilst *hundrad* (hundred: plural *hundruð*) is neuter. Note however *tvö hundruð þrjátíu og ein króna* where *tvö* is neuter to agree with *hundruð* but *ein* is feminine and singular to agree with *króna*.

Learning Icelandic

In theory, the Germanic roots of English and Icelandic, coupled with over two centuries of Norse influence in England during the Viking era should make Icelandic a fairly easy language for English speakers to learn. It doesn't – and any foreigner who has mastered even a smattering of the language will find Icelandic jaws dropping at his every turn. Conversely, most Icelanders speak excellent English, and young people in particular are only too keen to try out turns of phrase on you.

If you want to teach yourself **Icelandic**, however, your best bet is the widely available and excellent *Colloquial Icelandic* by Daisy L. Neijmann, a thoroughly contemporary and well constructed beginners' course accompanied by a couple of cassettes. There is only one Icelandic reference work in English on the subject of **grammar**, *Icelandic Grammar, Texts and Glossary*, by Stefán Einarsson. Originally published in 1945 and still printed today in paperback, it offers a very thorough, if somewhat stodgy analysis of the language.

Dictionaries and phrasebooks

Dictionaries are exceptionally thin on the ground outside Iceland, but the pocket sized *Icelandic–English, English–Icelandic Dictionary*, published by Hippocrene Books, New York, is good for basic reference and is fairly easy to get hold of. German-speakers have the best option, with *Universal-Wörterbuch Isländisch* (Langenscheidt), being by far the best small dictionary. Larger dictionaries are best bought in Iceland, where they're much less expensive – though reckon on at least 5000kr for an English–Icelandic or an Icelandic–English one, and double that for one referencing in both directions.

Of the **phrasebooks**, most useful is Berlitz's *Scandinavian Phrase Book and Dictionary*, which includes a hundred-page section on Icelandic.

Pronunciation

Stress in Icelandic is always on the first syllable. Below is a guide to the pronunciation of Icelandic vowels and consonants – some have no equivalent in English, but the nearest sound has been given to facilitate pronunciation.

Vowels

a	as is f*a*ther		ó	as in s*ow*
á	as in c*ow*		u	like u in c*u*te
e	as in g*e*t or *ai*r, depending on whether long or short		ú	as in f*oo*l
			y	see "i", above
é	like y*ea*h		ý	see "í" above
i	as in h*i*t		æ	as is *eye*
í	as in l*ea*n		au	as in French feu*i*lle
ö	as in f*u*r		ei	as in h*ay*

Consonants

As in English except:

j – as in *y*et

ll and rl – like the Welsh *ll*, or *dl* pronounced together in English
f before l or n – pronounced *b*, eg Keflavík
rn – pronounced as *dn*

Note that Icelandic Þ/þ is the same as English "th" in *th*ing
And Icelandic Ð/ð is the same as English "th" in *th*is

Useful words and phrases

Basic phrases

Yes	Já	Near/far	Nálægt/fjarlægt
No	Nei	This/that	Þetta/Það
Hello	Halló/hæ	Now/later	Núna/seinna
How are you?	Hvernig liður þér/hvað segirðú?	More/less	Meiri/minni
		Big/little	Stór/lítill/smár
Fine, thanks	Mér liður vel, takk; ég segi allt ágætt	Open/closed	Opið/lokað
		Men/women	Karlmenn/kvenmenn
Goodbye	Bless/bæ	Toilet	Snyrting
Good morning/ afternoon	Góðan dag	Gentlemen/ladies	Herrar/konur
		Bank	Banki
Good night	Gósa nótt	Post office	Pósthús
Today/tomorrow	Í dag/á morgun	Stamp(s)	Frímerki
Tonight	Í kvöld	Where are you from?	Hvaðan ertu?
Please	Afsakið	I'm from ...	Ég er frá ...
Thankyou	Takk fyrir	... America	... Bandaríkjunum
I'd like ...	Ég ætla að fá ...	... Australia	... Ástralíu
Excuse me	Fyrirgefðu	... Britain	... Bretlandi
Here you are	Gerið svo vel (plural)/gerðu svo vel (singular)	... Canada	... Kanada
		... England	... Englandi
Don't mention it	Ekkert að þakka	... Ireland	... Írlandi
Sorry? (as in "what did you say?")	Ha?/hvað sagðir þú?	... New Zealand	... Nyja sjálandi
		... Scotland	... Skotlandi
		... Wales	... Wales
Where/when?	Hvar/hvenær?	What's your name?	Hvað heitirðu?
What/why?	Hvað/hvers vegna?	My name is	Ég heiti
Who/how?	Hver/hvernig?	How do you say ... in Icelandic?	Hvernig segir maður ... á íslensku?
How much?	Hvað mikið?		
I don't know	Ég veit ekki	Do you speak English?	Talarðu ensku?
Do you know (a fact)?	Veistu ... ?		
Is there/are there ... ?	Er/eru ... ?	I don't understand	Ég skil ekki
		Could you speak more slowly?	Gætirðu talað hægar?
With/without	Með/án		
And/not	Og/ekki	How much is it?	Hvað kostar Þetta?
Something/nothing	Eitthvað/ekkert	Can I pay, please?	Ég ætla að borga?
Here/there	Hér/Þar	The bill/check, please	Reikninginn, takk

Getting around

How do I get to . . . ?	Hvernig kemst ég til . . . ?	When is the next bus to . . . ?	Hvenær fer næsta rúta (strætó) til ...?
Left/right	Vinstri/hægri	Can you let me know when we get to . . . ?	Gætirðu sagt mér þegar við komum til . . . ?
Straight ahead/back	Beint áfram/tilbaka		
Bus (in towns)	Strætó		
Bus (long distance)	Rúta	Is anyone sitting here?	Er þetta sæti laust?
Where is the bus station?	Hvar er biðstöðin?	Is this the road to . . . ?	Er þetta leiðin til . . . ?
Where is the bus stop?	Hvar er strætostöðin?	Where are you going?	Hvert ertu að fara?
		I'm going to . . .	Ég er að fara til . . .
Does this bus go to . . . ?	Fer þessi rúta (strætó) til . . . ?	Here's great, thanks	Hérna er ágætt, takk
		Stop here, please	Stansaðu hérna, takk
What time does it leave?	Hvenær fer hún?	Single ticket to . . .	Einn miða, aðra leiðina til . . .
What time does it arrive?	Hvenær kemur hún til?	Return ticket to . . .	Einn miða, báðar leiðir til . . .

Accommodation

Where's the youth hostel?	Hvar er farfuglaheimilið?	Can I see it?	Má ég sjá það
Is there a hotel/ guesthouse round here?	Er hótel/gistiheimili hér nálægt?	I'll take it	Ég ætla að taka það
		How much is it a night?	Hvað kostar nóttin?
I'd like a single/ double room . . .	Gæti ég fengið einsmanns herbergi/ tveggjamanna herbergi . . .	It's too expensive	Það er of dýrt
		Do you have anything cheaper?	Áttu eitthvað ódýrara?
. . . with a bath/ shower	. . . með baði/sturtu	Can I leave the bags here until . . . ?	Má ég geyma farangurinn hérna þangað til . . . ?
Bed	Rúm	Can I camp here?	Má ég tjalda hérna?

Days and months

Days and months are never capitalized. Days are declinable but months are not.

Monday	mánudagur	April	apríl
Tuesday	þriðjudagur	May	maí
Wednesday	miðvikudagur	June	júní
Thursday	fimmtudagur	July	júlí
Friday	föstudagur	August	ágúst
Saturday	laugardagur	September	september
Sunday	sunnudagur	October	október
January	janúar	November	nóvember
February	febrúar	December	desember
March	mars		

Numbers

1	einn	20	tuttugu
2	tveir	21	tuttugu og einn
3	þrír	22	tuttugu og tveir
4	fjórir	30	þrjátíu
5	fimm	31	þrjátíu og einn
6	sex	40	fjörutíu
7	sjö	50	fimmtíu
8	átta	60	sextíu
9	níu	70	sjötíu
10	tíu	80	áttatíu
11	ellefu	90	níutíu
12	tólf	100	hundrað
13	þrettán	101	hundrað og einn
14	fjórtán	110	hundrað og tuttugu
15	fimmtán	200	tvö hundruð
16	sextán	500	fimm hundruð
17	sautján	1000	þúsund
18	átján	1,000,000	milljón
19	nítján		

Numerals

Numerals 1–4 are all inflected as follows:

ONE	Masculine	Feminine	Neuter
Nominative	einn	ein	eitt
Accusative	einn	eina	eitt
Genitive	eins	einnar	eins
Dative	einum	einni	einu

TWO	Masculine	Feminine	Neuter
Nominative	tveir	tvær	tvö
Accusative	tvo	tvær	tvö
Genitive	tveggja	tveggja	tveggja
Dative	tveimur	tveimur	tveimur

THREE	Masculine	Feminine	Neuter
Nominative	þrír	þrjár	þrjú
Accusative	þrjá	þrjár	þrjú
Genitive	þriggja	þriggja	þriggja
Dative	þremur	þremur	þremur

FOUR	Masculine	Feminine	Neuter
Nominative	fjórir	fjórar	fjögur
Accusative	fjóra	fjórar	fjögur
Genitive	fjögra	fjögra	fjögra
Dative	fjórum	fjórum	fjórum

Glossary

Á river
Áætlun timetable
Ás small hill
Bær farm
Bíll car
Bjarg cliff, rock
Brú bridge
Dalur valley
Djúp deep inlet, long fjord
Drangur rock column
Ey island
Eyri sand spit
Fell/fjall mountain
Ferja ferry
Fjörður fjord
Fljót large river
Flói bay
Flugvöllur airport
Foss waterfall
Gata street
Gil ravine, gill

Gisting accommodation
Heiði heath
Herbergi room
Hnjúkur peak
Höfði headland
Hraun lava
Hver hot spring
Jökull glacier
Kirkja church
Laug warm pool
Lón lagoon
Reykur smoke
Rúta long distance coach
Staður place
Strætó city bus
Tjörn lake, pond
Vatn lake
Vegur road
Vík bay
Völlur plain, flatland

Rough
Guides

advertiser

Rough Guides travel...

...music & reference

small print and

Index

A Rough Guide to Rough Guides

In the summer of 1981, Mark Ellingham, a recent graduate from Bristol University, was travelling round Greece and couldn't find a guidebook that really met his needs. On the one hand there were the student guides, insistent on saving every last cent, and on the other the heavyweight cultural tomes whose authors seemed to have spent more time in a research library than lounging away the afternoon at a taverna or on the beach.

In a bid to avoid getting a job, Mark and a small group of writers set about creating their own guidebook. It was a guide to Greece that aimed to combine a journalistic approach to description with a thoroughly practical approach to travellers' needs – a guide that would incorporate culture, history and contemporary insights with a critical edge, together with up-to-date, value-for-money listings. Back in London, Mark and the team finished their Rough Guide, as they called it, and talked Routledge into publishing the book.

That first *Rough Guide to Greece*, published in 1982, was a student scheme that became a publishing phenomenon. The immediate success of the book – with numerous reprints and a Thomas Cook prize shortlisting – spawned a series that rapidly covered dozens of destinations. Rough Guides had a ready market among low-budget backpackers, but soon also acquired a much broader and older readership that relished Rough Guides' wit and inquisitiveness as much as their enthusiastic, critical approach. Everyone wants value for money, but not at any price.

Rough Guides soon began supplementing the "rougher" information about hostels and low-budget listings with the kind of detail on restaurants and quality hotels that independent-minded visitors on any budget might expect, whether on business in New York or trekking in Thailand.

These days the guides – distributed worldwide by the Penguin group – offer recommendations from shoestring to luxury and cover more than 200 destinations around the globe, including almost every country in the Americas and Europe, more than half of Africa and most of Asia and Australasia. Our ever-growing team of authors and photographers is spread all over the world, particularly in Europe, the USA and Australia.

In 1994, we published the *Rough Guide to World Music* and *Rough Guide to Classical Music*; and a year later the *Rough Guide to the Internet*. All three books have become benchmark titles in their fields – which encouraged us to expand into other areas of publishing, mainly around popular culture. Rough Guides now publish:

- Travel guides to more than 200 worldwide destinations
- Dictionary phrasebooks to 22 major languages
- History guides ranging from Ireland to Islam
- Maps printed on rip-proof and waterproof Polyart™ paper
- Music guides running the gamut from Opera to Elvis
- Restaurant guides to London, New York and San Francisco
- Reference books on topics as diverse as the Weather and Shakespeare
- Sports guides from Formula 1 to Man Utd
- Pop culture books from *Lord of the Rings* to Cult TV
- World Music CDs in association with World Music Network

Visit **www.roughguides.com** to see our latest publications.

Rough Guide credits

Desk editor: Geoff Howard
Layout: Umesh Aggarwal
Cartography: Rajesh Mishra, Animesh Pathak
Picture research: Sharon Martins, JJ Luck &
Mark Thomas
Proofreader: Antonia Hebbert
Indexing: David Abram
Editorial: **London** Martin Dunford, Kate
Berens, Helena Smith, Claire Saunders, Geoff
Howard, Ruth Blackmore, Gavin Thomas,
Polly Thomas, Richard Lim, Lucy Ratcliffe,
Clifton Wilkinson, Alison Murchie, Fran
Sandham, Sally Schafer, Alexander Mark
Rogers, Karoline Densley, Andy Turner, Ella
O'Donnell, Andrew Lockett, Joe Staines,
Duncan Clark, Peter Buckley, Matthew Milton;
New York Andrew Rosenberg, Richard Koss,
Yuki Takagaki, Hunter Slaton, Chris Barsanti,
Thomas Kohnstamm, Steven Horak
Design & Layout: **London** Helen Prior, Dan
May, Diana Jarvis; **Delhi** Madhulita
Mohapatra, Umesh Aggarwal, Ajay Verma

Production: Julia Bovis, John McKay,
Sophie Hewat
Cartography: **London** Maxine Repath, Ed
Wright, Katie Lloyd-Jones; **Delhi** Manish
Chandra, Rajesh Chhibber, Jai Prakash
Mishra, Ashutosh Bharti, Rajesh Mishra,
Animesh Pathak
Cover art direction: Louise Boulton
Picture research: Sharon Martins, Mark
Thomas, Jj Luck
Online: **New York** Jennifer Gold, Cree
Lawson, Suzanne Welles; **Delhi** Manik
Chauhan, Amarjyoti Dutta, Narender Kumar
Marketing & Publicity: **London** Richard
Trillo, Niki Smith, David Wearn, Chloë
Roberts, Demelza Dallow; **New York** Geoff
Colquitt, David Wechsler, Megan Kennedy
Finance: Gary Singh
Manager India: Punita Singh
Series editor: Mark Ellingham
PA to Managing Director: Julie Sanderson
Managing Director: Kevin Fitzgerald

Publishing Information

This second edition published March 2004 by
Rough Guides Ltd,
80 Strand, London WC2R 0RL.
345 Hudson St, 4th Floor,
New York, NY 10014, USA.
Distributed by the Penguin Group
Penguin Books Ltd,
80 Strand, London WC2R 0RL
Penguin Putnam, Inc.
375 Hudson Street, NY 10014, USA
Penguin Books Australia Ltd,
487 Maroondah Highway, PO Box 257,
Ringwood, Victoria 3134, Australia
Penguin Books Canada Ltd,
10 Alcorn Avenue, Toronto, Ontario,
Canada M4V 1E4
Penguin Books (NZ) Ltd,
182–190 Wairau Road, Auckland 10,
New Zealand
Typeset in Bembo and Helvetica to an original
design by Henry Iles.

Printed in Italy by LegoPrint S.p.A

© David Leffman and James Proctor

No part of this book may be reproduced in any
form without permission from the publisher
except for the quotation of brief passages in
reviews.

400pp includes index
A catalogue record for this book is available from
the British Library

ISBN 1-84353-2891

The publishers and authors have done their best
to ensure the accuracy and currency of all the
information in **The Rough Guide to Iceland**,
however, they can accept no responsibility for
any loss, injury, or inconvenience sustained by
any traveller as a result of information or advice
contained in the guide.

1   3   5   7   9   8   6   4   2

Help us update

We've gone to a lot of effort to ensure that
the second edition of **The Rough Guide to
Iceland** is accurate and up-to-date. However,
things change – places get "discovered",
opening hours are notoriously fickle,
restaurants and rooms raise prices or lower
standards. If you feel we've got it wrong or
left something out, we'd like to know, and if
you can remember the address, the price, the
time, the phone number, so much the better.

We'll credit all contributions, and send a
copy of the next edition (or any other Rough

Guide if you prefer) for the best letters.
Everyone who writes to us and isn't already a
subscriber will receive a copy of our full-
colour thrice-yearly newsletter. Please mark
letters: **"Rough Guide to Iceland Update"**
and send to: Rough Guides, 80 Strand,
London WC2R 0RL, or Rough Guides, 4th
Floor, 345 Hudson St, New York, NY 10014.
Or send an email to **mail@roughguides.com**

Have your questions answered and tell
others about your trip at
www.roughguides.atinfopop.com

Acknowledgements

James would like to extend grateful thanks to Kris Konrads of Arctic Experience for her superb planning and timetabling, plus expert knowledge of Flatey; also to Georgina Hancock whose good humour is always appreciated. In Iceland, thanks aplenty to Kristbjörn and Ólafur in Reykjavík for friendship, support and proud, if rainy, birthday celebrations on Laugavegur. Thanks too to the people and the ghost at *Hótel Tindastóll*, the guillemot at Lónkót, and especially the entire team at *Hótel Djúpavík* whose warm welcome was much appreciated, also to Áslaug in Ísafjörður who certainly knows a thing or two. Also to Lance for company along the way and for keeping things running so smoothly during this update in Montclus.

David would like to thank Njóla and Álfrun, champion potato farmers. Also Loftur and Meimei, Sue, Jim & Nik, and Aron and the Landsbankinn staff who had to put up with him on Laugavegur.

SMALL PRINT

Readers' letters

Thanks to all the readers who have taken the time and trouble to write in with comments and suggestions. Listed below are those who were especially helpful: apologies for any errors, omissions or misspellings.

Rune Amundsen; Alex Aquilina; A. Grady; Jane Horsfall; Susanna and Henry Long; Brendan O'Sullivan-Hale; Tinna Ottesen; Leo Vita-Finzi; Leesa Yeo.

Photo credits

SMALL PRINT

Index

Map entries are in colour.

A

accommodation.............31
Aðaldalshraun..............277
Aðalvík........................201
addresses (Icelandic)....362
airlines
  in Australia 14
  in Britain 10
  in Canada 12
  in Ireland 12
  in New Zealand 14
  in the US 12
AKRANES.............154–158
Akranes 157
  accommodation 156
  Akrafjall 158
  beach 157
  food and drink 158
  Glymur 158
  museums 156–157
Akurey 91
AKUREYRI 241–248
Akureyri 244
  accommodation.............. 242
  airport 242
  Akureyrarkirkja 245
  Akureyri museum 246
  Art Museum 245
  bars and nightlife 248
  botanical gardens 246
  Davidzshús 244
  eating and drinking 247
  Good Templars museum ...246
  harbour (Akureyrarhöfn) ... 245
  history 241
  information 242
  KEA 242
  Kjarnaskógur 247
  Listings 248
  Nonnahús 246
  Sigurhæðzir 245
  Skipgata.......................... 244
alcohol 35
Alþing, the.............106, 339
Arason, Jón.....................90
Arctic Circle, the 285
Arnarfjörður..................207
Arnarson, Ingólfur 90
Arnarstapi 186
Arnes............................119
Ásbergi 283
Askja route....................333
ATMs.............................21
Aurora Borealis (Northern
  Lights) 350

B

Bakkafjörður 287
Bakkahlaup 281
Barnafoss......................167
bars 35
Bergþórshvoll................129
Berserkjahraun..............180
Bifröst 169
Bíldudalur......................211
birdlife 100, 101, 137,
  140, 141, 146, 148, 158,
  201, 211, 214, 229, 252,
  256, 267, 273, 283, 303,
               352–354
Bjargtangar 213
Bjarkalundur..................216
Bjarnarflag.....................274
Bláfjöll 85
Blönduós 230
Blue Lagoon, the 98
Bolungarvík...................197
booking flights online 9
books....................355-358
bookshops......................45
Borg á Mýrum..............161
Borgarfjörður Eystri....304
Borgarnes 158–161
Bratthol farm.................113
Breiðdalsvík 310
Brjánslækur...................210
Brú 228
Búðardulur 170
Búðir 186
Búdahraun 186
Búrfell............................121
Búrfell 120
Búrstafell.......................288
buses 25

C

cafés 36
camping 33
car rental 26
chemists 22
Christianity 339
civil war.........................340
Cod Wars......................345
Cold War.......................345

credit cards....................21
crime 44
cycling............................29

D

Dalvík....................249–251
Deildatunguhver............165
Dettifoss.......................284
Dimmuborgir 271
disabled travellers...........18
Djúpalónssandur...........185
Djúpavík........................220
Djúpivogur.....................310
Drangajökull 200
Drangey 234
Drangsnes.....................219
drinking 35
Dritvík...........................185
driving 27
Dynjandi 210
Dyrhólaey.....................137

E

Eastfjords 303–311
Eastfjords and the
  Southeast 294
eating 34–36
Egill's Saga...................161
Egilsstaðir 295–297
Egilsstaðir.....................297
Eiðar.............................303
Einarsdottír, Thurídur 117
Eirík the Red (Eric the Red)
  ....169, 173, 339
Eiríksjökull 167
Eiríksson, Leif................339
Eiríksstaðir 170
Eldborgarhraun 187
Eldey 101
Eldhraun.......................323
electricity.......................45
embassies, Icelandic 16
English Century.............341
environmental issues 302
Eric Bloodaxe 161, 162
Eric the Red, see Eirík the
  Red

Erró 65
Eskifjörður 308
exchange 20
Eyjafjallajökull...............131
Eyjafjarðardalur Valley
....255
Eyjafjörður 248–255
Eyrarbakki 118
Eyvindur and Halla........333

F

Fagraskógarfjall 187
Fagrifoss 323
farms 32
Fáskrúðsfjörður.............309
Fellaær 299
ferries
from Britain 11
from Ireland.........................12
fishing 40, 128
Fjallabak routes, the 131
Flatey 179–180
Flateyri 205
flights
from Australia....................14
from Britain 10
from Canada.......................12
from Ireland.........................12
from New Zealand 14
from the US 13
in Iceland 25
Fljótsdalur 131
Flókalundur 210
flora...............................351
food................................34
Fosshóll.........................266
four-wheel-driving...........28
fuel 26

G

Garður.............................99
Gardur...........................272
gay and lesbian
Iceland 43, 82
geology...................347-349
geysers 349
Geysir............................111
Gilsfjörður 217
Gjástykki 276
Glaumbær 235
glossary 367
Golden Circle, the
............................103–113
Gorbachev, Mikhail 75

Grábrók..........................169
Grábrókarhraun..............169
Grænalón 321
Grænavatn 103
Grenivík 255
Grenjaðarstaður 276
Grettir's Saga 357
Grímsey.................256–259
Grímsey 257
Grímsvötn 321
Grindavík.......................101
Grótagjá 271
Grund............................256
Grundarfjörður 181
Guðmundsson,
Sigurður 72
Guðríður Þorbjardardóttir
....185
Gullborgarhraun 187
Gullfoss 112
Gunnarsson, Gunnar 299
Gunnarsstein................128

H

Hafnarfjörður 87
Hafnarfjörður 87
Hafnir 100
Hafragilsfoss 284
Hallbjarnarstaðir............281
Hallgrímsson, Jónas 108
Hallmundarhraun 166
Hallormsstaður..............298
Hamarinn 89
Hamragill.........................85
Hauganes......................250
Haukadalur....................112
health 21
HEIMAEY 142–148
Heimaey 143, 145
Blátindur 146
coastal trails....................147
Eldfell 146
Há 146
Heimaey town 142
Heimaklettur cliffs.............146
Helgafell 146
Herjólfsdalur.....................146
Landnámsbær...................146
lava flow...........................145
practicalities.....................144
Stórakliff...........................147
town 143
Hekla............................121
Helgafell 179
Hella 126
Hellissandur 182
Hellnar...........................185
Hengifoss......................299

Héraðsfloi......................303
Herðubreið route...........332
Herðubreiðarlindir 282
Herjólfsson, Bjarni 118
Hesteyri.........................201
hiking 41, 85, 115, 122,
124–125, 134, 136, 147,
166, 167, 183–184,
202–204, 239, 250, 254,
305, 312–313, 319, 332
history 337–346
hitching 30
Hjálparfoss....................119
Hjóðaklettar 283
Hlíðarendi.....................130
Höfði 272
Höfn 314
Hólar í Hjaltadal 236
Hólmatungur 283
Hólmavík 218
Home Rule 344
Hornstrandir 201–204
Hornstrandir 202
horse riding...............42, 84
Hosfsós.........................237
hospitals 22
hostels 32
hot pots...........................40
hotels 31
Hrafnagil.......................256
Hrafnkel's Saga 300
Hrafnkelsstaðir.............300
Hrafnseyri.....................208
Hraunfossar 167
Hraunhafnartangi 285
Hrauntún 109
Hredavatn 169
Hrísey 251
Hróarstunga 303
Hrolfssoon, Helgi 193
Húsafell 165
Húsavík 277-280
Húsavík 279
Hvalförður 154
Hvammsfjörður 169
Hvammstangi................229
Hvammur 171
Hvannadalshnúkur........317
Hvannalindir 334
hverabrauð ("steambread")*
....274
Hveragerði 114
Hverarönd 275
Hveravellir 277
Hverfjall 271
Hvolsvöllur 129

I

Ingjaldssandur (Sæból) ..205
Ingólfshöfði 317
insurance 17
Internet............................38
Ísafjarðardjúp 199–201
Ísafjörður..............193–197
Ísafjörður 196
Íslendingabók 340

J

Jökuladur 301
**Jökulsárgljúfur National
Park** 281–284
Jökulsárgljúfur National
Park 282
Jökulsárlón....................317
Jónsson, Ásgrímur 72
Jónsson, Einar 72

K

Kaldidalur interior route
......................................168
Kaldalón........................200
Kálfaströnd 272
Kárahnjúkar project,
the..............................302
Keflavík 98
Keldur 128
Kerlingarskarð...............179
Kirkjubæjarklaustur.......322
Kjarval, Jóhannes 73
Kjölur route, the 331
Kjölurvegur trek............332
Kleifarvatn 103
Kolbeinstangi
peninsula....................287
Kópasker........................284
Krafla.............................275
Kristínatindar.................320
Krísuvík 103
Krísuvíkurberg...............103
Króksfjarðarnes.............217
Kross.............................212
Kverkfjöll route, the.......334

L

Lagarfljótsormur............298

Lakagígar 323
Landmannalaugar 122
Langadalsströnd 200
Langanes peninsula......286
Langjökull......................167
language 361–366
Látrabjarg......................213
Látraströnd 254
Laufás 254
Laugar...........................267
Laugarhóll 219
Laugarvatn 110
Laugavegur (hiking trail)
......................................124
Laugur...........................172
laundry 45
Laxárdalur 171
Laxdæla Saga 172, 358
Laxness, Halldór 301
Leirhnjúkur 276
lesbian and gay Iceland
................................43, 82
literature 355
Lögurinn 298–299
Lón................................312
Lóndrangar 185
Lónsöræfi......................312
Lúdent...........................271
Lysuhóll.........................187

M

Mýrdalsjökull 136
Mývatn, Lake 265–276
Mývatn...........................266
Mývatn and the northeast
......................................264
Magnússon, Árni.............69
Magnússon, Skúli 91
mail 37
Malmey 237
mammals 351
Mánárayjar 281
maps 23
Markarfljót Valley 130
Möðrudalur 334
Móhálsadalur 103
money 20
mountain huts 33

N

Námafjall 275
names 362
nationalism....................343

NATO...............................98
Neskaupstaður..............308
Neslönd.........................273
newspapers 38
Njál's Saga 126
Norðurfjörður 220
Northern Lights (Aurora
Borealis) 350
Northwest Iceland
...........................226–227
Núpsstaðurskógur 322

O

Oddi 128
Okjökull 167
Ólafsfjörður 252
Ólafsvík 182
Öxarárfoss 107

P

package tours
from Australia...................12
from Britain 10
from New Zealand 12
from the US 12
Patreksfjörður 212
pharmacies 22
photography 45
post.................................37
price codes 31
(see also inside front cover)
public holidays................39
puffins 141

R

radio................................38
rafting..............................42
Rauðhólar 283
Rauðisandur..................214
Rauðuskriður
(Stóra-Dímon).............130
Raufarhöfn 285
Reagan, Ronald 75
Reformation, the 342
restaurants 35
Reyðarfjörður 307
Reykhólar......................216
Reykholt (west coast)
...........................162–165
Reykholt 111

Reykjafjörður 201
Reykjahlíð 268–274
Reykjanes 200
Reykjanesfólkvangur.....103
Reykjanes Peninsula,
the 97–103
Reykjanestá 101
REYKJAVÍK 47–92
Reykjavík 52, 56–57
Þjóðmenningarhúsið (Culture
House) 68
accommodation 58–61
Aðalstræti...........................64
airports.............................53
Altinghúsið 63
Árbæjarsafn Open-Air
Museum..........................76
Ásgrímur Jónsson Museum
..................................72
ASÍ Art Gallery 72
Ásmundur Sveinsson
Sculpture Museum 75
Austurstræti 63
Austurvöllur........................63
botanical garden................76
bus terminal 54
City Centre.........................62
city transport.....................54
clubs 81
Culture House 68
Dómkirkjan.........................64
eating and drinking 77–80
Einar Jónsson Museum 72
entertainment.....................80
Fálkahúsið..........................64
gay and lesbian Reykjavík
..................................82
Hafnarhúsið........................65
Hafnarstræti 64
Hallgrímskirkja 71
harbour 65
history 52
Iceland Phallological
Museum..........................71
information 54
Kjarvalsstaðir Art Gallery
..................................73
Lækjartorg.........................63
Listasafn Islands 67
listings...............................86
Museum of Natural History
..................................74
National Museum...............66
Norræna Húsið (Nordic
House) 67
Öskjuhlíð 73
Reykjavík City Hall 66
Saga Museum....................73
sports 83–85
Suðurgata 56
Tjörnin 66
tourist information..............54
Tryggvagata 65
zoo ....
Reynisfjall..........................137
Rif................................182

S

Sæból (Ingjaldssandur)
..................................206
Saga Age 339
sagas 68, 73, 126, 129,
159, 161, 171, 172, 287,
300
Sandgerði 100
Sandoddi 215
Sandvík 258
Sauðárkrókur......232–235
scuba diving 42
Selatangar....................102
Selfoss 116
Selfoss 284
Seljalandsfoss.................132
Seltún..........................103
Settlement....................338
sexual harassment..........44
Seyðisfjörður 305–307
Sigfússon, Sæmundur
..................................128
Siglufjörður...................238
Sigurðsson, Jón.....69, 208,
343
Skaftafell National Park
..................................315–320
Skaftafell National Park
..................................316
Skaftafellsheiði..............319
Skagafjörður 236
Skagaströnd 232
Skagi peninsula, the
..................................231–235
Skálafell 85
Skálafellsjökull 315
Skálavík 198
Skálholt 111
Skallagrímsson, Egil......159
Skeiðarájökull...............320
Skeiðarárjökull 319
skiing........................42, 85
Skógar 132
Skógarfoss....................133
Skógarkot 109
Skútusaðir....................272
Snæfell 301
Snæfellsjökull 183
Snæfellsnes Peninsula,
the....................173–187
Snæfellsnes Peninsula
..................................174–175
snowmobiling........84, 137,
167, 186
Sólheimajökull..............137
Southwest Iceland 96
Sólheimskáli.................137

souvenirs.......................45
sports............................40
Sprengisandur route 330
Stafafell 312
Stöðvarfjörður 310
Stokkseyri 117
Stöng 120
Stóra-Dímon
(Rauðuskriður)............130
Strandir coast, the
..................................217–221
Sturlung Age 340
Sturluson, Snorri.........162,
164
Stykkishólmur......174–178
Stykkishólmur 177
Súðavík 199
Súðureyri.......................205
Surtsey 147
Svartifoss 320
Sveinbjarnarson, Hrafn
..................................208
Sveinsson, Ásmundur.....75
Svínafell 317
swimming.......................40
Syðribú.........................110

T

Tálknafjörður 211
tax.................................20
telephones 37
television 38
thermal springs 348
time 38
Tindafjall.......................131
Tindafjallajökull 131
Tjörnes peninsula, the
..................................280
Tjörneshöfn 281
tourist offices, Icelandic...18
tours for disabled
travellers...................18
tours
from Australia.................15
from Britain 10
from Canada...................13
from Ireland....................12
from the US 12
travel agents
in Britain........................10
in Canada.......................13
in the US........................13
travel insurance 17
travellers' cheques.........21
Tröllkonuhlaup...............122
Tungnaá 124
Tungumuli 212

I N D E X

397

U

Unaðsdalur 201

V

Varmahlíð 235
Varmaland 168
VAT refunds....................20
Vatnajökull 311–323
**Vestmannaeyjar
(Westman Islands)**
.........................140–148
  ferries................................141
  history......................140, 147
Vesturdalur 283
Viðey 90
Vík 139
vikings.............69, 120, 337
Vilgerðarson, Flóki 210,
338
Vindbelgjarfjall...............273
visas...............................16

Viti 276
Vogar............................271
Voladstorfa...................281
volcanoes 121, 140, 146,
347
Vopnafjörður 287

W

Web sites, Icelandic........24
West Coast...................152
West Fjords 192
**Westman Islands, see
Vestmannaeyjar**
whale watching.......83, 278
whaling.................155, 346
whitewater rafting ..119, 235
World War II 344

Y

youth hostels 32

Þ

Þingeyrar......................229
Þingeyri 207
Þingskallar 126
Þingvallahraun 108
Þingvallavatn.................109
Þingvellir 107
Þingvellir...............105, 108
Þingvellir National
Park............................104
Þingvöllur 178
Þjórsárdalur...................119
Þjórsárdalur..................120
Þóðveldisbærinn 121
Þofafoss........................122
Þórshöfn 286
Þórsmörk 135
Þórsmörk......................135
Þórsmörk trail 134

Map symbols

Maps are listed in the full index using coloured text.

– – –	Chapter division boundary	◉	Accommodation	⌣	Bridge		
══	Major road	▣	Restaurant/pub	⚓	Golf course		
══	Minor road	⊔⊔⊔	Rift	⊛	Swimming pool		
··········	4 Wheel drive road	渐渐	Cliff	ⓘ	Tourist office		
- - - - -	Footpath	/||\	Hill	⊠	Post office		
———	Tracks	峦	Mountains	@	Internet		
♦	Point of interest	▲	Peak	©	Phone Office		
★	Bus stop	瀑	Waterfall	♱	Church (regional maps)		
✈	Airport	⇞	Spring	✚	Church (town maps)		
✗	Airstrip	⇟	Veiwpoint	■	Building		
⛽	Petrol station	/|\	Volcano	⊞	Cemetery		
P	Parking	⊕	Crater	▦	Park/National park		
	River/canal	♟	Fort	⠿	Forest		
⌂	Hut	∴	Ruins	⌇	Glacier		
⚠	Campsite	♟	Museum	⠂	Beach		
⚑	Lighthouse	⬭	Stadium	⫶⫶	Lava flow		